The *She* National Women's Directory

The *She* National Women's Directory

Loulou Brown

CASSELL
London and New York

Cassell
Wellington House, 125 Strand, London WC2R 0BB
370 Lexington Avenue, New York, NY 10017-6550

First published 1998

© Loulou Brown 1998

All rights reserved. No part of this publication may be reproduced or transmitted in any form or by any means, electronic or mechanical, including photocopying, recording or any information storage or retrieval system, without permission in writing from the publishers.

British Library Cataloguing in Publication Data
A catalogue record for this book is available from the British Library.
ISBN 0-304-33573-8

Printed and bound in Great Britain by CPD Wales, Ebbw Vale.

Contents

Acknowledgements	vii
Introduction	viii
NATIONAL	1
Accommodation	1
Agriculture	1
Armed forces	1
Arts and Crafts	2
Bereavement	4
Business support schemes	6
Carers	8
Centres for women	8
Child care and family	8
Computers/IT	15
Contraception/Well woman	15
Counselling and therapy	16
Disability	18
Education	20
Environment	22
Equal opps	22
Ethnic minorities	26
Finance	28
Girls/Young women	28
Health	29
International	40
Irish women	42
Jewish women	42
Legal matters	43
Lesbian and bisexual	43
Libraries/Archives	46
Media	46
Older women	47
Peace groups	49
Photography	50
Politics	51
Pregnancy/Childbirth	52
Prisoners/Prisoners' wives	55
Professional associations	56
Publishers/publications	60
Racial equality	64
Religious organisations	65
Rights	69
Services	71
Sexual abuse/rape crisis	71
Single parents	72
Social	74
Spirituality/ecofeminism	74
Sports and leisure	74
Support	76
Training	80
Transport	80
Violence against women	80
Women's Aid	81
Working women	81
ENGLAND	82
Bedfordshire	82
Berkshire	86
Birmingham and Midlands	88
Bristol and Bath	101
Buckinghamshire	110
Cambridgeshire	115
Cheshire	118
Cleveland	121
Cornwall	127
Cumbria	131
Derbyshire	132
Devon	135
Dorset	145
Durham	147
Essex	149
Gloucestershire	151
Hampshire & Isle of Wight	154
Hereford & Worcestershire	161
Hertfordshire	163
Hull and Humberside	165
Kent	167
Lancashire	170
Leicestershire	172
Lincolnshire	173
Liverpool and Merseyside	174
Manchester and Gtr. Manchester	182
Newcastle and Tyneside	192
Norfolk	201
Northamptonshire	204
Northumberland	209

CONTENTS

Nottinghamshire	210	Merton	356
Oxfordshire	215	Newham	358
Shropshire	219	Redbridge	364
Somerset	219	Richmond Upon Thames	366
Staffordshire	222	Southwark	368
Suffolk	223	Sutton	372
Surrey	224	Tower Hamlets	375
Sussex	225	Waltham Forest	382
Warwickshire	228	Wandsworth	385
Wiltshire	229	Westminster	388
Yorkshire	231		
		SCOTLAND	**393**
LONDON	**256**		
		Aberdeen and Grampian	393
Barking & Dagenham	256	Dumfries, Galloway &	
Barnet	258	Borders	397
Bexley	261	Dundee, Tayside & Fife	401
Brent	262	Edinburgh & Lothians	410
Bromley	264	Falkirk & Central	419
Camden	265	Glasgow & Strathclyde	427
Corporation of London	279	Inverness, H & I	445
Croydon	279		
Ealing	283	**WALES**	**451**
Enfield	285		
Greenwich	290	Aberystwyth and Mid Wales	451
Hackney	294	Bangor and North Wales	451
Hammersmith & Fulham	301	Cardiff and South Wales	453
Haringey	306		
Harrow	311	**EIRE**	**460**
Havering	314		
Hillingdon	318	Dublin	460
Hounslow	319	Outside Dublin	463
Islington	325		
Kensington & Chelsea	337	**NORTHERN IRELAND**	**468**
Kingston Upon Thames	340		
Lambeth	342	Belfast	468
Lewisham	352	Outside Belfast	472

Acknowledgements

First of all, thank you to the thousands of women who filled out questionnaires and thank you to over a thousand women who answered questions over the phone.

I particularly want to thank the following who worked on the Directory: Lee Bennett, Julia Clark, Hannah Franks, Helen Franks and Daphne Trotter.

I also want to thank the following friends who have been very supportive as well; many of them provided useful information: Astra Blaug, Elisabeth Brooke, Gillian Bull, Carolyn Faulder, Felicity Lawrence, Rachel Lever, Janice Markey, Angie Rivera and Ruth Stern.

The following people and organizations were helpful in many ways:

Jane Becker, Department of Sociology, University of Essex
Maria Craig, Profiles Directory
Christine Frizzier, Network 2000
Glasgow Women's Library
Health Education Board for Scotland (HEBS)
Geoffrey Leigh, Coordinator, Fair Play North West
London Feminist Library
Pat McCarthy, Fair Play South West
Married Women's Association
National Alliance of Women's Organisations (NAWO)
Neysa Moss
Pat Nicholl, National Coordinator, Fair Play
Dawn Nicholls, Coordinator, Fair Play West Midlands
Stella O'Donnell, Cornwall County Council
Frances Presley, King's Fund
Elizabeth Puttick
Elaine Roberts, Coordinator, Fair Play Merseyside
Maureen Roberts, North Tyneside Well Woman Centre
Jo Valks, Community Recreation Outreach Team, Hounslow
Sylvia Wardley, Fair Play East Midlands
Pauline Williams, Coordinator, Contact, Jedburgh
Women in Theology
Women Mean Business
Women's National Commission
Women's Resource and Development Agency, Belfast

Thank you to all the women who helped with my enquiries at the following women's centres:

Brighton Women's Centre
Cambridge Women's Resource Centre
Crossroads Women's Centre
Derby Women's Centre
Hillingdon Women's Centre
Hopscotch Asian Women's Centre
London Women's Centre (WHEEL)
Luton All Women's Centre
Nottingham Women's Centre
Tindlemanor
West Hampstead Women's Centre

Thank you to the librarians of over a hundred libraries that I contacted, and particularly to librarians in the following places that I visited: Barking, Bexley, Brent, Bromley, Camden, Fulham, Kensington, Lewisham, Luton, Merton, Newham, Northampton, St Albans, Tower Hamlets and Westminster.

Thanks to Roz Hopkins, my editor at Cassell, for commissioning this Directory and for giving me a free hand.

And thanks to Bradley, my husband, for tremendous technical input and for coping.

Loulou Brown
July 1998

Introduction

Today, although there is a mass of information available from many sources on very many subjects, women's organizations are not yet widely publicized. For the most part they are still difficult to locate and the information available is often too limited to be of much use. This directory seeks to remedy this.

To emphasize the diversity of women's experience and to ensure that the directory is truly national and that it reflects the wide diversity of the interests and concerns of women in different areas, no restrictions were placed on the variety of organizations listed.

The amount of information obtained varied considerably according to area in both amount and content. Some local authorities, libraries, individuals and phone books had a great deal more to offer than others. Occasionally, I quickly managed to find the relevant information, but more often the jackpot took time to access. Often I could not find the requisite information. Even so, the directory comprises by far the most comprehensive list of women's organizations yet published.

Organizations are described briefly. Each entry contains enough information for anyone wanting to find out more to be able to make contact for further details. It is hoped the way the book is set out allows for that information to be found quickly and easily. The Table of Contents at the beginning of the book provides easy access to national organizations by category and local organizations by area.

The directory lists over 4,800 organizations in England, Northern Ireland, Scotland and Wales, as well as the Republic of Ireland, listed as Eire. All are relevant to women and at least two thirds are specifically women's organizations. The directory is indispensable for:

- women who need immediate help
- basic facts about organizations
- information about products and services created or run by women
- women branching out into new activities
- women who want to contact other women with similar interests

The directory will be particularly useful for women who are:

- looking for organizations that are difficult to locate
- moving to a new area and wanting to find organizations relevant to their needs
- living in isolated areas and wanting to contact other women;
- already involved in a women's organization and wanting information about similar organizations

ARRANGEMENT

The directory is divided into two main sections. Part I comprises over 800 national organizations listed in categories. National organizations are those that have a head office with branches throughout the country, although some are autonomous with no branches. More usually there is the headquarters of an organizations with branches throughout the rest of the UK and sometimes Eire. In this case, only the HQ is listed in Part I; Part II may list some or all of the branch organizations.

Part II comprises nearly 4,000 local

INTRODUCTION

organizations listed under the following headings: England, London, Scotland, Wales, Eire, and Northern Ireland. Local organizations are specific to a given region. They may be branches of a national organization or an autonomous 'one-off' organization set up specifically to benefit women locally. Under these headings organizations have been listed in areas.

AREAS

Organizations in England, including those in the Home Counties outside the London boroughs, are listed either by county or metropolitan borough. For a complete list, see the Table of Contents. London, comprising Greater London, is divided into 33 boroughs. Some of the boroughs, such as Islington and Westminster, are within the inner London area, others exist within the Home Counties, such as Croydon in Surrey and Bexley in Kent. There are yet others, such as Hillingdon, that are in the nebulous area of Middlesex. In any event, all organizations with addresses in London boroughs are listed under London.

Scotland is divided into seven areas: Aberdeen and Gramplan; Dumfries, Galloway and Borders; Dundee, Tayside and Fife; Edinburgh and Lothians; Falkirk and Central; Glasgow and Strathclyde; Inverness, Highlands and Islands.

Wales is divided into three areas: Aberystwyth and Mid Wales; Bangor and North Wales; Cardiff and South Wales.

Both Eire and Northern Ireland are divided into two areas: Dublin and Outside Dublin and Belfast and Outside Belfast.

If you live in a rural area, your nearest town (likely to contain many more women's organizations than are available locally) may be in another area. It is always therefore worth checking areas adjacent to your own. Bear in mind that, if you do live in a rural area, there will be some organizations further afield that may be easier to access than those in, say, the next village.

CATEGORIES

Within areas the directory is arranged in 56 categories, listed in a table at the end of this Introduction. The categories allow for a search within a given area for organizations in particular fields of interest. For the most part these cater for specific interests, but there are some that are not so clear-cut and which overlap with other categories.

It is a damning indictment of the way we live now that there are so many organizations helping women who have suffered physical violence and/or sexual abuse. These have been divided into three categories: 'Women's Aid', 'Sexual Abuse/Rape Crisis' and 'Violence Against Women'. In addition, the 'Accommodation' category lists many refuges for women who have suffered violence that are neither Women's Aid nor Rape Crisis Centres. (Sometimes the information available for refuges is necessarily sparse to protect their anonymity.) Here it is important to note that 'Accommodation' lists only hostels and emergency accommodation for women. If you are looking for places to stay that cater for women on holiday, look under 'Places to Stay and Eat'. There are also many organizations that help women who have suffered mental abuse and these are to be found under the categories 'Counselling and Therapy' or 'Support'.

This directory, however, has not been set up only to help women who are victims of abuse but also to name and celebrate the wonderful diversity, inventiveness and creativity inherent in women's lives. Included within the 'Arts and Crafts' category, for instance, are very many arts, theatrical, dance and writing organizations. There were so many women's photography organizations that these were listed under a separate category, 'Photography'.

A very large number of entries eventually came to light, far more than had originally been anticipated, so

INTRODUCTION

saving space became important. Many local organizations were eventually deleted. In some instances the deletions were specifically requested by the national organizations themselves (for instance, La Leche League); in other cases it was thought sufficient to list only the national organization. Therefore, if you cannot find the local branch of an organization, look in Part I for the national organization and phone for details of your local branch. All local organizations that have no national head office or operate independently of their national organization have been retained.

A number of categories have been amalgamated. There are, for example, a very large number of health organizations relating specifically to women listed under 'Health'. These include women's cancer organizations, drugs (including alcohol) abuse, eating disorders, HIV/AIDS, and menopause organizations. Clinics and individuals specializing in alternative therapies are, however, listed separately, as are institutions and individuals providing counselling and therapy.

Contraception and well-woman clinics and centres are listed within one category because both services are usually provided in the same place, very often at the same time.

'Sports and Leisure' includes keep fit and self defence organizations.

'Ethnic Minorities' includes the following: Arab women, Asian women, Bangladeshi women, Black women, Chinese women, Cypriot women, Muslim women, Pakistani women and Turkish women.

Organizations listed under 'Education' cover a wide range. Women's Studies and other courses directly relevant to women, however, are not listed as information is widely available elsewhere. For example, an excellent list of Women's Studies courses was produced in *Women Making A Difference*, published in 1997 and details of women's courses are listed in *British Qualifications*, updated annually.

Very many organizations listed cater specifically for women – for instance, pregnancy and childbirth, and girls' and young women's organizations. There are also many businesses and services run by women listed under various headings such as 'Retailing' and 'Services' and sometimes more specifically under categories such as 'Alternative Therapies' and 'Finance'. These may cater for women only but more usually cater for both women and men.

CONCLUSION

The directory took a year and a half to compile. There were three main stages. The first was gathering the information, which was interesting and fairly easy. This information then had to be checked, a time-consuming and exhausting process; fortunately I had help with this. The third stage comprised typing the information into the database, again time-consuming and exhausting. I did this by myself but fortunately I have lots of stamina and patience. The length of time between gathering the entries and the directory being published has unfortunately been considerable, partly owing to technical difficulties. As with all reference books of this kind, by the time it is published, many entries will no longer be accurate. Check by telephone before visiting. In particular, e-mail addresses may not be accurate.

I hope the directory will prove a useful and practical guide.

Loulou Brown
July 1998

Categories

- Accommodation
- Accountancy
- Agriculture
- Alternative therapies
- Armed forces
- Arts and Crafts
- Bereavement
- Business support schemes
- Carers
- Centres for women
- Child care and family
- Computers/IT
- Contraception/Well woman
- Counselling and therapy
- Disability
- Education
- Environment
- Equal opportunities
- Ethnic minorities
- Finance
- Girls/Young women
- Health
- International
- Irish women
- Jewish women
- Larger/Taller women
- Legal matters
- Lesbian and bisexual
- Libraries/Archives
- Manual Trades
- Media
- Older women
- Peace groups
- Photography
- Places to stay and eat
- Politics
- Pregnancy/Childbirth
- Prisoners/Prisoners' wives
- Professional associations
- Publishers/Publications
- Racial equality
- Religious organisations
- Retailing
- Rights
- Services
- Sexual abuse/Rape crisis
- Single parents
- Social
- Spirituality/Ecofeminism
- Sports and leisure
- Support
- Training
- Transport
- Violence against women
- Women's Aid
- Working women

NATIONAL

ACCOMMODATION

National Homeless Alliance
5-15 Cromer Street
London WC1H 8LS
T 0171 833 2071 F 0171 278 6685
Campaigning & lobbying for single & homeless people. Works with member organisations & homeless people for better housing & services.

Refuge
Diane Church, Press & Information Officer
2-8 Maltravers Street
London WC2R 3EE
T 0171 395 7700 F 0171 395 7721
Runs 7 refuges for women & children subjected to domestic violence. Refers women across the UK. National 24-hours crisis line, 0181 995 4430, for women experiencing domestic violence. Counselling.

Richmond Fellowship
8 Addison Road
London W14 8DJ
T 0171 603 6373 F 0171 602 8652
Open Mon-Fri 9 am-5.30 pm. Housing association providing care/rehabilitation for people with mental health/learning disabilities, addiction, etc. Residential facilities. Work schemes, day centres, advocacy.

Shelter - National Campaign for the Homeless
88 Old Street
London EC1V 9HU
T 0171 253 0202 F 0171 505 2169
Open Mon-Fri 9.30 am-5.30 pm 24-hours emergency freephone London Line: 0800 446441. National campaign for homeless people & local housing aid. Housing advice & information.

AGRICULTURE

Farm Women's Club
Jean Howells
Quadrant House
The Quadrant
Sutton SM2 5AS
T 0181 652 4927
For all women in the UK connected with farming. Membership exclusive to 'Farmers' Weekly' readers. Clubs around the country meet informally.

Scottish Women's Rural Institutes
Mrs Anne Peacock
42 Heriot Row
Edinburgh EH3 6ES
T 0131 225 1724 F 0131 225 8129
To advance education & training of those who live/ work in the country, who like country life, home skills, family welfare & citizenship. Works for international cooperation/ understanding amongst women.

Women's Farm and Garden Association
Patricia Mchugh
175 Gloucester Street
Cirencester GL7 2DP
T 01285 658339
For people whose livelihood is connected with the land, agriculture, horticulture or allied industries. There is a training scheme aimed at women returners for gaining practical gardening skills.

Women's Farming Union
Mrs Meg Stroude
National Rural Enterprise Centre
National Agricultural Centre
Stoneleigh Park CV8 2LZ
T 01203 693171 F 01203 693181
Links food producers and consumers. Committed to promoting an understanding of, and confidence in, all aspects of quality British produce. 23 branches in England, Wales & Scotland.

ARMED FORCES

Altrusa International Inc
Mrs Pam Gammon
St Aubins
Bishops Close
Stoke Bishop
Bristol BS9 1JJ
T 0117 968 6597 F 0117 9686597
Oldest women's service association. Members meet twice a month. Meetings are a mixture of social, business, international links, service and literacy. An annual national conference.

Army Family Federation
the administrator
Trenchard Line
Upavon
Pewsey SN9 6BE
T 01980 615525
To benefit army wives & their children by improving social welfare, educational and recreational facilities. To help with finding employment and training schemes, etc.

NATIONAL - ARTS AND CRAFTS

Association of RAF Wives
Janet Sangster
Corridors RAF Insworth
Gloucester GL3 1HW
T 01452 712612   F 01452 712612

Association of WRENS
Mrs J Hardie
8 Hatherley Street
London SW1P 2YY
T 0171 932 0111
Charity for ex-WRNS. Preserving esprit de corps & WRNS traditions. 100 branches throughout UK, 12 abroad. Reunion usually every three years.

Royal British Legion - Women's Section
Miss Julia Simpson, National Secretary
Haig House
48 Pall Mall
London SW1Y 5JY
T 0171 973 7214   F 0171 839 7917
Improving the welfare of the ex-Service community, particularly ex-servicewomen, widows & dependants of past & present members of HM forces, etc. Weekly allowances to over 1,000 widows & ex-servicewomen.

Women's Royal Army Corps Association
Block 10
AGC Centre
Worthy Down SO21 2RG
T 01962 887 570
Aims to foster esprit de corps and to maintain comradeship amongst members. Helping members to obtain assistance if in need.

ARTS AND CRAFTS

Arts Council of England (ACE)
14 Great Peter Street
London SW1P 3NQ
T 0171 333 0100   F 0171 973 6590
Open Mon-Fri 8 am-7 pm. Library phone 0171 973 6517. Information about events & arts societies throughout England. Pubishes a directory of women's arts organisations.

Association of British Orchestras
Fiona Penny
Francis House
Francis Street
London SW1P 1DE
T 0171 828 6913   F 0171 931 9959
Represents collective interests of professional UK orchestras: conferences, seminars, training and general advocacy.

Cork Women's Poetry Circle
Maire Bradshaw
Tig Fili (Poets' House)
MacCurtain Street
Cork
T 021 509 274   F 021 509 274
'The Poetry Factory'. Open every day. Produces 10 titles per year. 18 regular workers. There is an annual event around the end of March with good food, wine, poetry, dance & music. A national organisation.

Crafts Council of Great Britain
44a Pentonville Road
London N1 9BY
F 0171 837 6891
Umbrella organisation for crafts in Great Britain. Reference library. Image store. Provides grants for crafts people. Events, seminars, training.

Embroiderers' Guild
Gale Williams
Appartment 41
Hampton Court Palace
Kingston Upon Thames KT8 9AU
T 0181 943 1229   F 0181 977 9882
For those interested in embroidery. Museum collection, library, workshops, courses, lectures, Embroiderers' Development Scheme, shop, tours, groups, exhibitions, etc. Phone for details of local groups.

Gay Sweatshop Theatre Co
Rose Sharp/Lois Weaver, Artistic Director
C/o Holborn Centre
3 Cups Yard
Sandland Street
London WC1R 4PZ
T 0171 242 1168   F 0171 242 3143
100255.2725@compuserve.com
National lesbian and gay touring theatre company. Open Mon-Fri 10.30 am-6.30 pm. Interested to hear from lesbian playrights, directors, designers, etc. Unsolicited scripts welcomed.

Impulse Music Consultants
Geraldine Allen
18 Hillfield Park
Muswell Hill
London N10 3Q5
T 0181 444 8587   F 0181 245 0358
impulse@cerbernet.co.uk

NATIONAL- ARTS AND CRAFTS

Advise, plan, project-manage & promote creative endeavours. Work includes feasibility studies, appraisals, publicity, advice on every aspect of classical music. Promotes classical music on the internet, etc.

International Network on Contemporary Women's Writing
Cath Stowers
Centre for Women's Studies
University of York
Heslington
York YO1 5DD
T 01904 433675 F 01904 433433
CCAS1@york.gc.uk
International network of writers, academics, research students, general public working in contemporary women's writing. No charge to join. Three newsletters per year. publications, conferences, readings, etc.

IX Arts
Francesca Piovano
P O Box 3103
Greenwich
London SE10 9SR
T 0181 692 4050 F 0171 490 0938
International agency for women artists and film makers. Promoting works by women artists through exhibitions and showing in international context. Agency fees on application.

Knitting and Crochet Guild
Anne Budworth, Membership Secretary
228 Chester Road North
Kidderminster DY10 1TH
T 01562 754367
100023.2353@compuserve.com
A society of enthusiasts with a creative need to turn yarn (of any kind) into a textile (of any kind) by means of hand knitting, machine knitting or crochet.

Museum of Women's Art (MWA)
Mae Keary/Belinda Harding
55-63 Goswell Road
London EC1V 7EN
T 0171 251 4881 F 0171 251 4883
Recovers, portrays & celebrates the work of women visual artists through the centuries. MWA intends to establish a centre of national/ international standing for the exhibition, research & study of women's art.

MUZE - Women Writers' Exchange
Stella Bellem
Kent County Council
Arts and Libraries
County Hall
Maidstone ME14 1XQ
T 01622 694454 F 01622 694465
stella.bellem@kent.gov.uk
Encourages & supports women writers through European exchanges.

National Campaign for the Arts
Jennifer Edwards
Francis House
Francis Street
London SW1P 1DE
T 0171 828 4448 F 0171 931 9959
nca@ecna.org
Independent advocacy organisation for all the arts. Membership open to individuals or organisations. Lobbies government & local government, produces research & briefings. Publishes Arts News.

New Playwrights' Trust
Angela Kelly
Interchange Studios
Dalby Street
London NW5 3NQ
T 0171 284 2818 F 0171 482 5292
upt@mail.ensyner.co.uk
National support & research network for new writing. Works with new writing in theatre, live art, performance poetry, television, radio, film & video. Advocates new writing, etc.

Royal School of Needlework, The
Mrs Elizabeth Elvin
Apartment 12a
Hampton Court Palace
East Molesey KT8 9AU
T 0181 943 1432 F 0181 943 4910
Open Mon-Fri 10 am-4 pm. Specialises in restoration of textiles & creation of new pieces of embroidery. Three-year apprenticeship scheme ensuring traditional skills of ornamental needlework are continued.

Sense of Sound
Jenny/Saphena/Juliet
33-45 Parr Street
Liverpool L1 4JN
T 0151 707 1050
Runs freelance singing workshops nationally. Focusses on improvisation & African music & looks at all areas of Black music. Aims to build up confidence. Acappella vocal workshops.

Sense of Sound Women's Vocal Agency
Jenny/Saphena/Juliet
33-35 Parr Street
Liverpool L1 4JN
T 0151 707 1050
Session singing agency specialising in female vocals. Provides singers for all forms of music, records & TV. All forms of pop, predominantly jazz, soul & blues. Represents singers nationally.

Society of Women Writers and Journalists
Jean Hawkes
110 Whitehall Road
Chingford
London E4 6DW
T 0181 529 0886
Encourages literary achievement, upholds professional standards & social contact with other writers. Lunchtime meetings held mainly monthly at Royal Scottish Corporation, 37 King street, Covent Garden.

Sphinx Theatre Company
Alison Gagen
25 Short Street
London SE1 8LJ
T 0171 401 9993 F 0171 401 9995
National touring theatre company specialising in new writing by women. One to two new productions annually to small & middle-scale venues. Annual conference for women in the arts organised by Sphinx.

Ulster Society of Women Artists
Gladys Maccabe
1A Church Road
Newtown Breda
Belfast BT8 4AL
T 01232 641189
Aims to promote & encourage a high standard of art in Ulster, to seek out & encourage talent, to maintain such a standard in exhibitions that election to membership be considered a mark of distinction.

Ulster Spinners and Weavers' Guild
The Hon Secretary
C/o Ulster Folk and Transport Museum
153 Bangor Road
Hollywood
County Down BT18 0EU

Visiting Arts
Melissa Naylor, General Enquiries
11 Portland Place
London W1N 4EJ
T 0171 389 3018 F 0171 389 3016
Facilitates in-coming foreign artists into the UK. Information, advice, publications, grants. Joint venture of Arts Councils, The British Council, The Foreign and Commonwealth Office and the Crafts Council.

Women's Playhouse Trust (WPT)
Jules Wright
6 Langley Street
London WC2H 9JA
T 0171 379 9700 F 0171 379 5936
Commissions and produces the work of writers, composers, choreographers, poets and visual artists. Note that it is NOT a grant giving body.

Women's Theatre Collection
Linda Fitzsimmons
Department of Drama, Uni of Bristol
Cantocks Close
Woodland Road
Bristol BS8 1UP
T 0117 928 8180 F 0117 928 7833
linda.fitzsimmons@bristol.ac.uk
The world's only archive & research collection dedicated to the preservation of a record of women's work in theatre. Holds international historical & contemporary material. Open Mon-Fri 9 am-5 pm

Workshop & Artists' Studio Provision - Scotland
Gillian Robertson/David Cook
256 Alexandra Parade
Glasgow G31 3AJ
T 0141 554 2499 F 0141 556 5340
Studios for visual artists & craftworkers, designers & cultural businesses. Not exclusively for women.

BEREAVEMENT

Child Bereavement Trust, The
Jennie Thomas, Director
Harleyford Estate
Henley Road
Marlow SL7 2DX
T 01628 488101 F 01628 488101
Cares for bereaved families by supporting the professional carer. Offers specialised training & support for all professionals caring for families in crisis. Helps bereaved families with information & resources.

Compassionate Friends, The
Rita Henshaw
9 Highfield Drive

Portishead BS20 8JG
T 01275 848130
Bereaved parents. Support through friendship, personal experience, etc. Publications. Help through group meetings & phone calls. Special groups for parents whose child has been murdered/committed suicide.

Cot Death Society, The
Geoff Noble
1 Browning Close
Thatcham RG18 3EF
T 01635 861771 F 01635 861771
socpil@aol.com
Support for parents who have suffered a cot death & advice on how to avoid risks of cot deaths.

Cruise Bereavement Care - Scotland
Hazel Walker, Co-ordinator
Baltic Chambers
50 Wellington Street
Glasgow G2 JHJ
T 0141 248 1602
Helpline: 0141 248 2199. Free service for anyone bereaved. One-to-one counselling, group support, practical advice. For people to work through grief in a safe environment. Phone for details of local groups.

CRUSE Bereavement Care
Elisabeth Linwood
Cruse House
126 Sheen Road
Richmond TW9 1UR
T 0181 940 4818 F 0181 940 7638
Provides free one-to-one counselling to anyone bereaved. Practical help, social support & publications. Bereavement helpline 0181 332 7227 open Mon-Fri 9.30 am-5 pm. Phone for details of local groups.

CRUSE Bereavement Care (Scotland)
Mrs Ruth Hampton
33-35 Boswall Parkway
Edinburgh EH5 2BR
T 0131 551 1511
Counselling for the bereaved; advice & information; social groups. Training. One-day seminars for lay people & professionals.

Foundation for the Study of Infant Deaths (FSID)
Kate Thomas
14 Halkin Street
London SW1X 7DP
T 0171 235 0965 F 0171 823 1986
fsid@dial.pipex.com
Provides information about cot deaths through a wide range of publications, special conferences & helpline. Monitors medical research & cot death issues worldwide. 24-hour helpline: 0171 235 1721.

Miscarriage Association
Ruth Bender Atik, National Director
C/o Clayton Hospital
Northgate
Wakefield WF1 3JS
T 01924 200799 F 01924 298834
Open 9 am-4 pm. Ansaphone out of hours. Provides information & support for women who have suffered a pregnancy loss. A network of local contacts around the UK with whom women can share their feelings.

Miscarriage Association - Scotland
23 Castle Street
Edinburgh EH2 3DN
T 0131 220 3841 F 0131 220 3841
Helpline: 0131 334 8883 - 24-hour ansaphone. Providing support during & after miscarriage. Support groups & befriending. For free information pack, send large sae to above address.

National Association of Widows
Lynne Davies, Information Officer
54-57 Allison Street
Digbeth
Birmingham B5 5TH
T 0121 643 8348
Advice & information provided to all widows, their families & friends. Friendly, supportive social life through nationwide branches. Contact lists, including one for young widows. Service free of charge.

National Child Death Help Line

T 0800 282986
Freephone on Wed 10 am-1 pm & evenings 7-10 pm

Northern Ireland Widows Association
Lilly Abbott
Primrose Hill
92 Derryloughan Road
Loughall
County Armagh
T 01762 891551

Umbrella organisation for various widows' associations in Northern Ireland acting as emotional support to counteract isolation. Meets once a month. Phone for further details.

Scottish Cot Death Trust
Mrs Hazel Brooke
Royal Hospital for Sick Children
Yorkhill
Glasgow G3 8SJ
T 0141 357 3946 F 0141 334 1376
Open Mon-Fri 9 am-5 pm. Aims to raise funds for research into cot death, improve support for bereaved parents & to help educate the public & healthcare professionals about cot deaths.

Stillbirth and Neonatal Death Society (SANDS)
28 Portland Place
London W1N 4DE
T 0171 436 7940 F 0171 436 3715
Helpline 0171 436 3715, open Mon-Fri 9.30 am-5.30 pm. Support through self-help groups & befriending to parents bereaved through neonatal death, stillbirth or miscarriages. Phone for details of local groups.

War Widows of Great Britain Association
17 The Earl's Croft
Coventry CV3 5ES
T 01203 503298
Formed to improve condition for all war widows & dependants. Works with government departments & service & ex-service organisations. Welfare support for members.

War Widows' Association of Great Britain
Mrs Irene Bloor
Bryn Hyfryd
1 Coach Lane
Stanton-in-Peak
Matlock DE4 2NA
T 01629 636374
Represents all war widows & service widows from 1914 to present day. Aims to improve conditions for widows & dependants. National & local meetings. Aims to provide comfort, friendship & support. Publications.

War Widows' Association of Great Britain - Wales
Mrs Hazel Murphy, Hon Secretary
54 West Street
Gorseinon
Swansea SA4 4AF
T 01792 896219 F 01792 896219
Working on behalf of all war widows for their welfare. Holds regional meetings. AGM usually held in last week in March in various venues throughout the UK. Fund raising activities.

BUSINESS SUPPORT SCHEMES

Business and Professional Women (BPW) International
Sylvia G Perry, President
Studio 16
Cloisters Business Centre
8 Battersea Park Road
London SW8 4BG
T 0171 738 8323 F 0171 622 8528
106261.1573@compuserve.com
International federation of business & professional women.

Business and Professional Women (BPW) UK Ltd
Rita Bangle
23 Ansdell Street
Kensington
London W8 5BN
T 0171 938 1729 F 0171 938 2037
A networking, training & lobbying organisation. Membership open to all working women or women on career breaks. Aim is to encourage women to achieve their full potential. Membership details from address above.

Business and Professional Women (BPW) UK Ltd - NI
Elaine McCrory
76 Forest Hill
Conlig
Newtownards
County Down BT23 3FL
T 01232 898183 F 01232 898169
A training, networking & lobbying organisation for working women. There are 18 clubs in Northern Ireland which meet on a monthly basis.

Club 2000
Irene Harris
4 Paddington Street
London W1M 3LA
T 0171 224 4388 F 0171 486 7681
Networking organisation for senior management women. Meets monthly, usually either last Wed or Thurs of each month in central London.

NATIONAL - BUSINESS SUPPORT SCHEMES

Federation of Business and Professional Women's Clubs
Dr Breda Scanlon
Church Street
Tullamore
County Offaly
T 0506 21170
Helping women to realise their potential; encouraging girls to speak & present themselves in schools. Arranges a competition for a young woman business entrepreneur.

International Training in Communication
Edna M Chapman
112 Oxbridge Lane
Stockton-on-Tees TS18 4HW
T 01642 673905
Training in communication & leadership skills. Preparing people for opportunities to move ahead in work/business/public life. Increases daily effectiveness. Stockton club meets twice monthly for two hours.

Network
Erica Groat
114b Cleveland Street
London W1P 5DN
T 0171 388 7383 F 0171 388 2290
106103.671@compuserve.com
For influential women. Offers an environment providing business, professional & development opportunities, with support from other women who have experienced the difficulties that are barriers to achievement.

NETWORK - The Organisation for Women in Business
19 Whitehall Road
Terenure
Dublin 12
T 01 455 6628 F 01 455 9400
National organisation for the advancement of women in business, professions & the arts. Helping women to develop formal & informal networks. Organises business seminars. Affiliated to the Small Firms Assn.

New Ways to Work
Margaret Ohren
309 Upper Street
London N1 2TY
T 0171 354 2978

Provides information & advice on flexible working arrangements; runs training seminars & conference workshops; provides advice for government & policy forums. Information packs; telephone help line.

Opportunity 2000
Pat Corcoran
44 Baker Street
London W1M 1DH
T 0171 224 1600 F 0171 486 1700
Open Mon-Fri 9 am-6 pm. A business-led campaign, part of the Business in the Community initiative, with the objective to increase the quality & quantity of women's employment opportunities.

Pepperell Network
C/o The Industrial Society
48 Bryanston Square
London W1H 7LN
T 0171 262 2401
A network for women within the Industrial Society.

Professional Women's Development Unit
Chris Garner
Staffordshire University
Unit 19
Hollies Avenue
Cannock WS11 1DW
T 01543 573054 F 01543 467947
Offering a comprehensive service of women's development & training to employers & individuals. Consultancy & research. Training & development in the form of in-house training, conferences, seminars, networking.

Soroptimist International
Kay Howard
127 Wellington Road South
Stockport SK1 3TS
T 0161 480 7686
For professional women active in business. Aims to maintain high ethical standards & to advance the status of women. Activities include education & health issues. Phone for details of local branches.

Training 2000
Sheena Briley
Dalian House
350 St Vincent Street
Glasgow G3 8XQ
T 0141 248 4486 F 0141 248 4489

Works to promote & support women's training in Scotland. Provides an extensive range of services to employers & women.

Women Entering Business (WEB)
Antonia Korrigan, Project Manager
512 Main Street
Tallagh
Dublin 24
T 01 459 0223 F 01 459 6183
webnow@aonad.iol.ie
Aims to encourage women who have been employed long-term to start up their own enterprises. Integrated framework of training & support. Enterprise development prgramme under the auspices of NOW.

Women In Management
Marian Watson
5th Floor
45 Beech Street
London EC2Y 8AD
T 0171 382 9978 F 0171 382 9979
Networking organisation for women managers of all levels. A chance to meet like-minded people. Offers relevant training & development. Supports those who wish to progress thier careers. Social events.

Women in the Public Sector
Pamela Whitford-Jackson
Morven Lodge
121 Welcomes Road
Kenley CR8 5HB
T 0181 645 0508 F 0181 645 0508
Networking for women in the public sector. Aim is to help women to fulfil their potential. Also aim to reduce sense of isolation which women managers often feel. Provides an information exchange. Publications.

Women Into Business
Jacqueline Russell-Lowe
Curzon House
Church Road
Windlesham GU20 6BH
T 01276 452010 F 01276 451602
SBB@compuserve.com
Aims to give successful businesswomen a higher national profile & greater visibility so as to publicise & acknowledge their achievements & contributions to the economy. Counselling service.

Women Mean Business
Jules Cranfield or Liz York
27 Poplar Court

Old Ruislip Road
Northolt
Middlesex UB5 6QG
T 0181 845 9945 F 0181 841 0802
Lesbian networking group. Regular meeting & social events.

CARERS

Carers' National Association
Gail Elkington
Ruth Pitter House
20-25 Glasshouse Yard
London EC1A 4JS
T 0171 490 8818 F 0171 490 8824
Carers' helpline: 0171 490 8898 open Mon-Fri 1-4 pm. The Association encourages carers to recognise their own needs, helps to develop appropriate support for carers, provides information and advice, etc.

Carers' National Association in Wales
Mrs O Melding, Coordinator
Pant Glas Industrial Estate
Bedwas
Newport NP1 8DR
T 01222 880176 F 01222 886656
Providing information & advice for carers in Wales; making carers aware of their role & status in society; encouraging them to recognise their own needs & helping them to achieve empowerment, control & choices.

Crossroads (Scotland) Care Attendant Schemes
John Thomas, Chief Executive
24 George Square
Glasgow G2 1EG
T 0141 226 3793 F 0141 221 7130
Providing respite care to carers. There are over 50 schemes spread throughout Scotland, currently supporting over 7,000 carers and their families.

CENTRES FOR WOMEN

West Indian Women's Association
Mrs Violet Smith, Chair
C/o William Morris Community Centre
Greenleaf Road
London E17 6QQ
T 0181 521 4456
Open 9 am-5 pm. Provides advice & information. Helps with families' welfare. Advice & counselling; training schemes. Holds discussions on family relationships & childcare.

CHILD CARE AND FAMILY

Action for Sick Children
Cheryl Hooper, Projects Director
Argyle House

29-31 Euston Road
London NW1 2SD
T 0171 833 2041   F 0171 837 2110
Open Mon & Wed 9 am-5 pm. Ansaphone at all other times. Aims to raise standards of health care for all children, whether in hospital or at home. There is a library & information service. Publications.

Action for Sick Children - Scotland
Josephine Ward, Coordinator
15 Smith's Place
Edinburgh EH6 8NT
T 0131 553 6553   F 0131 553 6553
Open Mon-Fri 9.30 am-1.30 pm. Supports sick children & their families & works to ensure that health services are planned for them. Promotes high quality health care for sick children at home & in hospitals.

Action on Child Expoitation (ACHE)
C/o British Assn of Social Workers
28 North Bridge
Edinburgh EH11 1QG
T 0131 225 4549   F 0131 220 0636
Educating the public about problems of paedophilia, child pornography & abuse in Britain.

AFASIC - Overcoming Speech Impairments
347 Central Markets
London EC1A 9NH
T 0171 236 6487   F 0171 236 8115
Promotes understanding, acceptance, equal opportunities & integration into society of children & young adults with speech & language impairments.

Anti-Bullying Campaign
10 Borough High Street
London SE1 9PP
T 0171 378 1446

Bristol Association for Neighbourhood Daycare Ltd
Paul Dielhenn
81 St Nicholas Road
St Pauls
Bristol BS2 9JJ
T 0117 954 2128   F 0117 954 1694
Promoting/supporting development of out of school clubs for school age children of working/training parents; acknowledging needs of single parent and/or low income families.

British Institute for Brain Injured Children
Mrs Caron Lane, Head of Clinic
Knowle Hall
Knowle
Bridgewater TA7 8PJ
T 01278 684060   F 01278 685573
For parents who want to give their children opportunities to develop ther full potential. Individual stimulatory programmes taught to parents during a week spent at BIBIC for child's assessment & evaluation.

Centre for Fun and Families, The
David Neville
25 Shanklin Drive
Knighton
Leicester LE2 3RH
T 0116 270 7198
To assist familes where parents are experiencing behaviour & communication difficulties with their children & young people; developing a constructive approach to parenting; networks of parent support groups.

Child & Family Trust, The
Heather Molloy
Fleming House
134 Renfrew Street
Glasgow G3 6ST
T 0141 353 2424   F 0141 353 2424
Supplies Fulton Mackay nurses working in the community with children and families. Special-needs children: sexually abused/with hyperkinetic disorder/will have tried to commit self-harm or suicide.

Child Accident Prevention Trust
4th Floor
Clerks Court
18-20 Farringdon Lane
London EC1R 3AU
T 0171 608 3828   F 0171 608 3674
Encourages investigation & research into accidents in childhood. Organises annual 'Child Safety Week' & provides information & advice to parents.

Childline
Valerie Howarth, Executive Director
2nd Floor
Royal Mail Building
Studd Street
London N1 0QW
T 0171 239 1000   F 0171 239 2300

NATIONAL - CHILD CARE AND FAMILY

Free national helpline - 0800 1111 24 hours every day for children & young people in danger & distress. Confidential phone counselling service. 0800 884444 open daily 6-10 pm childline for children in care.

Childline Scotland
18 Albion Street
Glasgow G1 1LH
T 0141 552 1123 F 0141 552 3089
Free & confidential national helplines: 0800 1111 (24 hours, 7 days a week); 0800 884444 for counselling for young people in care. For children & young people with any problem.

Children 1st
Melville House
41 Polworth Terrace
Edinburgh EH11 1NG
T 0131 337 8539 F 0131 346 8284
Aims to prevent the abuse & neglect of children & to protect children who may be at risk.

Children in Scotland
Annie Gunner
Princes House
5 Shandwick Place
Edinburgh EH2 4RG
T 0131 228 8484 F 0131 228 8585
Open 9 am-5 pm Mon-Fri. National agency for voluntary, statutory, professional organisations/ individuals working with children & their families in Scotland.

Children's Home-Based Education Association
14 Basil Avenue
Amthorpe
Doncaster DN3 2AT

Children's Legal Centre
University of Essex
Wivenhoe Park
Colchester CO4 3SQ
T 01206 873820 F 01206 874026
Advice line open Mon-Fri 10 am-12 noon & 2-5 pm. Campaigns for recognition of children & young people as individuals participating fully in all decisions affecting their lives. Free, confidential advice.

Concern for Family and Womanhood (CFW)
Mrs Yvonne Stayt, Hon General Secretary
Springfield House

Chedworth
Cheltenham GL54 4AH
T 01285 720454
Advancing education in, preserving, & promoting the proper (sic) man-woman relationship, masculinity, femininity, different sex roles, marriage & family unit according to natural (sic) sex differences, etc.

Contact A Family
parent advisers
170 Tottenham Court Road
London W1P 0HA
T 0171 383 3555 F 0171 383 0259
National charity for parents & professionals involved with or caring for a child with special needs. A network of local & national mutual support & self-help groups brings families together. Advice & guidance.

Council for Disabled Children
Wendy Beecher, Information Officer
8 Wakley Street
London EC1V 7QE
T 0171 843 6000 F 0171 278 9512
Represents wide range of professional, voluntary & statutory agencies with broad interest in services for children & young people with disabilities & special educational needs, & their families.

CRY-SIS Support Group
June Jordan, Admin
B M CRY-SIS
London WC1N 3XX
T 0171 404 5011 F 01634 710913
Self-help & support for families with excessively crying, sleepless & demanding young children. Support via helpline or post. Publications. Helpline (listed above) open 8 am-11 pm all week.

Daycare Trust
Lucy Lloyd
4 Wild Court
London WC2B 4AU
T 0171 405 5617 F 0171 831 6632
Generates & provides information & develops policy on children through advice, research, publications, conferences, campaigns & consultancy. Childcare hotline 0171 405 5617 open Mon-Fri 9.30 am-5.30 pm.

Disabled Children's Foundation
Leslie Henderson, Chief Executive
11/23 Royal Chambers
110 Station Parade

NATIONAL - CHILD CARE AND FAMILY

Harrogate HG1 1EP
T 01423 509863 F 014233 569020
Helps with provision of equipment for disabled children which statutory welfare organisations cannot fund, such as voice synthesizers, portable communication aids, light-weight manual & electric wheelchairs.

Education Otherwise
P O Box 7420
London N9 9SG
Supporting the right to educate children at home.

Exploring Parenthood
National Parenting Development Centre
4 Ivory Place
20a Treadgold Street
London W11 4BP
T 0171 221 4471 F 0171 221 5501
Aims to prevent stress & breakdown in family life by offering one-stop parents' support line.

Family Care
Linda Paterson
21 Castle Street
Edinburgh EH2 3DU
T 0131 225 6441 F 0131 225 6441
Provides Birthlink, the National Adoption Contact Register for Scotland. Counselling, search for birth relatives service, accessing court & adoption records, mediation, post reunion counselling, etc.

Family Education Trust
Valerie Riches
322 Woodstock Road
Oxford OX2 7NS
T 01865 556848 F 01865 552774
Carries out & promotes research into the social, medical, economic & psychological nature of family breakdown. Publications & videos to promote the welfare of the family founded on marriage.

Family Holiday Association
Jenny Stephenson
16 Mortimer Street
London W1N 7RD
T 0171 436 3304 F 0171 436 3302
Provides grants for holidays for families/women with children in great need of a break. Criteria are: low income, no holiday for a number of years, at least one child aged 2-18 years old. Referral necessary.

Family Information Network on Disability - Scotland
Jeanette Hodge
C/o Sparky Disability Awareness Project
Block 5, Unit A4
Templeton Business Centre
Glasgow G40 1DA
T 0141 554 2388
Parent-to-parent support. Group 2 network for families/carers of disabled children. Helpline. Parent-to-parent counselling. Workshops provided.

Family Mediation Scotland
Gay Cox, Publicity Officer
127 Rose Street
South Lane
Edinburgh EH2 4BB
T 0131 220 1610 F 0131 220 6895
Supports affiliated mediation services throughout Scotland to meet needs of children in separation & divorce. Enabling people to negotiate their own mutually acceptable resolutions to issues, etc.

Family Rights Group
The Print House
18 Ashwin Street
London E8 3DL
T 0171 923 2628 F 0171 923 2683
Open Mon-Fri. Advice line 0171 249 0008 open Mon-Fri 1.30-3.30 pm. To improve the law & practice around services for families with children, needing or receiving family support services. Free advice/advocacy.

Full Time Mothers
P O Box 186
London SW3 5RF
Promoting understanding of the child's need for a full-time mother; enhancing the status & self-esteem of mothers at home; campaigning for changes in the tax & benefits system & in employment policies; etc.

Gifted Children's Information Centre
Dr P J Congdon
Hampton Grange
21 Hampton Lane
Solihull B91 2QJ
T 0121 705 4547
Publishes & disseminates practical information about gifted & talented children, designed for teachers, parents & children. Runs advice/guidance service on special educational needs. Psychological assessments.

NATIONAL - CHILD CARE AND FAMILY

Hyperactive Children's Support Group (HACSG)
The Secretary
71 Whyke Lane
Chichester PO19 2LD
T 01903 725182 F 01903 734726
To help & support hyperactive children & their parents; to conduct research & promote investigation into the incidence of hyperactivity in the UK: its causes & treatments; to disseminate information.

I CAN (Invalid Children's Aid Nationwide)
Barbican City Gate
1-3 Dufferin Street
London EC1Y 8NA
T 0171 374 4422 F 0171 374 2762
Helping disabled children & young people & their families to live as full a life as possible, regardless of type of disability.

In Touch
Ann Worthington
10 Norman Road
Sale M33 3DF
T 0161 905 2440 F 0161 781 5787
Service available Mon-Fri 10 am-6 pm. Contacts & information for parents of children with special needs. Links parents of children with rare disorders. Referral to appropriate support groups. Publications.

Irish Pre-School Playgroups Association (IPPA)
Hilary Kenny
SPADE Centre
North King Street
Dublin 7
T 01 671 9245
Committed to enhancing the lives of children & their families by supporting the development of quality play-based early years services.

Kids' Club Network
Anne Longfield
Bellerive House
3 Muirfield Crescent
London E14 9SZ
T 0171 512 2112 F 0171 512 2010
The national organisation for out-of-school childcare. Provides publications, information, training & quality assurance to support the development of high quality kids' clubs. Campaigns for better childcare.

Kidscape
152 Buckingham Palace Road
London
T 0171 730 3300 F 0171 730 7081
Preventing abuse of children through education programmes. Parents' bullying helpline Tue & Wed on above number.

Kidscape
152 Buckingham Palace Road
London SW1W 9TR
T 0171 730 3300 F 0171 730 7081
Preventing child abuse through education programmes for parents & teachers.

National Association for Gifted Children
Park Campus
Boughton Green Road
Northampton NN2 7AL
T 01604 792300 F 01604 720636
Promoting the welfare of gifted children, their parents & families. Information, advice & support.

National Association for Gifted Children in Scotland
Mrs Susan Divecha, Information Officer
73 Castlehill Drive
Glasgow G77 5LB
T 0141 639 4797
Scottish charity run by volunteers bringing together teachers, parents & others interested in educational provision for gifted children, as well as their social & emotional development.

National Association for Maternal and Child Welfare
Valerie A Farebrother, Chair
40-42 Osnaburgh Street
London NW1 3ND
T 0171 383 4117 F 0171 383 4115
Aims to further education & training in relation to maternal & child welfare. Research, conferences, study days, meetings. Education & training for child care, nursery nurses & child minders.

National Association of Toy and Leisure Libraries
Glenys Carter, Director
68 Churchway
London NW1 1LT
T 0171 387 9592 F 0171 383 2714

Loans good quality toys to families with young children, including those with special needs. Aims to provide friendship & support for parents & other carers. Publishes booklets relating to toys & play; etc.

National Campaign for Nursery Education
Stephanie Collis, Hon Sec
BCM Box 6216
London WC1N 3XX
Campaigning for state provision of nursery education for all 3 & 4 year old children whose parents wish them to receive it. All nursery classes should be fully staffed by trained early years teachers; etc.

National Child Minding Association in Wales
Meryl Evans, Principal Officer
Offices 4 & 5
The Lighthouse Business Park
Bastion Road
Prestatyn LL19 7ND
T 01745 852995 F 01745 852995

National Childcare Campaign
4 Wild Court
London WC2B 4AU
T 0171 405 5618

National Childminding Association
8 Masons Hill
Bromley BR2 9EY
T 0181 464 6164 F 0181 290 6834
Promotes childminding as a quality childcare service. Supports childminders & parents & lobbies central & local government on childminding issues. Free information pack available on receipt of A5 sae.

National Children's Bureau
8 Wakley Street
London EC1V 7QE
T 0171 843 6000 F 0171 278 9512
Concerned with children's needs in the family, school & society.

National Children's Centre
Hazel Wigmore
Brian Jackson House
New North Parade
Huddersfield HD1 5JP
T 01484 519988 F 01484 435150
Small independent charity providing advice, information & services in the local area with dissemination of policy and practice nationally.

National Early Years Network
77 Holloway Road
London N7 8JZ
T 0171 607 9573 F 0171 700 1105
Information & practical support about children aged 5 & under regarding their education & childcare. National register & directories to help people keep in touch.

National Society for the Prevention of Cruelty To Children
National Centre
42 Curtain Road
London EC2A 3NH
T 0171 825 2500 F 0171 825 2525
Aims to prevent children suffering from significant harm resulting from ill-treatment; helps abused children; works to protect children from further harm. Free 24-hour phone helpline: 0800 800 500.

National Stepfamily Organisation
3rd Floor
Chapel House
18 Hatton Place
London EC1N 8RU
T 0171 209 2460 F 0171 209 2461
Counselling helpline: 0990 168 388 open Mon-Fri 2-5 pm & 7-10 pm. Provides support, advice & information for all members of stepfamilies & those who work with them. Increases awareness. Research.

NCH Action for Children
85 Highbury Park
London N5 1UD
T 0171 226 2033 F 0171 226 2537
Campaigns for the rights of children & families. Aims to improve the quality of life of some of Britain's most vulnerable children & their families.

NiPPA - The Early Years' Organisation
Helen Jenkins
Enterprize House
Boucher Crescent
Belfast BT12 6HU
T 01232 662825 F 01232 381270
info.nippa.cinni@nics.gov.uk
19 branches throughout Northern Ireland meeting locally and providing a forum for early years workers, parents & those interested in the care and education of young children & their families. Provides training.

NATIONAL- CHILD CARE AND FAMILY

Northern Ireland Childminding Association
Mrs Bridget Nodder
17a Court Street
Newtownards
County Down BT23 7NX
T 01247 811015 F 01247 820921
Supports childminders, parents & children. Promotes childminding as quality childcare & education service; provides training in child care & education; encourages legal childminding; provides support network.

OMEP (Ireland)
P O Box 2227
Dublin 1
T 01 821 6476 F 01 821 6476
aust@iol.ie
Irish branch of the World Organisation for Early Childhood Education. Umbrella organisation for organisations & individuals concerned with early childhood education. Regular meetings for members.

Parent Network
Room 2, Winchester House
Kennington Park
11 Cranmer Road
London SW9 6EJ
T 0171 735 4596 F 0171 735 4692
Groups for parents run by trained parents in local areas at reasonable cost. 13 weekly sessions offering parents ideas for handling daily problems of family life in new ways. Parent enquiry line: 0171 735 1214.

Parent Resource and Mother Support (PRAMS)
Pip Hughes
Churchgate House
96 Churchgate
Stockport SK1 1YJ
T 0161 477 0606 F 0161 477 0606
Open Mon-Thurs 9 am-4.45 pm; Fri 9.30 am-1 pm. Information & support for parents/carers of young children & professionals. Information held on local, regional & national self-help groups. Counselling.

Parentline
Endway House
The Endway
Hadleigh SS7 2AN
T 01702 554782 F 01702 554911
Helpline 01702 559900. Office open Mon-Fri 9 am-4 pm. Provides support for parents under stress & aims to prevent child abuse.

Parentline Wales/Cymru
Kay Griffiths
C/o St Illtyds Family Centre
Station Road
Llantwit Major CF61 1ST
T 01446 795595
Open Wed & Fri 1-3 pm. Helpline for parents/carers of children under stress. Listening service. Details of other agencies available when necessary.

Parents at Work
45 Beech Street
London EC2Y 8AD
T 0171 628 3591 F 0171 628 3591
Campaigns on behalf of working parents around issues such as childcare, leave, financial security for working parents.

Pre-School Learning Alliance
John Randall, Information Officer
61-69 King's Cross Road
London WC1X 9LL
T 0171 833 0991 F 0171 837 4942
To enhance the development and education of children primarily under statutory school age by encouraging parents to understand and provide for the needs of their children through community groups.

Reunite - National Council for Abducted Children
Samantha Edwards/Denise Carter
P O Box 4
London WC1X 3DX
T 0171 404 8357 F 0171 242 1512
reunite@dircon.co.uk
Advice, support, information given to parents who fear abduction of children or whose children have been abducted. Advice line open Mon & Fri 11 am-3 pm; Tue & Thurs 2-5 pm; Wed 1-8 pm 0171 404 8356.

Scottish Childminding Association
Maggie Simpson, National Development Officer
Room 7
Stirling Business Centre
Wellgreen
Stirling FK8 2DZ
T 01786 445377 F 01786 449062
Provides information and training to childminders. Promotes childminding as a quality child care service. Advice line: 01786 445063. Open Mon-Thurs 9 a.m-12 pm and 1-5 pm. Fri 9 am-12 pm; 1-4.30 pm.

NATIONAL- COMPUTERS/IT

Scottish Early Years and Family Network
Peter Lee, Director
Floor 4, St Andrew House
141 West Nile Street
Glasgow G1 2RN
T 0141 353 1710 F 0141 353 1443
Promotes quality childcare and education. Networks both nationally & locally.

Scottish Out of School Care Network
Shirley Norrie
Floor 9
Fleming House
134 Renfrew Street
Glasgow G3 6ST
T 0141 331 1301 F 0141 332 1206
Support, information, resources to all involved in out-of-school care. Telephone advice Mon-Fri 9 am-5 pm. Helps develop local out-of-school care networks. Holds training events. Liaises with local govt.

Scottish Pre-School Play Association (SPPA)
Mrs Elaine Smith
SPPA National Centre
14 Elliot Place
Glasgow G3 8EP
T 0141 221 4148 F 0141 221 6043
Committed to the development of quality care and education in pre-school groups which respect the rights, responsibilities and needs of all children and their parents. Open Mon-Fri 9 am- 4.30 pm.

Stepping Stones in Scotland
policy and information officer
55 Renfrew Street
Glasgow G2 3BD
T 0141 331 2828 F 0141 331 1991
Works to empower families with young children & young adults living in disadvantaged communities so they can effectively seek to improve their own lives & the communities in which they live.

Wales Pre-School Playgroups Association/PPA Cymru
Mrs Wendy Hawkins, National Executive Officer
2a Chester Street
Wrexham LL13 8BD
T 01978 358195 F 01978 312335
Open Mon-Fri 9 am-4.30 pm. Enhancing development, care & education of pre-school children in Wales by encouraging parents to understand & provide for their needs through high quality pre-school groups.

Women's Forum Northern Ireland
Sadie McClelland
3 Beechill Park Avenue
Belfast BT8 4PR
T 01232 701285
Promotes public welfare for women & children. Communicates & cooperates with voluntary organisations. Discussion of issues on public welfare & taking action where necessary in problem areas.

Working for Childcare
Scarlett Dewar, Information Officer
77 Holloway Road
London N7 8JZ
T 0171 700 0281 F 0171 700 1105
Promotes & develops quality affordable childcare for all working parents who need it. Information & advice provided on all aspects of employer-supported childcare. Publications, training for nursery staff, etc.

Working Mothers' Association
Spencer Walk
London SW15 1PL

COMPUTERS/IT

Equal Opportunties for Girls in Information Technology
Christine Whitehouse
School of Computing, P O Box 334
Staffordshire University
Beaconside
Stafford ST18 0DG
T 01782 294000 F 01785 353497
C.Whitehouse@soc.ac.uk
Set up to help educate young people to understand the opportunities & careers available to them within the computing industry & to remove gender sterotyping.

Women into Computing (WiC)
Judy Emms, Secretary
The Open University
4 Portwall Lane
Bristol BS1 6ND
T 0117 929 9641 F 0117 925 5215
jackie.archibald@sunderland.ac.uk
Encouraging women to study & undertake a career in computing & information technology. Pressure group concerned with gender discrimination within computing.

CONTRACEPTION/WELL WOMAN

Birth Control Trust
Ann Furedi
16 Mortimer Street
London W1N 7RD
T 0171 580 9360 F 0171 637 1378

NATIONAL - COUNSELLING AND THERAPY

bct@birthcontroltrust.org.uk
Educating women & men in procreation & contraception. Aims to prevent poverty & hardship caused by unwanted pregancies. Promotes medical & sociological research in contraception, sterilisation, legal abortion.

Brook Advisory Centres
Carole Study
165 Grays Inn Road
London WC1X 8UD
T 0171 833 8488 F 0171 833 8182
24 hour helpline: 0171 617 8000. To prevent & mitigate suffering caused by unwanted pregnancy by educating young persons in sexual & contraceptive matters.

Family Planning Association
Margaret McGovern, Information & Library Officer
2-12 Pentonville Road
London N1 9FP
T 0171 837 5432 F 0171 837 3034
Information service & helpline 0171 837 4044 open Mon-Fri 9 am-7 pm. Family planning & sexual health. Reference library, publications, research. Mail order service & training courses for professionals.

Family Planning Association Northern Ireland
113 University Street
Belfast BT7 1HP
T 01232 325488 F 01232 312212
Advice & information centre relating to contraception. Also pregnancy testing & counselling. Clinics on Mon-Thurs 9 am-5 pm; Fri 9 am-4.30 pm. Free service.

Family Planning Association Scotland
Jackie Nicholson
Unit 10
Firhill Business Centre
76 Firhill Road
Glasgow G20 7BA
T 0141 576 5088 F 0141 576 5006
Provides information around contraception via helpline (above) to all of Scotland. Open Mon-Thurs 9 am-5 pm (Fri 4.30 pm). Ansaphone at all other times. Publications & resource centre.

International Planned Parenthood Federation (IPPF)
Jeremy Hammond
Regent's College
Inner Circle
Regent's Park
London NW1 4NS
T 0171 487 7900
Initiates & supports contraceptive services worldwide. Promotes benefits for the family of spacing & planning births.

Irish Family Planning Association (IFPA)
4th Floor
Unity Building
16-17 Lower O'Connell Street
Dublin 1
T 01 878 0366 F 01 878 0375
Open Mon-Fri 9.30 am-5.30 pm. Has a list of main family planning clinics throughout the Republic of Ireland.

Marie Stopes International
Helen Axby, Director UK Clinics
153-157 Cleveland Street
London W1P 5PG
T 0171 574 7400 F 0171 574 7418
Pregancy advice (helpline 0171 388 4843); general healthcare/contraception (helpline 0171 388 0662); sterilisation services (helpline 0171 388 5554); well woman clinics; abortion clinics; menopause clinics; etc.

Population Concern
Kathy Siddle, Information Officer
178-202 Great Portland Street
London W1N 5TB
T 0171 631 1546 F 0171 436 2143
population.concern@ukonline.co.uk
Development projects in 20+ countries. Considers access to reproductive health information & services & improvement of women's status vital parts of development. Growing advocacy & education programme in UK.

Scottish Association for Natural Family Planning, The
Jean Carroll/Lucille McQuade
196 Clyde Street
Glasgow G1 4JY
T 0141 221 0858 F 0141 221 0858
Information about fertility, individual counselling on modern natural family planning methods. Contraceptive facts, STDs & HIV/AIDS available. 24-hour answer machine. Office open 13 hours a week. Free service.

COUNSELLING AND THERAPY

British Victims of Abortion
P O Box 91
Glasgow G1 2DB

NATIONAL - COUNSELLING AND THERAPY

T 0141 226 5407
Counselling & help offered to those experiencing physical/emotional difficulties after an abortion.

Careline
Gerry Burnikell
Cardinal Heenan Centre
326 High Road
Ilford IG1 1QP
T 0181 514 5444   F 0181 478 7943
0181 514 1177 counselling line open Mon-Fri 10 am-4 pm & 7-10 pm. Trained counsellors take calls nationally on issues such as child abuse, mental health & depression. For children, young people & adults.

Confederation of Scottish Counselling Agencies (COSCA)
64 Murray Place
Stirling FK8 2BX
T 01786 475140   F 01786 446207
The national professional body supporting counselling in Scotland. Advancing the development of, and supporting, organisations/individuals providing counselling.

Crisis Counselling for Alleged Shoplifters (CCAS)
Harry Kauffer
P O Box 147
Stanmore
Middlesex HA7 4YT
T 0181 958 8859
Two helpline numbers: 0171 722 3685 & 0181 202 5787. Provides crisis counselling & advice to people accused of shoplifting offences. Phone Mon-Fri between 9.30 am-6.30 pm

Divorce Mediation and Counselling Service
Faith Spicer
38 Ebury Street
London SW1W 0LU
T 0171 730 2422
Helps parents maintain workable arrangements for their children & themselves. Counselling to individuals pre or post divorce.

MIND
Angela Hendra
15-19 Broadway
London E15 4BQ
T 0181 519 2122   F 0181 522 1725

National information lines open Mon-Fri 9.15 am-5.45 pm (closed Tue am): 0181 522 1728 (inside London) & 0345 660 163 (outside London). Mental health charity. Phone for details of local groups for women.

Post Abortion Counselling Service (PACS)
Pat Garrard
340 Westbourne Park Road
London W11 1EQ
T 0171 221 9631
Counselling for women (& their partners) to talk about abortions. Maximum 10 sessions. Day & evening work. Counselling correspondence service with appropriate referrals. Wheelchair access.

Threshold Women's Mental Health Initiative
Sue Davis, Director
14 St George's Place
Brighton BN1 4GB
T 01273 626444
A women's community based drop-in service; counselling & therapy service; facilitation of self-help groups; training/consultancy on women & mental health issues; supportive contact with women; etc.

Women and Girls Network
Kim Thomas
P O Box 13095
London W14 0FE
T 0171 610 4678
Telephone/face to face counselling & complementary therapies for girls/women who have experienced any form of violence. Open Mon-Fri 10 am-5 pm. Counselling line Wed 12-4 pm: 0171 610 4345.

Women Unlimited
Sipora Levy
79 Pathfield Road
London SW16 5PA
T 0181 677 7503
Aiming to improve the working & personal lives of women by providing low cost workshops, short courses & individual counselling. Consultancy to voluntary organisations around the same issues.

Women's Therapy Centre, The
Siobhan Lanigan, Director
6-9 Manor Gardens
London N7 6LA
T 0171 263 6200   F 0171 281 7879

Provides psychoanalytic psychotherapy, education & training for women by women. It exists to enable women to make changes in their lives. Aims to provide an accessible, gender-conscious service for women, etc.

DISABILITY

Access for Disabled People to Arts Premises Today
Mrs Ann Packard, Director
Cameron House
Abbey Park Place
Dunfermline KY12 7P2
T 01383 623166 F 01383 622149
TheADAPTTrust@compuserve.com
Nationwide agency seeking to secure effective access at arts & heritage venues by 2001. Provides appraisals of plans, access audits of all types & size of premises & operates grant schemes.

Action for Blind People
Guy Neely, Director
14-16 Verney Road
London SE16 3DZ
T 0171 732 8771
Open Mon-Fri 9 am-5 pm. Services for visually impaired people. Information & advice, employment & training, accommodation, residential care, hostels, holidays. Grants for indidividuals.

Advisory Committee on Telecommunications for Disabled/Elderly
1st Floor
50 Ludgate Hill
London EC4M 7JJ
T 0171 634 8773 F 0171 634 8845
Minicom 0171 634 8769. Promoting better access to telecommunications networks for disabled & elderly people & providing a bridge between their needs & the telecommunications industry.

Anabledd Cymru/Disability Wales
Carol Thomas
Llys Ifor
Crescent Road
Caerphilly CF83 1XL
T 01222 887325 F 01222 888702
dw-ac@mcri.poptel.org.uk

Boadicea
C/o GLAD
336 Brixton Road
London SW9 7AA
T 0171 346 5800 F 0171 346 5810

Bi-monthly newsletter for disabled women and our women allies. Available in standard print, large print & on tape.

Break
Judith Davison
20 Hooks Hill Road
Sheringham NR26 8NL
T 01263 823170 F 01263 825560
Provides holidays, respite care & short-term breaks for children & adults with learning disabilities, & families with special needs. Facilities include: lift, indoor heated swimming pool, hoists, etc.

British Sports Association for the Disabled
Solecart House
13-27 Brunswick Place
London N1 6DX
T 0171 490 4919 F 0171 490 4914
Open Mon-Fri 9 am-5.30 pm. Minicom 1071 383 7332. Developed and coordinates sport and physical recreation for the disabled.

DIAL UK
Dorothy McGahan
Park Lodge
St Catherine's Hospital
Tickhill Road
Doncaster DN4 8QN
T 01302 310123 F 01302 310404
The national organisation for the DIAL network of disability advice centres. Contact DIAL UK on above phone number for details of local disability advice centres.

Disability Alliance Education and Research Association
Universal House
88-94 Wentworth Street
London E1 7SA
T 0171 247 8776 F 0171 247 8765
0171 247 8763 rights advice line. Open Mon-Fri 10 am-4 pm for general enquiries; Mon & Wed 2-4 pm for rights advice line, with help from trained adviser. Promotes wider understanding of needs of disabled.

Disability Awareness in Action (DAA)
11 Belgrave Road
London SW1V 1RB
T 0171 834 0477 F 0171 821 9539

NATIONAL- DISABILITY

Minicom 0171 821 9812. Open Mon-Fri 10 am-6 pm. An advice & information network for disabled people & their organisations worldwide, supporting self-help activities & ensuring equality of opportunity.

Disability Law Service
Room 241, 2nd Floor
49-51 Bedford Row
London WC1R 4LR
T 0171 831 8031 F 0171 831 5582
Open 9.30 am-5.30 pm. Free legal advice to disabled people, their families, carers & friends. Phone between 10 am-4.30 pm Wheelchair access. Nationwide service.

Disability Scotland
Princes House
5 Shandwick Place
Edinburgh EH2 4RG
T 0131 229 8632 F 0131 229 5168
The national umbrella organisation in Scotland concerned with disability. Campaigning, information, community care, etc.

Disabled Drivers' Association
Mrs Janet Rix, Office Manager
National HQ
Ashwellthorpe
Norwich NR16 1EX
T 01508 489449 F 01508 488173
Open Mon-Fri 9 am-4 pm. Run for & by disabled people. Encourages greater independence through enhanced mobility. Maintains full information service. Phone for details of local groups.

Disabled Living Foundation
380-384 Harrow Road
London W9 2HU
T 0171 289 6111
Advice/information on practical aspects of living with disability. Information line .

Handihols
Rhona M Thring
12 Ormonde Avenue
Rochford SS4 1QW
T 01702 548257
House exchange scheme for holidays for disabled people. Minimal costs.

Holiday Care Service
Derek Moore, Manager
2nd Floor
Imperial Buildings
Victoria Road
Horley RH6 7PZ
T 01293 774535 F 01293 784647
Free information about holidays for anyone who, because of disability or other special needs has difficulty finding suitable holidays. Promoting the needs of such people to the tourism & travel industries.

MENCAP
123 Golden Lane
London EC1Y 0RT
T 0171 454 0454 F 0171 608 3254
National organisation with seven divisional offices for adults & children with learning disabilities. For people with learning disabilities, their families & carers.

Mobility Information Service
Mrs J Griffiths, Information Officer
National Mobility Centre
Unit 2a Atcham Estate
Shrewsbury SY4 4UG
T 01743 761889 F 01743 761149
Open 10 a.m-5 pm. Accredited disabled driver assessment centre, providing information on mobility to all disabled persons.

OUTSET
Barrie Taylor, Chair
18 Creekside
London SE8 3DZ
T 0181 692 7141
National charity promoting training & employment for disabled people. Refers callers to a network of centres around the country offering office & computer skills. Runs a mobile training bus: 'Computer Tutor'.

ParentAbility
Lorna McLaughlin, Administrator
C/o National Childbirth Trust
Alexandra House
Oldham Terrace
London W3 6NH
T 0181 992 2616 F 0181 992 5929
Disabled parents supporting disabled people in pregnancy, chilbirth & parenthood. Newsletter. Open 9 am-5 pm.

Royal Association for Disability and Rehabilitation (RADAR)
12 City Forum
250 City Road
London EC1V 8AF
T 0171 350 3222

Minicom 0171 250 4119. Open Mon-Fri 10 am-5 pm. National campaigning & information-giving organisation, concerned with every aspect of disability: education, holidays, legal rights, access, employment, etc.

Sexual and Personal Relationships of the Disabled (SPOD)
Morgan Williams
286 Camden Road
London N7 0BJ
T 0171 607 8851
Counselling for people with disabilities having sexual or relationship difficulties. Information, support for carers/professionals. Open Mon-Thurs 9 am-5 pm & Fri 9 am-4 pm for telephone enquiries.

Wheelchair Loan Service Scotland (WLSS)
Paul Stapel, Chairman
3 Greenfern Avenue
Mastrick
Aberdeen AB2 6QR
T 01224 663180 F 01224 692913
Provides services for disabled people: DSS information & loan of wheelchairs to people who need them.

WinVisible
Crossroads Women's Centre
230a Kentish Town Road
London NW5 2AB
T 0171 482 2496 F 0171 209 4761
100010.2311@compuserve.com
Women with visible & invisible disabilites. Mail to: P O Box 287, London NW6 5QU. Support, information & campaigning. Wheelchair accessible. Phone Mon-Fri 10 am-12.30 pm & 1.30-4 pm; Thurs 5-7 pm.

EDUCATION

Advisory Centre for Education (ACE)
Aberdeen Studios
22-24 Highbury Grove
London N5 2EA
T 0171 354 8321 F 0171 354 9069
Helpline open Mon-Fri 2-5 pm. Campaigning for changes in state schools for them to become more responsive to needs of parents & children.

British Association for Early Childhood Education
Barbara Boon
111 City View House
463 Bethnal Green Road
London E2 9QY

T 0171 739 7594 F 0171 613 5330
Open Mon-Fri 9.30 am-4.30 pm. Promotes right of children to education of highest quality. Multi-disciplinary network of support/advice for everyone concerned with education & care of young children

British Federation of Women Graduates
4 Mandeville Courtyard
142 Battersea Park Road
London SW11 4NB
T 0171 498 8037 F 0171 498 8037
Representing women graduates in all professions; encouraging independent research by graduate women; stimulating the interest of graduate women in all spheres of public life. There are nearly 60 local branches.

Daphne Jackson Memorial Fellowships Trust, The
Mrs J Woolley
Department of Physics
University of Surrey
Guildford GU2 5XH
T 01483 259166 F 01483 259501
DJMFT@surrey.ac.uk
Providing Fellowships to scientists & engineers wishing to return to professions after career breaks for family reasons. Applicant to have first degree & submit substantial appropriate research proposal.

Educational Institute of Scotland
Veronica Rankin
46 Moray Place
Edinburgh EH3 6BH
T 0131 225 6244 F 0131 220 3151
The teachers' union contact is the equality officer who deals with all women's issues.

Equal Opportunities Higher Education Network
Berry Dicker, Membership Secretary
University of Wolverhampton
62-68 Lichfield Street
Wolverhampton WV1 1SV
T 01902 322930
For anyone in higher education. Ad hoc training events. Two conferences per year. Provides networking facilities.

European Forum of Left Feminists
Jane Pillinger (Chair of England Group)
16 Grahma Avenue
Leeds LS4 2LW
T 0113 278 0038 F 01226 284308

Europe-wide organisation of women academics & activists with aim of sharing ideas & experiences. Comes together in a once yearly conference & via newsletter. To join the England group contact Jane as above.

Girls' Public Day School Trust
26 Queen Anne's Gate
London SW1H 9AN
T 0171 222 9595 F 0171 222 8771
Owns & runs 26 schools nationwide. Provides private education for girls.

Irish Federation of University Women
Mary Horkan, President
7 Hollywood Park
Goatstown
County Dublin
T 01 298 4521 F 01 706 1197
For women graduates in Ireland. The council meets once a month.

National Association for Adult Education in Ireland (AONTAS)
Berni Brady, Director
22 Ealsfort Terrace
Dublin 2
T 01 475 4121 F 01 478 0084
aontas@iol.ie
Promotes a new opportunities project for women: Professional trainers for women managers.

National Union of Students - Women's Campaign
Alison Brown, Women's Officer
461 Holloway Road
London N7 6LJ
T 0171 651 6500 F 0171 263 5713
nusuk@nus.org.uk
Supports student union women's officers in their day-to-day work; helping with development of women's groups & local women's campaigns; fighting to combat sexism inside/outside education & students' unions.

National Union of Teachers
Ruth Blunt, Principal Officer, Gender Equality
Hamilton House
Mabledon Place
London WC1H 9BD
T 0171 388 6191 F 0171 387 8458

Represents all teachers including heads, deputies, supply & part-time teachers, providing support, advice & guidance. It plays a leading role in influencing education policies at national & local levels.

NUS Women's Campaign
women's officer
Manchester Metropolitan Students' Union
99 Oxford Road
Manchester M1 7EL
T 0161 273 1162 F 0161 273 7237

Schoolmistresses and Governesses Benevolent Institution
Mr L Baggott, Director and Secretary
Queen Mary House
Manor Park Road
Chislehurst BR7 5PY
T 0181 468 7997
Open Mon-Fri 9.30 am-5.30 pm. Helps women who have worked in all areas of education who find themselves in straitened circumstances or in temporary need. Helps those who are elderly and/or infirm.

Trinity Irish Women's Studies
Centre for Women's Studies
Trinity College
Dublin 4
T 01 660 9011 F 01 660 9828
pmmgmt@ecai.ie

University Women's Club
the secretary
2 Audley Square
South Audley Street
London W1Y 6DB
T 0171 499 2268 F 0171 499 7046
Pioneers higher education for women. Helps & encourages young women by providing networking opportunities at numerous club events. Open 24 hours a day. 24 bedrooms. Meals. A secure base for 1,200 members.

Women in German Studies (WIGS)
Dr Margaret Littler, Secretary
Department of German
University of Manchester
Oxford Road
Manchester M13 9PL
T 0161 275 3181 F 0161 275 3031
m.littler@man.ac.uk

Bringing together female Germanists in GB & Ireland & supporting them in all aspects of their professional life. Membership open to any woman currently teaching, studying or working in German studies.

Women's Studies Network (UK) Association
Diana Leonard, Co-Chair
Insittute of Education
University of London
20 Bedford Way
London WC1H QAL
T 0171 612 6322 F 0171 612 6177
There are about 400 members nationally involved in women's studies. Campaigning role for how women's studies is going to be geared in the future. Phone for details of UK women's studies courses in universities.

ENVIRONMENT

Green Network, The
9 Clairmont Road
Lexden
Colchester CO3 5BE
T 01206 546902
Umbrella organisation linking many campaigning groups involved with pollution & conservation of the environment. Promoting positive action.

Women in Design and Construction
Irena Bauman
Regent House
15 Hawthorn Road
Chapel Allerton
Leeds LS7 4PH
T 0113 294 4200
An all-women group involved in design/construction of buildings. Also planners & landscape architects. Raising the profile of women in design & construction. Meets on Mon or Thurs once a month.

Women's Design Service
Julie Christie, Coordinator
52-54 Featherstone Street
London EC1Y 8RT
T 0171 881 1302
Advice, information & training on issues concerning women & built environment. Promotes women's involvement & participation in design & planning process. Open Mon-Fri 10 am-6 pm. Publications.

Women's Environmental Network
Diana Cripps
87 Worship Street
London EC2A 2BE
T 0171 247 3327 F 0171 247 4740
WENUK@gn.apc.org
A campaigning organisation, WEN seeks to educate, inform & empower women & men who care about the environment to take positive action for a more sustainable lifestyle.

EQUAL OPPS

An Post Women's Network
Breda Trimble, Chairperson
GPO O'Connell Street
Dublin 1
T 01 705 7000 F 01 872 3553
Non-political equal opportunities project for women. Specifically for women who have received training, are in work & want to keep in touch - who might need reassurance about their new status.

British Housewives' League
Mrs A C Horsfield, Honorary Secretary
24 Liverpool Road
Kingston Hill KT2 7SZ
T 0181 546 3388
Information & advice to British housewives to provide them with an effective voice in all matters concerning themselves & their families.

CCL Education Fund
Mrs Sheila O'Reilly
14 Thistleworth Close
Isleworth
Middlesex TW7 4QQ
T 0181 737 3572 F 0181 568 2495
dgug@cix.compulink.co.uk
Helps to fund secondary school education of girls of high ability in own countries so they can complete secondary education. A major fund-raising event is the Commonwealth Fair. Only modest funds available.

City Centre Project
4th Floor
32-35 Featherstone Street
London EC1Y 8QX
T 0171 608 1338
Advice & information on employment related issues for office workers. Training on equal opps: race & sex discrimination, harassment, health & safety, VDUs, RSI, & stress. Publications.

Co-operative Women's Guild
Mrs Susan Bell
446 Hertford Road

Enfield
London EN3 5QH
T 0181 804 5905
Branches throughout England & Wales. Educating women in the principles & practice of cooperation in all its forms; working for the improvement of status of women, etc. Phone for details of local branches.

Commonwealth Countries League
Mrs Sheila O'Reilly
14 Thisleworth Close
Isleworth
Middlesex TW7 4QQ
T 0181 737 3572 F 0181 586 2495
dgug@cix.compulink.co.uk
A women's organisation with the aim of securing equal opportunities & status between women & men in the Commonwealth. Acts as a link between Commonwealth women's organisations.

Cynulliad Merched Cymru
Mair Stephens
The Coach House
Glanmorlais
Kidwally SA17 5AW
T 01267 267428 F 01267 267428
Wales Assembly of Women. Umbrella for women's organisations in Wales. Providing a voice for women in Wales enabling them through their languages to participate fully in local, national, international affairs.

Development Unit for Women: Science, Engineering and Technology
Dr Caroline Roberts
UG.B.36
1 Victoria Street
London SW1H 0ET
T 0171 215 0051 F 0171 215 0054
Has been established in the Office of Science & Technology in the DTI to promote the role of women in SET. The unit is charged with taking forward the recommendations accepted by the Government.

Employment Equality Agency
Kathleen Connolly
36 Upper Mount Street
Dublin 2
T 01 662 4577 F 01 662 5139
info@equality.ie
Open Mon-Thurs 9.30 am-1 pm & 2.15-5.30 pm; Fri 9.30 am-1 pm & 2.15-5.15 pm. Deals mainly with harassment in the workplace based on gender & marital status; equal pay for equal value.

Employment NOW
Ciara Mc Kenna
Co National Women's Council of Ireland
16-20 Cumberland Street South
Dublin 2
T 01 661 5268 F 01 676 0860
Aims to reduce unemployment & increase opportunities in the labour market for women & to improve position of those already in the labour force through promotion of equal opps strategies.

Equal Opportunities Commission
Overseas House
Quay Street
Manchester M3 3HN
T 0161 833 9244 F 0161 835 1657
Information centre open Mon-Fri 9 am-5 pm; advice lines open Mon-Fri 9.30 am-12 noon & 1-4 pm. To create equal opportunities for women & men, in work, education, consumer rights & welfare benefits.

Equal Opportunities Commission - Wales
Val Feld
Caerwys House
Windsor Lane
Cardiff CF1 1LB
T 01222 343552 F 01222 641079
Open Mon-Fri 9 am-5 pm Working towards elimination of unlawful sex & marriage discrimination; promoting equality of opportunity between men & women; keeping Sex Discrimination & Equal Pay Acts under review.

Equal Opportunities Commission for Northern Ireland
information officer
Chamber of Commerce House
22 Great Victoria Street
Belfast BT2 7BA
T 01232 242752 F 01232 331047
Works towards the elimination of discrimination, promoting equality of opportunity between women & men generally. Keeps relevant sex discrimination legislation under review. Advice & information, etc.

Equal Opportunities Commission for Scotland
Parveen Khan, Publications Officer
Stock Exchange House
7 Nelson Mandela Place
Glasgow G2 1QW
T 0141 248 5833 F 0141 248 5834

NATIONAL- EQUAL OPPS

Information & advice on the Sex Discrimination Act & the Equal Pay Act. Anyone who believes they are being discriminated against can use our service. Publications/leaflets, some of them free.

Fair Play
Pat Nicoll, National Coordinator
Department for Education and Employment
Caxton House
6-12 Tothill Street
London SW1H 9NF
T 0171 273 5205   F 0171 273 5124
Positive action equalities project. A government EOC initiative to stimulate partnerships which improve opportunities for women to realise their full potential in education, employment & the community.

Fair Play Northern Ireland
Department of Economic Development
Netherleigh
Massey Avenue
Belfast BT4 2JP
T 01232 529273   F 01232 529550
Positive action equalities project. A government EOC initiative to stimulate partnerships which improve opportunities for women to realise their full potential in education, employment & the community.

Fawcett Society, The
Charlotte Burt/Caroline Hepple
5th Floor
45 Beech Street
Barbican
London EC2Y 8AD
T 0171 628 4441   F 0171 628 2865
Campaigns for equality between women & men. Works to achieve equality for all women in all aspects of their lives by transforming attitudes & behaviour throughout society.

Federation of Women's Institutes of Northern Ireland
I A Sproule
209-211 Upper Lisburn Road
Belfast BT10 0LL
T 01232 301506   F 01232 431127
Approximately 9,000 members in Northern Ireland meeting monthly in their own Institute group & twice yearly at Council meetings.

Ffederasiwn Cenedlaethol Sefydliad y Merched - Cymru
Mrs L Rhiannon Beven, Head
19 Cathedral Road
Cardiff CF1 9LJ
T 01222 221712   F 01222 387236
National Federation of Women's Institutes (Wales). Aims to improve the quality of women's lives, especially those living in rural areas.

Irish Congress of Trade Unions - Women's Committee
Rosaleen Glackin, Equality Officer
19 Raglan Road
Ballsbridge
Dublin 4
T 01 668 0641   F 01 660 9027
RAGLAN@ ictu.iol.ie
Concerned with democracy, equality, negotiation, promotion, participation & cooperation.

Married Women's Association
Simone Grasse, Chair
16 Hollycroft Avenue
London NW3 7QL
T 0171 794 2884
Meets on last Wed on month 1.30-4 pm. To promote recognition of a wife as a legal & equal financial partner during marriage. Concerned with legislation & parliament.

National Alliance of Women's Organisations (NAWO)
Marie Louise Makris
Suite 44, 4th Floor
Diamond House
37-38 Hatton Garden
London EC1N 8E8
T 0171 242 0878
NAWO brings widely diverse women's organisations together to achieve true equality & justice for all women. Independent charity working at national level, accountable to its member organisations.

National Assembly of Women
1 Camden Hill Road
London SE19 1NX
T 0181 761 7532   F 0181 761 7532
megan@gn.apc.org
Promoting social, economic, legal, political & cultural equality for women.

National Council of Women of GB - Scottish Standing Cttee
Miss M J S Henderson
15 Shirra's Brae Road
St Ninians
Stirling FK7 0AY

T 01786 463512
Umbrella organisation in Scotland.

National Council of Women of Great Britain
Katy Lam, Office Manager
36 Danbury Street
London N1 8JU
T 0171 354 2395 F 0171 354 9214
Works to remove discrimination against women, to encourage effective participation of women in the life of the nation & to improve the quality of life for all. Phone for details of local branches.

National Federation of Women's Institutes
Jana Osborne, General Secretary
104 New Kings Road
London SW6 4LY
T 0171 371 9300 F 0171 736 3652
Membership comprises over 270,000 women in England, Wales, Channel Islands & Isle of Man. Aims to improve quality of life, particularly in rural areas, of women & families. Phone for details of local branches.

NUCPS - Women's Advisory Committee
women's officer
5 Great Southwark Street
London SE1 0NS
T 0171 928 9671
Advising the National Executive Council of the National Union of Civil and Public Servants negotiating issues of particular relevance to women.

Our Daughters' Charitable Trust
20-22 Craven Road
London W2 3PX
T 0171 402 5363 F 0171 402 5721
National organisers for the annual Take Our Daughters to Work Day which aims to remove barriers to personal development of girls & boys. Special packs for schools/students & employers available.

Scottish Co-operative Women's Guild
95 Morrison Street
Glasgow G5 8LP
T 0141 429 1457
Extending co-operation & stimulating thought on questions of reform; stimulating thought on all questions of social & political reform, etc.

Scottish Joint Action Group
Lorna Ahlquist, Chair
Holyrood
Innellan
Dunoon PA23 7SP
T 01369 830429
Designated the umbrella group for women's organisations in Scotland by the Women's National Commission. Consists of organisations, groups, individual women working on matters of concern to women in Scotland.

Standing Conference of Women's Organisations
Mrs Lynne Hoy, National Secretary
18 Slayleigh Avenue
Fulwood
Sheffield S10 3RB
T 0114 230 8215 F 0114 230 4098
Members of a local conference are the branches of national women's & family groups. Represent a range of interests addressing community issues & gaining representation. Phone for details of local groups.

Suffragette Fellowship
Sybil Gouldon Bach, Chairman
29 Vandon Court
Petty France
London SW1H 9HE
T 0171 222 2597
To perpetuate the memory of the pioneers & outstanding events connected with women's emancipation, & especially with the Women's Social and Political Union's campaign 1905-14.

Townswomen's Guilds
Mrs Pauline Wilkes
Chamber of Commerce House
75 Harborne Road
Edgbaston
Birmingham B15 3DA
T 0121 456 3435 F 0121 452 1890
To advance the education of women & enable them to make the best contribution towards the common good. Monthly guild meetings all over UK & Northern Ireland. Monthly magazine. Phone for local groups.

UNISON - Equal Opportunities Department
Gloria Mills, Director of Equal Opportunities
Civic House
20 Grand Depot Road
London SE18 6SF
T 0181 854 2244 F 0181 316 7770
g.mills@unison-gate.poptel.org.uk

Working for equal pay for work of equal value; for full-time rights for part-time workers; for better childcare facilities; for fairer pensions; against low pay; against sexual harassment & domestic volence.

Women's National Commission
Judith Bailey/Wanda Brown, Joint Secretaries
Dept for Education & Employment
Caxton House Level 4
Tothill Street
London SW1H 9NF
T 0171 273 5486 F 0171 273 4906
To ensure by all possible means that the informed opinion of women is given its due weight in the deliberations of govenment. Has 50 full and 30+ associate member organisations. Jointly chaired by two women.

ETHNIC MINORITIES

African Association for Maternal & Child Care International
the director
Community Health Resource Centre
Adunola House
13 Tatam Road
London NW10 8HT
T 0181 933 3767 F 0171 624 5002
To advance the education of women & children in London with particular regard to those of African origin. Activities focused on promoting/improving mental health of clients. Open Mon-Fri 10 am-6 pm.

African Council of Churches for Immigration & Social Justice
Unit 6-7
321 Essex Road
London N1 3PS
T 0171 704 2331
Open Mon-Fri 11 am-8 pm. Information, advice & support for people with immigration, asylum & refugee problems. Legal advice, computer skills training, drop-in Mon-Fri 1-5 pm. Prison visiting scheme, etc.

African Women's Welfare Group
Hadija Ahmed
Hesta Annex
301 White Heart Lane
Tottenham
London N17 7BT
T 0181 885 5822
Open Mon-Fri 9 a.m-4 pm. Creche, primary health care, community services, HIV/AIDS advice/counselling. Interpretation at GPs surgery. Works with Black women in Islington, Haringey & Hackney.

Akina Mama wa Afrika
Bisi Adeleye-Fayemi, Director
4 Wild Court
London WC2B 4AU
T 0171 405 0678 F 0171 831 3947
amwa@greenet.apc.org
An African women's organisation which coordinates local, regional & international initiatives taken by African women. Offers a resource & research forum on African women's issues.

Asian Family Counselling Service
Ms Kulbir Randhawa
74 The Avenue
West Ealing
London W13 8LB
T 0181 997 5749 F 0181 998 1880
Phoneline open Mon-Fri 10 am-4 pm. Marital & family counselling for the Asian community. Free service during the week, but a fee for evening & weekend appointments.

Association of Ukrainian Women in Great Britain
49 Linden Gardens
London W2 4HG
T 0171 229 8392 F 0171 792 2499
Meets irregularly. AGM.

Chinese Information and Advice Centre
68 Shaftesbury Avenue
London W1V 7DF
T 0171 494 3273
Open Mon-Fri 10 am-6 pm. Gives women advice on matrimonial issues, domestic violence, immigration & employment rights. Helps run Chinese women's support groups.

Eritrean Community in UK
Tekle Berhe
266-268 Holloway Road
London N7 6NE
T 0171 700 7995 F 0171 609 1539
Refugee community organisation. Provides advice & support on health matters, housing, welfare & education concerns. Open Mon-Fri 10 am-5 pm

FORWARD (Foundation for Wms Health Research & Development)
Mrs Rahmat Mohamad
Africa Centre
38 King Street
Covent Garden
London WC2E 8JT
T 0171 379 6889 F 0171 379 6199

NATIONAL - ETHNIC MINORITIES

FORWARD@dircon.co.uk
Open Mon-Fri 10 am-5 pm. Main aim is to eliminate practices of female genital mutilation. Also concerned with African women's health in general. Health information & contacts relating to health.

International Black Women for Wages for Housework
Sylvia Salley
Crossroads Women's Centre
230a Kentish Town Road
London NW5 2AB
T 0171 482 2496 F 0171 209 4761
100010.2311@compuserve.com
Mail to P O Box 287, London NW6 5QU.
Campaigning to get unwaged work valued & compensated, including pay equity & any issues affecting our diverse communities; immigration controls, police illegality, etc.

International Network of Women of Colour
C/o Crossroads Women's Centre
230a Kentish Town Road
London NW5 2AB
T 0171 482 2496 F 0171 209 4761

Muslim Women's Helpline
Unit 3, 1st Floor
GEC Estate
Wembley
London HA9 7PX
T 1081 908 3205
Helplines: 0181 904 8193 & 0181 908 6715 open Mon-Fri 10 am-4 pm. Provides confidential emotional support, a listening service, practical information & advice on where to find help for Muslim women.

National Network of Black Women's Organisations at Sia
Judith Lockhart
Winchester House
9 Cranmer Road
Kennington Park
London SW9 6EJ
T 0171 735 9010 F 0171 735 9011
GEO2@SIA-NDABUS
Open 9 am-5 pm. To raise awareness about the work of Black women's organisations; improve access to resources by Black women's organisations; promote information exchange. Produces a Black Women's directory.

Positively Women African Women's Support Group
347-349 City Road
London EC1V 1LR
T 0171 713 0222 F 0171 713 1020
Support group on Mon 5-9 pm. Creche, food & complementary therapies. For African women who have HIV/AIDS. Transport home. Book creche in advance.

Professional Afro-Asian Women's Association
Dr Stella Okonkwo
C/o Brunswick Park Health Centre
Brunswick Park Road
London N11 1EY
T 0181 368 1568
Aims to provide a forum for professional women of African, Asian & Caribbean descent nationally to achieve personal & professional development.

Refugee Council, The
Nish Matenjwa
3 Bondway
London SW8 1SJ
T 0171 820 3000 F 0171 582 9929
refcounciluk@gn.apc.org
Advice line 0171 582 1162; advisers' line 0171 582 9927. Open for advice: Mon, Tue, Thurs, Fri 9.30 am-1 pm; day centre open Mon-Fri 10 am-3 pm. Providing direct services to refugees and asylum seekers.

Union of Turkish Women in Britain
Gonul Akmackci
110 Clarence Road
London E5 8JA
T 0181 985 4072
Open Mon-Fri 2-8 pm. Helping Turkish speaking women in Britain. Advice, translation, interpretation, information. Social events. Seminars on issues such as women's health, immigration & racism.

Women's Council (Co-operating with Women of Asia)
Mrs E Pyke, Hon Secretary
82 London Road
Knebworth SG3 6HB
T 01438 811673 F 01438 811673
Ronkswood@msn.com
Education of British & Asian women with mutual exchange of cultural & social education. Annual scholarships to young women from Asia to study in Britian in relation to childcare & child development.

FINANCE

Low Pay Unit
27-29 Amwell Street
London EC1R 1IN
T 0171 713 7616 F 0171 713 7581
Helpline 0171 713 7583 open Mon-Fri 9.30 am-5.30 pm. Focusses on low pay issues & poverty. Information & advice to low paid workers. Acts as watchdog over government, employers, TUs, etc.

Money Advice Scotland
Yvonne Gallacher, Convenor
C/o Glasgow City Council
Strathclyde House 2
20 India Street
Glasgow G2 4PF
T 0141 227 3104 F 0141 227 3104
Promotes education about personal finance, encourages the development of free money advice services & provdes a forum for policy discussions between voluntary, statutory & finance industry organisations.

Money Management Council
John Moysey, Administrator
P O Box 77
Hertford SG14 2HW
T 01992 503448 F 01992 503448
Promoting education & understanding in personal & family finance. Operates through help/advice agencies, financial institutions & media. Free fact sheets on money topics. Does not offer individual counselling.

National Debtline
Meg van Rooyen, National Debtline Teamleader
Birmingham Settlement
318 Summer Lane
Birmingham B19 3RL
T 0645 500 511 F 0121 359 6357
Open Mon & Thurs 10 am-4 pm; Tue & Wed 10 am-7 pm; Fri 10 am-12 noon. Free, confidential & independent helpline for people with debt problems in England, Wales, Scotland & Northern Ireland.

Public Services Tax and Commerce Union (PTC)
Paulette Keating
5 Great Suffolk Street
London SE1 0NS
T 0171 960 2042 F 0171 960 2001
A trade union representing members in the civil service, public & private sectors. Works for improved pay & conditions of service for members, including childcare, maternity & paternity rights.

Scottish Low Pay Unit
Morag Gillespie
24 Sandyford Place
Glasgow G3 7NG
T 0141 221 4491 F 0141 221 6318
Information on pay/employment rights/training. Research/campaigning on low pay issues. Freepost address: Scottish Low Pay Unit, Freepost, Glasgow, Scotland G3 7BR; or phone. For low paid workers in Scotland.

TaxAid
Linburn House
342 Kilburn High Road
London NW6 2QJ
T 0171 624 3768
Free advice to individuals who have income tax problems & who cannot afford to pay an accountant. Helpline answered Mon-Fri 9-11 am. Face-to-face interviews can be arranged in Kilburn via helpline with appt.

GIRLS/YOUNG WOMEN

Girls' Friendly Society/Platform for Young Women
Mrs Hazel Crompton, General Secretary
Townsend House
126 Queen's Gate
South Kensington
London SW7 5LQ
T 0171 589 9628 F 0171 225 1458
Seeks to enable girls & young women to develop their whole potential, personally, socially & spiritually. Our work includes housing, youth & community work & branch membership.

Girls' Schools Association
Sheila Cooper
130 Regent Road
Leicester LE1 7PG
T 0116 254 1619 F 0116 255 3792
GSA@dial.pipex.com
Concerned with matters relating to the policy & administration of independent & direct grant girls' schools.

Girls' Venture Corps Air Cadets
Mrs M Rowland, Director
Redhill Aerodrome
Kings Mill Lane

South Nutfield
Redhill RH1 5JY
T 01737 823345 F 01737 823345
gvcac@ukonline.co.uk
For girls aged 11-18, providing training for them to develop into responsible adults giving service to the community. Outdoor activities such as camping, orienteering, canoeing, climbing & skiing.

Guide Association - Province of Ulster
Mrs Valerie Worthington
Lorna House
Station Road, Craigavad
Holywood
County Down BT18 0BP
T 01232 425212 F 01232 46025
Youth organisation for girls & young women aged 5-25.

Guide Association Scotland
16 Coates Crescent
Edinburgh EH3 7AH
T 0131 226 4511 F 0131 220 4828
Girls are encouraged to work together, to govern themselves & to make their own decisions, etc.

Guide Association, The
Hilary Williams, Chief Executive
17-19 Buckingham Palace Road
London SW1W 0PT
T 0171 834 6242 F 0171 828 8317
To enable girls to mature into confident, capable & caring women who are determined to realise their potential in their career, home & personal life & willing to contribute to their community & the wider world.

Sea Ranger Association
Vera Corner-Halligan
4 Grand Drive
Raynes Park
London SW20 0JT
T 0181 540 3694
For girls & young women aged 10-21. Cadets/sea rangers. Nautical activities & general good citizenship. Regional branches.

HEALTH

Action Against Breast Cancer
Bess Herbert
ABC, C2
Science & Engineering Centre
Culham OX14 3DB
T 01865 407384 F 01865 407065
abc-uk@dial.pipex.com
Funds research into secondary spread. Aim is to increase survival after breast cancer. Research in progress at UCL & Middlesex hospitals in London. Leaflets available.

Action on Pre-Eclampsia (APEC)
Isabel Walker, Director
31-33 College Road
Harrow
Middlesex HA1 1EJ
T 0181 863 3271 F 0181 424 0653
24-hour helpline 01923 266778. To raise awareness about pre-eclampsia & to support sufferers. To promote medical research relating to the disease.

Adult Children of Alcoholics (ACA)
P O Box 1576
London SW3 1AZ
T 0171 229 4587

Adult Children of Alcoholics (ACoA) - Ireland
C/o 21 Patrick Street
Dun Laoire
Dublin

AIDS Care Education and Training (ACET)
P O Box 3693
London SW15 2BQ
T 0181 780 0400 F 0181 780 0450
Providing home care to people with HIV/AIDS with doctors, nurses & volunteers.

AIDS Education and Research Trust (AVERT)
11-13 Denne Parade
Horsham RH12 1JD
T 01403 210202 F 01403 211001
avert@dial.pipex.com
Aims to prevent people from becoming infected with HIV, to improve quality of life for those already infected & to work to find a cure. Runs free information service for health professionals. Publications.

Al-Anon Family Groups/Alateen
61 Great Dover Street
London SE1 4YF
T 0171 403 0888
Help provided to families & friends of problem drinkers. Alateen is for young people aged 12-20 whose lives have been affected by someone else's drinking.

NATIONAL- HEALTH

Alcoholics Anonymous (AA)
P O Box 1
Stonebrow House
Stonebrow
York YO1 2NJ

Alcoholics Anonymous - Scotland
Ian Whyte, Scottish Secretary
Scottish Service Office
50 Wellington Street
Glasgow G2 6HJ
T 0141 226 2214
Counselling & advice for alcoholics, their friends & families. Helpline: 0345 697555.

Amarant Trust, The
11-13 Charterhouse Buildings
London EC1M 7AN
T 0171 490 1644 F 0171 490 2296
Administration centre. Write, phone or fax. NOT open for visiting. To promote a better understanding of the menopause & greater awareness of benefits of hormone replacement therapy (HRT). Helplines available.

Anaphylaxis Campaign, The
David Reading, Chairman
P O Box 149
Fleet GU13 9XU
T 01252 318723
To preserve the health of & relieve those persons who suffer anaphylactic reactions & associated disorders by advancing research; to advance education & general understanding of public concerning anaphylaxis.

Anorexia Anonymous
24 Westmoreland Road
London SW13 9RY
T 0181 878 9199
Helping people with bulimia & anorexia nervosa & other eating disorders. Phone between 7-9 pm for free advice & information.

Arthritis & Reumatism Council for Research
Kevin Hawes/Chris Gooderham
Copeman House
St Mary's Court
Chesterfield S41 7TD
T 01246 558033 F 01246 558007
info@arc.org.uk
A medical research charity, the main aim of which is to raise money to fund research into arthritis & rheumatism. Publications.

Arthritis & Rheumatism Council
Mrs C Baker
Melrose House
East Sleetburn
Bedlington NE22 7AT
T 01670 821146
Fundraising for research.

Arthritis Care
Janet Woolley, Information and Counselling
18 Stephenson Way
London NW1 2HD
T 0171 916 1500 F 0171 916 1505
Open 9 am-5 pm. Free helpline 12-4 pm. Support for arthritis sufferers & carers. Five specially designed hotels; nursing home. Young arthritis care section. Publications. Phone for details of local groups.

ASH - The Campaign for Freedom from Tobacco
Devon House
12-15 Dartmouth Street
London SW1H 9BL
Campaigning group. Provides literature specific to women: 'Women and Smoking: A Handbook for Action'; 'Teenage girls and smoking'; 'Smoke gets in her eyes'; 'Her Share of Misfortune', etc.

Ash yng Nghymru/Action on Smoking and Health in Wales
Mrs Naomi King, Director
372a Cowbridge Road East
Cardiff CF5 1HE
T 01222 641101 F 01222 641045
Promoting stopping smoking. Stopping young people from starting to smoke. Raising awareness of the harmful effects of the use of tobacco. Working towards comprehensive tobacco control measures.

Association for Prevention of Addiction
John Moore
67-69 Cowcross Street
London EC1M 6BP
T 0171 251 5860 F 0171 251 5890
Reducing the harm caused by drugs and alcohol in communities.

Birth Defects Foundation
Sheila Brown
Chelsea House
West Gate
London W5 1DR
T 0181 862 0198

National child health medical research charity concerned with prevention & treatment of all in-born conditions. Family helpline 01543 468400 open Mon-Fri 10 am-3 pm.

Body Positive
Micky Richards, Women's Worker
51b Philbeach Gardens
London SW5 9EB
T 0171 835 1045 F 0171 373 5237
Support, help, information for those living with/ directly affected by HIV/AIDS. Office Mon-Fri 9.30 am-5.30 pm; helpline 0171 373 9124 Mon-Fri 7-9 pm; Sat & Sun 4-10 pm Women's group Tue 6-9 pm.

Bodywhys
Helen McDaid, Chairperson
P O Box 105
Blackrock
County Dublin
T 01 288 9611
For people with eating disorders. Umbrella group for support groups in Dublin, Limerick & Ennis - a national network. Helpline: 01 283 5126. Open Tue 12.30-2.30 pm, Wed 7.30-9.30 pm, Thurs 10 am-12 noon.

Breakthrough Breast Cancer
P O Box LB25
London WC2B 6QW
T 0171 405 5111 F 0171 831 3873
Raising funds to create a breast cancer research centre to be based next to the Marsden Hospital & Insitute of Cancer Research.

Breast Cancer Care
Samila al Qadhi/Carolyn Faulder
Kiln House
210 New Kings Road
London SW6 4NZ
T 0171 384 2344 F 0171 384 3387
Free information, help & support for women affected by breast cancer. One-to-one support; confidential prosthesis fitting service; helplines staffed by breast care nurses. Nationwide freeline 0500 245 345.

Breast Care Campaign
Blytne Hall
100 Blytne Road
London W14 0HB
T 0171 371 1510 F 0171 371 4598

Information on benign breast disorders. Campaign to increase awareness & information about benign breast disorders & to promote better breast awareness amongst the public & professionals.

British Allergy Foundation
Siorbhan Hamilton
Deep Dene House
30 Bellegrove Road
Welling DA16 3BY
T 0181 303 8525
Helpline 0181 303 8583. Open Mon-Fri 10 am-3 pm. Information on household utensils claiming to reduce allergies. Food & cosmetics research. Information on registered NHS allergy clinics. Leaflets.

British Association of Cancer United Patients (BACUP)
Rebecca Powell
3 Bath Place
Rivington Street
London EC2A 3JA
T 0171 696 9003 F 0171 696 9002
Provides free information, counselling & support to anyone affected by cancer. Cancer information service: 0800 181199, lines open Mon-Fri 9 am-7 pm. Cancer counselling service: 0171 696 9000. Publications.

British Association of Cancer United Patients (BACUP) - Scotland
Jenny Whelan, Manager
30 Bell Street
Glasgow G1 1LG
T 0141 553 1553 F 0141 553 2686
Free helpline open Mon-Fri 9.30 am-5 pm: 0800 181119. Free counselling & support for anyone suffering from cancer. Publications. Write or phone for further details.

British Nursing Association (BNA)
Eileen Linsey
Rooms 16/18 2nd Floor
St Andrews House
59 St Andrews Street
Cambridge CB2 3BZ
T 01223 302377 F 01223 322528
A nurse & care assistant agency, supplying all grades of staff to hospitals, nursing homes, industry & people in their own homes. Countrywide with 129 branches.

Brittle Bone Society
Morna Wilson, Administrator
30 Guthrie Street

NATIONAL - HEALTH

Dundee DD1 5BS
T 01382 204446 F 01382 206771
Promoting research into causes, inheritance & treatment of osteogenesis imperfecta & similar disorders: excessive fragility of bones. Advice, encouragement, practical help for patients & relatives.

Cancer Relief Macmillan Fund
15-19 Britten Street
London SW3 3TZ
T 0171 351 7811
Open Mon-Fri 9 am-5 pm. National cancer charity with Macmillan nurses in hospitals & the community. Specialists in pain & symptom control & in emotional counselling. Financial help for patients in need.

Cancerkin
Gloria Freilich
The Cancerkin Centre
Royal Free Hospital
Pond Street
London NW3 2QG
T 0171 830 2323 F 0171 830 2324
Open Mon-Fri 9 am-5 pm, otherwise ansaphone. Provides breast cancer (non NHS) treatment, supportive care, rehabilitation, advice, information. Carries out clinical research. All services are free of charge.

CancerLink
11-21 Northdown Street
London N1 9BN
T 0171 833 2818 F 0171 833 4963
cancerlink@canlink.demon.co.uk
Cancer helpline 0800 132905 Mon-Fri 9.30 am-1 pm & 2-5 pm; Asian helpline 0800 590415 Mon & Fri 10 am-1 pm & Fri 2-4 pm; young people helpline 0800 591028 Mon-Fri 9.30 am-1pm & 2-5 pm. Free.

CancerLink - Scotland
9 Castle Terrace
Edinburgh EH1 2DP
T 0131 228 5567 F 0131 228 8956
cancerlink@cislink.demon.co.uk
Cancer helpline 0800 132905 Mon-Fri 9.30 am-1 pm & 2-5 pm; Asian helpline 0800 590415 Mon-Fri 10 am-1 pm & Fri 2-4 pm; young people helpline 0800 591028 Mon-Fri 9.30 am-1 pm & 2-5 pm. Free.

Centre for Eating Disorders (Scotland)
Mary Hart
3 Sciennes Road

Edinburgh EH9 1LE
T 0131 668 3051 F 0131 667 9708
mhart@globalnet.co.uk
Psychotherapy service to individuals & occasionally to couples & families. Appointments necessary. Open Mon-Fri 9 am-7 pm. Phone for up-to-date price list.

Childhood Cancer and Leukaemia Link (CALL)
Gill Denne/Elaine Trewhella
The Kerith Centre
Church Road
Bracknell RG12 1EH
T 01344 304080 F 01344 304080
Providing support & information to families affected by childhood cancer or leukaemia.

Coloplast Advisory Service
Peterborough Business Park
Peterborough PE2 6FX
T 01733 392000
Free helpline: 0800 220622. Free telephone advice on incontinence, ostomy & wound care. Run by nurse advisor with trained helpers.

Community Drug and Alcohol Initiatives
67-69 Cowcross Street
Smithfield
London EC1M 6BP
T 0171 251 5860 F 0171 251 5890
Aims to reduce harm caused by drugs & alcohol in communities. Advice, information, counselling, referral, HIV services, health care, needle exchange, free condoms. Raising awareness of risks of drug taking.

Community Health UK
6 Terrace Walk
Bath BA1 1LN
T 01225 462680 F 01225484238
Promotes & supports community health development in the UK. Acts as source of information & advice for those involved in community health; supports projects & provides forums for community health groups, etc.

Community Practitioners and Health Visitors' Association (CPHVA)
Jackie Carnell, Director
50 Southwark Street
London SE1 1UN
T 0171 717 4000 F 0171 717 4010

NATIONAL- HEALTH

Professional body & trade union for community practitioners, health visitors, school nurses & nurses working in the community.

CPHVA
Jackie Carnell, Director
50 Southwark Street
London SE1 UN
T 0171 717 4000 F 0171 717 4010
The professional organisation for primary health care nurses.

CRUSAID
Livingstone House
11 Carteret Street
London SW1H 9JD
T 0171 976 8100 F 0171 976 8200
Raising funds for the care & treatment of people with HIV/AIDS. Educating people about AIDS. Funding capital projects.

CRUSAID Scotland
25 Queensferry Street
Edinburgh EH2 4QS
T 0131 225 8918 F 0131 220 4033
Funds projects throughout Scotland, raising & distributing funds for HIV/AIDS prevention & care.

Cystitis and Candida
Angela Kilmarten
75 Mortimer Road
London N1 5AR
T 0171 249 8664 F 0171 249 8664
Provides information (classes and books), lectures & one-to-one counselling to help prevent & manage these problems. Offers telephone advice. Open Mon-Fri 9.30 am-5.30 pm.

Drink Crisis Centre - Women's Services
Bernie Cahill
56 Lordship Lane
East Dulwich
London SE22 8HJ
T 0181 693 9570 F 0171 252 6900
Drug & alcohol rehabilitation programmes for women. Resettlement project. Supportive housing service.

Drug & Alcohol Women's Network (DAWN)
C/o GLAAS
30-31 Great Sutton Street
London EC1V 0DX
T 0171 253 6221 F 0171 250 1627

A network open to women working, or interested in, the drug & alcohol field. Organises training events. There is a part-time worker in the office three days a week. Wheelchair accessible.

Eating Disorders Association
Sackville Place
44 Magdalen Street
Norwich NR3 1JU
T 01603 621414
Adult helpline above open Mon-Fri 9 am-6.30 pm. Also youth helpline for aged 18 years & under: 01603 765050 open Mon-Fri 4-6 pm. Offers help & understanding to people who have anorexia & bulimia nervosa.

Eating Disorders Wales (EDW)
Deborah Hill, Coordinator
Flat 15 Pavia Court
Craigwen Road
Pontypridd CF37 2TW
T 01443 491092
Supporting people overcoming their eating disorders through a self-help group for people suffering from eating disorders.

English National Board for Nursing, Midwifery & Health Visiting
Malcolm Crawford
Victory House
170 Tottenham Court Road
London W1P 0HA
T 0171 388 3131 F 0171 383 7276
Provides nurses, midwives & health visitors with nursing education. Responsible for all educational courses nationally as regards nursing, midwifery & health visitors.

Families Anonymous
The Doddington and Rollo Community Assn
Charlotte Despard Avenue
Battersea
London SW11 5JE
T 0171 498 4680
Open mon-Fri 1-4 pm; Sat & Sun 9 am-8 pm. Help for anyone who is troubled or distressed because of drug abuse or family. Groups meet regularly to share experiences & learn new ways of coping.

First Steps to Freedom
Sheila Harris
1 Castle Court
Park Road
Kenilworth CV8 2GF
T 01926 864873 F 01926 964873

106062.37@compuserve.com
Helpline 01926 851608 10 am-10 pm every day for people & their carers suffering from stress-related & anxiety conditions & phobias, obsessional compulsive disorders.
Publications, videos, relaxation tapes.

Food and Chemical Allergy Association
Mrs Ellen Rothera
27 Ferringham Lane
Ferring BN12 5NB
T 01903 241178
Advising people how to discover causes of their allergies, how to avoid allergies & how to stabilise their immune systems & regain good health. Can put people in touch with doctors & similar associations.

Health Rights
Frances Tufuor
Unit 405
444 Brixton Road
Brixton Small Business Ctr
London SW9 8EJ
T 0171 501 9856   F 0171 733 0351
Campaigns for more resources for the NHS, improving access to health care, improving local accountability, patients' rights, a better deal for health workers, making community care work, etc.

Herpes Viruses Association
Marian Nicholson
41 North Road
London N7 9DP
T 0171 609 9061
Information on herpes simplex virus to general public, media & health professionals; counselling for individuals affected physically/psychologically; advice on coping through helpline, post or face-to-face.

Hirsutism Society, The
C/O FACE
P O Box 484
Cambridge CB4 3TF

HIV and AIDS Centre for Support and Information (Solas)
David Cameron
2-4 Abbeymount
Edinburgh EH8 8EJ
T 0131 661 0982   F 0131 652 1780
mail@solas.demin.co.uk

Child care, arts programme, complementary therapy service, counselling service, emotional support. Advice services around welfare & housing rights, seminars & workshops for specific groups.

Hysterectomy Support Group
C/o Women's Health
52 Featherstone Street
London EC1Y 8RT
T 0171 251 6580
Encourages self help through informal sharing of experiences about hysterectomy. Pre-hysterectomy support for women & partners provided. Write or phone. Publications.

International Community of Women Living with HIV/AIDS
Leigh Neal, Chair
Livingstone House
11 Carternet Street
London SW1H 9DL
T 0171 222 1333   F 0171 222 1242
icw@qn.apc.org
Run by HIV + women for HIV + women. Support in setting up self-help & support groups; organisating international conferences for HIV + women; providing expert speakers; challenging discrimination, etc.

Interstitial Cystitis Support Group
Anthony Walker
76 High Street
Stony Stratford MK11 1AH
T 01908 569169   F 01908 569169
Supporting & supplying information on interstitial cystitis through quarterly newsletters & contact with local fellow sufferers. Videos, books & up-to-date information. Open Mon-Fri 9 am-5 pm.

Irish Nurses Organisation (INO)
11 Fitzwilliam Place
Dublin 2
T 01 676 0137   F 01 661 0466
The trade union for nurses. Negotiates pay & conditions. Also a professional educational centre. Has around 21,000 female members (& 2,000 male members).

ISSUE (National Fertility Association)
509 Aldridge Road
Great Barr
Birmingham B44 8NA
T 0121 344 4414   F 0121 344 4336

Open Mon-Thurs 9 am-4.30 pm; Fri 9 am-4 pm. Information & support to people with fertility difficulties. Answering service Mon-Thurs 8-9 am & 4.30-8 pm; Fri 8-9 am & 4-8 pm Sat 8 am-8 pm.

Macmillan Cancer Relief
Mr I Gibson
9 Castle Terrace
Edinburgh EH1 2DP
T 0131 229 3276 F 0131 228 6710
Promoting enhanced care & support for cancer patients & families; grants for patients & their families, etc. Helpline (CancerLink): 0800 132 905, phone free of charge.

Marce Society
Dr Trevor Friedman
Department of Psychiatry
Leicester General Hospital
Leicester LE52 4PW
T 0116 249 0490
Aims to improve understanding, prevention & treatment of mental illness related to child bearing.

Marie Curie Cancer Care
28 Belgrave Square
London SW1X 8QG
T 0171 235 3325
Offers 5000 Marie Curie nurses throughout UK giving free, practical nursing care at home to people with cancer. 11 Marie Curie hospice centres providing specialist medical & nursing care. Research & education.

Maya Project
14-16 Peckham Hill Street
London SE15 6BN
T 0171 635 5493
Residential rehabilitation service for women & their children, targeting women from ethnic communities. Children accommodated. Takes clients nationwide. Expert support & advice.

Medical Women's Federation
Tavistock House North
Tavistock Square
London WC1H 9HX
T 0171 387 7765
Membership organisation of UK women doctors, working for equal opportunities for women doctors & patients. Publication: 'Medical Woman' - quarterly.

Mental After Care Association (MACA)
Ms Parker
25 Bedford Square
London WC1B 3HW
T 0171 436 6194
Open Mon-Fri 9 am-5 pm. Offers a range of community-based services for people with mental health problems, including residential care, day care, respite care & general information.

Migraine Trust
45 Great Ormond Street
London WC1N 3HZ
T 0171 8331 4818 F 0171 831 5174

Multiple Sclerosis Society of GB & Northern Ireland
information officer
25 Effie Road
London SW6 1EE
T 0171 736 6287 F 0171 736 9861
Open Mon-Fri 9 am-5 pm. Helpline: 0171 371 8000 open Mon-Fri 10 am-4 pm to promote & fund research into MS to promote welfare & support services through local branches throughout the UK.

National Association for Children of Alcoholics (NACOA)
Hilary Henriques
P O Box 64
Fishponds
Bristol BS16 2UH
T 0117 924 8005 F 0117 924 8005
Free phone 0800 289061. Helpline open Mon-Fri 9 am-5 pm (extending to 7 pm). Support & advice to those who have or who are growing up in an alcoholic or disfunctional home.

National Association for Premenstrual Syndrome
Eve Browton , Office Manager
P O Box 72
Sevenoaks TN13 1XQ
T 01732 459378
Information line: 01732 741709. Provides personal support & advice to sufferers, their partners & families. Immediate help to sufferers through national helpline open five days a week. NAPS News newsletter.

National Asthma Campaign
Melinda Letts, Chief Executive
Providence House
Providence Place

NATIONAL- HEALTH

London N1 ONT
T 0171 226 2260 F 0171 704 0740
Information & advice to asthma sufferers: adults, children & schools. Videos in several Asian languages. Helpline: 0345 010203 - 24 hours; information line: 0171 971 0444.

National Asthma Campaign Scotland
21 Coates Crescent
Edinburgh EH3 7AF
T 0131 226 2544 F 0131 226 2401
Helpline 0345 010203 open Mon-Fri 9 am-7 pm. staffed by specialist nurses. Umbrella organisation for a network of branches. Providing information & support to those affected by asthma. Funding research.

National Autistic Society
276 Willesden Lane
London NW2 5RB
T 0181 451 1114
Offers families & carers information, advice & support to improve awareness amongst decision-makers, professionals & general public; providing training & promoting research into autism; etc.

National Bd Nursing, Midwifery & Health Visiting - Scotland
David Ferguson, Corporate Services Manager
22 Queen Street
Edinburgh EH2 1NT
T 0131 226 7371 F 0131 225 9970
Statutory body responsible for the education & training of nurses, midwives & health visitors in Scotland. Open Mon-Fri 8.30 am-4.30 pm.

National Eczema Society
163 Eversholt Street
London NW1 1BU
T 0171 388 4097
Improving quality of life for people with eczema & those caring for them. Empowering people with eczema to receive quality of treatment & care they have a right to expect. Information/advice on 0171 388 4800.

National Endometriosis Society
Sandra French
Suite 50
Westminster Palace Gardens
1-7 Artillery Row
London SW1P 1RL
T 0171 222 2781 F 0171 222 2786

National helpline 0171 222 2776 available every day 7-10 pm. Help & support available enabling self-help groups to exist. Informal clubs. Publications.

National Osteoporosis Society
Linda Edwards
P O Box 10
Radstock
Bath BA3 3YB
T 01761 471771 F 01761 471104
Helpline 01761 472721. Aims to make doctors & the general public more aware of osteoporosis. Publishes several self-help booklets. Send sae with 18p stamp for full list.

National Slimming Centres
Marilyn Russell
15 Crown Hill
Croydon CR0 1RY
T 0181 686 2111
Weight loss programme with consultations with doctor who advises on what to eat. Weekly check up with doctor with medication to help with diet. Self-referrals. Private - not part of NHS.

Nuffield Hospitals Health Screening
Lorna Young, Business Office Manager
Woodside House
Winchester Road
Eastleigh S05 2DW
T 01703 271288
Write for information about Nuffield hospitals, well woman screening & full health assessments for women at the above address. Phone for details of your nearest hospital.

Overeaters Anonymous
E Harrison
P O Box 19
Stretford
Manchester M32 9EB
T 0161 762 9348
For women & men affected by food/eating behaviours. Offers support & understanding. Meetings held throughout the UK. Applies principles of 12-Step Programme. Phone for details of local groups.

Patients' Association
Stephen Peebles, Information Manager
8 Guildford Street
London WC1N 1DT
T 0171 242 3460 F 0171 242 3461

sp@patients.demon.co.uk
Advice service & collective voice for patients. To present & further the interests of patients, provide information & advice & promote goodwill between patients & everyone in the medical profession.

Pelvic Inflammatory Disease Network
C/o Women's Health
52 Featherstone Street
London EC1Y 8RT
T 0171 251 6580
Support network for PID sufferers who can contact each other via women's health enquiry lines. Free leaflet. Twice-yearly newsletters.

PMS Help
Mrs Wendy M Holton
P O Box 83
Hereford HR4 8YQ
F 01432 760993
National postal organisation to help sufferers of pre menstrual syndrome (PMS) & postnatal depression (PND) & their families. Also helps medical health workers reach an understanding of these conditions.

PMS Help
P O Box 160
St Albans AL1 4UQ
Write for information about premenstrual syndrome (PMS), postnatal illness/postnatal depression or the menopause. Send large sae. Free leaflets.

Polycystic Ovary Syndrome Association
C/O FACE
P O Box 484
Cambridge CB4 3TF

Positive Youth
C/o Body Positive
51b Philbeach Gardens
London SW5 9EB
T 0171 835 1045 F 0171 373 5237
Helpline 0171 373 9124, phone Mon-Fri 7-10 pm; Sat & Sun 4-10 pm. Self-help group offering advice, information, support & social activities to young people aged 16-25 living with & affected by HIV/AIDS.

Positively Women
347-349 City Road
London EC1V 1LR
T 0171 713 0222 F 0171 713 1020

A national charity with support groups in various parts of London. A self-help organisation for women with HIV/AIDS. Helpline open Mon, Wed, Thurs & Fri 10 am-5 pm; Tue 10 am-12 pm. Free & confidential.

Pre-Eclampsia Society (PETS)
Dawn James
12 Monksford Drive
Hullbridge SS5 6D2
T 01702 230493
Support & information for anyone suffering or who has suffered from pre-eclampsia. Newletters, library service, telephone support.

Pre-Eclamptic Toxaemia Society (PETS)
Dawn James
Ty Iago
Carmel
Caernarvon LL54 7AD
T 01286 880057
Support for sufferers from pre-eclamptic toxaemia.

Premenstrual Society (PREMSOC)
Dr M C Brush
P O Box 429
Addlestone KT15 1DZ
T 01932 872560
Information & support to individual PMS sufferers; educational courses on PMS; helping individuals & organisations aiming to start self-help groups; supporting research on PMS in any way possible.

QUEST Cancer Research
Mrs Jean Pitt
Woodbury
Harlow Road
Roydon
Harlow CM19 5HF
T 01279 792233 F 01279 793340
Committed to funding the medical research necessary to develop new comprehensive methods of detecting cancer by combining screening, diagnosis & prognosis together. No animals used in research.

QUIT
Victory House
170 Tottenham Court Road
London W1E 0NS
T 0171 487 3000

NATIONAL- HEALTH

The above phone number is the QUIT smokers' quitline, offering advice & help on how to stop smoking. Free information packs & free telephone counselling. (Women counsellors can be asked for.)

Radiotherapy Injured Patients Support (RIPS)
Cindy Ricketts
194 Colchester Road
Lawford CO11 2BP
T 01206 395610
Support for those damaged by cancer radiotherapy treatment. Advice on benefits, disability allowance, care organisations/agencies. Medical negligence solicitor available. Phone 11.30 a.m-3 pm.

RAGE National
Vicky Parker
24 Lockett Gardens
Trinity
Salford
Manchester M3 6BJ
T 0161 839 2927
vicky @rage-ntl.demon.co.uk
Helping women & men with problems after radiotherapy. Phone & newsletter. Phone any time, also 0161 682 4255. Wanting more info for people about to have radiotherapy, proper pain control, compensation, etc.

Release
388 Old Street
London EC1V 9LT
T 0171 729 9904
Advice/information on drugs & drug-related legal problems. Above phone number is a helpline operating Mon-Fri 10 am-6 pm. Outside these hours phone 0171 603 8654 24-hour emergency helpline.

Repetitive Strain Injury Association (RSIA)
Chapel House
152-156 High Street
Yiewsley, West Drayton
Middlesex UB7 7BE
T 01895 431134
Helpline open Mon-Fri 12-4 pm. Information, help & advice for RSI sufferers. Information pack available on request.

Restricted Growth Association
Mrs Honor Rawlings, National Development Officer
P O Box 8
Coutesthorpe
Leicester LE8 5ZS
T 0116 247 8913
Aims to remove social barriers experienced by individuals of restricted growth; to improve quality of life & help alleviate fear & distress experienced by families when their child of restricted growth is born.

Royal College of Nursing
Jackie Mensah
20 Cavendish Square
London W1M 0AB
T 0171 409 3333 F 0171 495 6104
Open Mon-Fri 9 am-5 pm. Professional nursing body/trade union representing over 300,000 nurses. Advice, clinical development, higher education, career development for nurses & nursing students.

SAD Association (SADA)
the administrator
P O Box 989
Steyning BN44 3HG
T 01903 814942 F 01903 814942
Provides information about seasonal affective disorder (SAD). Meetings, light box hire scheme, newsletters, networking.

Schizophrenia A National Emergency (SANE)
Marjorie Wallace, Chief Executive
199-205 Old Marylebone Road
London NW1 5QP
T 0171 724 6520 F 0171 724 6502
A national telephone helpline for anyone coping with mental illness, whether sufferers, carers, concerned relatives, friends; Helpline 0345 678000 open 2 pm-midnight every day. Campaigns to change attitudes.

Scottish Association for Mental Health
Cheryl Minto
Atlantic House
38 Gardners Crescent
Edinburgh EH3 8DQ
T 0131 229 9681 F 0131 229 3558
Provides direct services to people with mental health problems. Campaigns for recognition of their fundamental human & citizens' rights.

Scottish Council on Alcohol
Mrs Ann Furst, Appeals Director
166 Buchanan Street
Glasgow G1 2NH
T 0141 333 9677 F 0141 333 1606

A network of 28 local agencies. Counselling, advice, support for women with alcohol related problems & for women living with someone with a drinking problem. Also available are self-help/educational materials.

Shingles Support Society
Marian Nicholson
41 North Road
London N7 9DP
T 0171 607 9661
Supplies information & advice on medical treatment & self help for post-herpetic neuralgia (PHN) which, particularly in older people, can follow shingles: a recurrence of chickenpox (herpes varicella-zoster).

Standing Conference on Drug Abuse (SCODA)
Waterbridge House
32-36 Loman Street
London SE1 0EE
T 0171 928 9500 F 0171 928 3343
Aims to improve health service provision for drug users by influencing policy at government & local levels. Advices on drug & HIV services. Up to date information on specialist services.

Tak Tent Cancer Support - Scotland
Carol Horne, Manager
Block C20
Western Court
100 University Place
Glasgow G12 6SQ
T 0141 211 1930 F 0141 211 1879
Support, information, practical help for patients, carers, friends & professionals affected by cancer - at resource centre, on phone (0141 211 1932) & in groups/communities around Scotland. Women only staff.

Terence Higgens Trust
52-54 Grays Inn Road
London WC1X 8JU
T 0171 242 1010
Helpline above open noon-10 pm daily. Administration 0171 831 0330; legal line 0171 1405 2381. Counselling & family therapy for people with HIV/AIDS or those concerned with it. Health education & advice.

Time Out (Scotland)
Sheena Mackinnon
C/o GCVS
11 Queen's Crescent

Glasgow G4 9AS
T 0141 337 2521
Provides support & information to sufferers of depression, past & present. Self-help groups, allowing opportunity to talk to & get support from others who have experienced depression. 24-hour ansaphone.

Toxic Shock Syndrome Association
24-28 Bloomsbury Way
London WC1A 2PX
T 0171 617 8040 F 0171 831 0752
Provides free leaflets, general information, etc to the general public & health professionals about toxic shock syndrome. The above telephone is a 24-hour pre-recorded advice line.

Toxoplasmosis Trust, The
Rachel Dyke
61 Collier Street
London N1 9BE
T 0171 713 0663 F 0171 713 0611
Helpline: 0171 713 0599. Provides information & support to anyone concerned about, or suffering from, toxoplasmosis. Publications. Helpline open Mon-Fri 9.30-5.30. Aims to provide an up-to-date advice centre.

UK Thalassaemia Society
107 Nightingale Lane
London N8 7QY
T 0181 348 0437
Counselling to Thalassaemia sufferers & carriers. Promotes research & educational work on problems of Thalassaemia. Leaflets & booklets. Some information & interpreting available.

WISH (Women in Special Hospitals)
Liz Mayne, Director
15 Great St Thomas Apostle
London EC4V 2BB
T 0171 329 2415 F 0171 329 2416
Supports & advocates on behalf of women in secure psychiatric units, in particular women in Special Hospitals.

Women in Gynaecology and Obstetrics (WIGO)
Dr M C Davies
78 Queen's Head Street
London N1 8NG
T 0171 226 9022 F 0171 226 9022

NATIONAL - INTERNATIONAL

For women doctors specialising in obstetrics & gynaecology. Aiming for greater influence for women doctors within the field, improvements in training & working patterns & improved care for women patients.

Women in Medicine
the secretary
21 Wallingford Avenue
London W10 6QA
T 0181 960 7446
A political voice for women medical doctors & medical students; to counteract adverse propaganda & stereotyping of women as users & providers of health care; to share information about women in medicine, etc.

Women in Optics
Sue Cutts, Secretary
7 Hall Orchard
Branshall
Uttoxeter
T 01889 566534
Support group for women working in the optical profession & students of optics. To promote cooperation among members; to provide information for women on aspects of their professional life, etc.

Women in Special Hospitals (WISH)
Annette Groom/Carole Rigby
15 Great St Thomas Apostle
London EC4V 2BB
T 0171 329 2415 F 0171 329 2416
Advocacy; befriending & supporting women in secure psychiatric containment.

Women's Cancer Detection Society
Mr G F Loble, Chairman
Breast Screening & Assessment Centre
Queen Elisabeth Hospital
Gateshead
Tyne & Wear NE9 6SX
T 0191 487 5646 F 0191 285 2547
Supports Breast Screening And Assessment Centre at Queen Elisabeth Hospital by purchasing equipment not available on NHS budget. Finances research into breast cancer. Supports initiatives for women's education.

Women's Health
52 Featherstone Street
London EC1Y 8RT
T 0171 251 6580 F 0171 608 0928

Committed to providing information in a supportive manner, helping women to make informal decisions about their health. Helpline open Mon, Wed, Thurs, Fri 10 am-4 pm. Publications.

Women's Health Concern
Mrs Joan Jenkins
93-99 Upper Richmond Road
Putney
London SW15 2TG
T 0181 780 3916 F 0181 780 3945
Helpline 0181 780 3007. Helps women to access information & free expert advice for all kinds of gynaecological, hormonal & associated health problems. Publications. Counselling services, video.

Women's Nationwide Cancer Control Campaign
Mary Button, Information Officer
Suna House
128-130 Curtain Road
London EC2A 3AR
T 0171 729 4688 F 0171 613 0771
wnccc@dial.pipex.com
Helpline: 0171 729 2229 open Mon-Fri 9.30 am-4.30 pm. Supports provision of facilities for early cancer diagnosis, primarily breast, cervical & ovarian. Publications, videos. Health days for homeless women.

Women's Nutritional Advisory Service
Maryon Stewart, Founder & Nutritionist
P O Box 268
Lewes BN7 2QN
T 01273 487366 F 01273 487576
Open 9 am-5.30 pm. Provides tailor-made dietary programmes for women suffering from a range of problems such as PMS, IBS, menopause, sugar craving & general health & nutritional deficiencies.

INTERNATIONAL

ACTIONAID
Antonella Mancini
Hamlyn House
MacDonald Road
London N19 5PG
T 0171 281 4101 F 0171 272 0899
Aims to tackle causes & effects of absolute poverty through integrated long-term development programmes. Links donors to ACTIONAID in UK to child sponsorship schemes.

Altrusa International Dublin Club
Mrs Lindy Colligan

Flat 1
225a Lower Kimmage Road
Dublin 6
T 01 492 1292
DEMPSEY@AM.ibec.team400.ie
An international organisation dedicated to community service; fostering the full personal & professional development of the businesswoman. Holds about two meetings per month, one business & one social.

Associated Country Women of the World
Anna Frost, General Secretary
Vincent House
Vincent Square
London SW1P 2NB
T 0171 834 8635 F 0171 233 6205
Aims to raise standards of living & education of women & their families worldwide through community development projects & training. Promoting goodwill, friendship & understanding between country women.

Corona Worldwide (Women's Corona Society)
C/o The Commonwealth Insitute
Kensington High Street
London W8 6NQ
T 0171 610 4407 F 0171 602 7374
Helps families to live in countries other than their own through a briefing service. Multicultural & secular; networks of branches & associated societies which are coordinated at London HQ.

European Women's Management Development International Network
Geraldine Upfold, Chair
4 Great Notley Avenue
Great Notley
Braintree CM7 8UW
T 01376 330459 F 01376 330459
EWDNetworkUK@Compuserve.Com
An international network of women in positions of responsibility in business, education & the professions, & women entrepreneurs. Enabling women to fully realise their potential.

International Women Count Network
Anne Neale
Crossroads Women's Centre
230a Kentish Town Road
London NW5 2AB
T 0171 482 2496 F 0171 209 4761
199919.2311@compuserve.com
Phone Mon-Fri 10 am-12.30 pm & 1.30-4 pm; Thurs 5-7 pm. Centre open Tue & Wed 12-4 pm & Thurs 5-7 pm Won UN decision that governments to measure & value unwaged work. Campaigning for implementation.

International Women's Week Collective
Viv Peto
61 Great Clarendon Street
Oxford OX2 6AX
T 01865 510066
Organises international women's festival annually in March coinciding with International Women's Day on 8 March (two-week festival in Oxford Town Hall). Holds events in poorer parts of the City.

National Women's Network for International Solidarity
83 Margaret Street
London W1N 7HB
T 0181 809 2388
nwnukwide@gn.apc.org
Network facilitating information exchange between groups & individuals. Feminist solidarity for women & women's organisations in UK & abroad. Campaigning for government policy changes.

Northern Ireland Women's European Platform (NIWEP)
Carol Conlin/Bronagh Hinds
52 Elmwood Avenue
Belfast BT9 6AZ
T 01232 682296 F 01232 682185
Umbrella body of groups with primary interest in matters of importance to women. A founding member of the UK Joint Committee on Women & of the European Women's Lobby.

Rhwydwaith Ewropeaidd Merched Cymru
Gabrielle Suff, Secretary
87 Dunvant Road
Killay
Swansea SA2 7NN
T 01792 208979
Wales Women's Euro Network is a non-party organisation working through women's voluntary organisations. Aims primarily to promote the interests of women in Wales with regard to European issues.

Womankind Worldwide
Simona Halambri, Information Officer
3 Albion Place
Galena Road

Hammersmith
London W6 0LT
T 0181 563 8607 F 0181 563 8611
womankind@gn.apc.org
Supports women in developing countries in their struggle for personal development & collective empowerment, for the eradication of poverty & want. Phone 1081 563 8609 for overseas programme.

Women of Europe Award (UK Association)
Alison Parry/Rebecca Hoar
Dean Bradley House
52 Horseferry Road
London SW1P 2AF
T 0171 233 1422 F 0171 799 2817
UK branch of the International Association. Annual selection & presentation of the women of Europe award to the UK woman of Europe. Supports occasional conferences. Creation of a network of active women.

Women Welcome Women
Frances Alexander
88 Easton Street
High Wycombe HP11 1LT
T 01494 465441 F 01494 465441
Aims to foster international friendship by enabling women of different countries to visit one another. Any woman may become a member, regardless of nationality, religion, home circumstances, etc.

Women Working Worldwide
Angela Hale
Centre for Employment Research
St Augustine's
Lower Chatham Street
Manchester M15 6BY
T 0161 247 1760 F 0161 247 6333
women-ww@mcrl.poptel.org.uk

Women's Development Agency
Matilda Nantogmah
109 Hicks Avenue
Greenford
Middlesex UB6 8HB
T 0181 813 0197 F 0181 575 8067
Promoting any charitable purpose to benefit women & children living in any part of the world, particularly to relieve poverty, distress & sickness & to advance education. Particularly related to Black women.

Women's Forum Scotland
C/o IPMS
18 Melville Terrace
Stirling FK8 2NQ
T 01786 465999 F 01786 465516
For women in Scotland in the European Women's Lobby to ensure the concerns, views & priorities of women are on the European agenda. Considering the lack of women on public bodies in Scotland, etc.

WomenAid International
Pida Ripley, Founder
3 Whitehall Court
London SW1A 2EL
T 0171 976 1032 F 0171 839 2929
International aid agency. Focusses on humanitarian issues such as aid to the former Yugoslavia. Funding grassroots organisations.

IRISH WOMEN

Irish Women's Defence Campaign
59 Stoke Newington Church Street
London N16 0AR
T 0171 249 7318
Campaigning against strip-searching

JEWISH WOMEN

35s Women's Campaign for Soviet Jewry
Margaret Rigal
Pannell House
779-81 Finchley Road
London NW11 8DN
T 0171 458 7148 F 0171 458 9971
Helps Jews in Russia, mainly the old, sick & children. A circular issued fortnightly giving news of FSU & Israel. Runs the One-to-One project which assists the disadvantaged among the new settlers in Israel.

Association of Jewish Women's Organisations in the UK (AJWO)
Mrs Joy Conway
4th Floor
24-32 Stephenson Way
London NW1 2JW
T 0171 387 7688 F 0171 387 2110
Furthers communal understanding & deliberates on matters of common interest & concern; works towards promoting unity among Jewish women of differing shades of opinion, etc.

League of Jewish Women
Marilyn Herman, Hon Secretary
24-32 Stephenson Way
London NW1 2JW
T 0171 387 7688 F 0171 387 2110

To unite Jewish women of every shade of opinion who are resident in Great Britain. To stimulate in Jewish women their sense of civic duty & to encourage expression of it by increased service to the country.

Legal Matters

Campaign Against Racist Laws (CARL)
G Cremer
15 Kenton Avenue
Southall
Ealing
London UB1 3QF
T 0181 571 1437 F 0181 571 9723
Campaigns & coordinates activities against racist immigration laws which can divide families & trap women in violent marriages.

Legal Action for Women
C/o Crossroads Women's Centre
230a Kentish Town Road
London NW5 2AB
T 0171 482 2496 F 0171 209 4761

Legal Services Agency (LSA)
Paul Brown, Chief Executive
11th Floor, Fleming House
134 Renfrew Street
Glasgow G3 6ST
T 0141 353 3354 F 0141 353 0354
National community law centre, user-controlled. Information about rights. Aims to tackle unmet legal needs. Deals with homelessness, domestic violence, race/sex discrimination, etc. Initial advice always free.

Lesbian and Bisexual

Acceptance
Mrs Jill Green
64 Holmside Avenue
Halfway Houses
Sheerness ME12 3EY
T 01795 661463
Helpline open Tue-Fri 7-9 pm. For parents & families of lesbians & gay men. Main purpose is to break down feelings of isolation & despair when told your child is lesbian or gay. Info pack (small fee).

Bisexuals Action on Sexual Health (BASH)
P O Box 10048
London SE15 4ZD
kcl@doc.ic.ac.uk
Promoting the sexual health of people who have sex with both men & women however they identify, & of people who are self-identified bisexuals.

Campaign for Homosexual Equality
P O Box 342
London WC1X 0DU
T 0171 833 3912 F 0181 743 6252
Aims for social & legal equality for homosexual & bisexual women & men. Drafts amendments to the law. Provides information to individuals. Line open Mon, Wed, Fri 12-6 pm. Otherwise an ansaphone.

Families and Friends of Lesbians and Gays (FFLAG)
Brenda Oakes/Cath Johnson
P O Box 153
Manchester M60 1LP
T 0161 748 3452
Support for parents of lesbian daughters, gay sons. Campaigns for equal rights. Additional phone number: 0161 747 0976.

Gay and Lesbian Humanist Association (GALHA)
George Broadhead
National Office
34 Spring Lane
Kenilworth CV8 2HB
T 01926 858450 F 01926 858450
galha@compuserve.com
Arranges humanist (non-religious) ceremonies for weddings, namings & funerals. Promotes a rational humanist approach to sexuality & gay/lesbian rights as human rights. Newsletter.

Gay Authors Workshop
Kathryn Byrd
BM Box 5700
London WC1N 3XX
T 0181 520 5223
Lesbian, gay & bisexual writers meet monthly in London to read work, share information & support. Quarterly newsletter.

GEMMA
Elsa Becket
BM Box 5700
London WC1N 3XX
National friendship & information group of disabled & non-disabled lesbians & bisexual women of all ages. Social events, pen tape, phone friends, newsletter. For enquiries send sae/tape/braille.

Happy Families
Glyn or Richard
P O Box 1060
Doncaster DN6 9QE

NATIONAL - LESBIAN AND BISEXUAL

T 01302 702601 F 01302 702601
Coordinators of Gay & Lesbian Parents Coalition - International in the UK. Open to any parent who is lesbian, gay or bisexual & their children. Helpline for enquiries. Aims to link similar families nationwide.

Kenric
B M Kenric
London WC1N 3XX
Nationwide organisation for lesbians. Non-political/independent organisation run by/for lesbians with age range of 18-80 from all walks of life. Social events & group details appear in monthly newsletter.

Lesbian and Gay Bereavement Project
Anne Raitt
The Vaughan Williams Centre
Colindale Hospital
Colindale Avenue
London NW9 5HG
T 0181 200 1511 F 0181 905 9250
Helpline 0181 455 8894 open 7 pm-12 am every day, inc. Bank holidays. Counselling service Sun in Islington (phone admin number above for details). Outreach educational work; HIV awareness; nurses' training.

Lesbian and Gay Coalition Against Racism
C/o National Assembly Against Racism
28 Commercial Street
London E1 6LF
T 0171 247 9907
Campaigns to create an anti-racist voice for lesbians & gay men, also to help forge unity needed to defeat racism, homophobia & bigotry.

Lesbian and Gay Employment Rights (LAGER)
Unit 1G
Leroy House
436 Essex Road
London N1 3QP
T 0171 704 8066
Helpline open Mon-Fri 11 am-5 pm. Advice to lesbians about employment issues & rights & discrimination & harassment at work.

Lesbian and Gay Police Association (LAGPA)
BM LAGPA
London WC1N 3XX
T 01462 943011

Advice & support to lesbian & gay police officers, special constables & civilian support staff.

Lesbian and Gay Postal Action Network (LAGPAN)
24 Briggs Street
Queensbury
Bradford BD13 2EW
T 01274 883845
Campaigning group writing letters about specific targets relating to lesbian/gay equality.

Lesbian Avengers
The Wheel
4 Wild Court
Kingsway
London WC2B 4AU
T 0421 326917
Campaigning & taking direct action relating to lesbian issues. Meets Tue 7.30 at above address.

Lesbian Education and Awareness
C/o LOT
5-6 Capel Street
Dublin 1
T 01 872 0460 F 01 872 0460
leanow@indigo.ie
Office open Mon-Fri 9 am-5 pm. Training programme for women throughout Ireland. Media skills, lesbian skills, computer skills, group work, facilitation. Outreach workers trained to combat homophobia.

Lesbian Equality Network
C/o LOT
5-6 Capel Street
Dublin 1
T 01 872 7770 F 01 872 0460
leanow@indigo.ie
Lobbying for law reform. Working around issues of equality.

Lesbian Parenting
C/o Rights of Women (ROW)
52-54 Featherstone Street
London EC1Y 8RT
T 0171 251 6576
Open Mon-Thurs. Telephone advice service on lesbian parenting issues. For lesbian mothers needing information & support around contested disputes for custody of children. Referrals to experienced solicitors.

NATIONAL - LESBIAN AND BISEXUAL

Lesbians Organising Together (LOT)
5-6 Capel Street
Dublin 1
T 01 872 7770 F 01 872 0460
leanow@indigo.ie
Drop in resource centre for lesbians. Umbrella organisation for other lesbian groups in the Republic of Ireland. Open Mon-Thurs 10 am-6 pm; Fri 10 am-4 pm.

Liberal Democrats for Lesbian and Gay Action (DELGA)
C/o 4 Cowley Street
London SW1P 3NB
T 01483 771042
Promoting lesbian, gay men & bisexuals' interests in & through the Liberal Democrats.

National Union of Students - Lesbian, Gay, Bisexual Campaign
416 Holloway Road
London N7 6LJ
T 0171 272 8900
Open Mon-Fri 9 am-6 pm. Supports student union lesbian, gay & bisexual groups. National campaigns. Supports individual students.

OutRage!
5 Peter STreet
London W1V 3RR
T 0171 439 2381 F 0171 439 3291
outrage@cygnet.co.uk
Highlighting issues affecting lesbians & gays. Countering homophobia by peaceful non-violent direct action. Open meetings every Thurs evening.

Outright Scotland
Alec Deary, Secretary/Ian Dunn, Convenor
Lesbian, Gay and Bisexual Centre
58a Broughton Street
Edinburgh EH1 3SA
T 0131 557 1662 F 0131 558 1683
alecd@divcon.co.uk
Non-party political organisation promoting civil & human rights of lesbian, gay, bisexual & transgendered people. Has drafted Equality 2000 reflecting their needs & opnions. Newsletter: SHOUT!

Parents' Friend
Joy Dickens
C/o Voluntary Action Leeds
Stringer House
34 Lupton St, Hunslet
Leeds LS10 2QW
T 0113 267 4627
A national lesbian, gay & bisexual helpline & support organisation for parents finding their child or other relation, including wife/husband. Helpline operates in the evenings between 8-10 pm.

Pride Trust, The
Suite 28
Eurolink Centre
49 Effra Road
London SW2 1BZ
T 0171 738 7644 F 0171 924 0325
INFO@pride.org.uk
Gets together the annual lesbian, gay, bisexual & trans-gender Pride march & festival.

Rank Outsiders
C/o Stonewall
16 Clerkenwell Close
London EC1 0AA
T 0171 336 8860
Helpline 0171 566 0044 open Wed 7-9 pm. Information, support & advice for all lesbians, gay men & bisexuals serving in the armed forces & who find themselves discharged on account of their sexuality.

Stonewall
Angela Mason
16 Clerkenwell Close
London EC1R 0AA
T 0171 336 8860 F 0171 336 8864
National lobbying & campaigning group for lesbian & gay equality. Deals with all issues affecting the legal & social position of lesbians.

Survivors of Lesbian Abuse (SOLA)
Petra and Laura
West Hampstead Women's Centre
55 Hemstal Road
London NW6 2AD
T 0171 328 7389
Weekly phoneline Thurs 7-9 pm for women who are being or have been abused by their female partners. Weekly self-help group. To support survivors & to raise awareness on lesbian domestic violence.

UNISON - Lesbian and Gay Section
National Lesbian and Gay Officer
20 Grand Depot Road
London SE18 6SF
T 0181 854 2244

Information & advice on discrimination & trade union rights for lesbians & gay men working in the public sector. Annual national conference. Newsletter.

Wages Due Lesbians
Crossroads Women's Centre
230a Kentish Town Road
London NW5 2AB
T 0171 482 2496 F 0171 209 4761
100010.2311@compuserve.com
Mail to P O Box 287, London NW6 5QU.
Multi-racial network campaigning for social, economic & legal rights for lesbian women. Pressing for recognition & compensation for all unwaged work.

LIBRARIES/ARCHIVES

Fawcett Library, The
Christine Wise/David Doughan
London Guildhall University
Old Castle Street
London E1 7NT
T 0171 320 1189 F 0171 320 1188
doughan@lgu.ac.uk
National research library for women's history. Open Mon 10.15 am-8.30 pm (term), 9 am-5 pm (vacation); Wed 9 am-8 pm (term), 9 am-5 pm (vacation), Thurs & Fri 9 am-5 pm (term & vacation).

Feminist Audio Books
Elizabeth Reiner
52-54 Featherstone Street
London EC1Y 8RT
T 0171 281 7838
Library of feminist, lesbian & women's books on tape for blind, partially-sighted or print-disabled people. Books stocked that are not available from mainstream talking book services.

Format Photographers
Maggie Murray/Sarah Potter
19 Arlington Way
London EC1R 1UY
T 0171 833 0292 F 0171 833 0381
All-women social documentary photo library & agency representing the social, political & economic life of Britain abroad. Specialises in images of women. B&W & colour. Open Mon-Fri 10 am-6 pm.

Lesbian Archive and Information Centre (LAIC)
Sue John/Kate Henderson/Adele Patrick
C/o Glasgow Women's Library
109 Trongate
Glasgow G1 5HD
T 0141 552 8345
The UK's largest collection of materials & information for lesbians. Open Mon-Sat 2-5 pm. A treasure trove of multi-media lesbian history from ancient times to today. All cultures, religions, races.

Women's Art Library, The
Althea Greenan, Librarian
Fulham Palace
Bishop's Avenue
London SW6 6EA
T 0171 731 7618 F 0171 384 1110
womensart.lib@ukonline.co.uk
Open Tue-Fri 10 am-5 pm. Offers practising women artists the opportunity to increase public awareness about their work via press exposure & possible selection for exhibitions & books.

MEDIA

Boxclever Communication Training
Elisabeth Hannah
The Maples Centre
144 Liverpool Road
London N1 1LA
T 0171 619 0606 F 0171 7002248
information@boxclever.co.uk
Media training: radio, TV, press. Crisis management, speech preparation, presentation. Open Mon-Fri 9 am-6 pm.

Boxclever Productions
Elisabeth Hannah
The Maples Centre
144 Liverpool Road
London N1 1LA
T 0171 619 0606 F 0171 700 2248
information@boxclever.co.uk
Independent women-run film & TV production company. Open Mon-Fri 9 am-6 pm.

Campaign for Press and Broadcasting Freedom (Women's Section)
Granville Williams
8 Cynthia Street
London N1 9JF
T 0171 278 4430 F 0171 837 8868
cpbf@architechs.com
Open 10 am-6 pm Tue & Fri or use ansaphone. For greater diversity in ownership & content of media. For representation of groups discriminated against by the media. Has published books on women's issues.

Cinenova - Women's Film & Video Distribution
Helen de Witt
113 Roman Road
London E2 0QN
T 0181 981 6828 F 0181 983 4441
admin@cinenova.demon.co.uk
Theatric & non-theatric distributor of films & videos directed by women, from features to documentary, experimental to animation. Catalogue available.

Women in Film and Television
Kate Norrish
Garden Studios
11-15 Betterton Street
Covent Garden
London WC2H 9BP
T 0171 379 0344 F 0171 379 1625
wftv@easynet.co.uk
For women with minimum one year's experience in the industry. To provide information & career support, act as educational forum, lobby & campaign to safeguard members' interests & champion women's achievements.

Women's Audio Visual Education Scheme (WAVES)
Jenni Israel, Administrator
4 Wild Court
Kingsway
London WC2B 4AU
T 0171 430 1076 F 0171 242 2765
Networking & training organisation concerned with giving women in the broadcasting industries & those aspiring to them access to industry level training & retraining for the different grades.

Women's Radio Group
Julie Hill
90 de Beauvoir Road
London N1 4EN
T 0171 240 1313 F 0181 995 5442
Provides training & information for women. Training in all areas of radio production. Runs frequent seminars with speakers from the industry. Membership open to all women interested in, or working in, radio.

OLDER WOMEN

Abbeyfield
Abbeyfield House
53 Victoria Street
St Albans AL1 3UW
T 01727 857536 F 01727 846168
Providing housing to older people. 1000 houses throughout the UK. A typical house offers resident housekeeper, call alarm systems, specialist facilities (eg assisted baths, lifts), two cooked meals a day; etc.

Age Concern Cymru
Debbie Meehan, Information Officer
1 Cathedral Road
Cardiff CF1 9SD
T 01222 371566 F 01222 399562
Information, support, advice & publications of specific interest to older women.

Age Concern England
1268 London Road
London SW16 4ER
T 0181 679 8000
Office open Mon-Fri 9.15 am-5.15 pm. Promoting well being of older people & positive attitudes towards older people & ageing. Fundraising, training, publications. Phone for details of local organisations.

Age Concern Scotland
Maureen O'Neill, Director
113 Rose Street
Edinburgh EH2 3DT
T 0131 220 3345 F 0131 220 2779
Promoting the welfare of oder people in Scotland. Information, training, campaining to improve services for older people, etc.

British Pensioners and Trade Union Action Association
Norman Dodds House
315 Bexley Road
Erith DA8 3EX
T 01322 335464
Open Mon-Fri 10 am-2 pm. Campaigning on questions affecting older people such as improvements in the NHS, free travel & a better deal in pension schemes.

Care Alternatives
Lucianne Sawyer
206 Worple Road
Wimbledon
London SW20 8PN
T 0181 944 9880 F 0181 944 9660
Provides flexible care at home for elderly or disabled people. Can assist with both personal care & domestic tasks. Care workers do induction training & are thoroughly vetted.

NATIONAL - OLDER WOMEN

Centre for Policy on Ageing
Gillian Crosby
25-31 Ironmonger Row
London EC1V 3QP
T 0171 253 1787 F 0171 490 4206
Aims to raise issues of public importance on matters to do with ageing & old age, to promote debate & influence policy in ways which further the interests of older people, etc.

Contact the Elderly
15 Henrietta Street
London WC2E 8QH
T 0171 240 0630 F 0171 379 5781
Encouraging older people living alone to develop social interests by bringing companionship into their lives. Monthly Sunday afternoon outings.

Contact the Elderly in Scotland
Elspeth Horsman
361 Albert Drive
Glasgow G41 5PH
T 0141 427 0827
Relieves loneliness among frail, elderly people by means of small group outings on Sun each month. Volunteers involved as drivers, collecting the same two older people by car each month, or as hosts.

Counsel and Care
Twyman House
16 Bonny Street
London NW1 9PG
T 0171 485 1566 F 0171 267 6877
Open Mon-Fri 10.30 am-4 pm. Free advice for older people, their families & professionals. Factsheets covering welfare benefits, domestic help at home, accommodation, etc. Telephone advice 10.30 am-4 pm

Edith Cavell and Nation's Fund for Nurses
Mrs Ann Rich
Flints
Petersfield Road
Winchester SO23 0JD
T 01962 860900 F 01962 860900
Also the Groves Trust for Nurses. The Funds are able to advise & help nurses in financial difficulty. Grants are paid to trained or auxiliary nurses who have retired on tiny pensions, etc.

Elderly Accommodation Council
46a Chiswick High Road
London W4 1SZ
T 0181 742 1182 F 0181 995 7714
Detailed information on all forms of accommodation for the elderly, nationwide, & advice on top-up funding for those in homes

EXTEND
Mrs Judith Holpin
22 Maltings Drive
Wheathampstead AL4 8QJ
T 01582 832760
Movement to music for over sixties & disabled of any age. To stimulate physical & mental health, increase mobility & independence, improve strength, stamina, posture & coordination, to overcome loneliness.

Fellowship Houses Trust
Clock House
Byfleet KT14 7RN
T 01932 343172
Accommodation for older women (& men) on low incomes. Women-only accommodation in Hove.

Friends of the Elderly and Gentlefolk's Help
42 Ebury Street
London SW1W 0LZ
T 0171 730 8263 F 0171 259 0154
Providing permanent residential homes for the elderly & grants to them in their homes.

Growing Old Disgracefully (GOD) Network
Barbara Tayler/Mary Cooper
C/o Piatkus Books Ltd
5 Windmill Street
London W1P 1HF
A network for older women who want to grow old with a sense of fun & optimism. Local groups offer support & friendship. National events are organised in different parts of the country.

Help the Aged
16-18 St James' Walk
London EC1R 0BE
T 0171 253 0253 F 0171 250 4474
h22p@www.helptheaged.org.uk
Open Mon-Fri 9 am-5 pm. Fund-raising charity for elderly people. Free helpline - 0800 650065 open Mon-Fri 10 am-4 pm offers information & advice. A range of free leaflets available.

NATIONAL - PEACE GROUPS

Help the Aged - Scotland
Heriot House
Heriothill Terrace
Edinburgh EH7 4DY
T 0131 556 4666 F 0131 557 5115
Free helpline: 0800 650 065 open Mon-Fri 10 am-4 pm. Working to improve the life of older people. The helpline is for older people, their relatives, friends & carers.

National Pensioners' Convention
Jack L Thain, General Secretary
4 Stevens Street
Lowestoft NR32 2JE
T 01502 565807 F 01502 565807
Campaigns for retention of NI Pension, equality of pension age, pensions for women, including those who give up part of their lives as carers. Membership open to all.

Older Feminists' Network
Astra
54 Gordon Road
London N3 1EP
T 0181 346 1900
Aims to counter negative stereotypes of older women in society. Contacts, mutual support, exchange of ideas & information. Meetings held on second Sat of each month 11.30 am-5 pm. Newsletter.

Outreach for the Elderly Housebound and Disabled
7 Grayson Close
Stocksbridge
Sheffield S36 2BJ
T 0114 288 5346
24-hour helpline (above). Improving conditions of life for those who are disabled & housebound. Promoting wider interests, new friendships & exchange of information. Advice & information on day-to-day problems.

Pensioners' Voice
Melling House
14 St Peter Street
Blackburn BB2 2HD
T 01254 52606
Aims to obtain reasonable pensions for retired people & provision of services to alleviate loneliness. Campaigning for national travel discount scheme.

REACH
Keith Galpin
Bear Wharf
27 Bankside
London SE1 9ET
T 0171 928 0452 F 0171 928 0798
REACH finds part-time, expenses only jobs for retired business or professional women (& men) to use their skills to help voluntary organisations with charitable aims. Free service for jobs throughout UK.

Relatives' Association
Jenny Stiles, Director
5 Tavistock Place
London WC1H 9SN
T 0171 916 6055 F 0171 387 7968
Relatives & friends of older people in residential & nursing homes/long-stay hospitals, offering advice/support about caring in a home. Advice line: 0171 916 6055 open Mon-Thurs 10 am-12.30 pm & 1.30-5 pm.

Royal Society for Relief of Indigent Gentlewomen of Scotland
Mabel M Douglas
14 Rutland Square
Edinburgh EH1 2BD
T 0131 229 2308 F 0131 229 0956
Assisting women of Scottish birth/education with professional business backgrounds who exist on low incomes with limited savings. Applications considered from spinsters & widows who have attained the age of 50.

Third Age Challenge Trust
Patrick Grattan
St James' Walk
Clerkenwell Green
London EC1R 0BE
T 0171 336 7477
Supporting projects tackling age discrimination. Creating opportunities for training & helping to secure employment for older people.

Third Age Network (TAN)
Friary Mews
28 Commercial Road
Guildford GU1 4SU
T 01483 440582
For people aged over 50. Providing employment & information on earning & learning.

PEACE GROUPS

Mothers for Peace
Beryl Milner
70 Station Road
Burley in Wharfedale
Ilkley LS29 7NG

T 01943 864577
Bridge-building between mothers of different countries as essential in pursuit of world peace.

Peace House
Old Manse
Greenloaning
Dunblane FK15 0NB
T 01786 880490
Large peace & justice library. Resources on non-violence. Researching the kinds of training UN peacekeepers get, the role of civilian peace teams. Offers training in non-violent action. Not residential.

Sellafield Women's Peace Camp
Kate and Rachel
Peace House
34 Byrom Street
Todmorden OL14 5HS
T 01706 812663
The camp is on the last full weekend of every second month outside Sellafield Visitors' Centre. The Camp can also be contacted at Department 66, 1 Newton Street, Manchester M1 1HW.

Women for World Disarmament
C/o 44 Upland Road
London SE22 9EF
T 0181 299 0352
Aims to abolish war throughout the world. Networks with other women's peace organisations.

Women Together For Peace
Anne Carr
62 Lisburn Road
Belfast BT9 6AF
T 01232 315100 F 01232 314864
Open Mon-Fri 9 am-4.30 pm. Aims to bring about cessation of sectarian violence in Northern Ireland; to support the victims of sectarianism; to give women a voice in society; to create a pluralistic society.

Women Working for a Nuclear Free & Independent Pacific
83 Margaret Street
London W1N 7HB
T 0181 809 2388

Women's International League for Peace and Freedom
Mrs Ruth Osborn, Secretary
10 Melbourne Way

Newport NP9 3RE
T 01633 251548
Working towards the end of the causes of war: economic, social, psychological, political. Monthly branch meetings. Speakers & discussions on issues of international interest: peace, women's rights, disarmament.

Women's Nuclear Test Ban Network
C/o Bristol Women's Centre
43 Dulcie Road
Bristol BS5 0AX
T 0117 935 1674

WoMenwith Hill Women's Peace Camp
Helen John
Menwith Hill US Spy Base
Kettlesing Head Laybye
A59 Road
Harrogate HG3 2RA
T 01943 468593
Green Style protest to expose illegal acts by the American National Security Agency re interception of telecommunications via satellite & ground link facilities.

Zoe
Di McDonald
30 Westwood Road
Southampton SO17 1DN
T 01703 554434 F 01703 554434
A women's European resource network against violence, intolerance, militarism & war. The aim is to link & stengthen women; to help ensure that we are not divided by movements tearing Europe apart.

PHOTOGRAPHY

International Association of Women Sports Photographers
Eileen Langsley
Wayside
White Lodge Lane
Baslow
Bakewell DE4 1RQ
T 01246 582376 F 01246 582227
Aims to attract more women into the profession, to encourage them to strive for high standards & to help beginners. Also aims to increase publicity about women's sports.

IRIS The Women's Photography Project
Catherine Fenily/Kate Newton
Staffordshire University
School of Design
College Road

NATIONAL- POLITICS

Stoke-on-Trent ST4 2DE
T 01782 294721   F 01782 2294873
iris@staffs.ac.uk
Recognises & celebrates contribution made by women practitioners to development of photographic theory & practice. Research into & promotion of contemporary women photographers & writers on photography.

POLITICS

300 Group
P O Box 353
Uxbridge
London UB10 OUN
T 01895 812229   F 01895 812229
Campaigning to bring more women into Parliament; encouraging more women to participate in decision-making in all areas of public life.

Campaign Against Pornography
Anne Mayne
11 Goodwin Street
London N4 3HQ
T 0171 263 1833   F 0171 263 7424
Open Mon-Fri 10.30 am-5.30 pm. A women-led campaign raising awareness about the coercion & violence behind the production of pornography & links between use of pornography & violence against women & girls.

Charter 88 Women's Group
Anna Killick
Exmouth House
3-11 Pine Street
London EC1R 0JH
T 0171 833 1988   F 0171 833 5895
Organisation promoting constitutional reform & civil rights.

Conservative Women's National Committee
Mrs Diane Clarke
32 Smith Square
Westminster
London SW1P 3HH
T 0171 222 9000

Emily's List UK
Valerie Price
P O Box 708
London SW10 0DH
T 0171 352 7759   F 0171 352 5168
100525.3275@compuserve.com

Aims to assist & support women members of the Labour Party who wish to stand for the European & Westminster parliaments by providing financial sponsorship, training, practical support, advice & information.

European Union of Women (British Section)
Mrs Frances Tubb
Chess Park
Berks Hill
Chorleywood WD5 5AJ
T 01923 490940   F 01923 490941
Open Mon & Tue 9 am-5 pm; Thurs 1-5 pm. An association of women who are members of centre & moderate right political parties in 20 European countries. Stands for safeguarding of human dignity & freedom.

Labour Party Women
Meg Russell, National Women's Officer
John Smith House
150 Walworth Road
London SE17 1JT
T 0171 277 3502   F 0171 277 3729
lp-women@geo2.poptel.org.uk
The women's organisation of the Labour Party exists to promote women's interests & involvement in the Labour Party & to support women Labour Party members.

Labour Women's Network
Valerie Price
P O Box 708
London SW10 0DH
T 0171 352 7759   F 0171 352 5168
100525.3275@compuserve.com
Aims to encourage, assist & support Labour women who wish to stand for public office by providing training, practical support, advice & information.

Women Against Fundamentalism
B M Box 2706
London WC1 3XX
Campaigning against religious fundamentalism.

Women for Electoral Reform
Sally Stepanian
9 Gwenbrook Road
Culwell
Nottingham NG9 4A2
T 0115 922 3733

NATIONAL - PREGNANCY/CHILDBIRTH

Affiliated to Labour Campaign for Electoral Reform, an organisation campaigning for a referendum on our voting system & change to proportional representation. Also provides information on women in politics.

Women's Communications Centre
3 Albion Place
Galena Road
Hammersmith
London W6 0LT
T 0181 563 8601   F 0181 563 8605
womentalk@easynet.co.uk
Putting female perspectives forward on a broad range of social issues. Research, multi-media campaigns, advocacy. To redefine gender politics for women & men. Aims to empower widows in developing countries.

PREGNANCY/CHILDBIRTH

Association for Improvements in Maternity Services (AIMS)
Maire O'Regan
18 Firgrove Drive
Bishopstown
County Cork
T 021 342 649   F 021 342 649
Emotional support, encouragement & information when having a baby. Publications. Aims for the recognition of childbirth as a normal physiological process & scientific evaluation of active management of labour.

Association for Improvements in the Maternity Services (AIMS)
Nadine Edwards
40 Leamington Terrace
Edinburgh EH10 4JL
T 0131 229 6259   F 0131 229 6259
Offers support and information to women on many aspects of pregnancy, birth and maternity services. Quarterly journals and other publications. Free publications list available. New members welcome.

Association for Improvements in the Maternity Services (AIMS)
Sandar Warshal
40 Kingswood Avenue
London NW6 6LS
T 0181 960 5585   F 01753 654142
A pressure group for consumers of the maternity services. Offers advice & support for parents who want home or water births, as well as advice on how to get individual care for NHS. Publications.

Association for Post Natal Illness, The
Clare Delpech
25 Jerdan Place
London SW6 1BE
T 0171 386 0868   F 0171 386 8000
Open Mon-Fri 10 am-5 pm. Ansafone outside office hours. Provides information leaflets to sufferers & medical professionals. Telephone support offered by past sufferers who have now fully recovered.

Association of Breastfeeding Mothers
P O Box 441
St Albans AL4 0AS
T 01727 859189
Offers information & support to breastfeeding mothers & all those interested in breastfeeding. Counselling via telephone & post. Also phone 0181 992 8637.

Association of Radical Midwives (ARM)
Ishbel Kargar, Administration Secretary
62 Greetby Hill
Ormskirk L39 2DT
T 01695 572776   F 01695 572776
ARM@radmid.demon.co.uk
Supports those having difficulty in getting or giving sympathetic, individualised NHS maternity care. Library of current midwifery-related texts on free loan to members. National & local meetings. Publications.

Baby Milk Action
Patti Rundall
23 St Andrews Street
Cambridge CB2 3AX
T 01223 464420   F 01223 464417
babymilkacti@gn.apc.org
We work to secure an infant's right to the highest level of health, a woman's right to informed choices about infant feeding, & the right of everyone to health care facilities free from commercial pressures.

BLISS - Baby Life Support Systems
Judy Kay
17-21 Emerald Street
London WC1N 3QL
T 0171 831 9393   F 0171 404 3811
blissbaby.lss@ukonline.co.uk
To supply neonatal care equipment, neonatal nurse training & to support parents of neonates.

Breastfeeding Promotion Group
C/o National Childbirth Trust
Alexandra House

NATIONAL- PREGNANCY/CHILDBIRTH

Oldham Terrace, Acton
London W3 6WH
T 0181 992 8637 F 0181 992 5929
Offers information, support & promotion of breastfeeding.

British Pregnancy Advisory Service (BPAS)
Marketing department
Austy Manor
Wootton Wawen
Solihull B95 6BX
T 01564 793225 F 01564 794935
30 branches throughout UK offering information, counselling & treatment. A range of services for contraception & unwanted pregnancy. Phone 0345 304030 seven days a week to make appointment at nearest branch.

British Pregnancy Advisory Service - Wales
B Neaves
Ocean Chambers
Dumfries Place
Cardiff CF1 4BN
T 01222 372389 F 01222 384320
Open Mon, Tue, Thurs & Fri 8.30 am-1 pm. Providing choice & support to women with unplanned pregnancies. Consultation & counselling.

Caesarean Support Network
Yvonne Williams/ Sheila Tunstall
55 Cooil Drive
Douglas IM2 2HF
T 01624 661269
Building a network of contacts offering one-to-one counselling; regular meetings for caesarian mothers; education & information on all matters relating to caesarian delivery. Phone after 6 pm.

Campaign for Rights in Breastfeeding (CRIB)
P O Box 67
Uckfield TN22 5ZY

Care
Griselda Gordon, Secretary
Stair House Farm
Stair
Mauchline KA5 5HW
T 01292 591741

Supporting parents who know their unborn baby has a severe abnormality & who have to decide whether or not to terminate the pregnancy. Also raises awareness of problem in the medical profession.

Care For Life
P O Box 389
Basingstoke RG24 9QF
T 01256 850111 F 01256 857528
cfl@care.org.uk
The HQ of crisis pregnancy centres. Networking over 100 centres around the UK, supported by training & conferences & providing free pregnancy testing & counselling services.

Centre for Pregnancy Nutrition
Fiona Ford
University of Sheffield
Clinical Sciences Centre
Northern General Hospital
Sheffield S30 35B
T 0114 242 4084 F 0114 261 7584
Provides nutritional information to women & health professionals on preconception & nutrition in pregnancy. Helpline open Mon-Fri 9 am-4 pm. Ansaphone at other times. Leaflets available.

CHILD
Clare Brown, Executive Director
Charter House
43 St Leonards Road
Bexhill-on-Sea TN40 1JA
T 01424 732361 F 01424 731858
office@email2.child.org.uk
24-hour answering service. National self-help network for those with infertitlity problems. Provides infertility education, counselling, newsletters, helplines.

Foresight Assn. for the Promotion of Pre-Conceptual Care
Mrs Peter Barnes
28 The Paddock
Godalming GU7 1XD
T 01483 427839
Aims to secure optimum health & nutritional balance in both parents before conception; to investigate research aimed at identification & removal of potential health hazards to developing baby.

Home Birth Association of Ireland
Monica O'Connor
Langford Cottages

NATIONAL - PREGNANCY/CHILDBIRTH

Summerhill
County Meath
T 0405 57795
Information/support to parents thinking of home births. Fostering awareness of childbirth as a natural event. Monthly events in Dublin. Newsletter. Lobbying for better services. List of domiciliary midwives.

Independent Midwives Association
Alice Coyle
94 Auckland Road
Upper Norwood
London SE19 2DB
T 0181 406 3172 F 0181 771 7143
Midwives working outside the NHS to give women more choice & independence when they give birth. For a list of independent midwives please send A5 sae.

La Leche League
B M 3424
London WC1N 3XX
T 0171 242 1278
73603.21@compuserve.com
Helpline open 24 hours. Support & information for women who wish to breastfeed their babies. Leaders available at any time to speak with mothers personally on the phone. Write for nearest leader & group.

La Leche League - Scotland
Tina Cooper
47 Muirton Place
Kinloss
Forres IV36 0VJ
T 01309 691065
Information & support to women wishing to breastfeed their babies. Monthly group meetings. The venue for meetings changes, so phone above number for details.

LIFE Pregnancy Care Service
Mrs Nuala Scarisbrick
LIFE House
Newbold Terrace
Leamington Spa CV32 7TE
T 01926 421587 F 01926 336497
life@lifehq.demon.co.uk
Helpline 01926 311511. Free pregnancy testing. Accommodation/advice on housing. Counselling: pregnancy & post abortion. Practical follow-up care. Help & advice on infertility. Phone for details of local groups.

Maternity Alliance
Christine Gowdridge, Director

45 Beech Street
London EC2P 2LX
T 0171 588 8582 F 0171 588 8584
Advice line available Mon, Tue, Thurs, Fri 10 am-1 pm; Wed 2-5 pm. Campaigning for improvement in health care & support currently offered to parents-to-be, mothers, fathers & babies. Legal rights advice.

Meet-A-Mum Association (MAMA)
Beryl Washington
Cornerstone House
14 Willis Road
Croydon CR0 2XX
T 0181 665 0357 F 0181 665 1972
Helps isolated mothers who are lonely by putting them in touch with other mothers for friendship & support. Offers infomation & support to mothers suffering post-natal illness.

Midwives Information and Resource Service (MIDIRS)
Professor Lesley Page, Chair
9 Elmdale Road
Clifton
Bristol BS8 1SL
T 0117 921 1791 F 0117 921 1791
Enabling midwives to keep up to date with information & thus to provide the best care possible for women & their babies.

Multiple Births Foundation
Queen Charlotte's and Chelsea Hospital
Goldhawk Road
London W6 0XG
T 0181 748 4666
Professional support for families with twins, triplets, etc. Educates professionals on the needs of families with multiple births. A media resource centre for research workers.

National Association of Nappy Services
Birmingham
T 0121 693 4949
Phone above number to find a local cotton nappy laundry service.

National Childbirth Trust (NCT)
enquiries department
Alexandra House
Oldham Terrace
Acton
London W3 6NH
T 0181 992 2616 F 0181 992 5929

Phone 0181 992 8637 for enquiries. Offers information & support in pregnancy, childbirth & early parenthood. Runs ante-natal classes. Also breastfeeding, counselling & post-natal support. 400 branches in UK.

National Egg and Embryo Donation Society
Regional IVF Unit
St Mary's Hospital
Whitworth Park
Manchester M13 0JH
T 0161 276 6000 F 0161 224 0957
Helps women who require treatment by IVF, using donated eggs or embryos, to overcome childlessness. Directs women who wish to donate eggs to centres nearest their homes.

Post Natal Distress Association of Ireland
Elizabeth Behan
Carmichael House
4 North Brunswick Street
Dublin 7
T 01 872 7172 F 01 873 5737
Friendship & support for women suffering depression after childbirth. Helpline open Mon-Fri 9 am-1 pm.

Preconception/Forsight
Mrs B Barnes
28 The Paddock
Godalming GU8 5PN
T 01483 427839
Promotes care for both parents before conception. Pre-conceptual consultation. Phone for further information.

Progress Educational Trust
Juliet Tizzard
16 Mortimer Street
London W1N 7RD
T 0171 636 5390 F 0171 637 1378
Researching into the earliest stages of human development & prevention of infertility, miscarriage & congenital handicap.

Royal College of Midwives
Karlene Davis, General Secretary
15 Mansfield Street
London W1M 0BE
T 0171 872 5100 F 0171 872 5101
Provides educational courses for midwives over a wide range of subjects such as maternity & child care, personal development; acts as a voice for all midwives to improve pay & working conditions, etc.

Scottish Independent Midwives
Linda Bryce
1 Morning Hill
Peebles EH45 9JS
T 01721 729601
Birth preparation & ante-natal classes. Hire of birth pool. Information on all aspects of birth. Mainly home birth service. Working towards obtaining contracts within the NHS in Scotland.

Twins and Multiple Births Association (TAMBA)
Gina Siddons
P O Box 30
Little Sutton
South Wirral
Merseyside L66 1TH
T 0151 348 0020 F 0151 200 5309
Twinline 01732 868000 available Mon-Fri 7-11 pm & Sat & Sun 10 am-11 pm. Supporting families with twins, triplets or more, individually, through local Twins Clubs & specialist support groups, etc.

WellBeing
Mary Stanton
27 Sussex Place
Regent's Park
London NW1 4SP
T 0171 262 5337 F 0171 7224 7725
mary.stanton@wellbeing.org.uk
Funds medical & scientific research for better health of women & babies. Promotes research in a wide range of gynaecological & obstetric problems.

PRISONERS/PRISONERS' WIVES

African Women Prisoners' Project
Gloria Ogunbadejo, Development and Outreach Officer
C/o Akina Mama wa Afrika
4 Wild Court
London WC2B 4AU
T 0171 405 0678 F 0171 831 3947
amwa@greenet.apc.org
Legal advice centre & counselling service for African women. Looks after welfare of African women in British prisons & their families. Ensures that basic human rights of African women prisoners are respected.

Black Female Prisoners' Scheme
Berverly Prowst
Room 29
Eurolink Business Centre
49 Effra Road
London SW2 1BZ
T 0171 733 5520

NATIONAL - PROFESSIONAL ASSOCIATIONS

Advice, support, family reunion, housing, training, employment. A service provided by a Black project for Black women.

Federation of Prisoners' Families Support Groups
Chief Olusegun Gbeleyi
C/o SCF
Cambridge House
Cambridge Grove
London W6 0LE
T 0181 741 4578 F 0181 741 4505
The national umbrella organisation founded to encourage the development of, & act as a voice for, organisations which provide assistance to the families of people in prison.

Female Prisoners' Welfare Project and Hibiscus
Olga Heaven
15 Great St Thomas Apostle
London EC4V 2BB
T 0171 329 2384 F 0171 329 23385
Providing welfare advice & support for female prisoners & their families. Visiting prisons. Providing reports for foreign nationals in Nigeria & Jamaica.

National Assn for the Care & Resettlement of Offenders (NACRO)
Selina Corkery, Publications and Information Officer
169 Clapham Road
London SW9 0PU
T 0171 582 6500 F 0171 735 4666
Information, advice & support to ex-prisoners offenders. Youth training programmes. Women prisoners' resource centres. Race unit. Training & Development Services. Publications.

Prisoners' Advice and Information Network (PAIN)
BM Pain
London WC1N 3XX
T 0181 542 3744
Links the following organisations: Black Female Prisoners' Scheme, Women in Prison, PROP & INQUEST - Deaths in Custody. Makes referral from prisoners or their families regarding all aspects of their treatment.

Prisoners' Advice Service
Fidelma O'Hagan
Unit 305
Hatton Square
16-16a Baldwin's Gardens
London EC1N 7RJ
T 0171 405 8090 F 0171 405 8045
Free, independent, confidential advice to prisoners concerning rights & application of prison rules. Takes up complaints & legal action if appropriate. Open Mon-Fri 9.30-5.30 for telephone enquiries. Ansaphone.

Prisoners' Families and Friends Service
20 Trinity Street
London SE1 1DB
T 0171 403 4091
Open Mon-Fri 10 am-5 pm or ansaphone. Information & advice to families of prisoners on any matters resulting from imprisonment. Information service available by telephone & letter to families throughout UK.

Women in Prison
3b Aberdeen Studios
22 Highbury Grove
London N5 2EA
T 0171 226 8180 F 0171 354 8005
Dealing with problems that affect women currently in prison. Open Mon-Fri 9 am-5 pm. Women in prison can phone for advice. Ground floor & toilet wheelchair access.

PROFESSIONAL ASSOCIATIONS

Association for Child Psychology & Psychiatry
Fred Wentworth-Bowyer
St Saviours House
39-41 Union Street
London SE1 1SD
T 0171 403 7458 F 0171 403 7081
Academic charity comprising membership of child psychologists/psychiatrists & any allied disciplines. Organises conferences. Publications.

Association for Women in Science and Engineering (AWISE)
Dr Christine Linfield, Administrator
One Park Square West
London NW1 4LJ
T 0171 935 3282 F 0171 935 0736
awise@wellcome.ac.uk
Looking for ways in which the potential, skills & expertise of women might best be secured in the fields of biology, science, engineering.

Association of Secretaries
Mrs S Dobbie
28 The Green
Elwick
Hartlepool TS27 3EF

T 01429 267394
Meets first Mon of each month at Grand Hotel, Hartlepool 7.30 pm. Social contact with secretaries. Branches throughout England & Scotland.

Association of Women Barristers
the chairwoman
P O Box 11750
London WC2A 3RX
To represent, support & further the interests of women barristers.

Association of Women Psychotherapists
167 Sumatra Road
London NW6 1PN
T 0181 202 0816
Group of psychoanalytically-trained psychotherapists affiliated to the Women's Therapy Centre. All fully trained & qualified. Consultation & referral services. Providing short- & long-term group work, etc.

Association of Women Solicitors
Judith McDermott
Communication Division
Law Society House
50 Chancery Lane
London WC2A 1SX
T 0171 242 1222 F 0171 405 9522
Promotes the professional & business interests of women solicitors. There are regional groups, meetings, courses & lectures, networking & a working party.

British Association For Counselling
1 Regent Place
Rugby CV21 2PJ
T 01788 578328 F 01788 562189
bac@bac.co.uk
Aims to promote counselling, develop & improve standards of counselling & training in counselling. Lists of counsellors in local areas available on recept of A4 sae. Information regarding training available.

British Association for Sexual and Marital Therapy
hon Secretary
P O Box 62
Sheffield S10 6T6
Advancing training of sexual & relationship therapists. Promoting sexual & relationship therapy. Providing information to the public about problems & treatments available.

British Association of Analytical Body Psychotherapy
the secretary
47 Dean Court Road
Rottingdean
Brighton BN2 7DL
T 01273 303382 F 01273 308020
Body-oriented analytical psychotherapy.

British Association of Women Entrepreneurs (BAWE)
Arline Woutersz, National President
114 Gloucester Place
London W1H 3DB
T 0171 935 0085 F 0171 224 0582
woutersz@msn.com
Brings together all women who own or control a manufacturing or services company or a retail business, whether operating alone, with co-directors or with members of their family.

British Women Pilots' Association
Valerie Cahill, Chairman
Vector House
Merle Common Road
Oxted RH8 0RP
T 01883 732102 F 01883 717924
To promote women in aviation. To arrage flying events. Training & careers advice.

Engender
Sue Robertson
C/o One Parent Families Scotland
Edinburgh EH1 3NX
T 0131 558 9596 F 0131 557 9650
engender@engender.org.uk
A research & campaigning organisation for women in Scotland. Publishes an annual gender audit on women's position in Scotland. Newsletter. Details of membership & publications from above address.

European Women in Mathematics (EWM)
Dr Catherine Hobbs
School of Computing & Math. Sciences
Oxford Brookes University
Gipsy Lane, Headington
Oxford OX3 0BP
T 01865 483686 F 01865 483666
cahobbs@brookes.ac.uk
Aims to encourage/support women in mathematics & to foster international scientific cooperation among women & men in mathematical community. Biannual conferences held in Europe & UK branch meets regularly.

NATIONAL - PROFESSIONAL ASSOCIATIONS

Gender and Mathematics Association (GAMMA)
C/o Assn for Teachers of Mathematics
7 Shaftesbury Street
Derby DE3 8YB
Evolving strategies & creating resources to reduce gender bias in mathematics. There is a national network for the exchange & sharing of ideas.

HERA
Hilary Barber
2 Valentine Place
London SE1 8QH
T 0171 928 6147 F 0171 401 2938
Hilary@hera.demon.co.uk
Recruitment agency for social housing sector. Promotes women's career development. Sponsors & runs the 'Women achievers in housing' awards & Women in Housing Network. Also provides careers counselling.

Institute of Home Economics
Sandra Holdsworth
21 Portland Place
London W1N 3AF
T 0171 436 5677 F 0171 436 5677
Promoting the interests, education & careers of its members. Embraces disciplines of both social & natural sciences & the arts. A journal - The Home Economist.

Institute of Qualified Private Secretaries (IQPS)
Jenny Jerrum, Membership Secretary
First Floor
6 Bridge Avenue
Maidenhead SL6 1RR
T 01628 25007 F 01628 24990
To facilitate & encourage training & continuing professional development of secretaries; to raise profile of qualified secretary; raise professional standards with continuing education. Encouraging/assisting.

National Association of Women Pharmacists
the secretary
C/o the Business Manager
Royal Pharmaceutical Society
1 Lambeth High Street
London SE1 7JN
T 0171 735 9141 F 0171 735 7629
To promote the careers of women in pharmacy & of women pharmacists in public life; to encourage continuing education & career development for women pharmacists; to represent pharmacy with other organisations.

National Consumer Council
20 Grosvenor Gardens
London SW1W 0DH
T 0171 730 3469 F 0171 730 0191
Representing the interests of the consumers of goods & services of all kinds, whether publically or privately supplied.

Prowess Ltd
Jo Cutmore, Director
118 Eaton Square
London SW1W 9AF
T 0171 245 6153 F 0171 823 1536
markscottatprowess@compuserve.com
Promoting people from under represented groups to position of non-executive director on public & public sector boards. Recruitment, nomination, selection, management development & training.

RELATE (formerly National Marriage Guidance Council)
Herbert Gray College
Little Church Street
Rugby CV21 3AP
T 01788 573241 F 01788 535007
relate@ukonline.co.uk
Counselling & psycho-sexual therapy for adults with relationship difficulties, whether married or not. To contact local RELATE centre, look in phone book under 'R' for RELATE or 'M' for marriage guidance.

United Kingdom Home Economics Federation
Miss Jane Lloyd Hughes, Hon Secretary
Dolwen
7 Conwy Crescent
Llandudno LL30 1NS
T 01492 581048 F 01492 581048
To advance public education in the science & practice of home economics for the benefit of the community. Promotes development of home economics & considers matters of common interest to its members.

Women Architects Group of the RIBA
Sue Carmichael
F 0151 427 9860
Promoting the interests of women architects.

NATIONAL- PROFESSIONAL ASSOCIATIONS

Women As Role Models (WARM)
Gail Waldman
Waldman and Jim Architects
383 Liverpool Road
London N7 8PG
T 0171 607 6416
Acting as role models to schoolgirls, women students & younger members of the construction professions.

Women Chemists Committee
Royal Society of Chemistry
Burlington House
Picadilly
London W1V 0BN
T 0171 437 8656 F 0171 437 8883
Advises Society's steering & coordinating cittee on development & coordination of Society policy regarding women engaged in chemisty surveys, professional symposia. Network of groups & bank of women chemists.

Women in Banking and Finance
Ann Leverett
43 Keswick Road
West Wickham BR4 9AS
T 0181 777 6902 F 0181 777 7064
Aims to develop & promote the role of women throughout the financial community. Bi-monthly newsletter. Monthly calendar of events. Training courses. Networking with other members. Speakers.

Women in Dentistry
Marion Press
609 Nelson House
Dolphin Square
London SW1V 3NZ
T 0171 798 8183 F 0171 798 5628
To help women dentists achieve their potential through the benefits of practical support & advice, personal contact & discussion & political representation. 24-hour ansaphone & fax.

Women in Direct Marketing
Chantal Butler
Prime Prospects Ltd
47 Wetherby Mansions
Earls Court Square
London SW5 9BH
T 0171 244 8888 F 0171 244 9916
Networking group for women working in all sectors of UK direct marketing industry. Social & training events to develop business & personal skills, directory, newsletters. Membership of WDM International.

Women in Fundraising Development
42 Middleton Drive
Pinner
Middlesex HA5 2PG
T 0181 868 0207 F 0181 868 0207
For women to share experiences & skills, non-competitively; to foster the professional growth of women in fundraising; provide an informal arena for the exchange of information & ideas; etc.

Women in Music
Lolita Ratchford
BAC
Lavender Hill
Battersea
London SW11 5TF
T 0171 978 4823 F 0171 978 7770
106224.2125@compuserve.com
Aims to raise awareness of women's contribution to all aspects of music. Bi-monthly news bulletin. Quarterly music information surgeries. Provides information about women's contribution to music.

Women in Physics Group
Mrs J Thomson, Hon Secretary
66 Upper Whatcombe
Frome BA11 3SE
T 01373 461213
Promoting equal opportunities for women physicists; supporting & encouraging women physicists in a career break & encouraging them to return to careers based on or involving physics, etc.

Women in Property
Fiona Alfred
24 St Ann's Villas
London W11 4RS
T 0171 603 4746 F 0171 603 2818
For women with established careers in the property industry. Sharing information; networking; tours of significant property developments; educational workshops & seminars; membership directory. Newsletter.

Women in Technology (WITEC)
Clare Manning
Sheffield Hallam University
Heriot House
Sheffield S1 1WB
T 0114 253 2041 F 0114 253 2046
witec@shu.ac.uk

European network of organisations working for development & support of women in science, engineering & technology. Student placement & short course programmes; database of women experts in SET, etc.

Women Into Science and Engineering
Marie-Noelle Barton, Manager
C/o The Engineering Council
10 Maltravers Street
London WC2R 3ER
T 0171 240 7891   F 0171 240 2517
MNBarton@engc.org.uk
Campaigning to encourage girls & women to consider careers within science & engineering. Mrs Barton manages this campaign & gives many talks. Publications posters & videos free of charge available to enquirers.

Women's Engineering Society, The
Imperial College
Dept of Civil Engineering
Imperial College Road
London SW7 2BU
T 0171 594 6025   F 0171 594 6053
wes@ic.ac.uk
Promotes the education, training, practice of engineering among women. Increases public awareness of the contribution women can make to engineering. Publications. Development fund. Local groups.

Women's History Network
Dr Gerry Holloway
Centre for Continuing Education
University of Sussex
Falmer
Brighton BN1 9RG
T 01273 606755   F 01273 678848
g.holloway@sussex.ac.uk
For all people concerned with promoting women's history & encouraging women interested in history. Annual national conference. Newsletter. Women's history notebooks.

Zonta International
Ruth Darr
6 Dundonald Road
London NW10 3HR
T 0181 969 6522
r.darr@ucl.ac.uk
Attached to international organisation with HQ in Chicago. Raising money for women's causes. Provides two scholarships: for women in aerospace to do postgraduate work & to eradicate violence against women.

PUBLISHERS/PUBLICATIONS

Attic Press
29 Upper Mount Street
Dublin 2
T 01 661 6128   F 01 661 6176
atticirl@iol.ie
Open 10 am-5.30 pm. Feminist press with books by women writers.

Bad Attitude
121 Railton Road
London SE24 0LR
T 0171 978 9057
Bimonthly radical women's magazine.

Dykenosis
Gudrun Limbrick
C/o Lesbewell
P O Box 4048
Moseley
Birmingham B13 8DP
A national bi-monthly journal for lesbians.

Equal Opportunities International
Nancy Wise, Editor
Barmarick Publications
Enholmes Hall
Patrington
Hull HU12 OPR
T 01964 630033   F 01274 547143
Journal with articles on equal opportunities & women's opportunities in the labour force.

European Journal of Women's Studies
Mary Evans, Editor
Sage Publications Ltd
6 Bonhill Street
London EC2A 4PU
T 0171 374 0645   F 0171 374 8741
market@sagepub.co.uk
Articles on women's studies in Europe.

Executive Woman Magazine
Angela Giveon, Editor
2 Chantry Place
Harrow
Middlesex HA3 6NY
T 0181 420 1210   F 0181 420 1691
Magazine for businesswomen: politics, conferencing, legal, fiscal, childcare, features on women in different industries, reviews, travel, fashion, beauty. Appears bi-monthly.

Fanny - Directory of Comic Strip Artists/Writers
Carol Bennett
Unit 6a
10 Acklam Road
London W10 5QZ
T 0181 969 2945 F 0181 968 7614
Collecting a database of all women cartoonists worldwide. Publishing women's comic art & exhibiting this art internationally.

Feminism and Psychology
Sue Wilkinson, Editor
Sage Publications Ltd
6 Bonhill Street
London EC2A 4PU
T 0171 374 0645 F 0171 374 8741
market@sagepub.co.uk
Articles relating to feminist theory & practice in psychology, representing concerns of women in a wide range of contexts across the academic divide.

Feminist Legal Studies
Deborah Charles Publications
173 Mather Avenue
Liverpool L18 6JZ
T 0151 724 2500 F 0151 729 0371
Journal relating to gender & legal relations concerning theoretical & practical issues.

Feminist Review
feminist review collective
Routledge
11 New Fetter Lane
London EC4 4EE
T 0171 583 9855 F 0171 842 2298
sample.journals@routledge.com
Socialist feminist journal covering topical problems.

Feminist Theology
Lisa Isherwood, Editor
Sheffield Academic Press
Mansion House
19 Kingfield Road
Sheffield S11 9AS
T 0114 255 4433 F 0114 255 4626
admin@sheffac.demon.co.uk
Providing a voice for women in the UK & Republic of Ireland in matters of theology & religion.

From the Flames
Vron or Maggie
42 Mapperley Road
Nottingham NG3 5AS
flames@codadata.demon.co.uk

'Radical feminism with spirit'. Poetry, articles, letters, illustrations & a comprehensive listing of feminist organisations & events. Irregular publication.

Gay Scotland
Dominic d'Angelo
11 Dixon Street
Glasgow G1 4AL
T 0141 204 0742 F 0141 204 0741
dominic@gayscotland.co.uk
Monthly magazine for lesbians, bi-sexual women, gay men & bisexual men with news & features of specific interest to men & women living & working in Scotland. Phone for up-to-date price list.

Gay Times
David Smith, Editor
Millivres Ltd, Ground Floor
Worldwide House
116-134 Bayham Street
London NW1 0BA
T 0171 482 2576 F 0171 284 0329
National lesbian & gay magazine. Above number is for editorial & advertising. Subscription & mail order 0171 267 0021.

Gender and Education
Carfax Publishing Company
P O Box 25
Abingdon OX14 3UE
T 01235 401000 F 01235 401550
enquiries@carfax.co.uk
Journal covering aspects of education in relation to gender.

Gender and History
Blackwell Publishers Ltd
108 Cowley Road
Oxford OX4 1JF
T 01865 791100 F 01865 791347
jnlinfo@blackwellpublishers.co.uk
Journal relating to the history of gender relations, men & masculinity & women & femininity.

Gender and Society
Sage Publications Ltd
6 Bonhill Street
London EC2A 4PU
T 0171 374 0645 F 0171 374 8741
market@sagepub.co.uk
Articles on gender as basic principle of social order & as a primary social category.

NATIONAL - PUBLISHERS/PUBLICATIONS

Gender, Place and Culture
Carfax Publishing Company
P O Box 25
Abingdon OX14 3UE
T 01235 401000 F 01235 401550
enquiries@carfax.co.uk
Journal on the study of geography & gender issues from a feminist perspective.

International Who's Who of Women
Europa Publications
18 Bedford Square
London WC1B 3JN
T 0171 580 8236 F 0171 636 1664
Directory listing details of the lives of some of the most notable women alive today.

Journal of Feminist Studies in Religion
Linda Woodhead, Editor
T & T Clark Ltd
59 George Street
Edinburgh EH2 2LQ
T 0131 225 4703 F 0131 220 4260
Journal on the study of religion from a feminist perspective.

Journal of Gender Studies
Jenny Hockey/Jenny Wolmarke, Editors
Carfax Publishing Co
P O Box 25
Abingdon OX14 3UE
T 01235 401000 F 01235 401550
enquiries@carfax.co.uk
Journal on gender perceived from a feminist perspective.

Letterbox Library
Gill Harris
Unit 2D
Leroy House
436 Essex Road
London N1 3QP
T 0171 226 1633 F 0171 226 1768
Open Mon-Thurs 10 am-5 pm & Fri 10 am-4 pm. Bookshop specialising in anti sexist & multicultural books for children, run by women's cooperative. Also book club with catalogue & newsletter. Workshops.

Medical Women
C/o Medical Women's Federation
Tavistock House North
Tavistock Square
London WC1H 9HX
T 0171 387 7765

Magazine of the Medical Women's Federation. Articles, medical news & activities. Items of interest to women doctors & patients.

National AIDS Manual (NAM)
16a Clapham Common South Side
London SW4 7AB
T 0171 627 3200 F 0171 627 3101
Provides information on HIV/AIDS in the UK. Publishes: National AIDS Manual, AIDS Directory, HIV/AIDS Treatment Directory, European Union Directory of AIDS Service Organisations. Undertakes research projects.

National Small Press Centre
Cecilia Boggis
BM Bozo
London WC1N 3XX
Provides help & advice to independent small press publishers. Has a database of independent publishers. Provides support to independent women publishers.

National Women's Network
83 Margaret Street
London W1N 7HB
Bimonthly newsletter with listings of women's events.

Onlywomen Press Ltd
Lilian Mohin
40 St Lawrence Terrace
London W10 5ST
T 0181 960 7122 F 0181 960 2817
100756.1242@compuserve.com
Independent lesbian feminist publishers. Publishes the radical edge of lesbian feminist literature: fiction, poetry, political theory, science fiction, crime fiction. Available from good bookshops & mail order.

Pandora Press
Belinda Budge
77-85 Fulham Palace Road
London W6 8JB
T 0181 741 7070 F 0181 307 4440
Feminist press housed within HarperCollins publishing house.

Piatkus Books
Judy Piatkus
5 Windmill Street
London W1P 1HF
T 0171 631 0710 F 0171 436 7137

NATIONAL- PUBLISHERS/PUBLICATIONS

Publishers of books on childcare, parenting, cookery, fiction, health, mind body & spirit, popular psychology & women's interests titles.

Pyramid Press
Rachel Lever
P O Box 10023
London E9 7UW
T 0181 533 7636
Publisher of books of women's poetry, prose & fine art illustrations. Titles include The West In Her Eye, Her Mind's Eye & To Her Naked Eye.

QWF Magazine
Jo Good, Editor & Publisher
80 Main Street
Linton
Swadlincote DE12 6QA
T 01283 761042
Bi-monthly magazine for best new female writing talent. 12-14 short stories per issue, readers' letters, two article slots. Stories should be a celebration of women & litarary. No formula romantic fiction.

Scarlet Press
Avis Lewallen
5 Montague Road
Hackney
London E8 2HN
T 0171 241 3702 F 0171 275 0031
Publishing house publishing non-fiction books on women's issues, ranging from art, photography & history to politics, sport & health books.

Social Politics
Oxford University Press
Oxford Journals
Walton Street
Oxford OX2 6DP
T 01865 267907 F 01865 267485
jnl.orders@oup.co.uk
Journal relating to gender studies & social policy.

Studies on Women Abstracts
Carfax Publishing Company
P O Box 25
Abingdon OX14 3U4
T 01235 401000 F 01235 401550
enquiries@carfax.co.uk
Bi-monthly publication. Abstracts & indices.

Theology and Sexuality
Elizabeth Stuart/Alison Webster
Sheffield Academic Press
Mansion House
19 Kingfield Road
Sheffield S11 9AS
T 0114 255 4433 F 0114 255 4626
admin@sheffac.demon.co.uk
Journal of the Institute for the study of Christianity & sexuality. Aims to address themes of constructions of masculinity & femininity; language of sexual identity & expression; etc. Published twice yearly.

Travel Her Way
Pat Bonner
17 Knotts Close
Dunstable LU6 3NY
T 01582 476905 F 01482 476905
Travel book for women listing holidays, B&Bs, places to eat, courses & activity holidays. Phone for further details.

Trouble and Strife
P O Box 8
Diss IP22 3XG
Radical feminist magazine.

Valian Publishing
Val Allen
Bow Patch
64 Browning Road
Leytonstone
London E11 3AR
T 0181 530 4494
Small publishing business & sharing of information & news (Information Exchange) between women craftworkers; sharing & exchange of skills/information in the field of creative crafts.

Violence Against Women
Sage Publications Ltd
6 Bonhill Street
London EC2A 4PU
T 0171 374 0645 F 0171 374 8741
market@sagepub.co.uk
Publishes empirical research & cross-cultural & historical analyses on all aspects of violence against women & girls.

Women and Literature
244a London Road
Hadleigh SS7 2DE
T 01702 552912 F 01702 556095
Journal relating to the literary treatment of women & women writers.

NATIONAL- RACIAL EQUALITY

Women in Publishing
12 Dyott Street
London WC1A 1DE
Promotes the status of women within publishing; encourages networking & mutual support among women; provides a forum for the discussion of ideas, trends & subjects to women in the trade. Training.

Women Making A Difference
Unit 3
1b Packington Square
London N1 7UA
T 0171 226 2160 F 0171 292 4139
A directory of women's organisations.

Women's History Review
Triangle Journals Ltd
P O Box 65
Wallingford OX10 0YG
T 01491 838013 F 01491 834968
journals@triangle.co.uk
Journal with articles on women's history.

Women's News
30 Donegall Street
Belfast BT1 2GQ
T 01232 322823 F 01232 237884
Irish feminist magazine. News on the state of the movement, cartoons, information, music, horoscopes ... and serious analytical articles. For older & younger women, mothers, dykes, community women's groups ...

Women's Press Bookclub, The
34 Great Sutton Street
London EC1V 0DX
T 0171 251 3007
Mail order bookclub. Women's writing at reasonable prices.

Women's Press, The
Kathy Gale, Editor
35 Great Sutton Street
London EC1V 0DX
T 0171 251 3007 F 0171 608 1938
Feminist publisher, women only books. Good backlist of radical feminist, lesbian, women's spirituality, SF publications. Also Livewire, books for girls/young women.

Women's Studies International Forum
Elsevier Science Ltd
P O Box 800
Kidlington OX5 1DX
T 01865 843000 F 01865 843010
nlinfo-f@elsevier.nl

Multi-disciplinary journal for publication of research & review articles in women's studies.

Women's Writing
Marie Roberts/Janet Todd, Editors
Triangle Journals Ltd
P O Box 65
Wallingford OX10 0YG
T 01491 838013 F 01491 834968
journals@triangle.co.uk
Journal on women's writing in English Literature before 1900.

Women: A Cultural Review
Dr Alison Mark
Department of English
Birkbeck College
Malet Street
London WC1E 7HX
T 0171 631 6070 F 0171 631 6072
Three issues per year. Explores the past & present role & representation of gender in the arts & culture. Phone for up-to-date price list.

World Who's Who of Women
Melrose Press Ltd
3 Regal Lane
Soham
Ely CB7 5BA
T 01353 721091 F 01353 721839
Directory listing profiles of around 6,000 women achievers.

RACIAL EQUALITY

Anne Frank Educational Trust
Gillian Walnes, Executive Director
P O Box 11880
London N6 4LN
T 0181 3340 9088
Aims to carry out Otto Frank's wish that, by helping to educate against all forms of prejudice, his daughter's diary be used as a general force for good.

Runnymede Trust, The
Sukhvinder Stubbs
133 Aldersgate Street
London EC1A 4JA
T 0171 600 9666 F 0171 600 8529
Independent think tank. Advice & information to policy makers. Undertakes applied & fundamental research. Supports project managers & employers on issues around race relations & cultural diversity.

Religious Organisations

Association for Inclusive Language
Ianthe Pratt
C/o Christian Women's Resource Centre
36 Court Lane
London SE21 7DR
T 0181 693 1438
To counterbalance the harm done within the churches by the use of language that excludes women. To stress the need to foster mutuality & equality between women & men; etc.

Association of Catholic Women
Mrs Ruth Real
22 Surbiton Hill Park
Surbiton KT5 8ET
T 0181 399 1459 F 0181 399 1459
100660.3574@compuserve.com
Expresses glad assent to the teachings of the Roman Catholic Church as proclaimed by the Magisterium. Works to ensure the teachings of the Church are made known to the wider public. Publications.

Baha'i National Women's Committee
Mrs Lois Hainsworth
Morants Court
Sevenoaks TN14 6HD
T 01732 462328 F 01732 462849
Currently represents some 3,000 women. Aims to develop throughout the UK an awareness of the Baha'i teachings on the emancipation of women & achievement of full equality between the sexes, etc.

Baha'i Women's Association of the Republic of Ireland
Caroline Smith
24 Burlington Road
Dublin 4
T 01 668 3150 F 01 668 9632
nsairl@iol.ie
Dedicated to pursuing the principle of the equality of the sexes on a practical & spiritual level. Irregular meetings; contact the Association for further details.

Catholic AIDS Link (CAL)
Tessa Sowerby
P O Box 646
London E9 6QP
T 0171 485 7298 F 0171 485 7298
Non-judgemental, practical help to people with HIV/AIDS; also spiritual & emotional help. Specific projects relating to refugees. Maintains network throughout England, Scotland, Ireland & Wales.

Catholic Association for Racial Justice (CARJ)
Molly Porter, Administrator
The Co-Op Centre
11 Mowll Street
London SW9 6BG
T 0171 582 2554
Office open part time, usually Tue, Wed & Thurs. National membership organisation of Black & white Catholics working for racial justice in Church & society.

Catholic Needlework Guild
Mrs Frances Ripper
Orchard House
High Street Green
Siblehedinghan
Halstead C09 3LG
T 01787 460234
Supplying new warm clothing for those who are unable to provide for themselves & their families.

Catholic Women's League
Mrs Breda Ford, General Secretary
164 Stockwell Road
London SW9 9TQ
T 0171 738 4894 F 0171 737 8053
A national, non-political organisation for the promotion of religious & intellectual interests & social work. Phone for details of local groups.

Catholic Women's Network
Veronica Readman
22 Wynyard Road
Wolviston
Billingham TS22 5LL
T 01740 644257
Providing support that empowers women to grow & mature in their spiritual life, encourage & enable women to engage in theology; work towards participation of women in every aspect of Church life, etc.

Catholic Women's Ordination (CWO)
Valerie Stroud, Administrator
P O Box 197
Rochester ME2 1ED
T 01634 713396
justitia@compuserve.com

NATIONAL- RELIGIOUS ORGANISATIONS

To achieve the ordination of women in the Roman Catholic church. To achieve a forum for examining, challenging, developing the present understanding of priesthood in the Roman Catholic tradition.

Catholics for a Changing Church (CCC)
the secretariat
14 West Halkin Street
London SW1X 8JS
T 0171 235 2841 F 0171 823 2110
To promote renewal of Catholic church in spirit of Vatican II & sharing of responsibilities within the Church; development of theology of sex & marriage & pursuit of truth & justice.

Christian Women's Resource Centre
Ianthe Pratt
36 Court Lane
Dulwich
London SE21 7DR
T 0181 693 1438
Works towards obtaining full equality of women & men in the field of religion & exploring its dimensions. Reference library including resource bank of inclusive language liturgies. Bookselling service.

Church of Scotland Woman's Guild
Lorna M Paterson, General Secretary
121 George Street
Edinburgh EH2 4YN
T 0131 225 5722 F 0131 220 3113
Movement within the Church of Scotland inviting & encouraging women to commit their lives to Jesus Christ & enabling them to express their faith in worship, prayer & action.

Girls' Brigade (Scotland), The
the secretary
Boys' Brigade House
168 Bath Street
Glasgow G2 4TQ
T 0141 332 1765 F 0141 331 2681
A Christian, uniformed organisation for girls, their homes, community & Church. Spiritual, physical, eucational & service subjects. Motto: seek, service & follow Christ. For 5-18-year-olds.

Girls' Brigade, The (England and Wales)
Mrs Sylvia Bunting, National Secretary
Girls' Brigade House
Foxhall Road
Didcot OX11 7BQ
T 01235 510425 F 01235 510429

Helping girls become followers of the Lord Jesus Christ through self-control, reverence & a sense of responsibility to find true enrichment of life. Offers fun, friendship, new skills & challenges.

Girls' Brigade, The (Northern Ireland)
Brigade House
16 May Street
Belfast BT1 4NL
T 01232 231157 F 01232 323633

Girls' Brigade, The (Republic of Ireland)
Brigade House
5 Upper Sherrard Street
Dublin 1
T 01 365 488

Institute for the Study of Christianity and Sexuality
Oxford House
Derbyshire Street
London E2 6HG

International Catholic Society for Girls (ACISJF)
Sheelah Clarke
St Patrick's International
24 Great Chapel Street
London W1V 3AF
T 0171 734 2156 F 0171 287 6282
info@st-patricks.org.uk
Language school. Runs a small au pair agency. Sends English girls abroad. Foreign girls are found families in the UK. Open Mon-Fri 10 am-4 pm.

Lesbian and Gay Christian Movement
Kate Hunt
Oxford House
Derbyshire Street
London E2 6HG
T 0171 739 1249 F 0171 739 1249
lgcm@churchnet.ucsm.ac.uk
Helpline 0171 739 8134 open Sun & Wed 7-10 pm. Encouraging friendship & support among lesbian & gay Christians; helping the church reexamine understanding human sexuality; maintaining links with other groups.

Mothers' Union Ireland
Mrs Margaret Mahon
The Mothers' Union Office
Christ Church Cathedral
Dublin 8
T 01 671 2475 F 01 671 2475

NATIONAL - RELIGIOUS ORGANISATIONS

Worldwide Anglican-led organisation whose purpose is to be concerned with all that strengthens & preserves marriage & Christian family life. Members worldwide are united in a daily 24-hour Wave of prayer.

Mothers' Union, The
Angela Ridler
24 Tufton Street
London SW1P 3RB
T 0171 222 5533 F 0171 222 1591
A worldwide Christian organisation within the Anglican church. Concerned with all aspects of Christian family life & supports all families through programmes & projects of social service & practical help.

National Board of Catholic Women
the Hon Secretary
39 Eccleston Square
London SW1V 1BX
T 0171 834 1186 F 0171 834 1186
Acts as a forum for women's concerns in the Catholic Church & as a channel of communication between them & the Bishops' Conference of England & Wales.

National Free Church Women's Council
Pauline Butcher
27 Tavistock Square
London WC1H 9HH
T 0171 387 8413 F 0171 383 0150
The Council unites Free Church women. Local groups run residential care homes for elderly people and, in Portsmouth, mother & baby accommodation.

Presbyterian Church of Wales - Women's Committee
Mrs Menna Lloyd Green
Y Coleg
Y Bala LL23 7RY
T 01678 520065
Women of the Presbyterian Church of Wales believe that God is calling us to proclaim the Gospel of His love & to show Christian concern for all. Our work is to present Christ & His Good News to others.

Seven Eleven
Anne Edwards
P O Box 521
Coventry CV5 6ZH
Support group for women in relationships with Catholic priests.

Society for the Ministry of Women in the Church
Iris Forrester
13 Sturges Field
Chislehurst BR7 6LG
T 0181 467 3843
Campaigns for the ordination of women to full Christian ministry. Ecumenical society supporting women ministers of all denominations. Encourages better deployment of women in wide spectrum of ministries.

St Joan's International Alliance (GB Section)
Anne Laishley
106 Thames Road
Chiswick
London W4 3RQ
T 0181 747 0313
A Roman Catholic organisation for women (& men) seeking the end of discrimination against women in both Church & society. Conferences & publications. Open to people who are not RCs but who agree with our aims.

Union of Catholic Mothers (Scottish National Council)
Mrs Anne O'Dowd
225 Balgreen Road
Edinburgh EH11 2RZ
T 0131 337 8118
To help Catholic women appreciate the sacramental characteristics, responsibilities & permanence of marriage. To assist them to bring up their children as practising Catholics.

Union of Catholic Mothers, The
Mrs Pat Durrant, National Secretary
1 Petersfinger Cottages
Clarendon Park
Salisbury SP5 3DA
T 01772 331449 F 01772 331449
A Christian-based organisation within the Roman Catholic Church offering support to marriage & family life. Emphasis on education regarding good citizenship & legislation affecting marriage & family life.

We Are Church
C/o Jubilee People
PO Box 12727
London SW1X 8FB

NATIONAL- RELIGIOUS ORGANISATIONS

A UK Roman Catholic organisation wanting the RC Church to be a Church of love in which all are equal; a church with a new attitude to women so that women have access to leadership & sacramental ministries, etc.

Womanspace
Hannah Ward/Jennifer Wild
T 01993 882348
Holds monthly meetings at St Martins in the Fields in the London borough of Westminster.

Women and the Church (WATCH)
Christina Rees, Chair
St John's Church, Waterloo
Waterloo Road
London SE1 8UF
T 01763 848822
Campaigning for inclusive ministry of women & men, lay & ordained, in the Church of England; justice & ending of discrimination against women in the Church of England; the appointment of women as bishops, etc.

Women in Theology
Janet Simpson, Membership Secretary
45 Morton Terrace
Gainsborough DN21 2RG
T 01427 617313
Aiming to build a women-centred community by empowering women to acknowledge & use their energies & strengths in a spiritual context, sharing support & information, exploring new ways of worship, etc.

Women's Auxiliary to the Baptist Union of Scotland
Mrs Margaret Brown
5 Barrie Terrace
Ardrossan KA22 8AY
T 01294 465886
Organises & coordinates work amongst Baptist women in Scotland & assists Baptist union in promoting schemes for advance of denomination & spread of the Gospel. National events throughout the year.

Women's Interchurch Council
Pauline Butcher
C/o Free Church Federal Council
27 Tavistock Square
London WC1H 9HH
T 0171 387 8413 F 0171 383 0150
A network of Christian women's organisations.

Women's Liturgy, The
Jo Garcia
15 Third Acre Rise
Botley
Oxford OX2 9DA
T 01865 862713
Meets at 11 Norham Gardens, Oxford on first Sat of each month (except January, August & September). Gives women the chance to gain experience in the preaching & planning roles & for leading worship.

Women's Network of the Methodist Church
Stella Bristow, Secretary
Methodist Church House
Network Office
25 Marylebone Road
London NW1 5JR
T 0171 486 5502 F 0171 935 2104
Encouraging, enabling, equipping women in the life of church & community. 'Magnet' magazine issued quarterly.

Women's Union of Scottish Congregational Church
Mrs Sheena Paul
11 Kennedy Street
Wishaw ML2 8LE
T 01698 384892
Religious meetings. Visits to elderly people at home & in hospitals. Providing meals on wheels when required.

Young Women's Christian Association - Scottish National Council
Isabel Carr, General Secretary
7 Randolph Crescent
Edinburgh EH3 7TH
T 0131 225 7592 F 0131 467 7008
101607.3174@compuserve.com
Open Mon-Thurs 9.30 am-4.30 pm. Working for the full participation of women & young people in society; believes in social justice & action; encourages & promotes women in decision-making & leadership.

Young Women's Christian Association of Great Britain (YWCA)
Gill Tishler
Clarendon House
52 Cornmarket Street
Oxford OX1 3EJ
T 01865 726110 F 01865 204805

Provides a range of youth, community & housing services to reach young women who are pregnant or have children, survivors of violence or abuse, those who are homeless, unemployed, etc.

Young Women's Christian Association of Ireland (YWCA)
Daphne Murphy
40 Main Street
Bray
County Wicklow
T 01 276 1648 F 01 276 1652
Inter-denominational Christian association serving the churches by encouraging young people to be active in their own denominations, through arranging programmes for young people.

RIGHTS

Amnesty International - Women's Network
Carolina Kaounides
Amnesty International
99-119 Rosebery Avenue
London EC1R 4RE
T 0171 814 6200
The women's branch of Amnesty International.

British Organisation of Non-Parents (BON)
R Cartwright, Chairman
B M Box 5866
London WC1N 3XX
T 01923 856177
For people choosing not to have children. Campaigns for greater tolerance for those making that choice; puts positive view of childfree life. Believes parenthood too important to be undertaken casually.

Campaign Against the Child Support Act (CASCA)
P O Box 287
London NW6 5QU
T 0171 482 2496 F 0171 209 4761
Campaigning against the Child Support Act & its Agency to be scrapped. Jointly coordinated by the Wages for Housework campagn & the Payday men's network.

Campaign For Freedom of Information
Maurice Frankel
Suite 102
16 Baldwin's Gardens
London EC1N 7RJ
T 0171 831 7477 F 0171 831 7461
admin@cfoi.demon.co.uk

Aims to obtain a Freedom of Information Act to eliminate unnecessary official secrecy & to give people legal rights to information affecting their lives. Publications.

Change
Georgina Ashworth
P O Box 824
London SE24 9JS
T 0171 277 6187 F 0171 277 6187
magnolia@dircon.co.uk
Aims to educate & alert public opinion to inequalities that impose on women through law, practice & custom. Encourages an international exchange of information on strategies to overcome discrimination, etc.

Child Poverty Action Group (CPAG)
Sally Witcher
4th Floor
1-5 Bath Street
London EC1V 9PY
T 0171 253 3406 F 0171 490 0561
Open 9.30 am-5.30 pm. Wheelchair accessible. Seeking to improve benefits & policies for low income familes to eradicate injustice of poverty. Promoting action for relief of poverty.

Fairshares
C Tomkins
15 Sandhurst Close
Croydon CR2 0AD
T 0181 657 3303
Encouraging an equitable division of all assets in the event of a divorce. Yearly AGM in Rugby. Newsletters.

Human Rights Society
Mrs Jennifer Murray
Mariners Hard
Cley
Holt NR25 7RX
T 01263 740404 F 01263 740404
Opposes the legalisation of euthanasia, because we can see no way in which a law could provide the necessary safeguards. Providing information about hospices, pain relief & educational material. Publications.

International Wages for Housework Campaign
Crossroads Women's Centre
230a Kentish Town Road
London NW5 2AB
T 0171 482 2496 F 0171 209 4761
100010.1211@compuserve.com

NATIONAL - RIGHTS

Phone Mon-Fri 10 am-12.30 pm & 1.30-4 pm; Thurs 5-7 pm. Centre open Tue & Wed 12-4 pm & Thurs 5-7 pm. Campaigning for recognition of & compensation for all the unwaged work women do.

Joint Council For the Welfare of Immigrants (JCWI)
115 Old Street
London EC1V 9JR
T 0171 251 8708 F 0171 251 8707
jcwi@mcrl.poptel.org.uk
Advice line: 0171 251 8706. Helps familes & refugees whose basic human rights are threatened by immigration law & practice. Free legal advice & assistance to families & refugees. Publications.

Justice for All Vaccine Damaged Children
Ivor and Enid Needs
Erins Cottage
Fussells Buildings
Whiteway Rd, St George
Bristol BS5 7QY
T 0117 955 7818
An in-touch service to parents of children damaged by vaccination. Advice on when to claim; tribunal procedures; contact with others in a similar situation. Send 254 x 178 mm sae with request for information.

Liberty - National Council for Civil Liberties
21 Tabard Street
London SE1 4LA
T 0171 403 3888 F 0171 407 5354
Telephone for free information pack. Advice on civil liberties & human rights issues affecting lesbians and/or gay men. Written enquiries only, answered within three weeks.

Mothers Apart from their Children (MATCH)
C/o BM Problems
London WC1N 3XX
Offers support, friendship & understanding to all women apart from their children. Informal meetings. sae to Box number above.

National Housewives Association
Mary Shelley, Secretary
12 Chestnut Drive
Pinner
Middlesex HA5 1LY
T 0181 866 2977

Aims to give housewives a chance to voice opinions to people such as MPs & services such as Water, Gas, etc. There are thousands of housewives, the backbone of Britain, & they should be listened to.

National Traveller Women's Forum
Brid O'Brien
Pavee Point
North Great Charles Street
Dublin 1
T 01 878 0255 F 01 874 2626
Network of Traveller women & settled women. For Traveller women to meet, discuss, share experiences & information to develop greater solidarity with each other & take action on their situation.

National Women's Council of Ireland
Ciara McKenna
16-20 Cumberland Street South
Dublin 2
T 01 661 5268 F 01 676 0860
nwci@aonad.iol.ie
The national representative body for women & women's organisations in the Republic of Ireland. Shaping society so that women can achieve their full potential; ensuring the law advances equality; etc.

Parents Against INjustice
Sue Amphlett
10 Water Lane
Bishop's Stortford CM23 2JZ
T 01279 656564 F 01279 655220
Office open from 8.30 am-4.30 pm. Advice & support to those who state they are mistakenly involved in investigations of alleged child abuse.

Positive Action
Mary O'Connor Bird
56 Fitzwilliam Square
Dublin 2
T 01 676 2853 F 01 662 0009
posact@indigo.ie
For women given contaminated anti-D (they being rh negative & their babies rh positive), & who developed hepatitis C as a result. A 1,000 women forced the government to provide a statutory compensation scheme.

Rights of Women (ROW)
Linda Diggin
52-54 Featherstone Street
London EC1Y 8RT
T 0171 251 6577 F 0171 608 0928

For free, sympathetic, quality legal advice call above number during the following times: Tue 12-2 pm; 7-9 pm; Wed 3-5 pm; 7-9 pm; Thurs 12-2 pm & 7-9 pm; Fri 12-2 pm.

Rights of Women: Lesbian Custody Group
52 Featherstone Street
London EC1Y 8KT
T 0171 251 6577
Open Tue, Thurs 12-3 pm & 7-9 pm Wed 3-5 pm & 7-9 pm. Advice & information for lesbian mothers. No wheelchair access.

Scottish Council for Civil Liberties
Catriona McCallum, Research & Information Officer
146 Holland Street
Glasgow G2 4NG
T 0141 332 5960 F 0141 332 5309
Campaigns for the defence & promotion of civil liberties in Scotland. We maintain a library of literature relating to civil liberties issues. Open Mon-Fri 2-5 pm.

Trade Union Congress
Kay Carberry, Head of Equal Rights
Congress House
Great Russell Street
London WC1B 3LS
T 0171 467 1266 F 0171 467 1333
kcarberry@tuc.org.uk
Affiliate organisation of over 70 trade unions representing some 7.5 million workers. Aims to campaign successfully for trade union aims & values & assists trade unions to increase membership & effectiveness.

Women Count Network
C/o Crossroads Women's Centre
230a Kentish Town Road
London NW5 2AB
T 0171 482 2496 F 0171 209 4761

SERVICES

Associated Nursing Services plc
1 Battersea Square
London SW11 3PZ
T 0171 924 4114 F 0171 924 3645
Owns & runs over 40 nursing homes. The largest provider of nursing beds in south London.

Careers Central Ltd
Mary McKellar
Enterprise House
Springkerse Business Park
Stirling FK7 7UF
T 01786 446150 F 01786 450582
Provides details of 5,000 local education & training courses, also 30,000 courses throughout Scotland. Supported by careers guidance for adults, offered by careers offices. Open Mon-Fri 9 am-5 pm.

Women's Resource and Development Agency
Geraldine Burns
6 Mount Charles
Belfast BT7 1NZ
T 01232 230212 F 01232 244363
Provides advice, information, support & resources for women about women's organisations & activities. Support & information to local women's groups. Provides training for members of groups.

SEXUAL ABUSE/RAPE CRISIS

Accuracy About Abuse
Marjorie Orr
P O Box 3125
London NW3 5QB
T 0171 431 5339 F 0171 433 3101
morr@aaastar.demon.co.uk
Disseminates information about child abuse to the media, mental health professionals & to legal & professional circles.

Action Against Abuse of Women and Girls
E Lambert, Hon Secretary
P O Box 124
Bognor Regis PO21 4SJ
Supporting groups/ individuals who are helping/wish to help girls & women who have been subjected to sexual abuse, domestic violence, female circumcision, forced prostitution, etc. Information provided by post.

Black Women's Rape Action Project
Cristel Amiss
Crossroads Women's Centre
230a Kentish Town Road
London NW5 2AB
T 0171 482 2496 F 0171 209 4761
100010.2311@compuserve.com
Open Tue & Wed 12-4 pm; Thurs 5-7 pm
Mail to P O Box 287, London NW6 5QU.
Counselling, advocacy, support to Black/immigrant women & other women of colour survivors of domestic violence, sexual assult, etc.

Campaign To End Rape
C/o 28 Eaton Road
Sale M33 9TZ

Campaigning for immediate action in three areas: increasing the conviction rate; ensuring better treatment & representation of victims in court; changing the law on consent.

Childwatch
Brenda or Diana
206 Hessle Road
Hull HU3 3BE
T 01482 325552
Counselling adults who have been abused in childhood either on phone or face to face. Information packs for victims of abuse. Campaigning for change in the law, larger sentencing & registering of pedophiles.

Childwatch and Kate Adams Crisis Centre
Kate Adams
443 Rainham Road South
Dagenham RM10 7XP
T 0181 593 9428
Helps abused children. One-to-one counselling.

Christian Survivors of Sexual Abuse (CSSA)
BM - CSSA
London WC1N 3XX
For adults who were sexually abused as children or teenagers. Run by survivors for survivors, their friends, families & Christian communities. No phone service but can reply by letter with care & advice.

Mothers of Abused Children
Chris Stickland
25 Wampool Street
Silloth CA5 4AA
T 016973 31432
Helpline open 6 pm on weekdays, otherwise ansaphone. Operates on a national basis for mothers of abused children & concerned fathers or men who have been abused in the past.

Rape Crisis Federation - Wales and England
C/o St Thomas Centre
Ardwick Green North
Manchester M12 6FZ
Recognises the importance of working from a feminist perspective; believes women have the right to the safety of women-only support; recognises that sexual violence is an act of male aggression & power, etc.

Reachout
Pat Marchbank/Sue Heimann
3 Broadfields Parade
Glengall Road
Edgware
Middlesex HA0 0TD
T 0181 905 4501 F 0181 905 4501
24-hour helpline for sexually abused women & men. Aims to provide help, guidance & support to those who have been sexually and/or physically abused & their families & friends. Appointments necessary.

Survivors' Network
Hazel Urquhart, Coordinator
CMHC
79 Buckingham Road
Brighton BN1 3RJ
T 01273 203380
Helpline 01273 720110 open Wed/Fri 7-9.30 pm. Drop in 251 Preston Road, Brighton, on first & third Thurs of each months. For women who were sexually abused in childhood. Holds list of independent counsellors.

Women Against Sexual Harassment (WASH)
4 Wild Court
London WC2B 4AU
T 0171 405 0430 F 0171 405 0429
Support & advice, including legal advice, & campaigning against sexual harassment in the workplace. Advice line: 0171 405 0430.

Zero Tolerance Justice Campaign
P O Box 13497
Edinburgh EH6 4ZF
A public education campaign using media to challenge male violence against women & children. Making the links between rape, child sexual abuse & domestic violence.

SINGLE PARENTS
CRISIS
Caroline Pickering, Acting Chief Executive
Challenger House
42 Adler Street
London E1 1EE
T 0171 377 0489 F 0171 247 1525
National charity for people who are single & homeless & who have no statutory rights to housing.

Gingerbread
Carole Anne Parker/Hilma Twentyman
19 Chester Street
Edinburgh EH3 7RF

T 0131 220 1585
Practical & emotional help to lone parent families via our information & advice centre open Mon-Fri 10 am-4 pm. After-school care & school holiday playschemes. Legal, counselling clinics. Self-help group.

Gingerbread
Kieron Murphy
16-17 Clerkenwell Close
London EC1R 0AD
T 0171 336 8183 F 0171 336 8184
ginger@lonepar-demon.co.uk
Open Mon-Fri 9 am-5 pm. Daily support & practical help for lone parents & their children. There is a national network of over 250 local self-help groups; phone for details. Publications.

Gingerbread (Ireland)
29-30 Dame Street
Dublin 2
T 01 671 0291 F 01 671 0352
Open Mon-Fri 9 am-5 pm. Mon 8-9 pm new members' night. Wed drop-in 6-9 pm. For single parents. Legal advice & counselling services & a mediation service.

Gingerbread Northern Ireland
Lesley Johnston
169 University Street
Belfast BT7 1HR
T 01232 231417 F 01232 240740
Open Mon-Fri 9 am-5 pm. Also an advice centre 01232 234568 open Mon-Fri 9 am-5 pm. Aiming to improve the social & economic circumstances of one parent families in need.

Holiday Endeavour for Lone Parents (HELP)
Jim Dooley
57 Owston Road
Carcroft
Doncaster DN6 8DA
T 01302 725315 F 01302 726959
Lone parent holidays run mainly by people who are or who have been single parents. High quality, low cost full- & half-board & self-catering accommodation. Over 95% of uptake are women. On call 24 hours.

Holidays One-Parents
Bill Softley
51 Hampshire Road
Droylsden
Manchester M43 7PH
T 0161 370 0337

Organises holidays for one-parents at discount prices. National camping holiday in Derbyshire separate from holiday centres. Befriending services, pen-pals for children. Holiday information. Publications.

National Council for One Parent Families
Ms A Fenn
255 Kentish Town Road
London NW5 2LX
T 0171 267 1361 F 0171 482 4851
To improve the economic, legal & social position of one parent families. Free information packs & publications to lone parents. Runs 'Lone parents into employment' projects nationwide, etc.

One Parent Families Scotland
Sue Robertson
13 Gayfield Square
Edinburgh EH1 3NX
T 0131 556 3899 F 0131 557 9650
maxwell@gn.apc.org
Open Mon-Fri 9 am-4 pm. Enables lone parents to achieve full potential by promoting public recognition of achievements & needs, working for supportive government policies, providing information, & support.

One Parent Family Holidays
Kildonan Courtyard
Barrhill
Girvan KA26 0PS
T 01465 821288
opfholiday@aol.com
Organises holidays for one parent families abroad, both with female & male parents.

One Plus - One Parent Families
Vicky Grandon, Development Officer
55 Renfrew Street
Glasgow G2 3BD
T 0141 333 1450 F 0141 333 1399
one-plus@com.co.uk
We campaign for equality of opportunities; offer advice/counselling for adults, youth, children; support for self-help groups; drama, writing & video projects; resource centre; training in childcare.

Single Parent Action Network (SPAN)
Annie Oliver, Information Worker
Millpond
Baptist Street
Easton
Bristol BS5 0XJ
T 0117 951 4231 F 0117 935 5208

NATIONAL- SOCIAL

A national multi-racial organisation run by single parents working to improve conditions of life for one parent families.

Single Parent Travel Club
Maggie Sharich
£1 Hatfield Close
Matchborough East
Redditch B98 0AD
T 01527 522409
Organising reasonably-priced short breaks & holidays for single & access parents & children. Newsletters. Phone in the evenings only.

SOCIAL

American Women's Club
Rosemarie Szilasi
68 Old Brompton Road
London SW7 3LQ
T 0171 589 8292 F 0171 823 9006
Open Mon-Fri 10 am-3 pm. Monthly meetings on fourth Tue of each month 10.30 am at The English Speaking Union, Dartmouth House, 37 Charles Street, London W1. Outings, bridge, book discussions, crafts, etc.

Assn of Inner Wheel Clubs in Great Britain and Ireland
Miss J Dobson
51 Warwick Square
London SW1V 2AT
T 0171 834 4600
Promoting friendship & service. Supporting charities through fundraising & personal service.

International Women's Organisation
Dawn Moore
9 Heron Court
North Circular Road
Limerick City
T 061 324 475
Aims to support women who are new to the Republic of Ireland & to counteract loneliness. Activities such as crafts, flower arranging and lunches. Outings. Also networking.

National Assn. of Ladies' Circles of Great Britain & Ireland
Mrs Marlene Sharkey
NALC HQ Office
Provincial House
Cooke Street
Keighley BD21 3NN
T 01535 607617 F 01535 662312

For women aged 18-45. Non party political, non sectarian. Motto: 'Friendhsip & Service'. Activities: fund-raising, community service, social. About 8,000 members in 750 clubs. All enquiries to above address.

National Association of Women's Clubs
Stella Nicholas, Secretary
5 Vernon Rise
King's Cross Road
London WC1X 9EP
T 0171 837 1434 F 0171 713 0727
The headquarters of a national network of 300 informal clubs, meeting the educational & social needs of women of all ages. Open 9 am-4 pm. Phone for details of local groups.

National Women's Register
3a Vulcan House
Vulcan Road North
Norwich NR6 6AQ
T 01603 406767 F 01603 407003
Offers women opportunities to meet informally, make new friends & enjoy stimulating discussions. Conferences, workshops, magazine, research bank, house exchange scheme, etc. Phone for details of local groups.

SPIRITUALITY/ECOFEMINISM

House of the Goddess
Shan Jayran
33 Oldridge Road
Wandsworth
London SW12 8PN
T 0181 673 6370
Teaching temple, both women & men, the the Craft/Goddess spirituality. Profoundly value female leadership & each person's independent way. Strong Celtic affiliation. National Clan, meetings festivals, etc.

Matriarchy Research and Reclaim Network (MRRN)
C/o The Wheel
4 Wild Court
Kingsway
London WC2B 5AU
Countrywide network of women who share a love of the Goddess & an interest in our matriarchal past & in women's spirituality in the present & future. Newsletter eight times a year.

SPORTS AND LEISURE

All England Netball Association (AENA)
Mrs E Nicholl, Chief Executive
Netball House
9 Paynes Park

Hitchin SGS 1EH
T 01462 442343 F 01462 442343
International matches; national competitions; inter-regional; inter-counties; English counties League. National clubs, leagues & competitions & championships. Further information from AENA.

Badminton Association of England
National Badminton Centre
Bradwell Road
Loughton Lodge
Milton Keynes MK8 9LA
T 01908 568822
Phone for details of women's badminton groups & associations throughout England.

Cumann Camegaiochta an Dun
Elizabeth Collins
1 Knocknagow
Portaferry
County Down BT22 1QL
T 012477 28532
Legislates for & promotes the game of Camogie, the largest field game for women in Ireland.

Disability Sport England
13-27 Brunswick Place
London N1 6DX
T 0171 490 4919 F 0171 490 4914
Aims to provide, develop & coordinate sports & recreation opportunities for people with disabilities.

English Hockey Association
The Stadium
Silbury Boulevard
Milton Keynes MK9 1HA
T 01908 689290 F 01908 241106
Phone for details of women's hockey clubs & associations throughout England.

English Lacrosse Association
Mr J D Shuttleworth - Chief Executive Officer
4 Western Court
Bromley Street
Birmingham B9 4AN
T 0121 773 4422 F 0121 753 0042
The English Lacrosse Association is the new joint Association for both men's & women's lacrosse nationally.

English Ladies' Golf Association
Mrs M J Carr
Edgbaston Golf Club
Church Road

Birmingham B15 3TB
T 0121 456 2088 F 0121 454 5542
Phone for details of local groups.

English Women's Indoor Bowling Association
Margaret Ruff
3 Scirocco Close
Mourton Park
Northampton NN3 6AP
T 01604 494163 F 01604 494434
Association for women's indoor bowls for England.

Football Association
Kelly Simmons, Coordinator
9 Wyllyotts Place
Potters Bar EN6 2JD
T 01707 651840
Phone for details of women's football clubs in England and Wales.

Health and Beauty Exercise
Val Augustine
52 London Street
Chertsey KT16 8AJ
T 01932 564567 F 01932 567566
Formerly The Women's League of Health and Beauty, a worldwide organisation with 600 classes in UK. Exercise, movement & dance. All teachers have two years' training. Phone for details of local groups.

Irish Women's Bowling Association
Mrs Vera Canning
1 Beach Road
Whitehead
County Antrim BT38 9QS
T 01960 378563
Promotes the game of Lawn Bowls for women & brings women into the World & Commonwealth standard of bowls.

Keep Fit Association
Francis House
Francis Street
London SW1P 1DE
T 0171 233 8898 F 0171 630 7936
Offers fitness through movement, exercise & dance. Is a national governing body supported by the Sports Council. Improving stamina, strength & suppleness; improved movement skills in balance, etc.

Ladies' Golf Union
Julie Hall, Secretary
The Scores

NATIONAL - SUPPORT

St Andrews KY16 9AT
T 01334 475811 F 01334 472818
The governing body of ladies' amateur golf. Phone for details of local groups.

Northern Ireland Netball Association (NINA)
Mrs Rosemay McWhinney
48a Balmoral Avenue
Belfast BT9 6NX
T 01232 666497 F 01232 682757
To promote, encourage & develop netball in Northern Ireland. Acts as sole governing body in NI. Membership consists of schools, clubs, youth clubs & registered participants.

Reebok/Runners' World Sisters' Network
Suzanne Rigg
P O Box 76
Warrington WA4 2HH
T 01925 269212 F 01925 269212
Aims to bring women together to run in a safe environment, to raise awareness levels of the benefits of running & other forms of exercise & to provide a social outlet for women whilst keeping fit.

Rugby Union Football for Women
Nicola Ponsford, National Development Officer
The House of Sport
De Montfort University
21 The Crescent
Bedford MK40 2RT
T 01234 261521
Phone for details of groups countrywide.

Scottish Women's Football Association
Maureen McGonigle
4 Park Gardens
Glasgow G3 7YE
T 0141 353 1162 F 0141 353 1823
Open 9.30 am-5 pm. Developing & promoting football for women in Scotland.

Welsh Ladies Indoor Bowls Association
Hilary King
Hillcrest Villa
Tynewydd
Treurchy
Rhondda, Cynon Taff CF42 5LU
T 01443 771618 F 01443 771618

Welsh Women's Bowling Association
Miss Linda Parker
Frydd Cottage
2 Ffrydd Road

Knighton LD7 1DB
T 01547 528331 F 01547 528331
Governing body for all ladies' outdoor bowls in Wales.

Women's Cricket Association
Barbara Daniels
Warwickshire County Cricket Ground
Edgbaston Road
Birmingham B5 7QX
T 0121 440 0567 F 0121 440 0567
National governing body of women's cricket in England, Scotland & Wales. It can advise on the setting up of new clubs & the establishment of girls' cricket in schools, etc. Phone for details of local groups.

Women's Sports Foundation
Lisa O'keefe, Development Support Officer
305-15 Hither Green Lane
London SE13 6TJ
T 0181 697 5370 F 0181 697 5370
Phone between 8 am-4 pm for information about women's sports organisations. A small library is available for members.

SUPPORT

Abortion Law Reform Association
Jane Roe
11-13 Charlotte Street
London W1P 1HD
T 0171 637 7264
Campaigns for a woman's right to choose on abortion, both in law & in practice. Membership is open to all who share our aims.

Alice Kilvert Tampon Alert
Peter and Jenny Kilvert
16 Blinco Road
Urmston
Manchester M41 9NF
T 0161 748 3123
Alerting people to symptoms of tampon related illnesses, particularly toxic shock syndrome. Providing support for sufferers & their families.

Befrienders International
23 Elysium Gate
126 New King's Road
London SW6 4LZ
T 0171 731 0101 F 0171 731 8008
Encouraging the establishment/development of national organisations & individual centres to befriend people who are suicidal, despairing or in distress.

NATIONAL- SUPPORT

Befriending Network, The
Alison Frankland/Diana Senion, Coordinators
11 St Bernards Road
Oxford OX2 6EH
T 01865 316200 F 012335 768867
Links trained volunteers to people at home with life-threatening illness. Free one-to-one support: practical, emotional, social. Enabling/standing alongside ill person. Office open Mon-Thurs 10 am-4 pm

Breast Implant Help and Information Service (BIHIS)
Sue
P O Box 15
Heanor DE75 7ZU
Provides independent & factual information to women about implants & related issues. Books, videos, medical reports, newsletters. Telephone support offered by women with breast implants & other volunteers.

Children Need Grandparents
Mr R C Fryer
2 Surrey Way
Laindon West
Basildon SS15 6PS
T 01268 456929
Telephone Mon-Sat 9 am-7 pm. Telephone & postal contact preferred. sae appreciated for information sheet. Aims to give comfort & advice to grandparents refused contact with their grandchildren.

Continence Foundation, The
David Pollock, Director
2 Doughty Street
London WC1N 2PH
T 0191 213 0050 F 0171 404 6876
Helpline as above available Mon-Fri 9 am-6 pm. Or write/fax as above. Extensive leaflets on various incontinence problems. Book order service. Recommended pelvic floor exercises.

Cult Information Centre
Ian Haworth
BCM Cults
London WC1N 3XX
T 0181 651 3322 F 0181 657 0204
Provides information & advice on cult groups & their methods. Help & advice for ex-members, family & friends. Information for researchers, students & community groups.

Depression Alliance
Anne Grant
35 Westminster Bridge Road
London SE1 7JB
T 0171 633 0557 F 0171 633 0559
Exists to provide support, information & help to sufferers of depression & those who care for them. Run by people with direct, personal experience of depression.

Enuresis Resource and Information Centre (ERIC)
Lizzie Chambers
34 Old School House
Britannia Road
Kingswood
Bristol BS6 6HB
T 0117 960 3060 F 0117 960 0410
Helpline available Mon-Fri 9.30 am-5.30 pm on bedwetting & day-time wetting in children & young adults. Sells useful literature, bedding protection & enuresis alarms, plus information pack.

Family Service Units
207 Old Marylebone Road
London NW1 5QP
T 0171 402 5175 F 0171 724 1829
Helps disadvantaged families unable to achieve full potential because of inadequate resources. Aims to prevent family & community breakdown. Units operate in over 20 areas.

Friends for Life
Laura Stevenson/Margaret Totten
Fifth Floor
52 St Enoch Square
Glasgow G1 4DH
T 0141 204 2202 F 0141 204 2203
friends.for.life@dial.pipex.com
Provides support to adults & children who are affected by a terminal or long-term chronic illness. Open Mon-Fri 10 am-5 pm. Advice, befrienders, bereavement counselling, home visits, respite care, etc.

Home-Start UK
2 Salisbury Road
Leicester LE1 7QR
T 0116 233 9955 F 0116 233 0232
Offers training, information & guidance to Home-Start schemes. Offers support & practical help to families with children aged under 5.

Irish Countrywomen's Association (ICA)
Maureen Holden, General Secretary
58 Merrion Road

Ballsbridge
Dublin 4
T 01 668 0453 F 01 660 9423
Open Mon-Fri 9.30 am-5 pm. Bringing women together in cooperative effort to develop & improve standard of rural & urban life in Ireland. Encouraging use of Irish language in affairs of Bantracht na Tuaithe.

Irish Feminist Information
C/o Attic Press
29 Upper Mount Street
Dublin 2
T 01 661 6128 F 01 661 6176
atticirl@iol.ie
Open 10 am-5.30 pm.

Manic Depression Fellowship
8-10 High Street
Kingston upon Thames KT1 1EY
T 0181 974 6550
Helping people with manic depression, their friends, relatives & others who care. Promoting, advising & supporting development of community based MD self-help groups across England.

Manic Depression Fellowship Scotland
7 Woodside Crescent
Glasgow G3 7UL
T 0141 331 0344
Helping people with manic depression, their friends, relatives & others who care. Promoting, advising & supporting development of community based MD self-help groups across Scotland.

Margaret de Sousa Deiro Fund
Mrs De E Hood/A P P Honigmann/W R I Crewdson
C/o Messrs Field Fisher Waterhouse
41 Vine Street
London EC3N 2AA
T 0171 481 4841 F 0171 488 0084
Funding provided for the care, rehabilitation & after-care of women in financial need suffering from any disease. Applications for assistance should be made in writing to secretaries & address listed above.

MATRIX
Carol Whitehouse
Careers Service
University of Leicester
Leicester LE1 7RH
T 0116 252 5230 F 0116 252 5230
cjwll@le.ac.uk

A women's career advice & support network holding the names of women who work willing to help female students at Leicester University. Women needed to join MATRIX; contacts needed in most fields of work.

Merched Y Wawr
Non Griffiths
34 Stryd Portland
Aberystwyth SY23 2DX
T 01970 611661 F 01970 626620
Open Mon-Fri 9 am-5 pm. Promoting any purpose for the benefit of women in Wales. Advancing education & promoting Welsh culture & the arts through the medium of the Welsh language.

National Abortion Campaign
The Print House
18 Ashwin Street
London E8 3DL
T 0171 923 4976 F 0171 923 4979
Campaigns for the right of all women to have equal access to safe, free abortion on request. Provides wide range of educational & campaigning materials & safer sex promotional products.

National Council for Divorced and Separated
Dorothy Squires
Box 519
Leicester LE2 3ZE
T 0116 270 0595 F 0116 270 0595
Membership open to all age groups of divorced & separated people. A small annual fee. Branches throughout the UK running social functions. Provides general help & support.

National Hospital of Aesthetic Plastic Surgery
Carol Millard
Stoney Lane
Tardebigge
Bromsgrove B60 1LY
T 01527 575123
Helpline with information on breast reduction surgery & breast augmentation surgery.

National Phobics Society, The
Ms N lidbetter
26 Kensington Road
Chorlton cum Hardy
Manchester M21 9QJ
T 0161 881 1937 F 0161 881 1937

NATIONAL- SUPPORT

Open Mon-Fri 9 am-5 pm. A national charity established to help people suffering with all anxiety disorders, particularly focusing on meeting the needs of sufferers who are usually marginalised by society.

Offshore Women's Link Support (OWLS)
Gina Sim, Chairwoman
PO Box 80
Falkirk FK2 0ZX
T 01324 717807 F 01324 713282
Provides support to families & friends of offshore workers, including anyone who works in the oil/gas industry. Currently a network of seven branches & 350 individual links throughout the UK & Ireland.

PAX
Alice Neville
4 Manorbrook
Blackheath
London SE3 9AW
T 0181 318 5026 F 0181 852 9772
Information/advisory service for those suffering from panic attacks, phobias & other anxiety disorders. Publications, contact with other sufferers, information on latest research & therapies.

Portia Trust
Portia Centre
Furnace Bank
Great Gate
Stoke-on-Trent ST10 4HE
T 0500 404025 F 01889 507394
Helpline (free phone) open Mon-Fri 9 am-5 pm. Helps disturbed women who may be in trouble with the law. Especially concerned with shoplifting & baby snatching.
Counselling & treatment programmes.

Pro-Choice Alliance
Jane Roe, Coordinator
11-13 Charlotte Street
London W1P 1HD
T 0171 636 4619
Campaigning for a woman's right to choose an abortion and for easy access to NHS abortion services.

Royal College of Psychiatrists
17 Belgrave Square
London SW1X 8PG
T 0171 235 2351

Open Mon-Fri 9 am-5.30 pm. Send sae for free leaflet explaining symptoms & treatment for anxieties, phobias, depression, anorexia, bulimia, postnatal depression, sleep problems, etc.

Samaritans, The
Paul Farmer
10 The Grove
Slough SL1 1QP
T 01753 532713 F 01753 775787
jo@samaritans.org
Phone 0345 90 90 90 local call rate anywhere in the UK at any time, day or night, any day of the year for help. For anyone passing through personal crisis & at risk of dying by suicide.

Scottish Befriending Development Forum
Lisa Fergusson
The Cabin
Rear of Cowane Centre
Cowane Street
Stirling FK8 1JP
T 01786 451203
Umbrella organisation for befriending schemes throughout Scotland.

Stresswatch Scotland
national coordinator
42 Barnweil Road
Kilmarnock KA1 4JF
T 01563 574144 F 01563 574144
stresswatch.scotland@ukonline.co.
Support, information, advice to those suffering stress, anxiety, phobias, panic attacks. Helping to set up local self-help groups throughout Scotland; encouraging research into anxiety, phobias, panic attacks.

Support Around Termination for Abnormality (SAFTA)
73 Charlotte Street
London W1P 1LB
T 0171 631 0280 F 0171 631 0280
Support & information to parents when abnormality is diagnosed in the foetus.
Helpline 0171 631 0285.

Triumph Over Phobia (TOP) UK
Joan Bond, Development Director
P O Box 1831
Bath BA2 4YW
T 01225 330353

Sets up structured self-help groups run by trained lay volunteers, most of whom have overcome a phobic problem, to teach sufferers from phobia or OCD self-management of their problem in supportive groups.

Women's Royal Voluntary Service (WRVS) - HQ
Lady Elizabeth Toulson, Chairman
National Head Office
234-244 Stockwell Road
London SW9 9SP
T 0171 416 0146 F 0171 416 0146
Volunteers welcome. Activities include: Meals on Wheels delivery, home support for elderly, Books on Wheels, creches, transport & holiday schemes. Phone for information about local groups.

TRAINING

Access 2000
Maeve O'Grady, Chairperson
4 Blenheim Heights
Waterford
County Waterford
T 051 855 474 F 051 841 564
Training organisation. A European-funded NOW (New Opportunities for Women) project. Monthly management committee meetings.

Society Promoting the Training of Women (SPTW)
Brian Harris
The Rectory
Main Street
Great Easterton
Stamford PE9 4AP
T 01780 764036
Interest-free loans (up to £1,250 for each year of study) to women aged 18-45 (approx) undertaking full-time education or training for a career. Must have been resident for at least 3 years in UK.

Women Returners' Network
Ruth Michaels, Director
100 Park Village East
London NW1 3SR
T 0171 468 2290 F 0171 380 0123
Seeks to facilitate the return of women to education, training & employment after a career break. Provides resource lists, evaluated models of custom-designed training & a source of information for women.

Women's Training Network (WTN)
Aizlewood's Mill
Nursery Street
Sheffield S3 8GG
T 0114 282 3172 F 0114 282 3174
An independent, non-profit making membership organisation promoting targeted vocational training for women. Raises awareness of women's training/ employment needs; represents interests of WTN members.

TRANSPORT

Scottish Association for Public Transport
the secretary
5 St Vincent Place
Glasgow G1 2HT
T 0141 639 3697
A pressure group to promote improvements in public transport in Scotland among users, operators, local & central government.

Sustrans Scotland
Les Tombs, Office Manager
53 Cochrane Street
Glasgow G1 1HL
T 0141 572 0234 F 0141 552 3599
Designing & building safe off-road routes for pedestrians, cyclists & disabled.

VIOLENCE AGAINST WOMEN

Campaign Against Domestic Violence (CADV)
Margaret Creear
P O Box 2371
London E1 5NQ
T 0181 558 6324
Also 0171 232 0348. Raises awareness of domestic violence; campaigns for women experiencing domestic violence; fights for legal reform & release of women imprisoned for defending themselves against violence.

Scottish Women's Access Network
Susan Moffat
23 Wellington Street
Edinburgh
T 0131 556 8704
For women sharing common approaches to the problems women face. Campaigning on issues around violence against women, linking with Women's Aid for Peace, Zero Tolerance & 16 Days Campaign Against Gender Violence.

Suzy Lamplugh Trust
Diana Lamplugh
14 East Sheen Avenue
London SW14 8AS

NATIONAL - WOMEN'S AID

T 0181 392 1839 F 0181 392 1830
For personal safety. A positive & pro-active approach to aggression & violence. Provides practical help: publications, videos, personal alarms, talks, courses. Campaigns for changes in the law.

Victim Support
Cranmer House
39 Brixton Road
London SW9 6DZ
T 0171 735 9166 F 0171 582 5712
Offers comprehensive information & support to victims of crime in England, Wales & Northern Ireland. Raises awareness of effects of crime. Promotes rights of victims of crime. Phone for details of local groups.

Victim Support Scotland
Elizabeth May
14 Frederick Street
Edinburgh EH2 2HB
T 0131 225 7779 F 0131 225 8456
Free confidential service to victims of crime. Practical help & emotional support. Victims receive home visit from trained volunteer visitors & appropriate action is taken. Phone for details of local groups.

Women Overcoming Violence and Abuse (WOVA)
Violence, Abuse & Gender Relations Research Unit, Uni of Bradford
21 Claremont
Bradford BD7 1BG
T 01274 385234 F 01274 385370
vagrru@bradford.ac.uk

Women's Local Authority Network
Steph Wilcock/Marilyn Taylor
Enterprise House
15 Whitworth Street
Manchester M1 5WG
T 0161 237 5077 F 0161 237 5077
Works to ensure that women's perspectives are included in work carried out by local authorities. Focusses on violence against women. Supports Zero Tolerance campaign. Meets 3 times a year. Open to all women.

WOMEN'S AID

Jewish Women's Aid
BM JWAI
London WC1N 3XX
T 0171 486 0860 F 0171 486 0600
Helpline 0800 591203. A service for Jewish women suffering domestic violence run by Jewish women. Provides the first Jewish refuge in Europe. The helpline is free of charge.

Northern Ireland Women's Aid Federation
129 University Street
Belfast BT7 1HP
T 01232 249041 F 01232 239296
24-hour helpline 01232 331818. Regional body setting up new women's aid groups, coordinating work of existing groups, providing information & training to groups. Accommodating approx 780 women & 1250 children.

Republic of Ireland National Women's Aid
Dublin
T 1800 341 900
National freefone helpline, available throughout the country.

Scottish Women's Aid
12 Torphichen Street
Edinburgh EH3 8JQ
T 0131 221 0401 F 0131 221 0402
scwomaid@atlas.co.uk
Phone open 10 am-1 pm. every day. Women's Aid in Scotland is the network of 39 groups & their national office, providing information, support & refuge to abused women & their children.

Women's Aid Federation of England
P O Box 391
Bristol BS99 7WS
T 0117 944 4411 F 0117 924 1703
wafe@wafe.co.uk
Working to end violence against women & children. Runs the Women's Aid National Helpline for women experiencing violence in the home: 0345 023468. Information, resources, support, training services, etc.

WORKING WOMEN

Josephine Butler Society
Mrs R M Cass
60 Rotherwick Road
London NW11 TDB
T 0181 455 1664
Aims to remove sex discrimination from laws relating to prostitution & enforcement of laws to penalise its exploiters. Opposed to legalisation/ official toleration of brothels & to registration of prostitutes.

ENGLAND

BEDFORDSHIRE

ACCOMMODATION

Bedford Women's Refuge
Jane Chohan, Centre Manager
Christian Family Care
P O Box 515
Bedford MK40 1XD
T 01234 353592
Refuge for women & their children fleeing violence.

CHARIS Mother and Baby Care
Jane Chohan, Centre Manager
Christian Family Care
P O Box 515
Bedford MK40 1XD
T 01234 353592
Residential supported independent living scheme for homeless pregant women or pregnant women needing support.

ALTERNATIVE THERAPIES

E Johnson
Ms E Johnson
4 Stewart Croft
Sutton Road
Potton SG19 2RR
T 01767 262174
Teaches The Alexander Technique. Individual and group sessions held in Bedfordshire and around Milton Keynes; other areas as requested. Aims to re-educate pupils to learn to employ F M Alexander's principles.

ARTS AND CRAFTS

Catherine Lacemakers
Dorothy Harris, Secretary
13 London Road
Biggleswade SG18 8ED
T 01767 314618
Workshops furthering interest in patchwork, tatting, needlelace, tapesty, etc. Meets every third Thurs of month (not June or December) at Weatherery Centre, Biggleswade 7.30-9.30 pm. Lacemaking demonstrations.

Chiltern Lacemakers
Jenny Kropelnicki
16 Poplar Road
Kensworth LU6 3RS
T 01582 873172
Aims to bring members together to enjoy their lacemaking. For new and experienced lacemakers. Members must be handicraft workers & bring equipment to all meetings.

Dunstable Machine Knitters' Club
Mrs Stella Coxhead
4 Saxon Close
Dunstable LU6 1TR
T 01582 666619
The club meets at Peter Newton Pavilion, Skimpot Road, Dunstable on first & third Thurs of each month from 10 am-12 noon. Speakers.

BUSINESS SUPPORT SCHEMES

Bedfordshire Businesswomen's Club
Janet Turley
13 Willmers Close
Bedford MK41 8DX
T 01234 262487 F 01234 262487
Promotes the interests of businesswomen in Bedfordshire. For women to meet & exchange ideas on a regular basis. Members meet for lunch monthly in Bedford. Speakers. Evening meetings in mid-Beds. Newsletter.

Business and Professional Women (BPW) - Chilterns
Mrs L M Stubbs
2 The Orchards
Eaton Bray
Dunstable LU6 2DD
T 01525 220731
Meets at Tilsworth driving range on first & third Wed of each month at 8 pm. The aims are to allow women to achieve their full potential in the workplace & in public life.

Hallwood Associates
Jayne Woodward
The Old Vicarage
37 Montrose Avenue
Luton LU3 1HP
T 01582 419026 F 01582 419026
Consultancy services for manufacturing, software & service companies.

Sheridan Secretarial Services
Mary Sheridan
28 Chestnut Hill
Linslade
Leighton Buzzard LU7 7TR
T 01525 852577 F 01525 852577

ENGLAND - BEDFORDSHIRE

A home-based secretarial service, offering professional support to local businesses as well as to private individuals.

CARERS

Luton Carers' Support Group
Mrs E I Knight
75 Ashcroft Road
Luton LU2 9AX
T 01582 35617
Sharing information; experiences in caring; mutual support; always listens. Guest speakers & outings. Meets first Tue in each month at Mixes Hill Court, Mixes Hill, Luton. Phone above no or Jean (01582 576930).

CENTRES FOR WOMEN

Luton All Women's Centre
Lorene Fabian
213 Birdsfoot Lane
Luton LU3 2HU
T 01582 505714
Open Mon, Tue, Thurs & Fri 10 am-12 pm; Tue & Wed 1-3 pm. Also at Gordon Street, Luton LU1 2QP. Women only drop in service for women who are seeking information. A referral service to the appropriate body.

CHILD CARE AND FAMILY

National Childminding Association - East Regional Office
55 Goldington Road
Bedford MK40 3LT
T 01234 211921
Promoting childminding as a quality daycare service; improving conditions for childminders; encouraging higher standards of daycare; keeping childminders, parents, employers & government informed.

COUNSELLING AND THERAPY

Centre for Counselling & Assertion Training
Peggy Simmons
68 Falcon Avenue
Bedford MK41 7DX
T 01234 268212
Assertion training, person-centred counselling, stress management & bereavement. I work with individuals, couples & groups & give talks. I have a special interest in disability awareness & HIV/AIDS.

Women's Assertiveness Group
Ayesha Kazi
341 Hightown Road
Luton
T 01582 453361
Meets once every three weeks at various venues. One-to-one counselling for women suffering psychological/emotional harassment. Advice for people feeling isolated. Conferences, outings, summer school, drama.

ENVIRONMENT

Luton Women's Environmental Network
Pat Woods
22 Rockley Road
Luton LU1 5RW
T 01582 26323
Local branch of Women's Environmental Network. An educational & campaigning organisation on a local level. Discouraging pollution packaging, unnecessary sanitary wear & disposable nappies.

ETHNIC MINORITIES

Afro-Caribbean Outreach Project
Ella Hughes
Luton All Women's Centre
213 Bordsfoot Lane
Luton LU3 2HU
T 01582 30708
Careers advice & information; projects funding; networking with other Black women's organisations.

Asian Girls' Club
Mrs F Z Islam
113 Cowper Street
Luton LU1 3SD
T 01582 22183
Meets at Denbigh High School, Alexander Avenue, Luton on Sat 11.30-2 pm (swimming) & Wed 6.30-8.30 pm. To help Asian girls overcome cross-cultural problems & problems arising at home & at school.

Colour Purple Foundation
Valma James
C/o Luton All Women's Centre
213 Birdsfoot Lane
Luton LU3 2HU
T 01582 30708
Meets last Wed of each month 5-7 pm. Targets Afro-Caribbean women & African women. Information, advice, support &

ENGLAND - BEDFORDSHIRE

counselling. Organises training, seminars & conferences.

Ghar Se Ghar
Mrs P Rashid
C/o Bury Park Community Centre
90 Dunstable Road
Luton
T 01582 450194
Meets on Fri at above address 9.30-11.30 am. Supporting Asian women. Advice on health & leisure issues, education, career & welfare rights.

Muslim Women's Association
Mrs N S Jaffari
38 Seamons Close
Dunstable LU6 3EQ
T 01582 606672
Information, advice & guidance to women who are disadvantaged in the community & ignorant of the services available. Seminars, summer schools for Asian girls & outings for women. Helpline for girls, etc.

Pragati Women's Group
Mrs U Bakshi
13 Oving Close
Luton LU2 9RM
T 01582 482524
For Asian women of any age. Phone for details of meetings. To encourage interest & participation by Asian women through education, health, arts & recreational programmes.

FINANCE

Jane Smith Independent Financial Services
Jane Smith
1 Manor Close
Carlton MK93 7LD
T 01234 7211400 F 01234 121191
Independent financial adviser specialising in women's needs in pension planning & investments.

LEGAL MATTERS

Luton Law Centre
2a Reginald Street
Luton LU2 7QZ
T 01582 482000
Advice line 01582 481000 open Mon-Fri 9.30 am-5.30 pm. Office open Mon & Fri 10.30 am-12.30 pm & Wed 2-4 pm. Free confidential legal services: housing, employment, welfare rights. Phone for appointment.

OLDER WOMEN

Bury Park Ladies Club
N L Chamberlain
Flat 1
The Shires
Old Bedford Road
Luton LU2 7QA
T 01582 28666
Meets at Bury Park Community Centre, Dunstable Road On Mon 2-4 pm. For women aged over 55. Bingo, raffles, lunches & outings.

Dallow Road Ladies Club
Mrs J Godfrey
5 Highbury Road
Luton LU3 1AD
T 01582 37345
Meets at Warwick Court, Warwick Road, Luton on Wed 1.45-3.45 pm. Lunches & social activities.

Friendship Home Carers
Mrs Naomi Mitchell
Seventh Day Adventist Church
1 North Street
Luton LU2 7QD
T 01582 36158 F 01582 36158
Care for the elderly within their own homes. Housework, fetching pensions & shopping; paying bills; preparing meals. Office hours Mon-Fri 10 am-4 pm.

Round Green Ladies Club
Mrs Bessie Bownes
41 Heywood Drive
Luton LU2 7AP
T 01582 27664
Meets at St Christopher's church hall, Felix Avenue, Luton on Fri 1.30-4 pm. Providing fellowship & friendship. Social activities & gentle exercise.

St Pauls Ladies Club
Mrs J M Gulliver
102 Park Rise
Harpenden AL5 3AN
Meets on Tue 2-4 pm at St Paul's Church, New Town Street, Luton. For women aged 60 & over for social activities.

RELIGIOUS ORGANISATIONS
Dunstable Ladies' Regnal Circle
Maureen G King

16 Hawthorne Close
Dunstable LU6 3BL
T 01582 607408
Meets second & fourth Thurs of each month 8 pm in the Wesley Chapel, Methodist Square Church, Dunstable. All women welcome, any age. The Regnal League works in all denominations within the Christian Church.

Services

Ad Hoc Marketing Services
Laina Freeman
8 Russell Avenue
Bedford MK40 3TF
T 01234 344174 F 01234 211164
101500.3076.compuserve
Helping a wide range of clients from international flavour technologists to independent opticians to increase their market awareness & find new customers. Telephone surveys; direct mail campaigns.

Bell Consultancy
Paula Grayson
The Old Chapel
Carlton Road
Turvey
Bedford MK43 8£G
T 01234 881708 F 01234 881708
Personnel consultancy working with individuals, organisations & government departments on good practice in recruitment, appraisal, development, investors in people & diversity issues.

Liz Taylor Interiors
Liz Taylor
35 Cooks Meadow
Edlesborough LU6 2RP
T 01525 222383
An interior design & soft furnishings service, concentrating on hand-finished products & personal service.

Sexual Abuse/Rape Crisis

Luton Rape Crisis
Luton
T 01582 733592
Providing counselling & support for any survivor of sexual abuse. 24-hour helpline.

Social

Bushmead Ladybird Club
Mrs June Bateman
12 Winton Close
Luton LU2 7BJ
T 01582 508024
Meets at Bushmead Community Centre, Hancock Drive, Luton on Wed 8-10 pm. Speakers & social activities.

Sports and Leisure

Bedfordshire County Women's Bowling Association
Mrs M Thorne, Hon Secretary
5 Holmewood Road
Greenfield
Bedford MK45 5DL
T 01525 712870 F 01525 712870
County ladies' bowling association. Helping to further the game of flat green bowling.

Bedfordshire Ladies' County Golf Association
Mrs Heddwen Molloy
Keepers Cottage
Beadlow
Shefford SG17 5PH
T 01525 861202
Promoting ladies' golf in the county & liaising/assisting clubs concerning the running of ladies' sections in golf clubs. Upholding rules of English Ladies' Golf Association. Organising county matches, etc.

Bedfordshire Women's Hockey Association
Miss E A Millson
21 Home Court
Leagrave
Luton LU4 9NP
T 011582 584424
Promoting women's hockey in Bedfordshire, organising tournaments & county teams.

Bedfordshire Women's Indoor Bowling Association
Mrs G Cousens
47 The Ridgeway
Bedford MK41 8ES
T 01234 347041
County level of bowls for women.

Chiltern Ladies' Hockey Club
Miss V Bryan
70 Heywood Drive
Luton LU2 7LP
T 01582 611699

SUPPORT

Family Groups (Bedford)
Janice Payne/Miriam Richardson
Westbourne Centre
Westbourne Road
Bedford MK40 4PQ
T 01234 325563 F 01234 344118
Runs six multicultural support groups for women, each meeting once a week for two hours during school term time. Creche. Crafts, food preparation, talks. Free of charge. Aims to build up support networks.

Luton Multicultural Women's Coalition
Dr Nazia Khanum, Chair
30 Knoll Rise
Luton LU2 7JA
T 01582 34532 F 01582 619715
nkhanum@aol.com
Voluntary organisation, open to all women living in Luton. Aims to develop support network & programme of action to enhance quality of life of women in Luton. Promoting positive changes in attitudes, etc.

RAGE
Rebecca Dodd
48 Elliott Crescent
Goldington
Bedford MK4 10J
T 01234 354436
Helping people with problems after radiotherapy treatment. Members (women & men) with injuries to any part of the body. Phone any time. Wanting more information for people about to have radiotherapy, etc.

TRAINING

Equlity in Diversity
Dr Nazia Khanum, Consultant
30 Knoll Rise
Luton LU2 7JA
T 01582 34532 F 01582 619715
nkhanum@aol.com
Independent management, research & training consultancy. Aims to integrate equal opportunities in policy & practice in education, housing, human resource management, etc. Raising the profile of equality.

WOMEN'S AID

Luton Women's Aid
Jenny Moody
144 Wardown Crescent
Luton LU2 7JU
T 01582 25045

Providing support, information, temporary accommodation for women escaping abuse at the hands of their partners. Also providing training & education for all groups regarding domestic violence.

BERKSHIRE

ARTS AND CRAFTS

Feet First Dance Theatre
Jackie Childs
42 Dolphin Road
Slough SL1 1TA
T 01753 536902
Small scale dance improvisation group, having completed several multicultural performance projects. Currently working on dance performance for all generations.

CENTRES FOR WOMEN

Reading Women's Information Centre
Alex Geldart, Project Coordinator
6 Silver Street
Reading RG1 2ST
T 0118 931 1939
Open Mon, Tue, Thurs 10 am-1.45 & 2.15-5 pm; Wed 10 am-2 pm. Free services in a women- only space. Legal advice sessions, pregnancy testing, library, drop-in, coffee/tea, meeting space, etc.

CONTRACEPTION/WELL WOMAN

HRH Princess Christian's Nuffield Hospital
12 Clarence Road
Windsor SL4 5AG
T 01753 853121
Well woman screen. Full female health assessment. Phone for up-to-date price lists.

Thames Valley Nuffield Hospital, The
Wexham Street
Wexham
Slough SL3 6NH
T 01753 662241
Well woman screen. Full female health assessment. Phone for up-to-date price lists.

Well Woman Association for West Berkshire
Greyfriars Centre
Friar Street
Reading RG1 1EH
T 0118 950 3157
Open Mon 10.30 am-1.30 pm & 6.30-9.30 pm. The following services are provided free of charge: counselling, self help groups,

workshops, events & courses, massage & reflexology. Doctor available. Library.

EDUCATION

Chiltern Association of Women Graduates
Mrs Jessica Houdret, Hon Secretary
Farnham Court
Church Road
Farnham Royal
Slough SL2 3AW
T 01753 643610
To foster friendship & promote the interests of women graduates. Monthly meetings & outings.

Reading Association of Women Graduates
Mrs E Cader
Donkey Pound Cottage
Beech HIll
Reading RG7 2AX
T 0118 988 2674
Bringing women graduates (& undergraduates in their final year) together locally, nationally & internationally for friendship, stimulus & support. Monthly meetings offering culturally diverse topics.

Women in Biology Working Group - Institute of Biology
Dr Jean Walsingham
Walnut Tree Cottage
Crays Pond
Reading RG8 7QQ
T 01491 680626
A working group within the Institute of Biology, 20-22 Queensberry Place, London SW7 2DZ, and trying to improve the status/role of women in biological careers & in the work of the Institute.

ETHNIC MINORITIES

Sahara Asian Women's Project
Reading
T 0118 926 6333
Phone shared by Reading Samaritans. Support given to Asian women for all needs. Providing a safe, non-judgemental & empowering environment for Asian women & their children who have suffered domestic violence.

HEALTH

Wyeth Laboratories
Sharon John, Customer services
Huntercombe Lane South
Taplow
Maidenhead SL6 0PH
T 01628 604377
Provides literature about women's health issues, eg coping with the menopause, hysterectomies, breast cancer, etc.

LARGER/TALLER WOMEN

Clothes by Jane John
Jane Shoebridge
Mayfield Studio
39 Pinehill Road
Crowthorne RG45 7JE
T 01344 771625
Open Mon only 10 am-4 pm, or by appointment & at venues throughout the south of England. Simple, flowing, unstructured clothes to flatter the more discerning woman. Free size.

Long Tall Sally
173 Friar Street
Reading RG1 1HE
T 0118 951 2300
Clothes for the taller woman sizes 12-20.
Open Mon-Sat 9.30 am-5.30 pm.

PEACE GROUPS

Aldermaston Women's Peace Camp
Aldermaston
T 0117 939 3746

Greenham Women
Blue Gate
Newbury

PREGNANCY/CHILDBIRTH

Thames Valley Independent Midwives
Melanie Milan
120 Straight Road
Windsor SL4 2SB
T 01753 841873
Independent midwifery practice. Mostly home births, including complete package of antenatal intrapartum & postnatal care. Continuity of carer & individual flexibility guaranteed. Phone for price list.

SOCIAL

Reading Business Women's Luncheon Club
Vicki Trigg
Barrett & Co

54 Queen's Road
Reading RG1 4AZ
T 0118 958 9711 F 0118 9393605
Lucheon club for business women meeting at different venues for lunch (or breakfast) six to eight times a year. The main purpose is social but it also provides valuable networking for its members.

Sports and Leisure

Fleet Morris
Yvonne Hallows
16 Lowry Close
College Town
Sandhurst GU47 0FJ
T 01276 31697
Female Cotswold Morris side. Practice nights are on Tue 8.15-10 pm, September-April. Dancing out at pubs, fetes, carnivals & festivals during summer months. Aims are to keep Morris alive, keep fit & have fun.

Mayflower Morris
Sarah Morland
21 King Street
Mortimer
Reading BG7 3RS
T 0118 933 2149 F 0118 933 1578
Women's north west clog Morris Dancing. Practice night Mon 8-10 pm from October to April, in Ash Vale near Aldershot. Dancing at festivals, events & pubs throughout the summer.

Reading Women's Self Defence Network
Gill or Debbie
C/o RISC
35-39 London Street
Reading RG1 4PS
T 0118 945 5394
Self-defence courses run for women by women. Sliding scale of course fees.

Women's Aid

Berkshire Women's Aid
P O Box 413
London Street
Reading RG1 4SF
T 0118 950 0182
Helpline: 0118 950 4003 open Mon-Fri 10 am-5 pm. Otherwise phone The Samaritans on 0118 926 6333. Supporting all women who experience cruelty or violence at home or in their relationships.

Birmingham and Midlands

Accommodation

Coventry Young Homeless Accommodation Project
Elemay Parkes
Unit 15 Arches Industrial Estate
Spon End
Coventry CV1 3JQ
T 01203 715113 F 01203 714302
29 housing places in Coventry set up by NACRO, including a quick access short stay hostel & separate provision for vulnerable women who are pregnant or have children.

Jyoti House
the manager
P O Box 1345
Birmingham B13 8ER
T 0121 624 490
Meeting the needs of women from the Asian communities. Shared home offering support to women escaping harassment or violence. Accommodation provides 4 family & 4 single rooms.

Sandwell Women's Refuge
Fiona Macdonald
370-2 High Street
Sandwell B66 3PJ
T 0121 552 9975 F 0121 544 7529
Women's refuge. Emergency helpline 0121 552 6448. Emergency crisis accommodation for women & their children escaping violence in the home. Open access. Asian languages, children's workers, disabled access, etc.

Alternative therapies

Donna Bissell MASC (Relax)
Donna Bissell
22 Hempole Lane
Queensgate
Great Bridge
Tipton DY4 0HQ
T 0121 557 6298
Qualified relaxation therapist using aromatherapy oils, colour therapy, crystal healing & creative visualisation.

Grosvenor Centre
Judith Wright
16 Grosvenor Avenue
Handsworth
Birmingham B20 3NR
T 0121 356 5886
Complementary therapies: reflexology, massage, aromatherapy, homoeopathy, Bach

ENGLAND - BIRMINGHAM AND MIDLANDS

flower remedies, acupuncture, Alexander Technique. Counselling for women to help with short-term crises & longer term problems.

S Billingham Chiropodist and Reflexologist
Mrs Sue Billingham
7a Bowstoke Road
Off Newton Road
Great Barr
Birmingham B43 5EB
T 0121 357 5348
Chiropody & reflexology. Home visits available for the housebound. Phone for price list.

Well Natural Health Centre, The
Sue Connolly
89 Institute Road
King's Heath
Birmingham B14 7EU
T 0121 443 1580
Appointments available six days a week, plus evenings. Therapies include acupuncture, aromatherapy, cranial sacral therapy, McTimony chiropractic, The Alexander Technique, homoeopathy, iridology, etc.

ARTS

Splinter Community Arts Ltd
Linda Merriman
Unit 5
Mayfield Workshops
19 Wednesbury Road
Walsall WS1 3RU
T 01922 725440
An arts co-op set up to increase arts access to members of the community who find arts access difficult. Working with people regardless of their disability at their own venue.

ARTS AND CRAFTS

Art Link West Midlands Ltd
Dawn Gelshinan, Acting Director
The Challenge Building
1 Hatherton Street
Walsall WS1 1YB
T 01922 616566 F 01922 616805
Regional access agency for the west Midlands, offering access into the arts for women and men with physical disabilities, learning disabilities and mental health problems.

Brumhalata Intercultural Storytelling Company
Dr Vayu Naidu, Storyteller/Artistic Director
Howard House
90 Granville Street
Birmingham B1 2LT
T 0121 248 4549 F 0121 248 4550
Storytelling from diverse cultures.Their literary/oral traditions recounted in terms of contemporary reality. Key visibility areas: performance, education, therapy, business & community, apprenticeships.

Foursight Theatre
Sheena Lucas
Newhampton Centre
Dunkley Street
Wolverhampton WV1 4AN
T 01902 714257
Women's theatre group. "Fulfilling scripts, fearsome acting, feisty women and a fertile imagination."

Liz Bayes Designs
Sheila Bayes-Clayton
69 Queensland Avenue
Chapelfields
Coventry CV5 8FF
T 01203 674375
Hand-made jewellery - one-off pieces made from recycled beads, paper, embroidery, etc. Embroidered & jewelled sachets, fruit & flowers. Sold by party plan, recommendation & craft stalls.

Polly and the Phonics
Karen/Kate/Heather/Alison
25 Hailstone Close
Rowley Regis
Warley B65 8LJ
T 01384 252632 F 01384 252632
All-female harmony quartet. Original, sometimes flighty, observations through song. Offer both formal & informal performances & music workshops, including 'finding your voice'.

SAMPAD
Piali Ray
C/o mac
Cannon Hill Park
Birmingham B12 9QH
T 0121 440 8667 F 0121 440 8667
Alternative phone no: 0121 440 4221 ext 273.
South Asian arts organisation aiming to increase awareness, access and opportunities for Asian people both in the classical and contemporary contexts.

Women and Theatre
J Adkins/Janice Connolly, Artistic Director
Friends Institute
220 Mosely Road
Highgate
Birmingham B12 0DG
T 0121 440 4203 F 0121 446 4280
Producing high quality drama which focuses on health and social care issues with particular reference to the Health of the Nation targets. Health and social care issues, work involving community groups.

WRPM (Women's Revolutions Per Minute)
Caroline Hutton
36 Newport Road
Birmingham B12 8QD
T 0121 449 7041 F 0121 442 2139
wrpm@mail.globalnet.co.uk
Mail order catalogue of music by women musicians and women composers, including CDs, cassettes and songbooks. All kinds of music. Phone calls welcome 10 am-10 pm. Visitors by appointment.

BUSINESS SUPPORT SCHEMES

Birmingham Women's Development Network
Lesley Pinder
C/o Birmingham TEC
Chaplin Court
80 Hurst Street
Birmingham B5 4TG
T 0121 622 4419 F 0121 622 1600
Promotes women's development in the city of Birmingham. The aim is to encourage key agencies to work together around 'equal participation of women in a high skill economy in Birmingham'. Produces a directory.

Business Team Ltd, The
Jenny Jones
West Midlands House
Gypsy Lane
Willenhall WV13 2HA
T 0121 609 7100 F 0121 609 7103
Provides courses for women in business.

Club Catering
Judi Gilbert
27 Merton Close
Warley B68 8NG
T 0121 552 6029
Caters for businesses: meetings; conferences; lunch plans. Daily sandwich deliveries; cold buffets for weddings & other functions. Open all week. All dietary requirements possible.

Golden Hillock Jobclub
Farzana Yousufzai
109 Golden Hillock Road
Small Heath
Birmingham B10 0DP
T 0121 753 0115 F 0121 753 0778
Open Mon-Thurs 10 am-3 pm. For women with language difficulties who find it difficult to use standard facilities. Free facilities: use of phone, stationery, photocopying, compiling cv, faxing, stamps, etc.

Just for Starters Ltd
Devi Sohanta
Waterlinks Enterprise Centre
69 Aston Road North
Aston
Birmingham B6 4EA
T 0121 359 2221 F 0121 359 2230
Aim is to contribute to long-term development & success of local small businesses. Provides training, advice on how to prepare business proposals, information about public sector loans & grants, etc.

Sandwell Women's Enterprise Development Agency
Gurminder Sehint
The Business Centre
Church Street
West Bromwich
Sandwell B70 8RP
T 0121 525 2558 F 0121 580 0103
Women's enterprise agency. Offers free advice, counselling, support & training for women going into businesses & helps established businesswomen.

Women in Business - Solihull branch
Rae Coton, Administrator
17 Dordon Close
Shirley
Solihull B90 1AH
T 0121 430 3213 F 0121 693 3818
100733.3151@compuserve.com
Meets at least once a month, rotating breakfasts, suppers & workshops to provide a range of opportunities for members to share views & experience with women in similar positions. 100+ members.

Women's Business Development Agency
Jennie Bryce
Enterprise House

ENGLAND - BIRMINGHAM AND MIDLANDS

Sheriff's Orchard
Coventry CV1 1QN
T 01203 633737 F 01203 632734
Enterprise centre for women providing business counselling & advice, training & outreach for women living in & around Coventry & Warwickshire. Business advice clinics held weekly. Phone for further details.

CENTRES FOR WOMEN

Birmingham Women's Advice and Information Centre Ltd
Carole Harte
Devonshire House
High Street
Digbeth
Birmingham B12 0LP
T 0121 773 6952 F 0121 604 0060
Offers a free service to all women. Open 10 am-4 pm. Information, support, support group for victims of domestic violence, crisis counselling, training. Offers a front line service & works for change.

Golden Hillock Women's Centre
Yvonne Bird, Centre Coordinator
113 Golden Hillock Road
Small Heath
Birmingham B10 0DP
T 0121 753 0086 F 0121 753 0086
Courses in English (City & Guilds or ONC), Urdu, maths, islamic Studies (GCSE), Introduction to Caring (British Red Cross), Business Administration (NVQ), Computer/Text Processing (RSA, CLAIT), etc.

Norton Hall Learning Area
Clare Jones or Suzanne Knipe
Ralph Road
Saltley
Birmingham B8 1NA
T 0121 328 3043 F 0121 327 9636
Open weekdays, day & evenings. For all women, especially those in local area. Aims to provide better chances of employment through provision of training in eg IT, English, fashion & design, embroidery.

Norton Hall Women & Children's Centre
Claire Jones, Coordinator
Norton Hall
Ralph Road
Saltley
Birmingham B8 1NA
T 0121 328 3043

Training for women, including computing, bi-lingual skills, sewing, design, health education; childcare provision for children & creche for all women's activities; girls' & young women's groups.

Osaba Women's Centre
Eileen Daley/Sonia Gordon
23 Victoria Street
Hillfields
Coventry CV1 5NA
T 01203 221816 F 01203 228223
osaba@covnet.co.uk
Open Mon-Fri 9.30 am-4.30 pm. Training, education & volunteering opportunities. Childcare & cultural activities for African Caribbean women & children.

UK Asian Women's Centre
Jeet Sohal
1 Stamford Raod
Handsworth
Birmingham B20 3PJ
T 0121 523 4910 F 0121 515 4245
Drop-in advice centre. Information, support & guidance is given on DSS benefits, housing, domestic & welfare, employment, training & education. Supplementary classes & playschemes for children.

Women's Health and Information Centre
Amy Corkish
Coventry Healthcare NHS Trust
Stoney Stanton Road
Coventry CV1 4FH
T 01203 844171 F 01203 844173
Information on women's health, pregnancy counselling, well woman & contraceptive services. Self-referral but please make an appt. Open Mon-Thurs 8.30 am-5.30 pm; Fri 8.30 am-4.30 pm.

Women's Therapy Centre
Amanda Richardson, Acting Coordinator
The Lodge
52 Queensbridge Road
Moseley
Birmingham B13 8QD
T 0121 442 2241
Counselling & psychotherapy service run by non-medical female therapists for women only. Self-referral. Committed to supporting development of services sensitive to women's needs.

ENGLAND - BIRMINGHAM AND MIDLANDS

CHILD CARE AND FAMILY

Acorns Children's Hospice
Brian Warr, Director of Care Services
103 Oak Tree Lane
Selly Oak
Birmingham B29 6HZ
T 0121 414 1741 F 0121 471 2880
Emotional & practical support given to life-limited children & their families. Aims to increase awareness of the condition and plight of these children. Respite care, bereavement friendship & counselling, etc.

Home Start Saltley
Raj Nepal, Organiser
Nansen Primary School
Naseby Road
Saltley
Birmingham B8 3HG
T 0121 327 1472
Help and support given to young families with at least one child under age 5. Befriending. Helping young families under stress.

Jigsaw Co-operative Ltd
Gail Taylor
30 Hen Lane
Holbrooks
Coventry CV6 4LB
T 01203 637925
First class affordable care in friendly, safe & caring atmosphere for children aged 2+. After school & holiday care for children aged 5-7 (both full- & part time). Open 8 am-5.30 pm

Sadwica Playgroup
Churchfields High School
Lee Community Building
Church Vale
West Bromwich
T 0121 588 4104

COMPUTERS/IT

Kalamazoo Computer Training Ltd
Rose Huish/Jennie Airyn
Mill Lane
Northfield
Birmingham B31 2RW
T 0121 478 1777 F 0121 476 0264
Computer training & consultancy contracted with TECs. Offers NVQ levels II & III.

CONTRACEPTION/WELL WOMAN

Bell Green Health Centre
Roseberry Avenue
Bell Green
Coventry
T 01203 844171
Well woman & contraceptive services. Free condoms, emergency contraception, pregnancy counselling, menopause clinic, cytology (smear testing). Clinic on Fri 9-11 am.

Birmingham Nuffield Hospital, The
22 Somerset Road
Edgbaston
Birmingham B15 2QQ
T 0121 456 2000
Well woman screen. Full female health assessment. Phone for up-to-date price lists.

Broad Street Health Centre
Broad Street
Coventry
T 01203 844171
Well woman & contraceptive services. Free condoms, emergency contraception, pregnancy counselling, menopause clinic, cytology (smear testing). Clinic on Wed 9-11 am.

Brook City Centre
12-22 Albert Street
Birmingham B4 7UD
T 0121 643 5341
Free confidential contraceptive advice. Help with emotional and sexual problems. Free condoms and other contraceptive supplies. Pregnancy tests and quick results, etc. Phone for opening times.

Edgbaston Brook Centre
9 York Road
Edgbaston
Birmingham B4 7UD
T 0121 643 5341
Free confidential contraceptive advice. Help with emotional and sexual problems. Free condoms and other contraceptive supplies. Pregnancy tests and quick results, etc. Phone for opening times.

Handsworth Brook Centre
102 Hamstead Road
Handsworth
Birmingham B19 1DG
T 0121 554 7553
Free confidential contraceptive advice. Help with emotional and sexual problems. Free condoms and other contraceptive supplies.

Pregnancy tests and quick results, etc.
Phone for opening times.

Jubilee Crescent Clinic
Community Centre
Jubilee Crescent
Coventry
T 01203 844171
Well woman & contraceptive services. Free condoms, emergency contraception, pregnancy counselling, menopause clinic, cytology (smear testing). Clinic on Thurs 9-11 am.

Saltley Brook Centre
3 Washwood Heath Road
Saltley
Birmingham B8 1SH
T 0121 328 4544
Free confidential contraceptive advice. Help with emotional and sexual problems. Free condoms and other contraceptive supplies. Pregnancy tests and quick results, etc. Phone for opening times.

Sandwell Brook Centre
Toll End Youth Centre
Toll End Road
Tipton DY4 0HP
T 0121 557 1937
Free, confidential contraceptive advice. Free condoms & other contraceptive supplies. Help with emotional & sexual problems. Pregnancy tests & quick results. Phone for opening times.

Tile Hill Health Centre
Jardine Crescent
Tile Hill
Coventry
T 01203 844171
Well woman & contraceptive services. Free condoms, emergency contraception, pregnancy counselling, menopause clinic, cytology (smear testing). Clinic on Wed 5-6.30 pm.

Willenhall Clinic
Stretton Avenue
Willenhall
Coventry
T 01203 844171
Well woman & contraceptive services. Free condoms, emergency contraception, pregnancy counselling, menopause clinic, cytology (smear testing). Clinic on second & fourth Tue of each month 1.30-3 pm.

Wolverhampton Nuffield Hospital, The
Wood Road
Tettenhall
Wolverhampton WV6 8LE
T 01902 754177
Well woman screen. Full female health assessment. Phone for up-to-date price lists.

Women's Health and Information Centre
Amy Corkish
Coventry Healthcare NHS Trust
Stoney Stanton Road
Coventry CV1 4FH
T 01203 844171 F 01203 844173
Well woman & contraception: Mon 10.50 am-12.30 pm, 1.50-3.40, 4.50-6.40 pm; Tue 9.15-11 am, 1.30-3.30, 4.50-6.40 pm; Wed 9-11 am, 4.50-6.40 pm; Thurs 1.50-3.40, 4.50-6.40 pm; Fri 9.30-11 am.

COUNSELLING AND THERAPY

West Midlands Counselling Association
Cathy Taylor
6 Foinavon Close
Rowley Regis
Warley B65 8QB
T 01384 235207 F 01384 235207
Provides training giving practical skills to be used at work or in the personal sphere. Training courses include: counselling skills, mental health counselling, bereavement counselling, stress management.

EDUCATION

Bournville College of Further Education
Maggie Dilloway
Bristol Road South
Northfield
Birmingham B31 2AJ
T 0121 411 1414 F 0121 411 2231
Offers daytime, evening & weekend provision. Special programmes available for women returners, organised to run during school term times only & within school hours. Child care assistance may be available.

Centre for the Study of Women and Gender
University of Warwick
Coventry CV4 7AL
T 01203 523600 F 01203 528170
c.wright@warwick.ac.uk
MA in Interdisciplinary Women's Studies; MA in Gender and International Development; MA in Gender, Literature and Modernity. The

Centre has two full-time academic staff & two half-time lecturers.

North Birmingham College
Information centre
Aldridge Road
Great Barr
Birmingham B44 8NE
T 0121 360 3543 F 0121 325 0828
Open Mon-Fri 8.30 am-9 pm. Mostly mature students. Nursery on site. Welfare, counselling, careers, basic skills support available free. Women only courses, eg Women's Access to Technology & Education.

Stone Hall Adult Education Centre
1083 Warwick Road
Acocks Green
Birmingham B27 6QT
T 0121 706 2744
Courses include the following: Child minders' support group (Mon); Embroidery/crochet/tatting (Mon); Introduction to massage (Mon); Moving on (free course for women, Tue); English for women only.

Women's Group Guild of Students
Jo Griffiths
University of Birmingham
Edgbaston Park Road
Birmingham B15 2TU
T 0121 472 1841 F 0121 471 2099
Meets Fri 1 pm in the women's room in term time. Workshops, meetings. Information & advice service. Woman-only place to chat, read or have a cup of tea. A pro-active group which campaigns regularly.

EQUAL OPPS

Fair Play West Midlands
Dawn Nicholls, Coordinator
Government Office for West Midlands
77 Paradise Circus
Queensway
Birmingham B1 2DT
T 0121 212 5429 F 0121 212 1010
Positive action equalities project. A government EOC initiative to stimulate partnerships which improve opportunities for women to realise their full potential in education, employment & the community.

ETHNIC MINORITIES

Asian Resource Centre
Kashmiro Kaur/Naghmana Kauser
101 Villa Road
Handsworth
Birmingham B19 1NH
T 0121 523 0580 F 0121 554 4553
Open Mon, Tue, Thurs 10 am-5 pm, Wed & Fri 10 am-1 pm. Free advice given in Bengali, Punjabi, Hindi, Gujerati & Urdu. Specialised counselling & support to Asian women & emercency sheltered accommodation.

Asian Women Adhikar Advice Association
Jatinder Kaur, Project Manager
15 Bright Street
Whitmorereans
Wolverhampton WV1 4AT
T 01902 29414 F 01902 28786
Advice, information, counselling, support, benefits, matrimonial problems, housing, immigration. Open Mon, Tue, Thurs 10 am-1 pm & 2-4 pm; Fri 10 am-1 pm. A social group on Tue afternoons.

Asian Women's Cookery Group
Mrs Lata
C/o Asian Welfare Centre
West Bromwich B70 6PJ
T 0121 525 9688 F 0121 525 9688
Meets Mon. Cookery classes in Asian foods. Also social activities.

Asian Women's Group
Munawar Khalil
C/o Norton Hall Learning Area
Ralph Road
Saltley
Birmingham B8 1NA
T 0121 328 3043 F 0121 327 9636
Open Mon-Fri 9 am-3 pm. For Asian women who want to combat the isolation & problems living in England. ESL, advice on form filling, advice on domestic violence. Sewing classes. Training in IT.

Asian Women's Job Club
Sarzana Yousufzai
109 Golden Hill
Oak Road
Small Heath
Birmingham B10 0DP
T 0121 753 0115
Open Mon-Thurs 10 am-1 pm. Free services for Asian women to help them find jobs. Help provided with cvs. Advice about training. ESL classes. Day centre for mentally ill Asian women on Tue.

ENGLAND - BIRMINGHAM AND MIDLANDS

Asian Women's Support Group
Caroline Leahy, Unit Manager
East Birmingham Family Service Unit
723 Coventry Road
Small Heath
Birmingham B10 0JL
T 0121 772 4217 F 0121 753 2375
Open Fri 10 am-1 pm. To give Asian women a chance to get out of their domestic environment. The aim is to encourage independece & self-sufficiency. Lessons on road safety & driving lessons.

Barnardos - Harmara Project
Perminder Paul
168 Birmingham Road
Oldbury
Warley B69 4EH
T 0121 544 1711 F 0121 544 1711
Aims to empower young Asian women who are at risk of becoming homeless in the Sandwell area. We counsel & support these women's decisions in a positive way. Generally open between 9-5 Mon-Fri.

Bengali Women's Group
Caroline Leahy, Unit Manager
East Birmingham Family Service Unit
723 Coventry Road
Small Heath
Birmingham B10 0JL
T 0121 772 4217 F 0121 753 2375
Meets Mon 10.30 am-12.30 pm. A self-support group of Bengali women who want to learn English.

Coventry and Warwickshire Asian Women's Business Club
Kala Patel
C/o Women's Business Development Agency
Enterprise House
Sheriff's Orchard
Coventry CV1 1QN
T 01203 633737 F 01203 632734

Foleshill Women's Training
Preet Grewal
70-72 Elmsdale Avenue
Coventry CV6 6E5
T 01203 637693 F 01203 662854
PREET.FWT@POP3.hiway.co.uk
Open 9 am-3 pm. A training centre for Asian women. Computer training, word processing, translating classes.

NAV-YUG - Training Project for Asian Women
Sharan Jit Walia
Barr's Hill School and Community College
Radford Road
Coventry CV1 4BU
T 01203 633903 F 01203 550941
Open Mon-Fri 10 am-12 noon & 1-3 pm. Free courses & free creche. Courses in computers, ESOL, spoken English, hair & beauty (the Asian way), fashion & design, etc. All courses are accredited.

Panahghar
Sobia Shaw
3 St Margarets Road
Stoke
Coventry CV1 5BT
T 01203 228952 F 01203 230886
For women & children suffering domestic violence in the home.

Roshni
Liz Tilly/Rajinder Bhara
Rounds Green Methodist Church Buildings
Newbury Lane
Oldbury B69 1HE
T 0121 544 6611 F 0121 544 6611
Part of Warley leisure & enabling services. Offers Asian women with learning disabilities opportunities for personal development by participating in community leisure activities such as cookery & needlework.

Sahil
Gurpal Matu
1st Floor
449a Foleshill Road
Foleshill
Coventry CV6 5AQ
T 01203 638754 F 01203 638762
A woman's group. Befriending; referral centre; support.

Walsall Black Sisters
Mrs Maureen Lewis
Black Women's Centre
17 Wednesbury Road
Walsall WS1 3RU
T 01922 616996 F 01922 725078
Advice & information for Black women living in or around Walsall. Saturday supplementary & cultural school; African Caribbean school & community project; after school project; education & training; etc.

ENGLAND - BIRMINGHAM AND MIDLANDS

GIRLS/YOUNG WOMEN

Young Parents Group, The
Yvonne Walton
South Birmingham Family Service Unit
45 Barratts Road
Pool Farm
Birmingham B38 9HU
T 0121 459 4232   F 0121 458 4323
For mothers under age 22. Creche. Drop-in. Women choose their own activities. Social workers available for information. Open Wed 1.30-3.30 pm. Has acted as stepping stone for further educational activities.

HEALTH

Longford Physiotherapy and Sports Injury Clinic
Mrs K Pabla
2 Pembry Avenue
Coventry CV6 6JT
T 01203 367918
Provides physiotherapy treatment for musculo-skeletal problems (back, neck, all joints) for stroke, multiple sclerosis, sports injuries, etc. Also a mobile service twice a week. Appts between 10 am-7 pm.

Menopause Clinic - Solihull
Mr D Sturdee, Consultant
Solihull Hospital
Lode Lane
Solihull B91 2JL
T 0121 711 4455
Clinic on Wed 9 am-1 pm with Mr Sturdee & two doctors who specialise in menopause & problems. Can also phone 0121 685 5055.

Menopause Helpline
Ros Roberts
Menopause Clinic
Solihull Hospital
Lode Lane
Solihull B91 2JL
T 0121 685 5355
Phone on Tue or Wed between 11 am & 1 pm. Two clinic nurse specialists are on hand to give advice & information about the menopause.

Menopause Support Group
Any Corkish
Women's Health and Information Centre
Coventry Healthcare NHS Trust
Stoney Stanton Road
Coventry CV1 4FH
T 01203 844171   F 01203 844173

Meets on first Tue of each month. Phone above number for further details.

Turning Point - Birmingham
Rita Knight
Dale House
New Meeting Street
Birmingham B4 7SX
T 0121 632 6363   F 0121 643 5904
Confidential information & advice on all aspects of drug use: effects of drugs, safer drug use, AIDS, legal & housing problems. Counselling & support, referral on, needle exchange scheme. Drop-in Fri 1-4 pm.

LARGER/TALLER WOMEN

Exersize 16+
Julie Morgan
14 Avenue Road
Warley B65 0LR
T 0121 559 5522   F 0121 559 5522
Exercise classes designed for women who are size 16 or over in an environment that is friendly, welcoming & non judgmental. To enable women to reap the long-term health benefits of regular exercise.

Julia-Michelle Knitwear
Miss Jilia Gready
20 Ravensdale Road
Wyken
Coventry CV2 5GQ
T 01203 443227
Designers & producers of exclusive hand- & machine-knitwear. All sizes catered for & no extra cost for the larger. Designs garments to orders at a reasonable price. Homebased. Phone also 01203 303820.

Long Tall Sally
3 North Western Arcade
Birmingham B2 5LH
T 0121 233 4563
Clothes for the taller woman sizes 12-20. Open Mon-Sat 9.30 am-5.30 pm.

LEGAL MATTERS

Adocks
Susan Howard
17-19 St Michael Street
West Bromwich B70 7AB
T 0121 553 7394   F 0121 500 6018
Solicitors & business advisors. Client base comprises predominatly small & medium-sized businesses in greater west Midlands.

ENGLAND - BIRMINGHAM AND MIDLANDS

Free initial legal audit. No extra charge for site visits. Pre-arranged fees.

LESBIAN AND BISEXUAL

Lesbewell
Gudrun Limbrick
P O Box 4048
Moseley
Birmingham B13 8DP
Covers lesbian health information & links all groups & health professionals working locally.

Lesbian and Gay Switchboard West Midlands
PO Box 3626
Birmingham B5 4GL
T 0121 622 6589
Telephone line open 7-10 pm every night of the year. Advice, information & counselling.

Lesbian Line West Midlands
P O Box 2405
Birmingham B5 4AY
T 0121 622 6536
Phone line open on Mon 7.30-9.30 pm (except on Bank Holidays). Offers information & support.

MANUAL TRADES

Lorraine's Painting and Decorating
Lorraine Howship
46 Anderson Crescent
Great Barr
Birmingham B43 2ST
T 0121 358 5826
A lot of work is for women on their own who are uneasy about having men in the house. Pricing is costing per job on an hourly rate. Best time to phone is after 6.30 pm

MEDIA

Ocean Video and Multimedia Productions
Gail Smirthwaite
Benson House
Lombard Street
Digbeth
Birmingham B12 0QR
T 017000 191920 F 017000 191921
OCEAN@oceanvid.demon.co.uk
Open Mon-Fri 9 am-5.30 pm. Producers of video productions from scripting to filming to editing/duplication. Producers of interactive CD-rom: programme design, authoring, filming live clips, duplication.

Second Sight (Birmingham) Ltd
Glynis Powell
Zair Works
111 Bishop Street
Birmingham B5 6JL
T 0121 622 4223 F 0121 622 5750
Specialises in arts or social issues projects. Video training/production company. Courses in video production from novice to advanced level for women-only groups. Most courses free to eligible unwaged.

OLDER WOMEN

Care Alternatives
Premier House
Darlington Street
Wolverhampton WV1 4ND
T 01902 23563 F 01902 717174
Provides flexible care at home for elderly or disabled people. Can assist with both personal care & domestic tasks. Care workers do induction training & are thoroughly vetted.

PREGNANCY/CHILDBIRTH

Crisis Pregnancy Centre - Birmingham
Mrs Bristow
168 Shenstone Road
Edgbaston
Birmingham B16 0NR
T 0121 429 9543
Open Tue & Fri 10 am-1 pm. Free pregnancy testing, counselling & support for women with unplanned pregnancies. Post abortion & miscarriage counselling. Phone for an appt. 24-hour ansaphone.

Crisis Pregnancy Centre - Stourbridge
Sharon Bradley
Living Springs Counselling Centre
105 High Street
Stourbridge DY8 1EE
T 01384 443446
Open Mon-Fri 9 am-5 pm. Free pregnancy testing, counselling & support for women with unplanned pregnancies. Post abortion/miscarriage counselling. Phone to check for availability. 24-hour ansaphone.

Gift of a Life - Infertility Support Group
Assisted Conception Unit, Ward M4
Walsgrave Hospital, Walsgrave
Clifford Bridge Road
Coventry CV2 2DX
T 01203 602020

Meets on last Mon of each month 7.30 at above address.

Kingstanding Pregnancy Help Centre
Emanuel Community Centre
Kettlehouse Road
Kingstanding
T 0121 355 8786
Open Mon 6-7 pm & Tue 1-3 pm. No appt is necessary. Free pregnancy testing, counselling & support for women with unplanned pregnancies. Post abortion & miscarriage counselling.

Pregnancy Assistance Centre
719 Stratford Road
Sparkhill
Birmingham B11 4DN
T 0121 778 3132
Telephone contacts available & telephone counselling. Phone for details. Free pregnancy testing, counselling & support for women with unplanned pregnancies. Post abortion & miscarriage counselling.

Wolverhampton Infertility Self Help (WISH)
infertility nurse specialist
Maternity Unit
Newcross Hospital
Wolverhampton WV10 0QP
T 01902 307999

PRISONERS/PRISONERS' WIVES

Help and Advice Line for Offenders' Wives (HALOW)
Summerfield Foundation
260 Dudley Road
Winson Green
Birmingham B18 4HL
T 0121 454 3615
Providing advice & practical support to any relatives of men in prison. Court escort service, etc.

PROFESSIONAL ASSOCIATIONS

West Midlands Association of Women Solicitors
Sue Bandalli, Chairman
Faculty of Law
University of Birmingham
Edgbaston
Birmingham B15 2TT
F 0121 414 3585
S.L.BANDALLI@bham.ac.uk
Group of solicitors. Several meetings yearly, educational & social. Newsletters. Aims to keep women solicitors in touch with each other & provide information to assist those in practice & at home with families.

PUBLISHERS/PUBLICATIONS

Wedge Co-operative
13 High Street
Coventry CV1 5RE
T 01203 225634
Substantial feminist list within a radical bookshop.

RETAILING

Coventry Sewing and Knitting Machine Centre
Pamela Neave
5 Central Buildings
Warwick Road
Coventry CV3 6AJ
T 01203 257266 F 01203 222134
Retailing, sewing & knitting machines, accessories, overlockers, cabinets, wool & some haberdashery. Tuition courses. Open Mon-Sat 9.15 am-5.30 pm.

Gamefreak
Miss C Deery
3 Salop Street
Wolverhampton WV3 0RX
T 01902 681212 F 01902 681212
Specilast independent retailers of computer games & consoles. Offical Sony centre. Open six days a week. New & secondhand. Part exchanges & swaps available. All prices below recommended retail prices.

Khaira Pharmacy
Mrs J K Khaira
214 Birmingham Road
West Bromwich B70 6QJ
T 0121 525 7201
Pharmacy.

SERVICES

Amanda Poyner Draughting Services
Amanda Poyner
36 Tower Hill
Great Barr
Birmingham B42 1LG
T 0121 358 7906
Professional, qualified draughtswoman offers comprehensive draughting service specialising in mechanical & electrical building services. Available for either manual or computerised drawings using Autocad.

ENGLAND - BIRMINGHAM AND MIDLANDS

Christina Ross Communications
Christine McCabe
20 Bellcroft
Ladywood
Birmingham B16 8EJ
T 0121 454 7692 F 0121 622 6150
Personal development.

Express Interpreting and Translation Service
Usha Chauhan
298 Rookery Road
Handsworth
Birmingham B21 9Q6
T 0121 554 1981 F 0121 554 7430
Interpreting & translation service in all Asian & European languages. Also provides typesetting, proofreading, voice-overs & a printing service.

Interior Elegance
Marilyn Cruckshank
5 Central Buildings
Warwick Road
Coventry CV3 6AJ
T 01203 257266 F 01203 222134
Professionally made-to-measure service for curtains & all soft furnishings. Retailing fabrics, wallcoverings.

It's A Snip!
Donna Bissell
127 Horseley Heath
Great Bridge
Tipton DY4 7EH
T 0121 557 2587
Unisex hair care at reasonable, affordable prices. Neck, shoulder & head massage. Open Mon 9 am-2 pm, Tue 9 am-4 pm, Wed & Sat 8 am-5 pm, Thurs 8.30 am-3 pm, Fri 8 am-6 pm.

Manipulations Ltd
Mrs Jane D Hastilow
Tasker Street
West Bromwich B70 0AY
T 0121 557 1757 F 0121 522 2417
Anodisers & polishers of aluminium. Price given as part of quotation. Open Mon-Fri 7 am-3.30 pm.

Meetings Company, The
Carol Wetton
85-89 Colmore Row
Birmingham B3 2BB
T 0121 236 8966 F 0121 233 9360
The.MEETINGS.Co@MSN.COM

Organises events throughout UK & Europe on behalf of clients. Conferences, meetings, workshops, corporate hospitality, full audio visual production, free venue funding service.

Sammy Rose Management Services
S Rose
186 Oldbury Road
Rowley Regis
Warley B65 0NW
T 0121 561 2800 F 0121 561 2700
Offers a full range of marketing services to all business types, including planning, research, promotional initiatives & training.

Solo Ltd
Mrs Tanya Ross
D5 Littleheath Ind. Centre
Old Church Road
Coventry CV6 7NB
T 01203 687119 F 01203 638521
Designers & manufactuers of executive incentives & awards.

Sylvana Training and Consultancy
Sue Wright
26 Rathbone Road
Bearwood B67 5JQ
T 0121 420 2951 F 0121 420 2951
Management development & training consultancy. Experience in course design & organisational development. Areas of expertise include women into management, equality assertiveness skills & managing change.

Tudor Translations
Tessa Cowie
46 Lyndhurst Road
Wolverhampton WV3 0AA
T 01902 560785 F 01902 560785
Translation of all languages, using mother tongue nationals. Aims to give quality, accuracy & integrity in translating & interpreting & to meet deadlines. Phone for up-to-date price list.

Type-write
Lynne Watkins
38 Kentmere Close
Potters Green
Coventry CV2 2GE
T 01203 611645 F 01203 602769
Typing for a wide range of companies, from engineering firms to estate agents. Work generally carried out within 24 hours.

ENGLAND - BIRMINGHAM AND MIDLANDS

Zakli International
Mrs Hemraj
249 Ladypool Road
Sparkbrook
Birmingham B12 8LF
T 0121 693 6622 F 0121 446 4453
Offers freight forwarding & typing services to companies & individuals. Open Mon-Fri 9 am-5 pm.

Sexual abuse/Rape crisis

Amazon Project
Brigitte Taylor, Project Manager
620-622 Warwick Road
Tyseley
Birmingham B11 2EX
For young female survivors of sexual abuse aged 12-21. The counselling catchment area is Birmingham. Office hours Mon-Thurs 9 am-5 pm & Fri 9 am-4 pm. Mother-daughter counselling & befriending.

Birmingham Rape and Sexual Violence Project
Libby Aston, Helpline Coordinator
P O Box 5876
Birmingham B44 0DF
T 0121 643 5600
Telephone helpline, counselling & support for women by women surviving rape & childhood sexual abuse. Limited face-to-face counselling service.

Coventry Rape and Sexual Abuse Centre
C/o CVSC
58-64 Corporation Street
Coventry CV1 1GF
T 01203 677229
Phoneline open Mon, Tues, Thurs & Fri 9.30-11.30 am; Mon & Wed 7-9 pm. Punjabi, patois speakers available. A service run by women for women who have been raped or otherwise sexually abused.

Sandwell Rape Crisis Centre
Pat McAllister
P O Box 2223
West Bromwich B70 8AH
T 0121 525 9981 F 0121 525 9913
Free, confidential face-to-face counselling service telephone helpline & drop-in support group. For women in Sandwell/Dudley. Line open Mon-Fri at varying times. Black women's line available Tue evening.

Social

Drop In, The
Sue Wiseman
South Birmingham Family Service Network
45 Barratts Road
Pool Farm Estate, Kings Norton
Birmingham B38 9HU
T 0121 459 4232 F 0121 458 4323
Meets Tue 10 am-12 pm. Drop-in for women local to the area. Women choose their own activities which can range from organising & drama group to discussions about particular problems. Creche.

Support

Deelands Hall Association
Rita Douglas
Deelands Road
Rubery
Birmingham B45 9RR
T 0121 453 7183
Women's craft club Tue 10 am; playgroup Mon, Wed, Fri 9.30-11.45 am; pensioners group Tue 1-3.30 pm. Playschemes during school holidays. Advice, back-up & support to individuals, families & groups.

Tuesday Support Group
Caroline Leahy, Unit Manager
East Birmingham Family Service Unit
723 Coventry Road
Small Heath
Birmingham B10 0JL
T 0121 772 4217 F 0121 753 2375
Meets Tue 1-3 pm. A multicultural women's self-support group discussing a wide range of topics relating to various different cultures. First aid classes & crafts.

Women's Group, The
Cornerstone Family Centre
Howard Street
Hillfields
Coventry CV1 4GE
T 01203 256611
Meets informally once a week on Thurs 12.30-2.30 pm

Training

Business Network Ltd and Training Opportunities
Dawn Bennett
93 Church Street
Bilston WV14 0BJ
T 01902 404500 F 01902 404545

ENGLAND - BRISTOL AND BATH

Free training, support & advice for women returners or set up in business. Training fits in with domestic responsibilites. Training advice & consultancy for women in work. Workshops for women owner managers.

Palm Training Ltd
Cathy Taylor
6 Foinavon Close
Rowley Regis
Warley B65 8QB
T 01384 235207 F 01384 235207
Training in clinical areas for community nurses to satisfy their professional registration with the UKCC. Includes update training days on diabetes, asthma, hypertension, women's health, coronary heart disease.

Women Acting in Today's Society (WAITS)
Joan Blaney, Director
Gala House
3 Raglan Road
Edgbaston
Birmingham B5 7RA
T 0121 440 1443 F 0121 440 1343
Providing training & support services for a network of women's groups & individual women. Helps local women to establish community-based projects & self-help groups increase participation in community affairs.

Women Print Ltd
Jesse Lyons, Coordinator
Devonshire House
High Street
Digbeth
Birmingham B12 0LP
T 0121 773 9065 F 0121 624 6800
A 40-week course. Attendance is 15 hours a week 10 am-3 pm. Only unemployed or unwaged women are eligible. Design, drawing, graphic design, 3d design, photography, computer skills, etc. The course is free.

Women's Help Centre Ltd
Mrs Usha Khera
321 Rookery Road
Handsworth
Birmingham B21 9PR
T 0121 551 2370 F 0121 551 1167
Training & advice centre. To empower women to help themselves in the job market. Free training in childcare, business administration & fashion design. ESOL classes. Creche. Open Mon-Fri 9 am-5 pm.

Women's Job Change
Christine Higgins
Birmingham Settlement
318 Summer Lane
Newtown
Birmingham B19 3RL
T 0121 359 3562 F 0121 359 6357
Free, independent service for women seeking a return to work or training. Low cost childcare on site. Open Mon-Fri 9.30 am-3 pm.

VIOLENCE AGAINST WOMEN

Sandwell Safer Cities Project
Linda Boys
C/o Sandwell Borough Council
P O Box 2374
Oldbury
Warley B69 3DE
T 0121 569 3078 F 0121 569 3079
Government-funded community safety partnership with NACRO promoting local initiatives to prevent crime & make places safer.

WOMEN'S AID

Asian Women's Refuge
Kash or Suki
C/o Asian Resource Centre
101 Villa Road
Handsworth
Birmingham B19 1NH
T 0121 523 0580 F 0121 554 4553
Open Mon-Fri 10 am-5 pm. Accommodates up to ten mothers & three to four children. Counselling, DSS, benefits, welfare rights, housing, immigration.

Birmingham Women's Aid
Sangita Mundy
P O Box 3039
Birmingham B20
T 0121 344 4889 F 0121 344 3661
Staff cover Mon-Fri 10 am-11 pm; Sat & Sun 10 am-5 pm. Refuge accommodation for women & their children (if any) suffering domestic violence.

BRISTOL AND BATH

ACCOMMODATION

Brighton Street Women's Hostel
Sally Gardner, Team Leader
30 Brighton Street
Bristol BS2 8XA
T 0117 942 1068 F 0117 942 0555
Hostel for women aged 16-30 requiring support. Self/professional referral. Key-work

ENGLAND - BRISTOL AND BATH

system available. Support & encourage self-confidence, self-value, self-empowerment. No facilities for children/wheelchairs.

Bristol Cyrenians Women's Direct Access Hostel
Sally Morrissen
11 Dean Crescent
Bedminster
Bristol BS3 1AG
T 0117 987 2055
Hostel for single homeless women aged 16+. Completely accessible. Lift to all floors. Accommodates cats & dogs. Accessible 24 hours a day, 365 days a year. Short stay; aims to re-house in three months.

Accountancy

Red Ledger
Helen Anderson, Tax Accountant
95 Effingham Road
St Andrew's Park
Bristol BS6 5AY
T 0117 983 6559 F 0117 983 6559
Non-suit wearing cheap accountant, specialising in tax and accounts for women. Sole traders and partnerships welcome. Childcare arranged at the office. Accounts for housing benefits & family credit purposes.

Arts and Crafts

Patchwork
Judith Gait
St Mary's Cottage
Hemington
Bath BA3 5XX
T 01373 834033
Traditional American designs, quilts, cushions & wearable art. Embroidered silk evening stoles, embroidered waistcoats, Victorian embroidered quilts.

Rive Gauche
Pat West
69 Lower Redland Road
Bristol BS6 6SP
T 0117 974 5106
Provides & promotes a platform for women's poetry in Bristol. Encourages women to write/perform their poetry. Has produced anthologies. Engaged in one major event each year.

Silly Muse
Sandra Stevens
4 Farm Cottages
Shoscombe
Bath BA2 8LT
T 01761 432546
Poetry and music performance group.

Woman's Woodwork Centre
Sandy Corke
Lambridge Mews
Bath BA1 6QE
T 01225 339482
New opportunity courses for unemployed women: Training for Trading - 2-day week vocational course in furniture making; Furniture Making & Restoration - 2-day week vocational course. Also recreational classes.

Women's Art Works
Denny Long
P O Box 854
Bristol BS99 5JA
T 0117 929 9234
Providing support/facilities to enable women from all economic, cultural & ethnic backgrounds & disabilities to publicly express the content & meaning of their lives through creative work of all kinds & media.

Word Works
Sandra Stevens
4 Farm Cottages
Shoscombe
Bath BA2 8LT
T 01761 432546
Offers a variety of services and opportunities for writers: courses, writing holidays, day workshops, critical feedback. Also tailor-made performances and workshops on request.

Business Support Schemes

Women in Business - Bedminster branch
Hebron House
Sion Road
Bedminster
Bristol BS3 3BD
T 0117 987 9444 F 0117 963 1770
Annual conference & variety of business seminars & workshops. Phone Mon-Fri 8.30 am-5.30 pm. Additional phone number: 0117 963 7634.

Women in Enterprise
Mollie Ward
Hebron House
Sion Road
Bedminster

Bristol B53 3BD
T 0117 987 9444 F 0117 963 1770
Membership includes free entry in the WIE directory, free seminars on subjects such as accounts, PR, time management, presentation skills, etc, annual conference, speakers, presentations & workshops.

CENTRES FOR WOMEN

Bristol Women's Centre
Jane Gregory
43 Dulcie Road
Barton Hill
Bristol BS5 0AX
T 0117 935 1674 F 0117 955 6971
Minicom 0117 935 1675. Open Mon, Tue & Fri 11 am-3 pm. Informal women's group Tue 8-10 pm 24-hour ansaphone. Information, advice, support for women. Level access for wheelchair users; loop system, etc.

St Paul's Asian Women's Group
Jamila Aftab
Community Flat
Halston Drive
St Paul's
Bristol BS2 9JN
T 0117 955 0895
Open Mon, Tues, Thurs 10 am-3 pm. Sewing & cooking classes. Discussion groups. Creche available Mon 1-3 pm. Advice provided on health issues. Young Asian women's group on Sat 1.30-3.30 pm.

CHILD CARE AND FAMILY

Avon Parents' Network
Jenny Craig
Unit 38
Easton Business Centre
Felix Road, Easton
Bristol BS5 0HQ
T 0117 941 3999 F 0117 941 5803
Telephone information service for parents, carers & workers caring for children. Helpline open Mon-Fri 11 am-3 pm. Information about registered childcare, parents & toddlers groups, playgroups, etc.

Bristol Children's Playhouse
Jackie Cutmore
Berkeley Green Road
Eastville
Bristol BS5 6LQ
T 0117 951 0037
Working against isolation, deprivation & poverty of families. Safeguarding & promoting the welfare of children in need within the family. Befriending & support in a crisis.

Bristol Homestart
St Matthew's Road
Kingsdown
Bristol BS6 5TT
T 0117 942 8399
Support in the home for young families with pre-school age children who are experiencing stress. Not only for women.

CONTRACEPTION/WELL WOMAN

Amelia Nutt Clinic
Queen's Road
Withywood
Bristol BS13
T 0117 940 5454
Contraception advice & supplies open access Wed 9-11.15 am 21s & under & emergency contraception only Thurs 4-6.30. Phone above number for an appointment.

Avon Brook Centre
1 Unity Street
Bristol BS1 5AH
T 01179 290090
Free, confidential contraceptive advice. Free condoms & other contraceptive supplies. Help with emotional & sexual problems. Pregnancy tests & quick results. Phone for opening times.

Central House Clinic
Tower Hill
Bristol BS2 0JD
T 0117 929 1010
Contraception: under 21s Mon 12-2.30 pm & 5.15-7.30 pm; Tue 9-11.15 am; Sat 10 am-12.30 pm. Open access Tue 5.15-7.30 pm; Wed 9-11 am & 5.15-7.30 pm; Thurs 5.15-7.30 pm; Fri 12.30-3 pm

Chesterfield Nuffield Hospital, The
3 Clifton Hill
Clifton
Bristol BS8 1BP
T 0117 973 0391
Well woman screen. Full female health assessment. Phone for up-to-date price lists.

Granby House
St John's Road
Bedminster
Bristol BS3
T 0117 966 5990

Open access (all ages) contraceptive advice & supplies Thurs 8.45-11 am Phone for an appointment.

Keynsham Clinic
Park Road
Keynsham
Bristol BS18
T 0117 986 2423
Open access (all ages) contraceptive advice & supplies Wed 6.30-8.30. Phone for an appointment.

Sawclose Clinic
Bridewell Lane
Upper Borough Walls
Bath
T 01225 466789
Contraception clinics by appt Mon 10 am-1 pm, Tue 6-9 pm, Thurs 9.15 am-12 noon. Young people's clinic drop-in Fri 3-5 pm. Free, confidential contraception & contraceptive advice & cervical cytology.

St John's Lane Health Centre
Wedmore Vale
Bedminster
Bristol BS3
T 0117 966 7681
Contraceptive advice and supplies for under 21s only Tue 4-6.30 pm. Phone for an appointment.

Stockwood Medical Centre
Hollway Road
Bristol BS14
T 01275 833103
Contraceptive advice & supplies for under 21s & emergency contraception only on Wed 5.30-7.30 pm. Phone for an appointment.

Wellwomen Information
6 West Street
St Philips
Bristol BS2 0BH
T 0117 941 3311
Health drop-ins for information & support. General service Tue & Wed 10 am-12.30 pm; Asian women Tue 10 am-12.30 pm (phone 0117 951 9500); counselling by arrangement. Workshops, talks, groups support.

William Budd Health Centre
Leinster Avenue
Knowle
Bristol BS4

T 0117 963 3152
Contraceptive advice & supplies for under 21s & emergency contraception only Tue 2-4 pm. Open access (all ages) contraceptive clinics Thurs 1.30-3.30. Phone to make an appointment.

COUNSELLING AND THERAPY

Avon Counselling and Psychotherapy Service
11 Orchard Street
Bristol BS1 5EH
T 0117 930 4447
Adult counselling & psychotherapy by appt. Short & long-term work available. Wheelchair access (but not toilet facilities). Sometimes funds to help people on benefit for short-term counselling/psychotherapy.

Touchstone Counselling Service
Su O'Dnnell/Jo Anning
NSPCC
85 North Street
Bedminster
Bristol BS3 1ES
T 0117 966 4283 F 0117 953 5396
Free counselling service for adults with children who are wanting to make sense of their own, or their children's, abuse. Open Mon-Fri 9 am-5 pm Run by NSPCC & staffed by trained volunteer counsellors.

Womankind
Suzi Sparham
76 Colston Street
Bristol BS1 5BB
T 0117 925 5207 F 0117 922 5236
Supporting women experiencing mental health problems/emotional distress. Daily telephone helpline. Weekly long-term therapy groups, short term (24 week) theme-based therapy groups; individual counselling; etc.

EDUCATION

Bath Association of Graduate Women
Mrs C M Faulkner, Hon Secretary
Milvidon
Evelyn Road
Weston
Bath BA1 3QF
T 01225 428029
Meets third Wed at 7.30 pm at the Environment Centre, 24 Milsom Street, Bath in October, November, March, April & May. Discussion meeting first Wed of month 10 am Lunch meetings in January & February.

ENGLAND - BRISTOL AND BATH

Environment

Sarah Wyatt Garden Design
Sarah Wyatt
16 Jubilee Road
St Werburghs
Bristol BS2 9RS
T 0117 955 7811
Qualified designer offering professional & comprehensive service, finding creative & practical solutions to help you get what you want out of your garden.

Susan JC Smith-Uncles Chartered Architect
Susan JC Smith-Uncles
25 Mervyn Road
Bishopston
Bristol BS7 9EL
T 0117 942 6225
Architectural practice with experience designing small & large buildings, including domestic, conversions, extensions, adaptions for disabilities, health & office buildings, conservation & refurbishment.

Ethnic Minorities

Asian Girls Youth Group
Jatinder Potiwal
C/o Sikh Resource Centre
114 St Mark's Road
Easton
Bristol BS5 6JD
T 0117 952 5023
Open Sun 3-6 pm. Mainly a discussion group on issues relevant to adolescent girls (eg problems at home). All discussion & information gained are confidential. Outings.

Asian Women's Music Group
Meher Rahman
C/o Bath Asian Council
27a Westgate Street
Bath BA1 1EP
T 01225 332231
Meets Fri 7-9 pm. For Asian women to learn music for vocal & instrumental Indian classical music.

Avon and Bristol Asian Women's Network
The Old Co-Op
42 Chelsea Road
Easton
Bristol BS5 6AT
T 0117 411 294
The link organisation for all Asian women's group in the Bristol & Bath area. Provides information & advice & details of local Asian women's organisations.

Awaz Htaoh
Simi Chowdhry
182 Stapleton Road
Easton
Bristol BS5 ONZ
T 0117 935 4528
Aims to reduce the fear of crime in the Asian community in Bristol by imparting knowledge to Asian women. Also aims to increase the rate of reporting crime.

Bangladesh Asian Women's Group
Lily Islam
C/o Bangladesh Association
539 Stapleton Road
Easton
Bristol BS5 6SQ
T 0117 951 1491 F 0117 952 5425
Open Sun 12-2 pm. Social gatherings, ESOL, supplementary Bengali classes.

Barton Hill Asian Women's Groups
Zahra Haq, Coordinator
Barton Hill Settlement
43 Ducie Road
Barton Hill
Bristol BS5 0AX
T 0117 955 6971
A service for young & elderly Asian women who are isolated. An exchange of ideas. An elderly Asian women's group meets on Mon & a young Asian mother's group meets on Thurs.

Bristol and Avon Chinese Women's Group
Rosa Hui, Project Manager
St Agnes Parish Church
Thomas Street
St Paul's
Bristol BS2 9LL
T 0117 935 1462 F 0117 935 1462
Supporting the welfare of Chinese women in Bristol & Bath & reducing isolation caused by language & cultural barriers. Drop-in day centre on Sun for Chinese parents & children.

Elderly Asian Women's Group
Jatindar Potiwal
C/o Sikh Resource Centre
114 St Marks Road
Easton
Bristol BS5 6JD
T 0117 952 5023

Open Wed 12-3 pm. Discussion group about health matters. Medication advice available. Massage on premises.

Khaas Asian Opportunity Group
Gurdarshen Dhanjal
St Werburgh's Community Centre
Horley Road
Bristol BS2 9TJ
T 0117 955 4070
Set up to provide help for Asian families with children who have special needs.

Maternity and Health Links
Shaheen Chaudhry
The Old Co-op
38-42 Chelsea Road
Easton
Bristol BS5 6AF
T 0117 955 8495 F 0117 955 8495
Open Mon-Fri 9 am-5 pm. For Asian women, enabling those with language & cultural difficulties to gain access to health services. Provides a linkworkers (interpreting & advocacy) service during pregnancy.

Raj Vidya Vihar
Yashu Amlani
Flat 2
5 Beaufort Road
Clifton
Bristol BS8 2JT
T 0117 923 9953
Meets Sat 10 am-12.30 pm. For Asian women & children. Educational, social, cultural activities. English taught & to improve relevant mother tongue (GCSE & A level courses provided). Building confidence.

Silai Project
C/o YWCA
101-104 Wells Road
Totterdown
Bristol BS4 2BS
T 0117 971 9432 F 0117 971 9432
Open Mon-Fri 9 am-4 pm. Provides training opportunities in sewing for Asian women. Trains women for two City & Guilds sewing certificates.

Totterdown Asian Women's Group
Floren Shamis
C/o YMCA
101-104 Wells Road
Totterdown
Bristol BS4 2BS
T 0117 971 9432

Aims to get Asian women together.

Women's Punjabi Class
Jatinder Potiwal
C/o Sikh Resource Centre
114 St Mark's Road
Easton
Bristol BS5 6JD
T 0117 952 5023
Open Tues 5.30-7.30, teaching women to write Punjabi.

GIRLS/YOUNG WOMEN

Young Mothers' Group Trust
Julia Nibloe
C/o Mill Youth Centre
Lower Ashley Road
Easton
Bristol BS5 0YJ
T 0117 955 5486
Barton Hill & Easton Young Mothers' group runs drop in for young mothers under age 21, creche & transport provided; Young Mothers' Information project trains & supports young mothers; a peer-led project.

HEALTH

Adult Health Service
Bath
T 01225 840132
Contraceptive advice & information, including emergency contraceptive advice; vasectomy service; advice on sexual problems. Phone Mon-Fri 10 am-3 pm

Avon Breast Screening Centre
Central Health Clinic
Tower Hill
Bristol BS2 0JD
T 0117 925 2867 F 0117 925 2867
Phone 0117 976 0195 for an appointment. Breast screening for women aged 50-64 once every three years. Open Mon-Fri 8.30 am-5 pm

Bath Area Drugs Advisory Service (BADAS)
Nanette Gregory, Administrator
32-33 Broad Street
Bath BA1 5LP
T 01225 469479 F 01225 429323
Free, confidential information, advice & services to those concerned about drug use. Open Mon, Tue, Thurs, Fri 10 am-1 pm & 2-4 pm; Thurs 5-7.30 pm Women-only drop-in Tue 10 a.m-1 pm. Counselling, etc.

ENGLAND - BRISTOL AND BATH

Bristol Crisis Service for Women
Hilary Lindsay
P O Box 654
Bristol BS99 1SH
T 0117 925 1119
Helpline for women in emotional distress. Focuses on self-injury. Training & publications about self injury. National helpline for women in distress Fri & Sat 9 pm-12.30 am Shout is a bi-monthly newsletter.

Eating Disorders Association - Bath and District Area
Brigid M Boardman
54 St James Park
Bath BA1 2SX
T 01225 311312 F 01225 313327
Helping all those with eating disorders, generally on a voluntary basis.

Genito-Urinary Medicine (GUM) Clinic
Royal United Hospital
Main Outpatients' Department
Bath
T 01225 824617
Free confidential information, advice & treatment for STDs & genito-urinary infections. Phone for appt. Health adviser for advice, counselling, information on HIV/AIDS, safer sex, etc. Phone 01225 824558.

Milne Centre Clinic
Bristol Royal Infirmary
Lower Maudlin Street
Bristol BS2 8HW
T 0117 928 3010 F 0117 928 2385
Women-only clinic Thurs 9 am-12 pm. Free, confidential screening & treatment for all STDs. HIV testing, counselling & medical care. Phone 0117 928 2580 for an appointment.

Sexual Health Advice for Women
Beverley Miller/Heather Devey/Tricia Mills
Royal United Hospital Bath
GUM Clinic
Main Outpatients' Dept
Bath
T 01225 824558
Appts Mon, Wed, Thurs 8.30 am-4.30 pm, Tue & Fri 8.30 am-7 p.m: 01225 824617. Free confidential advice, information on sex issues, & counselling: ectopic pregnancies, abortions, hysterectomies, etc.

LARGER/TALLER WOMEN

Long Tall Sally
3 New Market Row
Grand Parade
Bath BA2 4AN
T 01225 466682
Clothes for the taller woman sizes 12-20.
Open Mon-Sat 9.30 am-5.30 pm.

LESBIAN AND BISEXUAL

Bristol Lesbian and Gay Switchboard
Box 49
Greenleaf Bookshop
82 Colston Street
Bristol BS1 5BB
T 0117 942 5927
Helpline open every evening 7.30-10.30 pm. Information, support & advice to lesbians, gay men & those who are unsure of their sexuality. Also information about local groups, events, etc.

Bristol Lesbian Line
C/o Bristol Women's Centre
C/o Barton Hill Settlement
43 Ducie Road, Barton Hill
Bristol BS5 0AX
T 0117 907 7567
Telephone line open every Thurs evening 7.30-10 pm. 24-hour ansaphone. Information, confidential counselling & support for lesbians & women who are questioning their sexuality. Training; social events.

LIBRARIES/ARCHIVES

Feminist Archive, The
Liz Britton
Trinity Road Library
Trinity Road
St Philips
Bristol BS2 ONW
T 0117 935 0025
Houses national & international feminist material, including periodicals, books, pamphlets, photographs, posters, banners, records, stickers, postcards, drawings, clothing, diaries, conference papers, etc.

MANUAL TRADES

Bristol Women's Workshop
Anne Harding
Totterdown Centre
144 Wells Road
Bristol BS4 2AG
T 0117 9711672

Woodwork, furniture making and renovation courses for women; Introductory to City & Guilds Level; days, evenings and weekends.

Peace Groups

Women's International League for Peace and Freedom - Bristol
Barton Hill Settlement
43 Dulcie Road
Barton Hill
Bristol BS5 0AX
T 0117 955 2526

Places to Stay and Eat

Marco Polo Travel Advisory Service
Polly Davies
24a Park Street
Bristol BS1 5JA
T 0117 929 4123 F 0117 929 4123
Travel agency offering complete service to independent traveller, very sympathetic to needs of women travellers. Flights, tours, treks, safaris, overland expeditions, walking holidays, women & travel seminars.

Pregnancy/Childbirth

Bath Fertility Support Group
Bath Assisted Conception Clinic
Royal United Hospital
Combe Park
Bath BA1 3NG
T 01225 825566
Meets every second Mon of each month 7.30. Phone above number for further details.

Donor Insemination Patient Support Group
Dept of Obstetrics & Gynaecology
Level D St Michael's Hospital
Southwell Street
Bristol BS2 8EG
T 0117 928 5294 F 0117 927 2792
Meets at St Michael's hospital every 3-4 months.

Mothers for Mothers
Jo Griffiths
146a Redland Road
Redland
Bristol BS6 64D
T 0117 975 6006
Support group for mothers with post natal depression. Home & hospital visits; mothers & toddlers group; talks; runs crisis line; phone referrals.

Pregnancy Advisory Service
Dr S Bodard
Central Health Clinic
Tower Hill
Bristol B52 0JD
T 0117 927 6362
A service for women with unplanned pregnancies where they can discuss the issues & choices.

Sue Learner Independent Midwife
Sue Learner
58 Bellevue Cresecent
Clifton Wood
Bristol BS8 4TF
T 0117 927 6131
Offers full home-based ante-natal birth preparation, intra partum & post-natal midwifery care. Excellent links with obstetric unit, obstetricians, homeopaths, acupuncturists, yoga teachers, etc, if required.

Professional Associations

Network West Country
Julie Spence, Chair
96 Queen's Road
Clifton
Bristol BS8 1NF
T 0117 973 0517
Maintaining a forum in which women can develop professional & social contacts. Ensuring that women's contribution & influence is recognised as a vital force in the corridors of power.

Publishers/Publications

Green Leaf Bookshop
82 Colston Street
Bristol BS1 5BB
T 0117 921 1369
Radical bookshop with women's books, cards, tapes. Mail order.

Religious Organisations

Women's Fellowship
Mrs Queenie Thomas
497 Fishponds Road
Bristol BS16 3AL
T 0117 965 1113
Meets at the Easton Christian family centre, Beaufort Street, Stapleton Road, Easton, Bristol BS5 0PQ on Tue 12.30-2.15 (lunch club) & from 2.15-3.30 (social club with speakers).

ENGLAND - BRISTOL AND BATH

Retailing

Bishopston Trading Company
Carolyn Whitwell
193 Gloucester Road
Bishopston
Bristol BS7 8BG
T 0117 924 5598   F 0117 975 3590
A women's cooperative, committed to a fair deal for both producers & customers. Clothes for children up to age 14, clothes for women sizes 10-16 & men's shirts. Also sell earrings, necklances, scarves, etc.

Services

Bath Design Centre
Fiona Starkey
Monmouth Place
Bath BA1 2AY
T 01225 445800   F 01225 447244
fion@bathdesigncentre.demon.co.uk
Graphic design for print & publicity - commercial & industrial. Brochures to business cards - and back again!

Sexual Abuse/Rape Crisis

Avon Sexual Abuse Centre
Jo Chambers
P O Box 665
Bristol BS99 1XY
T 0177 935 1707
Offers short-term, in-depth counselling to women who have been sexually abused. Phone on Wed 12.30-2.30 pm. Otherwise 24-hour ansaphone. The staff are professionally trained counsellors & psychotherapists.

Bristol Women's Rape Helpline
Heather Pollard
Box 2
Greenleaf Bookshop
82 Colston Street
Bristol BS1 5BB
T 0117 987 3776
Helpline open Sun & Tue 7-10 pm. Confidential telephone counselling for women & girls who have been raped or sexually abused. Run by women for women.

Sports and Leisure

Women Alive Group
Linda Hawes, Barnardos
Lawrence Western Family Centre
Home Farm, Kingsweston Lane
Lawrence Weston
Bristol BS11 0JE
T 0117 982 4578
Drop-in facilities for women living in Lawrence Weston area of Bristol. Open Thurs term time. Women's preventative health group: keep fit 10-11 am; 11 am-12 pm discussion group; 12-1 pm lunch. Creche.

Support

Barton Hill Women's Group
Caroline Donald
Barton Hill Settlement
43 Ducie Road
Barton Hill
Bristol BS5 0AX
T 0117 955 6971   F 0117 955 6971
Maria Clarke@netgates.co.uk
Creche provided. A space for women away from their home & children so they can think about their own needs.

Brislington Neighbourhood Centre's Women's Group
Nancy Cole, Women's Support Worker
202 Allison Road
Brislington
Bristol BS4 4NZ
T 0117 977 2100
Meets Wed 10.30 am-2.30 pm. Outings. Training in First Aid, assertiveness, etc.

Bristol Family Mediation Service
25 Hobbs Lane
Bristol BS1 5ED
T 0117 929 2002
Mediation for divorcing/separating couples where there are unresolved issues arising from the breakdown of the couple's relationship. Not only for women.

For Acceptances and Care to Express Self Harm (FACES)
Diane
C/o 62 New Walls
3 Lamps
Totterdown
Bristol BS4 3TB
T 0117 971 1844
Offering women a safe place to explore issues related to self-harm. Offers support & an opportunity to share difficulties with other women.

Parents at Work - Bath
Alison Garcia Levy
Hillylands
Weston Lane

Bath BA1 4AA
T 01225 429647
Support for parents at work. Help with babysitting & arranging childcare. Monthly meetings on second Mon of each month 8 pm onwards. Speakers & social events.

Women of Henbury and Brentry (WHEB)
Helen Nobel
31 Marlwood Drive
Bristol BS10 6SH
T 0117 940 9528
Women's group for women in the local community providing informal support & contacts.

Women's Support Group
Louise Blowers
Windmill Hill City Farm
Bedminster
Bristol
T 0117 963 5783
Meeting place for women who feel isolated, depressed or just want a break from their young children. Meets Tue 12.45-2.45 pm. Creche.

TRAINING

Opportunities for Women in Lockleaze (OWL)
Pommy Harmar
C/o Lockleaze School
Romney Avenue
Lockleaze
Bristol BS7 9XT
T 0117 979 1207
Variety of educational, social & recreational activities for women. All courses run alongside a creche. The courses are subsidised. Phone for up-to-date information.

TRANSPORT

Bristol Community Transport
26 Bright Street
Barton Hill
Bristol BS5 9PR
T 0117 955 2260 F 0117 955 0971
Providing transport services for community-based groups. Serving many women's groups. Well maintained & affordable minibuses & cars.

WOMEN'S AID

Bath Women's Aid
J Knight

42 Bathwick Street
Bath BA2 6PA
T 01225 318343 F 01225 466990

Bristol Women's Aid
Una Harkin
248 Stapleton Road
Easton
Bristol BS5 0NT
T 0117 952 2393 F 0117 952 2393
Safe, temporary accommodation for women & children fleeing domestic violence. Four refuges, including refuge for Black & Asian women only. Helpline (above) open Mon-Fri 10 am-3 pm. Drop in centre at office.

Kingswood Women's Aid
Brenda Bishop/Margaret Cressey/Paula Hemming
Bristol
T 0117 957 5865 F 0117 904 0064
Office open Mon-Fri 9 am-4 pm. Provides accommodation, support & advice for women & their children (if any) suffering from domestic violence (physical, mental & sexual abuse).

BUCKINGHAMSHIRE

ACCOUNTANCY

Keens Shay Keens
Many Stewart, Audit Manager
Witan Court
295 Witan Gate
Milton Keynes MK9 2JL
T 01908 674484 F 01908 690371
Chartered accountants, open 9 am-5.30 pm.

ALTERNATIVE THERAPIES

Buckingham Natural Health Clinic
Christine Watson
Chantry House
West Street
Buckingham MK18 1HL
T 01280 823033 F 01280 700155
Open Mon-Fri 9 am-8 pm; Sat 9 am-12 noon. Osteopathy, herbal treatments, counselling, aromatherapy, reflexology, applied kinesiology, remedial massage. Female practitioners only; available as therapists.

INTEGRA - Life Skills
Pat Faith
1 Hunsman Grove
Blakelands
Milton Keynes MK14 5HS
T 01908 616317 F 01908 616317

To help people to achieve their maximum potential. Psychotherapy, hypnotherapy, stress management. Seminars on stress management, professional development and retirement lifestyle planning for businesses.

Arts and Crafts

Deni Bown Associates
Deni Bown
Belvoir House
Tattam Close
Woolstone
Milton Keynes MK15 0HB
T 01908 604535 F 01908 670368
Author, photographer, specialising in plants, flowers, herbs, botany and natural history. Consultancy, research, lectures, herb garden design. Tour leader, presenter. Slide library.

Musicians Unlimited Management (UK)
Dorothy Cooper
4 Medland
Woughton Park
Milton Keynes MK6 3BH
T 01908 670306 F 01908 674909
Represents artists. Provides backing music for functions - weddings & parties of all kinds. Schools work - teachers' workshops in jazz improvisation.

Out of the Woods
Chris Mottram-Wooster/Rosemary Wright
18 Hanmer Road
Simpson
Milton Keynes MK6 3AY
T 01908 674174
Artistic woodturners, selling through craft fairs & craft shops local to Milton Keynes. Products include bowls, vases, table lamps, platters. One-to-one training courses for women. Phone for further details.

Business Support Schemes

D & P Consultants
Sonia Coleman
44a High Street
Newport Pagnell MK16 8AQ
T 01908 617077 F 01908 210649
dandpcon@mag-net.co.uk
Consultants. Business management & staff recruitment.

Status Personnel Associates
Kala Solanki - Managing Director
215 Witan Gate East
Sovereign Court
Milton Keynes MK9 2DU
T 01908 200990 F 01908 200991
Fully accredited upmarket recruitment consultancy, specialising in commerce & industry. Open Mon-Fri 8 am-6 pm.

Strong Research International Ltd
Kathy Strong
The Strong Institute
Building 426
Westcott Venture Park
Westcott HP18 0XB
T 01296 655096 F 01296 655097
100724.323@compuserve.com
Neuro-linguistic programming training providers. Business communication, sales, disability awareness, information technology. Office hours Mon-Fri 9 am-5 pm. Aims to help people communicate effectively.

T L Marketing Services Ltd
Sally Barnes
Exchange House
494 Midsummer Boulevard
Milton Keynes MK9 2EA
T 01908 691013 F 01908 691013
Creative communication solutions provided for consumer & business to business markets. Full marketing support ranging from PR, sales, promotion, hospitality packages, to direct mail & copy writing.

Child Care and Family

Wellies Day Nursery
Mrs Helen Hobbs
1 Brook End
North Crawley
Newport Pagnell MK16 9HH
T 01234 391600
Open Mon-Fri 7.45 am-6.15 pm 49 weeks a year. Full- or part-time day care for children aged 0-5 years. Phone for up-to-date price list.

Contraception/Well Woman

Milton Keynes Brook Centre
Acorn House
355 Midsummer Boulevard
Milton Keynes MK9 3HP
T 01908 669215
Free, confidential contraceptive advice. Free condoms & other contraceptive supplies. Help with emotional & sexual problems. Pregnancy tests & quick results. Phone for opening times.

COUNSELLING AND THERAPY

Insight - Professional Counselling
Dr Magda-Pena Reeves
P O Box 1823
Winslow MK18 3ZX
T 01296 715001 F 01296 715001
Network of independent private counsellors. Confidential service for stress, anxiety, depression, bereavement, loss, separation, behavioural problems, drugs, alcohol, eating disorders. Mediation service, etc.

ENVIRONMENT

Lesley Keck Garden Design
Lesley Keck
4 Claremont Avenue
Stony Stratford
Milton Keynes MK11 1HH
T 01908 563385
Professional garden design service catering for the smallest courtyard to the country home owner or commercial business.

ETHNIC MINORITIES

Amal Ladies' Group
Firdus Khan
Multicultural Centre
Friar's Croft
Friarage Road
Aylesbury
T 01296 29364
For Pakistani women.

Asian Women's Project
C/o Milton Keynes Women & Work Group
Acorn House
365 Midsummer Boulevard
Milton Keynes MK9 3HP
T 01908 200186
Courses & individual guidance. Career information. Return to work course & training opportunities. Newsletter.

Asian Women's Training Project
Navrita Atwal
Milton Keynes Council
Saxon Court
Avebury Boulevard
Milton Keynes MK9 3HP
T 01908 253379
Open Mon-Fri 9 am-5 pm. Runs return to work courses & work experience placements. Individual advice & guidance. Runs partnership courses with local college. Assistance to women wanting to find employment.

Shakhti Women's Group
Ranjula Takodra
Multicultural Centre
Friar's Croft
Friarage Road
Aylesbury
T 01296 393173
For Asian women. Meets on Fri, once a month.

FINANCE

Prudential Assurance
Karen Wilson
15 Rixband Close
Walton Park
Milton Keynes MK7 7HU
T 01908 667187 F 01908 233931
Also phone 01908 233277. Financial consultant providing a free, no-obligation personalised service. Financial planning, pensions, mortgages, saving & investments. Any time Mon-Fri.

HEALTH

Marie Curie Cancer Care - Fundraising Office
Anne Dodds
68 High Street
Newport Pagnell MK16 8AQ
T 01908 616990 F 01908 616990
Open Mon-Fri 9 am-5 pm. Providing free nursing care & support for people with cancer & their families through 6,000 Marie Curie nurses & 11 hospice centres. The care is backed up by education & research.

LESBIAN AND BISEXUAL

Milton Keynes Lesbian Social Group
Milton Keynes
T 01908 666226
Phone Mon 7.30-9.45 pm for events list: meals, walks, theatre visits, music, games, discussions.

PHOTOGRAPHY

Tina Hadley Photography
Tina Hadley
College Farm House
School Lane
Oakley HP18 9PT
T 01844 2337525 F 01844 238694
Portrait & wedding photography specialising in informal portraiture & photo-journalistic wedding photography. Top portrait

photographer SE region (BIPP) 1996. Black & white protraiture.

PLACES TO STAY AND EAT

B&B - Sue Light
Sue Light
1 Glory Mill Lane
Wooburn Green HP10 0BX
T 01628 522472
B&B twin-bedded room. Phone for up-to-date price list.

Latini
Sally Fennemore
122 High Street
Newport Pagnell MK16 8EH
T 01908 617100 F 01908 617100
Italian restaurant & wine bar. Open Mon-Sat 12-2.30 & 6-11 pm. Lunch & dinner. Parties & weddings catered for.

PREGNANCY/CHILDBIRTH

Aylesbury Fertility Support Group
Aylesbury
T 01908 653306
Meets informally once a month at members' houses.

Bambino Mio
44 Montgomer Crescent
Bolbock Park
Milton Keynes MK15 8PR
T 01908 240484
Cotton nappies & accessories via mail order. Phone for brochure.

Concept - Infertility Support Group
The Health Matters/CHC Unit
The Food Centre
795 Avebury Boulevard
Milton Keynes MK9 3JS
T 01908 663800 F 01908 677301
Meets at above address on third Thurs of each month 8 pm. Couples & individuals welcome.

Crisis Pregnancy Centre - Milton Keynes
Mrs S Forbes
Neighbourhood House
1 Pencarrow Place
Fishermead
Milton Keynes
T 01908 608467
Open Mon-Fri 10.30 am-1.30 pm & Fri evening by appt only. Free pregnancy testing, counselling & support for women with unplanned pregnancies. Post abortion & miscarriage counselling.

Earthwise Baby
Aspley Distribution Ltd
P O Box 1708
Aspley Guise
Milton Keynes MK17 8YA
T 01908 585769 F 01908 585771
Provides reusable cotton nappies & sanitary pads.

PUBLISHERS/PUBLICATIONS

Milton Keynes Women's Newsletter
14 Gordale
Heelands
Milton Keynes MK13 7NQ
Bi-monthly. Contributions on all subjects welcome for all women.

RETAILING

Scotts Interiors
Helen Scott
24 Porlock Lane
North Derzton
Milton Keynes MK4 1JU
T 01908 503200
Makers of soft furnishings, curtains, blinds for domestic & commercial purposes. Upholstery, loose covers, painting and decorating. Wide range of fabrics and window accesseries. Delivery & fitting service.

SERVICES

Color Me Beautiful (CMB)
Margaret Macer
23 Parklands,
Great Linford
Milton Keynes MK14 5DZ
T 01908 605764 F 01908 605764
Image consultants. Through the correct use of colour & style in clothing & make-up application, we help you to develop your unique personal image. Helps to promote positive self-esteem & confidence.

Development At Work
Bridget Hogg, Director
42 Portland Drive
Willen
Milton Keynes MK15 9JP
T 01908 672506 F 01908 672506
Consultancy specialising in personal, careers & organisational development. Services &

ENGLAND - BUCKINGHAMSHIRE

advice concerning assessment & selction, development & training, opinion surveys & research.

First Impressions
Julia M Campion
Hollytree House
London Road
Broughton Village
Milton Keynes MK10 9AA
T 01908 691176   F 01908 691176
Personal & corporate image consultancy. Services designed to help clients to achieve their full potential in terms of personal presentation. Sessions range from colour & style to wardrobe assessment & shopping.

Impact Images International
Pat Ross-Woodford
1 Audley Mead
Bradwell Village
Milton Keynes MK13 9BD
T 01908 310080
Colour analyses, styles, image consulting - by appointment only. Seminars, workshops, image days, makeup & skincare lessons, special occasions makeup. Retail products for sale.

Kemp Professional Services (KPS)
Lesley Kemp
13 Colston Bassett
Emerson Valley
Milton Keynes MK4 2BU
T 01908 503930   F 01908 503930
RockyHorror@MSN.com
Typing & word processing service.

M H Business Support Services
Marilyn Howard
2 Lydiard
Great Holm
Milton Keynes MK8 9BE
T 01908 560558   F 01908 569911
Secretarial book-keeping services.

Olney Health & Beauty Salon
Deborah Sansom
11 Market Place
Olney MK46 4EA
T 01234 711741
Salon offering full range of treatments, including electrolysis, ear-piercing, aromatherapy, facial & body treatments. CIDESCO-qualified therapist, licensed with LA. Late-night opening Thurs and Fri.

SmallPrint MK
Zoe Sparks
5 Cowper Close
Newport Pagnell MK16 8PG
T 01908 216131   F 01908 216131
High quality design & print service for any size of business. In-house projects undertaken on request.

Sue Light Chair Caning
Sue Light
1 Glory Mill Lane
Wooburn Green HP10 0BX
T 01628 522472
Chair caning. Prices on request.

SEXUAL ABUSE/RAPE CRISIS

Aylesbury Vale Rape Crisis
C/o The Dove Centre
Greenhill United Reform Church
Rickfords Hill
Aylesbury HP20 2SA
T 01296 392468
Phoneline open Tue & Thurs 7-9 pm. Ansaphone checked daily. Counselling by appointment. Counselling for women who have experienced rape, sexual abuse, or sexual assault. Free & confidential service.

Milton Keynes Rape Crisis Centre
63 North Seventh Street
Milton Keynes MK9 2DP
T 01908 691969
Rape crisis counselling. Mon 7-9 pm; Wed 10 am-noon.

Wycombe Rape Crisis
Reb Tilbury
C/o The Priory Centre
11 Priory Road
High Wycombe HP13 6SL
T 01494 462222
Helpline open Tue & Thurs 7-9 pm. Free counselling service for women & young people who have experienced rape, sexual abuse & sexual assault. Information, practical help & support as necessary.

SPORTS AND LEISURE

Milton Keynes Women's Walking Network
Mary Balhatchet
C/o Milton Keynes Parks Trust
Milton Keynes
T 01908 233600
For all women, providing guided walks in Milton Keynes. Many suitable for wheelchairs

or pushchairs. Enabling women to meet others & be able to arrange walks themselves. Contact list available.

Training

Milton Keynes Women and Work Group
Mary Hopkins
Acorn House
365 Midsummer Boulevard
Milton Keynes MK9 3HP
T 01908 200676 F 01908 200979
Employment & training information for women, given by women. Drop-in advice & guidance sessions held at local bases. Specialist advice for Asian women. All services free. Phone for opening times.

Peak Performance Training
Jeannette Sloan
2 Telford Way
Blakelands
Milton Keynes MK14 5LB
T 01908 617532 F 01908 617532
Working for small groups to help individuals achieve greater sense of fulfilment, both in their personal & professional life. Topics include: Balancing Your Life, Understanding Self, Handling Difficult People.

Women's Aid

Aylesbury Women's Aid
St Mary's Centre
St Mary's Square
Aylesbury HP20 1JJ
T 01296 29499

High Wycombe Women's Aid
C/o The Priory Centre
11 Priory Road
High Wycombe HP13 6SL
T 01494 461367
24-hour helpline via the Samaritans: 01494 432000.

Milton Keynes Women's Aid
P O Box 790
Milton Keynes MK2 3YZ
T 01908 271900

Wycombe Women's Aid
Annie
C/o The Priory Centre
11 Priory Road
High Wycombe HP13 6SL
T 01494 432000

24-hour phone line seven days a week. Offers support, information & outreach to women experiencing abuse in their homes. Temporary, safe accommodation. Information & training around issues of domestic abuse.

Cambridgeshire

Alternative therapies

Hope Street Holistic Centre
Fara Begum-Baig, Owner
Hope Street
Cambridge CB1 3NS
T 01223 410571
Therapies provided include: acupuncture, aromatherpay, psychotherapy, food allergy testing, herbalism, homoeopathy, iridology, massage, reflexology, stress management, yoga & Polarity therapy.

Arts and Crafts

Dr Jennifer E Johnson
Jennifer Johnson
C/o Robinson College
University of Cambridge
Cambridge CB3 9AN
T 01223 311431
A writer, an academic and a researcher. Topics include 'Women in the arts', 'Women academics', 'Women's studies'.

Business support schemes

Cambridge Businesswomen's Network
Clare Benton
11 New Road
Melbourn
Royston SG8 6BX
T 01763 261928 F 01763 261928
Provides a forum for working women in the Cambridge area to make contacts & exchange ideas. We offer a programme of social & work-related events throughout the year.

Women in Management - Cambridgeshire
Shirely Jamieson, Branch Chairman
104 Hills Road
Cambridge CB1 1LH
T 01954 267639 F 01954 267639
Provides networking opportunities for women in business & supports those who wish to progress their careers. Offers advice to those who wish to start &/or develop a business. Relevant training provided.

CENTRES FOR WOMEN

Cambridge Women's Resources Centre
Francie, Sue, Derry, Margaret
The Wharf
Hooper Street
Cambridge CB1 2NZ
T 01223 321148 F 01223 321148
Open Mon-Fri 9 am-4 pm. Woman-only space run by women for women. Vocational training, guidance & counselling, creative courses, users & self-help groups, information, work resources room, creche, libraries.

Family Centre
Sue Lidgard
69a Queen's Road
Wisbech PE13 2PH
T 01945 582567
Fenland women's helpline: 01945 474422 for women suffering domestic violence. The centre provides a place for women to meet, hold lectures, demonstrations, etc. Counselling, mothers' & toddlers group, etc.

Peterborough Women's Centre
Jo Godwin
18 Crawthorne Road
Peterborough PE1 4AB
T 01733 311564 F 01733 311816
Open Mon-Fri 10 am-3 pm. Counselling, courses, activities, information, training, support. For Peterborough women to come together, support each other, learn about new opportunities & increase self-esteem.

CHILD CARE AND FAMILY

Cambridge City Council
Alison Kemp, Senior Personnel Manager
10 Downing Street
Cambridge CB2 3DS
T 01223 457000 F 01223 458109
Runs two childcare subsidy schemes, pre-school 0-5 & children aged 5-14, & a holiday play scheme for Cambridge City Council workers.

Studio Nursery School
Mrs Ann Cousins, Proprietor
The Old School
Church Hall
Granchester Road
Trumpington CB2 2LH
T 01223 840848
Nursery school for 2-5 year olds, offering structured activities. Open from 8.45 am-4 pm 46 weeks a year. Licensed for 28 children.

CONTRACEPTION/WELL WOMAN

Evelyn Hospital Health Screening Department
Dr Eleanor Birks, Director
4 Trumpington Road
Cambridge CB2 2AS
T 01223 303336 F 01223 316068
Only women work in this department of a private hospital. Well woman screening; full health & heart risk check up. Also menopause clinics. No free service. Direct phone line: 01223 370919.

North Cambridgeshire Hospital
Dr G Stuart
Wisbech PE13 3AB
T 01945 585781
Well woman clinic on Wed 2-3.30 pm. Breast checks, pregnancy testing, cytology (smear tests), blood pressure checks, weight checks, advice on menstrual problems & the menopause, etc. Free service.

EDUCATION

Cambridge Female Education Trust (CamFed)
Ann Cotton
25 Wordsworth Grove
Cambridge CB3 9HH
T 01223 362648 F 01223 362648
To enable more girls & women to benefit from education in rural communities in sub-Saharan Africa.

Lucy Cavendish College
Ruth Hawthorn, Admissions Tutor
Cambridge CB3 0BU
T 01223 332190 F 01223 332178
For mature women students aged 21 +. Three-year BA (Hons) courses offered & M.Phil & specialised certificates & diplomas. A level candidates are expected to have 'very good grades'.

New Hall
Huntingdon Road
Cambridge CB3 0DF
T 01223 351721 F 01223 352941
The college admits around 300 women undergraduates & there are female & male teaching staff. The normal conditional offer for A level students is three A levels, grades A, A & B.

Newnham College
Cambridge CB3 9DF
T 01223 335700 F 01223 357898
There are about 450 women undergraduates with women staff. Newnham provides a positive supportive community within a university in which women are still a minority.

Finance

Ellwood & Co, Financial Services for Women
Julie Byrne
The Mullards
16 Orchard Close
Harston
Cambridge CB1 5PT
T 01223 872758 F 01223 872919
An independent financial adviser. Working full time advising women on how best to manage their financial affairs. Flexible fee structure.

Health

Women's Health Concern - Peterborough
Jean Hunt
180 Crow Street
Peterborough PE1 3JA
T 01733 893586
Counselling clinics on women's health problems at the City Health Clinic, Wellington Street, Peterborough on Thurs 6-8 pm. Phone above number for an appointment.

Lesbian and Bisexual

Lesbian Line
Box CLL
12 Mill Road
Cambridge CB1 2AD
T 01223 311753
Telephone service offering advice, support & information to lesbians & bisexual women. Line open on Fri 7-10 pm. Information on local events. Confidential service.

Older Women

CareQuest
Primrose Taylor
3 Orwell Road
Barrington CB2 5SE
T 01223 872884 F 012233 872884
Runs home care agency specialising in needs for the elderly. Carers are sent into people's homes for up to an hour at a time. Fees are variable, according to specific needs.

Photography

Dumbleton Studios
Frances Dumbleton
4 Milton Road
Cambridge CB4 1JY
T 01223 358007 F 01223 316366
Social photographer, weddings & portraits. Would-be photographers trained in the business. Fees negotiated on an individual basis.

Services

Ann Reynolds Career Guidance and Development
Ann Reynolds
255 Dogsthorpe Road
Peterborough PE1 3AT
T 01733 62958
Career guidance for all ages. Individual guidance & help preparing an action plan to reach your goals. CV preparation. Psychometric testing of interests, aptitudes & career personality, etc.

Carpe Diem Associates
Glo Singer
26 Chesterton Hall Crescent
Cambridge CB4 1AP
T 01223 311483 F 01223 315976
Runs courses on how to sustain creative & sustaining relationships.

Mater Product Management
Mrs Julie Buck
Units 4-5 Mill Lane
Cotterstock
Oundle
Peterborough PE8 5HD
T 01832 226221 F 01832 226213
101334,462@compuserve.com
Marketing consultancy offering extensive range of marketing services on a cost-effectvie ad hoc basis, including customer focus groups, competitor analysis, promotional activities & market research.

Rosemarie Zamonski
Rosemaire Zamonski, Managing Partner
72 Girton Road
Girton
Cambridge CB3 0LN
T 01223 277810 F 01223 277983
Professional language training in interpreting & translation for business people & linguists.

Sexual abuse/rape crisis

Cambridge Rape Crisis Centre
Susan Turner
Box 6
12 Mill Road
Cambridge CB1 2AD
T 01223 358314
Open Wed 7-10 pm; Sat 11 am-5 pm. Free telephone support line. Free face-to-face support. Run by women for women. Offers training to other organisations if requested.

Peterborough Rape Crisis Counselling Group (PRCCG)
P O Box 409
Peterborough PE4 6WZ
T 01733 706700
Helpline (as above) open Tue 7.30-10 pm & Sat 10 am-12 pm. Otherwise ansaphone service. A women for women organisation. For all women survivors of any form of sexual abuse or sexual harassment.

Social

Talking With Women
Mrs Angela Woodward
34 Wingfield
Orton Goldhay PE2 5TH
T 01733 237025
Outings, occasional charity work, speakers. Meets Thurs 10 am-12 noon at Rangefield Community Centre, Orton Brimbles, Peterborough.

Sports and Leisure

Langford Ladies' Football Club (Bedfordshire)
Claire Tyrrell
100 Lindisfarne Close
Eynesbury
St Neots PE17 2UU
T 01223 273727 F 01234 345087
Girls under 10/12 & 14, plus two senior teams playing at local & national league levels. Training Wed: juniors 6-7.30 pm; seniors 7.30-9.15.

Women's Awareness and Self-protection Group
Julie
P O Box 29
Cambridge CB1 3HF
T 01223 565020 F 01223 565020
Runs workshops & training courses. Theory & practical skills. Regular courses in universities & regular classes at Coleridge Community College, Cambridge on Mon 7 pm.

Support

92 Stretten Avenue Project
92 Stretten Avenue
Cambridge
T 01223 313721
Drop-in facilities for familes & young children & women's groups. After school groups for under 5s.

Women's Aid

Cambridge Women's Aid
P O Box 302
Cambridge CB1 1EA
T 01223 460947
For all women in East Anglia escaping physical & mental abuse. Solicitors & rehousing provided if required.

CHESHIRE

Accommodation

Salvation Army - Warrington House
Captain D Lees, Officer in Charge
153 Old Liverpool Road
Warrington WA5 1A5
T 01925 415093 F 01925 230334
13-bed women's homelessness unit. Admissions either by self or agency referral. Short/medium term stay for women aged 18 +. Girls aged 16-18 ten short term with social work support.

Alternative therapies

Wilmslow Circle of Yoga
Miranda K Michaelides
6 Brent Close
Poynton SK12 1HS
T 01625 877596
Meets every last Fri of month at the Wilmslow Library from 7.30-9.30 pm. The aim is to lecture on every aspect of life.

Business support schemes

Business Link - Chester and Ellesmere Port
Ann Desormeaux
Hoole Bridge
Chester CH2 3NE
T 01244 674111 F 01244 310690
Training, counselling & ongoing support to help women prepare for self-employment. Six free training days from 9.45 am-3 pm with

childcare allowance & support group 'Women into business'.

Warrington Business Venture
Sandra Brusby, Director
Chadwick House
Warrington Road
Risely
Warrington WA3 6GX
T 01925 633309 F 01925 668041
Sandra@wbv.u-net.com
Registered women's enterprise centre offering friendly service to women: counselling, training & seminars designed specially for women. Offers free, practical help to exisiting businesses, etc.

Women in Business North West
Christine Lomas, Chair
121 Marsland Road
Sale M33 3NW
T 0161 969 2344
Providing a strong network of working women; helping women realise the opportunities available to them; promoting cooperation between members to achieve & maintain high business standards. Monthly meetings.

Computers/IT

CTS Training
Cindy Blight
11a Redhouse Lane
Disley
Stockport SK12 2EW
T 01663 765737
Woman owned company providing professional IT training for individuals & companies. Phone for further information between 8.30 am-6 pm.

Contraception/Well woman

Contraception and Well Woman Clinics
Knutsford & District Community Hospital
Knutsford
T 01565 652624
Contraception on Wed 7-8.30 pm. Contraception for young people Mon 3.15-4.30 in the ATTIC Knutsford Leisure Centre. IUD available by appointment. Well woman Mon 1.45-3 pm.

Contraception and Well Woman Clinics
Chapel Lane Clinic
Wilmslow
T 01625 526444
Contraception available on Tue 7-9 pm. IUD by appointment. Well woman once a month on Tue 9-11.30 am

Contraception and Well Woman Clinics
Dr Leslie Batchelor, Director
West Park Hospital
Macclesfield SK10 3BL
Open Tue 9-11.30 am & 2-4.30 pm; Mon & Thurs 6.45-8.30 pm. Contraception advice, info & supplies. IUD clinic first Fri on month 9-11 am Well woman Mon 9-11.30 am, breast checks, blood pressure checks.

Contraception and Well Woman Clinics
Park Lane Clinic
Poynton
T 01625 875618
Contraception on Tue 7-9 pm. IUD by appointment. Well woman 9-11 am second & fourth Thurs of each month.

Contraception Clinic
Bodywise
46 Colshaw Walk
Handforth
T 01625 548304
Contraception available on Wed 2-5 pm. Young people are welcome. Appointments are not necessary.

Contraception Clinic
Ely Court
Victoria Flats
Macclesfield
T 01625 616689
Contraception available on Tue 9.30-11 am Appointments are not necessary.

Contraception/ Well Woman Clinics
Congleton War Memorial Hospital
Canal Road
Congleton
T 01260 294832
Contraception on Mon and Thurs 7-9 pm. Contraception for young people on Wed 3.30-5.30 at 24 High Street, opposite the TSB (phone 01260 297297). IUD fitting by appointment only. Well woman Wed 1.30-3.30 pm.

Contraception/Well Woman Clinics
Carol Smith, Family Planning Nurse
Macclesfield District General Hospital
West Park Site
Victoria Road

ENGLAND - CHESHIRE

Macclesfield SK10 3BL
T 01625 661169
Contraception clinics on Mon & Thurs 6.45-8.30 pm; Tue 9-11.30 am& 2-4.30 pm; Sat 1-2 pm, emergencies only. Well woman Mon 9-11 a.m; IUD fitting second Fri of month 9-11.30 am

Grosvenor Nuffield Hospital, The
Wrexham Road
Chester CH4 7QP
T 01244 680444
Well woman screen. Full female health assessment. Phone for up-to-date price lists.

Weston Clinic
Earlsway
Macclesfield
T 01625 432208
Contraception available on Thurs 9-11.30 am IUD fittings by appointment only.

HEALTH

Amarant Trust - Chester
Drina Glyn-Jones
The Goldsmith's House
50 Hough Green
Chester CH4 8JQ
T 01244 679240
Information on HRT for menopause, hysterectomy, osteoporosis & heart disease. Group meets every third Mon of month 7.30 pm at Training Room, West Cheshire NHS Trust HQ, Countess of Chester Health Park.

Endometriosis Advice
Irene Walker
21 The Oval
Heald Green SK8 3JJ
T 0161 437 8718
Telephone support & information for women with endometriosis.

LARGER/TALLER WOMEN

All Woman
Jean Phelps
Unit 7
Clegge Street Workshops
Clegge Street
Warrington WA2 7AT
T 01925 652938
Outsize wear, sizes 26-36: leggings, swimsuits, T-shirts, briefs. Made to measure service at no extra charge.

Encore
Mrs J Farnworth
19 London Road
Alderley Edge SK9 7JT
T 01625 583031
Ladies' fashion outlet for larger sizes 16-26.

Florentyna Dawn
Dawn Gail Priestnall
327 London Road
Hazel Grove
Stockport SK7 4PS
T 0161 487 1679 F 0161 483 9478
Exclusive ladies' fashions sizes 8-28. Open 10 am-5 pm. Evenings & Sundays by appointment. Occasion wear for the discerning woman. 1996 retailer of the year.

PREGNANCY/CHILDBIRTH

Crisis Pregnancy Centre - Tameside Venture/Denton
Sue Dray
Image
P O Box 51
Hyde SK14 1PY
T 0161 320 7496
Above telephone number is the pregnancy helpline number open 24-hours a day. It networks six centres in the Tameside area. Phone to find out times/days of each centre. Free pregnancy testing & counselling.

PAC - Stockport
Chris
Hazlegrove Christian Centre
Station Street
Hazlegrove
Stockport SK7 4EX
T 0161 487 3709
Open Wed, Thurs & Fri 9.30-11.30 am; Wed 7.30-8.30 pm. Free pregnancy testing, counselling & support for women with unplanned pregnancies. Post abortion & miscarriage counselling. 24-hour ansaphone.

PRISONERS/PRISONERS' WIVES

Women Prisoners' Resource Centre
Ann Burgess
HMP and YOI Styal
Wilmslow SK9 4HR
T 01625 532141
Resettlement advice, information & support for women prisoners at Styal prison.

ENGLAND - CLEVELAND

Retailing

Jeanies Exercise and Dance Wear
Jean Phelps
Unit 7
Clegge Street Workshops
Clegge Street
Warrington WA2 7AT
T 01925 652938
Lycra wear: aerobic, keep fit, body building, children's gymnastic wear, dance outfits, slim wear, freestyle costumes. All with made to measure service at no extra charge.

Services

Muriel Cohen
Muriel Cohen
10 Marlborough Drive
Tytherington
Macclesfield SK10 2JX
T 01625 424317
Specialises in career change, working with all adults interested in exploring new avenues. Sees clients on a one-to-one basis. Also runs courses concerned with career development for organisations.

Sexual Abuse/Rape Crisis

Chester Rape Crisis
P O Box 280
St John's Street
Chester
T 01244 317922
Helpline (as above) open Sat 10 am-12 pm. Women for women who have been raped or otherwise sexually abused. Counsellors counselling women.

Halton Rape Crisis, Counselling and Research Group
Isobel Atkinson
P O Box 13
Halton General Post Office
Widnes WA8 9SR
T 0151 423 4251
Women's collective run by women for women. Alternative phone number: 0151 423 4192. Line open Tue 11 am-2 pm; Thurs 7-9 pm; Sun 11 am-2 pm

Sports and Leisure

Cheshire County Ladies Bowling Association
Mrs Mary Ashcroft
76 Wilmslow Crescent
Thelwall
Warrington WA4 2JE
T 01925 262712
Organises, encourages & develops the game of Crown Green Bowls.

Cheshire Keep Fit Association
Mrs Pam Young, Secretary
59 Ullswater Road
Congleton CW12 4JQ
T 01260 271429
Keep fit, dance, movement & exercise to music for women & men. Emphasis on safety & enjoyment. Classes taken by qualified teachers held throughout Cheshire. Private & at adult education establishments.

Cheshire Women's County Hockey Association
Tricia Mills
16 Stonehaven Drive
Fearnhead
Warrington WA2 0SR
T 01925 817468

Cheshire Women's Cricket Association
Barbara Sausbury
The Haven
Smithy Lane
Northop Hall
Flintshire CH7 6DE
T 01244 811430

Women's Aid

Chester Women's Aid
Sheila Brookes, Project Leader
P O Box 949
Chester CH2 3WA
T 01244 317929
Open Mon-Fri 9 am-5 pm. Temporary accommodation & support for women & their children (if any) who have experienced domestic violence. Accommodation for six families. Two move-on houses, one family each.

Deeside Women's Aid
6 High Street
Connahs Quay
Deeside CH5 4DA
T 01244 830436

CLEVELAND

Accommodation

Middlesbrough Refuge
advice line worker
P O Box 32

ENGLAND - CLEVELAND

Middlesbrough TS1 3YT
T 01642 225969 F 01642 225969
Support, advice & accommodation for women & children suffering domestic violence. Advice line as above open 9 am-5.30 pm. Accommodation 24 hours via police, samaritans, social services, etc.

ARTS AND CRAFTS

Cleveland Lace Guild
Mrs Sheila Walker, Secretary
41 Pinewood Road
Eaglescliffe
Stockton-on-Tees TS16 0AJ
T 01642 783783
Bobbin lace making. Four meetings, three workshops, one open Lace Day per year. Demonstrations on request. Aims to sustain & further bobbin lace skills.

Norton Flower Club
Mrs P M Kelsey, Secretary
4 Redwing Lane
Norton
Stockton-on-Tees TS20 1LL
T 01642 554290
Meets first Fri of each month (except January & August) 7.15 pm at Norton Community Centre, The Green, Norton. Visitors welcome. Aims to spread love & enjoyment of flowers with speakers & flower arrangers.

BUSINESS SUPPORT SCHEMES

Opportunities for Women
Tracy Elwin, Women's Opportunities Coordinator
Hartlepool Borough Council
Bryan Hanson House
Hanson Square
Hartlepool TS24 7BT
T 01429 523513 F 01429 523516
Assisting women to access training & employment opportunities. Women's training programme: free courses, free creche, etc; women's development fund: grants to assist women; women's business support network.

West View Advice & Resource Centre
Margaret Rae, Centre Coordinator
30 Miers Avenue
Hartlepool TS24 9HH
T 01429 271275 F 01429 265823
Offers New Opportunities for Women course: business administration, computer literacy, information technology & tourism. Free &

confidential advice service. Open Mon-Thurs 9 am-5 pm; Fri 9 am-4.30 pm.

CENTRES FOR WOMEN

South Bank Women's Centre
Sue Anderson
51b Passfield Crescent
South Bank
Middlesbrough TS6 6RJ
T 01642 468831 F 01642 468831
Aims to overcome barriers & help women access employment & training. Providing an informal support service to meet women's needs; lobbies and campaigns on women's issues & needs; educational opportunities.

CHILD CARE AND FAMILY

Mother & Toddler Group
Mandi Henderson/Keri Stewart
Robert Atkinson Youth & Community Centre
Thorntree Road
Thornaby
Stockton-on-Tees TS17 8AP
Open Mon & Thurs 9-11 am A chance for the children to learn to share & mix with other children, while mothers get a chance to meet other mothers & swap advice.

St Cuthbert Mother and Toddler Group
Mrs Beerley Morris
2 Milfoil Close
Marton Manor
Middlesbrough TS7 8SE
T 01642 327743
Informal meeting place for mothers/fathers with preschool children. Variety of toys & crayons, meet for an hour and half session once a week & charge a nominal fee only.

Youth and Community Centre
Donna Barrett
Duncan Place
Loftus
Saltburn by the Sea TS13 4PR
T 01287 640654
Mother and toddler group Mon mornings. Donna Barrett runs after school and holiday care schemes for children aged 5-12.

CONTRACEPTION/WELL WOMAN

Beresford Buildings
Thorntree
T 01642 240837
Free contraceptive advice & supplies & cytology (smear testing) service on first Tue

of each month 1.30-3 pm. Phone 01642 459583 for further information.

Carlow Street
Middlesbrough
T 01642 245799
Free contraceptive advice & supplies & cytology (smear testing) service on Tue 10-11.30 am & Fri 6.30-8 pm. Phone 01642 459583 for further information.

Cleveland Centre
Middlesbrough
T 01642 242128
Free contraceptive advice & supplies & cytology (smear testing) service. Clinic for under 20s on Mon 6-7.30 pm. Clinics for all ages Tue & Fri 6-7.30 pm. Phone 01642 459583 for further information.

Cleveland Nuffield Hospital, The
Junction Road
Norton
Stockton-on-Tees TS20 1QB
T 01642 360100
Well woman screen. Full female health assessment. Phone for up-to-date price lists.

Elizabeth Terrace
North Ormesby
T 01642 231500
Free contraceptive advice & supplies & cytology (smear testing). Clinics on Mon & Wed 6.30-8 pm. Phone 01642 459583 for further information.

Fabian Road
Eston
T 01642 453449
Free contraceptive advice/supplies & cytology (smear testing). Clinics Mon & Wed 6.30-8 pm & second Thurs of each month 10-11.30 a.m, with well woman clinic. Phone 01642 459583 for further information.

Hall Grounds, The
Loftus
T 01642 640583
Free contraceptive advice & supplies & cytology (smear testing) service. Clinic on Wed 6.30-8 pm. Phone 01642 459583 for further details.

Health Advice Centre
Wendy Francis, Women's Health Adviser
29-31 Yarm Lane
Stockton-on-Tees TS18 3DT
T 01642 607313
Advice, information & counselling on women's health issues on Tue 1-3.30 pm & Thurs 9.30-11.30 am Free needle exchange & condom service Mon-Fri 9.15 am-4.30 pm

Health Centre - Billingham
Queensway
Billingham
T 01642 558121
Free contraceptive advice/supplies & cytology (smear testing) service. Clinics on Tue 10-11.30 am & 6.30-8 pm. Over 30s clinic first Wed of each month 6.30-8 pm. Phone 01642 624274 for further information.

Health Centre - Guisborough
Guisborough
T 01642 635101
Free contraceptive advice & supplies & cytology (smear testing) service on Thurs 6.30-8 pm. Phone 01642 459583 for further details.

Health Centre - Hemlington
Hemlington
T 01642 597211
Free contraceptive advice & supplies & cytology (smear testing) service on Tue 4.30-6 pm. Phone 01642 459583 for further information.

Health Centre - Redcar
Coatham Road
Redcar
T 01642 478431
Well woman clinic on third Wed of each month 2.30-4 pm. Free cytology (smear testing), breast checks, urine & blood pressure tests, menopause advice & counselling, etc. Phone 01642 459583 for further details.

Health Centre - Stockton-on-Tees
Lawson Street
Stockton-on-Tees
T 01642 613444
Free contraceptive advice/supplies & cytology (smear testing). Clinics Mon 6.30-8 pm, Wed 10-11.30 am & 6.30-8 pm. Over 30s clinic first Thurs morning of each month. Phone 01642 624274 for further details.

ENGLAND - CLEVELAND

Health Centre - Thornaby
Trenchard Avenue
Thornaby
T 01642 765781
Free contraceptive advice & supplies & cytology (smear testing) services. Clinics on Thurs 2-3.30 pm & 6.30-8 pm. Phone 01642 624274 for further information.

Maternity Block
North Tees Hospital
Stockton-on-Tees
T 01642 617617
Free contraceptive advice & supplies & cytology (smear testing) services. Clinics on Thurs 6.30-8 pm & Fri 2-3.30 pm. Phone 01642 624274 for further information.

Neighbourhood Centre
Ragworth
T 01642 606591
Free contraceptive advice & supplies & cytology (smear testing) services. Clinics on first Fri of each month 10-11.30 pm. Phone 01642 624274 for further information.

Neighbourhood Centre
Grangetown
T 01642 483166
Free contraceptive advice & supplies & cytology (smear testing) service. Clinic on second Wed of each month 2-3.30 pm. Phone 01642 459583 for further details.

Overdale Road
Park End
Middlesbrough
T 01642 314560
Free contraceptive advice & supplies & cytology (smear testing) service on Wed 10-11.30 am - also well woman clinic. Contraceptive clinic also on Thurs 6.30-8 pm. Phone 01642 459583 for further information.

Roseberry Square
Lakes Estate
Redcar
T 01642 485736
Free contracetive advice & supplies & cytology (smear testing) service. Clinics on Mon 6.30-8 pm & Thurs (first & second Thurs of each month) 2.30-4 pm. Phone 01642 459583 for further information.

Skelton Health Centre
T 01642 650430
Free contraceptive advice & supplies & cytology (smear testing) service on second Mon of each month 5-6.30 pm. Phone 01642 459583 for further information.

South Bank Health Shop
T 01642 459583
Free contraceptive advice & supplies & cytology (smear testing) service on first Tue of each month 6.30-8 pm. Phone 01642 459583 for further details.

The Clinic
Bath Street
Saltburn
T 01642 622894
Free contraceptive advice & supplies & cytology (smear testing) service on Tue 6.30-8 pm. Phone 01642 459583 for further information.

The Clinic
The Avenue
Nunthorpe
T 01642 314132
Free contraceptive advice & supplies & cytology (smear testing) service on second & fourth Tue of each month 2-3.30 pm. Phone 01642 459583 for further information.

The Clinic
Worsall Road
Yarm
T 01642 558121
Free contraceptive advice & supplies & cytology (smear testing) services. Clinics on Wed 6.30-8 pm. Phone 01642 624274 for further information.

The Clinic
High Street
Lingdale
T 01642 650406
Free contraceptive advice & supplies & cytology (smear testing) service on first Wed of each month 2-3.30 pm. Phone 01642 459583 for further information.

The Clinic
Birtley Avenue
Acklam
T 01642 813568
Free contraceptive advice & supplies & cytology (smear testing) service on Sat 10-

11.30 am - also well woman clinic. Phone 01642 459583 for further information.

The Clinic
Hall Close
Marske
T 01642 483817
Free contraceptive advice & supplies & cytology (cervical smear) service Mon 10-11.30 am Phone 01642 459583 for further information.

EDUCATION

Teesside Association of Women Graduates (TAWG)
Mrs Sheila M Young
27 Grisedale Crescent
Egglescliffe
Stockton-on-Tees TS16 9DS
T 01642 652861
Meets at Stockton library on third Thurs of months. Usually an invited speaker at these meetings. Also an annual dinner, Christmas lunch and summer outing. Promoting a professional network for support, etc.

EQUAL OPPS

Fair Play for Women (North East)
Jan Sinclair, Chair
Policy Unit, Chief Executive's Dept
Middlesborough Borough Council
P O Box 99a Municipal Building
Middlesbrough TS1 2QQ
T 01642 263520 F 01642 263827
To improve access to training & education for all women in the north east of England; to encourage employers to develop their female staff and to assist women who wish to develop their skills, etc.

ETHNIC MINORITIES

Asian Ladies
Lesley Sinclair, Head Teacher
Ayresome Infant School
Worcester Street
Middlesbrough TS1 4NT
T 01642 244961
Groups run on Thurs afternoons.

Victoria Asian Ladies' Group
Mrs Niaz
1 Albert Terrace
Middlesbrough TS1 3PA
T 01642 230545

Meets at Health House, 169 Victoria Road, Middlesbrough. Education & training; courses on health issues; social events.

HEALTH

Breast Cancer Support Group
Mrs Susan Greenwood, Chairperson
1 Mill Court
Greatham
Hartlepool
T 01429 872339
Meets at Central Library, York Road, Hartlepool in the community room on first Tue of each month. Informal support group.

Cleveland Aids Support
Barry Kelly, Service Manager
61 King's Road
North Ormesby
Middlesbrough TS3 6EP
T 01642 254598 F 01642 244558
Offers befriending, support & help to people infected or affected by HIV/AIDS, their families, carers & friends.

LESBIAN AND BISEXUAL

Cleveland Lesbian Line
the collective
C/o St Mary's Centre
82-90 Corporation Road
Middlesbrough
T 01642 217955
Line open Mon 8-10 pm. Help & support for gay women or those who are unsure of their sexuality. Organising women only social events in the Cleveland area.

Gender and Sexuality Alliance (G&SA) - Cleveland
Kate More
Box 8
St Mary's Centre
Corporation Road
Middlesbrough TS1 2RW
T 01642 224617 F 01642 224617
CousinKat@aol.com
Local chapter of non-sectarian national group working on the politics of gender/sexuality & their transgression.

RELIGIOUS ORGANISATIONS

Ladies' Group
Mrs P Szabo
345 West Dyke Road
Redcar TS10 4PS

ENGLAND - CLEVELAND

T 01642 470301
Christian-based fellowship group meeting Fri 7.30-9 pm Wheelchair access. Speakers, visits to theatre, discussions, banner-making & devotional meetings.

Women Together
Grace Counter
53 Rosebury Crescent
Great Ayton
Middlesbrough TS9 6EW
T 01642 724178
Meets from September-May at Methodist Church, Great Ayton on second, third & fourth Tue of each month. Speakers.

SEXUAL ABUSE/RAPE CRISIS

Cleveland Rape and Sexual Abuse Counselling Service
Laureen Ditchburn
P O Box 31
Middlesbrough TS4 2JJ
T 01642 223885
01642 225787 - counselling line. Open Mon & Thurs 9 am-8 pm; Tue & Wed 9 am-4.30 pm; Fri 9 am-4 pm 24-hour ansaphone. Confidential service: counselling, support & advice for women & girls aged 12+.

SOCIAL

Grangefield Ladies' Club
Mrs Marianne Brooks
25 Kirkdale Close
Newham Grange Estate
Stockton-on-Tees
T 01642 612238
Talks, slide shows, speakers. Pooling skills. Part of National Association of Women's Clubs. Meets second and fourth Wed of each month 8-10 pm at The Insitute, Grays Road, Grange Estate, Stockton on Tees.

St Mary's Ladies' Luncheon Club
Jean Tinkler
12 Castle Wynd
Nunthorpe
Middlesbrough TS7 0QB
T 01642 319912
Meets third Wed in each month (except July, August, December) at 12.45 for lunch followed by speaker at St Mary's Church Hall, Nunthorpe. Providing St Mary's Parish church with some regular income.

St Peter's Ladies' Wednesday Group
Mrs Dorothy Falconer, Chairlady/Secretary

70 Wheatlands Park
Redcar TS10 2PF
T 01642 484396
Meets in Zetland Rooms, St Peter's Church, Redcar Lane, Redcar on first & third Wed 7.30-10 pm. Speakers, social events - theatre trips, walks, treasure hunts. Supports charities & community projects.

Yorkshire Country Women's Association
Mrs Elsie Breckon, President
67 Hutton Lane
Guisborough TS14 6QP
T 01284 633914
Meetings held at Guisborough Hall, Whitby Road, Guisborough, TS14 6PT on first Tue of each month 7.30-9.30 pm. Talks, slides, demonstrations, outings. Walks, meals out, theatre. No meetings in August.

SPORTS AND LEISURE

Keep Fit
Mrs Niaz
1 Albert Terrace
Middlesbrough TS1 3PA
T 01462 230545
Meets at Abingdon School, Abingdon Road, Middlesbrough on Tue 10-11.30 am & Thurs 10.30 am-12 pm

Middlesborough Ladies Football Club
Marrie Wieczorek
41 Wentworth Street
Middlesbrough TS1 4ET
T 01642 231201
Ladies' football team for ages 14-40. Plays Sun September-May/June. Training twice a week.

New Marske Ladies' Hockey
Nance Wrigley
27 Severn Grove
Skelton TS12 2LU
T 01287 652558
Ladies' hockey club playing Sun afternoons outdoor & Mon evenings when indoor league is on. There is a match fee charge to cover cost of club euqipment, petrol & hiring of pitch when necessary.

Park Ladies' Bowling Club
Mrs P Tweddle
50 Greta Avenue
Hartlepool TS25 5LE
T 01429 864718

Play league matches Tue afternoons from April to September. Also play almost every day during these months.

Roseberry Women's Hockey Club
Jill Instone
3 Barkston Avenue
Thornaby TS17 0LE
T 01642 762185 F 01642 612865
Promoting women's hockey. Training sessions 7.30 every Thurs at Acheson Sports Centre.

South Durham & Cleveland Netball Association
Mrs D Covell
50 Cleveland Avenue
Stokesley
Middlesbrough TS9 5HB
T 01642 710984
Promoting & developing netball in the area by providing leagues, coaching & umpiring courses - entry to AENA national netball competitions & youth development work.

Teeside Ladies' Bowling League
Mrs H N Parnell
1 Mallard Lane
Norton
Stockton-on-Tees TS20 1NE
T 01642 890370
Bowling for Teesside & surrounding areas. 20 clubs are registered. Plays during the season.

Support

Marske Ladies' Lifeboat Guild
Mrs J McBurney
18 Inglewood Avenue
Marske by the Sea
Redcar TS11 6DU
T 01642 486313
Raising funds for the Royal National Lifeboat Institution & promoting the good name of the institution locally.

Cornwall

Accommodation

YWCA Truro Young Women's Centre
Mari Eggins, Coordinator
Union Place
Truro TR1 1EP
T 01872 260847 F 01872 262570
Accommodation for 6 young women aged between 14-25. Counselling, training, young women's groups. Trips, activity days, residential weekends, childcare. Drop-in centre open Mon 12.30-4 pm & Fri 2-5 pm.

Arts and Crafts

Arts Support Club
Mrs Sandra Holmes
Briars End
Perrancoombe
Perranporth TR6 0HZ
T 01872 573423
For mature, trained, committed women artists to recharge their batteries, discuss ideas, plan projects, make contacts. Two accredited courses, ten sessions per term. Details on request; phone after 10 am

ECC International Ladies' Choir
Mrs J Hubbard, Secretary
3 Palace Road
St Austell PL25 4BP
T 01726 66140
Rehersals are at John Keay House, St Austell on Mon at 7.30 pm. The choir is available for concerts, weddings and festivals.

Taking Space
Mary Fletcher
23 Tregwary Road
St Ives TR26 1BL
Aims to bring together contemparary women artists living & working in the Penwith area of Cornwall; to enable women artists to exhibit art work free of selection by others; etc.

Business Support Schemes

Camborne Redruth Business and Professional Women's Club
Mrs Frieda Curnow
St Anthony
Redruth Road
Helston TR13 8LP
T 01326 572497
Women working for women. Meets on first & third Wed of each month (except August) at the Lowenac hotel, Camborne at 7 pm. New members welcome.

Enterprise Tamar
Mary Gleeson, Assistant Director
National School
St Thomas Road
Launceston PL15 8BU
T 01566 775632 F 01566 775632
To encourage women to explore, develop & utilise unrecognised skills & rebuild their

confidence after a career break. Advice, information, training, premises, visits.

CONTRACEPTION/WELL WOMAN

Cornwall Brook Advisory Centre
60 Station Road
Pool
Redruth TR15 3QG
T 01209 710088
Open Tue 3.30-6 pm; Thurs 5-7 pm; Sat 1-3.30 pm. Telephone enquiries Mon 9.30 a.m-1 pm; Wed 3.30-7 pm. Free confidential service for under 25s. Contraception, pregancy tests with immediate results.

Cornwall Women's Refuge Trust
T 01872 77814
Refuge with 4 family rooms and 2 single rooms. Shared living facilites. For all women suffering from physical or severe mental abuse. 24-hour one-to-one telephone service. Help, information, advice.

EDUCATION

Cornwall Women in Engineering, Science and Technology (CWEST)
Dr Lesley Atkinson
Camborne School of Mines
University of Exeter
Redruth TR15 3SE
T 01209 714866 F 01209 716977
L.Atkinson@csm.ex.ac.uk
Encouraging girls & women into SET. Support network for women in SET.

ENVIRONMENT

West Cornwall Women's Land Trust
T 01736 331864
Land to be held in trust for women in perpetuity. An opportunity for ecological land use, gendening, vegetable growing, tree planting, wet-land area, quiet space. Any woman can come & work on the land.

Women's Environmental Network - Cornwall
Jayne
T 01736 711976
Local group meets on third Mon of each month at 8 pm at Dandelions cafe, Causeway Head, Penzance. New members and children welcome. Articles for a newsletter are needed.

EQUAL OPPS

Fair Play South West
Pat McCarthy
No 5 Elizabeth House
Church Street
Liskeard PL14 3AR
T 01579 347107 F 01579 347627
fairplaysw.co.uk
Positive action equalities project. A government EOC initiative to stimulate partnerships which improve opportunities for women to realise their full potential in education, employment & the community.

GIRLS/YOUNG WOMEN

Redruth Methodist Young Wives Club
Mrs M J Trewen, Secretary
Outlook Club
Galanthus
Pednandrea
Redruth TR15 2EE
T 01209 218341
Meets first Fri of each month at 7.30 at Redruth Methodist Church, Redruth. Fundraises for community organisations. Talks & demonstrations.

Young People Cornwall
Nicky Davey
The Old School
Daniell Road
Truro TR1 2DA
T 01872 222447 F 01872 260099
Various projects for young women, including 'Young women & change' sexual health peer education project; 'Young women & children group'; women's work at 'Zebedees venue for young people'.

HEALTH

Breast Cancer Support Service
Sue Ferguson
C/o Treliske Hospital
Truro TRS 3LJ
T 01872 252691
Advice, information & counselling are provided & prosthesis fitting. Development of self-help groups are encouraged; information leaflets provided. Meetings held in Diabetic Centre at Treliske hospital.

Hysterectomy Support Network - Torpoint
Mrs M Lawson
Newhaven
Sunnyside
Polbathic

ENGLAND - CORNWALL

Torpoint PL11 3HA
T 01503 230889
Helpline support & advice for women who are about to have, or have had, a hysterectomy.

Redruth Health Club
Mrs M Turner, Secretary
14 Clijah Close
Southgate
Redruth TR15 2NS
T 01209 214348
Meets at Redruth Clinic, Redruth every Tue at 7.45 pm apart from school holidays. For women of all ages. Talks, demonstrations, slide shows & trips.

LESBIAN AND BISEXUAL

Cornwall Lesbian Line
Kate de Wreede
P O Box 41
Penzance TR18 2XY
T 01736 753709
Phone Thurs 8-10 pm. Advice, helpline, referral & information.

Out in Cornwall
T 01209 711211
Helpline run by young people who are available to talk through any issues around being lesbian or bi-sexual. Helpline open on Thurs between 7-9.30 pm. Telephone at this time or leave a message on ansaphone.

LIBRARIES/ARCHIVES

Hypatia Trust, The
Dr Melissa Hardie, Secretary to Trustees
The Old Post Office
Newmill
Penzance TR20 8XN
T 01736 360549 F 01736 330704
101546.2430@compuserve.com
Created to collect & make available published & personal documents about the achievements of women. Cares for & develops Hypatia Collection, books & achives by & about women.

Jamieson Library, The
Dr Melissa Hardie
The Hive
The Old Post Office
Newmill
Penzance TR20 8XN
T 01736 360549 F 01736 330704
101546.2430@compuserve.com

Private research library of books, ephemera & fine art, focussing on the history, literature & arts of women & their artistic & scientific contributions to society & culture. Supported by arts events.

MEDIA

Passing Light Syndicate
Lee Berry & Co
3 Mount Edgcombe Terrace
Falmouth TR11 2BS
T 01326 313818
Phone between 11 am-4 pm Mon-Fri (no opening times). Multi-media constantly changing organisation: art-based film, video, installation, 2D-3D, works, etc. Networking & fundraising.

PLACES TO STAY AND EAT

Capistrano
Sylvia
1 Chy-An-Dour Square
Penzance TR18 3LW
T 01736 64189
Woman-owned cottage. Women only. 1 double bedroom & washbasin. Shared bathroom. No children or pets. Car park. Vegetarians welcome. Open from March to October. Prices to be agreed on application.

Dolphin Cottage
Kate Wilson/Sara Clayton
Newtown
St Buryan
Penzance TR19 6BQ
T 01736 810394
B&B near Land's End in 17th-century granite cottage. Ancient sites. Run by women for women only. Three rooms, one double, one single & one twin. Vegetarian meals. No smoking. Phone for up-to-date price list.

Penryn House Hotel
Christine Kay
The Coombes
Polperro PL13 2RG
T 01503 272157 F 01503 273055
Women-run hotel in fishing village; ensuite accommodation. Open October-March for women only holidays & March-October for everyone. Gay & lesbian murder mystery weekends. Phone for up-to-date price list.

Wild Rose Women's Holidays
Sheila Gwyn
2 Blerrick Cottages

ENGLAND - CORNWALL

Antony
Torpoint PL11 3BA
T 01752 822609
Small-group holidays for women based on special interests, particularly walking. Also singing, drumming, writing, pot-luck, etc. Holidays in various venues in Cornwall, Devon & Gozo (Maltese island).

York House
Jean Fletcher or Ingrid Allen
Fore Street
Goldsithney
Penzance TR20 9LG
T 01736 711129
Double room only. Full beakfast. Vegetarian or vegan meals available. Parking space available. Phone for up-to-date price list.

PREGNANCY/CHILDBIRTH

Nappi Nippas
P O Box 35
Penznace TR18 4YE
T 01736 351263
Waterproof pants for babies. Also a plastic nappy fastner which is a useful & safe alternative to nappy pins.

PUBLISHERS/PUBLICATIONS

Alternatives
Sue Bonnick
49 Vyvyan Street
Camborne TR14 8AS
T 01209 716557
Women's second-hand books - lesbian, feminist, women's studies, auto/biographies, health, fiction, music, etc. Mail order but also stalls (eg Women's Craft Fair in Brixton). Viewing by appointment.

Outback
Sue Bonnick
P O Box 41
Penzance TR18 2XY
T 01209 716557
Newsletter for lesbians in Cornwall & the far south west. News, reviews, features, book & film reviews, gardening tips, listings, what's on & where to go.

SEXUAL ABUSE/RAPE CRISIS

Women's Rape and Sexual Abuse Centre
P O Box 39
Bodmin PL31 1XF
T 01208 77099

Helpline (above) open Mon 7.30-10 pm. 24-hour ansaphone. Free, confidential service run by women for women & teenage girls who have experienced/ are experiencing any form of sexual abuse or sexual violence.

SPORTS AND LEISURE

Cornwall Ladies County Golf Association
Mrs A Eddy
Penmester
Hain Walk
St Ives TR26 2AF
T 01736 795392 F 01736 752996
For women golfers resident in Cornwall & members of the Association. There are county golf competitions.

Keep Fit: Heamoor
Mrs M Worledge
8 Holly Terrace
Heamoor
Penzance TR18 3EJ
T 01736 69187
A keep fit group which meets on Thurs 7.15-9 pm at the Wesley Rock School Room, Heamoor.

Keep Fit: St Austell
Mrs Sidey
30 Sea Road
Carlyon Bay
St Austell PL25 3SF
T 01726 813149
A keep fit group which meets at Charlestown Church Hall on Wed 10-30 am-12 noon from October to Witsun.

Launceston Leisure Centre
Coronation Park
Launceston PL15 9DQ
T 01566 772551
Women only classes at the leisure centre: swimming Wed & Thurs 9-10 pm; keep fit Mon 11 am-12 noon.

Wellbeing Workshops for Women
Jaye Tabbner
Oakhurst
South Road
Strithians
Truro TR3 7AD
T 01209 860801
Exercise & dance to teach ways of coping with problems such as stress, relationships, menopause, etc.; to improve health &

confidence. Mobile workshops; available on Sundays. Residential weedends.

SUPPORT

Padstow Ladies Guild
Mrs Joan Lowe, Chairman and Secretary
St Pirans
8 Cross Street
Padstow PL28 8AT
T 01841 5323341
Fundraising for the RNLI.

WOMEN'S AID

Penzance Women's Aid
P O Box 94
Penzance TR18 ZXP
T 01736 50319
Helpline advice & support. One-to-one counselling & outreach group & survivors of sexual abuse group. Children's worker. Benefits, legal & housing advice. There are 11 bedspaces in the refuge.

CUMBRIA

ALTERNATIVE THERAPIES

Delcia McNeil
Delcia McNeil
Laundry Cottage
Whitbarrow Lodge
Witherslack
Grange Over Sands LA11 6ST
T 015395 52047 F 015395 52047
Psychotherapist & healer & specialises in working with women around the issues of self-esteem, personal crisis, relationship & work problems. Runs a women's therapy group. Also runs courses (not women only).

CHILD CARE AND FAMILY

Cumbria County Council's Childcare Information Service
Anne Quilter
Corporate Services Under 8s
The Courts
Carlisle CA3 8NA
T 01345 125737 F 01228 606322
Free service to parents, carers & professionals looking for information & advice on providers of childcare in Cumbria. Telephone enquiries open office hours Mon-Fri. Detailed up-to-date information provided.

COUNSELLING AND THERAPY

Fawcett Mill Fields - Counselling & Psychotherapy
Sue Wallace
Gaisgill
Tebay
Penrith CA10 3UB
T 01539 624408
Women-run workshops, mainly for women, eg psychodrama, colour therapy, expressive therapy, etc. Phone for further details.

EQUAL OPPS

Carlisle Women's Forum
Jeanette Harold/Linda Mark
Carlisle City Council
Civic Centre
Rickergate
Carlisle CA3 8QG
T 01228 23411 F 01228 511216
Aims to enhance the general well being of women in Carlisle; to raise awareness on issues affecting women; to positively challenge discriminatory practice against women, etc.

LESBIAN AND BISEXUAL

Peers
P O Box 48
Kendal LA9 5JG
Introduction & networking agency for discerning lesbians. Write to the above address for a discreet service to help you meet like-minded women for genuine friendships and/or relationships.

PLACES TO STAY AND EAT

Fawcett Mill Fields - Accommodation
Sue Wallace
Gaisgill
Tebay
Penrith CA10 3UB
T 01539 624408 F 01539 624408
Women-run accommodation can sleep up to 22 guests. Divided into four areas & the group size/holiday needs determines which areas will be used. Minimum stay is two nights. Catered & self-catering accomodation.

Keswick
Jacqui Best
Wootton Grove
Sherborne DT9 4DL
T 01935 814369
B&B in quiet house in Sherborne with women's history books etc to read. Walk the Sylvia Townsend Warner/Valentine Ackland walks & visit their tombstone.

ENGLAND - DERBYSHIRE

Self Catering Bungalow
S Kelly
T 01539 730340 F 01539 730340
Woman-owned self-catering accommodation in Kendal, gateway to the Lakes. Sleeps 4, linen provided, no smoking, no children, no pets. For further details & up-to-date price list phone above number.

Skadi Women's Walking Holidays
Paula Day
High Grassrigg Barn
Killington
Sedbergh LA10 5EW
T 015396 21188
Walking holidays for women based at above address between Lake District & Yorkshire Dales. Dates from February-November. Vegetarian food. Sauna. Phone for up-to-date price list.

PREGNANCY/CHILDBIRTH

Barrow Pregnancy Crisis Centre
2 Dalton Road
Barrow-in-Furniss LA14 2HD
T 01229 431926
Mobile Phone: 0468 842492. No set times of opening. Phone for an appt. Free pregnancy testing, counselling & support for women with unplanned pregnancies. Post abortion & miscarriage counselling.

RELIGIOUS ORGANISATIONS

Salvation Army - Cumbria
the commanding officer
Nelson Street
Millom LA18 SDS
T 01229 772775
Mon 2.30-3.30 pm women's meeting: spiritual & educational; Fri 9.30-11.30 am guardian & toddler group; Wed 9.30 am-1 pm drop-in for friendship & food.

SEXUAL ABUSE/RAPE CRISIS

Cumbria Rape Crisis Group
P O Box 34
Carlisle CA3 1EZ
T 01228 36500
Free, confidential helpline for survivors of rape & sexual abuse. Open Wed 7-10 pm. Ansaphone at other times which is checked regularly.

South Cumbria Rape and Abuse Service
92 Stricklandgate

Kendal
T 01539 734734
Helpline open Mon 7-9 pm.

DERBYSHIRE

ACCOMMODATION

NACRO Housing in Derby
Helen Scatcherd
The Spot Chambers
43-45 Osmaston Road
The Spot
Derby DE1 2JF
T 01332 200244 F 01332 297474
31 housing places in Derby, including separate provision for Black ex-offenders & young women leaving care. Self-build housing & employment training project for young people.

ALTERNATIVE THERAPIES

Creative Dreamwork
Lorna Dexter
Quarry Garden
Farnah Green
Belper DE56 2UP
T 01773 822732
Workshops and individual sessions to explore your own dreams, through action, art and writing.

BEREAVEMENT

National Association of Widows - City of Derby branch
Sigrid Linthwaite
43 Sydenham Road
Mackworth
Derby DE22 4EJ
T 01332 733982
Run by widows for widows providing help, comfort & advice; offering a social & educational life & ensuring the voice & needs of the widow are never forgotten. Meets twice monthly. Advisory centre open most Fri.

CENTRES FOR WOMEN

Derby Education Centre for Asian Women
Nasreen Akhtar/Yasmeen Akhtar
275 Normanton Road
Derby DE23 6UU
T 01332 363179
Accredited training for Asian women in traditional, non-traditional skills. To improve employment prospects. Training in IT. Job clubs. English. Women returners. Help with cv. Open Mon-Thurs 9 am-3 pm.

Derby Women's Centre
Kim Barlow
4 Leopold Street
Derby DE1 2HE
T 01332 341633
Open Mon-Sat 10.30 am-3 pm. Support, information, training for women in Derbyshire. Free counselling. Free legal advice Wed 12-1 pm. Aromatherapy Mon eves & Sat 12-3.30 pm. Creche. Free pregnancy tests.

Hadhari Nari Women's Project
Charlene Henry
36 St James Road
Normanton
Derby DE23 8QX
T 01332 270101 F 01332 769790
Women's aid; refuge accommodation; pregnancy testing Mon 10.30 am-12.30 pm & Thurs 3-6 pm; counselling; outreach service; training; information & advice Mon-Wed & Fri 10 am-4 pm & Thurs 10 am-5 pm.

CHILD CARE AND FAMILY

Childcare Options
Wendy Haynes
C/o Manor College
Ashgate Road
Chesterfield S40 4AA
T 01246 558070 F 01246 558180
Support service for providers of childcare services. Also a database which may be accessed by parents in the north Derbyshire area.

CONTRACEPTION/WELL WOMAN

East Midlands Nuffield Hospital, The
Rykneld Road
Littleover
Derby DE23 7SN
T 01332 517891
Well woman screen. Full female health assessment. Phone for up-to-date price lists.

EDUCATION

Derby and District Association of Women Graduates
Mrs Cynthia Marks
249 Duffield Road
Allestree
Derby DE22 1ET
T 01332 557214
Promotes interests of women graduates & makes their views known. Meetings on topics of current interest. Open to all women who hold degrees of universities or who have been accredited by universities.

ETHNIC MINORITIES

Asian Women's Counselling Service
C/o Karma Nirvana
Derby Women's Centre
4 Leopold Street
Derby DE1 2HE
T 01332 297677
A counselling & befriending service. Phone for further details between 9 am-5 pm

HEALTH

Karma Nirvana
Derby Women's Centre
4 Leopold Street
Derby DE1 2HE
T 01332 297677
A women's health project. Open 9 am-5 pm. Aims to bring down language & cultural barriers & to eliminate inequalities in health care & information obtained. A women's health information recource centre.

LESBIAN AND BISEXUAL

Gals - Lesbian Support Group
P O Box 8
Chesterfield S40 1NY
T 01246 559431
Line open Tue 7.30-9.30 Confidential support, advice & information to lesbian women & women who are unsure of their sexuality. Details of social group available.

LIBRARIES/ARCHIVES

Derby Women's Centre Library
Derby Women's Centre
4 Leopold Street
Derby DE1 2HE
T 01332 341633
Open Mon & Wed 12-2 pm, Thurs 5.30-7.30 pm Wide selection of books.

Supersport Photographs
Eileen Langsley
Wayside
White Lodge Lane
Baslow
Bakewell DE45 1RQ
T 01246 582376 F 01246 582227
Sports photography library. Specialist areas include coverage of a wide range of sports for women & girls.

ENGLAND - DERBYSHIRE

PHOTOGRAPHY
Lu Jeffery Photographer
Lu Jeffery
Providence Mill
Gorsey Bank
Wiksworth DE1 1AD
T 01629 825222 F 01629 825022
lu@provmill.demon.co.uk
Freelance photographer specialising in interiors & gardens for all national women's magazines. Also craft & home/garden books.

PLACES TO STAY AND EAT
Hide, The
T 01629 636189
Woman-owned studio/barn. Cooking facilites, shower, TV. Sleeps 1/2. No smoking. Renting by the week. Weekend breaks by arrangement. Phone for up-to-date price list.

Old Station House, The
Cheryle Coyne
4 Chatsworth Road
Rowsley
Matlock DE4 2EJ
T 01629 732987
Women run B&B. Open all year. 3 Bedrooms. CH. No smoking in bedrooms or bathrooms. TV. Traditional, vegetarian or continental breakfasts. Packed lunches. Vegetarian evening meals. Phone for price lists.

PREGNANCY/CHILDBIRTH
HIS - Derby
Val Turner
YMCA
London Road
Wilmorton
Derby DE24 8UT
T 01332 572076
Open Tue & Thurs 10.30 am-12.30 pm. Free pregnancy testing, counselling & support for women with unplanned pregnancies. Post abortion & miscarriage counselling.

SERVICES
Ariginal Fayres
Val Bacon
Unit 7
Butterly Croft Business Centre
Whitley Way, Peasehill
Ripley DE5 2QL
T 01773 603187 F 01773 749696
Exhibition organisers, mainly weddings & ladies' day exhibitions. Also hires screen & staging.

SEXUAL ABUSE/RAPE CRISIS
Derby Rape Crisis
Trish Cox
P O Box 142
Derby DE1 2HF
T 01332 342255
Helpline: 01332 372545 open Mon 10 am-12 pm, Thurs 7.30-9.30 pm, Fri 1-3 pm 24-hour ansaphone. Messages responded to promptly. To help relieve suffering & distress of persons raped or sexually abused.

One in Four Women's Group
Lisa
C/o Derby Women's Centre
4 Leopold Street
Derby DE1 2HE
T 01332 345633
Meets fortnightly on Thurs 7.30-10 pm. One-to-one counselling & support for women who have been sexually abused given by women survivors.

Seremis
Shelah Eisenberg
P O Box 119
Derby DE22 122
T 01332 758244
Therapy group for women survivors of sexual abuse. !2-week groups for up to 8 women. Caring environment for women to explore feelings about sexual abuse & patterns of behaviour. Also drop-in group.

Sexual Abuse and Incest Line (SAIL)
P O Box 8
Chesterfield S40 1NY
T 01246 556114
Helpline: 01246 559889 open Tue 7-9 pm & Wed 1-3 pm. Face-to-face counselling for women by women who have been sexually abused or raped as adults.

SUPPORT
Osmaston Women's Project
Helen Scatcherd
30 Varley Street
Allenton
Derby DE24 8DE
T 01332 384414

Community project on the Osmaston estate set up by NACRO, providing advice, a drop-in centre & creche for local women.

Take A Break
Nasreen Shahid
3 Young Street
Derby DE23 6NB
T 01332 736866
An all-women's group providing monthly health talks, short courses, speakers, drop-in on Fri 9.30 am-12 p.m, yoga class Mon 9.30-11 am All activities are free with free creche.

TRAINING

Canopy Training
Helen Bovey
7 Jackson Tor Road
Matlock DE4 3JS
T 01629 584600 F 01629 584600
Consultancy, research & training in the voluntary & community sectors, with particular expertise in rural issues.

Derwent Stepping Stones Nursery & Community Training Centre
Romi Jones
St Marks Road
Chaddesden
Derby DE21 6RW
T 01332 372245 F 01332 372245
Open Mon-Fri 8 am-6 pm. Free training courses & creche for trainees. Otherwise nursery costs are £15 per day. Aims to identify & facilitate community-based training schemes which meet local women's needs.

TRANSPORT

Aristocrat Chauffeured Cars
Val Bacon, Senior Partner
Unit 7
Butterly Croft Business Centre
Whitley Way, Peasehill
Ripley DE5 2QL
T 01773 603187 F 01773 749696
Chauffeuring company for business hire, races, airports, civic functions, corporate entertainment, films, weddings & special occasions. Provides chauffeur only service. Women drivers on request.

DEVON

ACCOMMODATION

Young Women's Christian Association (YWCA) - Plymouth
Dee McClenaghan
9-13 Lockyer Street
Plymouth PL1 2QQ
T 01752 660321 F 01752 229476
Provides safe & affordable accommodation for 78 young people, 13 young mothers & their babies. Priority given to women. Support given by providing intense housing support, life skills, budgeting, etc.

ALTERNATIVE THERAPIES

Mary Booker - Dramatherapist
Mary Booker
1 Hill Budge Terrace
Park Street
Crediton EX17 3ED
T 01363 777564
Dramatherapy aims to facilitate positive change, promote healing and develop personal potential. It reunites your body with your thoughts, feelings and imagination. Phone for up-to-date price list.

Psychodrama
Sandra Wooding
Lower Cator Farmhouse
Widecombe-in-the-Moor TQ13 7TX
T 01364 621239
Sandra Wooding runs psychodrama groups/weekends for both clients and staff who experience or who work with people with eating problems. She also works with women only groups.

ARMED FORCES

Association of Wrens - Exeter Branch
Mrs Ethel F Harris
59 Blackthorn Crescent
Exeter EX1 3HQ
T 01392 465206
Meet first Thurs in month 7.30 pm at Exeter White Ensign Club, South Street, Exeter (except in August when we go out for a meal). To maintain comradeship for those in the Women's Royal Naval Service.

Association of Wrens - Plymouth Branch
Miss Della Jackson
14 Ronsdale Close
Pomphlett
Plymouth PL9 7QZ
T 01752 484019
For past and present members of WRNS, QARNNS and WRNR. To maintain friendship enjoyed in WRENS. This branch mainly Wrens serving in Second World War. Meets Wed afternoon once a month.

ENGLAND - DEVON

Women's Royal Army Corps Association - Exeter Branch
Mrs Margaret D Cranmer
Viva Neuva, 2 Moon Ridge
Newport Park
Topsham Road
Exeter EX2 7EW
T 01392 875885
Meets third Tues of month at noon. Speakers, coffee. Fundraising. Aims are to foster esprit de corps and to maintain comradeship amongst members. To help members obtain assistance if in need.

Arts and Crafts

Barnstaple Ladies Choir
Mrs Mary Chant
12 Allenstyle Gardens
Yelland
Barnstaple EX31 3EA
T 01271 860500

Chulmleigh Ladies Choir
Mrs Elizabeth Andrew
Culverhayes
East Street
Chulmleigh EX18 7DD
T 01769 580363
Meets Thurs 7.30 pm at Chulmleigh Town Hall. Choir open to women who wish to sing and includes children from aged 6 upwards. No audition. Choir sings at local events. Social events organised.

Elizabeth Aylmer Pottery
Elizabeth Aylmer
Widgery House
20 Market Street
Hatherleigh
Okehampton EX20 3JP
T 01837 810624
Pottery workshop and showroom open Mon-Sat 10 am-5 pm. Large range of kitchen ware for sale, glazed in wood ash.

Fool's Paradise
Jo Burgess and Nicky Street
Sentry Farm
Exminster
Exeter EX6 8DY
T 01392 832268 F 01392 833122
fools@avel.co.uk
Entertainment agency specialising in cabaret and street entertainment. A policy of actively promoting women performers as there are not enough of them working either in comedy or outdoor entertainment.

Jubilee Singers of North Devon
Mrs Maureen Sobey, Secretary
Bella Vista
Ashleigh Crescent
Barnstaple EX32 8LA
T 01271 78719
Ladies' choir. Rehersals are on Wednesday evenings. We entertain anyone who likes to listen - residential homes, churches, charities, music festivals, etc.

Ladies of Letters and Write On Writing Groups
Denise Couch
10 Short Park Road
Peverell
Plymouth PL3 4P2
T 01752 661367
Meets Tue 1-3 pm in term time at Mutley Plain, Plymouth. To share ideas and information and to encourage women writing at all levels and of all types. Members are both published and unpublished women writers.

Margaret Morris Movement
Mrs Janice Evans
The Old Station
Briston
Plymouth PL8 2BH
T 01752 491433
Dance organisation. Suitable for women of all ages and abilities.

Pyworthy Ladies Choir
Clare Cook
Stockenden
Trevalgas Cross
Poughill
Bude EX23 9HH
T 01288 353235
The choir meets in the village hall of Pyworthy, near Holsworthy, Devon on Wed 7.30-9 pm. Extensive repertoire ranging from folk music and music hall to sacred music and modern songs.

South West Women in the Arts
Sarah Dawson
South West Arts
Bradninch Place
Gandy Street
Exeter EX4 3LS
T 01392 218188 F 01392 413554
sarah.dawson.swa@artsf6.org.uk
Ad hoc grouping of professional women working in various areas in the arts who undertook a creative women's project with

BEREAVEMENT

North Devon Miscarriage Support Group
Sue Luscombe
Hillhead
Chittlehampton
Umberleigh EX37 9RG
T 01769 540431
Both one-to-one & group support for women experiencing the loss of a baby through miscarriage. Support group meetings held every first Thurs of month at Victoria House, Victoria Road, Barnstaple.

Support After Miscarriage
Gill Watson
2 Brim Brook Court
Veille Park
Torquay TQ2 7RY
T 01803 613100
Meets first Mon of month 7.30-9 pm at Meeting Room 6, Central Church (side entrance - in Morgan Avenue), Tor Hill Road, Torquay. Group offers support following miscarriage in an informal atmosphere.

Widows' Social Club
Mrs M E Cridland
71 Park Road
Exeter EX1 2HT
T 01392 216965
Provides friendly help to any widow. Weekly meetings of varying activities: trips, parties, & dinners. Open to any widow.

BUSINESS SUPPORT SCHEMES

Business and Professional Women (BPW) - North Devon
Mrs Joan Clark, Administration Officer
9 Style Close
Bumsam
Barnstaple EX32 9EZ
T 01271 45696
Meetings held on first Thurs of every month at 7.30 pm at the Cedars Lodge Inn, Bickinston Road, Barnstaple, tel 01271 71784, fax 01271 25733. A branch of the Business and Professional Women UK Ltd.

Network 2000
Christine Fraser
Eastgate House
Princesshay
Exeter EX1 1LY
T 01392 494210 F 01392 413163
christinenet2000.zynet.co.uk
Committed to training, upskilling & 'learning for life' activities as the key to individual development. Recognises the changing nature of work in society & the need for new strategies to achieve skills.

Southern Ladies in Commerce
Patsy Stidwill
46 Molesworth Road
Plympton
Plymouth PLY 4NU
T 01752 344588
Meets every second Wed of each month at 7 pm. A meal follows at 8 pm & then a speaker. Meetings held at the Duke of Cornwall Hotel. For employed or self-employed women.

Women Mean Business - Exeter
Angela McTiernan/Judith Reynolds
DCDA, 2nd Floor
Eastgate House
High Street
Exeter EX4 3JT
T 01392 410222 F 01392 410022
To promote economic activity amongst unemployed women in Devon through providing part-time, nationally accredited training in setting up a cooperative or small business.

CENTRES FOR WOMEN

Margaret Jackson Centre
Eve Lane
1st Floor
4 Barnfield Hill
Exeter EX1 1SR
T 01392 256711
Women's health information centre; telephone help line; resource centre; specialist bookshop. Details of self-help groups, counselling agencies available. Middle years counselling; menopause support group.

Plymouth Women's Resource Centre
Ginny Lee
Room 7 All Saints' House
Harwell Street
Stonehouse
Plymouth PL1 5BW
T 01752 257765
Houses Wider Opportunities for Women which runs a two-year women's studies course. Free childcare for under 5s, plus

ENGLAND - DEVON

refreshments. Occasional day workshops for women, all with free childcare.

CHILD CARE AND FAMILY

Devon & Cornwall Playlines
Judith Mcmahon
The Polsham Centre
Higher Polsham Road
Paignton TQ3 2SZ
T 01803 551448 F 01803 665735
Aimed at setting up quality after-school child care in Devon and Cornwall to encourage parents to return to work.

Kings Nympton Mother and Toddler Club
Mrs Sue Down
Deer Park
Chumleigh EX18 7AN
T 01709 581165
Meets Tue afternoons at Kings Nympton Parish Hall. For mothers and children aged 0 to school age.

CONTRACEPTION/WELL WOMAN

Beacon Heath Family Centre
139 Beacon Lane
Exeter
T 01392 76892
For information & free contraception. Free condoms. All the staff are women. Open every day except Sunday, both day & eve. Drop in on Saturday (no appointment required).

Exeter Nuffield Hospital, The
Wonford Road
Exeter EX2 4UG
T 01392 276591
Well woman screen. Full female health assessment. Phone for up-to-date price lists.

North Devon Family Planning Service
Mary Metcalf, Family Planning Coordinator
The Health Centre
Vicarage Street
Barnstaple EX32 7BT
T 01271 71761 F 01271 321586
Free contraceptive service & advice; psychosexual clinics; well women clinics; pregnancy testing & referral; counselling for unplanned pregnancy issues. Available at six clinics in north Devon.

Plymouth Nuffield Hospital
health screening department

Derriford Road
Plymouth PL6 8BG
T 01752 775861 F 01752 768969
Open Mon-Fri 8.30 am-4.30 pm. Various screening tests are available, including menopause screening tests. Phone for up to date price list.

Well Woman Clinic - Barnstaple
Mary Metcalf
Barnstaple Health Centre
Vicarage Street
Barnstaple EX32 7BT
T 01271 71761
There are two clinics each month on alternate Tue 9.30 am-1 pm. Services offered include advice, support, screening & treatment for women with concerns relating to the menopause.

Well Woman Clinic - Bideford
Bideford Hospital
Abbotsham Road
Bideford EX39 3AF
T 01237 472692
There is a well women clinic every third Tuesday afternoon of each month. Advice on contraception every Tuesday afternoon.

Well Woman Clinic - Okehampton
Okehampton Medical Centre
East Street
Okehampton EX20 1AY
T 01837 52233
There are well women clinics on Wed mornings with a practice nurse & clinics with doctors on Mon & Thurs afternoons. Advice on contraception available on Thurs afternoons.

FINANCE

Money Services for Women
Margaret Sandow
Eastgate House
Princesshay
Exeter EX1 1LY
T 01392 210603 F 01392 413163
Educational, counselling service on all financial matters. Independent financial adviser regulated by the personal investment authority.

HEALTH

Breakthrough Breast Cancer (Devon and Cornwall)
Mrs Lyn Brown

ENGLAND - DEVON

264 Blandford Road
Efford
Plymouth PL3 6HX
T 01752 775357
Support & self-help group for breast cancer victims & their families. Leaflets. Information, practical & emotional help provided (eg babysitting, befriending). Trained counsellor available.

East Devon Breast Screening Service
Dr J Brennan, Clinical Director
Royal Devon and Exeter Hospital
Barrack Road
Exeter EX2 5DW
T 01392 402480
Offers mammography to women aged 50-64 on a three-yearly basis. Office hours are from 8.30 am-5 pm. Phone for an appointment.

Pre Menstrual Self Help
Daphne Appleton
Tremore Cottage
Ianivet
Bodmin PL30 5JT
T 01208 831773
Will send out leaflet on PMS & self-help advice on receipt of 80p. Advice via telephone, or will meet individuals on a one-to-one basis. Would appreciate not being contacted Sunday lunchtime!

West Devon Breast Screening Service
M A Worrall, Programme Manager
X-ray Department
Level 6
Dernford Hospital
Plymouth PL6 8DH
T 01752 792700
For women aged 50-64. HQ of the programme for calling women in West Devon to the National Breast Screening Service. Office hours are from 8.30 am-5 pm.

LARGER/TALLER WOMEN

Long Tall Sally
19 Princesshay
Exeter EX1 1NQ
T 01392 413636
Clothes for the taller woman sizes 12-20.
Open Mon-Sat 9.30 am-5.30 pm.

Masey's
Linda Bertram
1 St Andrew Street
Plymouth PL1 2AH

T 01752 222141 F 01752 222141
Open Mon-Sat 9.30-5.30. Beautiful clothes for every occasion in sizes 18-28.

LESBIAN AND BISEXUAL

Plymouth Organisation of Lesbians (POOL)
T 01752 603839
Phone in on Thurs 7-9 pm. Otherwise an ansaphone service. A voluntary service run by lesbians for lesbians.

PEACE GROUPS

Spiral Women's Camp
Al
90 Langham Way
Ivy Bridge PL21 9BY
T 01752 892 881
Runs one camp per year somewhere in England. Women & children (girls & boys) are welcome. No fixed costs. Donations welcome.

PLACES TO STAY AND EAT

Hillview Guest House
Jackie Bosley
The Woodlands
Coombe Martin EX34 0AT
T 01271 882331
A B&B run by women & women-friendly. Open from Easter to October. Sheltered garden, covered veranda, varied breakfast menu, non smoking, en-suite rooms, large car park. TV. Phone for up-to-date price list.

PREGNANCY/CHILDBIRTH

Active Birth Plymouth
Kassandra Clemens
6 Bellows Park
Brixton
Plymouth PL8 2AS
T 01752 880031
Active birth teacher covering childbearing year: ante-natal classes from three months; couples classes; post-natal classes with baby massage. Holistic approach to pregnancy & special yoga for childbearing.

Exeter Crisis Pregancy Centre
Heather Sears
33 Longbrook Street
Exeter EX4 6AW
T 01392 412332

Open Tue and Wed 1-3 pm, Thurs 5.30-7.30 pm, Fri 5-6 pm. Free pregnancy testing & counselling. Offers information to women with unplanned pregnancies, to help them make decisions right for them.

Exeter District Maternity Unit
Head of Midwifery
R D & E Hospital
Heavitree
Gladstone Road
Exeter EX1 2ED
T 01392 411611 F 01392 405106
Four consultants run ante-natal clinics. Day care unit & drop-in from 8.30 am-5 pm. There is also a sub-fertility clinic.

Exeter Fertility Clinic
Dept of Obstetrics & Gynaecology
Royal Devon & Exeter Hospital
Gladstone Road
Exeter EX1 2ED
T 01392 405051 F 01392 405106

Exeter Pregnancy Testing Service
Sandie Hicks
Play Training & Resource Centre
Clifton Hill
Exeter
T 01392 79989
Free pregnancy test; immediate result; no appointment necessary. Support & confidentiality. Information on pregnancy, abortion, adoption & contraception. Open Tues 6-8 pm & Sat 10 am-12 noon.

Exeter Twins Club
Sarah Card
6 Woodbury View
St Thomas
Exeter EX2 9JT
T 01392 499578
Support group for mothers & pregnant women of twins, triplets & more. £5 annual sub. Monthly meetings, coffee mornings, trips, parties. Practical advice & friendship. Second-hand baby equipment available.

Exeter Unplanned Pregnancy Service
4 Barnfield Hill
Exeter
T 01392 426943
Offers free information, counselling & pregnancy testing. No appointment needed. Open Wed 9.30 am-12 noon & Sat 10 am-12 noon.

National Childbirth Trust - Torbay and South Devon branch
Sally Shoolbraid
19 Shiphay Avenue
Torquay TQ2 7ED
T 01803 613819
Aims to provide information to enable women to make informed & appropriate decisions about childbirth. Promotes breastfeeding. Offers post-natal support.

Postnatal Depression Support
June Dickinson
114 Westcliff Park Drive
Dawlish EX7 9EL
T 01626 866306
Confidential information & advice relating to postnatal illness/depression. Ongoing individual telephone support. Leaflets & booklets produced by the Association For Post-Natal Illness available.

RELIGIOUS ORGANISATIONS

Bideford Baptist Women's Guild
Mrs E G Phillips
20 Hillgarden Close
Lower Gunstone
Bideford EX39 2RS
T 01237 473067
Meets on Thurs 3 pm. January to May & September to December. Devotional meetings only.

East & West Buckland Women's Fellowship
Mrs H Pickard
Farm View
Brayford
Barnstaple EX32 7PZ
T 01598 710715
A small group which has a monthly meeting on third Wed to help members in the aim to increase an interest in our Methodist church.

Ladies' Fellowship
Mrs Margaret Lake
2a Belvedere Road
Exmouth EX8 1QN
T 01395 264128
Meetings held Tue 2.45-3.45 pm (except Bank holidays & August). Singing, hymns, choruses, Bible talk. Tea & home-made cakes afterwards. Meetings held at Exmouth Chapel, Exeter Road, Exmouth.

Peverell Park Methodist Church Wives' Club
Mrs Maureen Sings (Leader)
4 Barrie Gardens
Manadon
Plymouth PL5 3DW
T 01752 783179
Meetings on Thurs afternoons throughout term time. Speakers; fundraising; friendship & fellowship. Affiliated to the Women's Network of the Methodist Church.

Plymouth Women's Theology Group
Kathy Gilbert/Christine Avery
1 Ronald Terrace
Ford
Plymouth PL2 1JT
T 01752 569252
Discussion group/support group for feminists with an interest in or commitment to religious or spiritual experience & exploration. Meets last Sat of each month. Free vegetarian meal provided.

St Budeaux Methodist Sisterhood
Mrs D Gardiner
4 Trelawney Avenue
St Budeaux
Plymouth PL5 1RH
Friendly ladies endeavouring to show what the love of Christ means to them. Bible-based talks, followed by tea & biscuits. Once a month a bring-and-buy table for the Women's Network of the Methodist Church.

Wives and Friends
Mrs A J Wheatley
Okehampton United Church
16 Abbey Rise
Okehampton EX20 1PJ
T 01837 54723
A fortnightly meeting of women on Thurs at 7.30 pm, aimed at providing interesting speakers, prayer & social time for members & non-members of the Church.

Women's Christian Fellowship
Miss Jean Reader
St Peter's Church
1 West Hill Gardens
Budleigh Salterton EX9 6BL
T 01395 443409
Meets once a fortnight, offering fellowship to church members & others from local churches. Speakers & occasional open meetings when support is engendered for a given society.

RETAILING
Green Shoes
Alison Hastie
Station Road
Totnes TQ9 5HW
T 01803 864997
A women's business which designs & makes shoes. Non-leather as well as leather shoes made.

SERVICES
HGS Research
Jo Elliott
28 North Street
Witheridge
Tiverton EX16 8AG
T 01884 860043 F 01884 861162
Market research specialising in door-to-door, streets, product placements, mystery shopping & telephone research. Field interviews, ad hoc projects.

SEXUAL ABUSE/RAPE CRISIS
Exeter Rape & Sexual Abuse Support Services
P O Box 123
Exeter EX4 3RR
T 01392 430817
Telephone line open Mon, Fri 1.30-4 p.m; Thurs, Sun & alternate Tue 8-11 pm. An answerphone at all other times. Face to face counselling by arrangement. Information, support & counselling.

Judy Shaw
Judy Shaw
T 01398 331004
One-to-one counselling & psychotherapy for men & men. Therapy group supervision working in the field of survivors of childhood sexual abuse.

Plymouth Rape Crisis
P O Box 227
Plymouth PL4 0YX
T 01752 263600
Helpline: 01752 223584 open Wed & Fri 7-9.30 pm. Telephone & face-to-face counselling for women who have been sexually abused at any time of their lives. Self-help group on Tue 7.30-9.30 pm.

ENGLAND - DEVON

SOCIAL

Chagford Ladies' Evenings Out (CLEO)
Mrs Margaret Marsh
Wayebrook
Manor Road
Chagford TQ13 8AS
T 01647 433225 F 01647 433225
Open to all women. Meets second Thurs of each month at 7.45 p.m at Endecott House unless otherwise stated. Outings, speakers, arts & crafts.

Friendly Circle
Mrs Elsie Gage
1 Glebe Close
Littleham
Exmouth EX8 2QU
T 01395 271065
Meetings held on first & third Thurs of each month at Exmouth Chapel, Exeter Road, Exmouth, at 8 pm. Demonstrations, cookery, handwork, talks. Light refreshments.

Plymouth Ladies Day Out Club
Mrs J Yates
Plymouth YWCA G K Centre
Alfred Street
Plymouth PL1 2RP
T 01752 268458
Open 11 am-1.45 pm. Meet new friends; listen to interesting speakers. Free creche.

Torbay Homemakers
Mrs Joan B Mansell, Secretary
Manington
22 Broadsands Bend
Paignton TQ4 6JH
T 01803 844282
Branch of the Women's Guild of Friendship. Programmes related to the home in its widest aspect. Meets at the Kistor Hotel, Belgrave Rd, Torquay on second Thurs of each month at 8 pm.

Tower Club Torquay, The
Mrs Joy L Smith
1 Purbeck Avenue
Livermead
Torquay TQ2 6UL
T 01803 605737
Meets on third Mon of each month apart from July & August 10.30 am-12 noon. Numbers are limited to 50 women. Fundraising financial assistance given to Rowcroft Hospice, Torquay.

Tuesday Club, The
C Ainsworth
Caplecombe
Kingsnympton
Umberleigh EX37 9TG
T 01760 072401
Club for women meeting second Tue of each month at 7.30 pm. Kingsnympton Village Hall. Speakers & light refreshments.

SPORTS AND LEISURE

Braunton Ladies Netball Club
Sally Sawyer
45 Davids Hill
Georgeham EX33 1QF
T 01271 890741
A netball club with three teams in the North Devon netball league. Open to women & girls aged 14 plus. Training nights; regular matches played.

Dawlish Ladies Hockey Club
Anne Tait
Penicoe
Stockton Villas
Dawlish EX7 9NN
T 01626 864853
Women's hockey club. There are two teams which play on Sat & Sun. In the West Clubs Women's Hockey League.

Devon County Women's Hockey Association
Jackie Oaw
10 Claymans Pathway
Woodlands
Ivybridge PL21 9UZ
T 01752 893772
We co-ordinate the hockey clubs within the county, organise competitions, tournaments, etc. We run a number of schoolgirl (u16 & u18), u21 & senior county representative teams.

Devon Violets Ladies Clog Dance
C Newns
10 South View
Chaddiford Lane
Barnstaple EX31 1RD
T 01271 45985
Ladies Morris dancing team. We dance north-west Morris.

Exeter Exiles Netball Club
Mrs Jan Howard
17 Attwyll Avenue

Heavitree
Exeter EX2 5HN
T 01392 71090
Aims to provide a good standard of netball for team players. Plays in the south west's Super League & the Exeter & District Netball League. New members are always welcome.

Exeter Ladies Hockey Club
Deborah Barrett, Secretary
78 Granary Lane
Budleigh Salterton EXG 6ER
T 01395 443672
Trains Thurs evening throughout the season at Exeter School 6.30-8.00 pm on Astro turf. The Club runs three senior teams playing league hockey. There is a junior section. Also involved in indoor hockey.

Ilfracombe Red Petticoats
Mrs S A Hesman
15 Queen's Avenue
Ilfracombe EX34 9LN
T 01271 862421
Ladies' clog dance team. Practice every Thurs evening 7.30-9.30 pm. During the summer we dance out in the local villages. On Thurs nights we attend folk festivals & support local charities with collections.

ISCA Ladies Hockey Club
Trina Lake
25 Radford Road
St Leonards
Exeter EX2 4EU
T 01392 422752
Club runs three teams, two in competition in West Clubs Women's Hockey League & a third playing social hockey. Train on Tue at Exeter School. Also a junior section training on Tues evenings.

Ladies First
Gaynor Daniels
St Annes Well Brewery
18 Lower North Street
Exeter EX4 3ET
T 01392 214169
Health & fitness centre for women only. Open Mon-Fri 10 am-8 pm; Sat 9 am-1 pm. Facilities include sunbeds, jacuzzis, sauna, beauty room & toning tables. Phone for up-to-date price lists.

North Devon Leisure Centre
Seven Brethren Bank
Barnstaple EX31 2AP
T 01271 73361 F 01271 73234
Water-based ante- & post-natal exercise class on Wed 11-12 noon; parents & babies swimming Mon 11.45-12.30 pm & Wed 10.30-11.15 am Creche Mon-Fri 10-12 noon & Mon & Wed 1-3 pm. Open all year.

North Devon Netball League (1)
Kay Albery
27 Ashley Terrace
Bideford EX39 3AL
T 01237 479330
Winter league from September to March playing at Bideford School & Community College, Abbotsham Road, Bideford on Mon evenings 7-9.30 pm. Fees are set before each season.

North Devon Netball League (2)
Mrs Celia Mathews, Secretary.
9 Highbury Road
Newport
Barnstaple EX32 9BY
T 01271 75757
Plays during summer season from May to July on Mon eves 6.45-9 pm at Pilton School & Community College, Chaddiford Lane, Barnstaple, or the Park School, Barnstaple. Fees set before each season.

Okehampton Columbines Ladies Hockey Club
Jane Jones
School House Cottage
Inwardleigh
Okehampton EX20 3AN
T 01837 52217
Hockey club playing from September to April. Training continues throughout the summer. All standards & ages welcome.

Okehampton Netball League
Mrs A Herrod-Taylor
16 Oaktree Park
Sticklepath
Okehampton EX20 2NB
T 01837 840742
Matches played at Okehampton College on Tues evenings, 8 pm & 8.20 pm. Phone for up-to-date fees.

Plym Valley Ladies Hockey Club
Wendy Salsbury
2 Leyford Close
Wembury
Plymouth PL9 0HX
T 01752 862820 F 01752 862820

Ladies' hockey club with two teams. Training is on Tue evenings, with matches on Sat & Sun. Many social events with various evenings out. A very friendly club.

Plymouth Ladies Hockey Club
Elaine Edwards
59 Stuart Road
Pennycome quick
Plymouth PL1 5LW
T 01752 564344
ese@wpo.nerc.ac.uk
Four teams play on Saturdays & Sundays; all teams play in a league. Train on Wed 7-9.30 pm. Home ground is College of St Mark & St John, Derriford, Plymouth. Over 60 members with an age range of 14-48.

Rugby Football Union for Women - Exeter
Sue Eakers
33 Rices Mews
St Thomas
Exeter EX2 9AY
T 01392 221754

Saltash Essanians Women's Hockey Club
Viv Horton
Hazeldon Mews
Wallabrook
Tavistock PL19 0JR
T 01822 612141 F 01822 613851
Matches: Sat afternoons; practice Tue evenings. Friendly, sociable club - welcomes new members of all standards. Ist XI play in South West Women's League; 2nd XI play in Plymouth & District league.

Taw Valley Ladies Hockey Club
Heather Dolan
Church Street
Braunton
T 01271 816704
Ladies' hockey club open to all ages with both senior & junior membership, playing at Park School all weather pitch, Barnstaple.

SUPPORT

Ilfracombe Ladies Circle
Mrs K Irvine
Hollybrow
Crofts Lea Park
Ilfracombe EX34 9PN
Mainly concerned with raising funds for charities.

Paignton Ladies Group
Mrs June W Edwards, Secretary
Broadwater House
Preston Down Road
Paignton TQ3 1DT
T 01803 523154 F 01803 523154
Meets monthly 10 am at the Palace Hotel, seafront, Paignton. Provides friendship, companionship & assistance in times of difficulty or illness. Formal meetings, lunches, outings, coffee mornings.

Watch Ashore - Plymouth & District Branch
Mrs Lynda Payne, Hon Sec
71 Church Road
Wembury
Plymouth PL9 0JJ
T 01752 862654
Support group for merchant navy wives, widows, daughters, etc. Meets second Wed of each month (except August and December) at the Duke of Cornwall Hotel, Plymouth.

Women's Royal Voluntary Service - South West Division
Christine Cribb, Divisional Director
Elizabeth House
Emperor Way
Exeter Business Park
Exeter EX1 3QS
T 01392 203292 F 01392 203294
Provides care to those in need in the local community. Meals on wheels; lunch club meals; clubs for the elderly; holidays; hospital services; mobile library; residential homes; projects for offenders, etc.

TRAINING

Plymouth Returners Ltd
Gill Thomas
40 Tavistock Place
Plymouth PL4 8AX
T 01752 673466 F 01752 673466
Open 9.30 am-3.30 pm. Training in personal effectiveness, confidence building, job seeking skills, CLAIT & work experience. All courses are free.

Project Anna - WEA
Liz Barker
Martinsgate
Bretonside
Plymouth PL4 0AT
T 01752 664989 F 01752 254195

To enable women who have started a business or who have a business plan the opportunity to further develop their businesses into Europe through export training & qualifications.

Women's Aid

Exeter Women's Aid
Emma, Lynne, Anna, Kim
P O Box 121
Exeter EX4 6BJ
T 01392 52486
Runs a refuge for women & children escaping domestic violence. Telephone support offered.

North Devon Women's Aid
T 01271 75896
Provides a safe house for women & children who are victims of domestic violence & abuse. Provides advice & information to women.

Plymouth Women's Refuge
Maggie Horne, Coordinator
Plymouth Guild of Community Service
Ernest English House
Buckwell Street
Plymouth PL1 2DA
T 01752 562286 F 01752 562286
Advice & information for women suffering from domestic violence. Safe accommodation for families made homeless. Counselling provided. Can also phone 01752 665084 or fax 01752 254818

South Devon Women's Aid (1)
P O Box 65
Totnes TQ11 0YF
T 01364 644088
The above phone line is a helpline. For all other enquiries other than for immediate help phone 01364 643866. Offers therapeutic groups for women who have experienced or who are experiencing domestic violence.

South Devon Women's Aid (2)
P O Box 82
Torquay
T 01803 315154
Secure accommodation for women & children escaping domestic violence. This line is answered 24 hours a day every day by another woman.

Dorset

Accommodation

Bournemouth Women's Refuge
Mags Smith
P O Box 2028
Bournemouth BH1 3YN
T 01202 547755
24-hour helpline. Safety & support for women & children escapting domestic violence. 24-hour care.

Weymouth Women's Refuge
J Russell
P O Box 2530
Weymouth DT4 7YW
T 01305 772295
Providing temporary space in a non-judgemental environment. Helping women & children to regain control over their lives. Open during office hours. Otherwise a 24-hour contact via pager.

Arts and Crafts

Ros Huxley
Ros Huxley
137 Victoria Grove
Bridport DT6 3AG
T 01308 423360 F 01308 423360
Quantitive & qualitative research relating to women & the arts. Published 'Women and Jazz'. Working on similar projects relating to women.

Business Support Schemes

Business and Professional Women (BPW) - Poole
S Wilson
2 Marshwood Avenue
Poole BH17 9EP
T 01202 600151
Meets fortnightly on Thurs 7.30 pm at Poole Day Centre, 12a Commercial Road, Poole. To enable business & professional women to achieve their potential in public life, work & any other opportunities available.

Business and Professional Women (BPW) - West Dorset
Mrs Carolyn Golds
8 South Lawns
Bridport DT6 4DS
T 01308 422215
Works for all women's issues within the workplace & for personal issues. Meets on first & third Mon of each month at Lyme

ENGLAND - DORSET

Regis, Bridport & Beaminster in rotation at 7.30. Part of an international federation.

Network for Executive Women
Jane Kistner
9 Charborough Road
Broadstone BH18 8NE
T 01202 697909 F 01202 657465
A local organisation for business & professional women. Meets about once every two months for social activities.

CONTRACEPTION/WELL WOMAN

Bournemouth Nuffield Hospital, The
67 Lansdowne Road
Bournemouth BH1 1RW
T 01202 291866
Well woman screen. Full female health assessment. Phone for up-to-date price lists.

HEALTH

Women in MIND
Cheryl, Coordinator
Mind Office
11 Shelley Road
Boscombe
Bournemouth BH1 4JQ
T 01202 392910
A project of the local branch of MIND, the national mental health association. Self-help groups in Bournemouth & Poole for women who suffer from depression & anxiety. Meet every week for two hours. Free.

LARGER/TALLER WOMEN

Different Approach, The
Desiree Lyon
123 Poole Road
Westbourne
Bournemouth BHH 9BG
T 01202 768070
Women's dress shop. Middle market. Sizes 12-28. Mature & elderly women catered for by trained, helpful, friendly & knowledgeable staff.

LESBIAN AND BISEXUAL

Communicate Services
Jacqui Best
Keswick
Wootton Grove
Sherborne DT9 4DL
T 01935 814369

Lesbian counsellor: relationships, sexual abuse, bereavement. Trained therapist, for women only: lymphatic drainage, massage, assertiveness training. Workshops: celebrating our sexuality & strengths.

PREGNANCY/CHILDBIRTH

Crisis Pregnancy Centre - Bournemouth
Rachel Pringle
32 Palmerstone Road
Boscombe
Bournemouth
T 01202 300750
Mobile 0378 300750. Open Mon, Tue, Thurs, Fri 10 am-12 noon. Otherwise by appt. Free pregnancy testing, counselling & support for women with unplanned pregnancies. Post abortion & miscarriage counselling.

SERVICES

Dorset and Hampshire Heatcare
Norman Hulse
34-36 Sterte Avenue
Poole BH15 2AP
T 01202 667633 F 01202 661345
Insulation & energy efficiency services for low income households in Dorset, Hampshire & Wiltshire.

SEXUAL ABUSE/RAPE CRISIS

East Dorset Rape Crisis Line
P O Box 877
DT9 4DL
T 01202 547445
Helpline open Mon 1-3 pm; Tue 10 am-noon; Wed, Thurs & Fri 8-10 pm; Sat 4-6 pm

RAIL (Rape, Abuse & Incest Line)
Deborah McLennan/Colleen Gallager
12 Porre Hill
Bournemouth BH12 5PS
T 01202 311431
Telephone help line & free professional counselling to those who have suffered abuse. Both women & men operate the helpline service.

SOCIAL

Bridport Ladies Club
Mrs J M Williams, Secretary
8 North Hill Way
Bridport DT6 4JX
T 01308 4233593

ENGLAND - DURHAM

Monthly meeting for women of all ages meeting at the WI Hall, Bridport on second Thurs of month at 7.30 pm (except August). Speakers, outings, events, fundraising.

Dorchester Ladies Circle
Miss Liz Grassby
5 Jubilee Court
Colliton Street
Dorchester DT1 1XH
T 01305 251416
A social club for women aged 18-45. Meets fourth Thurs of each month in the evening.

Gillingham Wives
Helen Covell
5 Jesop Close
Gillingham SP8 4SJ
Monthly evening meetings giving an opportunity for informal discussion & friendship.

Petwyn Ladies' Club
Mrs E Dallison
55 Sarum Avenue
West Moors
Ferndown BH22 0ND
T 01202 892510
Meets at West Moors Memorial Hall, Station Road, West Moors on fourth Wed of each month at 2.15. Speakers, outings & fund raising for a named charity.

SPORTS AND LEISURE

Hampshire Ladies' County Golf Association
Mrs S O'Shea
134 Carbery Avenue
Southbourne
Bournemouth BH6 3LH
T 01202 424651
For women golfers belonging to a Hampshire golf club. Competition run for players with a LGV handicap of 24.

SUPPORT

Poole Women's Group
Veronica Clanchy
42 Winifred Road
Poole BH15 3PU
Women's Liberation Group. Flexible meeting times. Free.

VIOLENCE AGAINST WOMEN

Bournemouth Safer Cities Project
Corinne Brewer
Third Floor (Environmental Health)
Bournemouth Town Hall
St Stephen's Road
Bournemouth BH2 6DY
T 01202 451165 F 01202 451011
Government-funded community safety partnership with NACRO promoting local initiatives to prevent crime & make places safer.

Dorset Women's Outreach Porject
Sue Rothwell
P O Box 41
Weymouth DT4 8YL
T 01305 821111
Supporting survivors of domestic violence in the Dorset Community (excluding Bournemouth & Poole). Helpline & one-to-one counselling & advice.

DURHAM

ARTS AND CRAFTS

Keep Fit and Chatter Box
Muriel Peters
12 Marcia Avenue
Shotton Colliery DH6 2JN
T 0191 526 1671
Meets Mon in St Saviour's church hall to make a number of crafts, to chat & have cups of tea. All that is sold goes towards the church funds. Occasional meals out.

HEALTH

Durham and District Women's Cancer Group
Jo McLaughlin
25 Browning Hill
The Woodlands
Coxhoe
Durham DH6 4HB
T 0191 377 0541
For women with cancer, their friends & family, meeting emotional needs & practical help. Individual telephone counselling & home & hospital visiting. Library. Meets at Committee Room, Dryburn Hospital, Durham.

LEGAL MATTERS

Alison Stott Solicitors
Mrs A M Stott
Aykley Vale Chambers
Durham Road
Aykley Heads

ENGLAND - DURHAM

Durham DH1 5NE
T 0191 384 7210 F 0191 384 4882
alisonstott@ukbusiness.com
Solicitors, undertaking family & childcare, conveyancing & general work. Disabled access. Aim to maintain high quality of service with reasonable fees.

LESBIAN AND BISEXUAL

Gender and Sexuality Alliance (G&SA) - Co Durham
Caroline Bavin
C/o 6-9 Cynthia Street
London N1 9JF
T 0171 498 5965
GayGnSA@aol.com
Local chapter of non-sectarian national group working on the politics of gender/sexuality and their transgression.

PREGNANCY/CHILDBIRTH

Options Pregnancy Crisis Centre
1 Chester Street
Bishop Auckland DL14 7EN
T 01388 450950
Open Tue 6.30-8.30 pm & Fri 11.30 am-1.30 pm. Free pregnancy testing, counselling & support for women with unplanned pregnancies. Post abortion/miscarriage counselling. Phone for appt. 24-hour ansaphone.

RELIGIOUS ORGANISATIONS

Salvation Army Ladies' Fellowship
Mrs I V Ward
3 Grosvenor Terrace
Consett DH8 6BD
T 01207 505649
Meets first Mon of each month 7.30 pm Wheelchair access. Speakers, demonstrations, outings, fundraising, meals out. For young & old to meet in Christian fellowship; encouraging people to attend church.

Wives' Club, The
Mrs V Fisher/Mrs H Robinson
26 Kendrew Close
Newton Aycliffe DL5 4JB
T 01325 318567
Meets in Christian fellowship from all denominations from around the town on Mon 7.30-9.30 pm. Age range 35-80+. Speakers, slide shows, crafts, outings, visits to theatre.

SEXUAL ABUSE/RAPE CRISIS

Durham County Rape Crisis Centre
P O Box 106
Darlington DL3 7YS
T 01325 369933
Telephone helpline open Thurs 7.30-10 pm. Ansaphone at other times. Also face-to-face counselling for women or young girls who have experienced any form of sexual abuse at any time in their lives.

SOCIAL

Chester-Le-Street Ladies' Meeting Point
Mrs M S Cayeill
27 Lywdhurst Avenue
Chester-Le-Street DH3 5AS
T 0191 388 3818
Meets first Wed of each month except Jan & August in Civic Centre, Chester-Le Street at 7.15 pm. Promoting friendship & helping local charities. Speakers, discussions, social events & outings.

Ladies 7.30 Club
Mrs E Watson, Secretary
1 Western Terrace North
Murton
Seaham SR7 9AZ
T 0191 526 1690
Meets Mon 7.30 at Fellowship Room of St Paul's Methodist Church, Murton. Speakers, demonstrations, musical evenings, etc. Supports church & charities. Primarily Methodist but members from other churches.

Shotley Bridge Women's Forum
Mrs D Greves
3 Sherwood Close
Shotley Bridge
Consett DH8 0TX
T 01207 509566
Meets on second & fourth Tue of every month during term time in each other's houses. Talks, discussions, outings, treasure hunt, barbecue, Christmas party. No age limit.

St Aidan's Ladies' Club, Blackhill
Mrs A M Howe
1 Derwent Mews
Blackhill
Consett DH8 8TU
T 01207 502127
Social group with interests in local matters, the environment, crafts & charities. Meets on first & third Thurs of each month (not August)

at Community Centre, Derwent Street,
Blackhill at 7.15. Speakers.

Support

Women's Royal Voluntary Service - North East Division
1st Floor
Enterprise House
Valley Street
Darlington DL1 1GY
T 01325 465848 F 01325 381707
Services are divided into family, hospital, food & emergency services. They include meals on wheels, hospital shops, tea & coffee bars, contact centres, family holidays & lunch clubs.

Violence against women

East Durham Safer Cities Project
Tony Hodgson
Yoden House
30 Yoden Way
Peterlee SR8 1AL
T 0191 586 5885 F 0191 586 0266
Government-funded community safety partnership with NACRO promoting local initiatives to prevent crime & make places safer.

Essex

Alternative therapies

Joyrani Health Centre
34 Cleveland Road
South Woodford E18 2AL
T 0181 530 11146
Hypnotherapy; waterbirths.

Arts and Crafts

London Writers' Circle
Margaret Owen
15 Lower Park Road
Loughton IG20 4NB
Monthly talks at the Conway Hall, Red Lion Square, Holborn WC1 on fourth Mon of each month 6.30. Group meeting for short stories, articles & poetry also held monthly.

Contraception/Well woman

Essex Nuffield Hospital, The
Shenfield Road
Brentwood CM15 8EH
T 01277 263263
Well woman screen. Full female health assessment. Phone for up-to-date price lists.

Harlow Well Women Centre
Vivienne Wachenje, Centre Manager
Latton Bush Centre
Southern Way
Harlow CM18 7BL
T 01279 411330
Helping women to help themselves to health via information, advice, support groups. Health adviser sessions & individual counselling.

Education

BFWG - Colchester & District Association
Elisabeth Baines
37 Valley Road
Wivenhoe
Colchester CO7 9LZ
T 01206 823523
Usually meets on second Tue of month at 8 pm in members' homes. National networks of BFWG provide links for those in each profession & for those with similar interests.

British Federation of Women Graduates - Brentwood & Chelmsford
Mrs A Dwyer-Joyce
176 Hanging Hill Lane
Hutton CM13 2HE
T 01277 222883
Monthly meetings usually held in the evenings in members' homes.

Equal opps

Fair Play Eastern Region
Melanie Newton
Essex Returners' Unit
Abacus Ctr, Chelmsford College
Moulsham Street
Chelmsford CM2 0JG
T 01245 280949 F 01245 280949
Positive action equalities project. Tackling barriers facing women in eonomic & social life. Aims to encourage competitiveness, equality of opportunity & partnerships.

Finance

Christine Sharpe
Christine Sharpe
Maypole Close
Saffron Walden CB11 4DB
T 01799 527531 F 01799 521977
Accountant & financial adviser. Specialises in being a 'GP' in dealing with small businesses that don't have their own financial adviser.

ENGLAND - ESSEX

GIRLS/YOUNG WOMEN

Young People's Counselling Service
Jan Carter
Brescia House
3 Eastfield Road
Brentwood CM14 4HB
T 01277 830831
Counselling for young people of both sexes aged 13-25 on issues such as relationships, family breakdown, separation, bullying, drug abuse, depression, etc. Pre- & post abortion counselling. Referrals.

HEALTH

Women's Support Project
Sheila
C/o South Essex Rape & Incest Centre
The Mall
West Street
Grays RM17 6LL
T 01375 381322 F 01375 381322
tcvs.tc@gtnet.gov.uk
Service run for women by women providing sexual health information.

LARGER/TALLER WOMEN

Long Tall Sally
14 Short Wyre Street
Colchester CO1 1LN
T 01206 579084
Clothes for the taller woman sizes 12-20.
Open Mon-Sat 9.30 am-5.30 pm.

Robita Fashions
Mrs Rita Thorn
519 London Road
Westcliff-on-Sea SS0 9LJ
T 01702 334266
Open Mon, Tue, Thurs, Fri, Sat 9.30 am-5 pm. Bright & welcoming large showroom displaying fashions from UK, Germany, Finland, Sweden & Denmark for women. Size range 12-28, price range medium-high.

Sized Up
Mrs J Stock
11 Headingham Road
Halstead CO9 2DA
T 01787 472633
Selling larger-sized ladies' fashion (14-26) in high quality English & continental styles. Open Mon, Tue, Thurs, Fri, Sat 10 am-4 pm or by appointment.

MEDIA

Take One
Mena Digings
12 Haven Avenue
Holland On Sea OO13 5TX
T 01255 812706 F 01255 812706
mena@takeone.keme.co.uk
Making film, video & multi-media available/accessible to children, young people & women. Workshops, activities & events organised by negotiation. Media research.

PREGNANCY/CHILDBIRTH

Crisis Pregnancy Centre - Dovercourt
Frances Langlands
7 The Ridgeway
Dovercourt CO12 4AT
T 01255 508492
Open 1st & 3rd Thurs of each month 10 am-12 noon. Offers a listening ear to women who are pregnant or those connected with a pregnancy. No pregnancy testing. Post abortion & miscarriage counselling.

Lighthouse Family Trust
Mackmurdo House
Springfield Road
Chelmsford
T 01245 494838
Free pregnancy testing, counselling & support for women with unplanned pregnancies. Post abortion, still birth & miscarriage counselling available.

SEXUAL ABUSE/RAPE CRISIS

Chelmsford Rape and Sexual Abuse Counselling Centre
Mary-Ann Taylor
P O Box 566
Chelmsford CM6 3EU
T 01245 356260
Helpline: 01245 492123. Telephone, face-to-face counselling for any women or girl who has been sexually abused, recently or in the past. Telephone line open Tue & Fri 7.30-9.30 pm. Face-to-face by appt.

Colchester Rape Crisis
P O Box 540
Colchester CO3 3TX
T 01206 769795
Helpline (as above) open Wed 7.30-9.30 pm & Sun 2-4 pm. For women & girls who have suffered rape or other sexual assault. Run by women for women.

South Essex Rape and Incest Centre
Sheila
The Hall
West Street
Grays RM17 6LL
T 01375 381322 F 01375 381322
tcus.tc@gtnet.gov.uk
Free, confidential support & counselling service for women & girls over aged 13 who are suffering/ have suffered sexual violence. Crisis line 01375 380609 open Tue 8-10 pm, Thurs 12-4 pm & Fri 10-12 pm

Southend Rape and Sexual Abuse Support Line
15 Weston Road
Southend on Sea SS1 1AS
T 01702 347933
Open Fri 12-2.30 pm & Tue 7-10 pm. 24-hour ansaphone. Face-to-face counselling & group work & telephone helpline for women who have been raped or sexually abused.

SPORTS AND LEISURE

Essex Women's Hockey Association
Miss P Nisbet
Great Blunts
Stock
Ingatestone CM4 9PL
T 01277 840285

Women's Adventure Project
Sheila
C/o South Essex Rape & Incest Centre
The Mall
West Street
Grays RM17 6LL
T 01375 381322 F 01375 381322
tcvs.tc@gtnet.gov.uk
Women only outdoor activities.

GLOUCESTERSHIRE

CHILD CARE AND FAMILY

Gloucestershire Childminding Association
Mrs Shirley Crandon
30 Hillview Drive
Hucclecote
Gloucester GL3 3LL
T 01452 610376

CONTRACEPTION/WELL WOMAN

Cinderford Family Planning Clinic
The Health Centre
Cinderford GL14 2AN
T 01594 822279
Free contraceptive advice & supplies & well woman clinics on Thurs 5.30-7.30 pm. All forms of contraception/free condoms; pregnancy testing; cytology (smear tests); menstrual problems; etc.

Coleford Family Planning Clinic
The Health Centre
Coleford GL16 8RH
T 01594 832567
Free contraceptive advice & supplies & well woman clinics Tue 9-11.30 am (1st Tue 1-3 pm); Fri 4-6 pm. All forms of contraception/free condoms; pregnancy testing; cytology (smear tests); etc.

Cotswold Nuffield Hospital, The
Talbot Road
Cheltenham GL51 6QA
T 01242 232351
Well woman screen. Full female health assessment. Phone for up-to-date price lists.

Dursley Family Planning Clinic
Sandpits Clinic
Norman Hill
Dursley GL11 5QF
T 01453 542550
Free contraceptive advice & supplies & well woman clinics on Mon & Tue 6-8 pm. All forms of contraception/free condoms; pregnancy testing; cytology (smear tests); menstrual problems; menopausal problems; etc.

Gloucester Family Planning Clinic
Hope House
Gloucester Royal Hospital
Great Western Road
Gloucester GL1 3NN
T 01452 394201
Free contraceptive advice & supplies & well woman clinics On Mon 10 am-12 pm & 5-7 pm; Tue 12-2 pm; Wed 5-7 pm; Thurs 3.30-5.30 pm; Fri 1-3 pm. All methods of birth control/free condoms; etc.

Lydney Family Planning Clinic
Physiotherapy Department
Lydney Hospital
Lydney GL15 5JS
T 01594 842033
Free contraceptive advice & supplies & well woman clinics on Mon 6-8 pm. All forms of contraception/free condoms; pregnancy testing/cytology (smear tests); menstrual problems; menopausal problems; etc.

ENGLAND - GLOUCESTERSHIRE

Stonehouse Family Planning Clinic
The Health Clinic
High Street
Stonehouse GL10 2NG
T 01453 822622
Free contraceptive advice & supplies & well woman clinics on 2nd, 4th & 5th Tue of each month 5.45-7.30 pm. Phone during clinic hours. All forms of contraception/free condoms; pregancy testing; etc.

Stroud Family Planning Clinic
Beeches Green Health Centre
Stroud GL5 4BH
T 01453 766331
Free contraceptive advice & supplies & well woman clinics. Clinics on Thurs 11.30 am-1.30 pm & 5.45-7.30 pm. All methods of contraception & free condoms; pregnancy testing; cytology (smear tests); etc.

Wotton-Under-Edge Family Planning Clinic
Symn Lane Clinic
Wotton-Under-Edge GL12 7BD
T 01453 842236
Free contraceptive advice & supplies & well woman clinics. Clinics on 1st & 3rd Tue of each month. Phone between 9 am-12 noon. All forms of contraception/free condoms; pregnancy testing; etc.

EDUCATION

Cotswold Association of Women Graduates
Mrs H M Sackett
Upland House
Chalford Hill
Stroud GL6 8QF
T 01453 883072
Aiming to provide, in the Cotswold area, friendship with women of like mind & a variety of experience. We give help to local girls going into higher education. Meetings are on a variety of topics.

ETHNIC MINORITIES

Gloucestershire Chinese Women's Guild
Mew Ning Chan-Edmead
First Floor
75-81 Eastgate Street
Gloucester GL1 1PN
T 01452 332088
Open Mon-Fri 12-4 pm. For urgent needs phone for appointment any time. Home visiting; advocacy; transportation; interpretation service; advice on benefits. Cantonese, Hakka, Mandarin & English spoken.

HEALTH

Forest Breast Cancer Support Group
Liz Knowles
Macmillan Centre
Belle Vue Centre
Cinderford GL14 2AB
T 01594 826368 F 01594 824752
Meets last Wed of each month at above address 6.30-8 pm. Support, information, advice. An opportunity for women with breast cancer to meet & discuss relevant issues.

South Gloucestershire Cancer Support Group
Mrs Lorraine Wilkinson
24a Everlands
Cam
Dursley GL11 5NL
T 01453 542973
Meetings held on first Wed of each month at Dryleaze House, Wotton-Under-Edge 2-4 pm. Support for cancer patients & their relatives. Meeting others in a similar position. Talks, leaflets, social evenings.

LARGER/TALLER WOMEN

Extra Special
Jean Cross
2 Chipping Court
Tetbury GL8 8ES
T 01666 505474 F 01666 505474
Open Mon-Sat 9.30-5 pm. Fashion retail specialising in large sizes (16-30). Aiming to give a wide choice of quality fashionable clothes to the larger women - a forgotten area in fashion retailing generally.

Long Tall Sally
32 Cambray Place
Cheltenham GL50 1JP
T 01242 243001
Clothes for the taller woman sizes 12-20.
Open Mon-Sat 9.30 am-5.30 pm.

PHOTOGRAPHY

Abbey Studios
Deborah Bristow
5 Whitworth Road
Querns Business Centre
Cirencester GL7 1RT
T 01285 653069 F 01285 622364

ENGLAND - GLOUCESTERSHIRE

Professional photographic studio. Weddings, portraits, etc.

Sand Partnership, The
Sandra Ireland
The Rectory
Avening GL8 8PE
T 01453 835466 F 01453 835466
zand2000@aol.com
Freelance photography for publishing companies. Botanical still life, architecture, gardens, abstracts & illustration work.

Politics

Cotswold Ladies' Luncheon Club
Mrs E M Finlayson, Secretary
2 Moorcourt Drive
Cheltenham GL52 2QL
T 01242 528192
Affiliated to the Conservative Association. Lunches 7 times per year at the Carlton hotel in Cheltenham on first Thurs of each month, except for May meeting which is held on second Thurs.

Pregnancy/Childbirth

Cirencester Pregnancy Crisis Centre
The Fountain
Bigham House
1 Dyer Street
Cirencester GL7 2PP
T 01285 640445
24-hour ansaphone checked regularly. Free pregnancy testing, counselling & support for women with unplanned pregnancies. Post abortion & miscarriage counselling.

Crisis Pregnancy Centre - Gloucester
29a Spa Road
Gloucester GL1 1VY
Open Mon 12-1 pm; Tue 6-7 pm; Wed 11.30 am-12.30 pm; Fri 2-3 pm. Free pregnancy testing, counselling & support for women with unplanned pregnancies. Post abortion & miscarriage counselling.

Forest Pregnancy Crisis Care
Janet Adams
Upper Room
1 Woodside Street
Cinderford GL14 2NL
T 01594 824474
Phone for times of opening. 24-hour ansaphone. No appt necessary. Free pregnancy testing & confidential counselling & support for any woman with an unplanned pregancy. Post abortion & miscarriage counselling.

Gloucester Fertility Support Group
Hope House
Gloucester Royal Hospital
Great Western Road
Gloucester GL1 3NN
Meets on second Thurs alternate months at above address 7-9 pm. Providing an opportunity for people in a similar position to meet informally & discuss relevant issues. Speakers. Offers support to new couples.

Services

Gloucester and Wiltshire Heatcare
Tony Sproston
Unit 17
Lansdowne Insudstrial Estate
Gloucester Road
Cheltenham GL51 8PL
T 01242 238838 F 01242 238868
Insulation & energy efficiency services for low income households in Gloucestershire & Wiltshire.

Zebra
Mary Wright
37 Copt Elm Road
Charlton Kings
Cheltenham GL53 8AG
T 01242 244007 F 01242 244027
zebra@coptelm.demon.co.uk
Graphic design consultancy, specialising in typographic design, logos, brochures, annual reports, leaflets, books.

Sexual Abuse/Rape Crisis

Gloucestershire Rape Crisis Centre
Candice
P O Box 16
Gloucester GL4 0RU
T 01452 526770
Free, confidential support, information, counselling to women/girls who have been raped/sexually assaulted in their lives. Phone answered by women Mon, Tue, Wed, Fri 7.30-8.30 pm; Thurs 11.30 am-12.30 pm

Kinergy
41 Britannia Road
Kingswood BS15 2BG
T 0117 908 7712
Free counselling service for women living in south Gloucestershire who have been

ENGLAND - HAMPSHIRE & ISLE OF WIGHT

sexually abused or raped. Open Tue 10 am-1.30 pm & Thurs 6.30-9 pm.

TRAINING
Springboard Consultancy, The
Liz Willis or Jenny Daisley
P O Box 69
Stroud GL5 5EE
T 01453 878540 F 01453 872363
100732.1462@compuserve.com
Women's training & development consultancy. Offers wide range of training & development activities for employers & women from all sectors. Springboard Programme & workbook.

HAMPSHIRE & ISLE OF WIGHT

ACCOMMODATION
Andover Crisis and Support Centre
the staff team
17 New Street
Andover SP10 1EL
T 01264 366122
Hostel offers medium-term accommodation (to six months) for women with/without children needing supportive environment. Staffed 24 hours. Drop-in open six days a week: crisis counselling, pregnancy testing.

Portsmouth Housing Trust
Helen Brafield, Service Manager
Homelessness
C/0 247 Fratton Road
Fratton
Portsmouth PO1 5PA
T 01705 291155 F 01705 814725
HBRAFIEL@pha.co.uk
The housing trust manages a women's refuge & move-on, as well as two projects for single homeless women & a 24-hour domestic violence helpline.

Portsmouth Women's Refuge Service
Helen Brafield, Service Manager
Homelessness
C/o 247 Fratton Road
Fratton
Portsmouth PO1 5PA
T 01705 291155 F 01705 814725
HBRAFIEL@pha.co.uk
The refuge provides temporary accommodation to women & children escaping domestic violence.

Shakti-Bhavan
Kish Bhatti-Sinclair
C/o Department of Social Work Studies
University of Southampton
Highfield
Southampton SO17 1BJ
T 01703 592022 F 01703 581156
KBS@soc.sci
A refuge project providing for the housing & related needs of Asian women & children affected by domestic violence & abuse.

Young Women's Christian Association (YWCA)
Mrs J O'Brien
Bellvue Road
Southampton SO15 2YE
T 01703 227155
66 bed hostel for women. Direct access. No drink or drugs.

ARMED FORCES
Ex Wrens Association
Mrs V Reeves
4 Wellington Grove
Porchester PO16 9RX
T 01705 791583
Meets third Tue of each month 7-9 pm at Porchester Community Centre, Westlands Grove, Porchester.

Women's Royal Army Corps Association - Hampshire
Miss Doreen Pledge
Flat One
47 Blenheim Avenue
Highfield
Southampton SO17 1DQ
T 01703 556069
Meets first Wed of each month at the Ex-Servicemen's Club, Archers Road, Southampton, 7.30 pm. Also area reunions. To keep serving & ex-serving women in touch & to help them in times of hardship & trouble.

ARTS AND CRAFTS
Dot To Dot
Anna Potten
Paulsgrove Community Centre
Marsden Road
Paulsgrove
Portsmouth PO6 4JB
T 01705 200317
Community arts organisation committed to working with people who would not otherwise have access to the arts. Much of our work is with women & children. Work is with groups & free in our revenue-funded areas.

ENGLAND - HAMPSHIRE & ISLE OF WIGHT

Romsey Machine Knitting Club
Maureen Lord
8 High Firs Road
Romsey SO51 5PZ
T 01794 513798
Meets third Tue of each month (except December) 7.30 in lounge at Gainsborough court, Willis Avenue, North Baddesley. Beginners to very experienced members, using Japanese/European machines, etc.

Solent Singers
Sandra Hann, Secretary
34 Warsash Road
Warsash
Southampton SO31 9HZ
T 01489 574702
Solent singers is a women's choir based at Warsash. Many successes in local music festivals. Performs concerts. Has raised thousands of pounds for charities.

BUSINESS SUPPORT SCHEMES

Business and Professional Women (BPW) - New Milton
Evelyn Lamb
Newlands
Christchurch Road
New Milton BH25 6QQ
T 01425 613593
Meets on first & third Tue of each month at 7.30 pm at the Community Centre, Osborne Road, New Milton, Hampshire.

Business and Professional Women (BPW) - Portsmouth
Mrs Mavis D Burton
Portsmouth Club
Redmile
6 Abbey Hill
Netley Abbey SO31 5FB
T 01703 453228
Meets at Sorrell Dial, Prince Albert Road, Southsea, Hampshire on second & fourth Thurs of each month (not August) at 7.30 pm. Wheelchair access. An organisation for working women.

Business and Professional Women (BPW) - Southampton
Miss Doreen Pledge
Flat One
47 Blenheim Avenue
Highfield
Southampton SO17 1DQ
T 01703 556069

Meets second & fourth Mon of each month at different venues. Phone for details 7.30 onwards. Enabling business & professional women to achieve their full potential, etc.

CONTRACEPTION/WELL WOMAN

Wessex Nuffield Hospital, The
Winchester Road
Chandler's Ford
Eastleigh SO53 2DW
T 01703 266377
Well woman screen. Full female health assessment. Phone for up-to-date price lists.

COUNSELLING AND THERAPY

Counselling and Therapy Centre for Women
Sally Saunders
168 Northam Road
Southampton SO14 0QF
T 01703 233763 F 01703 233763
Aims to provide an easily accessible low-cost counselling & therapy service for women. Sessions are daytime or evenings during the week.

Susan Jane Hale
Sue Hale
Greenacres
SO11 1PR
T 01264 889260
Mediation for divorce, counselling, psychotherpay, relationahips, bereavement, stress, anger, abuse. For indlviduals, couples, family, workshops, courses.

EDUCATION

Southampton Association of Women Graduates
Mrs F Attwood
22 Kellett Road
Southampton SO15 7PR
T 01703 773221
For friendship; promoting the interests of women; supporting & encouraging women in all their endeavours.

GIRLS/YOUNG WOMEN

Hampshire County Council - The Centre
Sue Willis
Tunstall Road
Thornhill
Southampton SO19 6RD
T 01703 402909

Young women aged 16-21 with/without children meet in the Centre on Fri 10 am-3 pm supported by youth workers. Creche. Providing an opportunity for women to learn new skills, eg self-defence, using a video.

Health

Cancer Care Society - Romsey Centre
Kim Fielder
Jane Scarth House
39 The Hundred
Romsey SO51 8GE
T 01794 830374
For cancer patients, family & friends. Open Mon-Fri 10 am-5 pm & Sat mornings. Befriending, free, confidential counselling, complementary therapies, group meetings, sitting service, relaxation, car service.

Larger/Taller Women

Long Tall Sally
80-81 High Street
Winchester SO23 9AP
T 01962 840058
Clothes for the taller woman sizes 12-20. Open Mon-Sat 9.30 am-5.30 pm.

Libraries/Archives

Billie Love Historical Collection
Billie Love and Anna Shepherd
3 Winton Street
Ryde
Isle of Wight PO33 2BX
T 01983 812572   F 01983 811164
Historical picture library.

Older Women

Care Alternatives
5 High Street
Sandown
Isle of Wight PO36 8DA
T 01983 402069   F 01983 408436
Provides flexible care at home for elderly or disabled people. Can assist with both personal care & domestic tasks. Care workers do induction training & are thoroughly vetted.

Lychpit Ladies' Group
Norma Tarling, Secretary
14 Little Fallow
Old Basing
Basingstoke RG24 8UN
T 01256 818534

A social group of older women aged 50-65 who have mostly moved into this 'newish' area to be nearer family. Meets second Wed in each month 2-4 pm. Speakers, quizzes, craft days, etc.

Peace Groups

Women's Aid to Former Yugoslavia
Sian Jones
20 Tennyson Road
Portswood
Southampton SO17 2GW
T 01703 551094   F 01703 554434
waty@gn.apc.org
A women's anti-war non-sectarian aid group, providing humanitarian aid to refugees & displaced women in former Yugoslavi; supporting refugee groups & women's projects; working with women refugees.

Photography

Billie Love
Miss Billie Love
3 Winton Street
Ryde
Isle of Wight PO33 2BX
T 01983 812572   F 01983 811164
Photographer supplying illustrations for books, magazines & television. Picture librarian.

Places to Stay and Eat

Florida
Christine O'Brien/Wendy King
17 Cliff Path
Lake
Isle of Wight PO36 8PL
T 01983 408474   F 01983 408474
A guest house catering exclusively for women. All rooms are heated. Colour TV, hairdryer, tea/coffee-making facilities. Licensed bar, residents' car park. Open all year. Phone for up-to-date price list.

Loft Restaurant, The
Jules Cranfield and Alex Ross
The Edge
Compton Walk
Southampton SO14 0BH
T 01703 366163   F 01703 630186
Open Mon-Fri 11 am-11 pm & 11 am-2 am at weekends. Women-only events. Nightclub available for hire. Women-only discos Sat night with own in-house DJ. Also book launches, birthday parties, etc.

Politics

European Union of Women
Miss Jacquie Welch, Chairman
14 Hiltingbury Road
Chandler's Ford
Eastleigh SO53 5ST
T 01703 252574 F 01703 274382
Political group of women, Conservative paid-up members, pro-Europe & promoting links with all Europe. Exhange visits, particularly with women from former Eastern bloc. Fundraising, speakers, social functions.

Pregnancy/Childbirth

Active Birth Classes, Winchester
Marion Symes
4 Webster Road
Teg Down
Winchester SO22 5NT
T 01962 864823
Six-week courses, Wed afternoon or Thurs Evening. Emphasis on natural ways of coping with labour & includes yoga-based stretching, breathing & relaxation techniques.

Alton Pregnancy Crisis Centre
8 Normandy Street
Alton GU34 1BX
T 01420 541620
Open Fri 10 am-1 pm 24-hour ansaphone. A counsellor all available to phone on Tue 10 am-1 pm. Free pregnancy testing, free & confidential counselling, practical support & post-abortion counselling.

Borders Birth Practice, The
Gwyneth Watts
2 Lawford Crescent
Yately GU46 7JU
T 01252 879723
Provides independent midwifery services.

Bordon Pregnancy Crisis Centre
Rear of 16 Chalet Hill
Borden GU35 0TQ
T 01420 475646
Office open Mon & Thurs 11 am-2 p.m, or 24-hour ansaphone. An appt can be made any time by request. Free pregnancy testing & confidential counselling & support for any woman with an unplanned pregnancy.

Crisis Pregnancy Centre - Gosport
Mrs G Payce
2 Bemisters Lane
Gosport
T 01329 221795
Helpline open Mon-Fri 9 am-3 pm. Phone for an appt. 24-hour ansaphone. Free pregnancy testing, counselling & support for women with unplanned pregnancies. Post-abortion & miscarriage counselling.

Firgrove Crisis Pregnancy Centre
107 Firgrove Road
Southampton SO15 3ET
T 01703 783134
Open Mon, Tue, Wed & Fri 9.30 am-2.30 pm. Free pregnancy testing, counselling & support for women with unplanned pregnancies. Post abortion & miscarriage counselling.

National Childbirth Trust - Portsmouth & Southsea branch
Sue Cregan
143 Langstone Road
Copnor
Portsmouth PO3 6BT
T 01705 730393
Information about pregnancy, childbirth & early parenthood. Ante-natal classes. Breastfeeding counsellors, postnatal support including postnatal exercise & discussion classes.

National Childbirth Trust - Southampton branch
Amanda Hames
10 Bankside
Southampton SO18 2JW
T 01703 480710 F 01703 480710
Breastfeeding counsellor, providing information & support on breastfeeding. Also a breast pump agent, providing an electric breast pump hire scheme.

Wessex Maternity Centre
Kate Walmsley
Mansbridge Road
West End
Southampton SO30 3SF
T 01703 464721 F 01703 470735
Pre- & post natal care. Birth at the Maternity Home. Classes, medical insurance, midwifery & medical care, complementary/alternative therapies. Phone for up-to-date price list. (NB not part of NHS.)

ENGLAND - HAMPSHIRE & ISLE OF WIGHT

RELIGIOUS ORGANISATIONS

Basingstoke & Deane Bahai Community Women's Group
Zarin Hainsworth Fadaei
16 Horwood Gardens
Basingstoke RG21 3NR
T 01256 350187
Meets Tue 10 am-12 noon; also evening meetings on Wed 8 pm. Offers friendship & regular meeting for any woman interested in life issues, especially from a spiritual point of view. Free.

Ropley Women's Fellowship
Mrs A Wood, Secretary
4 Rowdell Cottages
Ropley
Alresford SO24 OBU
T 01962 772613

Woman's Bright Hour
Mrs E E Deverill
154 King's Road
Gosport PO12 1PZ
T 01075 584091
Ladies' meeting attached to Stoke Road Baptist Church, Stoke Road, Gosport, held to bring the gospel to any woman, whether or not a church goer. Meets at the church Mon 2.30. Hymns, scripture reading, etc.

Women's Fellowship - Hedge End Methodist Church
Miss H Rhodes
38 Monarch Way
West End
Southampton SO30 3JQ
T 01703 360196
Meets on Wed 2.30-3.45 pm in hall of Methodist Church, St John's Road, Hedge End. Wheelchair accessible. Christian organisation formed to bring women together for friendship & awareness of Christian values.

SEXUAL ABUSE/RAPE CRISIS

Andover Rape Crisis Helpline (ARCH)
Philippa King
P O Box 1608
Andover
T 01264 336222
Helpline open Tue 7-9 pm & Sat 2-4 pm. Otherwise ansaphone. Counselling service for victims of sexual abuse. Telephone or face-to-face counselling available.

Basingstoke Rape & Sexual Abuse Centre
Jan Ross
T 01256 843810
Crisis line: 01256 843810. Information, support, accompanying to court, F-to-F telephone/counselling for those affected by or surviving sexual violence. Female/male crisis line open Tue, Wed, Thurs 7-10 pm

Parasol
Mrs Ann Dibden
Desborough House
1 Desborough Road
Eastleigh SO50 5NY
T 01703 615729 F 01703 629182
For women who have been sexually abused.

Portsmouth Area Rape Crisis
P O Box 3
Portsmouth
T 01705 669513 F 01705 669512
Offers a free, confidential counselling service for women who have been raped &/or sexually abused at any time in their lives. Women's crisis line 01705 669511. (A similar service provided to men.)

Rapport
Caroline Love
T 01705 861675
Counselling for women by experienced volunteer counsellors covering the south east area of England. For women who have been sexually abused & who have children of their own. Phone Mon-Wed 9 am-5 pm.

Southampton Rape Crisis and Sexual Abuse Counselling Service
Rose/Jo
P O Box 50
Head Post Office
High Street
Southampton
T 01703 701213
Helpline open Sun & Mon 7-10 pm, Tue 10 am-1 pm, Thurs 1-4 pm. Face to face counselling by appt. Black/Asian counsellors available. Free services. For women/girls who have been sexually assaulted/abused.

SOCIAL

Anton Ladies' Group
Mrs J A Taylor
22 Conholt Road
Andover SO10 2HR
T 01264 352962

Meets 7.30-9.30 pm in Anton Infants' School, usually on first Tue of each month. Social meetings, speakers, garden party, skittles, etc.

Ashley Wives
Lynda Henderson
2 St John's Road
Bashley
New Milton BH25 6SB
T 01425 628181
Meets on first Wed of each month at St Peter's Church, Ashley Common Road, Ashley, New Milton. Speakers, quizzes, demonstrations, outings.

Cameo at Romsey
Mrs Marian Gibbs
Lugano
113 Botley Road
Romsey SO51 5RQ
T 01794 512719
Meets on third Tue of each month at Crossfield Hall, Romsey. Coach trips, coffee mornings, barbecue, strawberry teas. Fundraising for charities.

Cameo in Southampton
Mrs Jean Bot, Secretary
36 Bitterne Road West
Bitterne Manor
Southampton SO18 1AP
T 01703 224175
Meets on Third Wed of each month 7.30 pm in the Founder's Room, La Sainte Union College of Further Education, The Avenue, Southampton SO17 1BG; 01703 228761. A social group for ladies.

Cameo in Waterlooville
Mrs Jacqueline Robbins
34 Ferndale
Waterlooville PO7 7PA
T 01705 262619
Speakers, outings, theatre trips. Good laughs; we enjoy ourselves. Go to France & meet up with other women's groups. Meets in Community Centre on Third Tue of each month at 10 am Fundraising for charities.

Chandlers Ford Widows' Social Club
Mrs E Lidstone
7 Pitmore Close
Allbrook
Eastleigh SO50 4JL
T 01703 269101

Meets second Thurs of each month for cup of tea, chat & speakers or entertainment. Outings. Aim is to give companionship & friendship to widows.

Chiltern Ladies
Mrs H Boyling
223 Kenilworth Road
Windlebury 3
Basingstoke RG23 8JP
T 01256 420325
Weekly meetings on Wed 8 pm (except school holidays) at Worting Junior School, Chiltern Way, Basingstoke, Hampshire. Speakers once a month, quizzes, discussions, keep fit, etc.

Doyle Ladies' Club
Mrs R Corless, Hon Sec
7 Bursledon Road
Purbrook
Waterlooville PO7 5NJ
T 01705 256342
Meets Wed (Except August & Christmas) 7.30 pm at Oddfellows' Hall, 356 London Road, North End, Portsmouth. Parties, outings, talks, slide shows. Raffle each week. Meetings end about 9.15 pm

Dragon Ladies' Club
Mrs M R Tomlinson
14 Cheshire Way
Southbourne
Emsworth PO10 8PU
T 01234 374569
Meets on second Mon of each month in Southbourne Village Hall, First Avenue, Southbourne, Emsworth 7.30 pm. Skittles, barbecues, outings, coach trips, cultural & educational activities.

Inner Wheel Club of Andover
Mrs Dee Humphries
1 St Mary's Meadow
Abbotts Hill
Little Ann
Andover SO11 7SZ
T 01264 710803
Meets once a month, alternating between a lunch & evening meeting. Aim is friendship, fellowship & fun. Fund raising.

Locks Heath Wives
Mrs Maureen Jarvis
47 Laurel Road
Locks Heath
Southampton SO31 6QG

ENGLAND - HAMPSHIRE & ISLE OF WIGHT

T 01489 583932
Friendly, informal group meets at St John's Church Hall, Locks Heath Park Road, Locks Heath, Southampton 1st & 3rd Mon of each month 7.30 pm. Speakers, beetle drives, quizz nights, outings. Fundraising

Mums' Morning
Pip Warner and Nessie Scales
98 Sussex Street
Winchester SO23 8TH
T 01962 840518

Shedfield Parish Wives
Linda Hobley
Loyes
Upper Church Road
Shedfield
Southampton SO32 2JB
T 01329 833765 F 01329 833765
For women of all ages. Meets once a month usually on first Wed of each month 8-10 pm in village reading room. Speakers & theme evenings on eg alternative therapies, make up, car maintenance.

St Thomas' Wives' Club
Mrs Penny Fergus
232 Elson Road
Elson
Gosport PO12 4AO
Women's group open to all women. Speakers, social afternoons, local fundraising events. Meets Wed 1.30-3 pm. Creche.

SPORTS AND LEISURE

Atherley Bowling Club
Marion Collins
1 Trearnan Close
Millbrook
Southampton SO16 4NH
T 01703 787981
Ladies meet Tue 2 pm for outdoor bowling & cups of tea. Competitions. Indoor bowling green open 8 am-10 pm.

Banister Park Bowling Club
Mrs H Schwodler, Ladies' Secretary
C/o Banister Park Bowling Club
Stoneham Lane
Eastleigh SO50 9HT
T 01703 643477
Indoor & outdoor bowling club. There is a separate ladies' bowling section - contact Mrs Schwodler (home phone number 01703 601510). Teaching arrangement for under 17s & disabled bowlers.

Hamble Old Girls' Hockey Club
Jasmine Bennett
21 Hunt Avenue
Netley Abbey
Southampton SO31 5BD
T 01703 561170
Hampshire 3rd division club, playing in the Hants league. All ages welcome. Runs with Hamble Old Boys. Own club house & Astro pitch, on Hamble school campus site.

Hampshire Women's Cricket Association
Sharon Eyers
Flat 2
139 Avenue Road
Portswood
Southampton SO14 6BD
T 01703 397705
Aims to offer all women & girls an opportunity to play cricket & progress according to their own abilities.

Hampshire Women's Hockey Association
Mrs Sue Barnett
110 Weston Lane
Woolston
Southampton SO19 9HG
T 01703 449633
County member of the English Hockey Association.

Moneyfield Ladies' Bowls Club
Mrs S Eaton
Threeways' Court Lane
Cosham
Portsmouth PO6 2LG
T 01705 375443
Play on Copnor Green, Tangiers Road, Portsmouth.

Portsmouth FC Ladies
Di Summers
78 Stamsaaw Road
Portsmouth PO2 8LT
T 01705 617139 F 01705 618769
Women's/girls' football club, ages from 8 onwards. Four teams all playing league football. U15, U16, First Team & Reserve Team. Continued development of girls'/women's football.

Southampton Running Sisters
Ann Dukes
15 Bassett Row
Bassett
Southampton SO16 7FT
T 01703 768643
Running club for women of all levels of ability. Main club night Wed 7 pm at Southampton Institute. Ten-week beginners course held annually starting first week in May.

Southsea Castle Women's Bowling Club
Mrs C Reynolds
298 Fawcett Road
Southsea PO4 0LG
T 01705 818728
Share three bowling greens at Southsea Castle with the men's bowling club.

SUPPORT

Portsmouth Harmony Group
Mrs Jagjit Frewall
Social Service Department
Merefield House
Nutfield Place
Portsmouth PO1 4J2
T 01705 839111 F 01705 875503
SS05JG@hanst.gov.uk
To promote cultural identity for women from ethnic minority backgrounds. Meets Thurs 12.30-3 pm at Wesby Centre, 128 Fratten Road, Portsmouth. Creche. Discussions on women's health issues, etc.

Women Hurt By Abortion
Tracy Joynes
42 Chessel Avenue
Southampton SO19 4DX
T 01703 394890
Provides a phone line & referral to therapy for any woman distressed or confused by her own or some other woman's abortion.

HEREFORD & WORCESTERSHIRE

ACCOMMODATION

Droitwich Women's Refuge
Dr J N Bulman, Committee Chair
P O Box 23
Droitwich WR9
T 01905 797537

ALTERNATIVE THERAPIES

Christina Coole Natural Therapiost
Christina Coole
7 Rosemary Road
Kidderminster DY10 2SW
T 01562 639467
Mobile therapist offering aromatherapy, therapeutic massage, reflexology, Reiki, Bach flower remedies & nutritional & diet advice. Offering a tailor-made holistic treatment for all clients.

Coopers Complementary Health Care
Christine Cooper
Bothy Cottage
Lower Hergest
Kington
Hereford HR5 3EN
T 01544 231417
Aromatherapy massage, Shiatsu, sotai, ear acupressure, advice on lifestyle diet & herbs & psychotherapy by qualified practitioners for women in the Border region in their own homes. Reasonably priced.

Diana Pardoe Consultant Hypnotherapist
Diana Pardoe
Pixie Cottage
47 Churchfields
Bromsgrove B61 8DX
T 01527 870085
Practising hypnotherpist treating a wide range of problems such as how to stop smoking, stress, how to slim. Flexible times. Has been a self-employed hypnotherapist for the past 17 years.

Jenni Stuart-Anderson
Jenni Stuart-Anderson
The Birches
Middleton-on-the-Hill HR6 0HN
T 01568 750229
Reiki healing; spiritual healing; distant healing. Also takes commissions on rag rugs. Workshops.

ARTS AND CRAFTS

Green Woodworking Courses
Gudrun Leitz
Hill Farm
Stanley Hill
Ledbury HR8 1HE
T 01531 640125 F 01531 640125
Tutors two- to nine-day courses in green woodworking. Makes greenwood furniture. Courses include Weekend Introduction to Green Woodwork; Make & Use a Polelathe & 9-day Chairmaking Workshop.

CHILD CARE AND FAMILY

First Stop Nursery
Ms V Roberts
70 Bromsgrove Road
Redditch B97 4RN
T 01527 450781
Nursery open 8 am-6 pm 51 weeks of the year. Creche. For children aged 0-5 years old. Phone for up-to-date prices.

Tudor Hall Nursery
Mrs K Ananthram
168 Birmingham Road
Enfield
Redditch B97 6EN
T 01527 61692
Private day care for children aged 0-8 years old. Out of school care for 5-8 year olds. Open Mon-Fri 7.30 am-6.30 pm. Ballet, tap, music, French, German tuition. Qualified teacher.

CONTRACEPTION/WELL WOMAN

Wye Valley Nuffield Hospital, The
Venns Lane
Hereford HR1 1DF
T 01432 355131
Well woman screen. Full female health assessment. Phone for up-to-date price lists.

EDUCATION

Wocestershire Association of Women Graduates
Mrs Ruth M Simpson, President
Wyre House
Wyre Piddle
Pershore WR10 2JD
T 01386 552516
We meet in members' homes usually once a month on various days at 7.30 pm. A discussion group focusing on modern novels meets monthly between September & April.

ETHNIC MINORITIES

All Women's House
June Sutherland, Co-ordinator
Sandycroft
West Avenue
Reddich B98 7DH
T 01527 595135
Open Mon-Fri 9.30 am-2.30 pm. For ethnic women. Drop in centre. English classes. Nursery. Creche. Flower arranging, sewing classes, sign languages for deaf women. Writing classes. Cooking.

PLACES TO STAY AND EAT

Strathmore
Mrs M C Matthews
Strathmore
West Malvern Road
Upper Wyche
Malvern WR14 4EL
T 01684 562245 F 01684 562245
Woman-owned women-friendly B&B. Open throughout the year except for Christmas/New Year. 1 double and 1 twin/double room. TV; coffee/tea-making; advanced booking essential. Phone for up-to-date price list.

PREGNANCY/CHILDBIRTH

Cedar Tree Pregnancy Crisis Centre
4 Barbourne Terrace
Worcester WR1 3JT
T 01905 616166
24-hour ansaphone, phone for an appointment. Free pregnancy testing, counselling & support for women with unplanned preganancies. Post abortion & miscarriage counselling.

RETAILING

Classy Numbers/Classy Kids
Ros Clayton
37 Rosehall Close
Oakenshaw
Redditch B98 7YD
T 01527 403436
High street fashions at affordable prices. By direct sale or party plan.

Mobile Pet Supplies
Karen Foort
Four Oaks
Cottage Farm
Gorcott Hill, Beoley
Redditch B98 9EP
T 01564 742851 F 01564 742851
Free delivery service of all animal feeds, retail & wholesale, in a twenty-mile radius around Redditch.

Wiggly Wigglers
Heather Gorringe/Louise Hayes
Lower Blakemere Farm
Blakemere HR2 9PX
T 01981 500391 F 01981 500432
wiggly@atlas.co.uk
Worms & worm composting kits for gardeners & recyclers. Worm shop open Mon-Fri 9 am-5.30 pm. There are a few open days

throughout the year & trips can be organised for groups to look around.

SERVICES

Jaybee Secretarial Services
Mrs Jacqui Mills
19 Jersey Close
Church Hill North
Redditch B98 9LS
T 01527 63236 F 01527 63236
Open Mon-Fri 10 am-5 pm. Access by appt only. Aims to produce first-class professional documents for those wishing to maintain high standards of presentation. Estimates given having seen the original work.

Personal Shopping Service
Sandy Warren
16 Lightoak Close
Walkwood
Redditch B97 5NQ
T 01527 403100
Door-to-door shopping service aimed at professional couples with young families.

SEXUAL ABUSE/RAPE CRISIS

Worcestershire Rape and Sexual Abuse Support Centre
P O Box 240
Worcester WR1 2LF
T 01905 424282
Helpline open Mon & Thurs 7.30-9.30 pm. Free advice, information & counselling for women over the age of 16 who have been raped or sexually abused at any time in their lives.

TRAINING

Redditch Women's Enterprise Development Agency
Anne Allen
54 South Street
Redditch B98 7DQ
T 01527 60919 F 01527 597107
Free business advice, training & support to local women. Flexible training & on-site creche.

Training for Excellence
Michelle Dale
De Salis Court
Hampton Lovett
Droitwich SR9 0NX
T 01905 795185 F 01905 797666

A training consultancy dealing in all aspects of training. Sometimes runs free supervisory management NVQ programme for unemployed women in the area: 'Women into Management'.

WOMEN'S AID

Wyre Forest Women's Aid
P O Box 152
Kidderminster DY11 7YY
T 01299 828200
24-hour helpline, supporting women with advice, counselling & advocacy.

HERTFORDSHIRE

BEREAVEMENT

Not Out Of Mind
Althea Hayton
P O Box 396
St Albans AL3 6NE
T 01727 761719 F 01727 765832
Promoting prayer & support when a baby dies during pregnancy or at birth. Three publications, published by Wren Publications, & more to follow. Leaflet available for books. Available through mail order only.

BUSINESS SUPPORT SCHEMES

Business Women's Network
Phil Stafford
P O Box 85
Hertford SG14 1TL
T 01992 501601 F 01992 551950
An active forum for business & professional women of all ages living or working in Hertfordshire & surrounding area. Meets once a month in various locations.

CENTRES FOR WOMEN

Watford Women's Centre
Sylvia Harvey
18b Clarendon Road
Watford WD2 7BJ
T 01923 816229
Open Mon-Fri 10 am-3 pm. Drop-in advice sessions Wed 12-2 pm. Counselling service, support, courses, workshops. Library. Rape crisis & sexual abuse line.

CONTRACEPTION/WELL WOMAN

Family Planning Clinic
Dr B Bean
Queensway Health Clinic
Hatfield AL10 0LF

ENGLAND - HERTFORDSHIRE

T 01707 264577
Open Mon 7-9 pm. Contraception advice, information and supplies.

EDUCATION

Potters Bar Association of British Assn of Women Graduates
Yasmin Shariff
1 Woodcock Lodge
Epping Green
Hertford SG13 8ND
T 01707 875253 F 01707 875286
Support network for women; contact with women across a wide range of disciplines; recognised platform for women concerned with improving the status of women & girls.

Women Graduates Association
Margaret Morgan
1a New Barnes Avenue
St Albans AL1 1TG
T 01727 856388
Hertfordshire association for women graduates aiming to promote friendship. Meetings, roughly monthly, of an intellectual, informative or social nature; bookgroups. Raises funds to support students from abroad.

HEALTH

Menopause Clinic - Hatfield
Dr B Bean
Queensway Health Centre
Hatfield AL10 0LF
T 01707 264577
Open first Fri in month 9.30 am-12 pm.
Advice & information about menopause & HRT.

UK Nursing Care Agency International Ltd
Porie Mahmood
26 Ivinghoe Close
Garston
Watford WD2 4SX
T 01923 496 699 F 01923 496 699
Nursing agency in Radlett, Hertfordshire supplying qualied nurses & care works to nursing & residential homes, hospitals, community & private patients. Office open 24 hours.

Women's Health Information Services
Project worker
Suite 3a
30 Bancroft
Hitchin SG3 1LE

T 01462 440674 F 01462 457298
To improve the physical & mental health of women in the community. Information on a broad range of topics with a mobile service. Counselling by women for women on low incomes.

LARGER/TALLER WOMEN

Long Tall Sally
21 George Street
St Albans AL3 4ES
T 01727 834250
Clothes for the taller woman sizes 12-20.
Open Mon-Sat 9.30 am-5.30 pm.

LESBIAN AND BISEXUAL

Women's Link
P O Box 13
Ware SG12 7TS
Social group for lesbians in Hertfordshire & surrounding areas.

PREGNANCY/CHILDBIRTH

Active Birth Classes
Billie France
5 Meldreth Road
Shepreth
Royston SG8 6PS
T 01763 262683 F 01763 262683
Weekly yoga-based pre- & post natal exercise classes. Also childbirth preparation classes for women & their partners & birth support by arrangement. Main aims of classes are to augment good body & breathing.

North London and Hertfordshire Independent Midwives
Jane Evans
90 Cravells Road
Harpenden AL5 1BG
T 01582 769408
Group practice of independent midwives covering N & W London, Herts, Harrow & Beds. Provides individualised care for women seeking home or hospital births. Experience in homoeopathy, birth education, yoga, etc.

Porie Mahmood
Porie Mahmood
26 Ivinghoe Close
Garston
Watford WD2 4SX
T 01923 681 924

ENGLAND - HULL AND HUMBERSIDE

Independent midwife. Member of IMA. Offers home, hospital, waterbirth, pre-conceptual care & counselling. Adheres to mothers wishes during pregnancy, labour & post-natally. Covers area up to 25 miles from home.

SERVICES

Felicity Cooper
Felicity Cooper
The Old Surgery
High Street
Much Hadham SG10 6DA
T 01279 842567
Podiatrist/chiropodist specialising in biomechanics & sports injuries. Phone during office hours for up-to-date price list.

SEXUAL ABUSE/RAPE CRISIS

Herts Area Rape Crisis
P O Box 21
Ware SG12 1ZA
T 01707 276512
Helpline open Thurs 7.30-9.30 pm. Women only counselling/talking to women only about rape, sexual abuse, child abuse, ritual abuse - whatever clients want to talk about.

Rape Crisis and Sexual Abuse Line
C/o CVS
149 The Parade
Watford WD1 1NA
T 01923 241600
Line open Mon 10 am-12 noon; Wed 8-10.30 pm; Sat 10 am-12 noon. Ansaphone with messages responded to within 24 hours. Free & confidential telephone helpline offering support & information to women.

SOCIAL

J-E (Japan-England) Japanese Women's Club
Ms C Izuka
6a Oxley Road
Watford WD1 4QE
T 01923 817860 F 01923 817860
Japanese women's club. Meets regularly. Members visit schools to provide an introduction to Japanese culture.

SPORTS AND LEISURE

Bedfordshire Lace Ladies Morris Dancers
Gill Goodman
54 Ickleford Road
Hitchin SG5 1TR
T 01462 456811
Female Morris side with members in Beds & across borders. Dancing in the 'Cotswold' style at fetes, festivals & for different associations, usually for a fee to cover expenses.

Hitchin Ladies' Cricket Club
Jenni Grove
1 Ostlers Cottage
Wood End
Ardeley SG6 7AX
T 01438 869434
Players of all ages & abilities welcome. All equipment provided & training available. Reduced membership & match fees are available for students.

WOMEN'S AID

Watford Women's Aid
C/o Watford Women's Centre
18b Clarendon Road
Watford WD2 7BJ
T 01923 816229

HULL AND HUMBERSIDE

ARTS AND CRAFTS

Hull Time Based Arts
Gillian Dyson
8 Posterngate
Hull HU1 2JN
T 01482 216446 F 01482 589952
htba@htba.demon.co.uk
For female & male artists: film guides, performance, installation & new media arts. AUDLAB & training workshops include women only training online video, non linear editing, internet, web page design, etc.

CENTRES FOR WOMEN

Hull Women's Centre
Janey Turner
First Floor
Queen's Dock Chambers
Queen's Dock Avenue
Hull HU1 3DR
T 01482 226806
Drop-in Mon-Fri 1-3 pm. Free creche Tue 1-3 pm; Wed & Thurs 10 am-12 noon & 1-3 pm for children aged 0-5. Courses (eg assertiveness, self-defence). Provides an information service. All services are free.

ENGLAND - HULL AND HUMBERSIDE

Open Door, The Bransholme Women's Centre
Nicky Williams
Bude Park
Cookbury Close
Bransholme
Hull HU7 4EY
T 01482 828755 F 01482 822096
Open Mon-Fri 9 am-4 pm. A safe meeting place for women. Groups, courses, leisure activities, health activities. Low cost quality childcare. All activities are free. Confidential counselling service.

Well Woman Centre - Grimsby
Eleanor Centre
Eleanor Street
Grimsby DN32 9EA
T 01472 3554113
Open Thurs 7-9 pm. Advice centre run by women for women. For women to talk through problems. Confidential advice, information & counselling. Creche. Free legal advice. Relaxation groups, etc.

Willow, The North Hull Women's Centre
Celia Wangler
32 Etton Grove
North Hull Estate
Hull HU6 8JY
T 01482 858057 F 01482 803367
Open Mon-Fri 9.30 am-4 pm Most activities, run in term time, are free. Creche. Confidence building, drop-in 1.30-3.30 pm; counselling; youth work training; money management; creative writing; etc.

CONTRACEPTION/WELL WOMAN

Hull Nuffield Hospital, The
81 Westbourne Avenue
Hull HU5 3HP
T 01482 342327
Well woman screen. Full female health assessment. Phone for up-to-date price lists.

LARGER/TALLER WOMEN

Long Tall Sally
26 Paragon Street
Hull HU1 3ND
T 01482 327646
Clothes for the taller woman sizes 12-20.
Open Mon-Sat 9.30 am-5.30 pm.

LESBIAN AND BISEXUAL

Hull Lesbian Line
P O Box 26
Hull HU1 2RX
T 01482 214331
Confidential, non-judgemental telephone helpline, open for any woman on Mon 7-9 pm. 24-hour ansaphone at all other times. Offers someone to talk to, information, someone who will listen, befriending, events.

PREGNANCY/CHILDBIRTH

Crisis Pregnancy Centre - Bridlington
White Cliffe Lane
Bridlington YO15 2AU
T 01262 401902
Office open Mon-Fri 9 am-12 noon, otherwise 24-hour ansaphone. Free pregnancy testing & confidential counselling & support for any woman with an unplaned pregnancy. Post abortion/miscarriage counselling.

PUBLISHERS/PUBLICATIONS

Page One Books
9 Princes Avenue
Hull HU5 3RX
T 01482 341925
Feminist section within a radical bookshop.

SEXUAL ABUSE/RAPE CRISIS

Grimsby and Scunthorpe Rape Crisis
Mrs J P Rilatt
Nunsthorpe & Bradley Resource Centre
Second Avenue
Grimsby DN33 1NU
T 01472 322111 F 01472 322111
Confidential counselling service for female victims of rape/sexual abuse (& male victims of rape/sexual abuse). Helpline open Wed (in Grimsby) 7-9 pm & Thurs (Scunthope) Mon 7-9 pm & Thurs 8-10 pm

Hull Rape Crisis (SAVES)
P O Box 40
Hull
T 01482 329990
Free, confidential counselling, support & information for women who have been raped or sexually abused. Line open Mon 6-8 pm, Thurs 5-10 pm, Sat 3-5 pm 24-hour ansaphone.

VIOLENCE AGAINST WOMEN

Great Grimsby Safer Cities Project
Anne Lawtey
Nunsthorpe/Bradley Park Resource Ctr

ENGLAND - KENT

2nd Avenue
Grimsby DN33 1NU
T 01472 311611 F 01472 311612
Government-funded community safety partnership with NACRO promoting local initiatives to prevent crime & make places safer.

KENT

ACCOMMODATION

Canterbury Women's Refuge
Janet & Helly
P O Box 123
Canterbury
T 01227 451238
Women's refuge, self-referral. Provides all immediate needs & women may stay for as long as necessary. Counselling, legal & housing advice, welfare rights information. Play & art therapy for children.

Iden Manor
Sister Rosemary, Director
Iden Manor
Staplehurst TN12 0ER
T 01580 891261
Registered nursing home for treatment & rehabilitation of women with difficulties, particularly associated with alcohol & drug dependency. Twelve-step abstinence-based programme. Self-referral.

AGRICULTURE

NFU Canterbury Ladies' Group
Alison Hume, Secretary
Southlands Farm
Molland Lane
Ash
Canterbury CT3 2EE
T 01304 812253
Monthly meetings held at 7.30 pm at Greenfields Clubhouse, Sturry. Aims to provide an opportunity for women connected to the farming community to meet & socialise to share experiences.

ARMED FORCES

WRAC and ATS Association
Maria Power
Dominican Priory
St Peter's Lane
Canterbury
T 01843 296373
For ex-servicewomen. Meets first Wed or each month 2 pm at Dominican Priory, Canterbury. Social forum & support for women who have served in the armed forces.

BUSINESS SUPPORT SCHEMES

Canterbury Business and Professional Women's Club
Mrs J Henley
Endeavour
2 St Mary's Grove
Seasalter
Whitstable CT5 4BH
T 01227 262452
Meets second Tue of each month at Slatters Hotel, Canterbury. Encouraging women to take their place in business & public life & to achieve their potential.

CENTRES FOR WOMEN

Women's Resource Centre
Lorraine Vincent
56a Dover Street
Canterbury CT1 3HD
T 01227 451753 F 01227 451753
Advice, information & support for women by women. Support groups, workshops, meeting space & specialist advice clinics. Drop-In sessions Tue & Thurs 11 am-2 pm.

CONTRACEPTION/WELL WOMAN

Tunbridge Wells Nuffield Hospital, The
Kingswood Road
Tunbridge Wells TN2 4UL
T 01892 531111
Well woman screen. Full female health assessment. Phone for up-to-date price lists.

EDUCATION

Canterbury & District Association of Women Graduates
Mrs Barbara Leeming
8 Lanfranc Gardens
Harbledown
Canterbury CT2 8NJ
T 01227 456537
Member of British Federation of Women Graduates. Aims to perfect the art of friendship through a varied programme of intellectual & social activities. Meets on third Thurs evening of each month.

Sevenoaks Association of Graduate Women
Lorna Lee
25 St George's Road
Sevenoaks TN13 3ND
Local branch of the British Federation of University Women.

ENGLAND - KENT

Environment

Canterbury Women's Environment Network
Jan Stewart
Canterbury Environment Centre
St Alphege Lane
Canterbury CT1 2EB
T 01227 457009 F 01227 457009
Group meets on Sat mornings once a month to discuss local issues of concern & to campaign & focus on action for change. Creche.

Finance

L M B H
Lorrie Harte Benwell
Clock Cottage
Shoreham Place
Shoreham
Sevenoaks TN14 7SA
T 01959 524363
Financial services, corporate communications consultancy, advice on strategy & implementation. For communications, both internal & external, on PR, press, sponsorship.

Health

Medway Women's Health Information and Support Service
Marian Gordon
The White House
The Riverside
Chatham ME4 4SL
T 01634 407281
Health information & support to women. Free service & drop-in. Health reference library, leaflets, information on groups & health organisations. Open Mon 7.45-9.45 pm, Tue 12-3 pm, Wed 11 am-2 pm.

Naomi Project, The
Peter Brook, Trust Administrator
C/o Kenward Trust
Kenward House
Yalding ME18 6AH
T 01622 814187
Residential groupwork programme for women only housed in Dartford for women recovering from chemical addition. Age limits 21-60. 24-week (minimum) programme based on 12 steps of AA/NA.

Turning Point - Canterbury
Annie Linton, Community Outreach, Women's Officer
63 Whitstable Road
Canterbury CT2 8DG
T 01227 452001
Community outreach service. Sees clients in home, GP's surgery, by appt. Service is free & confidential. Also runs support groups. Advice, information, support & counselling to deal with alcohol/drugs.

Larger/Taller Women

Long Tall Sally
13 Chapel Place
Tunbridge Wells TN1 1YQ
T 01892 534131
Clothes for the taller woman sizes 12-20. Open Mon-Sat 9.30 am-5.30 pm.

Places to Stay and Eat

Acacia House B&B
Jackie and Ann
1 Linton Road
Loose ME15 0AE
T 01622 741943 F 01622 745311
Women only B&B. 2 double rooms & 1 twin room. Open all year. Detached country house in Kent countryside. Welcomes all women as couples, singles or as friends. Phone for up-to-date price list.

Pregnancy/Childbirth

Crisis Pregnancy Centre - Leigh
Mary Lavelle
King's Park Christian Centre
Leigh Road
Leigh WN7 1AX
T 01942 745512
Open Tue 6-7 pm. Free pregnancy testing, counselling & support for women with unplanned pregnancies. Post abortion & miscarriage counselling. Phone for an appointment.

National Childbirth Trust - Deal branch
Mrs Harris
57 Circular Road
Betteshanger
Deal CT14 0LT
T 01304 611166
Regular get-togethers where mums can meet for relaxation & support & where they can obtain up-to-date information on topics such as pregnancy, labour, healthy eating, home births, antenatal check ups, etc.

ENGLAND - KENT

Pregnancy Crisis Centre
32 Cheriton Road
Folkestone
T 01303 242777
Phone for opening times. Free pregnancy testing, counselling & support for women faced with unplanned pregnancies. Post-abortion/miscarriage counselling. Phone for appointment. 24-hour ansaphone.

Pregnancy Crisis Centre
1 Grosvenor Hill
Margate CT9 1UU
T 01843 295222
Open Mon 5-7 pm; Wed & Sat 10 am-12 noon. Free pregnancy testing, counselling & support for women with unplanned pregnancies. Post-abortion/miscarriage counselling. Phone for appt. 24-hour ansaphone.

Pregnancy Crisis Centre
35B Broad Street
Canterbury
T 01227 785410
Open Wed 2-4 pm; Sat 10 am-12 noon. Free pregnancy testing, counselling & support for women faced with unplanned pregnancies. Post-abortion/miscarriage counselling. Phone for appointment. 24-hour ansaphone.

Recurrent Spontaneous Miscarriage Clinic
Pembury Hospital
Pembury
Tunbridge Wells TN2 4QJ
T 01892 823535
Provides free immunotherapy treatment.

SEXUAL ABUSE/RAPE CRISIS

East Kent Rape Line
Canterbury
T 01227 766911
Helpline 01227 450400. Open Mon-Thurs 6-9 pm.

Merrywood Counselling
Rosina Godfrey
No 5 Highfield Road
Rainham ME8 0EG
T 01634 378399
All women counsellors specialising in sexual abuse. Open 9 am-10 pm.

Sanctuary
Rosina Godfrey
64 High Street
Rainham ME8 7JF
T 01634 378300
Open 9 am-10 pm six days a week. One-to-one counselling & support to all who have suffered sexual abuse. Helpline. Support groups for women only.

SOCIAL

Deal and District Lioness Club
Mrs Gladys Hall
Churchfield Farm
30 The Street
Sholden
Deal CT14 0AL
Meets second Thurs of each month. Aims to fundraise, help others & have fun.

Medway Women's Group
Mrs Nina Drongin
39 Kingsdale Court
Hopewell Drive
Chatham ME5 7NN
T 01634 402515
Open to all women. Meets monthly for discussion on any subject of special interest to women. Phone for details of time & place of next meeting.

Streets Apart Mobile/Club Discos
Karon Hope
41 Thanet Road
Ramsgate CT11 8EH
T 01843 586834
Mobile 0421 994776. Works as a mobile DJ. Runs a women only club/social evening 8.30 am-1 pm every first Sat of each month in Canterbury. Also does furniture/rubbish removals & painting/decorating.

University of Kent at Canterbury Women's Club
Gill Rickayztn
27 Ross Gardens
Rough Common
Canterbury CT2 9BZ
T 01227 464996
For staff or students & open to any women with an interest in the University. Meets Thurs 10.30 am-12 noon in members' houses.

SUPPORT

Tranx Helpline
Peggy Watkinson
32 Halstead Close
Canterbury CT2 7UD
T 01227 457205

Helpline for women withdrawing from tranquilisers. Self-help, information & support. There is no charge.

LANCASHIRE

ARTS AND CRAFTS

Tache Painted Furniture
Angela Jaynes
3 Victoria Street
Wheelton
Chorley PR6 8HG
T 01254 831450
Takes mass-produced furniture and makes them into individually designed decorative yet still utilitarian pieces. Commissions welcome.

CENTRES FOR WOMEN

Pendle Women's Centre
the coordinator
21 Market Square
Nelson BB9 7LP
T 01282 696100
Open Mon-Fri 10 am-12 noon; Wed & Thurs 1-3 pm. Drop-in. Counselling. Self-harmers' group; writers' group; diabetics' group. Encourages women to have a say in the care & control of their bodies & lives.

Women's Centre
55 Clifford Street
Chorley PR7 1ER
T 01257 265342
Open Tue & Fri 10 am-4 pm.

Women's Centre, The
Catherine Jones
25 Wellington Street
St John's
Blackburn BB1 8AF
T 01254 583032
Open Mon-Fri 10 am-3 pm. Health information, support groups, counselling, education, personal development courses, library, creche, drop-in, referrals. Prices for courses vary with a woman's income.

Women's Resource Centre
Glenda Sutcliffe
C/o The Refugee Assurance Building
Ground Floor
Ainsworth Street
Blackburn BB2 6AZ
T 01254 260736 F 01254 261015
Open Mon-Thurs 10 am-12 noon & 12.30-4 pm. Fri & Sat morning by appointment only. To help & support women to better themselves into employment, education & training.

CONTRACEPTION/WELL WOMAN

Blackburn Brook Centre
54-56 Darwen Street
Blackburn BB2 2BL
T 01254 692546
Free, confidential contraceptive advice. Free condoms and other contraceptive supplies. Help with emotional and sexual problems. Pregnancy testing and quick results. Phone for opening times.

Lancaster and Lakeland Nuffield, The
Meadowside
Lancaster LA1 3RH
T 01524 62345
Well woman screen. Full female health assessment. Phone for up-to-date price lists.

North East Lancashire Brook Centre
Top Floor
79 Church Street
Burnley BB11 2RS
T 01282 416596
Free, confidential contraceptive advice. Free condoms & other contraceptive supplies. Help with emotional & sexual problems. Pregnancy testing & quick results. Phone for opening times.

Preston Well Women Centre
Pat Elliott, Centre Administrator
18-20 New Hall Lane
Preston PR1 4DU
T 01772 702397
Open Mon-Wed 10 am-4 pm; Thurs-Sat 10 am-1 pm. Promoting positive health care for women. Health, education & supportive services: counselling, doctor, health visitor, self-help & therapy group, etc.

Rochdale Well Woman Centre
Mrs D Forshaw
2 Roach Place
Rochdale OL16 2DD
At Health Education Unit, Penn Street, Rochdale on Tue 6-8 pm. Drop-in. Informal & confidential counselling service, advice, information & free pregnancy tests. No cytology or medical examinations.

ENGLAND - LANCASHIRE

PLACES TO STAY AND EAT

Amalfi Licensed Hotel
M Elmore
19-21 Eaves Street
Blackpool FY1 2NH
T 01253 22971
Women-run hotel, minutes from promenade, clubs & Golden Mile. One minute from sea front. All bedrooms on first floor. Full English breakfast served 9 am Phone for up-to-date price list.

Kingston Hotel, The
Ann Jackson-Blanchard, Proprietor
12 Cocker Street
Blackpool FY1 1SF
T 01253 24929
Licensed hotel for holiday & residential. Open all year. Special offers on request. Phone for up-to-date price list.

Mount Hotel, The
Tracey or Vanessa
30 Exchange Street
Blackpool FY1 2DU
T 01253 25659
Women-owned & women-friendly B&B. 12 rooms available. Open all year (except Christmas day). Phone for up-to-date price list.

Prospect Cottage
Louraine Palmeri
Prospect Cottage
Ingleton
Carnforth LA6 3HE
T 015242 41328
Vegetarian/vegan B&B in a centre of crags, caves, fells, glens & waterfalls. Comfy, inexpensive accommodation. Wonderful walks & views. Phone for details of up-to-date prices.

PREGNANCY/CHILDBIRTH

Crisis Pregnancy Centre - Rochdale
Hebrom Pentecostal Church
Falinge Road
Rochdale
T 01706 42772
Open Tue & Fri 2-3 pm. 24-hour ansaphone. Free pregnancy testing, counselling & support for women with unplanned pregnancies. Post abortion & miscarriage counselling. Phone for an appt.

Crisis Pregnancy Centre - St Helens
Norelle Tout
Well Come Inn
63 Park Road
Fingerpost
St Helens WA9 1DS
T 01744 611093
Open Tue, Wed & Thurs 2-3 pm & also by appt. 24-hour ansaphone. Free pregnancy testing, counselling & support for women with unplanned pregnancies. Post abortion & miscarriage counselling.

Lighthouse Pregnancy Centre, The
Joan Littlewood Coordinator
155 Scotland Road
Nelson BB9 7YS
T 01282 693333
Helpline open Mon 6.30-7.30 pm & Fri 12-1 pm. 24-hour ansaphone. Free pregnancy testing & confidential counselling. Support for any woman with an unplanned pregnancy. Post-abortion/miscarriage counselling.

RELIGIOUS ORGANISATIONS

Salvation Army Home League
Mrs Mary Taylor
Women's Fellowship
1 London Street
Fleetwood FY7 6JE
T 01253 874350
Meets Mon 2 pm. A gathering of women but also open to men, run by women. For worship, education, fellowship & service.

SEXUAL ABUSE/RAPE CRISIS

Preston Survivors' Group
C/o Preston Well Women Centre
18-20 New Hall Lane
Preston PR1 4DU
T 01772 702397
For women who have suffered childhood rape or sexual abuse. Phone above number for further details.

Women Survivors' Group
C/o The Women's Centre
25 Wellington Street
St John's
Blackburn BB1 8AF
T 01254 583032
For women who have suffered childhood rape or sexual abuse. Phone above number for further details.

ENGLAND - LEICESTERSHIRE

Sports and Leisure

Lancashire Women's Cricket Association
Mrs Sue Lever
50 Lulworth Avenue
Ashton on Ribble
Preston PR2 2BE
T 01772 731883

Training

Business Link Fylde Coast Ltd
Julia Stickley
Unit 6a-10a
Marsh Mill Village
Fleetwood Road North
Thornton Cleveleys FY5 4JZ
T 01253 897000 F 01253 897001
A women's enterprise centre. Business link. Counselling for women. Free creche. Self-esteem courses.

Women's Aid

Blackburn and Darwin District Women's Aid
P O Box 120
Blackburn BB1 8RP
T 01254 260465
Helpline open Mon-Fri 10 am-4 pm. Refuge & accommodation for women & their children (if any) fleeing domestic violence. 24-hour ansaphone.

Lancaster and District Women's Aid
P O Box 23
Lancaster LA1 4GP
T 01524 383636
Office open Mon-Fri 11 am-1 pm. 24-hour ansaphone. Offers safe & temporary accommodation to women & children fleeing domestic violence. Also offers outreach services.

Leicestershire

Arts and Crafts

Mad Dog Design
Jenni Robson
178 Avenue Road Extension
Clarendon Park
Leicester LE2 3EJ
T 0116 274 5256
Dimensional design service, ranging from surface decoration including illustration to display work, ie props, for shop interiors. Supplying galleries & shops with decorative papier mache & ceramic mirrors, etc.

Nilmani Kathak Kendra
Rajesh Bhavsar/Nilima Devi
48-50 Churchill Street
Leicester LE2 1FH
T 0116 255 2862 F 0116 285 4472
The Institute of Classical Indian Dance. Aims to develop knowledge, understanding & cultural awareness of Indian classical dance. Training and diplomas.

Centres for Women

Shama Asian Women's Centre
Mrs Sumansingh
39-45 Sparkenhoe Street
Leicester LE2 0TD
T 0116 251 4747 F 0116 251 4747
Classes, dressmaking, keep fit classes, swimming. Creche. Outings & other social events.

Contraception/Well Woman

Leicester Nuffield Hospital, The
Scraptoft Lane
Leicester LE5 1HY
T 0116 276 9401
Well woman screen. Full female health assessment. Phone for up-to-date price lists.

Ethnic Minorities

Leicester Asian Ladies' Circle
Mrs S Arolker
40 Spencefield Lane
Leicester LE5 6HF
T 0116 241 2723 F 0116 253 1568
Meets once every 4-6 weeks. Providing socal, cultural, physical, religious & educational activities & fostering/preserving Asian culture & traditions. Fundraising activities.

Sexual abuse/Rape Crisis

Leicester Rape Crisis
Chris or Denise
C/o 70 High Street
Leicester LE1 5YP
T 0116 270 6990
Provides support for women by women who've been raped or sexually abused by telephone or face-to-face counselling. Phone Tue-Fri 10 am-4 pm or Wed 6.30-9.30 pm.

Mothers' Group
Leicester Family Services Unit
26 Severn Street

ENGLAND - LINCOLNSHIRE

Leicester LE2 0NN
T 0116 254 3352 F 0116 275 5216
For mothers with children who have been sexually abused. Both self-referrals & referred women. An occasional group.

Women's Group, The
Leicester Family Service Unit
26 Severn Street
Leicester LE2 0NN
T 0116 275 5216
For women who have been sexually abused as children & who are now mothers. Both self-support & advice given. For both self-referrals & referred women. Meets occasionally.

SOCIAL

Minerva Ladies' Discussion Group
Mrs L A Lawson
Granary Cottage
9 Church Street
Cottingham
Market Harborough LE16 8XG
T 01536 771559
We meet in each other's homes once a fortnight on Tue 8 pm. A set programme to discuss the topics of the day.

SUPPORT

Company of Women
Vivian Flower
Charnwood Community Council
John Stoner House
Ward End
Loughborough LE11 3HA
T 01509 230131
Meets first Wed of each month 7.30-10 pm to discuss issues relevant to women: health, self-esteem & social events.

TRAINING

Re-Source
Vida Pearson
22 Main Street
Hoby LE14 3DT
T 01664 434451 F 01664 434451
Consultant, trainer & personal development coach, interested in self-empowerment, creativity & managing change. Works with public service agencies. Author of 'Women and Power' & 'The Causes of Aggression'.

LINCOLNSHIRE

EDUCATION

Lincoln and Lincolnshire Association of BFWG
Mrs M Sexton
Fen Farm
Burton
Lincoln LN1 2RE
T 01522 522776
Holds regular meetings offering the opportunity to meet fellow graduates, listen to speakers & make social & professional contacts. Briging women graduates together worldwide.

EQUAL OPPS

Fair Play East Midlands
Sylvia Wardley
Lincolnshire TEC
Beech House
Witham Park, Waterside South
Lincoln LN5 7JS
T 01522 567765 F 01522 510534
Positive action equalities project. A government EOC initiative to stimulate partnerships which improve opportunities for women to realise their full potential in education, employment & the community.

FINANCE

FMW Financial
Mrs Flora M Winter
32 High Street
Brant Broughton
Lincoln LN5 0SL
T 01400 273395 F 01400 272733
Independent financial adviser.

PREGNANCY/CHILDBIRTH

Crisis Pregnancy Centre - Grantham
Judy McGibbon
Upper Room Care Centre
Baptist Church
Wharf Road
Grantham
T 01476 573050
Open Tue 12-4.30 pm. Free pregnancy testing, counselling & support for women with unplanned pregnancies. Post abortion & miscarriage counselling. Phone for an appt.

Midwives Together
Paulette Walker
Shepherd's Pasture
3 Chancery Close

Lincoln LN6 8SD
T 01522 520225
An independent midwife, working with local midwives as back up. Offers personal service & continuity of care to pregnant women. Member of IMA & RCM. Most clients have home births; delivers where women want.

WOMEN'S AID

Lincoln Women's Aid
P O Box 125
Lincoln LN1 1HA
T 01522 510041   F 01522 510041

LIVERPOOL AND MERSEYSIDE

ACCOMMODATION

Women's Alliance
Shelagh McLinden
Imagine
25 Hope Street
Liverpool L1 9BQ
T 0151 709 2366   F 0151 709 9790
Supported housing scheme for women with mental health problems. A forum to debate issues around women's mental health & challenge the lack of appropriate services.

Women's Refuge Wirral
Eddy Shallcross, Project Leader
P O Box 14
Birkenhead L41 6PX
T 0151 652 6300
Assists women & children in trouble, involved in domestic violence. Accommodation for women & children fleeing violence. Counselling. A helpline (see above) & self-help group. Leaflets available.

ARTS AND CRAFTS

Cassandra McDonough
Sandra McDonough
Flat 5
6 Lorne Road
Oxton L43 1XB
T 0151 653 7433
Freelance community artist, both solo & as part of team; graphics instructor, designs/assesses projects, teaches artwork techniques; self employed artist - portraitist in oils, making/selling hatboxes, etc.

Susan Kam
Susan Kam
8 Pine Court
Dardigan Avenue
Wirral

Merseyside L41 TF4
Freelance artist/designer: painting, drawing, portraits, landscapes, 2-D design (cards, murals), illustration, posters, leaflets (graphics).

Theatre Resource Centre
Maria Barrett/Fi Kellett
Graphic House
Duke Street
Liverpool L1 4JR
T 0151 708 5818   F 0151 708 9819
Helps development of small-scale theatre in north west England. Optimises its contribution to artistic & cultural life & to economic regeneration of region. Offers access to equipment, information & training.

Women - A Network of Professional Women Artists
Jean Grant
Liverpool
T 0151 727 1074
Run by collective of practising women artists: dance, performance, film, video, visual arts, fine arts, etc. Meets monthly at Bluecoat Gallery & sometimes at Tate (Liverpool). To exchange ideas & skills.

BEREAVEMENT

St Helens Bereavement Service
Joan Ashcroft, Co-ordinator
First Floor, Corporation Buildings
Corporation Street
St Helens
Merseyside WA10 1DZ
T 01744 451793
Open Mon, Wed & Fri 9 am-1 pm. Free counselling & befriending service for bereaved. Confidential counselling & practical, emotional support. Develops awareness & understanding of the nature of grief.

BUSINESS SUPPORT SCHEMES

Train 2000
Colette Russell
C/o Blackburne House Centre for Women
Hope Street
Liverpool L1 9JB
T 0151 709 7898   F 0151 709 7898
Open Mon-Fri 9 am-6 pm. Mon-Fri. New Opportunities for Women business enterprise training & counselling services for women. MOCF accredited business enterprise training courses; business counselling.

CENTRES FOR WOMEN

'The Attic' Young Women's Resource Centre
Diane Rimmer
6th Floor
Crane Buildings
Hanover Street
Liverpool L1 3DZ
T 0151 707 2433
For young women aged 13-25. Support & friendship. Practical activities, courses, workshops. Library. Training. Magazine production. Young lesbian group Thurs 7.30-9.45 pm; young women's forum Wed 7-9.45 pm.

Blackburne House Centre for Women
Claire Dove, Director
Hope Street
Liverpool L1 9JB
T 0151 709 4356   F 0151 709 8293
bhcfw@mail.cybase.co.uk
Open Mon-Thurs 9 am-9 pm; Fri 9 am-6 pm. Provides training & education for women. Training in electronics, computing, telematics, health courses, European languages, etc. Training allowances & childare.

Leasowe Women's Centre
Edwina Doyle
46 Shakleton Road
Leasowe
Merseyside L46 2RT
T 0151 637 1812
Education & information for women to preserve & protect health & well being. All services free. Open Mon-Fri 9 am-5 pm. Disabled access. Free Creche. Courses include computer studies, maths for fun, etc.

Sefton Women's Advisory Network
Mrs Ann Crotty, Project Manager
King George V1 Centre
Knowsley Road
Bootle
Liverpool L20 5DE
T 0151 933 3292
Open Mon-Fri 9 am-4 pm. Offers information on all aspects of women's health & well-being. Offers support to women who suffer from depression, anxiety or loneliness & isolation. Also a counselling service.

Women & Girls' Information & Resource Centre
Mary McLoughlin/Marie Appleton
Peter Street
St Helens
Merseyside WA10 2EQ
T 01744 454062
To empower women & girls to fulfil potential & develp skills. Drop-in Wed 1-4 pm; counselling; girls' groups Mon & Wed 7-10 pm; training, complementary therapies; assertiveness training. All free.

Women's Enterprising Breakthrough
Lucy Holbrook, Centre coordinator
176 Corporation Road
Birkenhead L41 8JQ
T 0151 653 3771
Education & training. Good health & well-being of all women in area. Drop-in service, relaxation room, courses, library & information leaflets, meeting room, creche, wheelchair access. All services are free.

Women's Health Information & Support Centre (WHISC)
Chris James, Manager
120 Bold Street
Liverpool L1 4JA
T 0151 707 1826   F 0151 709 2566
Run by women for women. Information, support & training. Drop in service. Well-established women's health courses. Mobile health information service via a double-decker bus. Short courses.

YWCA Parr Women & Girls' Centre
Lorraine Mason
Nunn Street
Parr
St Helens
Merseyside WA9 3SF
T 01744 25813   F 01744 25813
Training in computer skills & business administration; complementary therapies provided; young women's art project; Mum & tots; social club; Morris dancing; basic child care skills. Creche. Coffee bar.

CHILD CARE AND FAMILY

Cheshire Childminding Association
Elaine Clarke
3 Tynesdale
Whitby
Ellesmere Port
Merseyside L65 6RB
T 0151 355 9688
Supports childminders in Cheshire. Provides training & networking facilities. Shares inforamtion. Social events.

ENGLAND - LIVERPOOL AND MERSEYSIDE

Crosby Childminding Group
Christine Bates
65 Seafield Avenue
Crosby L23 0TG
T 0151 476 8541
Offers access to training for local childminders. A childminders' support group. Monthly meetings; drop in.

Huyton Childminders' Group
Christine Landry, Coordinator
74 Church Road
Roby
Huyton
Merseyside L36 9TR
T 0151 482 1188
Offers friendship and support to childminders. Informal drop-in Wed 9.45-11.30 am at Huyton Voluntary Service Building, Lathom Road, Huyton.

Liverpool Childminding Association
Heather Garnett, Secretary
3 Earlsfield Road
Liverpool L15 5BZ
T 0151 475 0062
Aims to improve recognition of childminding as an important & valuable form of childcare, & employment, in Liverpool. Provides support network for childminders & promotes good childminding practice.

Parent and Toddler Group
Mrs Joan Petrie
Salvation Army Community Centre
140a Earle Road
Liverpool L7
T 0151 734 2556
Runs on Wed 9.45-11.45 am.

Parent School Partnership (PSP)
Lyn Carey
C/o Blackburne House Centre for Women
Hope Street
Liverpool L1 9JB
T 0151 708 6339 F 0151 708 6339
Open Mon-Fri 9 am-5 pm. Closed during school holidays. Aims is to work with parents of children at schools. Family support; involvement in children's education through workshops & structured courses.

Wirral Childminding Association
Mrs Lynn Henry, Chair
15 Kingsway
Wallasey
Merseyside L45 4PL

T 0151 637 1069
Promoting provision of facilities for daily care, recreation & education of children under 8. Advancing education & training of childminders & other persons providing day care for children under 8.

COMPUTERS/IT

Women's Technology Training
Julie Rushton
Blackburne House Centre for Women
Hope Street
Liverpool L1 9JB
T 0151 709 4356 F 0151 709 8293
electra@MCRI.poptel.org.uk
For times of opening & details of courses see under Blackburne House Centre for Women.

CONTRACEPTION/WELL WOMAN

Family Planning Services
St Catherine's Hospital
Derby Road
Birkenhead
Merseyside L42 0LQ
T 0151 678 5111
Free pregnancy testing & counselling, emergency contraception, smear tests, HIV prevention advice, free condoms, IUDs fitted. Drop-in clinics, no appointments necessary. Speakers available for women's groups.

Merseyside Brook Centre
104 Bold Street
Liverpool L1 4HY
T 0151 709 4558
Free confidential contraceptive advice. Help with emotional & sexual problems. Free condoms & other contraceptive supplies. Pregnancy tests & quick results etc. Phone for opening times.

Well Woman Clinic - Wallasey
Pauline Robertson, Administrator
Under 5s Centre
St Paul's Road, Seacombe
Wallasey
Merseyside
T 0151 691 0399
Open Thurs 9.30 am-12 pm. Free & confidential NHS service run by & for women. Various examinations (smear tests, breast & vaginal examinations, blood pressure, weight). Publications. No appointment needed.

Well Women Centre - Birkenhead
Pauline Robertson, Administrator
St Catherine's Hospital
Derby Road
Birkenhead
Merseyside L42 0LQ
T 0151 670 1223 F 0151 670 1223
Wed 9.30 am-12.30 pm & Thurs 1-3 pm. Free & confidential NHS service run by women for women. Information, medical examinations (smear tests, breast & vaginal examinations, blood pressure). Publications.

Wirral Brook Centre
14 Whetstone Lane
Charing Cross
Birkenhead
Merseyside L41 2QR
T 0151 670 0177
Free, confidential contraceptive advice. Help with emotional & sexual problems. Free condoms & other contraceptive supplies. Pregnancy tests & quick results, etc. Phone for time of opening.

EDUCATION

Liverpool Association of Graduate Women
Evelyn C Smith
28 Ferguson Avenue
Greasby
Wirral
Merseyside L49 1RP
T 0151 678 1620
Two meetings per month in people's homes. To promote understanding & friendship amongst graduate women of the world. To help women take opportunities for education, training & research.

Opportunity Development Unit
Pamela Matfin
University of Liverpool
P O Box 147
Liverpool L69 3BX
T 0151 794 3287 F 0151 794 2852
matfin@liverpool.ac.uk

West Lancashire Association of Women Graduates
Mrs Carmena Newey, Secretary
2 Eshe Road North
Blundell Sands
Liverpool L23 8UD
T 0151 924 3367
Meets once a month in each others' houses with speakers. Promoting friendship, mutual interests, social contacts.

Women's Educational Training Trust
Dorothy Mathews
Blackburne House Centre for Women
Hope Street
Liverpool L1 9JB
T 0151 709 43356 F 0151 709 8293
electra@MCRI.poptel.org.uk
For times of opening & details of courses see under Blackburne House Centre for Women.

Women's Research Group
Dr Mairead Owen, School of Social Science
Liverpool John Moores University
Trueman Building
15-21 Webster Street
Liverpool L3 2ET
T 0151 231 4077 F 0151 258 1224
m.owen@INjm.ac.uk
Meets first Wed of month in term time 4-6 pm at Trueman Building, Liverpool John Moores University. Informal group for women interested in research - interdisciplinary, academic, or otherwise, based anywhere.

EQUAL OPPS

Fair Play Merseyside
Elaine Roberts, Coordinator
Cunard Building
Piers Head
Liverpool L2 7XR
T 0151 224 2910 F 0151 224 2904
Positive action equalities project. A government EOC initiative to stimulate partnerships which improve opportunities for women to realise their full potential in education, employment & the community.

University of Liverpool Guild of Students' Women's Group
Women's officer
University of Liverpool Student's Guild
P O Box 187
160 Mount Pleasant
Liverpool L69 7BR
T 0151 794 4153 F 0151 794 4174
To promote women's equality within the university; to provide a safe place for women to discuss issues; to provide women only social events; to campaign nationally on women's issues as a group, etc.

ETHNIC MINORITIES

Liverpool Black Sisters
Norma Stoddart
34 Princes Road
Liverpool L8 1TH

ENGLAND - LIVERPOOL AND MERSEYSIDE

T 0151 709 8162
Provides advice & support around training/education & employment opportunities; advocacy project; childcare provision for children aged between 5-12; free short courses with creche; keep fit sessions, etc.

Mary Seacole House (MSH)
Melissa Kponou/ Karen Small
91 Upper Parliament Street
Toxteth
Liverpool L8 7LB
T 0151 707 0319 F 0151 709 6661
Open Mon 9 am- 7.30 pm; Tue-Thurs 9 am-4.30 pm; Fri 9 am-4 pm. Drop-in day centre mainly for Black communities of Liverpool 8. The women's group provides mutual support focusing on mental distress.

Wirral Chinese Association
Sadie Ning, Chair
Wirral Multicultural Centre
111 Conway Street
Birkenhead, Wirral
Merseyside L41 4AF
T 0151 666 4552
ESOL Mon 10 am-12 noon; WCALC Wed 12.30-2 pm; employment/education Wed 9 am-5 pm. For further details of activities for Chinese women, phone above number.

Women's Independent Cinema House (WITCH)
Ann Carney
C/o Blackburne House Centre for Women
Hope Street
Liverpool L1 9JB
T 0151 707 0539 F 0151 709 8293
Offers media training to young Black women: production skills, script writing, photography, camera skills, lighting, sound & editing in a twelve week course which includes a two-week placement.

Young Women's Multi-Cultural Association
Noreen Hameed, Chair
47 Windsor View
Liverpool L8 0UN
T 0151 709 9654 F 0151 709 9654
Primarily, but not exclusively for young Muslim women. To enhance their educational skills provide job opportunities, information & advice. Support forum. Activities for children aged 5-7.

HEALTH

Allerton Healthcare Clinic
Ursula M Thompson
119 Allerton Road
Liverpool L18 2DD
T 0151 724 5788
Physiotherapy & sports injuries clinic. By appointment only. At very reasonable cost.

Breast Screening Unit
St Catherine's Hospital
Derby Road
Birkenhead
Merseyside L42 0LQ
T 0151 653 7686
Open Mon-Fri 8.30 am-5.30 pm. Women aged 50-64 are given free appointments every three years for screening. Any abnormalities found are followed up by the highly qualified specialist breast team.

Cercan Women's Health Group
Lily Hopkins, Chair
6 Landford Avenue
Liverpool L9 6BR
T 0151 525 2848 F 0151 523 4266
Supporting women who have had an abnormal smear &/or cervical cancer. Phone any time for information & literature. A group of women meet four or five times a year.

Lift Up
Barbara Blundell, breast care nurse
Southport & Formby DGH
Town Lane
Kew
Southport PR8 6HJ
T 01704 547471
Offers support & encouragement to women being treated for breast cancer. Social & support group. Meets last Thurs in month at St George's Church Hall, Lord Street, Southport at 8 pm.

Liverpool Women's Hospital
Crown Street
Liverpool L8 7SS
T 0151 708 9988
Gynaecological emergency service, menopause clinic, breast screening clinic, contraception, miscarriage clinic, fetal wellbeing assessment centre, preconceptual clinic, multiple pregancy clinic, midwifery, etc.

Mersey Positive Women
Many O'Brien
c/o Merseyside AIDS Support Group

P O Box 11
Liverpool LG9 1SN
T 0151 708 9080 F 0151 707 1716
For women with HIV/AIDS in the Mersey Regional Health Authority area. Helpline 0151 709 9000.

St Helens & Knowsley Bosom Friends
Mrs Doreen Jones
16 Kelsall Avenue
St Helens
Merseyside WA9 4DQ
T 01744 811198
Gives support to women who have had or are about to have surgery or treatment for breast cancer. Meets on the first Tue of each month at St Julie's Church Hall, Eccleston, St Helens.

LARGER/TALLER WOMEN
Claire's 26 to 40 Plus
Mrs Claire Houghton/Mrs Pauline Beattie
16a Ormskirk Road
Rainford Village
St Helens
Merseyside WA11 8BT
T 01744 884688
A small firm manufacturing & retailing ladieswear for the larger woman. Sizes 26-40. Also a mail order facility with sizes up to 48. Very reasonable prices.

LEGAL MATTERS
Silverman Livermore (Solicitors)
Eleanor King
Silverman Livermore
11-13 Victoria Street
Liverpool L2 5QQ
T 0151 227 1871 F 0151 255 0216
Eleanor King - litigation. Runs drop-in for women at Blackburne House on Tue. Phone for appt. Sandra Todd - matrimonial & family law; Karen Wishart - family; Lyn Coventry - family & child care; etc.

LESBIAN AND BISEXUAL
Friend Merseyside
Kim Singleton
36 Bolton Street
Liverpool L3 5LX
T 0151 708 9552
Confidential help, information, support to lesbians, gay men, bisexuals, transvestites, transsexuals & those unsure of sexuality. Lesbian line Tue & Thurs 7-10 pm on 0151 708 0234.

Women's 30+ Group
Eileen Calder
C/o Friend Merseyside
36 Bolton Street
Liverpool L3 5LX
T 0151 708 9552
Informal social group for lesbian/bisexual women. Sat from 8-10 pm. Age limit is not strictly adhered to - the group offers an alternative to the pub/club scene & will welcome all.

LIBRARIES/ARCHIVES
June Henfrey Library
Kim Meacher, Library Coordinator
C/o Blackburne House Centre for Women
Hope Street
Liverpool L1 9JB
T 0151 709 4356 F 0151 709 8293
bhcfw@mail.cybase.co.uk
Open to women who are members of Blackburne House Mon-Fri 9.15 am-5 pm. A woman only space providing a welcoming, safe environment in which they can study, relax & find information. Exhibitions, discussions.

Tropix Photo Library
Veronic Birley
156 Meols Parade
Meols
Wirral
Merseyside L47 6AN
T 0151 632 1698 F 0151 632 1698
Specialist photographic library focusing on developing nations & environmental issues. Supplies publishers, press, designers worldwide. Second prize Women's Enterprise Network Businesswoman of the Year 1990.

POLITICS
Merseyside Socialist Women
Cathy Wilson
11 Dovey Street
Liverpool L8 8BT
T 0151 727 6933
Broad-based, political campaigning body for women to fight the present economic system & promote socialist ideas around women's equality & liberation. Meets bi-monthly locally & 3 times per year nationally.

PREGNANCY/CHILDBIRTH
ElliePants
The Ellie Nappy Company
P O Box 16

South Wirral
Merseyside L66 2HA
T 0151 200 5012
Waterproof coverings for terry nappies. No pins.

Link Support Group
P O Box 30
Liverpool L15 9HZ
T 0151 722 8139 F 0151 709 9462
Meets at 7.30 on second Wed of each month in Urodynamics Teaching Room on ground floor of Liverpool Women's Hospital, Crown Street, Liverpool L8 7SS. Self-help infertility patient support group.

PRISONERS/PRISONERS' WIVES

Merseyside Specialist Training Agency
Val Metcalf
Room 414
Tower Building
22 Water Street
Liverpool L3 1BA
T 0151 231 1355 F 0151 227 4014
Vocational guidance, assessment & information for unemployed adults, ex-offenders, ex-prisoners set up by NACRO in partnership with Merseyside probation service.

Merseyside Women's Group
Nora O'Shaughnessy, Group Coordinator
13 North View
Edge Hill
Liverpool L7 8TS
T 0151 281 1245 F 0151 281 1246
Meets Tue 5.30-7.30 pm at Walton FSU, 5-6 Tetlow Way, Lagham Industrial Estate, Walton, Liverpool L4 4QS; phone 0151 207 1302. Offers friends & partners of prisoners a chance to meet & share information.

PROFESSIONAL ASSOCIATIONS

Institute of Qualified Private Secretaries - NW branch
Elaine Wallwork, PR coordinator
16 Penny Lane
Hadock
St Helens
Merseyside WA11 0QS
T 01942 720714
Regular events/meetings held approximately every six weeks in venues around the region on a variety of topics. New members welcome. A branch of the national organisation.

Merseyside, Chester and North Wales Assn of Women Solicitors
Rosemary Dale
Maxwell, Entwistle and Byrne
12 Newtown Gardens
Kerkby
Merseyside L32 8RR
T 0151 548 7370 F 0151 546 2836
Supports women solicitors. Meets about six times a year in various venues in the north west of England.

Women As Role Models (WARM) - North West
Fiona Crehan
C/o EEP Ltd
The View, 6th Floor
32-36 Hanover Street
Liverpool L1 4LN
T 0151 708 7103 F 0151 708 7103
Raising awareness of how women can & do achieve in non-traditional areas of employment. Women working/ training in non-traditional areas of work as role models for boys, girls & adults. Challenges stereotypes.

PUBLISHERS/PUBLICATIONS

News From Nowhere
96 Bold Street
Liverpool L1 4HY
T 0151 708 7270
Open Mon-Sat 9.45 am-5.45 pm. Radical & feminist bookshop & women's collective committed to social change. A wide range of books, particularly literature. Also magazines & posters.

RELIGIOUS ORGANISATIONS

Presbyterian Tuesday Women's Meeting
Mrs Edna Davey, Hon Sec
16 Fairmead Road
Moreton
Wirral
Merseyside L46 8TX
T 0151 677 0963
A one-hour devotional meeting: hymns, prayers & a Bible reading. A speaker (20-25 minutes) every week from October to Easter. Keeps members in touch; always ready to encourage & help. Average of 30 women.

Salvation Army - Southport Citadel
Women's Home League
59 Shakespeare Street
Southport PR8 5AJ

ENGLAND - LIVERPOOL AND MERSEYSIDE

T 01704 547805
Meets for worship & education on Mon & is part of the Salvation Army's outreach programme. Transport is provided.

SERVICES

Pat McCourt Originals Designer Knitwear
Pat McCourt
158 Park Road
Formby
Liverpool L37 6ES
T 01704 875111
Design & manufacture of exclusive knitwear - suits, dresses & separates (including clubwear) to retailers. Also designs for yarn producers & knitwear magazines. Private commissions undertaken.

SEXUAL ABUSE/RAPE CRISIS

Umbrella Centre, The
Maureen Boyd
Lower Ground Floor
111 Mount Pleasant
Liverpool L3 5TF
T 0151 708 0415
Support service for women survivors of child sexual abuse. Open Mon-Fri 9.30 am-4.30 pm. Self-referral or referral through DHS/GPs. Information/support for people experiencing mental health problems.

Wirral Rape Crisis Counselling Service
Helen Lancaster
P O Box 35
Birkenhead L42 4RX
T 0151 650 0155   F 0151 666 1392
Helpline: 0151 666 1392 open Sun 2-5 pm; Mon 7-9 pm; Wed 2-5 pm; Thurs 7-9 pm. Face-to-face counselling & court/hospital support available. Free service to women survivors of sexual violence.

SOCIAL

Luncheon Club for Women
Mrs Joan Petrie
Salvation Army Community Centre
140a Earle Road
Liverpool L7
T 0151 734 2556
Mon & Fri 12.15-1.15 pm.

SPORTS AND LEISURE

Liverpool & District Keep Fit Association
Mrs Dorothy Bush, Secretary
14 Beechdale Road
Liverpool L18 5EL
T 0151 475 0542
The umbrella organisation for the many keep fit branches in the area, both within the aegis of the LEAs & those sponsored privately. Phone above number for details of your nearest local branch.

Sports & Health Unit - Blackburn House
Gill Mackay, Coordinator
C/o Blackburne House Centre for Women
Hope Street
Liverpool L1 9JB
T 0151 709 4356   F 0151 709 8293
electra@mcr1.poptel.org.uk
Circuit training, Alexander Technique, step aerobics, reflexology, holistic massage, Latin American dance, etc. Steam & weights rooms. Also Liverpool Women's Outdoor Activities Group: camping & walking.

SUPPORT

Merseyside Anxiety/Agoraphobia Support & Information Network
Barbara Kingman, Mental Health Officer
C/o Merseyside CVS DRU
Mount Vernon Green
Hall Lane
Liverpool L7 8TF
T 0151 709 0990
Advice, information & support for those suffering from anxiety disorders. One-to-one support & referral to other agencies, if necessary.

Newton Family and Community Association
Judi Lunt
Park Road South
Newton Le Willows
Merseyside WA12 8EX
T 01925 224731
The following groups are run by women: women's group (women only) Mon 1-3 pm; keep fit Mon 7-8 pm; aerobics Mon 8.15-9.15 pm; flower arranging Wed 10 am-12.30 pm; single parents Fri 7-9 pm (creche).

Women's Community Action Group
Maureen Dunwoody
C/o St Mark's Church Hall
Brookhey Drive, Northwood
Kirkby
Merseyside L33 9TE
T 0151 289 9692   F 0151 289 9694
wcag.mersinet.co.uk

Open Tue, Wed, Thurs 10 am-3 pm. Self help goup. Drop-in. Information & advice. Skill sharing. The group was set up with the aim to provide a space for women to organise around community matters.

Training

R R Consultancy/Training
Rita Roberts
20 Thames Road
Sutton
St Helens
Merseyside WA9 4HB
T 01744 821387
Equal opportunities training/consultancy. Business English (TEFL).

Transport

Mersey Travel
Paulette Howe
24 Hatton Garden
Liverpool L3 2AN
T 0151 330 1300 F 0151 330 1222
Open Mon-Fri 8.30 am-5 pm. Phone: 0151 227 5181. Coordinates public transport on Merseyside. Funds socially necessary bus services, the Merseyrail Network. Provides free travel for elderly & disabled.

Violence against women

Merseyside Campaign Against Domestic Violence (CADV)
Cathy Wilson
11 Dovey Street
Liverpool L8 8BT
T 0151 727 6933 F 0151 727 6933
Aims to promote discussion, argue for more resources in benefits, wages, refuges & housing & to achieve a change in the law on provocation & self-defence. Meets locally, public campaigns, street stalls, etc.

Merseyside Safer Cities Project
Kevin Wong
Room 417
Tower Building
22 Water Street
Liverpool L3 1AB
T 0151 227 4130 F 0151 227 4014
Government-funded community safety partnership with NACRO promoting local initiatives to prevent crime & make places safer.

Women's Aid

Sefton Women's and Children's Aid
Lesley Paterson
100 Bridge Road
Litherland
Liverpool L21 6PH
T 0151 920 6072 F 0151 920 6072
Support services for women & children victims/survivors of domestic violence. Refuge accommodation, advice centres, outreach services, counselling & self-help groups. Training for statutory/voluntary groups.

St Helens District Women's Aid
Eileen Taylor, Director
42 Hardshaw Street
St Helens
Merseyside WA10 5JN
T 01744 454438
Drop-in centre for women Mon-Fri 9 am-5 pm. Offers short-term accommodation to women & their children (if any) who are or who may be at risk from domestic violence. A support network offered for women.

Manchester and Gtr. Manchester

Accommodation

Beeches, The
6 Wilbraham Road
Fallowfield
Manchester M14 6JZ
T 0161 224 8300
Accommodation for 21 single homeless women. Support offered when moving to permanent accommodation. 24-hour staffing. Referrals mainly from Direct Access hostel but referrals from other agencies welcome.

CONTACT - Norwood
339 Wilbraham Road
Whalley Range
Manchester M16 8GL
T 0161 861 9806
Long-stay accommodation for homeless girls aged 14-21. 24-hour support.

Stop Over
Manchester
T 0161 224 8594
Provides immediate access to accommodate 10 young women aged 16-25 with 24-hour staffing. Also eight move-on beds in self-contained flats with low level support.

ACCOUNTANCY

Slade & Cooper
Janet Slade and Sue Cooper
5th Floor
Fourways House
57 Hilton Street
Manchester M1 2EJ
T 0161 236 1493 F 0161 228 7239
There are two female partners who specialise in voluntary grant-aided organisations as well as more general work.

ARTS AND CRAFTS

Black Arts Alliance
SuAndi, performance artist
111 Burton Road
Withington
Manchester M20 1HZ
T 0161 445 4168 F 0161 448 0335
101651.2770@compuserve.com
To promote Black art and culture on a non-profit basis to all members of the community at large. Work includes showcases, performances, seminars, exhibitions, workshops in education, community & prisons.

Cultureword
Cathy Bolton
C/o Commonword
Cheetwood House
21 Newton Street
Manchester M1 1FZ
T 0161 236 2773
cathy.bolton@mcr1.poptel.org.uk
Acts as a focus for Afro-Caribbean, Chinese & Asian writers in the north west of England. Provides a range of activities, including workshops & performances.

Salford Women Writers
Pat Winslow
8 Mount Pleasant
Darcy Lever
Bolton BL3 1RZ
A creative writing group that has published an anthology of poetry & prose. Meets on Wed. Write for further details.

Womanswrite
Cathy Bolton
Commonword
21 Newton Street
Manchester M1 1F2
T 0161 236 2773 F 0161 236 2773
Workshop for women writers providing support and critical feedback, as well as performance and publishing opportunities. Meets Tue 11 am-1 pm.

Women Writers' Network North
Manchester
T 0161 929 0894
Contact with other women writers & editors. Over 200 members with range of writing interests - jouranlism, fiction, non-fiction, children's writing, poetry, drama, etc. Monthly meetings with editors & agents.

BUSINESS SUPPORT SCHEMES

Salford Way Project, The
Ann Whittam/Kim Jones
Salford Opportunities Centre
Churchill Way
Pendleton
Salford M6 5PL
T 0161 737 0634
Helping Salford women overcome barriers to personal/career development. Open to employed & unemployed women. Can help find right training, edcuation, employment. Help with childcare, travel, books, equipment.

CENTRES FOR WOMEN

Opportunities for Women Centre
Sarah Bell/Cari Ryan
Block B
Brunswick Square
Union Street
Oldham OL1 1DE
T 0161 628 9294 F 0161 628 9957
100667.1412@compuserve.com
Open Mon-Fri 9 am-5 pm drop-in information on training & education; grants & benefits; etc. Free to unemployed women: cv preparation; women into teleworking, etc; training for employed women in eg telework.

Pankurst Centre
Rachelle Warburton, Administrator
60-62 Nelson Street
Chorlton on Medlock
Manchester M13 9WP
T 0161 273 5673
Open Mon-Fri 10 am-3 pm Women's resource centre. Meeting rooms, space for exhibitions. Rents out offices for counselling sessions.

Salford Women's Centre
Gill Stanton/Sam Priestley
Halton Bank
Langworth Road

Salford M6 7AB
T 0161 736 3844
Promoting well being of women who live or work in Salford. Training, adult education courses, one-to-one counselling, support groups, meeting space. Free creche. Snack bar. All women welcome.

CHILD CARE AND FAMILY
Fun Club
Seline Downey
Miles Platting Community Assembly
39 Varley Street
Miles Platting
Manchester M40 8EE
T 0161 205 1860
Play scheme for children Tue 6-8 pm. Also runs activities for children at other times during school holidays.

COMPUTERS/IT
Chorlton Workshop Electronic Village Hall
Jak Radice
Chorlton Central Church
Barlow Moor Road
Manchester M21 8BF
T 0161 860 6238   F 0161 881 5189
chorlton-ws@mcr1.poptel.org.uk
Adult education centre for unwaged/unemployed adults who don't have further/higher education qualifications. Open Mon-Thurs 10 am-12 pm & 1-3 pm. Free courses & free creche. Wheelchair accessible.

Manchester Women's Electronic Village Hall
Emma Healey/Clem Herman/Martha Walker
23 New Mount Street
Manchester M4 4DE
T 0161 953 4049   F 0161 953 4051
women-evh@mcri.poptel.org.uk
Open Mon-Fri 10 am-3 pm. Computer training for unwaged women returning to work. Courses include NVQ1, NVQ2 teleworking & NVQ2 computer networks. Wheelchair access. Free courses. Part of WEBIN project.

CONTRACEPTION/WELL WOMAN
Abbey Hey Clinic
Constable Street
Manchester
T 0161 223 4193
Free contraceptive advice, information & supplies Mon 6.30-8.30 pm; Tue 9.30-11.30 am

Alexandra Park Health Centre
2 Whitswood Close
Alexandra Park
Manchester
T 0161 226 0101
Free contraceptive advice, information & supplies on Fri 1.30-3.30 pm

Ancoats Community Clinic
The Old Casualty Department
Old Mill Street
Ancoats
Manchester M4 6EB
T 0161 203 4033
Well woman clinics first & third Thurs of each month 9.30-11.30 am & fourth Tue 6-8.30 pm. Drop-in. Blood pressure checks, urine tests, etc. Free contraceptive advice/supplies Fri 6.30-8.30 pm

Baguley Clinic
Hall Lane
Baguley
Manchester
T 0161 998 6071
Free contraceptive advice, supplies & information on Wed 6.30-8.30 pm

Brunswick Health Centre
Hartfield Close
Brunswick Street
Manchester
T 0161 273 4901
Free contraceptive advice, supplies & information on Tue 9.30-11.30 am

Charlestown Health Centre
Charlestown Road
Manchester
T 0161 740 7786
Free contraceptive advice, supplies & information on Mon 9.30-11.30 am & Thurs 6.30-8.30 pm

Cheetham Clinic
1 Smedley Street
Cheetham
Manchester
T 0161 205 1704
Free contraceptive advice, supplies & information on Mon 1.30-3.30 pm.

Chorlton Health Centre
1 Nicholas Street
Chorlton
Manchester
T 0161 861 8888
Free contraceptive advice, supplies & information on Tue 6-8 pm & Thurs 9.30-11.30 am

Clayton Health Centre
89 North Road
Clayton
Manchester
T 0161 231 1151
Free contraceptive advice, supplies & information on Wed 9.30-11.30 am & Tue 6.30-8.30 pm

Crumpsall Clinic
Margaret White
Humphrey Street
Cheetham
Manchester
T 740 9973
Well woman clinics on first Wed of each month 9.30-11.30 am Drop-in. Blood pressure checks, urine tests, pregnancy tests, weight checks. Advice & information about the menopause. Free services.

Eccles Health Centre
Corporation Road
Salford M30 0EQ
T 0161 789 5135
Free contraceptive advice & supplies. Clinics on Thurs 6.30-8.30 pm.

Format 131 Under 25s Only
131 Cleggs Lane
Little Hulton
Salford
T 0161 799 4001
Free contraceptive advice & supplies for under 25s. Clinics on Mon, Tue & Thurs 8.30-10.30 am &3-5 pm; Wed 8.30-10.30 am & 3-6 pm; Fri 8.30-10.30 am

Gorton Clinic
Blackwin Street
Gorton
Manchester
T 0161 223 3025
Free contraceptive advice, supplies & information on Tue 1.30-3.30 pm

Harpurhey Health Centre
1 Church Lane
Harpurhey
Manchester
T 0161 205 5063
Free contraceptive advice, supplies & information on Mon 6.30-8.30 pm & Fri 9.30-11.30 am

Higher Broughton Health Centre
Bevendon Square
Salford M7 0UF
T 0161 792 6969
Free contraceptive advice & supplies. Clinics on Wed 6.30-8.30 pm; Fri 10 am-12 pm.

Hulme Clinic
217 Hulme Walk
Hulme
Manchester
T 0161 226 5211
Free contraceptive advice, supplies & information on Mon 1-3 pm

Irlam Health Centre
Macdonald Road
Salford M44 5LH
T 0161 775 2902
Free contraceptive advice & supplies. Clinics on Mon 10-11.30 am; Wed 6.30-8 pm.

Lance Burn Health Centre
Churchill Way
Salford M6 5PN
T 0161 745 8855
Free contraceptive advice & supplies. Clinics on Tue 1-2.30 pm.

Langworthy Clinic
451 Liverpool Street
Salford M6 5QQ
T 0161 737 6036
Free contraceptive advice & supplies. Clinics on Tue 6.30-8 pm.

Levenshulme Health Centre
Dunstable Street
Levenshulme
Manchester
T 0161 225 4343
Free contraceptive advice, supplies & information on Wed & Thurs 9.30-11.30 am

Little Hulton Health Centre
Haysbrook Avenue
Salford M38 0AY

ENGLAND - MANCHESTER AND GTR. MANCHESTER

T 0161 790 4283
Free contraceptive advice & supplies. Clinics on Tue 6.30-8 pm.

Longsight Health Centre
526-528 Stockport Road
Longsight
Manchester
T 0161 225 9274
Free contraceptive advice, supplies & information on Wed 6-8 pm

Manchester Brook Centre
Faulkner House
Faulkner Street
Manchester M1 4DY
T 0161 237 3001
Free, confidential contraceptive advice. Free condoms & other contraceptive supplies. Help with emotional & sexual problems. Pregnancy testing & quick results. Phone for opening times.

Marie Stopes Centre
Joan Pilsburg, Manager
St John Street Chambers
2 St John Street
Manchester M3 4DB
T 0161 832 4260
Pregancy advice (helpline 0171 388 4843); general healcare/contraception (helpline 0171 388 0662); sterilisation services (helpline 0171 388 5554); well woman clinics; abortion clinics; menopause clinics; etc.

Moss Side Health Centre
Monton Street
Moss Side
Manchester
T 0161 226 5031
Free contraceptive advice, supplies & information on Tue 6-8 pm.

Neesa Well Women Drop In Project
Zhara Hussain
Woodville Community Resource Centre
Shirley Road
Cheetham Hill
Manchester M8 7NE
T 0161 740 2995
Drop-in Tue, Wed, Thurs 1.15-3.15 pm
Mother & toddler club; social events; outings.

Ordsall Health Centre
Belfort Drive
Salford M5 3PP

T 0161 872 2004
Free well woman & contraceptive advice & supplies. Well woman clinic only on fourth Fri of each month 1.30-3 pm. Contraception clinics on all other Fri 1.30-3 pm.

Palatine Centre
63-65 Palatine Road
Withington
Manchester
T 0161 434 3555
Free contraceptive advice, supplies & info Mon-Fri 10 am-12 noon; 1.30-3.30 pm; 6-8 pm. Please make an appt for the first session. Emergencies seen at any session. Well woman clinic Thurs 1-4 pm

Plant Hill Clinic
Plant Hill Road
Manchester
T 0161 740 8004
Free contraceptive advice, supplies & information on Tue 9.30-11.30 am Also phone 0161 740 7909.

Rusholme Health Centre
Walmer Street
Manchester
T 0161 681 0940
Well woman clinic Wed 1.30-3.30 pm. Drop-in. Woman doctor available. Free services. Blood pressure checks, urine tests, pregnancy tests, etc. Contraceptive clinic Thurs 1.30-3.30 pm. Free services/supplies.

Salford Brook Centre
55 Regent Street
Eccles
Manchester M30 0BP
T 0161 707 9550
Free, confidential contraceptive advice & supplies. Pregancy testing. Clinics on Mon 6.30-8.30 pm.; Wed 3.15-5.15 p.m; Fri 6.30-8.30 pm (under 25s only), Sat 12-2 pm (under 25s only).

St Mary's Hospital
Hathersage Road
Manchester
T 0161 276 6406
Free contraceptive advice, supplies & information on Wed 1.30-3.30 pm

Swinton Clinic
Partington Lane
Salford M27 3WN

T 0161 794 7521
Free contraceptive advice & supplies. Clinics on Mon 6.30-8 pm.

Varley Street Clinic
Farnborough Road
Miles Platting
Manchester
T 0161 205 6111
Free contraceptive advice, supplies & information on Wed 1.30-3.30 pm & Fri 9.30-11.30 am

West Penine Brook Centre
8 Manchester Chambers
Manchester Street
Oldham OL8 1LF
T 0161 627 0200
Free, confidential contraceptive advice. Free condoms & other contraceptive supplies. Help with emotional & sexual problems. Pregnancy testing & quick results. Phone for opening times.

Woodhouse Park Clinic
Simonsway
Wythenshawe
Manchester
T 0161 437 2228
Free contraceptive advice, supplies & information on Tue 9.30-11.30 am & Thurs 6-8 pm. Also phone 0161 437 4502.

Wythenshawe Health Care Centre
Stancliffe Road
Sharston
Wythenshawe
Manchester
T 0161 946 0065
Free contraceptive advice, supplies & information on Wed 9.30-11.30 am Well woman clinics Tue 1-4 pm. Doctor available at all sessions. Phone or drop in to make an appointment.

COUNSELLING AND THERAPY

Newton Heath Health Centre
2 Old Church Street
Newton Heath
Manchester M10 6JF
T 0161 681 0940
Drop-in first & third Tue of each month 9.30-11.30 am Also second Thurs of each month 6-8 pm. On second, fourth & fifth Tue of each month a relaxation session for women only 10-11 am

EQUAL OPPS

Fair Play North West
Geoffrey Leigh, Coordinator
Government Office for the North West
Washington House
New Bailey Street
Manchester M3 5ER
T 0161 952 4474 F 0161 952 4169
Positive action equalities project. A government EOC initiative to stimulate partnerships which improve opportunities for women to realise their full potential in education, employment & the community.

Policy & Equality Unit
Monaza Luqman, Principal Policy Officer
Tameside Metropolitan Borough Council
Wellington Road
Ashton-Under-Lune Ol6 1DL
T 0161 342 3542 F 0161 342 2148

ETHNIC MINORITIES

African Women's Arts and Development (AWAD) 2000
Mrs Toro Kane
C/o West Indian Centre
Carmoor Road
Chorlton-on-Medlock
Manchester M13
T 0161 257 2092
Set up to assist African women in developing their art & culture, language, etc. A platform for promotion of continued progression of the 'Arts of Africa'. For women born in & living outside of Africa.

Bangladesh Welfare and Community Project
Mr Chaudri
Bangladesh House
19a Birch Lane
Longsight
Manchester M13 0NW
T 0161 225 4012
Women & children's groups; day nursery; computer training for development of office skills. Every Fri women only. Badminton, table tennis, pool, fitness centre, kitchen, aerobics women only Fri 5-6 pm.

Manchester Bangladeshi Women's Project
Slade Lane Neighbourhood Centre
642 Stockport Road
Longsight
Manchester M13 0RZ
T 0161 257 3867

Open Mon-Fri 9 am-3 pm Runs regular ESOL classes; mother & toddler group; young women's group; keep fit class; well woman drop-in clinic; advice sessions on DSS, housing, employment, education, etc.

Noor-ul-quran
Mrs Shahzada
24 Polygon Avenue
Arwick
Manchester M13 9FX
T 0161 224 0774
General & specific advice for women. Play schemes & transport for children; computing classes; counselling for drugs users. Children & adults are taught Urdu, Bengali, English, & Arabic. Physical education.

Opportunity for Women Bus
Habidah Usman/Samima Ahmed
Oldham
T 0161 627 2409
Mobile 0831 597 258. Open Mon, Tue, Wed & Fri 9.30 am-3.30 pm; Thurs 9.30 am-1.30 pm Mobile information, guidance & training service for women in ethnic minority communities in Oldham. Creche on bus.

Pakistan Community Centre
481 Stockport Road
Longsight
Manchester M12 4NN
T 0161 224 5235
Centre for the Pakistani community in Manchester, offering vocational help & advice, play schemes, women's activities (keep fit, discussions on health matters, etc). Activities for women during summer holidays.

GIRLS/YOUNG WOMEN

42nd Street
Alistair Cox
2nd Floor
Swan Buildings
20 Swan Street
Manchester M4 5JW
T 0161 832 0170 F 0161 839 5424
Mental health service for young people aged 15-25. Individual support for women (befriending, counselling & psychotherapy). Women's groups including survivors' group, women's group & support for lesbians.

Barlow Moor Community Centre
Julie Mrozek, Centre Coordinator
23 Merseybank Avenue
Chorlton
Manchester M21 7NT
T 0161 434 1538
Girls & young women's group (aged 13-25) Tue 6.30-9.30 pm; playgroup for children aged 2½-5 Mon-Fri 9.30 am-12 noon; parents & toddlers Mon 1-3 pm.

Girls' Work Unit
Olalunde Spence
Manchester Youth Service
The Ardwich Centre
100 Palmerstone Street
Manchester M12 6PE
T 0161 273 1763 F 0161 445 7266
Providing support, advice, information & resources to develop work with girls & young women on issues affecting women. Training. Supporting/developing work on issues of sexuality & challenging homophobia.

Manchester Girls and Young Women's Project
Michelle Walmsley and Chiara Vagnarelli
The Ardwick Centre
100 Palmerston Street
Ardwick
Manchester M12 6PE
T 0161 273 1763 F 0161 273 2059
Evening phone: 0161 445 7266. Offers support, resources, contacts, training & networking opportunities to youth & community workers & others responding to young people's needs.

Manchester Youth and Community Service (MYCS)
Lynne White, Coordinator
Greenacres
2 Moor Lane, Northern Moor
Wythenshawe
Manchester M23 0LT
T 0161 945 1032
Young women & children group Tue afternoon; young women group Tue evening, safe transport; Playbus for whole of Wythenshawe area; drop-in pregnancy testing Tue & Thurs mornings; counselling; free condoms, etc.

HEALTH

Body Positive North West
Chris Brown
Body Positive Centre, 3rd Floor
4 Ways House
18 Tariff Street
Manchester M1 2EP

T 0161 236 9669 F 0161 237 9412
Open Mon 11 am-8 pm; Tue 11 am-5 pm; Fri 11 am-4 pm. Helpline available on Tue & Thurs 7-10 pm, always staffed by people who are HIV positive & experienced counsellors. Alternative therapies.

Cheetham & Crumpsall Women's Health Drop-in
Margaret White
Neighbourhood Offices
Cheetham Hill Road
Cheetham Hill
Manchester
T 0161 740 9973
Drop-in for women only on Wed 9.30-11.30 am Supervised play area for children. Run by local community workers & volunteers.

North Manchester Breast Care and Mastectomy Group
Joyce Bell
Community Care Department
North Manchester Gen Hospital
Crumpsall
Manchester M8 6RB
T 0161 720 2533
Support & self-help for women who have had treatment for breast cancer. Practical information & mutual support provided.

Women's Health Team
Newton Heath Health Centre
2 Old Church Street
Newton Heath
Manchester M10 6JF
T 0161 681 0940
Provides information about well woman clinics & contraception clinics throughout Manchester. Advice & information for women about health problems.

Y-Wait
Maggie Flint
Moston Youth Centre
Hough Hall Road
Manchester M40 9NJ
T 0161 205 4128
Open Mon 4-8 pm. For young women up to age 25, run by young women volunteers, health workers & a doctor. Health advice, information & time to talk. Pregancy testing, contraceptives. Creche. Free services.

LEGAL MATTERS

Cheetham Hill Advice Centre (CHAC)
Jane Eberhart/Maggie Foley
24 Alderford Parade
Waterloo Road
Manchester M8 7TN
T 0161 708 9901 F 0161 708 9662
Drop-in Tue 10-1; Thurs 1-3. Fri morning appts only. Also Mon 1-3 pm drop-in & Fri afternoons home visits Woodville Resource Centre, Shirley Road, Manchester. Free appointments with solicitor. Free advice.

Robinson King Solicitors
Jane Robinson
Grosvenor House
22 Grafton Street
Altrincham WA14 1BH
T 0161 929 8686 F 0161 929 8787
RK@robinsonking.co.uk
Solicitors practice specialising in personal injury work. Mainly female organisation (non matrimonial). Open normal office hours & outside office hours by arrangement. Woman friendly.

MEDIA

WFA Media and Cultural Centre
Fiona Johnson
9 Lucy Street
Old Trafford
Manchester M15 4BX
T 0161 848 9782 F 0161 848 9783
Educational cooperative. Low cost access to video equipment/facilities for production, editing, duplication, exhibition, video training, unionised video production unit, bookshops, access to media workstations.

PLACES TO STAY AND EAT

Cafe des Femmes
Rachelle Warburton, Administrator
Pankhurst Centre
60-62 Nelson Street
Charlton on Medlock
Manchester M13 9WP
T 0161 273 5673
Women-only vegetarian restaurant.

Home From Home
Sue or Janette
13 Oswald Road
Chorlton-cum-Harray
Manchester M21 9NL
T 0161 291 0637

Women only B & B. A ten-minute bus or car ride from Manchester's gay scene. Come & relax with us. Phone for details of up-to-date prices.

Pregnancy/Childbirth

Crisis Pregnancy Centre - Bolton
Mary Waller
Rainbow Pregnancy Advice Centre
Bolton Pentecostal Church
Bury New Road
Bolton BL2 2BD
T 01204 522002
Open Mon-Fri 9 am-3 pm. Free pregnancy testing, counselling & support for women with unplanned pregancies. Post abortion & miscarriage counselling.

Crisis Pregnancy Centre - Oldham
Joyce Jepsom
236 Rochdale Road
Royton
Oldham
T 0161 624 3563
Open Wed 10 am-1 pm. Helpline (as above) open mon-Fri 9 am-5 pm. Free pregnancy testing, counselling, support for women with unplanned pregnancies. Post abortion & miscarriage counselling. Phone for appt.

Crisis Pregnancy Centre - Salford
Pearl King
26 Saxby Street
Salford M6 7RG
T 0161 736 5748
Open Fri 12-1 pm.; Tue 6.30-7.30 pm. Free pregnancy testing, counselling, support for women with unplanned pregnancies. Post abortion/miscarriage counselling. 24-hour ansaphone. Also out of hours if needed.

Pregnancy Advisory Service
Mrs Avril Dunn
3rd Floor
43-45 Picadilly Gardens
Manchester M1 2AP
T 0161 228 1887 F 0161 236 2368
Open Mon-Fri 8.30 am-4.30 pm. Pregnancy testing, problems relating to women & pregnancy, counselling & advice. Abortions, sterilisation, sterilisation reversal. 24-hour ansaphone.

Prisoners/Prisoners' Wives

Campaign Against Double Punishment
C/o POPS, St Marks Cheetham
Tetlow Lane
Cheetham
Manchester M8 7HF
T 0161 740 8600 F 0161 740 4181
Supporting families & prisoners who are concerned about deportation in conjunction with a custodial sentence.

Partners of Prisoners and Families Support Group (POPS)
Diane Curry
St Marks Cheetham
Tetlow Lane
Cheetham
Manchester M8 7HF
T 0161 740 8600 F 0161 740 4181
Open Mon-Fri 9 am-4 pm; drop-in Wed 10 am-2 pm. For prisoners' families. Support & information. Practical help. Pre-release training to prisoners' wives: assertiveness training, etc. Welfare rights.

Publishers/Publications

Commonword - Community Writing and Publishing Project
Cathy Bolton
Cheetwood House
21 Newton Street
Manchester M1 1FZ
T 0161 236 2773
cathy.bolton@mcr1.poptel.org.uk
Non-profit cooperative, producing books by writers in the north west of England, providing support & development. Writers' workshops, including Womanswrite. Crocus imprint. Manuscript reading service.

Subversive Sister
Department 33
1 Newton Street
Piccadilly
Manchester M1 1HW
Manchester's radical women's magazine.

Rights

UNISON - North West Region
regional women's officer
3-5 St John Street
Manchester M3 4DL
T 0161 832 5025 F 0161 833 1614
Public sector trade union. Working for equal rights at work and in the community.

Services

Building Positive Action
Annie Hopley
C/o Tung Sing Housing Association
Richmond House
15 Bloom Street
Manchester M1 3HZ
T 0161 236 6277 F 0161 237 3447
Raising profile of minority-led firms in social housing. If business is owned/manged by women, Black, ethnic minority people, people with disabilities apply to be included in skills directory free of charge.

Sexual Abuse/Rape Crisis

Black Women's Service Helpline
C/o Manchester Rape Crisis
P O Box 336
Manchester M60 2BS
T 0161 839 8379
Free, confidential service for Black & Asian women who have been raped/sexually abused/ sexually assaulted. Staffed by Black women & trained volunteers. Helpline open Wed 9 am-12 noon & Fri 6-9 pm

Manchester Rape Crisis
Kath Dimmelow
P O Box 336
Manchester M60 2BS
T 0161 839 8379
Free, confidential support, advice, counselling for women & girls who have been raped/sexually abused/sexually assaulted. Helpline: 0161 834 8784 open Tue & Fri 2-5 pm; Wed & Thurs 6-9 pm

Mothers of Sexually Abused Children
Liz Green, Group Worker
Manchester Family Service Unit
Varley Street
Miles Platting
Manchester M40 7AH
T 0161 205 7402 F 0161 205 7825
A self-support group for women whose children have been sexually abused. Meets occasionally. Both self-referral & referred.

Sexual Assault Referral Centre
St Mary's Centre
St Mary's Hospital
Hathersage Road
Manchester M13 0JH
T 0161 276 6515 F 0161 276 6691

Women's Survivors' Group
Liz Green, Group Worker
Manchester Family Service Unit
Varley Street
Miles Platting
Manchester M40 7AH
T 0161 205 7402 F 0161 205 7825
For women who have experienced sexual abuse. Meets occasionally. Both self-referral & referred.

Sports and Leisure

Water Adventure Centre
Lilian Pons, Centre Manager
The Old Boathouse
Fairfield Locks
Maddison Rd, Droylsden
Manchester M35 6ES
T 0161 301 2673 F 0161 301 5972
Open seven days a week. Water-based activities, camps, etc. Women only days once every three months & in March for International Women's Day. Free creche. Young women only space (under age 25) Wed 4.30-8 pm.

Support

Moss Side and Hulme Women's Action Forum
97 Princess Road
Moss Side
Manchester M14 4TH
T 0161 232 0545 F 0161 232 0546
Open Mon-Fri 9 am-5 pm; advice sessions & open drop-in Tue 10 am-1 pm & 2-4 pm & Thurs 2-4 pm (otherwise make an appointment). Facilitating improvement of women's skills, qualifications, etc.

Positively Women
Julie Mrozek, Centre Coordinator
Barlow Moor Community Centre
23 Merseybank Avenue
Chorlton
Manchester M21 7NT
T 0161 434 1538
Meets Thurs 1-3 pm. Creche. Aiming to develop women's self-esteem. Health oriented: aromatherapy demonstrations & keep fit classes.

Women's Royal Voluntary Service - North West Division
597 Stretford Road
Old Trafford
Manchester M16 9BX
T 0161 872 7492 F 0161 877 8023

ENGLAND - NEWCASTLE AND TYNESIDE

Services are divided into family, hospital, food & emergency services. They include meals on wheels, hospital shops, tea & coffee bars, contact centres, family holidays & lunch clubs.

VIOLENCE AGAINST WOMEN

Justice for Women - Manchester
28 Eaton Road
Sale M33 9TZ
Campaigning for changes in the law so that it recognises & takes seriously women's experience of male violence; monitoring & raising awareness around response of criminal justice system to male violence, etc.

Open Door
Carol Helm, Manager
35-37 Princess Road
Moss Side
Manchester M14 4TE
T 0161 226 1751 F 0161 226 1751
Open Mon, Tue, Thurs, Fri 9.30 am-5 pm; Wed 9 am-1.30 pm. Support for women, particularly for those who have not received help from statutory services, on domestic violence issues. Creche.

Women's Domestic Violence Helpline
Geraldine Flanagan, Coordinator
P O Box 156
Newton Street
Manchester M60 1DB
T 0161 839 8574
Minicom 0161 834 4496. Open Mon-Fri 10 am-4 pm; Sat 10 a.m-1 pm. Advice, support information to women suffering domestic violence, or whose children have been abused, or who wish to leave home.

WORKING WOMEN

Manchester Action on Street Health (MASH)
Sarah Crosby, Service Manager
Unit 201 Ducie House
37 Ducie Street
Manchester M1 2JW
T 0161 228 3433 F 0161 236 1458
Aims to reduce incidence of HIV infection & other STDs & to reduce unwanted pregnancies in prostitutes. Provides free condoms, needle exchanges, GUM service, pregnancy testing, advice & information.

NEWCASTLE AND TYNESIDE

ACCOMMODATION

Norcare Ltd
Team Manager
Cumberland House
172 Westgate Road
Newcastle upon Tyne NE4 6AL
T 0191 230 2090
Provides temporary supported accommodation for single homeless women aged 17-60 years. Staff available in office hours. On-call system. Support geared to individual needs. Networking with specialist agencies.

PANAH
the workers
P O Box 27
Newcastle upon Tyne NE3 1EU
T 0191 284 6998 F 0191 284 6998
Black women's refuge & outreach service. Provides safe, secure, temporary accommodation for Black single women & women with children fleeing from domestic violence.

Wearside Women in Need
Claire Phillipson, Coordinator
1st Floor, The Elms
19 Front Street, Concord
Washington
Tyne & Wear NE37 2BA
T 0191 416 3550 F 0191 416 3888
Refuge accommodation for women & children fleeing/who have experienced psysical, sexual or emotional abuse. Staff available 24 hours. Hotline nos: 0191 415 1506 or 0191 514 1972. Young women's project.

AGRICULTURE

British Women's Land Army Society - Sunderland
Mrs Evelyn S Elliott
26 Srley Street
Millfield
Sunderland
Tyne & Wear SR4 7UU
T 0191 565 9232
Meets annually on first Sat in March. Aim is to keep all ex women's land army and timber corp members in touch with each other.

ALTERNATIVE THERAPIES

Arden Aromatherapy
Leigh Clarke

14 Arden Avenue
Brunton Park
Newcastle upon Tyne NE3 5TS
T 0191 236 3306
Professional holistic aromatherapy treatments for stress, PMS, aches & pains, etc. Essential oils & vegetable-based cruelty free creams & lotions for sale.

ARTS AND CRAFTS

Artists' Agency
Esther Salamon/Lucy Milton, Co-Directors
18 Norfolk Street
Sunderland
Tyne & Wear SR1 1EA
T 0191 510 9318 F 0191 565 2586
artistsagency@artab.demon.co.uk
Working across Northern region aiming to offer artists opportunities to extend scope of work in new environments, facilitating exchange of ideas knowledge & skills leading to greater appreciation of the arts.

Kathleen McCreery
Kathleen McCreery
19 Wandsworth Road
Heaton
Newcastle upon Tyne NE6 5AD
T 0191 276 2550
rik@stc.ac.uk
Playwright & theatre director with extensive experience of teaching creative writing & drama. Welcomes enquires re commissions, workshops & directing. Particularly enjoys working with women & girls.

Poetry Virgins
Ellen Phethean
5 Bentinck Road
Newcastle upon Tyne NE4 6UT
T 0191 273 5326 F 0191 273 5326
A five-woman performance poetry group. Available for readings and workshops. Their aim is to encourage others to write. Writing and performance workshops. Publications and broadcasts.

South Tyneside Arts Studio
Clare Gee
The Old Synagogue
25 Beach Road
South Shields
Tyne & Wear NE33 2QA
T 0191 454 4004 F 0191 454 7638
Open Mon-Fri 10 am-5 pm. Arts and mental health project. Women only on Tue, otherwise open access to anyone from South Tyneside on all other days.

Them Wifies
Veronica Addison, Administrator
109 Pilgrim Street
Newcastle upon Tyne NE1 6QF
T 0191 261 4090 F 0191 261 4091
A women's collective. To encourage traditionally silenced groups in the local community to gain control over and make use of the arts in order to speak for themselves and effect change.

BUSINESS SUPPORT SCHEMES

Women in Business - Gateshead branch
Caroline Watson
16 Manor Gardens
Gateshead
Tyne & Wear NE10 8UZ
T 0191 477 2271 F 0191 478 6536
Meets first Mon of each month 7.30-10 pm. Providing a strong network of working women; helping women realise the opportunities available to them; promoting cooperation between members, etc.

CARERS

North Tyneside Carers' Centre
Carole Card
Neptune House
Neptune Road
Wallsend
Tyne & Wear NE28 6DG
T 0191 295 4321 F 0191 295 0050
Practical & emotional support to carers, ex-carers & those working with & for carers. Encourages all carers to recognise their own needs. Information & training. Aims for recognition for carers' contribution.

South Tyneside Sitting Service
Lily Shields
South Tyneside Voluntary Project
Victoria Hall, 119 Fowler St
South Shields
Tyne & Wear NE33 1NU
T 0191 456 9551 F 0191 456 0603
Provides free carer relief to those families caring for a relative at home who should not be left alone. Operates 7 days a week, 52 weeks a year. Morning, afternoon & evening sessions (sits) up to 3 hours.

ENGLAND - NEWCASTLE AND TYNESIDE

CENTRES FOR WOMEN

Bridge Women's Education Centre
Sheila Davidson
Grassmere Place
Columbia
Washington
Tyne & Wear NE38 7LP
T 0191 417 2445 F 0191 416 4183
Accessing women into education & training. Specialised confidence-building courses & wide range of GCSEs, C&G courses, etc. Childcare for all courses in women-friendly hours. Counselling/support service.

Sunderland Women's Centre
Willa Allan
8 Green Terrace
Sunderland
Tyne & Wear SR1 3PZ
T 0191 567 7495
Provides educational opportunities & access to educational guidance; creche for under 5s; offers resources, meeting space & information to further develop opportunities for women.

Women's Health in South Tyneside (WHIST)
Angela Oxberry
25 Beach Road
South Shields
Tyne & Wear NE33 2QA
T 0191 454 6959
Open Mon-Fri 9.30 am-3.30 pm. Courses to improve self-confidence, self-esteem, health & well-being; self-help groups, free creche; information & resources; counselling related to sexual abuse.

CHILD CARE AND FAMILY

Children's Warehouse, The
Ray
109 Pilgrim Street
Newcastle upon Tyne NE1 6QF
T 0191 232 1606 F 0191 232 1355
The children's warehouse/artstore provides low cost materials, training, information & hire equipment to organisations involved in play/youth work, education & childcare (including registered childminders).

Families in Care
Joan Mills/Kath Swan
St Andrews Church Hall
Newgate Street
Newcastle upon Tyne NE15 7SR
T 0191 230 0977 F 0191 230 0977
Meets Wed 2-4 pm. St Andrews Church Hall, Newgate Street, Newcastle upon Tyne NE1 5SS. Supports parents & relatives with children in care or trying to keep their children out of care. Advocacy. Practical help.

Millers Dene Family Centre
Debbie Carey, Family Suport Coordinator
Shields Road
Walkergate
Newcastle upon Tyne NE6 4XW
T 0191 295 5220
Provides a safe environment for families with young children from local community to play, learn & socialise. Playgroup, parent, toddler & baby groups, holiday play schemes, courses, family support/outreach.

CONTRACEPTION/WELL WOMAN

Newcastle Nuffield Hospital, The
Clayton Road
Newcastle upon Tyne NE2 1JP
T 0191 281 6131
Well woman screen. Full female health assessment. Phone for up-to-date price lists.

North Tyneside Well Woman Centre
Hazel Parrack/Maureen Roberts
Albion Road Clinic
Albion Road
North Shields
Tyne & Wear NE29 0HG
T 0191 252 2548 F 0191 251 1212
Offers help & support for all women through talks, discussion groups, videos, one-to-one listening & a counselling service. Open Wed 7-9 pm.

COUNSELLING AND THERAPY

Women's Outreach Project
Christine Burns, Women's Outreach Worker
C/O NECA Gateshead
203 High Street
Gateshead
Tyne & Wear NE8 1AS
T 0191 490 1045
Offers a safe, confidential advice, support & counselling service. Helps women to make decisions, be in control, make choices, obtain support systems, achieve things, be assertive, learn to express themselves.

DISABILITY

Deaf Mother and Toddler Group
Mrs Angela Thorpe

8 Thropton Terrace
High Heaton
Newcastle upon Tyne NE7
T 0191 266 3134
Self-help support for deaf mothers, babies & children under school age in Gateshead, Newcastle, North & South Tyneside. Access to information on health education & parentcraft topics through BSL.

Disabled Women's Action and Support
Dorothy Mallon
40 Park Lane
Shiremoor
Newcastle upon Tyne NE27 0TJ
T 0191 252 9127 F 0191 417 0218
Minicom 0191 478 4082 Mon-Fri 9.30 am-4.30 pm. Exists to support disabled women & to campaign on issues that affect our lives. Operates in Tyne & Wear, Durham & Northumberland.

Newcastle Disability Forum
Ruth Abrahams
The Dene Centre
Castles Farm Road
Gosforth
Newcastle upon Tyne NE3 1PH
T 0191 285 4556
Office open Mon-Fri. Minicom number: 0191 284 53313. Represents all people with disabilities living in Newcastle. To provide support, encouragement, information. Provides platform for airing opinions & ideas.

EDUCATION

North Eastern Association of Women Graduates (NEAWG)
Miss Valerie Masterman, Secretary
Prospect View
Seaton Delaval
Whitley Bay
Tyne & Wear NE25 0DY
T 0191 237 0530
Part of BFWG. Supports women's education, political, career & home-maker roles. Affiliated to International Federation of University Women & promotes international friendship. Usually meets monthly on Fri.

Workers' Educational Association - Northern District
Anne Staines
51 Grainger Street
Newcastle Upon Tyne NE1 5JE
T 0191 232 3957 F 0191 230 3696

Education & training for women: confidence-building, health, study skills, matriarchal studies, etc. Part-time courses run in school terms in daytime often with creche. Free for those receiving benefits.

EQUAL OPPS

Fair Play North East
Lorraine Marais
Employment Service
Broadacre House
Market Street (East)
Newcastle upon Tyne NE1 6HQ
T 0191 211 4359 F 0191 211 4433
Positive action equalities project. A government EOC initiative to stimulate partnerships which improve opportunities for women to realise their full potential in education, employment & the community.

ETHNIC MINORITIES

Angelou Centre, The
the workers
2 Brighton Grove
Fenham
Newcastle upon Tyne NE4 5NR
T 0191 226 0394 F 0191 272 2984
Open 9 am-5 pm. We provide training services for Black women to enable them to get into employment. All of our services are free.

Apna Ghar
Vimla Storey
124 Ocean Road
South Shields
Tyne & Wear NE33 2JF
T 0191 456 5326
ko26@netscape.com
Provides educational, social & recreational opportunities for ethnic minority women in the borough of south Tyneside.

Asian Girls' Group
Kameljit/Sopna
C/o Roshni
10 Dilston Road
Fenham
Newcastle upon Tyne NE4 5NP
T 0191 273 0972 F 0191 272 3134
Meets Fri 5.30-8.30. Self-defence, keep fit, discussion groups on topics of importance to girls. Outings.

Carers' Support Group
Tamanna Salam

C/o Dekh Bhal Project
4 Callerton Place
Fenham
Newcastle upon Tyne NE4 5NQ
T 0191 272 2877 F 0191 226 1596
Mothers & their children meet monthly for support, exchange of information & raising of awareness. An awareness-raising course is held over a period of about eight weeks. Topics of interest are discussed.

Meetali Group
Sakia Chowdhury
Ethnic Minorities Team
Callerton House
4 Callerton Place, Fenham
Newcastle upon Tyne NE4 5NQ
T 0191 273 3264 F 0191 226 1596
A meeting place where women from ethnic minorities, mainly Bangladeshi, can meet on an informal basis, in a non-threatening, safe environment. Group activities include sewing, knitting, keep fit, ESOL, etc.

Milna Julna
Vijay Nayyar
C/o Age Concern Newcastle
MEA House
Ellison Place
Newcastle upon Tyne NE1 8XS
T 0191 232 6488 F 0191 261 1574
A club for Asian older women aged 50+. Activities include outings, videos, talks. Information provided. Vegetarian lunch & transport provided. Interpreter available. Meets daily 11 am-2.30 pm.

Roshni (Asian Women's Association)
Narjis/Kamaljit/Usha
10 Dilston Road
Fenham
Newcastle upon Tyne NE4 5NP
T 0191 273 0972 F 0191 272 3134
Open five days a week. Help, advice & support. Advice sessions. Outreach work, free childcare support for courses & activities arranged at the centre. Courses include first aid & child care. Library.

Saheli
Justine King
4a Callerton Place
Fenham
Newcastle upon Tyne NE4 0NQ
T 0191 272 2574
Acts as support group for Black women. Challenges attitudes in white society about position & role of Black women. Enables Black women to achieve an equal voice. Highlights existence of all forms of inequality.

Shathi Project
Zakia Chowdhury
Ethnic Minorities Team
Callerton House
4 Callerton Place, Fenham
Newcastle upon Tyne NE4 5NQ
T 0191 273 3264 F 0191 226 1596
Active in west end of Newcastle, with unemployed & low income families living in a racially tense area. Targeted at Bangladeshi women. A safe meeting place where women can make friends & break isolation.

FINANCE

Byker Advice and Information Project
Joe Nicholson
21 Raby Cross
Byker
Newcastle upon Tyne NE6 2FF
T 0191 224 2194 F 0191 224 2194
Open Mon & Wed 10 am-2 pm; Fri 1-3 pm. Free & impartial advice, information & support through trained volunteers enabling local people to maximise their income & enhance the quality of their lives.

GIRLS/YOUNG WOMEN

Elswick Girls' Project
Huffty
Ground Floor, Stephenson Building
173 Elswick Road
Elswick
Newcastle upon Tyne NE4 6SQ
T 0191 273 4942
Asian Girls' group Mon 5-7 pm; mixed girls' group Tue 6-8 pm; women's group Wed 7-9 pm. Meeting needs of women & girls in the west end of Newcastle. Creche support.

HEALTH

AIDS Care Education and Training (ACET) North East
Cath Campbell
P O Box 161
Newcastle upon Tyne NE99 1QN
T 0191 273 5200 F 0191 273 5277
Church-based organisation offering free practical support, such as transport, cooking, shopping, decorating, day or night sitting, friendship, to anyone suffering or affected by HIV or AIDS.

Body Positive North East
J Flaherty, Client/Volunteer coordinator
SIDA Centre
12 Princess Square
Newcastle upon Tyne NE1 8EG
T 0191 232 2855   F 0191 2220514
Support, care, information & advice to anyone affected by HIV/AIDS. Open Mon-Fri 9 am-6 pm. Advice surgeries, advocacy, needle exchange system, housing, SIBS groups, volunteering, complementary therapies.

Breast Care & Mastectomy Support Group
Linda Kerrigan
C/o Coping with Cancer North East
4 Clarence Walk
Newcastle upon Tyne NE2 1AL
T 0191 230 4424
Meets third Tue of month 7-9 pm. Nuffield Hospital, Clayton Road, Jesmond, Newcastle. Offers emotional/practical support to women with breast cancer, their families, friends & carers. Phone between 7-10 pm.

Depression, Anxiety, Tension, Agoraphobia (DATA)
Brian Istead
26 Ribble Walk
Calfclose Estate
Jarrow
Tyne & Wear NE32 4BT
T 0191 489 9325
To create an environment which welcomes & supports people who suffer the effects of depression, anxiety, tension & agoraphobia with a view to self-improvement & personal development. Promotes self-learning.

M D Awareness North East
Mrs Lynn Arkless
42 Wedmore Road
Westerhope
Newcastle upon Tyne NE5 5NR
T 0191 267 0272
Self-help Manic Depression Awareness NE. Self-therapy, exchanging knowledge & gaining strength & experience. Library relevant to our problems. videos, contact names.

Mastectomy Counsellor
Joan Beautyman
76 Melness Road
Brunswick Green South
Wideopen
Newcastle upon Tyne NE13 7BL
T 0191 236 6787

One-to-one counselling for mastectomy patients, partners & families. Visiting hospitals & homes where needed. Phone any time. No charge. Non-medical counselling.

N E Council on Addictions - Women's Service
Barbara Mehan
Bridge View House
15-23 City Road
Newcastle upon Tyne NE1 2AF
T 0191 222 1262
Open Mon, Wed, Thurs, Fri 9 am-4.30 pm for both sexes; Tue 2-9 pm for women only. Free & confidential support & counselling for women experiencing drug/alcohol related problems.

NHS Health Information Service
Ann Purvis, Manager
3rd Floor
Lombard House
4 Lombard Street
Newcastle upon Tyne NE1 3AE
T 0800 665544   F 0191 232 3296
100412.2573@compuserve.com
Part of a national network of services providing information on health & NHS. Free & confidential. Available Mon-Fri 9 am-7 pm. Health information includes medical conditions & treatments, self-help groups.

North East Council on Addictions (NECA) - Gateshead
Avril Christie, Senior Worker
203 High Street
Gateshead
Tyne & Wear NE8 1AS
T 0191 490 1045   F 0191 490 1673
Open Mon 9 am-7 pm, Tue-Thurs 9 am-5 pm, Fri 9 am-4.30 pm. Free, confidential services promoting prevention, recognition & treatment of problems relating to use of drugs. Counselling, group work.

North Tyneside Community & Health Care Forum
Mrs Michele Spencer
Neptune House
Neptune Road
Wallsend
Tyne & Wear NE28 6DG
T 0191 295 4233   F 0191 295 0050
Aims to include service users, carers, advocates & voluntary groups in planning & delivery of health/ social care in north Tyneside. Sepcifically concerned with people with HIV/AIDS, learning difficulties, etc.

ENGLAND - NEWCASTLE AND TYNESIDE

Northern Initiative on Women and Eating, The
Annemarie Norman
2nd Floor
1 Pink Lane
Newcastle upon Tyne NE1 5DW
T 0191 221 0233 F 0191 222 0919
Offers support to women experiencing problems in their relationship to food. It is NOT a healthy eating or slimming organisation. Telephone helpline. All services are free & confidential.

Streetlevel
Gill Horner
Stanhope Parade
South Shields
Tyne & Wear NE33 4BA
T 0191 455 3027 F 0191 456 8009
Open mon, Tue, Fri 10 am-4.30 pm, Wed 10 am-12.30 pm, women only 12.30-4.30 pm, needle exchange only 5-6.30 pm, Thurs 12.30-4.30 pm. For those affected by drug use & those affected with HIV & AIDS.

Turning Point - Tyne & Wear
Clare Stokes
61 Marine Avenue
Whitley Bay
Tyne & Wear NE26 1NB
T 0191 251 1725 F 0191 297 1799
Outreach daycare support to women with substance dependencies. A women's activity group is based at the workshop. Accommodation provided.

Tyneside Women's Health Project
Lynn Edmonds
Swinburne House
Swinburne Street
Gateshead
Tyne & Wear NE8 1AX
T 0191 477 7898
Believes women have right to make informed choices about their own health. Offers support/information to enable women to do this. Leaflets; working with groups on special issues; working one-to-one.

LEGAL MATTERS

Advocacy in Gateshead
Mrs Maureen Coloman
The Old Bank
Swinburne Street
Gateshead
Tyne & Wear NE8 1AN
T 0191 478 6472 F 0191 477 8559

Open Mon-Thurs 9 am-4 pm. Services are free to people with learning disabilities. Provides an advocacy service for people with a learning disability who reside in Gateshead.

Newcastle Law Centre
Ms M Foster
51 Westgate Road
Newcastle upon Tyne NE1 1SG
T 0191 230 4777 F 0191 233 0295
Open door advice sessions: Mon, Wed, Fri 10 am-12 noon. Telephone advice Mon-Fri 10 am-4.30 pm. Legal advice & representation in specialist areas of the law. Criminal injuries compensation, housing, etc.

LESBIAN AND BISEXUAL

Bi Women
Kath Arrowsmith
P O Box 1JR
Newcastle upon Tyne NE99 1JR
A social support group for bisexual women in the north east of England. We offer individual support & hold regular social events. All women welcome, regardless of their sexual orientation & identity.

Lesbian Line
P O Box 1HT
Newcastle upon Tyne NE99 1HT
T 0191 261 2277
Telephone line open Tue 7-10 pm. Provides confidential support & information for lesbians & women questioning their sexuality.

Tyneside Young Lesbian Project
C/o The Friday Group
P O Box 1HT
Newcastle upon Tyne NE99 1HT
T 0191 261 2277
Mon 6-7 pm. Ansaphone at other times. Supports the work of the Young Lesbian Group, a social & support group for young women under 25 years of age who are, or who think they might be, lesbian.

OLDER WOMEN

Northern Ladies Annuity Society
Mrs J Davies, Secretary
178 Portland Road
Shieldfield
Newcastle upon Tyne NE2 1DJ
T 0191 232 1518
Assists single/ widowed ladies over retirement age on low incomes. No one-off grants. Help is given by payment of small,

regular annuities. Applicants must reside or have been born in north of England.

PREGNANCY/CHILDBIRTH

Caesarean Support Network
Ann Carruthers
16 Devonshire Place
Jesmond
Newcastle upon Tyne NE2 2ND
T 0191 281 1566
A phoneline providing information, contacts, support & advice to women in the Gateshead, Newcastle, North Tyneside & South Tyneside areas who are having, or who have had, a caesarean section.

Heartbeat Pregnancy Crisis Centre
Dr Whitford
Abbey House
7/9 Bigg Market
Newcastle upon Tyne NE1 1UN
T 0191 261 7111
Open Tue-Fri 11 am-1 pm; Thurs 6-8 pm. Free, confidential pregnancy testing. Post-abortion & miscarriage counselling. An opportunity for women with unwanted /unplanned pregnancies to consider options.

National Childbirth Trust - Newcastle & Gateshead branch
Alison Priestley
20 Ivy Road
Gosforth
Newcastle upon Tyne NE3 1DB
T 0191 232 4322
Offers information & support in pregnancy, childbirth & early parenthood. Aims to enable every parent to make informed choices. Ante natal classes, breastfeeding support, post natal drop-in & exercise classes.

Post Natal Illness Support Line
Linda Wilson or Petra Crichton
28 Strawberry Gardens
Wallsend
North Tyneside
Tyne & Wear NE28 8AZ
T 0191 263 8020 F 0191 263 8020
Help & support to women, their families & anyone else in the Gateshead, Newcastle, North & South Tyneside areas in need of post natal support. To enable them to get correct, direct action for their needs.

PUBLISHERS/PUBLICATIONS

Writing Women
Unit 14
Hawthorn House
Forth Banks
Newcastle upon Tyne NE1 3SG
Publishes poems & short stories by women.

RELIGIOUS ORGANISATIONS

AGLOW International (Sunderland)
Mrs Ardyn E Pearson
Rosemount
48 Woodville Crescent
Sunderland
Tyne & Wear SR4 8QG
T 0191 528 5953
Christian women meet in fellowhip together and worship God. Speakers. Meets 7.15 p.m on Third Wed of each month at The Rosedene, Queen Alexandra Road, Sunderland for a meal and coffee.

SEXUAL ABUSE/RAPE CRISIS

Ellis Fraser Centre
Tracey Cole, Manager
District General Hospital
Kayll Road
Sunderland
Tyne & Wear SR4 7TP
T 0191 565 3725 F 0191 569 9221
Counselling & support to women aged 16 and over who have been raped or sexually assaulted. A free service to women living in the area.

Gateshead Women Survivors' Resource Centre
the workers
Swinburne House
Swinburne Street
Gateshead
Tyne & Wear NE8 1AX
T 0191 478 1800
Open Mon-Thurs 10 am-4 pm. An advice, information & resource centre, also providing free short-term counselling to female survivors of sexual abuse who live in Gateshead.

Justice for Abused Children
Trish Paxton/Dawn Harkness
JAC 3rd Floor
Marseilles Chambers
45-47 Groat Market
Newcastle upon Tyne NE1 1UG
T 0191 221 1919

ENGLAND - NEWCASTLE AND TYNESIDE

We run a self-help group for women survivors of any form of abuse. A one-to-one listening service for women & men. Meetings to promote awareness & enlighten people about child abuse. Gives talks to groups.

Tyneside Rape Crisis Centre
Newcastle upon Tyne
T 0191 222 0271
Rape: 0191 232 9858; incest: 0191 261 5317. Helplines open Mon-Fri 10 a.m-5 pm. Free women-centred counselling, by women for women. Support/information for women who have been sexually abused or raped.

Social

Social Service Women's Club
Mrs Marie McGrath, Chairman
10 Kew Gardens
Whitley Bay
Tyne & Wear NE26 3LY
T 0191 252 5886
Open to any woman over 18 for education, friendship & fun. Meets Thurs at 2 pm at Voluntary Service Centre, Whitley Bay. Speakers, demonstrations, etc.

Washington Ladies Social Group
Mrs V Sixsmith
6 Model Dwellings
Columbia
Washington
Tyne & Wear NE38 7AS
Meets weekly 7-9 pm. Speakers. Fund-raising for cancer charities, etc.

Sports and Leisure

Sandgate Women's Morris
Miss Hilary Forster
2 Okehampton Court
Cromer Avenue, Low Fell
Gateshead
Tyne & Wear NE9 6UQ
T 0191 487 8502
A women's Morris dance team, danding north west Morris - & looking for new members. Meets Mon 7.45 pm at Community Centre, Trevhitt Road, Heaton, Newcastle. Dance at folk festival weekends, ceilidhs, etc.

Support

Women and Girls (WAG)
Marion Simpson
Gladstone Terrace Community Centre
12 Gladstone Terrace

Gateshead
Tyne & Wear NE8 4DX
T 0191 478 2780
Working with women & girls in Gateshead. For women who promote women & girls' issues. Meets monthly. Support network, identifying issues affecting girls & women, sharing knowledge of available resources, etc.

Training

Women Into Work
North Tyneside Council
Suite G2, Howard House
Howard Street, North Shields
Tyne & Wear NE30 1AR
T 0191 200 6080
0191 200 6142
Open 10 am- 3 pm. Drop in Mon 1-3 pm. Free taster courses & free creche. The courses are short, normally lasting for 6-8 days. Subjects include: bricklaying, sign language, first aid, counselling, etc.

Violence Against Women

DIVA - Newcastle Domestic Violence Forum
Pummi Mattu
C/o NCVS, 2nd Floor
MEA House
Ellison Place
Newcastle upon Tyne NE1 8XS
T 0191 232 7445 F 0191 230 5640
An inter-agency forum concerned with domestic violence. Main aims are training, policy development & developing community-based initiatives.

Getting There
Karen Weaver
Probation Centre
Cornwallis Street
South Shields
Tyne & Wear NE33 1BB
T 0191 456 1000 F 0191 427 6922
Informal support group provides support for women victims of domestic violence who may be in a violent relationship. An informal setting & total confidentiality provide an outlet for escape from pressures.

Newcastle Safer Cities Project
Marion Talbot
Portland House
New Bridge Street
Newcastle upon Tyne NE1 8AL

T 0191 244 2477 F 0191 244 2009
Government-funded community safety partnership with NACRO promoting local initiatives to prevent crime & make places safer.

WOMEN'S AID

Newcastle Women's Aid
the workers
Box 32
Heaton
Newcastle upon Tyne NE6 1HZ
T 0191 265 2148 F 0191 276 2366
24-hour emergency phoneline: 0191 265 1848. 24-hour emergency accommodation for women fleeing domestic violence. Advice, support & counselling. Help with housing & legal issues. Outreach services.

North Tyneside Women's Aid
P O Box 12
Whitley Bay
Tyne & Wear NE26 1ET
T 0191 251 3305 F 0191 251 2848
Offers support, advice & information & temporary accommodation for women & children fleeing domestic violence.

South Tyneside Women's Aid
Wynne Giles
P O Box 29
South Shields
Tyne & Wear NE33 1DL
T 0191 454 8257 F 0378 284 881
Provides temporary emergency safe accommodation for women & children fleeing domestic abuse. Staff on duty in refuge Mon-Fri 9 am-8 pm. On-call staff available at all other times.

NORFOLK

ACCOMMODATION

Archway Housing Project
staff team
23 West Parade
Norwich NR2 3DN
T 01603 616950
Provides accommodation for single homeless young women aged 16-23. Resettlement programme for residents acquing skills they feel they need to live independently. One 8-bed hostel & 3 x 2-bed 'move on' flats.

Great Yarmouth Young Women's Housing Project
Valerie Cudmore
24a South Quay
Great Yarmouth NR30 2RG
T 01493 853933

ARMED FORCES

Royal British Legion Women's Section - Norfolk
Mrs E Corston, County Secretary
The Retreat
38 Back Lane
Wymondham NR18 0LB
T 01953 605473 F 01953 605473

ARTS AND CRAFTS

Janet Hegarty School of Ballet
Janet Hegarty
Meadow Cottage
Rectory Road
Tivetshall St Mary
Norwich NR15 2AL
T 01379 676426
Teaching cecchetti ballet to children aged 3+. Performances & exams.

Wells School of Dance
Sheila Owen
28 Waveney Close
Wells Next The Sea NR23 1HT
T 01328 710745
Children's ballet & tap classes; adult tap; line dancing; gentle exercises.

BUSINESS SUPPORT SCHEMES

Business and Professional Women (BPW) - Swaffham
Janet Furniss
11 Captains Close
Swaffham PE37 8HQ
T 01760 721073
A club for working women in business. Aims to develop a greater understanding of issues concerning women, working or not. To give members self-confidence & heighten self-esteem, etc.

CHILD CARE AND FAMILY

Family First
Angie Dent
Fourways Centre
Stevenson Road
Norwich NR5 8TN
T 01603 456678
Supports families in North Earlham. Befriending service. Drop-in & creche Mon, Wed & Fri 9 am-noon; parent & toddler group

Tue 9.45-11.45 am & Wed 12.45-2.45 pm; women's health group Wed 12.30-2.30 pm.

CONTRACEPTION/WELL WOMAN

Women's Health Information and Support Service (WHISS)
Jordan House
7a St Benedicts Street
Norwich NR2 4PE
T 01603 623835 F 01603 623835
Open Mon & Wed 10 am-4 pm; Fri 10 am-1 pm. An information & resource centre for women on health topics. Well woman clinic - cytology, contraception, HIV/AIDS, menstrual problems, free pregnancy testing.

DISABILITY

Deaf Women's Health Project
Julie Tufnail
24 Woodward Road
Norwich NR3 2LQ
T 01603 403083
Minicom only.

EDUCATION

Norfolk and Norwich Association of Women Graduates
Mrs Marie N P McKeown, Membership Secretary
4 Judges Walk
Norwich NR4 7QF
T 01603 453982
Meeting with speakers at St Giles Rooms, 47 St Giles Street, Norwich, 7 pm. Coffee mornings 10 am Social events, discussion groups, outings.

ENVIRONMENT

BTCV Women Working for the Environment
Lottie Carlton
BTCV
Royal Oak Court
Horns Lane, Ber Street
Norwich NR1 3EP
T 01603 767300 F 01603 763711
floris@btcv.org.uk
Women only group carrying out practical conservation projects at a variety of interesting sites throughout Norfolk. Meets Mon 9.30 am-2.30 pm. No previous experience necessary - come & join us!

ETHNIC MINORITIES

Norwich Black Women's Group
Kirat Randhawa
The Advice Arcade
4 Guildhall Hill
Norwich NR2 1JH
T 01603 661779
Meets third Wed of each month 7.30 pm at different venues. Support network for all Black women in Norwich; celebrating the great variety of cultures within the group; heightening awareness; etc.

GIRLS/YOUNG WOMEN

Great Yarmouth Young Women's Project
Karen Harvey
24a South Quay
Great Yarmouth NR30 2RG
T 01493 852253 F 01493 857306
Open Mon-Fri 9 am-5 pm.

HEALTH

Norfolk Eating Disorders' Association
Linda Hurley, Administrator
Wensum House
103 Prince of Wales Road
Norwich
T 01603 767062
Helps anyone involved with anorexia, bulimia, compulsive eating who lives in Norfolk. Individual counselling sessions, open self-help group, helpline, information/support to families, friends & professionals.

LARGER/TALLER WOMEN

Long Tall Sally
8 Bedford Street
Norwich NR1 1AR
T 01603 660544
Clothes for the taller woman sizes 12-20.
Open Mon-Sat 9.30-5.30; Sun 11 am-5 pm.

LEGAL MATTERS

Norwich and District Legal Services Committee
Victoria Daines
The Advice Arcade
4 Guildhall Hill
Norwich NR2 1JH
T 01603 661779 F 01603 616116
Equality in employment, part of Norwich & District Legal Services Committee, provides advice, assistance & sometimes representation on matters related to gender

ENGLAND - NORFOLK

equality in the workplace. Phone for appointment.

LESBIAN AND BISEXUAL

Lesbian Line
(GMHP) 69 Bethel Street
Norwich NR2 1NP
T 01603 628055
Helpline open Tue 7-9 pm. Befriending service. Monthly socials, first Sun of each month in the Castle pub, Norwich.

MEDIA

Cinewomen
Jaune Morgan, Festival Director
Cinema City
St Andrews Street
Norwich NR2 4AD
T 01603 632366 F 01603 767838
j.h.morgan@uea.ac.uk
Promoting all aspects of women's film making, primarily through annual festival held in Norwich. Aimed at practitioners, academics, students & general public.

OLDER WOMEN

Anglian Older Feminists' Network
Valerie Macfarlane
The Barn
114 The Street
Ashwellthorpe
Norwich NR16 1EZ
T 01508 489411 F 01508 489411
101677.23351@compuserve.com
Meets on first Sat of each month 1-5 pm at Greenhouse Trust, 42-48 Bethel Street, Norwich. Aims to validate wisdom & creativity, celbrate diversity & supportiveness of each other, etc.

PLACES TO STAY AND EAT

Old Exhchange, The
Jean Clitheroe
45 Freeman Street
Wells-next-the-Sea NR23 1BQ
T 01328 711362
Woman-run guest house open all year. No smoking. Dogs welcome. 200 year old cottage with some exposed beams & brickwork, 500 yards from quayside. Phone for up-to-date price list.

PREGNANCY/CHILDBIRTH

Norfolk Fertility Support Group
Shelagh and Steve Wragg
5 Kimberley Road
North Walsham
T 01692 500961

PUBLISHERS/PUBLICATIONS

Raging Dykes Newsletter
P O Box 468
Norwich NR5 8ES
For lesbian separatists & lesbian feminists.

RETAILING

Flamedragon Belts
Felicity Seaman
Minns Farm
Ranworth Road
Blofield Heath
Norwich NR13 4PW
T 01603 714378 F 01603 713553
Wholesale/retail fashion belts & accessories. Any colour; any size. Open any time (phone first).

SERVICES

Norfolk Heatcare
Martin Howe/Patricia Davison
18 Twickenham Road
Fifers Lane Industrial Estate
Norwich NR6 6NG
T 01603 488724 F 01603 485351
Insulation & energy efficiency services for low income households in Norfolk.

Quillpower
Christine Whitfield
22 Marguerite Close
Bradwell
Great Yarmouth NR31 8RL
T 01493 661958
Commissions for all types of calligraphy undertaken.

SEXUAL ABUSE/RAPE CRISIS

Norwich Rape Crisis Resource Centre
P O Box 47
Norwich NR31 1HA
T 01603 667687
Helpline open Tue 7-9 pm; Fri 12-2 pm. 24-hour ansaphone. Offers face-to-face counselling & support for women who have been sexually abused at any time in their lives.

SOCIAL

Norwich Ladies' Luncheon Club
Mrs Margaret Thompson
Applecross
Woodland Drive
Thorpe End
Norwich NR13 5BH
T 01603 433561
Social luncheon club. No fundraising. A group of ladies (250) who meet for an 'after luncheon' talk on any subject (non political). Two-and-a-half-year waiting list.

Norwich Tangent No 233
Mrs Christabel Bennett
1 The Glade
Old Costessey
Norwich NR8 5EB
T 01603 743228   F 01603 743228
Meets third Mon of each month at different venues. Meetings with speaker usually begin at 7.45 pm. The object is fellowship.

Professional and Business Executive Ladies' Luncheon Club
Miss Marian C Shackleton
4 Curzon House
Albemarle Road
Norwich NR2 2DF
T 01603 455215
Opportunity for ladies who lead busy lives to meet once a month for lunch as purely social occasion - no responsibilities, no hassle, no fund-raising, no commitments, no speakers - just relaxation.

SPORTS AND LEISURE

Fiddlesticks
Susan Holt
9 Lavender Grove
Toftwood
Dereham NR19 1JZ
T 01362 693942   F 01842 750125
North west Morris dancing. Women dancers, female or male musicians, based in Norwich.

TRAINING

Women's Employment, Enterprise & Training Unit (WEETU)
Erika Watson/Louise Richmond
The Music House
Wensum Lodge
King Street
Norwich NR1 1QW
T 01603 767367   F 01603 666693
Develops women's access to quality employment, education & training. Free advice & guidance at Norwich Advice Arcade (drop-in) on Tue 10 am-12.30 pm & 1-3.30 pm. Main office (see above) open office hours.

VIOLENCE AGAINST WOMEN

Justice for Women - Norfolk
Louise Smith
C/o The Advice Arcade
4 Guildhall Hill
Norwich
Providing women-only space to encourage women to discuss views, concerns & options on domestic violence. Supporting campaigns of individual women who are discriminated against by the legal system, etc.

Norwich Safer Cities Project
Tony Carter
4th Floor
St James Yarn Mill
Whitefriars
Norwich NR3 1SU
T 01603 618975   F 01603 664019
Government-funded community safety partnership with NACRO promoting local initiatives to prevent crime & make places safer.

NORTHAMPTONSHIRE

ACCOUNTANCY

Anne Falkner Chartered Accountant
Mrs Anne Falkner
Temple Cottages
Horton
Northampton NN7 2BH
T 01604 870876   F 01604 870876
Chartered accountant specialising in affairs of small businesses and individuals. Free initial meeting with no obligations.

Moneybox Accounting Services
Clare Elsby
8 Bell End
Wollaston NN29 7RN
T 01933 270171   F 01933 441657
Freelance company account service for small businesses. Management accounts, forecasts & business plans, budget & targets for motivational purposes, year end accounts, VAT, bookkeeping, etc.

Ros Munton Bookkeeping & Accounts Service
Ros Munton

16 Aviemore Gardens
West Hunsbury
Northampton NN4 9XJ
T 01604 764701
Computerised bookkeeping. Production & analysis of management accounts/financial reports.

Alternative Therapies

Nene Valley Complementary Therapies
Linda Parrott
41 Park Avenue South
Northampton NN3 3AB
T 01604 881390
Open Mon-Thurs 10 am-4 pm & occasional Sat. Holistic treatments include aromatherapy, reflexology & massage. Aim is to relax client, provide stress relief, improve circulation, skin texture, etc.

Vanessa Horne Ltd
Vanessa Horne
846 Watling Court
Towcester NN12 7BS
T 01327 359088 F 01327 359088
Health & beauty centre, specialising in seaweed, aromatherapy & reflexology. 95 % of treatments involve skin care & electrolysis. Open for day packages 10 am-4 pm. Also private tuition in beauty therapy.

Arts and Crafts

E K Pollard Artist
E K Pollard
42 East Park Parade
Northampton NN1 4LA
T 01604 37932 F 01604 37932
Fine art portraits. Pastels, acrylics, oils & murals - any subject & size.

Lynne Evans Calligraphy
Lynne Evans
Greenhills
4 Northampton Road
Denton
Northampton NN7 1DL
T 01604 890134
All types of calligraphy (illustrated or plain) for organisations or individuals. Certificates, commemorative scrolls, decorated poetry or prose. Designs for greetings cards, leaflets, brochures, etc.

Pam Gardner (Hand Spinning, Knitting and Crochet)
Pam Gardner

1 Norton Crescent
Towcester NN12 6DW
T 01327 350025
Spins long-haired cat & dog combings, angora rabbits, angora goats (mohair) & sheep fleeces for their owners to knit into garmets. Keeps large stock of white & coloured fleeces. Phone for further details.

Poppies Fun Jewillery
Julia Laffite
41 Newtown Road
Lt Irchester
Wellingborough NN8 2DX
T 01933 225087
Manufacturing children's earrings, bracelets, fun hair things, necklaces and in general anything that makes you laugh. Events, local fairs in Northamptonshire.

Business Support Schemes

NEW Network, The
Rachel Mallows
Arch Villa
23 High Street
Bozeat NN29 7NF
T 01933 664437 F 01933 664556
Professional women's group only for women who run their own businesses. Opportunities for networking, inter-trade, discount facilities for members, member directories, newsletter & monthly meetings.

Northamptonshire Women's Network, The
Rachel Mallows
Arch Villa
23 High Street
Bozeat NN29 7NF
T 01933 664437 F 01933 664556
To help women who are looking to return to work or for retraining. Support, information about employment & training. Opportunities for networking & publications. Also a telephone helpline service.

Profitable Learning Ltd
Carmel Capewell
Forest Lodge
Hazelborough Forest
Syresham NN13 5TU
T 01327 857657 F 01327 857777
plltd@intonet.co.uk
Management training & development. Equal opportunities training. Special development centre for women managers who wish to progress their careers. Skills analysis for women managers.

ENGLAND - NORTHAMPTONSHIRE

Rachel Mallows Services to Business
Rachel Mallows
Arch Villa
23 High Street
Bozeat NN29 7NF
T 01933 664437   F 01933 664556
rachel.mallows@totnet.co.uk
A range of services to business, including print & design, secretarial & bookkeeping, recruitment & training. Examples of training: secretarial skills, management, teleworking & business administration.

Tricia Adams, Business Services (TABS)
Tricia Adams
2 Denford Ash Cottages
Denford
Kettering NN14 4EW
T 01832 734425   F 01832 734425
TAdams3894@aol.com
Information broker. Tenders alerting service for business; general word processing of academic articles, essays, etc; desk research; newsletter preparation; editing; proofreading; professional puzzle compiling.

Wellingborough Business Centre
Caire Elsby, Administrator
Everitt Close
Denington Estate
Wellingborough NN8 2QE
T 01933 440448   F 01933 441657
Comprising 20 small units of workshop & office accommodation for people starting up a business available on flexible terms with on site management & support to enable a move to more permanent premises later.

Wellingborough Ladies' Lunch Club
Rachel Mallows
Arch Villa
23 High Street
Bozeat NN29 7NF
T 01933 664437   F 01933 664556
Professional women's group providing opportunities for monthly meetings for working & inter-trade. The meetings encourage debate. Speakers at a local venue. Newsletter & directory of members.

Wings Business Services
Shena Mackaness
4 Blisworth Road
Gayton NN7 3HL
T 01604 859639   F 01604 859639
Corporate hospitality & event organising. Tailor-made packages for small & large groups, employees or clients.

CENTRES FOR WOMEN

Women's Health Information & Support Centre (WHISC)
3-7 Hazelwood Road
Northampton NN1 1LG
T 01604 39723
Drop in & telephone sessions Mon & Wed 10 am-3 pm; Thurs 5.30-8 pm by appt. Free daytime creche. Wheelchair access. Free pregancy testing. Information on eg abortion, contraception, abuse, etc.

COUNSELLING AND THERAPY

Manor House Counselling Service, The
Denise Moth
St Giles Street
Northampton NN1 1JW
T 01604 33304
Counselling in all areas, especially emotional, marriage, depression, sexual abuse & eating disorders.

ENVIRONMENT

Janet Thomas Quality Garden Design
Janet Thomas
Mulberry Cottage
Collswell Lane
Blakesley
Towcester NN12 8RB
T 01327 860523   F 01327 860523
Quality garden design. Full design service from survey through to specification, master plants, planting plans & construction drawings.

ETHNIC MINORITIES

Dostiyo Asian Women & Girls Organisation
Kalpana Desai
26 Cloutsham Street
Northampton NN1 3LN
T 01604 601097
Attacks barriers that isolate women; enables Asian women to access services with linguistic support & religious sensitivity in all services; empowers Asian women through self-help, training, advocacy, etc.

HEALTH

Advanced Hygiene Distribution Ltd
Vannessa Tennant
Aspen House
14 Station Road
Kettering NN15 7HE
T 01536 513501   F 01536 513562

Manufacturers of ladies' sanitary units, incinerated in their entirety, thus reducing risk of infection. The only units with instructions in braille. Also service these units.

Eating Disorders Group
Denise Moth
C/o Manor House Counselling Service
St Giles Street
Northampton NN1 1JW
T 01604 33304
Meets on Tue fortnightly 5.45-7 pm. Mixed group of anorexics, bulimics & compulsive eaters. Self-help group with a support system. Phone any time to leave message on ansaphone. Contact will be made.

LEGAL MATTERS

Shoosmiths & Harrison
Lisa Dunn
517 The Lakes
Northampton NN4 7SH
T 01604 29977 F 01604 543543
Solicitors. Switchboard open 8.30 am-7 pm. Sympathetic to women.

MEDIA

Lauren Associates Video Productions
Jean Rowton
Haybarn
High Street
Yardley
Hastings NN7 1ER
T 01604 696246 F 01604 696246
Video production for product promotion, education or training. All sizes of project tackled, broadcast & non-broadcast.

OLDER WOMEN

New Horizons Ladies' Club, The
Mrs J Richmond
29 Wolfe Close
Kettering NN15 5DA
T 01536 81364
Meets second & fourth Thurs of each month 7.30-10 pm at Carey Church, Kettering. Activities, speakers & discussions of interest to ladies aged 45 & over.

RELIGIOUS ORGANISATIONS

Home League (Salvation Army)
Joyce Hill
28 Resthaven Road
Wootton
Northampton NN4 6LB
T 01604 767555
For women of all ages. League meetings Tue 2-3 pm. Fellowship, service & worship.

Methodist Ladies Fellowship
Mrs Joyce Hefford
22 Kingsley Road
Rothwell NN14 6HU
T 01604 710775
A mainly devotional meeting for older ladies. We aim to provide warmth, friendship, local information & a cup of tea. We run a limited number of outings throughout the year. Choir.

Women's Fellowship
Muriel Edwards
48 Sherwood Drive
Daneholme Estate
Daventry NN11
T 01327 77343
Meets 2.30 fortnightly at Daventry Methodist Church. Seeks to make the Christian faith relevant to our lives today so as committed Christians we may work out our responsibilities in the home & community.

RETAILING

Artouche
Lema Townsend
P O Box 438
Sywell
Northampton NN6 0SP
T 01604 647379
Network marketing company selling amber & silver jewellery imported from Eastern Europe direct to customers via a network of consultants. All items are hallmarked.

Toolsafe Ltd
Lesley Russell
P O Box 33
Rushden NN10 6YE
T 01933 410770 F 01933 311490
Rechargeable power tools & safety equipment. By mail order.

SERVICES

Alison Gilbert
Alison Gilbert
11 Lakeside Drive
Ecton Brook
Northampton NN3 5EL
T 01604 413425
Provides chiropody treatments for clients in their own homes. Day, weekend & evening appointments by arrangement.

ENGLAND - NORTHAMPTONSHIRE

Elite Screen Printers and Embroiderers
Pauleen Soderquist
Top Floor
45 Sartcris Road
Rushden NN10 9TL
T 01933 315930 F 01933 418364
EliteTex@aol.com
Embroidery & screen printing on to clothing & all promotional items. Friendly & personal service. Advice given. Quick turnaround, competitive prices. Open Mon-Fri 8 am-6 pm.

Hansons Autocentre
Mrs Patricia Prigmore
242 Bedford Road
Rushden NN10 0SE
T 01933 312473 F 01933 413551
Open Mon-Fri 9 am-6 pm; Sat 9 am-2 pm; Sun 10 am-12 pm (tyres only). MOTs, servicing, brakes, clutches, tyres, exhausts, batteries.

Hawthorn Marketing and Language Services
Helen Pilkington
123 Hawthorn Road
Kettering NN15 7HU
T 01536 416450 F 01536 414785
Providing language services in main European languages, covering translation, interpreting, tuition, plus telemarketing in English. French & German covering telesales, market research, appointment setting.

Julia Thorley Editorial Services
Julia Thorley
191 Kingsley Avenue
Kettering NN16 9ET
T 01536 81841 F 01536 81841
Caters for all editorial needs, including copywriting, proofreading, project management, company literature, including newsletters brochures & press releases. Any writing job undertaken.

Juniper House Interiors
Mary Halsey
231 Abington Avenue
Northampton NN1 4PU
T 01604 720198 F 01604 720198
Interior design company with own curtain workshop. Specialises in show houses & upgrading offices, particularly reception areas. Private work also undertaken.

Trade Flooring Ltd
Mrs Dianne Lang
8 St James Mill Road
Northampton NN5 5JW
T 01604 751821 F 01604 755600
Supply & fitting floor coverings (carpet, vinyl, wood, rugs & tiles). Open Sun 11 am-4 pm; Mon-Sat 9 am-5.30 pm. Company converting from private ownership to a workers' cooperative.

SEXUAL ABUSE/RAPE CRISIS

Northampton Women Survivors Network Group
Denise Moth
C/o The CSA Survivors Group
Council for Voluntary Service
13 Hazelwood Road
Northampton NN1 1LJ
T 01604 24121
Women are referred from various organisations & their GPs. One-to-one counselling & psychotherapy. A group of 8-10 women survivors meets fortnightly on Tue 3.45-5 pm.

Northamptonshire Rape & Incest Crisis Centre
P O Box 206
Northampton NN1 1NF
T 01604 250721
Confidential support for women & children who have suffered rape, incest, sexual abuse. Telephone helpline usually available 9 am-9 pm. Also centre at Kettering on this number. Support/assistance to carers.

SOCIAL

Ecton Brook Ladies' Circle
Joyce M Gater
5 Sharrow Place
Ecton Brook
Northampton NN3 5AJ
T 01604 415741
Meets Tue 2-4 pm at Ecton Brook Community Centre. Cards, Scrabble, outings, talks, etc. General social afternoons.

Kettering Ladies Cameo
Mrs J D Webb
23 Bayes Street
Kettering NN16 8EH
T 01536 514832
Meets third Tue of each month at the Corn Market Hall 2 pm. Speakers, outings & visits

to places of interest. We try to promote friendly meetings for ladies of all ages.

Kettering Trefoil Guild
Mrs D Humphrey
34 Masefield Road
Kettering NN16 9LE
T 01536 85602
We are former girl guides & meet on second Tue of each Month. We do badge testing & help at the local guide shop. There is a speaker at most meetings, also a bring & buy sale.

Ladybirds
Ms S Wells
108 Regent Street
Kettering NN16 8QQ
T 01536 415375
A friendship group for women of all ages. Puts women in touch with each other & gives them opportunities to increase their social circle. Monthly newsletter provides details of events & activities.

Lively Minds
Cynth Howe
26 Washington Street
Northampton NN2 6NL
T 01604 791983
Women's discussion group in informal surroundings. Meets alternate Thurs 8 pm to discuss a wide range of topics. To get away from domestic issues.

SPORTS AND LEISURE

Northampton Ladies' Badminton Club
Mrs Doreen Brydon
12 Favell Way
Weston Pavell
Northampton NN3 3BZ
T 01604 408647 F 01604 402845
Plays on Thurs afternoons. Good standard of play.

Town & County Diamonds Ladies Football Club
Glenda Bird, Secretary
11 Bibury Crescent
Boothville
Northampton NN3 6AG
T 01604 412116
Ladies & girls football club. Training Thurs 8-10 pm Match days Sun 2 pm. National league status.

TRAINING

Janet Thomas Communication Skills Training
Janet Thomas
Mulberry Cottage
Collswell Lane
Blakesley
Towcester NN12 8RB
T 01327 860523 F 01327 860523
Communication skills training. In-house & one-to-one training on speaking in public, speaking on radio & TV, writing speeches, etc.

Supporting Customer Care
Kathy Stiff
14 Lakeside
Irthlingborough NN9 5SW
T 01933 631807 F 01933 631807
Consultancy & training in customer care, including complaint handling.

WOMEN'S AID

Northampton Women's Aid
Michelle Batchlor
P O Box 315
Northampton NN1 1LS
T 01604 39099
24-hour telephone helpline (after office hours ansaphone regularly checked). Advice sessions at The Abbey, Market Square, Daventry. Help, support & advice for women victims of domestic violence. Accommodation.

NORTHUMBERLAND

CENTRES FOR WOMEN

Women's Health Advice Centre
Tracey Morrison/Cath Carnaby
1 Council Road
Ashington NE63 8RZ
T 01670 853977
One-to-one counselling on issues such as bereavement, anxiety, sexuality, domestic violence; courses on eg astrology, creative writing, assertiveness. Open Mon-Thurs 9 am-4.30 pm; Fri 9 am-4 pm.

PHOTOGRAPHY

Crest Photography
Helen J Card
3 Lambton Court
Bedlington NE22 5YQ
T 01670 828956 F 01670 821716
Wedding & portrait photography.

ENGLAND - NOTTINGHAMSHIRE

PREGNANCY/CHILDBIRTH

ISIS Northern Region Fertility Support Group
119 Milburn Road
Ashington NE63 ONA
T 01670 523600 F 01670 523600
Confidential support for those undergoing infertility treatment. Meetings & newsletters. Areas covered are: Northumberland, Tyne & Wear, Durham, Sunderland, Cleveland & north east Cumbria.

RELIGIOUS ORGANISATIONS

Women's Meeting - Cramlington
Mrs Lilian Brown
Station Terrace Methodist Church
52 Evesham Place
Beacon Lane
Cramlington NE23 8JJ
Meets fortnightly on Mon 2-2.45 pm. Hymn singing, prayer & readings.

SEXUAL ABUSE/RAPE CRISIS

ACT Abuse Counselling & Training
Mrs B Gaines
Halforton House
29 Katherine Street
Ashington NE63 9BU
T 01670 521111
Also on 01670 852971. Helpline runs Tue & Fri 10 am-12 pm & Tue 7-9 pm. Ansaphone for both lines. Counselling & self-help groups for children, adult survivors of child abuse, partners, parents & carers.

VIOLENCE AGAINST WOMEN

Wansbeck Safer Cities Project
Colin Anderson
C/o Choppington Police Station
46-47 The Square
Choppington NE62 5BY
T 01670 530135 F 01670 821514
Government-funded community safety partnership with NACRO promoting local initiatives to prevent crime & make places safer.

WOMEN'S AID

Northumberland Women's Aid
P O Box 82
Ashington NE63 0DU
T 01670 521775
Office hours Mon-Fri 9 am- 4.30 pm.
Emergency number 0378 455894 - 24 hours.
Offers safe, secure temporary accommodation to women & children fleeing domestic violence.

NOTTINGHAMSHIRE

ACCOMMODATION

Asante Sana
P O Box 226
Nottingham NG1 5LJ
T 0115 958 0873
Nottingham Black Women's Housing & Support Project. Temporary accommodation for Black women & their children who are vulnerable or are at risk. Seven self-contained flats. Staff cover Mon-Fri 9 am-5 pm.

Caravan in Skegness
Roshni Nottingham Asian Women's Aid
Nottingham Women's Centre
30 Chaucer Street
Nottingham NG1 5LP
T 0115 948 3450
Caravan to be used by Roshni's own residents as well as residents of other refuges around the country who are affiliated to Women's Aid Federation. Minimal charge. Phone above number or 0115 924 2864.

Second Base
Faye Lindsay-Booker
25 Vivian Avenue
Sherwood Rise
Nottingham NG5 1AF
T 0115 985 7744 F 0115 985 7397
181 housing places in Nottingham & north Nottinghamshire, including separate provision for women, Black people, people with mental health problems & people leaving prison. Set up by NACRO.

ARTS AND CRAFTS

Angel Row Gallery
Ruth Lewis/Angela Watts
3 Angel Row Gallery
Nottingham NG1 6HP
T 0115 947 6340 F 0115 947 6335
Open Mon-Sat 11 am-6 pm (Wed stays open until 7 pm) Contemporary art space in the centre of Nottingham.

Expansions Unlimited
Christine Michael
54 Kingswood Road
West Bridgford
Nottingham NG2 7HS
T 0115 981 9397 F 0115 982 6839

ENGLAND - NOTTINGHAMSHIRE

Correspondence club for creative writers, mainly open to newsletter, poetry competitions, small press. Organising body for Community Expansions In Literature (CEIL) - festival of literature of the arts.

Gwendoline E Grant
Gwendoline E Grant
3 Cottage
84 Shireoaks Road
Shireoaks
Worksop S81 7NA
T 01909 484213
Writer. Has worked with women's groups on creative writing. Committed to helping women find their own voice. Helps women with poetry, stories, novels, etc. Phone for up-to-date fees & times available.

Mulhouse Design Co
Caroline Newton
Mulhouse
Loughba
Orston NG13 9NJ
T 01949 850115 F 01949 850058
Distributing a wide range of quality giftware to retailers within the UK & export markets.

My Sty Crafts
Margaret Stone
14 Weedon Close
Nottingham NG3 7DE
T 0115 9582476
Craft items in wool & wood. Dolls' clothes, knitted novelties & knitted jumpers with pictures/catchphrases for children & adults. Other items made using pyrography - the burning of a design on to wood, etc.

Nikki McKay - Artist
Nikki McKay
Studio
Swallow Farm
43 Farndon Road
Newark NG24 4SQ
T 01636 700474
Artist/animator. Permanent show at local French restaurant (Cafe Bleu, Newark). Commissions for large canvases & murals taken. Ongoing experiments in animation. Studio visits by appointment.

Rachel Frost - Design and Print
Rachel Frost
The Attic Studio
42-48 Carrington Street
Nottingham NG1 7FG
T 0115 950 6895

Provides printed designs for fashion fabrics, children's wear, T-shirts, cards & giftwrap to various companies. Open Mon-Fri 9 am-6 pm

Rowena Edlin-White
Rowena Edlin-White
The Grebes
89 Morley Avenue
Mapperley
Nottingham NG2 5FZ
T 0115 960 4240
Writer/speaker/ researcher. Licensed Reader in Church of England. Key-note speaker on 'Women's spitituality, Re-discovering the Foremothers' (history of women in the church), feminist theology/women's ministry.

Sue Sareen, Fine Artist
Sue Sareen
92 Loughborough Road
West Bridgford
Nottingham NG2 7JH
wjsl@innotts.co.uk
An artist painting independently or on commissions. Runs watercolour painting courses & day/weekend courses for adults organised from her studio. Writes articles on painting for art magazines.

BUSINESS SUPPORT SCHEMES

Business Women's Network
Shirley Hoyland
16 Stable Close
Worksop S81 0UL
T 01909 501515 F 01909 470400
shirley.hoyland@virgin.net
Hold six weekly meetings throughout north Notts. Very informal & friendly atmosphere. Heightens profile of women-led businesses; provides opportunity to share common problems; etc.

Training Employment and Development Project
Pauline Dorey
C/o Nottingham Women's Centre
30 Chaucer Street
Nottingham NG1 5LP
T 0115 924 0041
Open Mon-Fri 9 am-5 pm. Training courses women only; training information; supports women starting up businesses; business advice sessions; free careers advice & counselling. Six work spaces available.

CENTRES FOR WOMEN

Ashfield Women's Centre
Jackie Frith/Mary Stephenson
Kirkby Folly School
Diamond Avenue
Kirkby-in-Ashfield NG17 7GN
T 01623 723836 F 01623 723836
Women only single storey renovated primary school. Social space with cafe, training rooms, ongoing courses, laundry & showers. Free childcare on site for users, with playground.

Nottingham Women's Centre
reception
30 Chaucer Street
Nottingham NG1 5LP
T 0115 941 1475
Drop-in for women, open Mon-Fri 10 am-4 p.m: lesbian centre, bisexual room, room for black women, free pregnancy testing, room of computers. Training courses & events. Creche for children aged 2-5.

Ollerton and Boughton Women's Centre
Jo-Anne Baker
Stepnall Heights
Boughton
Newark NG22 9HL
T 01623 836106 F 01623 836106
Open Mon-Fri 9.30 am-4 pm. Most services are free. Counselling, training, free pregnancy testing, listening service, advice & information, free legal service, creche, playgroup, cafe, social events, etc.

EDUCATION

Nottingham Association of Women Graduates
Mrs Barbara M Brooke
57 Westerlands
Stapleford
Nottingham NG9 7JE
T 0115 939 4979
Local association of BFWG. Talks, discussion, study groups & social events. Monthly evening meetings & informal Saturday lunches at members' homes. Raises funds to sponsor education of an African schoolgirl.

ETHNIC MINORITIES

Asian Women's Project
Parveen Mirza
1 Sturton Street
Forest Fields NG7 6HU
T 0115 978 3945 F 0115 979 0238

Offers information & advice on training, education, employment, domestic violence, immigration & homelessness to Asian women in Nottingham. Open Mon-Fri 9 am-5 pm.

Black and Asian Sexual Health (BASH)
Shashi Nijran
The Health Shop
Broad Street
Hockley
Nottingham NG1 3AL
T 0115 9475414 F 0115 955 4990
Free, confidential drop-in for Black & Asian women & men promoting sexual health & safer drug use to prevent HIV transmission & related problems.

Nai Sindagi Project
Mrs Raqbir Virdee
South/West Community Mental Health Team
19 Regent Street
Nottingham NG1 5BS
T 0115 941 8370 F 0115 947 0393
Offers support through counselling, advice & information for Asian women with mental health difficulties. Support given on a one-to-one basis & also in group work, conducted in the appropriate Asian language.

HEALTH

Health Shop, The
Broad Street
Hockley
Nottingham NG1 3AL
T 0115 947 5414
Free, confidential drop-in service in Nottingham's city centre, promoting sexual health & safer drug use to prevent HIV transmission & related problems. Needle exchange; hepatitis B & C screening; contraception.

Open Doors
3 Newcastle Chambers
Angel Row
Nottingham NG1 6HQ
T 0115 950 8887
Drug advice & information, counselling, needle exchange, healthcare & outreach programme. Crack awareness team (CAT): freephone advice & information helpline, drop-in centre, 24-hour emergency outreach service.

LARGER/TALLER WOMEN

Long Tall Sally
6-8 King's Walk
Nottingham NG1 2AE
T 0115 924 1073
Clothes for the taller woman sizes 12-20.
Open Mon-Sat 9.30 am-5.30 pm.

LESBIAN

Nottingham Black Lesbians Group
C/o Nottingham Women's Centre
36 Chaucer Street
Nottingham NG1 5LP
T 0115 941 1475
Providing a safe & supportive space for lesbians of colour to meet; information & advice; aiming for lesbians of colour to have equal access to women's groups, rescources, etc. Ansaphone 0115 958 8010.

LESBIAN AND BISEXUAL

Banna Housing Co-op
C/o 42 Mapperley Road
Nottingham NG3 5AS
T 0115 960 5469
Small housing co-op for lesbians & their children. Single person flats & small houses. Attending co-op meetings once a month is obligatory.

Nottingham Lesbian Line
C/o Nottingham Women's Centre
30 Chaucer Street
Nottingham NG1 5LP
T 0115 941 0652
Helpline open Mon & Wed 7-9 pm. Otherwise an ansaphone which is regularly checked. Minicom service available. Confidential advice, information & support to lesbians & women questioning their sexuality.

Nottingham Women's Bisexual Group
C/o Nottingham Women's Centre
30 Chaucer Street
Nottingham NG1 5LP
T 0115 916 1532
Meets each month at the women's centre (top floor, through the library). The women in the group cover a broad spectrum of sexuality, regardless of lifestyle, racial origin, language or disability.

LIBRARIES/ARCHIVES

Women's Library, The
Chloe Griffiths

Nottingham Women's Centre
30 Chaucer Street
Nottingham NG1 5LP
T 0115 941 1475
Open Mon 12-2 pm; Tue 12-2 pm & 5.30-7.30 pm; Thurs 11 am-3 pm; Fri 7-9 pm; Sat 11 am-2 pm. Fiction, lesbian, Jewish, Celtic & world literature. Lending library open to all women.

MANUAL TRADES

Purrfect Painters
Lyn Bowen
Flat 14, Althea Court
Poyser Close
New Basford
Nottingham NG7 7LB
T 0115 979 2519
Interior/exterior decorating. Aims to offer high quality decorating service at competitive price. Work is clean, tidy, efficient & can offer added security to clients who may prefer a tradeswoman in their home.

PREGNANCY/CHILDBIRTH

Nottingham Self-Insemination Group
The Women's Centre
30 Chaucer Street
Nottingham NG1 5LP
T 0115 941 1475
Meets every second Tue of each month. For all women considering or using self or donor insemination. A group for support, for talking about issues involved, & for sharing information. Write or phone as above.

PUBLISHERS/PUBLICATIONS

Mushroom Bookshop
10-12 Heathcote Street
Nottingham NG1 3AA
T 0115 958 2506 F 0115 959 0971
Feminist, lesbian & books on women's health issues sections.

RETAILING

Oodles Fancy Dress
Mrs Sheila Jean Whalley
335 Berry Hill Lane
Mansfield NG19 7EE
T 01623 29491
Open mon-Sat 10 am-5 pm (Closed Sun & Wed). Hire of costumes & wigs. Sales of dance shoes, etc. Sales of helium balloons, accessories, etc.

ENGLAND - NOTTINGHAMSHIRE

RIGHTS

Women's Centre Welfare Rights Advice Group
30 Chaucer Street
Nottingham NG1 5LP
T 0115 941 8968
Open Tue 10 am-4 pm. Aims are to ensure that women have access to welfare rights advice, information & representation so they can make informed choices.

SERVICES

Able Wordsmith - European Language Services
Cynthia Howell
20 Ridgeway
Southwell NG25 0DU
T 01636 814619 F 01636 814619
Teaching, translating & interpreting, typing & WP. Languages offered: English, French, German & Spanish.

Bubbles Balloons & Bubbles Promotions
Mrs Barbara McLillitte
5 Lea Road
Ravenshead NG15 9EG
T 01623 793182
Balloon decorations, garlands, gifts in boxes for weddings, parties, balls, other events. Full wedding or party consultations. Coordinator for everything for the events from flowers to cars.

Carol Walker & Co
Carol Walker
3 Lamb Close
Newark NG24 4RT
T 01636 77569 F 01636 77569
Specialist in advertising, property development/management. Aim is to offer quality, advice & service at a realistic price.

Groundworks Architects
Alison Davies
Unit 4
NCDA
Dunkirk Road
Nottingham NG7 2PH
T 0115 942 4388 F 0115 970 2290
Cooperatively structured architectural practice. Recent projects include women's centres, community centres, village halls. High quality, accessible, robust & energy efficient buildings built on time to budget.

Jenny Wright Designs
Jenny Wright
Tudor Cottage
New Road
Oxton NG25 0SL
T 0115 965 2329 F 0115 965 2329
Graphic design for all printing requirements.

Making A Difference
Lesley Jackson
64 Astley Drive
Hazelwood
Mapperley
Nottingham NG3 3EU
T 0115 948 0810
Human resource consultancy specialising in equal opportunity & diversity, recruitment & selection, personal development & stress management. Helps organisations to develop & implement policy & practice.

Wildflower
Michelle Blenkinsopp
Studio 6
35 Warser Gate
Nottingham NG1 1NU
T 0115 9550021 F 0115 9550021
Designer of women's clothing, clubwear/streetwear, aimed at young market 18-35. Supplier of independent designer outlets. All enquiries welcome. Trade only.

SEXUAL ABUSE/RAPE CRISIS

Nottingham Rape Crisis Centre (NRCC)
C/o Nottingham Women's Centre
30 Chaucer Street
Nottingham NG1 5LP
T 0115 941 0440
Helpline open Mon, Wed, Thurs & Fri 10 am-1 pm & Tue 10 am-8 pm. 24-hour ansaphone checked every morning with calls answered. One-to-one counselling. For girls & women who have been sexually abused.

SOCIAL

Women's Room Cafe Group
Jennifer Moore
C/o Nottingham Women's Centre
30 Chaucer Street
Nottingham NG1 5LP
Organises a women-only cafe night in Nottingham town centre once a month.

TRAINING

Nottinghamshire Women's Training Scheme
Albion Close

Worksop S80 1RA
T 01909 474029 F 01909 530335
Open 9.45 am-2.45 pm term time only. For women aged 18 + living in Notts with no or few qualifications. Free training in painting, decorating, motor mechanics, carpentry & joinery, computer studies, etc.

Women in Training (WIT)
Lesley Cramman
12 Denmark Grove
Alexandria Park
Nottingham NG3 4JG
T 0115 960 6615 F 0115 960 6615
Training & management consultancy, organisation & development. Women in management. Women's leadership development programmes.

WOMEN'S AID

Roshni Nottingham Asian Women's Aid
Mrs S Hindocha
C/o Nottingham Women's Centre
30 Chaucer Street
Nottingham NG1 5LP
T 0115 948 3450 F 0115 985 8766
Providing refuge for Asian women & children suffering physical, sexual, mental, financial pressures. Open Mon-Thurs 9 am-5 pm; Fri 9 am-4 pm. Confidential counselling. Welfare rights & legal advice.

Women's Aid Advice Centre
Pat Stafford
C/o Nottingham Women's Centre
30 Chaucer Street
Nottingham NG1 5LP
T 0115 947 6490
Open Tues-Fri 10 am-3 pm. Ansaphone with emergency refuge number. During busy periods helpline may be on ansaphone; checked regularly. Also an outreach number 0115 947 5257 open Tues-Fri 10 am-3 pm.

OXFORDSHIRE

ALTERNATIVE THERAPIES

Well Being Clinic, The
Sandy Fleming, Proprietor
6 Kingston Road
Oxford OX2 6EF
T 01865 311704
Naturopathic clinic: 17 disciplines, 52 therapies, including acupuncture, Traditional Chinese Medicine, chiropractic, shiatsu, osteopathy, The Alexander Technique, reflexology, kinesiology, nutrition, etc.

ARTS AND CRAFTS

Cyndy Silver, Goldsmith
Cyndy Silver
19 Cumnor Rise
Oxford OX2 9HD
T 01865 862295 F 01865 862295
A goldsmith, silversmith & jewellery designer-craftswoman, making jewellery, small boxes, bowls & spoons, small animal sculptures in silver & gold. Pieces made for exhibition or commission.

Sarah More
Sarah More
6 Meadside
Dorchester on Thames OX10 7JX
T 01865 858154 F 01865 858154
Letter cutter & stone carver. Inscription & lettering in stone & wood for architectural purposes; gravestones, stones in gardens & for work in exhibitions. Works to commission. Phone for further details.

BEREAVEMENT

National Association of Widows - Oxford branch
Mrs J Howe
53 Plantation Road
Oxford OX2 6JE
T 01865 559081
Run by widows for widows. Offers advice & information on queries/problems following the loss of a husband. Advice on pensions, benefits, housing, legal matters, etc, & support & help with emotional problems.

S & R Childs Funeral Services
Sandra Homewood
Pharmacy House
69 London Road
Headington
Oxford OX3 9AA
T 01865 427272 F 01865 437373
Open 9.30 am-4.30 pm. Independent family-run funeral service under personal supervision of proprietor, Sandra Homewood. 24-hour service, day or night for the bereaved.

BUSINESS SUPPORT SCHEMES

Oxford Business and Professional Women
Miss Margaret Norman
3 Lime Court
Lime Walk

ENGLAND - OXFORDSHIRE

Headington
Oxford OX3 7AF
T 01865 762252
Meets at Oxford Academy, Bardwell Road, 2nd Tue of each Month at 7.30 pm. Part business part social meetings. Promoting a free & responsible society in which women take an active part in decision-making, etc.

CARERS

Oxfordshire Carers' Forum
5 Bullindon House
174 Cowley Road
Oxford OX4 1UE
T 01865 209191 F 01865 295040
Promoting carers' interests & helping them to get the support they need. Helping carers explain what types of support they need from health, social services & other agencies.

COMPUTERS/IT

Computency Ltd
Doreen Pechey
Jays Lodge
Crays Pond
Goring Heath RG8 7QG
T 01491 681236 F 011491 682025
doreen@cix.compulink.co.uk
Consultancy & training in datacommunications, PC-related topics, mathematics & statistics.

Oxford Women's Training Scheme
Jane Butcher
The Northway Centre
Maltfield Road
Oxford OX3 9RF
T 01865 741317 F 01895 742199
Courses in computing, computing training, introductory woodwork, introductory painting & decorating, computing for speakers of languages other than English, basic maths, ESOL. Free courses & childcare.

CONTRACEPTION/WELL WOMAN

Acland Hospital, The
Banbury Road
Oxford OX2 6PD
T 01865 404142
Well woman screen. Full female health assessment. Phone for up-to-date price lists.

Well Woman Holistic Advisory Service
Sandy Fleming, Proprietor
The Well Being Clinic

6 Kingston Road
Oxford OX2 6EF
T 01865 311704
Offers help for a wide range of problems. Promoting balance of hormones through changing food consumption. Experienced practitioner available for consultations, diagnosis & treatment.

COUNSELLING AND THERAPY

East Oxford Women's Counselling (EOWC)
111 Magdalen Road
Oxford OX4 1RQ
T 01865 725617
Office open Wed morning or 24-hour ansaphone. Low cost or free counselling for women run by women. Offers counselling to women who might not otherwise have access to it. A friendly non-threatening service.

EDUCATION

Oxford Association of Graduate Women
Mrs N K Trenaman
4 Fairlawn End
Oxford OX2 8AR
Meets on first Fri of month at noon at The Friends' Meeting House, 43 St Giles, Oxford. Readings, discussions, speakers. Working for conditions in which women can combine careers & domestic responsibilities.

EQUAL OPPS

Oxford City Council Women's Sub-Committee
St Aldate's Chambers
St Aldate's
Oxford OX1 1DS
T 01865 252414
Promoting the welfare & interests of women in Oxford; implementing policies to promote equal opportunities for women; increasing opportunities for women who are employed by the city council; etc.

ETHNIC MINORITIES

Asian Girls' and Young Women's Group
Nhila
C/o Asian Cultural Centre
Old Cowley Road Hospital
Manzila Way
Oxford
T 01865 793087
Social group that meets on Sat. Parties & outings.

Asian Young Women's Group
Nhila
East Oxford Youth Centre
Union Street Complex
Oxford OX4 1JP
T 01865 248521
An Asian young women's group. Meets on Sat mornings. Social activities, outings, parties.

Sahara Asian Women's Support Group
The Carers' Centre
179a Cowley Road
Oxford OX4 1UE
T 01865 295176
Meets Mon 1.30-3 pm.

HEALTH

Libra Project
St Lukes
Oxford Road
Cowley
Oxford
T 01865 749800
A counselling service for anyone worried about drink or drug use. Support & information to anyone concerned about the alcohol or drug use of a family member or friend. All services are free & confidential.

Mental Health Resource Centre
19 Paradise Street
Oxford OX1 1LD
T 01865 728981
Open Tue 9.30 am-4.30 pm, Wed 1.30-4.30 pm, Thurs 9.30 am-6.30 pm, Fri 9.30 am-3 pm. Drop-in centre for information & advice on all matters connected with mental health.

Oxford Radcliffe Hospital - Women's Centre
Headington
Oxford OX3 9DU
T 01865 221530
Self-referral (appt only) to see specialist physiotherapists about bladder problems, back or plevic pain before/after birth & painful scarring after delivery; gynaecological surgery advice & information; etc.

Vita Clinic
health adviser
Harrison Department
The Radcliffe Infirmary
Woodstock Road
Oxford OX2 6HE
T 01865 246036
Open alternate Fri 9.15-10.30 am Lesbian sexual health clinic. Free, confidential clinic offering routine screen tests, including cytology (smear tests) & treatment for STDs. HIV pre- & post-test counselling.

LARGER/TALLER WOMEN

Narda Fashion Studios
Mrs Narda Dalgleish
67-68 High Street
Oxford OX1 4BA
T 01865 793082
Open Mon-Sat 10 am-6 pm "We fashion clothes for the woman whose beauty is determined not by the perfection of one or a few attributes she may possess, but by the whole of her original purpose."

LESBIAN AND BISEXUAL

Oxford Lesbian Line
Oxford
T 01865 242333
Oxford lesbian line provides a unique & confidential telephone helpline & meeting service to all women in the Oxfordshire area who may have questions about their sexuality.

PEACE GROUPS

Women's International League for Peace and Freedom - Oxford
Jean Kaye
5 Annesley Road
Oxford OX4 4JH
T 01865 771046
Consultancy status with the UN. Peace is the main focus. An international organisation coordinated by the Geneva office. Around 300 members in the UK. Head office in south Wales.

PHOTOGRAPHY

Bloomin Arts Ltd
Maria Jurd
East Oxford Community Centre
Princes Street
Oxford OX4 1HU
T 01865 245735 F 01865 724317
Women Photographers Group meets every Wed 10 am-1 pm. Creche 11 am-1 pm. To provide an inspiring & supportive environment in which to encourage women to express themselves through the photographic medium.

ENGLAND - OXFORDSHIRE

PREGNANCY/CHILDBIRTH

Crisis Pregnancy Centre - Witney
33b High Street
Witney
T 01993 779396
Open Mon, Thurs, Fri 11 am-1.30 pm & Sat 10 am-12 noon appt only. Special appts available - phone Rosemary: 01367 810612. Free pregnancy testing, counselling, support for women with unplanned pregnancies.

PUBLISHERS/PUBLICATIONS

Oxford Women in Publishing
Sue Bennett/Corinne Miley-Smith
C/o Training Matters
15 Pitts Road
Headington Quarry
Oxford OX3 8BA
T 01865 766964 F 01865 60637
Provides forum for women working in, studying, interested in publishing & allied professions (bookselling, printing). Training, speakers, meetings. Courses are held on Sat 9.30 am-5.30 pm. Directory.

RETAILING

Willowbrook Antiques
J Lacey
84 Fernhill Road
Begbroke
Kidlington OX5 1RR
T 01865 376827
Retailer of furniture, collector's items & sporting goods at Unit 39, Station Mill Antique Centre, Chipping Norton, Oxfordshire.

SERVICES

Pathfinder International Freight Forwarding
Erica Tyler
6 Grove Street
Wantage OX12 7AA
T 01235 760825 F 01235 760 826
Worldwide freight forwarding by air & by sea. European freight forwarding by road. Parcel service door to door. Commercial & industrial freight.

SEXUAL ABUSE/RAPE CRISIS

Oxford Sexual Abuse and Rape Crisis Centre
P O Box 20
St Aldate's Post Office
Oxford OX1 1HQ
T 01865 726295
Centre open Sun 6-8 pm, Mon 7-9 pm, Wed 4-6 pm, Thurs 7-9 pm. Telephone counselling & free face-to-face counselling by women for women who have suffered any form of sexual abuse & or rape.

SUPPORT

Oasis
C/o MIND
Micklewood House
331 Cowley Road
Oxford OX4 2AQ
T 01865 511702
Open Mon 5-9 pm & Fri 11 am-3 pm. Drop-in centre for women only in distress; all women welcome; run by women for women. Creche for under 5s; friendly safe place to be & find support & listening ear.

Redbridge Traveller Women's Support Group
CEC Office
Union Street Complex
Oxford OX4 1JP
T 01865 727148 F 01865 201755
Develops community links with women travellers & their families from the Redbridge Oxford site. To expose & combat discrimination against travellers. To give travelling community access to wider society.

TRANSPORT

Oxford Women's Night Bus, The
Oxford
T 01865 270777
The above number is for phoning during office hours. After 8 pm phone 0831 227908 (mobile phone). The bus runs on Thurs, Fri & Sat 11 pm-2 am

VIOLENCE AGAINST WOMEN

Oxford Safer Cities Project
Ruth Cane
C/o Chief Executive's Department
Oxford City Council
St Aldate's
Oxford OX1 1DS
T 01865 252304 F 01865 252256
Government-funded community safety partnership with NACRO promoting local initiatives to prevent crime & make places safer.

ENGLAND - SHROPSHIRE

WOMEN'S AID

Oxfordshire Women's Aid
Deborah Schofield
P O Box 255
Oxford OX2 6BB
T 01865 791416
Helpline open Mon-Fri 9.30 am-5 pm. Refuge for women & their children (if any) facing domestic violence.

SHROPSHIRE

CONTRACEPTION/WELL WOMAN

Shropshire Nuffield Hospital, The
Longden Road
Shrewsbury SY3 9PD
T 01743 353441
Well woman screen. Full female health assessment. Phone for up-to-date price lists.

EDUCATION

Shropshire Association of Women Graduates
Miss A Hunt
73 Preston Street
Shrewsbury SY2 5PN
T 01743 355349
Meets monthly, usually to hear speakers on a wide range of topics. Objectives are mainly social or educational. Opportunities to meet other women graduates at regional, national & international level.

LARGER/TALLER WOMEN

Long Tall Sally
66 Wyle Cop
Shrewsbury SY1 1UX
T 01743 271878
Clothes for the taller woman sizes 12-20. Open Mon-Sat 9.30 am-5.30 pm.

LESBIAN AND BISEXUAL

Border Women
Pauline
P O Box 42
Ludlow SY8 1WD
T 01584 873181
Organisation for lesbians in Wales & the border counties of Shropshire, Hereford & Worcester. Newsletter once a month containing diary of events, small ads, personal ads, articles, letters, opinions & news.

SEXUAL ABUSE/RAPE CRISIS

Shropshire Rape Crisis Centre
P O Box 89
Wellington
Telford TF1 1TZ
T 01952 248444
Free, confidential face-to-face or telephone counselling for women who have been raped or otherwise sexually abused at any time during their lives. A service run by women for women.

SOCIAL

Female 77
Brenda Ray
16 Wenlock Drive
Newport
T 01952 812207
For young women with children. Courses, cookery demonstrations. Meets Wed 8 pm during term time.

SOMERSET

ACCOUNTANCY

Julie Wakeford Chartered Accountant
Julie Wakeford
7 The lawns
Yalton BS19 4BG
T 01934 834969
Specialising in small businesses operating as sole traders & partnerships. Offers complete accountancy & taxation service. Evening & daytime appointments available. All services at reasonable rates.

AGRICULTURE

Women's Farming Union - Somerset Branch
Mrs Jane Small
Charlton Orchards
Creech St Michael
Taunton TA3 5PF
T 01823 412979
Committed to promoting an understanding of, and confidence in, all aspects of quality British produce.

ALTERNATIVE THERAPIES

Terrace, The
Jane Gotto
Therapy and Natural Health Centre
35 Staplegrove Road
Taunton TA1 1DG
T 01823 338968

ENGLAND - SOMERSET

Office hours 9 a.m-1 p.m and 2-4 pm.
Therapies in daytime and some in evening, including acupuncture, Alexander Technique, homoeopathy, ayurveda, counselling, herbal medicine. There is a women's group.

ARTS AND CRAFTS
Chard Festival of Women in Music
Angela Willes
1 Hope Terrace
Combe Street
Chard TA20 1JA
T 01460 66115 F 01460 66115
A festival held in May in and around Chard promoting music composed by women of all music types. A working committee meets every month.

MiniMax Productions
Alex, Administration/Business Manager
100 Bove Town
Glastonbury BA6 8JG
T 01458 831327 F 01458 831327
Recording & distribution company specialising in women's music. Aims to create a conducive & supportive environment for the recording of music backed by experienced production team.

Wild Women
Jana Runnalls/Katrina Brown
C/0 MiniMax Productions
100 Bove Town,
Glastonbury BA6 8JG
T 01458 831327 F 01458 831327
Jana Runnalls vocals & Katrina Brown bass & guitar. World music drawing from jazz/blues, reggae & Afro-Carribean styles to acoustic fold ballads.

BEREAVEMENT
Somerset Baby Lost Support Group
Kate Makin, Social Work Department
Musgrove Park Hospital
Taunton TA1 5DA
T 01823 333444
Support, comfort & information for parents who have suffered stillbirth, miscarriage or termination owing to foetal abnormailities or death of a baby in the first 28 days of life.

BUSINESS SUPPORT SCHEMES
Business and Professional Women (BPW) - Somerset
Mrs Ann O'Brien

17 Baker's Close
Bishops Hull
Taunton TA15HD
T 01823 286547
To help women realise their full potential in the workplace & public life. This organisation meets every second & fourth Wed in the month.

CHILD CARE AND FAMILY
Albys Playgroup
Deborah Clifford
The Albermarle Centre
Albermarle Road
Taunton TA1 1BA
T 01823 289332
Playgroups for children aged two-and-a-half to five Mon-Fri 9.15 a.m-12.15 pm; rising 5s Wed 12.30-3 pm. Snacks and drinks provided. All staff are experinced and are registered with social services.

CONTRACEPTION/WELL WOMAN
Somerset Nuffield Hospital, The
Staplegrove Elm
Taunton TA2 6AN
T 01823 286991
Well woman screen. Full female health assessment. Phone for up-to-date price lists.

Taunton & Somerset NHS Trust
Jean Pottage, Administrator - Family Planning
Family Planning Service
East Reach Centre
East Reach
Taunton TA1 3HQ
T 01823 331121 F 01823 326867
Free contraception, confidential counselling. Free pregnancy tests, cevical smears, well women clinics, emergency contraception and sexual health advice. Clinics in seven towns; young persons' walk-in clinics.

Taunton Well Women Centre
Eileen
Ante-natal Clinic
Musgrove Park Hospital
Taunton TA1 5DA
T 01823 252077
Talk to a woman doctor about your problems. Every Fri 2-4 pm. Free & confidential service. No appointment needed. Advice, information, simple treatments: blood pressure, breast examinations, urine tests.

ENGLAND - SOMERSET

Yeovil Well Women Centre
Barbara McAulay, Chairwoman
Out-Patients' Department
Yeovil District Hospital
Higher Kingston
Yeovil BA21 4AT
T 01935 23871
Open Mon 7-9 pm. A meeting place for women in relaxed & friendly atmosphere. Literature available. Advice & information from doctors & nurses. Routine examinations. Pregnancy testing, cervical smears, etc.

Environment

Friends of Bride's Mound
Serena Roney-Dougal
Box 23
5 High Street
Glastonbury BA6 8HN
Aims to protect Bride's Mound from inappropriate development & supports a proposal to recreate a women's sanctuary on this ancient site. Donations welcome.

Girls/Young women

Tauton Detached Youth Work Team
Helen Macdonald/Sarah Stevens
Somerset County Youth Service
TYCC
Tangier
Taunton
T 01823 324790 F 01823 351325
Detached@mplc.co.uk
Delivering youth work to marginalised young people across Taunton. Developing work with girls & young women aged 13-25. Advice & information, personal & social education, social contact, support.

Health

Hysterectomy Support Network
Teena Carberry
35 Newlands Road
Ruishton
Taunton TA3 5JZ
T 01823 442446
Provides information & support & links up women who have had hysterectomies.

Somerset Mastectomy and Breast Cancer Group
Anne Dibble, Breast Care nurse
Musgrove Park Hospital
Taunton TA1 5DA
T 01823 333444

Support for women both pre- & post-operation. Questions answered. Group meets once a month socially. Trips and speakers. Anne Dibble can also be contacted on 01823 342453 or Maureen Hancock on 01823 283507.

Publishers/publications

Just Women
Avril Silk
Rainbow Cottage
3 Rowcliffe's Cottages
Ashbrittle
Wellington TA21 0LF
T 01823 672131
Feminist quarterly cooperative magazine for & by women, providing a platform for opinions, fiction, poetry, reviews, news from women. Supportive editorial policy. Meets weekly on Wed in/around Taunton.

Retailing

Material World
Babs Humphrey
53 Station Road
Taunton TA1 1NZ
T 01823 335553 F 01823 335553
Fabric (soft furnishing) shop. Curtain & soft furnishing making-up service. Loose covers, fixed upholstery fitting, hanging service. Free help, advice, measuring service. Open Mon-Sat 9.30 am-5.30 pm.

Toucan Wholefoods
Sally Eveleigh/Jane Hart
7 Floyds Corner
The Parade
Minehead TA24 5UW
T 01643 706101
A wholefood & completely vegetarian shop, also selling a comprehensive range of supplements. Advice on nutrition. Organic vegetables & take away foods. Open 8.30 am-5.30 pm six days a week.

Sexual abuse/rape crisis

Mrs Barbara Moss
T 01460 242795
Offers counselling/therapy to women on a one-to-one basis, specialising in adult survivors of abuse, sexual/emotional/physical. Pre-menstrual syndrome, menopausal problems, addictions - alcohol, food, sex.

Personal Recovery Service
Jo Keohane, Office Manager
Island House
Huntspill Road
Highbridge TA9 3DD
T 01278 794448 F 01278 795552
Counselling/ therapy to help recovery from all forms of sexual, physical, mental and/or emotional abuse. Special expertise in sexual abuse. Telephone hours: Mon-Fri 9 am-4 pm. Ansaphone outside these hours.

Support Group for Mothers
Pam
Somersaetas
Wedmore BS28 4DU
T 01934 713362
Telephone support for mothers of abused children & survivors. Phone at any time.

SOCIAL

Chard Ladies' Afternoon Guild
Mrs L Ball, Secretary
19 St Gildas
Millfield
Chard TA20 2AF
T 01460 65339
For all women, irrespective of race, colour or creed, to serve as a group of women interested in subjects concerning the well being of home & community. To encourage friendship. Meets fortnightly Tue afternoon.

WOMEN'S AID

South Somerset Women's Refuge
Jan or Pat
P O Box 1923
Yeovil BA21 4YD
T 01935 27594 F 01935 27594
We aim to provide refuge space for women & children escaping mental, physical or sexual abuse 24 hours a day, 365 days a year.

STAFFORDSHIRE

ALTERNATIVE THERAPIES

Athena School of Natural Therapy
Lynn Davies
2 Osprey Grove
Heath Hayes
Cannock WS12 5YE
T 01543 271278
Training company specialising in natural therapies/complementary medicine. Recognised qualifications offered (part-time) in: massage, aromatherapy, reflexology, nutrition, Reiki & Indian head massage.

New Perspectives: Counselling and Training for Health
Ann Mason and Kate Kirk
Prospect Villa
20 Newton Street
Basford
Stoke-on-Trent ST4 6JL
T 01782 713581
To enable women to improve upon current levels of well being in physical, emotional, sexual, relationship areas of health through reflexology, aromatherapy, psychotherapy, counselling. Workshops & training.

CONTRACEPTION/WELL WOMAN

North Staffordshire Nuffield Hospital, The
Clayton Road
Newcastle-under-Lyme ST5 4DB
T 01782 625431
Well woman screen. Full female health assessment. Phone for up-to-date price lists.

COUNSELLING AND THERAPY

Potential Unlimited
Amanda Parkyn
1 Church Farm Close
Penkridge
Stafford ST19 5AP
T 01785 716068 F 01785 716068
Individual career counselling; organisational development for equality; women's development programmes; equal opportunities awareness training; training for women & men in effective working & communications.

EDUCATION

Manchester Association of Women Graduates
Professor B R Heywood
Department of Chemistry
Keele University
Keele ST5 5BG
T 01782 583507 F 01782 583508
cha42@keele.ac.uk
Network for graduate women. Career advice. Awards, scholarships & emergency funds for postgraduate research through BFWG, the parent body.

PREGNANCY/CHILDBIRTH

Stafford Christian Life Trust
84 Marston Road
Stafford ST16 3BY
T 01785 241798

Free pregnancy testing, counselling & support for women with unplanned pregnancies. Post abortion & miscarriage counselling. Phone for an appt. 24-hour ansaphone. Mother & baby home for pregnant women.

Sexual Abuse/Rape Crisis

Rape Crisis - North Staffs & South Cheshire
Angela or Jakki
P O Box 254
Hanley
Stoke-on-Trent ST1 4RE
T 01782 214733 F 01782 214733
Counselling line: 01782 204177. Free, confidential counselling & information by women for women & girls who have been sexually assualted. Line open Mon-Fri 10 am-4 pm; Tue 5.30-7 pm. Otherwise ansaphone.

Sexual Abuse and Rape Advice Centre
P O Box 3
Burton-on-Trent DE14 1ZT
T 01283 535110
Counselling helpline: 01283 517185. Face-to-face & phone counselling & some outreach services.

Suffolk

Girls/Young Women

Girls' Friendly Society Platform
Mrs Jill Eaton
Rozel
5 Kensington Road
South Lowestoft NR33 0H7
T 01502 565815
Area representative for Suffolk & Norfolk, dealing with branch work. Age range 6-15 years, & youth & community work from aged 15 onwards.

Health

Halesworth Women's Health Information Centre
C/o Waveney Local Office
London Road
Halesworth IP19 8LW
T 01986 875360
Information on health & specifically problems affecting women throughout their lives. Phone for details of opening times.

Waveney Women's Health Information Centre
Dawn Coleman
21 Milton Road East
Lowestoft NR32 1NT
T 01502 561816
Open Mon 10 am-4 pm; Wed 10 am-1 pm; Thurs 10 am-4 pm. Information on health, specifically problems affecting women throughout life. Support groups, stress management, pregnancy testing, etc.

Larger/Taller Women

Blake House
Mrs Pat Blakeburn
2a Earsham Street
Bungay NR35 1AG
T 01986 893131
Retailer of clothes for the larger woman, ie 14-34+. Open daily 9 am-5 pm (except Wed & Sun). Medium prices. Wheelchair access & nearby parking.

Retailing

Tight Fit Ltd
Helen Elliot
P O Box 48
Beyton
Bury St Edmunds IP30 9HS
T 01359 271629 F 01359 271629
tight.fit@dial.pipex.com
Supply of vending machines for hosiery & hygiene products & the products to sell through them. Also breath freshener products & travel/overnight packs.

Services

EURAG International Ltd
Hortense Hargreaves
P O Box 3464
Sudbury CO10 6DY
T 01787 881242 F 01787 881242
Export company, sourcing & supplying specialist products. Shipping & freight forwarding. Aims to facilitate UK companies to find right partners in markets & help with export/freight forwarding documentation.

Sexual Abuse/Rape Crisis

Christine Boatwright
Christine Boatwright
Little Hickbush
Great Henny
Sudbury CO10 7LU
T 01787 269694
Counselling BAC accredited/UKRC registered. Person-centred counselling/therapy. For general anxiety, depression. Works with adults who have

suffered child abuse. Line open Mon-Fri 9 am-9 pm. Ansaphone.

Suffolk Rape Crisis Centre
P O Box 135
Ipswich IP1 2QQ
T 01473 715333
Helpline open Mon & Fri 7-9 pm. Otherwise 24-hour ansaphone. A support service run by women for women with a listening ear who've suffered sexual abuse, rape and/or sexual harassment.

WOMEN'S AID
Waveney Women's Aid
Lowestoft
T 01502 519801
Provides safe, temporary accommodation for women & their children (if any) escaping from domestic violence, whether physical or emotional abuse. Women may stay overnight or for several months in the refuge.

SURREY

BEREAVEMENT
South Thames Cot Death Support Group
Morag Bean
52 Blake Hall Road
Carshalton Beeches SM5 3EZ
T 0181 647 7248
Offers befriending & support, both for individuals & in groups. Free service. 24-hour national helpline 0171 235 1721.

CONTRACEPTION/WELL WOMAN
Woking Nuffield Hospital, The
Shores Road
Woking GU21 4NY
T 01488 763511
Well woman screen. Full female health assessment. Phone for up-to-date price lists.

DISABILITY
Us in a Bus
Janet Gurney
Kingsfield Resource Centre
Philanthropic Road
Redhill RH1 4DP
T 01737 783240
Small mobile project working with people with learning disabilities. Activities offered to people in their home environment by two project workers. 24-hour ansaphone: 01737 763591.

EDUCATION
Farnborough and District Assn of University Women
Mrs W R Hynd
Frensham Grove
46 Frensham Vale
Lower Bourne
Farnham GU10 3HT
T 01252 792602
Meets third Mon of each month. Topics of interest to local members. Social events throughout the year: lunches, annual dinner, evening get-togethers, Christmas party. Encourages friendship & discussion.

West Surrey Association of Women Graduates
Dr Mary Hunter
9 Ennismore Avenue
Guildford GU1 1SP
T 01483 823229
To perfect the art of friendship; promote the interests of all women; support & encourage women in all their endeavours. Provides friendship with women graduates of widely differing backgrounds & interests.

EQUAL OPPS
Fair Play South East
Janet Dallas
Government Office for the South East
Bridge House
1 Walnut Tree Close
Guildford GU1 4GA
T 01483 882274
Positive action equalities project. A government EOC initiative to stimulate partnerships which improve opportunities for women to realise their full potential in education, employment & the community.

LARGER/TALLER WOMEN
Long Tall Sally
23 Tunsgate
Guildford GU1 3QY
T 01483 451099
Clothes for the taller woman sizes 12-20. Open Mon-Sat 9.30 am-5.30 pm; Sun 11 am-5 pm.

MANUAL TRADES
Inside and Out Decorators
Jane Marshall
3 Wilton Road
Redhill RH1 6QR
T 01737 762756

Qualified female decorator established in business for 10 years. Domestic & small contract work. Interior & exterior decoration. Some special decorative effects.

Sexual abuse/Rape Crisis
Friday Night Group
C/o South West Surrey Family Centre
The Park
St James Avenue
Farnham GU9 9QN
T 01252 733855
Self-help group for survivors meets on Fri evenings. Can be contacted through the family centre.

Spelthorne Open Space
Jeanne
Staines
Middlesex
T 01784 210661
Crisis helpline 9 am-12 am Self-help group for women once a fortnight.

Sussex

Alternative therapies
Gillian Smith Complementary Therapist
Gillian Smith
38 Quebec Close
Bexhill-on-Sea TN39 4HX
T 01424 215646
Works Mon-Fri 9 am-7 pm concentrating on light touch therapies addressing the energetic aspects of the body: Bowtech, Bach Flower Remedies, reiki & aromatherapy. Metaphysical workshops held on Sat.

Marion Eaton Aromatherapist & Reiki Master and Healer
Mrs Marion Eaton
The Professional Centre
50 High Street
Old Town
Hastings TN34 3EN
T 01424 465050 F 01424 436573
Using essential oils in aromatherapy treatments to improve physical/emotional wellbeing. Healing through hands in Reiki therapy, an effective method for prevention & treatment of diseases & energy imbalances.

Professional Centre for Holistic Health
50 High Street
Hastings TN34 3EN
Group practice of qualified professional complementary therapists committed to working holistically. Nutrition, podiatry & chiropody, geng shui, aura soma, etc.

Arts and Crafts
Acabellas, The
Julia Lynn
GFF
33 Wilbury Road
Hove BN3 3PP
T 01273 774917
An A Capella women's singing group, singing a wide range of songs from around the world. Available to perform at benefits.

Business support schemes
Women in Business - Horsham Branch
Jackie Charman, Co-ordinator
23 Arun Vale
Coldwaltham,
Pulborough RH20 1LP
T 01798 872887 F 01798 872887
101557.3332@compuserve.com
Monthly evening meetings to provide workshops of interest, talks & presentations on a wide range of topics. Breakfast & lunch meetings. A business & social networking group for women who work for themselves.

Women in Business - West Sussex branch
Caroline Brannigan
Keeper's Cottage
East Mascalls Lane
Lindfield RH16 2QJ
T 01444 483311 F 01444 483311
Networking support organisation primarily aimed at women running their own businesses. Proving a support network, sharing information, exchanging ideas, promoting each others' activities.

Centres for women
Brighton Women's Centre
Lettice House
10 St George's Mews
Brighton BN1 3EU
T 01273 600526
Open Mon, Wed, Thurs, Fri 10.30 am-3.30 pm; Sat 11 am-1 pm. 24-hours ansaphone. Counseling, health services, legal advice (Wed 10.30 am-12.30 pm; Thurs 2.00-3.30 pm), drugs project, creche.

Contraception/Well woman
Family Planning Clinic
Sue Ward, Service Manager

Morley Street
Brighton BN2 2RA
T 01273 693600
Open Mon, Wed & Thurs 10 am-12 noon & 2-4 pm; Tue 10 am-12 noon & 2-3.30 pm; Mon, Wed & Thurs 6-7.15 pm. Advice and information about contraception and supplies.

Sussex Nuffield Hospital, The
Warren Road
Woodingdean
Brighton BN2 6DX
T 01273 624488
Well woman screen. Full female health assessment. Phone for up-to-date price lists.

COUNSELLING AND THERAPY

Springfield Centre for Holistic Health
Jen Popkin
4 Springfield Road
St Leanards TN38 0TU
T 01424 428470
Personal development & counselling service, providing training & therapy in eating disorders, alcohol abuse problems. Art therapy. Aims to help people attain their personal best. Disability access.

EDUCATION

West Sussex Association of Women Graduates
Maria Martin, Secretary
58 Littlehaven Lane
Horsham RH12 4JB
T 01403 270707 F 01403 257850
Part of the British Federation of Women Graduates which is a non-governmental national organisation with neither political nor religious bias, bringing women together worldwide.

ENVIRONMENT

Countryside Management Consultancy
Ruth M Tittensor
Walberton Green House
The Street
Walberton
Arundel BN18 0QB
T 01243 542431 F 01243 555963
barnham.telecottage@dial.pipex.co
Concerned with rural landscapes, their history & management. Appraising the ecological status of the areas under investigation. Offers advice & prepares plans for ongoing management of the countryside.

ETHNIC MINORITIES

Sussex Muslim Ladies' Circle
Mrs Jamila Sajid
8 Caburn Road
Hove BN3 6EF
T 01273 722438 F 01273 279438
Regular ladies' meetings & get togethers. Social club - religion & cultural activities. Discussion of women's issues. Health care. Mother & toddler group.

HEALTH

Crawley Drug Advice Centre
The Annex
103 High Street
Crawley RH10 1DD
T 01293 548350
Provides a wide range of care, advice & helpline services for drug & alcohol users & their families. Particularly successful in attracting women & people from ethnic communities.

Hatherley Road Day Programme
Hatherley Road
St Leonards on Sea TN37 6JR
T 01424 441548
Community rehabilitation programme for drug using offenders. Drop-in centre, needle exchange, advice, counselling.

Horder Centre for Arthritis, The
Mr J E Ball, Chief Executive
St John's Road
Crowborough TN6 1XP
T 01892 665577 F 01892 662142
Specialist assessment & treatment of patients suffering from arthritis & locomotor disorders. Facilities include surgical joint replacement operating theatre, medical nursing, osteoporosis screening, etc.

Menopause and PMS Clinic - Brighton
Sue Ward, Service Manager
Morley Street
Brighton BN2 2RA
T 01273 693600
Open Fri 9.30-11.30 am Advice & counselling on menopause & HRT.

Southwater Advice Centre
Hatherley Road
St Leonards on Sea TN37 6JR
T 01424 441548
Drug advice and information. Tranquilliser support.

ENGLAND - SUSSEX

Trinity Project
6 Trinity Street
Hastings TN34 1HG
T 01424 426375
Drug advice & information, counselling, needle exchange, healthcare & outreach programme. Drop-in.

LARGER/TALLER WOMEN

Emma Plus Ltd
Emma Hayes
16 Church Street
Brighton BN1 1RB
T 01273 327240
Larger-sized women's designer clothes in younger, fashionable styles, ranging in sizes 18-32. Featuring a wide, unique mix of mid-price items & a friendly, professional service.

Long Tall Sally
10 East Street
Brighton BN1 1HP
T 01273 731791
Clothes for the taller woman sizes 12-20. Open Mon-Sat 9.30 am-5.30 pm; Sun 11 am-5 pm.

Splash Out
Maureen Smyth
100 Brighton Road
Worthing BN11 2EN
T 01903 230861
Specialises in lycra wear. Personal fitting for fuller busted women, taller women. Now working with Worthing hospital & have produced a range of mastectomy swim & aerobics wear. All individually produced.

LEGAL MATTERS

Marion Eaton Lawyer Mediator
Mrs Marion Eaton
The Professional Centre
50 High Street
Hastings TN34 3EN
T 01424 465050 F 01424 436573
A voluntary process of alternative dispute resolution. Where realism & common sense combine in a cost-efficient method of resolving disputes.

PLACES TO STAY AND EAT

Bannings Guest House
Geoff or Steve
14 Upper Rock Gardens
Kemptown
Brighton BN2 1QE
T 01273 681403
Women only. 3 double, 3 twin bedrooms. Vegetarians catered for. Dining room & two bedrooms non smoking. No children or pets. Closed December to February. Phone for a brochure of up-to-date prices.

Only Alternative Left, The
Monica Crowe
39 St Aubyn's
Hove BN3 2TH
T 01273 324739
Women's guesthouse. Open all year. Feminists/lesbians welcome. Two minutes to the sea; secluded walled garden. Smoking area. Lesbian & gay tea garden. Phone for up-to-date price list.

PREGNANCY/CHILDBIRTH

Alternatives Pregnancy Counselling Service
City Gate Centre
84-86 London Road
Brighton BN1 4QA
T 01273 687687
Open Mon, Wed, Thurs & Fri 10 am-2 pm. Free pregnancy testing, counselling & support for women with unplanned pregnancies. Post abortion & miscarriage counselling. Phone for an appt. 24-hour ansaphone.

PROFESSIONAL ASSOCIATIONS

Women's History Network (Southern)
Dr Gerry Holloway
Centre for Continuing Education
University of Sussex
Falmer
Brighton BN1 9RG
T 01273 606755 F 01273 678848
g.holloway@sussex.ac.uk
Regional network mainly covering Hampshire, Surrey & Sussex. Three day conferences per year around the region to talk about women's hisotry, past & present. Annual conference. Research databank.

PUBLISHERS/PUBLICATIONS

Out! Brighton
4-7 Dorset Street
Kemp Town
Brighton BN2 1WA
T 01273 623356

Lesbian & gay bookshop.

RETAILING

Brighton Badges
Monica Crowe
39 St Aubyn's
Hove BN3 2TH
T 01273 324739
Button badges. Minimum order 50. Write or phone for details.

SERVICES

Career Profiles
Mrs P V Jones, Proprietor
First Floor
12a Marine Square
Brighton BN2 1DL
T 01273 695095 F 01273 695095
Career profiles, computer-aided career guidance, counselling sessions, cvs & job applications, mock interviews. For older married women making fresh career start, those about to leave school/college, etc.

SEXUAL ABUSE/RAPE CRISIS

Brighton Rape Crisis Project
Karen Leenders
P O Box 323
Brighton BN2 2TY
T 01273 323027
Helpline: 01273 203773 open Mon & Wed 6-9 pm; Fri 9.30 am-12.30 pm. Confidential non-judgemental counselling service by women for women by phone & face-to-face in the Sussex region. Free service.

TRAINING

Brighton, Hove and Lewes Enterprise Agency
Jean Cranford
23 Old Steine
Brighton BN1 1EL
T 01273 688882 F 01273 604023
Open 9 am-5 pm. A women's enterprise centre. Courses for women in business. Women counsellors & women trainers.

Olufemi Ah'ssociates Training and Consultancy
L Olufemi Hughes
4 Westhill Street
Brighton BN1 3RR
T 01273 323524
jonas@pavilion.co.uk

Training, facilitation & consultancy in personal & professional development related to equality & diversity issues. Many of these services are targeted at women from various backgrounds & ethnic identities.

VIOLENCE AGAINST WOMEN

Brighton Safer Cities Project
Julia Carrette
2nd Floor
3 St George's Place
Brighton BN1 4GA
T 01273 692693 F 01273 679797
Government-funded community safety partnership with NACRO promoting local initiatives to prevent crime & make places safer.

WARWICKSHIRE

ALTERNATIVE THERAPIES

Debbie Collins
Debbie Collins
21 Aylesford Street
Leamington Spa CV31 2AL
T 01926 337409
Acupuncture & counselling - humanistic integrative approach & groupwork. Objective is empowerment, enabling health & awareness. Workshops for women/girls exploring positive approach to menstruation.

CHILD CARE AND FAMILY

Rainbow Nanny Agency
Valerie Norman
25 Long Street
Bulkington
Nuneaton CV12 9J2
T 01203 643211 F 01203 643211
Placing nannies in private homes & nurseries. Also provides creche workers and temporary nursery staff to nurseries & hotels & baby sitting service.

CONTRACEPTION/WELL WOMAN

Family Planning Clinic
Kenilworth Clinic
Smalley Place
Kenilworth CV8 1QG
T 01926 852087
Clinics on first, third and fifth Wed of each month from 7-9 pm. Contraception advice, information and supplies. Phone for an appointment.

Warwickshire Nuffield Hospital, The
Old Milverton Lane
Leamington Spa CV32 6RW
T 01926 427971
Well woman screen. Full female health assessment. Phone for up-to-date price lists.

EDUCATION

Warwickshire Association of University Women
Mrs S Lynch
Greville House
8 Northumberland Road
Leamington Spa CV32 6HQ
Friendship with women graduates of widely differing backgrounds & interests who enjoy meeting & working together. Meetings with speakers. Social events & outings.

ETHNIC MINORITIES

Warwickshire African Caribbean and Asian Women's Network
Anita Kumari
C/o WDREC
28 Hamilton Terrace
Leamington Spa CV32 4LY
T 01926 421447
Open Mon-Fri 9 am-5 pm. To network & support development of organisations & services to Black women. Challenging racial & sexual discrimination. Promoting positive images of Black women.

HEALTH

Menopause Advice Clinic - Kenilworth
Kenilworth Clinic
Smalley Place
Kenilworth CV8 1QG
T 01926 852087
Clinic on second Wed of each month 9.30 am-12 pm. Phone to make an appointment. Advice & information about menopause and HRT.

LARGER/TALLER WOMEN

Long Tall Sally
The Regency Arcade
154-156 Parade
Leamington Spa CV31 4BQ
T 01926 885175
Clothes for the taller woman sizes 12-20.
Open Mon-Sat 9.30 am-5.30 pm.

PLACES TO STAY AND EAT

Meg Rivers Traditional English Tea Room
Meg Dorman
2 High Street
Shipston-on-Stour CV36 4AS
T 01608 664099 F 01295 680799

Stonehouse Farm B&B
Mrs K Liggins
Cubbington Heath
Leamington Spa CV32 6AZ
T 01926 336370 F 01926 336370
Grade 4 listed Queen Anne farmhouse in countryside close to Leamington Spa, Warwick & Stratford upon Avon. Bed & breakfast. Phone for up-to-date price list.

PREGNANCY/CHILDBIRTH

Crisis Pregnancy Centre - Nuneaton
Jane Brown
1a Bond Gate Chambers
Bond Gate
Nuneaton CV11 4AL
T 01203 381878
Open Mon, Wed & Fri 10 am-2 pm. Other times by appt only. Free pregnancy testing, counselling & support for women with unplanned pregnancies. Post abortion & miscarriage counselling.

RETAILING

Meg Rivers Cakes
Meg Dorman
2 High Street
Shipston-on-Stour CV36 4AS
T 01608 664099 F 01295 680799
Mail order cakes, made from the finest ingredients, hand decorated & slow baked in small batches. Iced cakes available to order.

WILTSHIRE

BUSINESS SUPPORT SCHEMES

BusinessWomen's Breakfast Club
Dee McVey
3 Cricklade Court
Cricklade Street
Swindon SN1 3EY
T 01793 423169 F 01793 496631
101377,3711 (Compuserve)
Creating business opportunities through networking. Gaining value from high calibre speakers at regular breakfast meetings. Sharing business ideas & experiences. Maintaining consistent standards of membership.

CONTRACEPTION/WELL WOMAN

Health Clinic - Calne
Coleman's Close
Calne
T 01249 812821
Free, confidential contraception/contraceptive advice & cervical cytology clinics on first & third Tue of each month 6-9 pm

Health Clinic - Chippenham
Goldney Avenue
Chippenham
T 01249 653184
Free, confidential contraception/contraceptive advice & cytology clinics on Mon 6-9 pm. Phone during these hours for free emergency contraceptive advice.

Health Clinic - Devizes
New Park Street
Devizes
T 01380 722318
Free, confidential contraception/contraceptive advice & cytology clinic on Thurs 6-9 pm

Health Clinic - Melksham
Lowbourne
Melksham
T 01225 702443
Free, confidential contraception/contraceptive advice & cervical cytology clinics Tue 9.15 am-12 noon.

Health Clinic - Trowbridge
The Halve
Trowbridge
T 01225 766161
Free, confidential contraception/contraceptive advice & cervical cytology clinics Thurs 6-9 pm. Phone during these hours for free advice about emergency contraception.

Health Clinic - Warminster
The Avenue
Warminster
T 01985 218945
Free, confidential contraceptive advice/cytology clinics on second & fourth Wed of each month 6-9 pm

Salisbury and District Well Woman Centre
Sylvia Wright
49 Castle Street
Salisbury SP1 3SP
T 01722 326966
Open Tue 11 am-1.30 pm & 6.30-9.30 pm; Thurs by appointment only; Fri 12-4 pm. Free creche on Fri. Run by women for women to discuss health issues, seek information & advice. One-to-one counselling

Well Women Centre
Claire Drinkwater
Health Hydro
Milton Road
Swindon SN1 5JA
T 01793 511064
Drop-in for medical sessions Mon 5.30-7.30 pm & Wed 12.30-2.30 pm. For information & advice, library, etc Fri 10 am-12 noon. Medical services, information, self-help/support groups, library. Free creche.

EDUCATION

Wessex AWISE
Dr Jacqueline Akhavan
SEAS
Cranfield University
RMCS, Shrivenham
Swindon SN6 8LA
T 01793 785324 F 01793 783192
akhavan@rmcs.cranfield.ac.uk
Association for Women in Science and Engineering, covering Wiltshire. Main objectives are to encourage women to continue or go into science & engineering & technology subjects. Networking & mentoring.

HEALTH

Menopause Group
C/o Well Woman Centre
49 Castle Street
Salisbury SP1 3SP
T 01722 326966
Meets monthly on Tue evenings. Information & advice provided about problems related to the menopause.

Midlife Group
C/o Well Woman Centre
49 Castle Street
Salisbury SP1 3SP
T 01722 326966
Deals with issues relating to the menopause, HRT, diet, relationships & stess.

LARGER/TALLER WOMEN

Rubenesque
Mrs Christine Cooper

22 Bath Road
Devizes SN10 2AU
T 01380 728972
Ladies' size 16+ fashion shop. Everyday wear at everyday prices. Special occasion wear at discount prices. Sizes 16-38 available. Open Thurs, Fri, Sat & Sun 10 am-4 pm

LESBIAN AND BISEXUAL

Lesbian Support Group
C/o Well Woman Centre
49 Castle Street
Salisbury SP1 3SP
T 01722 326966
For lesbian women & women who think they might be lesbian to give them the opportunity to meet & share experiences, exchange information & discuss relevant issues.

MEDIA

Media Arts
Farideh Camyab
Town Hall Studios
Regent Circus
Swindon SN1 1QF
T 01793 463224 F 01793 611181
Public media centre. You can make, watch, enjoy products of film, video, photography & sound. Experienced team available to help with requirements to utilise the modern television & sound recording studios.

SEXUAL ABUSE/RAPE CRISIS

Rape Support Group
Theresa
Well Woman Centre
49 Castle Street
Salisbury SP1 3SP
T 01722 326966
Meets Thurs 7 pm. For more information phone Theresa on above number.

SUPPORT

Relationships Anonymous for women
C/o Well Woman Centre
49 Castle Street
Salisbury SP1 3SP
T 01722 326966
A self-help group offering mutual support to women who want to recover from unhealthy past relationships & improve existing ones with, for example, families, men, women, friends, & colleagues.

ENGLAND - YORKSHIRE

YORKSHIRE

ACCOMMODATION

Blenheim Project
14 Oak Lane
Bradford BD9
T 01274 495834
Accommodation for homeless women with or without children. Average stay six-nine months. Self contained, mainly shared fully furnished flats. 24-hour cover is provided. Urdu, Punjabi & English are spoken.

Bradford City Centre Project Ltd
YMCA Building
Little Horton Lane
Bradford BD5 OJG
T 01274 736507
Open Mon 10 am-4 pm, Tue 2-6 pm, Thurs 1-4 pm, Fri 10 am-1 pm. Helps young single homeless (both sexes) aged 16-25 years find accommodation. Housing support & benefits advice. Freephone 0800 220 102.

Bradford Life House
T 01274 225823
Accommodation for pregnant homeless women &/or with small children. Under 16s also catered for. Five beds, including large family room. No male visitors or drugs. Counselling, housing, legal & DSS advice.

Bradford Nightstop
49 Aireville Road
Frizinghall
Bradford BD9 4HH
T 01274 776888
For single homeless 16-25 year olds. For referral phone 01274 499094 - no self-referrals. Emergency accommodation throughout Bedford, Shipley & Keighley. Length of stay: one night at a time. Evening meal, B&B.

City Centre Project - Bradford branch
Little Horton
Bradford
T 01274 736507
For young, single & homeless people of both sexes aged 16-25. Eight single bedrooms with shared facilities. Advice & support on housing. Assistance in securing a move on accommodation.

City Centre Project - Shipley branch
1 Wharf Street
Shipley BD17 7DW

ENGLAND - YORKSHIRE

T 01274 530763
For young people aged 16-25 who are homeless at at risk or vulnerable under Children/Housing Act. Single person accommodation for six months. Help with maintaining independent living, benefits, budgeting.

Doncaster Young Women's Housing Project
C/o Community House
7 Netherhall Road
Doncaster DN1 2PH
T 01302 364729
24-hour ansaphone. Residential project accommodation for young women aged 16-25 who are homeless & who are at risk or who have suffered from some form of abuse, either physical, including sexual, or emotional.

Fairweather Project
P O Box 21
Bradford BD15 7XW
T 01274 480092
For homeless women with/ without children. No boys over age 14. Immediate short-stay accommodation. Two shared bedrooms, eight single bedrooms, seven single bedrooms in two houses. Support services provided.

Harrogate Homeless Project Ltd
Liz MacKenzie
7 Bower Street
Harrogate HG1 5BQ
T 01423 566900 F 01423 566900
Short stay emergency hostel for local people of both sexes over 18 who have just become homeless. Open 7 pm-9 am every day.

Isis Housing Co-op
Maggie Somers
55 Sholebroke Avenue
Leeds LS7 3HP
T 0113 262 2064
To provide single women & women with children suitable housing in good condition at a fair rent. 3 houses divided into 1 or 2 bedroomed self-contatined flats. Regular tenants' meetings about running of co-op.

Key House Project
General Buildings
2nd Floor
91 Kirkgate
Bradford BD1 1SZ
T 01274 728205

Open Mon-Wed & Fri 10 am-3 pm, Thurs 2-6 pm. For anyone seeking housing advice, accommodation information and/or benefits advice. Free telephone service. Languages spoken: Punjabi, Urdu, Hindi.

Keyhouse Project Hostel
20 Low Street
Keighley BD21 3PN
T 01535 600890
For young people aged 16-25 in need of housing until suitable alternative accommodation has been secured. Also housing advice & support. Contact above phone number or address.

Kirklees Asian/Black Women's Welfare Association
Sarah Lala
P O Box B68
Huddersfield HD1 4QW
T 01484 426390 F 01484 426390
Provides temporary supported accommodation to Asian, African & Caribbean women & children fleeing domestic violence. Also provides advice, support & counselling for women not wishing to come to the refuge.

Leigh House
T 01274 371277
For women with severe & enduring mental health problems. Five single bedrooms with shared kitchen, bathroom, living room & laundry facilites. Emotional & practical support, eg housing, benefits, budgeting, etc.

North British Housing Association
65 Vicar Lane
Bradford BD1
T 01274 721463
16-25-year-olds of both sexes requiring support. 11 fully furnished bedsits.

North Kirklees Women's Refuge
Janet Woodhead/Sue Scott
P O Box 6
Dewsbury WF13 3TB
T 01924 465238
Women's refuge with emergency accommodation for women & children fleeing violence. Staff hours 9 am-6 pm 24-hour service. Pager system after 6 pm 10 private rooms, shared communal rooms, kitchen, etc.

ENGLAND - YORKSHIRE

Sahara Black Women's Refuge
Nasreen Khan
P O Box 94
Wellington Street
Leeds LS1 2EE
T 0113 230 5087
Provides safe, secure accommodation to women & children fleeing violence. Confidential advice, support, counselling. Ansaphone 24 hours. Workers available during office hours. Access via self-referral.

ALTERNATIVE THERAPIES

Healing Clinic, The
June Tranmer
33 Fulford Cross
York YO1 4PB
T 01904 679868 F 01904 679868
Open most weekdays 8.30 am-8 pm. Home visits where possible. Telephone service over the weekends so people can call for advice. Large range of complementary therapies available.

Healing Shiatsu
Maggie Barton
Ch'ien Clinic
296 Tadcaster Road
York YO2 2ET
T 01904 709688
Individual sessions of Healing-Shiatsu which aims to re-balance energy in the body by bringing energy to areas in need & dispersing energy from areas of congestion, thereby restoring vitality & calmness.

Healing Shiatsu Qualified Practitioner
Maggie Barton
14 St Olave's Road
Bootham
York YO3 7AL
T 01904 652574
Individual sessions of Healing-Shiatsu that aims to re-balance energy in the body by bringing energy to areas in need & dispersing energy from areas of congestion, thereby restoring vitality & calmness.

Herbaria Aromatherapy and Dramatherapy
Anita Furness
39 Sutton Street
Norton
Malton YO17 9AW
T 01653 693364
Aromatherapy, both clinical & relaxation & Swedish massage carried out by a fully qualified nurse practitioner. Psychotherapy: specialist area survivors of sexual abuse & personal growth. Training courses.

ARMED FORCES

Association of WRENS - York branch
Miss Marie Taylor
3 St Wulstan Close
Fossway
York YO3 7SJ
T 01904 425751
Association for the welfare & fellowship of serving & ex-service members of the WRNS, WRNR, QARNNS, WRNVR & naval VADs.

Royal British Legion - Women's Section - York
107 Chaloners Road
Dringhouses
York YO2 2TG
T 01904 337647
Meets fourth Tue of each month at Cranes Working Men's Club at 7.30 pm. Aims to help others.

ARTS AND CRAFTS

Arabesque
Elaine Leeming
17 Cross Flatts Avenue
Leeds LS11 7BE
T 0113 277 4001
For all women to practice and promote Arabic dance. No previous experience necessary. Meets Thurs and Sun evenings 7.30 pm at Horsforth Club, New Road Side, Horsforth, Leeds.

Bradford Community Arts Ltd
Caro Blount-Shah/ Sharon Hayden
Arts and Resources Centre
17-21 Chapel Street
Bradford BD1 5DT
T 01274 721372 F 01274 390725
Open Tue-Fri 10 am-4 pm. Women only Wed 1-4 pm. Arts & media courses & projects. To increase access to arts facilities in photography, desktop publishing, digital imaging, drama & textiles.

Bradford Women Singers
Mary Dowson
Park Cottage
9 Randall Place
Bradford BD9 4AE
T 01274 543415
8-women acapella singing group, performing hard-hitting, inspiring, funny & moving songs.

Fees for performances negotiable. 2 recent cassettes. Organises 'Women Take Note' days of singing workshops for women.

Chapeltown Black Women Writers' Group
Mrs O Otoule, Treasurer
7 Pasture Road
Leeds LS8 4JJ
T 0113 249 2735
Meets on Thurs at Roseville Centre, Gledhow Road, Leeds 8. Encourages Black women, particularly older Black women, to write in an informal setting. Links with other writing groups in the community.

Christy Adair - Writer
Christy Adair
17 Levisham Street
York YO1 4BL
T 01904 643195
Reviews/articles concerned with dance & feminism. Author of Women and Dance (Macmillan, 1992). Presenter: illustrated talks concerned with dance and feminism. Reviews for radio.

Hot Promotions
Rachel Anstis
The Hot Hole
P O Box TR69
Leeds LS12 5TJ
T 0113 256 6733
hothole@hotcott.demon.co.uk
Global music & dance music, dancers, DJs, cabaret, magicians, jugglers, event management, publicity, launches, promotions, arts administration.

Knitting and Crochet Guild - Leeds
Liz Gillett
5 Roman Mount
Roundhay
Leeds LS8 2DP
Promotes the craft of hand- & machine-knitting & crochet. Participates in textile & craft exhibitions. Promotes development of local groups. Classes, workshops, lectures & seminars. Library of books & patterns.

Loud Mouthed Postcards
Chet Cunago
The Workstation
Grinders Hill
15 Paternoster Row
Sheffield S1 2BX
T 0114 275 3175 F 0114 249 4328
loud@eg-g.demon.co.uk

An all women print service. Computer-designed images on postcards. For photographers, artists, music & arts industries & media women.

One To One Productions
Judi Alston
Cultural Industries Centre
Redhill Avenue
Glasshoughton
Castleford WF10 4QH
T 01977 603431 F 01977 512819
Production company specialising in documentary, arts & issue-based work from community projects to braodcast television commissions.

Track 29
Caroline Vaughan
2 Pavillian Cottages
Shipton Road
York YO3 6RD
T 01904 637801
Female choir. Non-music readers. Unaccompanied four-part harmony. Sings locally at charity events, old people's homes, stately homes, busking, etc. Meets weekly and sometimes purely for fun.

Yorkshire Dance
box office
3 St Peter's Buildings
St Peter's Square
Leeds LS9 8AH
T 0113 243 8765 F 0113 259 5700
admin@yorkshiredance.org.uk
Community dance classes & workshops, including a number for women only, such as Arabic & Raqs Sharqi. Wheelchair access. Phone, fax, e-mail or call in to collect a programme of activities.

Yorkshire Women Theatre
Julie Courtney
Unit 10
231-5 Chapeltown Road
Leeds LS7 3DX
T 0113 262 6900
Produces and performs plays of immediate relevance to the lives of women today. Touring theatre in health education performance.

BEREAVEMENT

Bradford Bereaved Parents Link
Kathy Kenure
Bradford Link Centre

7 Southbrook Terrace
Bradford BD7 1AB
T 01274 309909
Support group for bereaved parents, run by bereaved parents. Meets first Thurs of each month at the Link Centre at 7.30 pm.

Foundation for the Study of Infant Deaths (FSID) - York branch
Lin Roche
73 Burnholme Avenue
York YO3 0NA
T 01904 431187 F 01904 431187
Supporting all members of a family affected by cot death. Raising funds for research. Newsletters. Befriending & group support.

Leeds Miscarriage Association Support Group
Sue Lefley
6 South View
Guiseley
Leeds LS20 9AY
T 01943 873704
Meets second Tue of each month 7.30 pm at St James Hospital, clarendon Wing, LGI. Support for those who have suffered a pregnancy loss. Safe environment where feelings & experiences can be shared.

Widows' Advisory Service
14 Great George Street
Leeds LS1 3DW
T 0113 245 0533
For all widows in Leeds. Open Mon-Thurs 10.30 am-3 pm. Offers information & support to widows & those concerned with their problems. Meets at above address & Centenary House, North Street.

BUSINESS SUPPORT SCHEMES

Business and Professional Women (BPW) - York
Judith Wynne-Jones, External Affairs Coordinator
12 Matmer Court
Melrosegate
York YO1 3TY
T 0113 274 4444 F 0113 280 4406
A branch of Business & Professional Women UK Ltd, encouraging women to realise & fulfil their potential. Meets on third Tue of each month at 7.30 pm

Harrogate Business Development Centre Ltd
J Kennett

Conyngham Hall
Knaresborough HG5 9AY
T 01423 799100 F 01423 799101
Helps people starting a business to obtain enterprise grants by training, advice & counselling. Also help & advice given to people with existing businesses.

Leeds Business and professional Women's Club
Mrs Ann Franckel
C/o Flat 1
Fernbank Villas
Half Mile Lane
Leeds LS13 1DA
T 0113 255 1754
For women working in business, commerce & the professions. Meets first & third Wed of each month 7-9.30 pm. Business metings with speakers, social activities, training opportunities.

New Working Women
Blaize Davies
Suites 16-19, 2nd Floor
Munroe House
Duke Street
Leeds LS9 8AG
T 0113 243 2474 F 0113 234 2117
Free business training for Leeds women residents. Childcare & travel expenses provided. Courses run for 12 weeks, 14 hours per week. Other training arrangements for outside Leeds.

CARERS

Carers' Resource, The
Anne Smyth, Director
11 North Park Road
Harrogate HG1 5PD
T 01423 500555 F 01423 507777
Information, advice & support for carers & all those who work with them. Guidance through 'the system' to support needed, links with other carers. Information about eg holidays, transport, long term care, etc.

CENTRES FOR WOMEN

Asian Women and Girls' Centre
Nasreen Butt
Scout Hut
St Paul's Road
Mannighan
Bradford BD8 7LS
T 01274 490353
Open Mon-Fri 9 am-5 pm 1-3 pm girls' group.

ENGLAND - YORKSHIRE

Black Women's Resource Centre
Janette Brown/Sofia Bibi
72a Burngreave Road
Sheffield S3 9DD
T 0114 276 0996 F 0114 276 0996
Aims to empower Black women to ensure their full participation in the local community at all levels. Creating a space where women can meet without threat or intimidation. Open Mon-Fri 9.30 am-3.30 pm.

Castleford Women's Centre
Averil J Birch
2-4 Wesley Street
Castleford WF10 1AE
T 01977 511581 F 01977 603158
Provides education & childcare. Most courses are free with a small charge for administration.

Harrogate Women's Centre
Jane Jewitt
West Park Centre
7 Raglan Street
Harrogate HG1 1LE
T 01423 527615
Open Tue 9.30 am-12.30 pm, Wed 1.30-4 pm, Thurs 7-9 pm. Run by women for women. Advice, information & support on a range of subjects. Referral when relevant to appropriate agencies.

Keighley Asian Women and Children's Centre
Eastwood Centre
Marlborough Street
Keighley BD21 3HU
T 01535 667359
Open Mon-Fri 8 am-4.30 pm. Creche and full day-care nursery. Self-help goups. Training in English, sewing, typing, beauty therapy. Help with referrals from DHS in connection with domestic violence.

Keighley Women's Centre
Jean O'Keeffe, Coordinator
1st Floor
Central Hall
Alice Street
Keighley BD21 3JD
T 01535 681316
Open Mon, Thurs, Fri 10 am-4 pm; Wed by appointment only. Courses, groups, workshops, events. Well women's centre. Education, training, health, women's studies, domestic violence unit, etc.

Milan Centre
Pam Hardisty, Coordinator
Victor Street
Manningham
Bradford BD9 4RA
T 01274 480619
Open 9.30 am-3 pm. Education & training for all women. GCSEs in maths & English. Free computer training & exercise classes. Creche for children aged two-and-a-half. Cooking & sewing classes. Advice sessions.

Roshni Gar Asian Women's Centre
Gyan Dass
13 Scott Street
Keighley BD21 2JH
T 01535 691758 F 01535 691758
Day centre for Bangladeshi & Pakistani women with mental health problems. Open Mon-Fri 9 am-4 pm. Four groups per week.

Roshni Sheffield Asian Women's Resource Centre
444 London Road
Sheffield S2 4HP
T 0114 250 8898 F 0114 258 4008

Sheffield Women's Cultural Club
Joella Bruckshaw
Workstation
Grinders Hill
Sheffield S1 2BX
T 0114 272 1866 F 0114 279 6522
Safe place for all women, particularly disadvantaged women, to relax, learn & be entertained. Bar & cheap vegetarian food. Children welcome to 8 pm. Nappy-changing facilities. Open 11 am-11 p.m; closed Sun.

Women's Centre
Mandy Willis
21 Cleveland Street
Doncaster DN1 3EH
T 01302 326749
Open Mon-Fri 9 am-3 pm. Providing educational, social & leisure activities for women & acting as a resource & information centre. Courses, classes & support groups. Assertiveness-training, Yoga, art, etc.

Womenspace
Erica Simmonds/Maureen Telemacque
Room 51
Estate Buildings
Railway Street
Huddersfield HD1 1JY
T 01484 536272

ENGLAND - YORKSHIRE

Open Mon, Tue, Thurs 12-3.30 pm Women only & run by women. Advice, counselling & long term support to all women. Group work, pregnancy testing, day trips, informal setting, library. Lift for wheelchairs.

York Women's Centre
the collective
11 Holgate Road
York YO2 4AA
T 01904 647530
Open Mon-Fri 10 am-1 pm. Information, support & counselling for all women. Free services, including one-to-one counselling, aromatherapy sessions & evening support groups. Drop-in Thurs 10 am-12 pm.

CHILD CARE AND FAMILY

Bradford Under-Fives Association
19-25 Sunbridge Road
Bradford BD1 2AY
T 01274 308725
To enhance development/ education of children under age 5. Playgroups, toddler groups. Fieldworkers provide advice and support to established groups. Training for adults about children's play. Toy library.

Women's Technology Centre Play Group
Melody Hudson
Chandos Street
Off Bolling Road
Bradford BD4 7BB
T 01274 733116
Open 9.15 am-4 pm for children of mothers who attend Women's Technology Centre. 12 children aged 3-5 cared for free. No food provided. Parents are responsible for care of children between 12.30-2 pm.

COMPUTERS/IT

Core Key Boarding Skills
Angela Timbers
Burley Lodge Centre
12 Burley Lodge Road
Leeds LS6 1QP
T 0113 244 3335
For women whose second language is English. Wordprocessing skills, keyboarding & machine functions, letter & envelope layout; manuscript typing. Two groups. Phone for further details.

Women's Technology Centre
Pat Olifer, Senior Training Officer
1st Floor
Broomfield House
Bolling Road
Bradford BD4 7BG
T 01274 752139   F 01274 305445
IT 35-week courses; Administration NVQ levels 1, 2, 3. Electronics training NVQ levels 1, 2, 3. Playgroup attached to WTC is free to women attending courses at the Centre (open Mon-Fri 9 am-4.30 pm.)

Women's Technology Centre
Centre Manager
38 Sweet Street
Leeds LS11 9AJ
T 0113 243 5511
Full-time training for women, funded by Leeds City Council/TEC & ESF. Provides training in information technology up to Level III. Recruitment throughout the year.

CONTRACEPTION/WELL WOMAN

British Pregnancy Advisory Service (BPAS) - Leeds
2nd Floor
8 The Headrow
Leeds LS1 6PT
T 0113 244 3861
Open Tue, Wed and Fri 9.30 am-2.30 pm. Pregnancy testing, counselling, abortion, contraception.

Calderdale Well Woman Centre
Clare Hyde
Harrison House
10 Harrison Road
Halifax HX1 2AF
T 01422 360397
Open Mon 10 am-1 pm; Tue 11.30 am-2.30 pm; Wed 5.30-7.30 pm; Thurs 12-3 pm; Sat 10 am-12 pm. All services free. A nurse, creche & interpreter available. Emphasis on preventative medicine.

Children's Society Beckhill Family Centre - Women's Group
Pam Lythe
17 Beckhill Avenue
Meanwood
Leeds LS7 2RE
T 0113 268 5819
For women mainly from Beckhill/Mileshill estates. Meets Mon 1-3 pm at above address. Informal discussions, mutual support and information from service providers.

Duchy Nuffield Hospital, The
Queen's Road
Harrogate HG2 0HF
T 01423 567136
Well woman screen. Full female health assessment. Phone for up-to-date price lists.

Harrogate District Well Woman Project
women at the centre
C/o The Women's Centre
West Park Centre
7 Raglan Street
Harrogate HG1 1LE
T 01423 527615
Free service run by women for women. The Centre is open Tue 9.30 am-12.30 pm, Wed 1.30-3.30 pm, Thurs 7-9 pm 24-hour ansaphone. Workshops & talks on a range of health matters. Book loans, videos, etc.

Huddersfield, Nuffield Hospital, The
Birkby Hall Road
Huddersfield HD2 2BL
T 01484 533131
Well woman screen. Full female health assessment. Phone for up-to-date price lists.

Marie Stopes Centre
Sue Firth, Manager
10 Queen Square
Leeds LS2 8AJ
T 0113 244 0685 F 0113 244 8865
Pregnancy advice (helpline 0171 388 4843); general healcare/contraception (helpline 0171 388 0662); sterilisation services (helpline 0171 388 5554); well woman clinics; abortion clinics; menopause clinics; etc.

Mid Yorkshire Nuffield Hospital, The
Outwood Lane
Hornsforth
Leeds LS18 4HP
T 0113 258 8756
Well woman screen. Full female health assessment. Phone for up-to-date price lists.

COUNSELLING AND THERAPY

Susan Evasdaughter
Susan Evasdaughter
Vixen House
5 Huntsman Close
Beaumont Park
Huddersfield HD4 7BR
T 01484 667385
Psychotherapy for women. Experienced psychotherapist & art therapist offers woman-centred eclectic therapy & support to women who experience problems or who wish to change their way of relating to the world.

Women's Counselling and Therapy Service
Caroleen La Pierre
Oxford Chambers
Oxford Place
Leeds LS1 3AX
T 0113 245 5725
Provides a range of psychotherapy services for women in Leeds. Innovates & develops therapy services which actively assist disadvantaged groups to benefit from the service. Individual & group therapy.

DISABILITY

Time-Together
Mary Scurr
34 Victoria Avenue
Harrogate HG1 5PR
T 01423 521522 F 01423 530388
Support for people with learning disabilities. This support extends to people enabling them to enjoy & benefit from their leisure time. Also provides an activity break, respite, holiday service.

Work-able
Jean Nicol/Pauline Cauender
Keighley Disabled People's Centre
Temple Road
Keighley BD21 2AH
T 01535 618161 F 01535 618163
Working with people who are disabled or who have general health problems. Free training in word processing, information technology, job search, NVQ business administration. Open Mon-Fri.

EDUCATION

Harrogate Association of Women Graduates
Mrs Joyce Line, Secretary
10 Blackthorn Lane
Burn Bridge
Harrogate HG3 1NZ
T 01423 872984 F 01423 879349
Meets monthly on Mon. Around 30 members. Speakers. Also coffee mornings, music group meetings, theatre & garden visits. Has a particular interest in supporting women in developing countries.

ENGLAND - YORKSHIRE

Huddersfield Association of Women Graduates
Miss Nina Nicholson
10 Slead Grove
Brighouse
Huddersfield HD6 2JF
T 01484 714401
Exists to promote friendship among women graduates, to sponsor the education of some African schoolgirls, & to promote women's interests.

Leeds Association of Women Graduates
Y J Reedman
36 Birkdale Drive
Alwoodley
Leeds LS1 1RU
T 0113 268 1536
For all women graduates. Meets regularly at St Micael's Parish Hall, Headingley. To provide friendhsip & promote matters affecting women, especially women's education. Talks, discussions, interest groups.

Sheffield Association of Women Graduates
Ruth Naish, Secretary
9 Oakburn Court
Broomhall Road
Sheffield S10 2DR
T 0114 266 3438
Group of 41 women graduates holding monthly meetings. Speakers on a wide variety of topics. Several social events each year. The group makes small grants to women graduates working for higher degrees.

EQUAL OPPS

Fair Play Yorkshire and Humberside
Geoff Sutcliffe
Gvmnt Office for Yorkshire & humberside
P O Box 213, City House
New Station Street
Leeds LS1 4US
T 0113 2835230 F 0113 2835452
Positive action equalities project. A government EOC initiative to stimulate partnerships which improve opportunities for women to realise their full potential in education, employment & the community.

Women's Section - Equal Opportunities Unit
Any staff
Leeds City Council

Civic Hall
Leeds LS1 1UR
T 0113 247 4742
Open Mon-Fri 9 am-5.15 pm. To promote equality of opportunity for all women in Leeds. Grants to women's groups, promotion of International Women's Day, networking, advice, publications.

ETHNIC MINORITIES

African Caribbean Women's Disability Project
Phil James
Unit 4
Ray Street Enterprise Centre
Ray Street
Huddersfield HD1 6BL
T 01484 455252

Asha Neighbourhood Project
Zaheda Khanam/Helen King
43 Stratford Street
Leeds LS11 6JG
T 0113 270 4600
For Bangladeshi women & children in Beeston & Holbeck. Open Mon-Fri 9 am-5 pm. English classes, sewing classes, baby clinics, mothers' & babies' group, counselling & advice, craft group. Creche.

Asian Women's Drama Project
Anna Ashby, Drama Development Worker
C/o Yorkshire Women's Theatre
Unit 10
231-235 Chapel Town Road
Leeds LS7 3DX
T 0113 262 6900
A drama group for Asian women

Bangladeshi Porishad Organisation - Women's Section
Shafia Chowdry
C/o Bangladesh Porishad Community Centre
31 Cornwall Road
Manningham
Bradford BD8 7JN
T 01274 722069
Open Mon-Fri 9 am-5 pm. Advice & training for Asian women. Drop-in centre & advice & information on a wide range of issues, including housing & benefits. Day care for women only.

Bengali Women Support Group
Dr Debjani Chatterjee
C/o DLP

ENGLAND - YORKSHIRE

69 Division Street
Sheffield S1 4GE
T 0114 276 2578
Meets each month usually on Sat in Sheffield or Donacster or Rotherham. Promotes Bengali languages & culture & celebrates festivals. Promoting bilingual women's anthologies: 'Barbed Lives' & 'Sweet and Sour'.

Black Women's Project (BWP)
P O Box 230
Huddersfield HD1 1AA
T 01484 450040
Free, confidential service, by phone & face-to-face, to Black women & girl survivors, by Black women counsellors. Patois, Urdu, Hindi, Punjabi & English spoken. Women can be accompanied to outside agencies.

Bradford Moor Asian Women & Girls Association
Mrs Krishna Dlal, Development Worker
C/o Laisterdyke Youth & Community Centre
Manse Street
Bradford BD3 8RP
T 01274 669387 F 01274 667649
Open Mon 9.30 am-6 pm; Wed 9.30 am-3 pm; Sat 10 am-2.30 pm. Activities include typing, wordprocessing, keep fit, health & safety, sewing, counselling, English, Urdu, craft exchange. Drop in on Wed.

Hooner Kelah Asian Women's Training Project
Jasbinder Saimbhi
The Roseville Centre
Gledhow Road
Leeds LS8 5ES
T 0113 235 0484 F 0113 240 8250
Training provided in the areas of clothing technology, computing/office skills & English language support. Full childcare provision. Training & travel allowances provided. Open Mon-Fri 9.30 am-4 pm.

Jamaica Society (Leeds) Women's Group
Mrs L S Powell
Jamaica House
277 Chapeltown Road
Leeds LS7 3HA
T 0113 262 6435
For Jamaican women. Meets every second Wed of each month. To maintain Afro-Caribbean culture: talents, thoughts, art, drama, folksong, cooking. Also to create awareness of women's health issues.

Kiren - Asian Women's Association
Shahida Johnson
Firth Park Library
Firth Park Road
Sheffield S5 6WS
T 0114 242 1231
Open Mon & Wed 10 am-7 pm (general activities); Tue 10 am-3 pm (training sessions). Providing Asian women with space/facilities to deal with day-to-day problems. Most services free. Disabled access.

Ladies Sanjh Group
Mrs P K Shahid, Chairperson
46 Manor Grove
Leeds LS7 3LS
T 0113 262 8263
Aims to broaden outlook towards life in UK of all Asian women. Activities include keep fit, fabric painting, badminton, netball & social gatherings. Events to celebrate International Women's Day.

Leeds Black Women's Forum
C/o Leeds Interagency Project
Unit A3
26 Roundhay Road
Leeds LS7 1AB
T 0113 234 9090
For Black women to give support to other Black women & to exchange information. Meets third Wed of each month 10 am-12 noon at above address.

Leeds Chinese Women's Group
C/o Chinese Advice Centre
Harehills Middle School
Harehills Road
Leeds LS8 5HS
T 0113 235 9006
For all Chinese women in Leeds. Meets Sun 2-4 pm in term time at Shakespeare Primary School, Stoney Rock Lone, Leeds 7. To raise awareness & offer training; to assist women to gain access to services.

Leeds Latin American Women's Support Group
Florinda Henderson
45 Lincombe Drive
Leeds LS8 1PS
T 0113 266 5932
For Latin American women living in Leeds & English women interested in Latin American culture. Meets once a month either Fri evening or Sun afternoon at different members' houses.

ENGLAND - YORKSHIRE

Mary Seacole Nurses Association
Mrs L Crumbie
C/o 52 Gledhow Park Avenue
Leeds LS7 4JN
T 0113 262 3313
Aims to secure a nursing home for Black elderly people. Meets at the Unity Housing Association. Various activities such as health seminars, lunch clubs, drop in health sessions, visiting the elderly.

Milun Women's Centre
Fauzia Bhatti/Rukhsana Hussain
31 Hilton Road
Leeds LS8 4HB
T 0113 237 4150
For Asian women in postal areas of Leeds 7, 8, 9 & 17. Meets Mon-Fri 9.15 am-3.15 pm; Sun 2.30-5 pm. Activities: keep fit, language support, weight training, antenatal classes, aqua aerobics, sauna.

Muslim Women's Association
Zohra Qureshi
42 Roxholme Place
Leeds LS7 4JQ
T 0113 262 3221
For all Muslim women who are lonely or isolated at home. Help, advice, counselling, information about education, careers, marital problems.

Nari Ekta
Harinder Kaur
14 Great George Street
Leeds LS1 3DW
T 0113 243 4023 F 0113 2434023
Open Mon-Fri 8.30 am-5 pm. Vocational training given to unemployed Asian women aged 18+ in computing, finance & business administration. The courses are free with a travel allowance. Creche.

Naya Ujala Asian Women's Group
Rose Stead
West Leeds Family Service Unit
3 Chiswick Street
Leeds LS6 1QE
T 0113 275 7600 F 0113 278 9990
Naya Ujala (New Light) acts as a support group for Asian women having difficulties coping with their lives & families & with the alien English culture & as a group providing information & health checks.

One In Four Project
C/o Bradford Resource Centre
17-21 Chapel Street
Bradford BD1 5DT
T 01274 305276
Open Mon-Thurs 10 am-4 pm. For Asian women with or without children fleeing any form of domestic violence. Referral system. Also counselling service set up for all women who are survivors of sexual abuse.

Sikh Girls' Group
I K Hunjan
10 Allerton Grove
Moortown
Leeds LS17 6RD
T 0113 269 6436
For all Sikh women aged 13 to 25. Meets Tue 7-9 pm at Lady Pitt Lane. Discussions, issue-based workshops, woodwork, outdoor pursuits, video, photography, drama, creative arts.

Sistas
Rose Stead
West Leeds Family Service Unit
3 Chiswick Street
Leeds LS6 1QE
T 0113 275 7600 F 0113 278 9990
Meets fortnightly on Mon 5.30-7.30 pm. For African & Caribbean women. Aims to project positive feedback & images for women who may feel alienated & discriminated against. Outings.

FINANCE

Diane Saunders Financial Adviser
Diane Saunders
351 Harrogate Road
Leeds LS17 6PZ
T 0113 268 9102 F 0113 237 0695
An all-women team provides independent financial advice on mortgages, pensions, insurances & investments. Happy to work on fee or commission basis.

Women & Money
Yvonne Rose
351 Harrogate Road
Leeds LS17 6PZ
T 0113 266 9595 F 0113 237 0695
Provides training on main aspects of personal finance. Enables women to take control of their financial planning. A minimum of six students required to run courses. Phone for up-to-date price list.

Girls/Young Women

Belle Isle Young Women's Group
Low Grange House
6-8 Low Grange Crescent
Leeds LS10
T 0113 271 6139
For women aged 16 & over in the Belle Isle area. The groups meets in the evenings at the above address. Discussion groups, crafts, local issues, social events, job search. Creche provided.

Getaway Girls
Scott Hall Resources Centre
Poternewton Lane
Leeds LS7 3DR
T 0113 237 4754
For all girls & young women. Challenging outdoor activities to increase confidence, empower, etc. Accessible to women with disabilities. Canoeing, climbing, abseiling, orienteering, skiing, camping, etc.

Trevor Stubbs House (YWCA)
Sally Deane
256-262 Sissons Road
Middleton
Leeds LS10 4JG
T 0113 270 6935
For all women aged 16-25 in Middleton to build up self-confidence & learn new skills. Meets Mon and Thurs evenings at address above & at Upstone Centre, Middleton. Discussions, sports, photography, etc.

Young Women's Christian Association (YWCA) - Leeds
Youth and Community Worker
Upstone Centre
80 Throstle Lane
Leeds LS10
T 0113 270 0874
Offers educational opportunities to the local community, targeting young women particularly but not exclusively. Playgroup, mums and tots, support groups, toy library, holiday playschemes, youth clubs.

Young Women's Housing Project
Sarah Hoyle/Jo Meagher/Theresa Wilding
P O Box 303
Sheffield S1 1YD
T 0114 268 0580
Safe/supportive accommodation for young women aged 16-25 who have left home because of sexual abuse. Counselling available to women of all ages. Staff available Mon-Thurs 10 am-5 pm; Fri 10 am-4 pm.

Health

Eating Problems Project
Helen Murdoch
4 Brantford Street
Leeds LS7 4LE
To inform sufferers & the general public of the nature of eating problems (anorexia, bulimia, binge eating) & prospects for treatment. To provide a voice for sufferers as opposed to 'experts'.

Liberty Bells (Eating Disorders Group)
Jane Naton-Dunham
16 House Hill Close
Proppleton Road
York YO1 37G
T 01904 603397
Diet breaking self help group.

Mastectomy Association Self Help (MASH)
Oxford Place Methodist Centre
Oxford Place
Leeds LS1
For women with breast problems. Meets first & third Mon of each month 7.30-9.30 pm at Woodhouse Street Day Centre, Leeds LS6; second & fourth Wed of each month 2-4 pm at Oxford Place Methodist Centre.

Menopause Group
York Women's Centre
11 Holgate Road
York YO2 4AA
T 01904 647530
Support group meeting Wed 7.30 onwards every third Wed of each month.

Tranquilliser Advice and Support Services
Sue Tollemache
15 Bridge Street
York YO1 1DA
T 01904 647474
Support group for tranquilliser dependency & withdrawal, on Thurs 7-8.30 pm. Providing support & advice for those experiencing dependency &/or withdrawal symptoms.

Women's Health Matters
Carol Burns
Room 8C, First Floor
Vassalli House
20 Central Road
Leeds LS1 6DE
T 0113 242 1070
Information & support to women on health matters. Telephone enquiry service, drop in

(in south Leeds, Chapeltown & Gipton). Free pregnancy service. Meets in various venues.

Women's Health Policy Group
Ann Bilous
KHFA
St Luke's House
Blackmoorfoot Road
Huddersfield HD4 5RH
T 01484 466173 F 01484 466184
Aims to improve women's health in Kirklees. Collecting information on women's health needs, services available; finding out what women in area say about needs; making women's health needs more widely known.

York AIDS Action
Yvette Turnbull, Manager
11-12 Stonebow House
The Stonebow
York YO1 2NP
T 01904 640024 F 01904 620424
Provides practical/emotional support for people living with HIV/AIDS, their families, carers, partners, friends. Befriending, social activities, driving, etc. Free services. Phone Mon-Fri 10 am-4 pm

York Drug Dependency Clinic
Jane Payling, Project Manager
28 High Petergate
York YO2 2EH
T 01904 637121 F 01904 67300
Prescribing service for drug users, offering prescribing/detoxification to opiate users. Aims to reduce physical/mental drug-related harm & to improve social, legal & financial status. Phone for opening times.

York Drugs Resource Scheme
Kathy Stone
15 Bridge Street
York YO1 1DA
T 01904 647474 F 01904 639192
Free confidential service. Advice, information & support on matters related to use/misuse of drugs. Women only sessions Wed 1-4 pm. Specialist worker from family centre available for input on parenting skills.

INTERNATIONAL

Manantial (International Women's Link)
45 Grange View
Leeds LS7 4ER
T 0113 240 6977

To develop links between women's groups in Leeds & women's groups in Third World countries as the basis for joint action to improve the lives of women. Workshops, conferences.

IRISH WOMEN

Irish Women's Support Group
Eileen Sailes
Vale Day Centre
Pottery Vale
Hunslet
Leeds LS10 2AP
T 0113 271 3337
For women to support each other, sharing experiences in problems around anxiety & depression & obtaining a better insight into their lives. Meets at the above address.

JEWISH WOMEN

Leeds Rosh Chodesh Group
Janette Madar
3 Sandhill Grove
Leeds LS17 8ED
T 0113 266 5751
For Jewish women to explore cultural roots & history, building on identity as Jewish women. Meets at new moon in members' homes. Annual open event for International Women's Day.

LARGER/TALLER WOMEN

Long Tall Sally
25 King Edward Street
Leeds L31 6AX
T 0113 245 5791
Clothes for the taller woman sizes 12-20. Open Mon-Sat 9.30 am-5.30 pm; occasionally open on Sun.

Long Tall Sally
44 Fossgate
York YO1 2TF
T 01904 640374
Clothes for the taller woman sizes 12-20. Open Mon-Sat 9.30 am-5.30 pm.

LEGAL MATTERS

Advocacy and Interpreting Service
Nuzhut Mahmood
Advocacy and Interpreting Service
101 Roundhay Road
Leeds LS8 5AG
T 0113 235 1877

ENGLAND - YORKSHIRE

Open Mon-Fri 9.30 am-5 pm. Drop in. Women-only sessions on health/social care. The needs of women from the Chinese, Pakistani and Bengali communities are prioritised.

LESBIAN AND BISEXUAL

Bradford Lesbian Line
Jenny Pickles
C/o Bradford Resource Centre
17-21 Chapel Street
Bradford BD1
T 01274 305525
Helpline open Thurs 7-9 pm. 24-hour ansaphone at all other times, & this is checked regularly.

Doncaster Gay Support
Janet, Saul & Rennie
C/o 21 Cleveland Steet
Doncaster DN1 3EH
T 01302 789151
Meets last Thurs of each month at the Vine pub, Kelham St, Doncaster 7.30 pm. Providing support to the lesbian, gay & bi-sexual community of Doncaster.

Lesbian Information Service & Lesbian Youth Support Service
Jan Bridget
P O Box 8
Todmorden OL14 5TZ
T 01706 817235 F 01706 817235
Information, support, publications, training, advocacy. Aimed at isolated lesbians, especially young lesbians. Aims to prevent/reduce harmful behaviours amongst lesbians; to change homophobic attitudes, etc.

Sheffield Lesbian Link
C/o Sheffield Women's Cultural Club
Grinders Hill
Paternoster Row
Sheffield S1 2BX
T 0114 272 1866
For women new to the area wanting to meet like-minded women or for women questioning their sexuality. Meets on first & third Tue of each month at above venue for an informal social evening.

York Lesbian Line
P O 225
York YO1 1AA
T 01904 646 812

Helpline open Fri 7-9 pm 24-hour ansaphone. Information & support service, eg information on friendly places to stay in York, social events, etc.

Young Lesbian Drop In (Youthreach)
Youthreach Hennymoor House
Ground Floor
7 Manor Row
Bradford BD1 4PB
T 01274 720196 F 01274 739706
Open 9 am-5.30 p.m, also evenings & weekends for groups. Youth project work with young lesbians. Counselling, residentials, courses, support networks. Publication.

LIBRARIES/ARCHIVES

Feminist Archive North
H510
Leeds Metropolitan University
Calverley Street
Leeds LS1 3HE
T 0113 283 6774 F 0113 283 6709
A collection of grassroots materials from the Women's Liberation Movement. Collecting & preserving the history of women's organising. Women are wlecome to use the collection for research purposes. By appt only.

MANUAL TRADES

Amazon Nails
Barbara Jones
554 Burnley Road
Todmorden OL14 8JF
T 01706 814696 F 01706 812190
An all-women roofing & general building firm. Large & small contracts undertaken. Straw bale building. Teaching & consultancy. Training & on-site support to women in non-traditional skills.

East Leeds Women's Workshop
Newton Hill House
Newton Hill Road
Leeds LS7 4JE
T 0113 237 4718
For women aged 23 + who have been unemployed for over six months. Open 9 a.m-5 p.m at above address. Free year-long courses in carpentry/joinery, electronics & computer programming. Childcare & travel free.

Women In Manual Trades - Leeds
Sue Hall
C/o East Leeds Women's Workshop

ENGLAND - YORKSHIRE

Newton Hill House
Newton Hill Road
Leeds LS8 4JE
T 0113 237 4718
To give information & support to women working in manual trades.

MEDIA

Campaign for Press and Broadcasting Freedom (North)
Kirklees Media Centre
7 Northumberland Street
Huddersfield HD1 1RL
T 01484 454184 F 01484 454185
For greater diversity in ownership, control & content of media & equal opps & representation of groups discriminated against by the media. Campaigns for reform on secrecy, free access & accountability.

Foot-in-Mouth Productions
Jacqui Bellamy
68 Machon Bank
Netheredge
Sheffield S7 1GP
T 0114 258 8229
Skilled group of female film-makers in sheffield available to productions coming into the area, ranging from sound & camera technicians, locations & production managers.

Joanna Dunn
Joanna Dunn
C/o 19 Banstead Terrace East
Leeds LS8 5PX
T 0113 248 5559 F 0113 248 4997
Animator & independent director. Rostrum camera operator specialising in 2D painted animation & abstract work. Commissions & comercials.

Leeds Animation Workshop
Terry Wragg
45 Bayswater Row
Leeds LS8 5LF
T 0113 248 4997 F 0113 248 4997
Open Mon-Thurs. Women's collective producing & distributing short animated films of social issues relevant to women. Provides short courses for women & demonstrations on techniques of animation.

NETWORKING for women in film, video and television
Jane Howarth/Al Garthwaite
C/o Vera Productions
30-38 Dock Street
Leeds LS10 1JF
T 0113 242 8646 F 0113 245 1238
networking@vera-media.demon.co.uk
Membership organisation for women working in, seeking work in, or studying film, video or TV. Quarterly newsletter & members' index.

Sheffield Women's Printing Co-Op Ltd
Jess Osborn
111a Matilda Street
Sheffield S1 4QF
T 0114 275 3180 F 0114 275 3180
A cooperative print & design business, serving mainly the voluntary & not-for-profit sector.

Vera Productions
Al Garthwaite/ Catherine Mitchell
30-38 Dock Street
Leeds LS10 1JF
T 0113 242 8646 F 0113 245 1238
vera@vera-media.demon.co.uk
An all-women video production, training & development organisation with feminist aims. Runs a membership organisation called Networking for women in, or seeking work in, film, video & television.

OLDER WOMEN

59 Centre - Women's Group
J Noble
59-65 Belle Isle Circus
Leeds LS10 3DU
T 0113 270 1220
For women in Belle Isle aged 60 & over. Meets daily at above address. Adult education classes, arts, outings, bingo, hairdressing. Refreshments provided. Opportunities to socialise, combat loneliness.

Older Women of Leeds (OWL)
Ros Shepperd
C/o 1st Floor
Headingley Community Centre
North Lane
Leeds LS6
T 0113 261 0874
For women aged 50 & over. Meets every third Fri at above address 11 am-1.30 pm. Aims to improve the quality of older women's lives in a safe, confidential space for personal growth.

PHOTOGRAPHY

Pam Rhodes Photographer
Pam Rhodes
75 Sapgate Lane
Thornton
Bradford BD13 3HB
T 01274 832852
106677.3511@compuserve.com
Freelance photographer.

Pavilion, The
Julie Courtney/Sue Ball/Azar Emdadi
2 Woodhouse Square
Leeds LS3 1AD
T 0113 243 1749
For all women in Leeds & west Yorkshire. Open Mon-Thurs 10.30 am-5 pm. A women's photography centre, providing training & workshops in photography; City & Guilds training, darkroom available.

PLACES TO STAY AND EAT

Ellis House
Ms J Hunt
51 Queen Street
Withernsea HU19 2AR
T 01964 615538
Accommodation for women. Quiet seaside village. Cliff-top walks. Beach 200 yds from house. Pleasant drives out to nearby villages. Lounge/dining romm. Double, single & twin bedrooms available.

Jerry & Ben's Holiday Cottages
Judith M Joy
Hebden
Skipton BD23 5DL
T 01756 752369 F 01756 753370
Women owned & women friendly. Seven holiday cottages & flats open all year. New brochure & prices out each November for the following year. Phone for further details.

Women's Holiday Centre
Donna Smith
The Old Vicarage
Horton-in-Ribblesdale BD24 0HD
T 01729 860207
Holidays for women & children in the Yorkshire Dales. Group bookings, couples, singles, special weekends, camping. Reasonable rates for all. Phone for up-to-date price list.

POLITICS

Leeds Labour Women's Council
Chris Gunter
C/o 39 Sutherland Avenue
Leeds LS8 1BY
T 0113 266 7449
For women who are members of the Labour Party. Meets last Tue of each month 7.30-9 pm at the Civic Hall, Leeds. Aims to promote women's participation & organisation in the Labour Party.

PREGNANCY/CHILDBIRTH

Assisted Conception Unit, The
Mrs V Sharma
Consultant Obstetrician & Gynaecologist
St James's Univ. Hospital
Beckeet Street
Leeds LS9 7TF
T 0113 206 4612 F 0113 242 6496
Provides information & treatment for women who wish to conceive through IVF or GIFT. Also collects eggs from donors who want to help another woman conceive.

Crisis Pregnancy Centre - Sheffield
Janet Pike
12 Hartshead
Sheffield S1 2EL
T 0114 279 6734
Open Wed 12-2 pm & Sat 10 am-12 pm. Free pregancy testing, counselling & support for women with unplanned pregnancies. Post abortion & miscarriage counselling. Phone for an appt. 24-hour ansaphone.

Foresight Assn. for the Promotion of Pre-Conceptual Care
Val Kearney
2 Ridge Villas
Forest Moor Road
Knaresborough HG5 8JP
T 01423 864358
Aims to give babies best possible start by ensuring both parents are healthy & well nourished before conception by improving nutrition, combating pollution, treating allergies, discouraging use of poisons, etc.

Infertility Research Trust
Department of Obstetrics and Gynaecology
Jessop Hospital for Women
Leavygreave Road
Sheffield S3 7RE
T 0114 276 6333 F 0114 275 2153

The group meets monthly at the clinic. Individual & couple counselling also available.

National Childbirth Trust - Leeds branch
Janet Cartwright
6 Barfield Avenue
Yeadon
Leeds LS19 7SH
T 0113 250 5446
Information & support in pregnancy, childbirth & early parenthood. Antenatal classes, breastfeeding, counselling, postnatal exercises, discussions, postnatal support networks.

Pregnancy Service - Bradford
Barbara Gaskin
The Abundant Life Centre
Wapping Road
Bradford BD3 0EQ
T 01274 308171
Open Mon-Fri 10 am-3.30 pm & 24-hour ansaphone. Free pregnancy testing, counselling & support for women with unplanned pregnancies. Post abortion, bereavement, miscarriage & other counselling services.

York Lifeline
Tina Klar
11 Priory Street
York YO1 5ET
T 01904 492299
Helpline open Mon 7-9 pm 24-hour ansaphone. Appointment system. Free pregnancy testing & confidential counselling & support for any woman with an unplanned pregnancy. Post abortion counselling.

York NCT Home Birth Support Group
Helen Sugrue
36 Acomb Road
York YO2 4EW
T 01904 782598
Support group of parents interested in home births. Meets monthly. Publications & videos. Share information & specialist knowledge. Also offer support on an individual basis.

York Storks
Chris Warren
Eagle Farm House
Cundall
York YO6 2RN
T 01423 360 324

Independent midwifery service providing continuity of midwifery care throughout pregnancy, birth & post-natal period. Advice & consultation to empower women to get what they want from NHS maternity service.

PRISONERS/PRISONERS' WIVES

Women Prisoners' Resource Centre
Jackie Lowthian
Wakefield Branch
Outwood Hall
Victoria Street
Wakefield WF1 2NN
T 01924 820970
Staff visit prison to meet the needs of women prisoners. Queries relate mainly to housing, but can advise or refer on queries about education, training welfare, benefits, health, legal rights, etc.

PUBLISHERS/PUBLICATIONS

Aireings Publications
Jean Barker
Flat 3
24 Brudenell Road
Leeds LS6 1BD
T 0113 278 5893
Aireings, a poetry magazine, is published twice a year by a group of women writers who aim to publish accessible poetry & prose of a high standard. Poetry readings are done as a group or as individuals.

In Yer Face
Norrina Rashid
C/o Young Lesbian Drop In (Youthreach)
Youthreach Hennymoor House
Ground Floor, 7 Manor Row
Bradford BD1 4BP
T 01274 720196 F 01274 739706
A magazine for young lesbians. Free to lesbians but organisations have to subscribe. Phone for up-to-date price list.

RACIAL EQUALITY

Asian Racial Harassment Group
Rose Stead
West Leeds Family Service Unit
3 Chiswick Street
Leeds LS6 1QE
T 0113 275 7600 F 0113 278 9990
Meets Tue mornings. For Asian women who experience racial harassment. To provide support & empowerment. Two workers are available to give advice, particularly with problems relating to language.

Rights

Leeds University Union Women's Affairs Committee
Women's Officer
C/o Leeds University Union
P O Box 157
Leeds LS1 1UH
T 0113 231 4225
Campaigning for women's rights during term time between 1-2 pm at the Leeds University Union Women's Centre, Flat 14, 23 Cromer Terrace, Leeds University.

West Yorkshire Homeworking Unit
Linda Devereux/Amrit Choda
C/o Leeds Industrial Mission
Salem Church
Hunslet Road
Leeds LS10 1JW
T 0113 244 4937
Aims to improve pay & conditions of homeworkers. Open 9 am-4.30 pm. Two outreach workers give practical help & support to women working at home, help with benefits. Health & safety equipment loan scheme.

Women Against Fundamentalism - Leeds branch
Angela Dale
C/o New Working Women
3 St Peters Building
York Street
Leeds LS9 8AJ
T 0113 243 2474
Meets monthly. Provides a forum where women can challenge & organise against fundamentalism in all religions. Challenges racism; defends individual women; disseminates information.

Services

NACRO Heatcare
John Turner
Unit 1
Horbury Bridge Mills
Wakefield WF4 5RW
T 01924 281882 F 01924 281883
Insulation & energy-efficiency services for low-income households provided by NACRO.

Sexual Abuse/Rape Crisis

Barnsley Sexual Abuse and Rape Crisis Helpline
P O Box 72
Barnsley S70 1EU
T 01226 298560
Open Mon, Tue, Fri 10 am-12 noon; Wed 7.30-9.30 pm. Free helpline, listening service & counselling by women for women. Free appointments for further counselling, face-to-face if required.

Bradford Rape Crisis Centre
C/o 17-21 Chapel Street
Bradford BD1 5DT
T 01274 308270
Telephone lines open Mon & Wed 1-4 pm, Tue 5.30-7.30 pm, Thurs 7.30-9.30 pm, Fri 1.30-4 pm. On Wed Black women only answer the phone. Free & confidential counselling service for women/girls raped/abused.

Doncaster Rape and Sexual Abuse Counselling Centre
C/o Community House
7 Netherhall Road
Doncaster DN1 2PH
T 01302 341572
Helpline: 01302 360421 open Mon 1-4 pm & Wed 6-8 pm. 24-hour ansaphone. For women & men. Free face-to-face counselling available to women only, individual or group, for survivors & mothers of survivors.

Kirklees Rape Crisis Centre
Tracy Mulleague
P O Box 230
Huddersfield HD1 1AA
T 01484 450040
Women only free & confidential telephone helpline &/or face-to-face counselling for women & girls who have been raped, sexually abused, sexually assaulted, etc. Line times Mon-Wed 1-5 pm; Thurs 3-7 pm

Leeds Incest Survivors Action (LISA)
C/o 13 Gilpin View
Armley
Leeds LS12 1HJ
T 0113 231 0949
Open Mon-Fri 9 am-5 pm. Run by women survivors of child sexual abuse. Free, confidential phone or face-to-face counselling for women only. Supports women who might want to go to the courts, the police, etc.

Leeds Rape Crisis Centre
P O Box 27
Wellington Street
Leeds LS2 7EG
T 0113 244 1323

ENGLAND - YORKSHIRE

24-hour answerphone & one-to-one woman-to-woman offering emotional & practical support non-judgementally. Support, counselling for female survivors of sexual abuse & rape. (Helpline 0113 244 0058.)

MOSAIC
Linda Colclough
117 Little Horton Lane
Bradford BD5 0HT
T 01274 736932 F 01274 394646
Support group for mothers of sexually abused children. Helpline open Wed mornings. Holds two groups per week. One-to-one support & home visits if required. Works with police, probation, social services, etc.

Sheffield Rape Counselling Service
P O Box 34
Sheffield S1 1UD
T 0114 244 7936
Helpline open Tue & Wed 1-3 pm & Thurs 6-8 pm.

Sheffield Women's Counselling and Therapy Service
Teri Connolly
44 Daniel Hill
Upper Thorpe
Sheffield S6 3JF
T 0114 275 2157
Free individual or group therapy for women in Sheffield who are survivors of child sexual abuse.

SURVIVE (York Women Survivors of Child Sexual Abuse)
Tricia Walker
10 Priory Street
York YO1 1EZ
T 01904 638813 F 01904 630361
01904 642830 helpline. Offers advice & support to adult women survivors of child sexual abuse. Helpline, visiting service, free counselling, book loan service, information & self-help groups.

Survivors - Harrogate
women at the Centre
C/o The Women's Centre - Harrogate
West Park Centre
7 Raglan Street
Harrogate HG1 1LE
T 01423 536425
Women survivors of child sexual abuse. A contact point for anyone who has been sexually abused by someone in a position of trust. Self-help groups; information. 24-hour ansaphone. Call direct Mon 7-9 pm.

York Rape Crisis
York
T 01904 610917 F 01904 613869
YRC@langwork.demon.co.uk
Counselling, support, information to women who have been raped/sexually abused. All counselling & support is one-to-one by trained YRC counsellors. Helpline on Thurs 6.30-10 pm. Ansaphone.

SINGLE PARENTS

Bradford Gingerbread Centre
Sue Adsetts
45 Darley Street
Bradford BD1 3HN
T 01274 720564
Support & self help for lone parents & their children providing adult education classes with free creche, pregancy testing, used clothing store, supported housing project, before & after school care, etc.

Gingerbread Housing Project
Liz Eastwood
56 Boldshay Street
Bradford BD3 OAJ
T 01274 734285
Temporary supported accommodation for lone parents & their children. Staff available office hours Mon-Fri (not staffed for 24 hours). Not women only as applications accepted from lone parent fathers.

SOCIAL

Alwoodley Women's Group
Mrs J Lacy
C/o 5 Wentworth Way
Alwoodley Park
Leeds LS17 7TG
T 0113 269 8077
For all women. Meets Tue 9.15-11.15 am in term time. (No set meeting place.) Creche. Couses on confidence building, stress management, homoeopathy, aromatherapy, etc.

Brudenell Tuesday Women's Group
Clare Dowgill
Brudenell Centre
Welton Road
Leeds LS6
T 0113 244 3335

For all women to have fun, gain information & receive support, if necessary. Meets Tue 12 noon-2.30 pm at above address. Free refreshments, creche & activities.

Burley Ladies Group
Mrs Fletcher
Burley Parish Hall
St Matthias Street
Leeds LS4
T 0113 278 7988
Meets first & third Thurs of each month 1.45-3.45 pm. Provides friendship & help. Speakers, outings, theatre visits, coffee mornings.

Middleton Women's Group
Pamela Graham
10 Acre Street
Middleton
Leeds LS10
Meets Wed 1-3 pm at Middleton Clinic, Acre Close, Middleton Park Avenue, Leeds LS10 4HT. Social interaction with other women, education, fun, summer trips, speakers.

New Wortley Community Centre - Women's Group
40 Tong Road
Leeds LS12 1LZ
T 0113 279 3466
For women of all ages for community contact. Meets at above address Mon-Fri 9.30-11.30 am & 1-4 pm. Mums & tots group, playgroup, health & fitness for women over 50, ante-natal group. Coffee bar.

Tuesday Luncheon Club York
Patricia Brisbane, Hon Secretary
3 Fulfordgate
Heslington Lane
York YO1 4LY
T 01904 633424
Social events with meals at York Racecourse. Speakers. Meets nine months of the year from October to June.

SPORTS AND LEISURE

Durham County Ladies' Golf Association
Mrs R Foy
Jolby Manor
Stapleton
Darlington DL2 2QS
T 01325 377500 F 01325 377500

Leeds Women's Self Defence Group
Jackie Boland
10 Blenheim Avenue
Leeds LS2 9AX
T 0113 244 9873
To promote self-defence for women of all ages & levels of physical ability in women-only classes. Self-defence instructors teach courses in many settings, including community centres, colleges, youth clubs.

Yorkshire County Women's Bowling Association
Anita Haw
24 Finsbury Avenue
York YO2 1LW
T 01904 623438

SUPPORT

Chas Housing Aid
Sedgefield Terrace
Bradford BD1 2RU
T 01274 726790
Open Mon-Fri 9.30 am-12.30 pm, Mon & Tue 1.30-3.30 pm. Advice on housing, homelessness, debt, etc. Money management scheme. Furniture service (01274 731909). Clothing/household goods store.

Cottingley Women's Group
Sandie White/Janine Lawley
Cottingley Community Centre
115 Cottingley Approach
Leeds LS11 0HH
T 0113 270 2109
Meets Wed 9.30-11.30 am term times. Mixed weekly programme including: coping with stress, healthy eating, supporting women prisoners of conscience. Also a Cottingley girls' group (ages 11-14 years).

Fairfield Women's Group
Diane Law/Sandy Crossland
Fairfield Community Centre
Fairfield Terrace
Bramley
Leeds LS13
T 0113 255 6907
For all women around the Fairfield estate. To encourage other relationships with women, build up self-esteem & confidence, raise issues affecting young women. Speakers on welfare, first aid. Outings.

ENGLAND - YORKSHIRE

Kirkstall Ladies
Mrs J Storey/Mrs L Longbottom
144 Argie Avenue
Kirkstall
Leeds LS4 2TZ
T 0113 275 5177
Meets Fri 1-3 pm in term time at Kirkstall Hill Community Centre, Eden Mount, Leeds 4 (0113 787 367). Creche provided with NNEB qualified staff. Speakers & activities.

Langbar Women's Group
Vanessa Hawkins/Liz Mchale
Langbar Family Nursery Centre
Langbar Road
Swarcliffe
Leeds LS14 5ER
T 0113 232 3571
Open 10 am-12 noon Thurs. For women from Stanks/Swarcliffe/Whinmoor estates & any who have a connection with the centre. Creche staffed by qualified workers. Meets at above address. Discussions, outings.

Leeds Home Start
Ann Pemberton
Oxford Place Care Centre
Oxford Place
Leeds LS1 3AX
T 0113 244 2419
For women in Leeds with young children, helped by volunteer women. To provide support & befriending to young families in times of stress or difficulty. Volunteers visit families in their homes regularly.

Leeds MIND Women's Group
Gillian Berresford
Leeds Mind Social Centre
157 Woodhouse Lane
Leeds LS2 3ED
T 0113 245 1662
For women who suffer from or who experience mental health problems. Meets at above address on Wed 12-4 pm. Information, advice & support on women's issues. An opportunity to combat isolation.

Leeds Travellers Women's Group
Jacky Glass
Travellers' Education Service
C/o Swinnow Primary School
Swinnow Lane
Leeds LS13 4PG
T 0113 236 1942
For all women travellers. Meets Mon 1-3 pm in term time at above address. Sewing, cooking, outings. Transport & creche facilities.

Link Drop-in Women's Group
Liz Kitching
Roundhay Road Day Centre
79 Roundhay Road
Leeds LS7 4AA
T 0113 247 7309
For all women who have experienced mental health problems. Meets at above address on Thurs 10.30 am-12 noon. Friendship, outings, art, pottery, use of day centre facilities. Tea or coffee available.

Making Space Yorkshire
Jennifer Campbell-Robson
111a Otley Road
Headingley
Leeds LS6 3PX
T 0113 274 6010
For women with long term mental health problems & for their carers, offering support, advice, counselling & practical help. A self-help befriending group.

Middleton Clinic Women's Group
Karen Wallis/Wendy White
Middleton Clinic
Acre Close
Leeds LS10
T 0113 270 0773
For all women in Leeds. Meets Wed 1.15-3 pm at above address. Speakers, trips, time to chat. Creche facilities.

Palace Youth Project - Women's Group
Patricia Joseph
90-92 Shepherd's Lane
Chapeltown
Leeds LS7 4DZ
T 0113 262 0093
For all women living in the Chapeltown & Harehills area. Open Mon-Fri 9 am-5 pm. Meeting place, base for activities, drop in, resource centre, women's groups, youth work, hostel service for single women.

Pudsey Time Out Group
Margaret Illingworth
South Pudsey Training, Ed. & Com. Centre
Kent Road
Pudsey
Leeds LS28
T 0113 236 0756
For all women in the area, to give women time out from being a wife & mother. Meets

ENGLAND - YORKSHIRE

Fri 9.30-11.30 am in term time at above address. Talks; days & nights out.

Sandford Women's Afternoon
Chris Coates
Sandford Church Hall
Broad Lane/Outgang
Bramley
Leeds LS13
T 0113 255 9582
For women living around the Bramley area. A space for themselves & a place of safety for their children. Creche. Meets at above address 12.45-2.45 pm in term time. Activities to suit the women.

Selby Daytime Projects
Vera St Paul
The Cygnet Centre
Union Lane
Selby YO8 0AU
T 01757 700131
Aims to encourage women & girls to participate in their own programmes in women's groups; to help women develop new skills, grow in confidence, independence & self-esteem & to value their friendship networks.

Swillington Women's Group
Ann Mason
C/o 35 Millcrest
Swillington
Leeds LS26 8DL
T 0113 286 8057
Meets Mon 1.30-3.30 pm term time only at Swillington Community Centre. Provides a meeting place for women of all ages to develop skills. Creche, crafts, health issues, keep fit, speakers. Lunch, tea, coffee.

Two Willows Women's Group
Jane Russell
Two Willows Family Nursery Centre
Cardinal Square
Beeston
Leeds LS11 8HF
T 0113 270 6166
Meets Thurs 9.30 am-12 noon. For women to support each other. Speakers, events, confidence building, welfare rights, drama group, etc. Creche, refreshments.

West Leeds Family Service Unit - Women's Group
Helen Sharpe
3 Chiswick Street

Leeds LS6 1QE
T 0113 275 7600
Open Mon-Thurs 9 am-5 p.m; Fri 9 am-4.30 pm. Open access services: women's groups: women & violence, Asian Women, parents of special needs children, playgroups, after-school playshemes, drop in.

Women's Forum
Sue Stark
Sansbury Place
Duke Street
Settle BD24 9AS
T 01729 823840
A small group of women meet in Settle once a month. We explore issues affecting women's lives & well-being. We learn new skills & introduce new ideas. We offer friendship & support to women of all ages.

Women's Helpline
Sara Everatt
C/o Doncaster Women's Centre
21 Cleveland Street
Doncaster DN1 3EA
T 01302 361527
Confidential listening service for women offering support & reassurance in crisis. Operates Mon-Fri 5 pm-midnight.

York Family Mediation Service
Catharine Morris
82 Bootham
York YO3 7DF
T 01904 646068
Helping parents at any stage of divorce & separation who are having difficulties coming to agreement over arrangements for the children once the family has split up. Open Mon-Fri 9.30 am-12.30 pm.

TRAINING

Active Women Group
Ele Jarrett
C/O Halton Information Centre
Neville Road
Leeds LS15 0NW
T 0113 260 8901
For all women in the Halton Moor/Osmondthorpe area. Meets Mon 1-3 pm in term time at East Leeds Leisure Centre, Halton Moor, Leeds 15. (Also outings.) Free creche. Groupwork skills, sports, video making, etc.

ENGLAND - YORKSHIRE

Activities for Women - 16+
Joan Beattie
Richmond Hill Community Centre
Long Close Lane
Leeds LS9 8NP
T 0113 248 7496
For all women over the age of 16. Meets Wed 1-3 pm at above address in term time only. Varaious skills offered such as aromatherapy, silk screen printing, video recording, canoeing, abseiling, exercise.

Auto Engineering for Women
Karen Griffiths/Annette Williams
Bradford and Ilkley Commercial College
Auto Section
Randall Well
Bradford BD7 1AY
T 01274 753026 F 01274 741060
One-year, four-day week course for women only to gain skills in maintaining their vehicle or acquiring C&G qualifications to enter the motor industry. Course is free & childminding & travel expenses paid.

Burley Lodge Women's Group
Carol Ciplinski/Amanda Philpotts
Burley Lodge Centre
12 Burley Lodge Road
Leeds LS6 1QP
T 0113 244 3335
Meets Thurs 1-3 pm at above address. Sewing classes & open college certificates. Aims to support women, provide confidence & new skills.

Cynet Centre
Vera St Paul, Daytime Projects Coordinator
Union Lane
Selby YO8 0AU
T 01757 700131
Short courses for women Mon 9.30-11.30 am Cyget Centre Craft Group (women) Tue 1-3 pm. Allsorts after school club: affordable after-school & holiday care for 5-11 year olds. Creche Mon 9.30-11.30 am

First Net
Liz Thomas
41 Low Petergate
York YO1 2HT
T 01904 613869 F 01904 613869
firstnet@langwork.demon.co.uk
Run by women providing training, research, supervision & consultancy around women's issues, in particular rape, sexual abuse, domestic violence & social issues.

Skills for Women
Lindsey Fraser/Julia Gardner
Harehills Ex-Middle School
Harehills Road
Leeds LS8 4HD
T 0113 235 1718
Open to women with little or no post-16 education in areas of high social need. Courses include: management committee skills, group skills, oppression awareness, confidence building, where to next?

West Bowling Community Advice & Training Centre
Jane Binns
Clipstone Street
West Bowling
Bradford BD5 8EA
T 01274 392896
Advice & training centre for women, particularly single parents & disabled, unemployed or elderly. Men also train at the Centre. No discrimination allowed on the grounds of sex, colour or creed.

Women's Motor Vehicle Course
Rosalind Wollen
Sheffield College
Granville Road
Sheffield S2
T 0114 260 2182
Women's motor vehicle courses. Three days a week, leading to NVQ 1.

TRANSPORT

Harrogate District Community Transport Ltd
Lyn Costelloe
2 Mornington Terrace
Harrogate HG1 5DH
T 01423 526655
Voluntary organisation using accessible mini-buses & cars, driven by paid staff & volunteers to transport anyone frail, disabled, elderly or in need of care & who cannot easily access public transport

Keighley Community Transport
Allan Harrison
Unit One
Holycroft Street
Keighley BD21 1PT
T 01535 609278
Bookings for minibuses Mon-Fri 9 am-5 pm. For people whose access to transport is limited by physical, financial or social

ENGLAND - YORKSHIRE

constraints. Session times are: 9 am-12.30 pm; 12.30 -6 pm; 6 pm-12 am

Nightlink
Carolyn James
C/o The Secretary
Oakdene
Houghley Lane
Leeds LS13 2DT
T 0113 235 1289
Aims to provide direction & develop policies for the Nightlink service, a safe transport bus service for women. Meets first Tue of every second month at Leeds Civic Hall.

Shopmobility
Steve Ward
Town Hall
Bow Street
Keighley BD21 3PA
T 01535 618225
Electronically powered scooters helping disabled people use town centre facilities & shops. At Cook Street, Keighley, John Street Market, Bradford City Centre & Asda store, Shipley. Phone for further details.

Women's Wheels
Frances
Leeds
T 0113 274 7135
Private hire for women & children. Phone bookings in advance of journeys wherever possible. Babyseat available. Open Mon-Thurs 7 am-11 pm; Fri & Sat 7 am-2 to 3 am (bookings in advance).

VIOLENCE AGAINST WOMEN

AWARE
Christina Hanson
22 Brownroyd Avenue
Rawthorpe
Huddersfield HD5 9PP
T 01484 535148
Self-help group for women who are/have been in abusive relationshops, mental or physical abuse from their partners. Meets Town Hall, Huddersfield, Wed 7-9 pm. Support, self-confidence, self-esteem, etc.

Justice for Women - Leeds
Jude Boyle/Chris Hoy
C/o Leeds inter-Agency Project
CHEL
26 Roundhay Road
Leeds LS7 1AB
T 0113 262 0293
Meets fortnightly Wed 7.30 pm. (Phone for location.) To assist & campagn on behalf of women who kill their violent/abuse partners. To protest about the inequality of the law. To publicise women's cases.

Justice For Women - West Yorkshire
Jude Boyles
Bradford Resource Centre
17-21 Chapel Street
Bradford BD1 5DT
T 0113 262 0293
Campaigns for & supports women who have killed/fought back against men who have abused them or someone in their family. Campaigns for changes in the law to accept women's experiences of male violence.

Keighley Domestic Violence Forum
P O Box 79
Keighley BD21 2UD
T 01535 690458
For women & children experiencing/fleeing domestic violence. Referral/ self-referral. Self-help support or personal support. Structured support for children experiencing violence. Punjabi/Urdu speaking workers.

Leeds Safer Cities Project
Cath Mahoney
Selectapost 29
Merrion House
110 Merrion Centre
Leeds LS2 8DR
T 0113 247 6373 F 0113 247 6911
Government-funded community safety partnership with NACRO promoting local initiatives to prevent crime & make places safer.

Scunthorpe Safer Cities Project
Geoff Ogden
58 Oswald Road
Scunthorpe DN15 7PQ
T 01724 276066 F 01724 846185
Government-funded community safety partnership with NACRO promoting local initiatives to prevent crime & make places safer.

Sheffield Safer Cities Project
Julie Tasker
5 Orchard Chambers
31 Church Street
Sheffield S1 2FB
T 0114 276 9150 F 0114 276 9155

ENGLAND - YORKSHIRE

Government-funded community safety partnership with NACRO promoting local initiatives to prevent crime & make places safer.

York Safer Cities Project
Sarah Loftus
1a Whip-ma-Whop-ma Gate
York YO1 2BL
T 01904 611188 F 01904 673011
Government-funded community safety partnership with NACRO promoting local initiatives to prevent crime & make places safer.

Young People and Community Safety Project
Gwen Barrell
C/o Education Department
Leopold Street
Sheffield S1 1RJ
T 0114 273 5829 F 0114 273 5655
Development of partnerships, policies and programmes to address issues of community safety with young people across Sheffield.

WOMEN'S AID

Bradford Women's Aid
P O Box 124
Bradford BD1 1AA
T 01274 660052 F 01274 669937
Refuge for women & their children (if any) who have been or are suffering domestic violence from their partners.

Harrogate and District Women's Aid
West Park Centre
7 Raglan Street
Harrogate HG1 1LE
T 01423 530078 F 01423 526386
Temporary, safe accommodation for women & their children (if any) who have suffered sexual abuse/domestic violence from their partners. Helpline open Mon-Fri 9 am-5 pm. Can accommodate up to 8 families.

Keighley Women's Aid
P O Box 46
Keighley BD20 6UA
T 01535 210067
Above number ususably available 24 hours a day. For women & their children (if any) fleeing domestic violence. Emergency accommodation provided.

Leeds Women's Aid
Kathryn Shaw
P O Box 89
Wellington Street
Leeds LS1 2EE
T 0113 246 0401 F 0113 2468377
Practical/ emotional support. Emergency accommodation for women & children experiencing violence. Office open 9.30 am-4.30 pm. A worker can be paged for emergency admissions at any time.

Shipley Women's Aid
T 01274 530124
Phone above number at any time to make contact. For women & their children (if any) fleeing domestic violence. (Male children up to age 16 only.) Emergency accommodation provided vacancies permitting.

York Women's Aid
S Lonsdale
C/o CVS
10 Priory Street
York YO1 1EZ
T 01904 646630 F 01904 622994
Provides temporary accommodation for women & children suffering domestic violence. Also offers help & advice through telephone service available Mon-Fri 9 am-5 pm

WORKING WOMEN

Bradford Working Women's Project
Sarah Chapple/Katherine Fraser
11 Hallfield Road
Bradford BD1 3RP
T 01274 741357 F 01274 730559
Open Mon, Tue, Wed, Fri 10 am-5 pm., Thurs 10 am-midnight. Working with women involved in prostitution. Free condoms, works, family planning, pregnancy testing available. Advice & support on sexual health.

Genesis Leeds Project
Kathy/Sue/Julia
Oxford Chambers
Oxford Place
Leeds LS1 3UA
T 0113 245 0915
Female prostitutes aiming to improve services for working women, to support & empower working women. Drop in Wed evenings. One-to-one advice & support on legal, health, HIV/AIDS issues. Advocacy.

LONDON

Barking & Dagenham

Arts and Crafts

Barking Flower Arranging Classes
Mrs Evans
Eastbury House
Eastbury Square
Barking IG11 9SN
T 0181 591 3892
Meets at above address on Thurs 7.30-9.30 pm.

Romford and West Essex Embroiderers' Guild
Pat Hamlin
43 Beam Way
Dagenham RM10 8XR
T 0181 595 1572
Meets once a month on Sat 2-4 pm at United Reform Church, Romford. Holds workshops.

Bereavement

Grief and Bereavement Service
Oxlow Lane Clinic
Oxlow Lane
Dagenham RM10 7YU
T 0181 593 5035
Offers caring & emotional support to anyone who has lost a relative or friend.

Contraception/Well Woman

Barking Brook Centre
Central Clinic
Vicarage Drive
Barking IG11 7NF
T 0181 507 2776
Open Sat 12-2 pm. To make an appointment outside opening hours, phone 0171 580 2991. Free confidential contraceptive advice. Help with emotional & sexual problems. Free condoms & other contraceptive supplies.

Five Elms Health Centre
Five Elms Road
Wood Lane
Dagenham
T 0181 593 7241
Comprehensive contraceptive and cytology services available. Emergency contraception, pregnancy testing, condoms, the pill, coil, cap, etc. Smear tests. Clinic on Wed 6-9 pm

Ford Road Clinic
Ford Road
Dagenham
T 0181 592 0925
Blood pressure checks, urine tests, pregnancy testing, weight checks, cervical cytology (smear tests). Female doctor/nurse available. Clinics on first Mon of each month 1.30-4.30 pm.

Julia Engwell Clinic
Woodward Road
Dagenham
T 0181 592 2588
Comprehensive contraceptive and cytology services available. Emergency contraception, pregnancy testing, condoms, the pill, coil, cap, etc. Smear Tests. Clinic on Thurs 6-9 pm

Marie Stopes Fairfield Clinic
Liz Davies, Manager
Buckhurst Hill IG9 5QB
T 0181 505 4641   F 0181 504 1494
Pregancy advice (helpline 0171 388 4843); general healcare/contraception (helpline 0171 388 0662); sterilisation services (helpline 0171 388 5554); well woman clinics; abortion clinics; menopause clinics; etc.

Medical Centre, The
92 Hedgemans Road
Dagenham
T 0181 984 1008
Comprehensive contraceptive & cytology services available. Emergency contraception, pregnancy testing, condoms, the pill, coil, cap, etc. Smear Tests. Clinics on Wed 11 am-noon; Fri noon-1 pm.

Orchard Health Clinic
Gascoigne Road
Barking
T 0181 594 1311
Contraceptive & cytology services available. Emergency contraception, pregnancy testing, condoms, the pill, coil, cap, etc. Cytology (smear testing). Direct line 0181 594 9818. Clinic on Wed 4-7 pm.

Oxlow Lane Clinic
Oxlow Lane
Dagenham
T 0181 592 3588
Emergency contraception, pregnancy testing, condoms, the pill, coil, cap, etc. Smear tests. Clinics on first, third & fourth Thurs of each

LONDON - BARKING & DAGENHAM

month 1.30-4.30 pm & second Thurs of each month 9 am-noon.

Thames View Clinic
Bastable Avenue
Barking
T 0181 594 4233
Emergency contraception, pregnancy testing, condoms, the pill, coil, cap, etc. Smear tests. Women's health service. Clinics on first & third Tue of each month 6.15-8.15 pm.

Vicarage Field Health Centre
Vicarage Drive
Barking IG11 7NR
T 0181 591 5466
Thurs 9 am-12 noon. A nurse is available. A fully comprehensive contraceptive, cytology (smear testing) & women's health service available.

Young People's Sexual Health Project
39-41 Axe Street
Barking IG11 7LX
T 0181 507 9777
Free advice/ information; free pregnancy testing; free condoms. Contraception. HIV/AIDS, relationships, lesbian counselling. Fully confidential for all under the age of 21. Open Wed 4-6 pm. Drop-in.

ETHNIC MINORITIES

Muslim Parents Association
Mrs H Sarwar
C/o 5 Wilmington Gardens
Barking IG11 9TW
T 0181 591 0165
Working towards improvement of educational performance of children of Islamic faith; promoting better access to educational provision.

GIRLS/YOUNG WOMEN

Young Women's Drop In
Wendy Casselden
Community Concern for Young People
39-41 Axe Street
Barking IG11 7LX
T 0181 594 7227
Meets on Mon 4-6 pm. Drop-in for young women aged 11-18.

Young Women's Project
Lynn Money/Michele Lucas
The Vineries

321-329 Heathway
Dagenham RM9 5AF
T 0181 593 3931
Information, support, advice, leisure facilities for women aged 16-25. Creche. Drop-in sessions. Mums & toddlers Wed 10 am-12 noon; babywatch Wed 1-3 pm; sexual health project Wed 4-6 pm.

HEALTH

Barking and Havering Health Authority
women's development manager
The Clock House
East Street
Barking IG11 8EY
T 0181 591 9595

Women Only Drug Advice Sessions
Community Drug Advice Service
Oxlow Lane Clinic
Dagenham RM10 7YU
T 0181 592 7748
A female counsellor is offered to any woman who drops in.

SINGLE PARENTS

Lonepac
Mrs J Brandon
Faircross Community Complex
Hulse Avenue
Barking IG11 9UP
T 0181 594 9418
Advice & support given to lone parents.

SOCIAL

Chequers Women's Club
Mrs Taylor
St Peters Hall
Goresbrook Road
Dagenham RM10
T 0181 252 7682
Meets Tue 8 pm at above address. To combat isolation. Speakers & games for women who work for two charities a year.

Eastbrook Women's Club
Pat Van Doorn
49 Osborne Road
Hornchurch RM11 1EX
T 01708 446148
Meets on Tue 8 pm at Wantz Community Hall off Rainham Road North, Dagenham. Non political group. Speakers, weekends away, fun nights.

LONDON - BARNET

Mayesbrook Women's Club
Elsie Bailey
Ted Ball Memorial Hall
Neasham Road
Dagenham RM8 2LL
T 0181 594 0716
Meets on Wed 7.30 at above address. For women aged 18-80. Bingo, dominoes, speakers, harvest festival activities, Chinese auctions.

SPORTS AND LEISURE

Women's Activity Morning Programme
Abbey Sports Centre
Axe Street
Barking IG11 7NA
T 0181 594 1818
For women only on Thurs 10 am-12 noon. Badminton, weights, squash, keep fit. Play area for children.

WOMEN'S AID

Barking and Dagenham Women's Aid Drop-in Service
The Orchards Health Centre
Gascoigne Road
Barking IG11 7RS
T 0181 594 2242
An advice surgery for women in Barking & Dagenham. A place where women can meet other women who have suffered physical & mental abuse. Information on legal options, housing issues, etc. Wed 12.45-2.45 pm.

BARNET

ACCOMMODATION

Young Women's Christian Association (YWCA) - Barnet
the director
Clarendon House
69 Gainsborough Road
Finchley
London N12 8BL
T 0181 446 2550
Offers studio-type flats for young women in low paid employment. Open 9 am-5 pm, otherwise ansaphone always operating.

ARTS AND CRAFTS

Scarlet Theatre Company
Marie Remy
Studio 8
Old Bull Arts Centre
68 High Street
London EN5 5SJ
T 0181 441 9779 F 0181 441 9779
London-based women's theatre company. Aims to entertain by presenting & touring vibrant, original theatre created from a female perspective. Opportunities for women in all aspects of theatre.

CENTRES FOR WOMEN

Asian Women's Resource Centre
134 Minet Avenue
Harlsden
London NW10 8AP
T 0181 961 6549
Drop in, phone for advice/counselling for Asian women/girls across London on any problem. Activities, classes, training, counselling, advocacy. Information on benefits, health, domestic violence, housing, etc.

CHILD CARE AND FAMILY

Handicapped Children's Aid Committee
Mrs Beverley Emden
11 Fairholme Gardens
London N3 3ED
T 0181 349 2829
Assisting provision of equipment to handicapped children, at home or in hospital.

CONTRACEPTION/WELL WOMAN

East Barnet Health Centre
149 East Barnet Road
New Barnet
London EN4 8RB
T 0181 440 1251
Well woman & contraception clinics on Mon 12.30-3 pm; Tue 7-9.30 pm; Wed 9-11.30 am; Wed 6.30-9 pm. Domiciliary & hospital liaison. Menopause counselling. Free services.

Edgware Clinic
Rear of Post Office
Station Road
Edgware
London
T 0181 952 2500
Well woman & contraception clinics on Tue 5.45-8.15 pm; Wed 1.30-4 pm. Youth Advisory services Mon 5-7 pm. Intrauterine device (IUD) fittings Wed 1.30-4 pm. Free services.

Finchley Memorial Hospital
Outpatients' Department
Granville Road

Finchley
London N12
T 0181 349 3121
Well woman & contraception clinics on Fri 9.30 am-12 pm & 1.15-3.45 pm. Intrauterine device (IUD) fittings 9.30 am-3.45 pm. Breast screening, contraceptive advice & supplies. Free services.

Grahame Park Health Centre
The concourse
Grahame Park
London NW9 5XT
T 0181 205 6204
Telephone 0181 200 2539 during clinic times. Well woman & contraception clinics on Tue 5.45-8.15 pm. Intrauterine device (IUD) fittings Tue 5.45-8.15 pm. Free services.

Hendon Central Clinic
Rear of Library
The Burroughs
London NW4 4BH
T 0181 202 6101
Well woman & contraception clinics on Wed 6.30-9 pm. Breast screening, smear tests, blood pressure & urine tests; contraceptive advice & supplies. Free services.

Holly Park Clinic
Holly Park Road
London N11 3HB
T 0181 368 3812
Well woman & contraception clinics on Mon 1-3.30 pm. Breast screening, smear tests, blood pressure & urine tests, etc; contraceptive advice & supplies. Free services.

Mill Hill Clinic
Hartley Avenue
Mill Hill
London NW7 2HX
T 0181 959 3005
Well woman & contraception clinics on Thurs 6.30-9 pm. Breast screening, smear tests, blood pressure & urine tests etc; contraceptive advice & supplies. Free services.

Oak Lane Clinic
Oak Lane
East Finchley
London N2 8LT
T 0181 346 9343
Contraception & well woman clinics on Mon 10 am-12.30 pm; Tue 6.45-9.15 pm; Thurs 6.45-9.15 pm. Breast screening, smear tests, etc; contraceptive advice & supplies. Free services.

Sutton Road Clinic
Sutton Road
Muswell Hill
London N10 1HE
T 0181 883 7150
Contraception & well woman clinics on Tue 9.30 am-12 pm. Breast screening, smear tests, blood pressure & urine tests etc; contraceptive advice & supplies. Free services.

Temple Fortune Health Centre
23 Temple Fortune Lane
Golders Green
London NW11 8TE
T 0181 458 8844
Contraception & well woman clinics on Mon 6.30-9 pm. Breast screening, smear tests, blood pressure & urine tests etc; contraceptive advice & supplies. Free services.

Torrington Park Health Centre
16 Torrington Park
Finchley
London N12 9SS
T 0181 446 4201
Contraception & well woman clinics on Mon 6.30-9 pm; Wed 10 am-12.30 pm & 6-8.30 pm; Thurs 12.30-3 pm; Sat 10 am-12.30 pm. Vasectomy counselling; psychosexual counselling. Free services.

Vale Drive Clinic
Vale Drive
Barnet
London EN5 2ED
T 0181 440 1417
Contraception & well woman clinics on Tue 6.30-9 pm; Thurs 1.30-4 pm & 6.30-9 pm. Youth advisory services 5-7 pm. Intrauterine device (IUD) fittings Thurs 1.30-4 pm. Free services.

Watling Clinic
36 Cressingham Road
Burnt Oak
London HA8 0RW
T 0181 959 2188
Well woman & contraception clinics on Mon 1.30-4 pm. Breast screening, smear tests, blood pressure & urine tests, etc;

LONDON - BARNET

contraceptive advice & supplies. Free services.

West Hendon Clinic
215 The Broadway
West Hendon
London NW9 7DG
T 0181 202 8514
Contraception & well woman clinics on Tue 1.45-4.15; Wed 6-8.30 pm. Intrauterine device (IUD) fittings Tue 1.45-4.15 pm. Breast screening, smear tests, etc; contraceptive advice & supplies. Free services.

COUNSELLING AND THERAPY
Women's Therapy Group
C/o MIND in Barnet
2 Schoolway
North Finchley
London N12 0RY
T 0181 446 1654 F 0181 446 3724
Also 0181 446 6470. Meets Thurs 10.30 am-12 noon at Greenhill New Church, 177 Leicester Road, New Barnet. For women with mental health problems who feel lonely, anxious, depressed, stressed, etc.

DISABILITY
Age and Disability Unit
BT Colindale House
London NW9 6HH
T 0800 671504
Information about BT's services for disabled people. Home visits & demonstrations can be arranged. Catalogue available on request.

ETHNIC MINORITIES
Barnet Asian Women's Association
Farida Bhaloo
1 Friern Park
London N12 9DE
T 0181 446 9897 F 0181 446 5036
Open Tue & Fri 11.30 am-4.30 pm. For Asian women to help combat isolation. General advice on practical problems. Religious activities. Gujarati classes for children on Sat. Gujarati, Punjabi, Hindi spoken.

HEALTH
Barnet General Hospital
Clare Simpson House
3-5 Wellhouse Lane
London EN5 3DL

T 0181 732 4110
Clinics on Mon, Wed, Thurs & Fri 9-11 am HIV/AIDS clinic Tues 2-5 pm. HIV testing & counselling. Free contraceptive advice & supplies. Advice on sexual health. Screening for STDs.

Eating Distress Support Group
C/o MIND in Barnet
2 Schoolway
North Finchley
London N12 0RY
T 0181 446 1654 F 0181 446 3724
Also 0181 446 6470. Meets Fri 10.30 am-12 noon at Greenhill New Church, 177 Leicester Road, New Barnet. Offers help, understanding, care & respect to people with eating disorders. Sharing personal issues.

JEWISH WOMEN
Jewish Bereavement Counselling Service
P O Box 6748
London N3 3BX
T 0181 349 0839

League of Jewish Women - Barnet branch
Mrs V Ferber, Chairman
5 Downes Court
London N21 3PT
T 0181 886 4463
Providing voluntary social care: visiting, befriending, meals on wheels & transport to day centre, catering for people in need regardless of race or religion who live in Barnet & Enfield.

League of Jewish Women - Hendon branch
Mrs Helen Adam, Secretary
20 Edgeworth Crescent
Hendon
London NW4 4HG
T 0181 202 7961
Services include visiting housebound people, providing transport, helping at day centre. There is a visiting welfare officer. For everyone, regardless of race or religion.

LESBIAN AND BISEXUAL
Barnet College Gay, Lesbian and Bisexual Befriending Group
Peter/llech
T 081 366 5136
Or 0181 361 8661. Meets first Thurs of each month at Barnet College.

LONDON - BEXLEY

Lesbian and Gay Bereavement Project - Barnet
Unitarian Rooms
Hoop Lane
London NW11 8BS
T 0181 455 8894
For information/admin phone 0181 200 0511 Mon-Fri 10.30 am-4.30 pm. Telephone bereavement counselling for lesbians & gay men. Callers are referred to volunteers available every evening 7 pm-midnight.

OLDER WOMEN

Sir Thomas Lipton Memorial Hostel
Mrs M Trahar
151 Chase Side
Southgate
London N14 5HE
Residential home for elderly women, primarily retired nurses. 25 residents at any one time. Five acres of land. Registered with Barnet Council.

RELIGIOUS ORGANISATIONS

Friendship Club
Mrs A Johnson
59 Ventnor Drive
Totteridge
London N20 8BU
Meets at Union Church (Free church), Northiam, London N12 on Thurs 2.15-3.15 pm. Talks on various topics. Holiday films.

SERVICES

Amanda Shribman, Event Planning and Management Services
Amanda Shribman
56 Manor Park Road
London N2 0SJ
T 0181 444 1110 F 0181 444 1110
shribman@easynet.co.uk
Professional organiser; conferences & special events.

SOCIAL

Acorns
Lorna
T 0181 346 7378
For mothers with children. Meets Wed 10.45-11.30 am in term time at St Paul's Church Hall, Long Lane, Finchley N3. Informal talks, creche, baby sitting circle, half term holiday outings. Wheelchair access.

Springwell Club
Mrs M Cairns
11 Salisbury Road
London EN5 4JW
T 0181 441 5104
Meets at Stephen's Hall, Bells Hill, Barnet on Tue 8 pm. Speakers, DIY, outings. A branch of the National Association of Women's Clubs.

SPORTS AND LEISURE

Barnet Copthall Sports Centre
Great North Way
Hendon
London NW4 1PS
T 0181 457 9900
Women-only gym sessions Mon (with instructor) 11 am-1 pm; Wed 8.30-9.30 pm Women only Tue 9.30-10.30 am water aerobics; 11 am-12.30 pm women & children only swimming; Wed 1-2 pm water aerobics.

Hendon Youth Sports Centre
Marble Drive
Hendon
London NW2 1XQ
T 0181 455 0818
Women-only keep fit Tue 10.30-11.55 am Women's weights Sun 10-11.30 am; Thurs 7.30-9 pm.

Women's Recreation Group
Helen Hooper
96 Ashurst Road
Friern Barnet
London N12 9AB
T 0181 445 3118
For women aged 18+. Sports activities such as football, basketball, volleyball, kwik kricket, etc (sometimes with a coach). Meets Mon 8-10 pm. Phone for further details.

BEXLEY

CONTRACEPTION/WELL WOMAN

Broadway Clinic
315 Broadway
Bexleyheath
T 0181 303 7319
Contraceptive advice & supplies Mon & Wed 7-9 pm. Drop-in youth advisory service Thurs 7-9 pm. Emergency contraception also available.

Erith Health Centre
Queen Street
Erith
T 01322 339248

Contraceptive advice & supplies. Youth advisory service Mon 7-9 pm. Contraception for all ages Tue 7-9 pm. Emergency contraception also available.

Queen Mary's Hospital
Frognal Avenue
Sidcup DA14
T 0181 302 2678
Contraceptive advice & supplies Wed 7-9 pm. Emergency contraception also available.

COUNSELLING AND THERAPY

Stress and Anxiety Management Group
Anne Sargent
C/o Family Service Unit
2 Maran Way
Thamesmead
Erith DA18 4BP
T 0181 310 6570 F 0181 312 4277
Meets Thurs 9.30 am-1 pm. An all-women's group with a counsellor set up to help manage stress & anxiety. By referral only.

PREGNANCY/CHILDBIRTH

Independent Midwifery Practice
Sharon Batty
63 Hatherley Road
Sidcup DA14 4AR
T 0181 308 9221
Mobile: 0973 516643; pager 01523 104926.
Two midwives provide total midwifery care in south east London & local Kent area. Happy for home or hospital births. Bathing pool for clients' use. Phone for price list.

RELIGIOUS ORGANISATIONS

Christchurch Women's Fellowship
Christchurch
The Broadway
Bexleyheath
T 0181 304 4303
Two groups: (a) meets first & third Thurs in each month; (b) meets second Tue afternoon in each month. Church-based women's groups, not necessary to be congregation member. Speakers, outings, wheelchair access.

SOCIAL

Bexley Village Ladies' Club
E Jeffrey
13 Ascot Court
Parkhill Road
Bexley DA5 1HS
T 01322 523275
Meets third Thurs in each month at John Fisher Roman Catholic Church Hall, Thanet Road, Bexley. Speakers each month. Outings.

TRANSPORT

Lady Birds
Bexley
T 0181 295 0101
Taxi service with women drivers operating in Bexley area.

WOMEN'S AID

Bexley Women's Aid
P O Box 25
Bexleyheath DA7 4BB
Office open Mon-Fri 9 am-5 pm. Otherwise a 24-hour helpline ansaphone service. Nine bedrooms for women & children available.

BRENT

ARTS AND CRAFTS

Shoe String Club
Mrs Lavinia Reynolds
Northolt Village Community Centre
Manor House
Ealing Road, Northolt
Middlesex UB5 6AD
Sewing club making soft toys, cushions, tea cosies. Stalls at fetes. Members are mostly retired ladies.

CENTRES FOR WOMEN

Asian Women's Resource Centre
108 Craven Park
London NW10 8QE
T 0181 961 6549 F 0181 838 1823
Open Mon-Fri 10 am-5 pm. Advice sessions on Wed 10 am-1 pm & Thurs 3-7 pm. Confidential advice on welfare rights, domestic violence, immigration, the police, etc. Advice line 0181 838 3462.

COUNSELLING AND THERAPY

Family Outreach Project
34 Craven Park
Harlesden
London NW10 8QN
T 0181 965 5480
Daycentre providing counselling, advice & practical experience to women experiencing boredom, depression. Open Tue-Thurs 10

am-5.30 pm; Fri 10 am-4 pm. Information technology Mon-Fri 9.30 am-4.30 pm.

EDUCATION

Shordene Women's Club
Mrs Edith Keen
80 Elton Avenue
Greenford
Middlesex UB6 0PR
T 0181 426 4763
Meets Wed 8-10 pm. Concerned with further education of women. Yearly conference; resolutions submitted re government legislation. Social events: discussions, speakers, craft work.

ETHNIC MINORITIES

All Muslim Women Association
Mrs Q Qureshi
57 West Ella Road
London NW10 9PT
T 0181 965 0894
Advice, support & information for Muslim women, girls & children. Special help for the disabled. Education, welfare, assistance, etc.

An-Nisa Society
Khalida Khan
Bestways Complex
2 Abbey Row
Park Royal
London NW10 7BW
T 0181 838 0311 F 0181 838 0311
A women-managed group catering for Muslim families. To regain harmony & balance. Encouraging natural ways of living. Health sessions Mon 10 am-1 pm. Free creche. Also women's health issues.

Asian People with Disabilities Alliance - Women's Forum
Disability Alliance Centre
Central Middlesex Hospital
The Old Refectory, Acton Lane
London NW10 7NS
T 0181 961 6773 F 0181 961 2797
Open Mon-Fri 9.30 am-5 pm. Highlights cultural/social needs of Asian people with disabilities. Campaigns for rights. Organises social events. Advocacy. Women's forum covers all women's issues as carers.

Family Connections/AAMCCI
Ronke Jomo-Coco
Community Health Resource Centre
Adunola House
13 Tatam Road
London NW10 8HT
T 0181 961 0268 F 0181 961 4142
Cultural services for those of African origin, especially for mental health & HIV/AIDS. Organises training & weekend clubs for affected children. Open Mon-Fri 10 am-6 pm; alternate Sat 10.30 am-5 pm.

Muslim Women's Association
Mrs Venish
63 Windermere Avenue
Wembley
London HA9 8QU
T 0181 904 1489
Promoting the educational needs of Muslim women. Training courses, outings, activities. Offers advice in a number of areas.

Navnat Vanik Bhagini Samaj
Mrs Roopal Pramod Punater
153 Chalklands
Wembley
Middlesex HA9 9DU
T 0181 908 0833 F 0181 908 0833
For Navnat women. Providing services, holding monthly meetings, organising cultural & religious programmes. Outings.

JEWISH WOMEN

League of Jewish Women - Edgware branch
Mrs Ruth Aharoni, Chairperson
59 Wood Lane
Kingsbury
Middlesex NW9 7PD
Meets at Edgware synagogue once a month. A voluntary organisation providing services such as meals on wheels, hospital visiting to people regardless of race or creed.

LARGER/TALLER WOMEN

Delia Marketing Ltd
Diana Whiston
24 Craven Park Road
London NW10 4AB
T 0181 965 8707 F 0181 965 4261
Special sized lingerie by mail order & in the shop.

PHOTOGRAPHY

Michele Photography
Michele Martinoli
152 Rucklidge Avenue
London NW10 4PR

T 0181 961 5207 F 0181 961 5207
Fashion & portrait photographer for models, actors, media people or anyone who needs professional pictures to enhance their business. Advertising & private commissions welcome.

RACIAL EQUALITY

Women's Development Group
Carol Thompson, Coordinator
C/o Brent Family Service Unit
60 Nicholl Road
London NW10 9AS
T 0181 453 0969 F 0181 961 9340
Meets approximately every three months to promote & develop anti-sexist practices & policies with the Brent FSU.

WOMEN'S AID

Brent Women's Aid
P O Box 2492
London NW10 5AF
T 0181 459 5414
A refuge for women suffering from domestic violence. Helpline open seven days a week 9 am-6 pm.

BROMLEY

BUSINESS SUPPORT SCHEMES

South London Training and Enterprise Council (Solotec)
Customer services
Lancaster House
7 Elmfield Road
Bromley BR1 1LT
T 0181 313 9232 F 0181 313 9245
Open Mon-Fri 9 am-5 pm. Offers free services for people starting up a business. Training for work programme. Support available for women on the SAFe scheme. Women in business forum.

CONTRACEPTION/WELL WOMAN

Downham Clinic
24 Churchdown
Downham
Bromley BR1 5PT
T 0181 695 6644
Free contraceptive advice/supplies. Clinics Tue 6.30-9 pm; Thurs 1.45-4.15 pm Well woman on alternate Tue 9.15-11.45 am Free, confidential service for women run by women. Advice/info on health topics.

COUNSELLING AND THERAPY

Beckenham MIND
Seamus Kelleher
20b Hayne Road
Beckenham BR3 4HY
T 0181 650 9540 F 0181 650 8372
A women's group meets on Mon 11 am-1 pm to discuss topical issues & discussion of women's issues.

MIND - Orpington
Anchor House
5 Station Road
Orpington BR6 0RZ
T 01689 811222 F 01689 816666
Women-only relaxation group on Mon 11 am-12.30 pm; women-only discussion group on Fri 11 am-12.30 pm (issues, topics, guest speakers).

Valerie J Bucknall
Valerie J Bucknall
26 Burnt Ash Lane
Bromley BR1 4DH
T 0181 290 6817
A psychoanalytic psychotherapist registed with the UKCP. Offers a safe place where people who have been abandoned or abused in childhood can explore their inner life & recover from trauma.

EDUCATION

North West Kent Graduate Women
Gwen Howell
9 Redroofs Close
The Avenue
Beckenham BR3 5YR
T 0181 663 1822
Meets for social & intellectual support & activities. Open to graduate women or women of equivalent status. Meets once a month in people's homes.

PREGNANCY/CHILDBIRTH

Bethesda (Pregnancy Advice)
Marion Osgood
21a The Mall
Bromley BR1 1TR
T 0181 313 9041 F 0181 313 9039
Helpline 0181 313 9893. Free pregnancy testing, counselling & support for women with unplanned pregnancies. Post abortion & miscarriage counselling. Phone for an appt. 24-hour ansaphone.

LONDON - CAMDEN

SPORTS AND LEISURE

Fitness Unlimited
Dawn Foreman
21 St David's Road
Hextable BR8 7RJ
T 01322 666822
Step, bums 'n tums, aerobics classes mainly around the Bexley area. Phone for further details.

TRANSPORT

Lady Birds
Bromley
T 0181 295 0101
Taxi service with women drivers operating in Bromley area.

South East London Dial-A-Ride
Unit 2 Lagoon Road
St Mary Cray
Orpington BR5 3QX
T 01689 896333
Door to door service for people with disabilities unable to use public transport. Seven days a week 8.30 a.m-11.30 pm. Fares similar to bus fares. Operating in Southwark, Lewisham, Greenwich, Bexley & Bromley.

CAMDEN

ACCOMMODATION

Chinese Women's Refuge Group
Swee Ling Yeow, Project Worker
209-215 King's Cross Road
London WC1X 9DB
T 0171 837 7297
Safe accommodation for Chinese women/children fleeing from domestic violence &/or sexual abuse. Advice, support & advocacy. Informal counselling. Access to legal information/assistance. Recreational activities.

Frontline Housing Advice
Sheron Carter
67-69 Chalton Street
London NW1 1HY
T 0171 388 2175 F 0171 388 2181
Open Mon-Fri 9.30 am-5.30 pm for telephone enquiries & appointments only; Mon & Thurs 2-4 pm drop-in. Housing advice agency aimed mainly at ethnic minority users. Languages offered.

Girls Alone Project (GAP)
Heather Petch

GAP House
76 Oakley Square
London NW1 1NH
T 0171 383 4103
Hostel for homeless women aged 16-21. Takes women from throughout London, with initial referral only, from social services, housing, voluntary organisations, etc. Stay is a year-18 months with support workers.

Shelter London
Kingsbourne House
229-231 High Holborn
London WC1V 7DA
T 0171 404 7447 F 0171 404 7771
Open Mon-Fri. 9 am-5.30 pm. Emergency advice for homeless on the night, people in priority needs & families. Free phone for all housing related problems: 0800 446 441. Publications. Training courses.

St Ursula's Hostel
P O Box 22, Official Division
London EC1A 1DD
T 0171 404 5443 F 0171 831 6132
Refuge for single women who are fleeing emotional, physical or sexual violence/sexual abuse. Advice & support provided. 30-bed refuge in Camden. No children. Phone 0171 831 3927/9616.

ALTERNATIVE THERAPIES

Feminist Aquarian Consciousness Tapes (FACT)
Jean Freer
BM-Liberation
London WC1N 3XX
Cassette tapes to assist in personal development. Visualisations for chakra cleansing, meeting your spirit guides & other meditations.

Royal London Homoeopathic Hospital
60 Great Ormond Street
London WC1N 3HR
T 0171 837 8833 F 0171 833 7269
Open Mon, Wed, Thurs, Fri 9.30-11.45 am & 2-4.45 pm. Referral from GP/hospital consultant only. Homoeopathic remedies for infertility, pregancy conditions, menstrual problems, endometriosis, cystitis, etc.

Women and Health Travelling Therapies Team
4 Carol Street
London NW1 0HU

LONDON - CAMDEN

T 0171 482 2786
Provides a course of complementary therapies for women who are housebound at low cost.

ARTS AND CRAFTS

Asian Women Writers' Collective
Kiran
C/o The Wheel
4 Wild Court
London WC2B 5AU
T 0171 793 0589
Phone the above number for enquiries. A group to support the growing number of Asian women writers seeking publication of their work.

Clean Break Theatre Company
Vedette Samuels
37-39 King's Terrace
London NW1 0JR
T 0171 383 3786 F 0171 388 7252
A theatre company for women who have experienced imprisonment or who have been before the courts.

Drill Hall Theatre
Julie Parker
The Drill Hall
16 Chenies Street
London WC1E 7EX
T 0171 631 1353 F 0171 631 4468
admin@drilhall.co.uk
Presents many shows that are of interest to women and lesbians in particular.

Ovatones
Lesley Wood
14 Lambs Conduit Passage
London WC1R 4RH
T 0171 404 6006 F 0171 404 6006
24-hour track recording studio, PA hire/live recording facilities, mainly for women. Training in all aspects of music technology; live & studio sound engineering for women. Music technology for schools.

Pascal Theatre Company
Julia Pascal
35 Flaxman Court
Flaxman Terrace
London WC1H 9AR
T 0171 383 0920 F 0171 383 0920
A theatre-producing company funded by Camden. Performs throughout Europe. Aim is to create and produce new writing. Particular encouragement is given to new women writers.

Single Bass
Jennifer Moore
BOM Material
London WC1N 3XX
T 0115 978 3489
jennifer@material.demon.co.uk
Singer/songwriter/electric bass guitarist. "One woman and her bass guitar". CD "Be Your Friend" released 1991.

BEREAVEMENT

Camden, City & Islington Bereavement Service
Neil Arnold
Instrument House
207-215 King's Cross Road
London WC1X 9DB
T 0171 833 4138 F 0171 837 5731
Free, confidential bereavement counselling to anyone in Camden, Islington & the City of London Corporation. Unlimited time framework.

BUSINESS SUPPORT SCHEMES

Camden Enterprise Ltd
Hane Howden, Director
Britannia House
4-24 Britannia Street
London WC1X 9JD
T 0171 278 5757 F 0171 278 3466
Open Mon-Thurs 8.30 am-5.30 pm; Fri 8.30 am-5 pm. Helping businesses employing less than 10 people & for those wishing to start a business in Camden.

CARERS

KIDS - Support Group for Carers
Mary Kells
Kingsgate Community Centre
107 Kingsgate Road
London NW6 2JH
T 0171 328 9480 F 0171 624 8067
Open Thurs 1-3 pm. Support group for mothers of children with disabilities. The women talk amongst themselves and bring advice and support for others.

CENTRES FOR WOMEN

Camden Young Women's Centre
Theresa Thomas and Liz Corder
4 Caversham Road

LONDON - CAMDEN

London NW5 2DU
T 0171 267 2898
Mon African/Caribbean Women's Group 3-6 pm; Tue drop-in 11 am-6 pm; Wed Young Mother's 12.30-2.30 pm (creche);Thurs Young Mothers & Young Carers Group 4-6 pm; Fri drop-in 10.30 am-12 noon, etc.

Church Army Women's Day Centre
1-5 Cosway Street
London NW1 5NR
T 0171 262 3818 F 0171 402 8752
Open Mon-Thurs 9.30 am-3.30 pm; Fri 9.30 am-2 pm. Day centre for women only. Hot & cold food, hot showers, career & employment guidance, legal advice, counselling, women's health sessions, craft groups.

Crossroads Women's Centre
230a Kentish Town Road
London NW5 2AB
T 0171 482 2496 F 0171 209 4761
Previously the King's Cross Women's Centre. Open Tue & Wed 12-4 pm & Thurs 5-7 pm. The base for 11 women's groups. Wheelchair accessible and accessible toilet facilities.

Hopscotch Asian Women's Centre
Sandra Machado, Project Coordinator
42 Phoenix Road
London NW1 1TA
T 0171 388 6200 F 0171 383 0963
Provides an opportunity for women to meet & give support to each other; outreach support; advice, counselling & information; health sessions; a range of adult classes; Family Literacy Project; etc.

West Hampstead Women's Centre
Jean Cross/Rukhsana Chishti
55 Hemstal Road
London NW6 2AD
T 0171 328 7389
Resource & information centre. Open Tue & Thurs 10 am-12.30 pm & 2-4.30 pm. Housing & social welfare advice & other women's groups.

WHEEL (Women's Health Education Entertainment Leisure)
Linda Eziquiel, Centre Manager
4 Wild Court
Kingsway
London WC2B 4AU
T 0171 831 6946 F 0171 831 6632
Open Mon-Fri 8 am-10 pm; Sat 8.30-10 pm. Meeting space for many women's groups, including lesbians. Regular events. Wheelchair access to all floors, including toilets. Induction loop.

CHILD CARE AND FAMILY

Alpha Beta Nursery
16 Kentish Town Road
London NW1 8NH
T 0171 482 2263
Open Mon-Fri 8.30 am-4.30 pm. Primarily for children of Greek Cypriot origin living in Camden. Phone for further details.

Parents & Co
Lucy Draper
St Margarets
25 Leighton Road
London NW5 2QD
T 0171 482 2593 F 0171 482 5014
Support for families & children under 5. Creche; playschemes; parenting skills; parents of special needs' children welcome. Support group for very young mothers. Open Mon-Fri 10 am-5 pm. Wheelchair access.

COMPUTERS/IT

Microsyster
The Wheel
4 Wild Court
London WC2B 4AU
T 0171 430 0655
Open Mon-Fri. Offers computer services for women working in the voluntary sector & women's groups. Offers training, consultancy, DTP. Mainly workplace training & one-to-one. Phone for up-to-date price list.

Women's Computer Centre Ltd
Erin Power
The Wheel
Third Floor
4 Wild Court
London WC2B 5AU
T 0171 430 0112
Computer training for women only open Mon-Fri 10 am-5 pm. Offers facilities in central London for women to learn about, use & expolore IT. Computer courses offered at reasonable prices. Drop-in facility.

CONTRACEPTION/WELL WOMAN

Belsize Priory Health Centre
208 Belsize Road
London NW6 4DJ
T 0171 530 2600 F 0171 530 2652

Free contraceptive advice & supplies. Clinics on Mon 5.15-7 p.m; Wed 5.15-7 pm; Thurs 1.45-3.30 pm & Fri 9.45-11.30 am (appointment necessary).

Crowndale Health Centre
59 Crowndale Road
London NW1
T 0171 530 3800
Free contraceptive advice & supplies. Clinics on Mon 5.30-7.00 pm; Wed 9.30-11.30 am & 1.30-3.30 pm (appointment required); Thurs 5.30-7 pm; Fri 9.30-11.30 pm (appointment required).

Daleham Gardens Health Centre
5 Daleham Gardens
London NW3
T 0171 530 4600
Free contraceptive advice & supplies. Clinic on Mon 5.15-7 pm. Appointment necessary.

Elizabeth Garrett Anderson Hospital
144 Euston Road
London NW1 2AP
T 0171 387 2501 F 0171 388 3197
Appts 0171 387 4598. Contraceptive advice & supplies Wed 9-11.30 am; well woman (by appt) Tue 3.30-6 pm; mamograms (by appt) Mon-Fri. Well woman drop-in Fri 9 am-12 noon & 1.30-3.30 pm.

Gospel Oak Health Centre
Lismore Circus
London NW5 4QF
T 0171 530 4600 F 0171 530 4629
Free contraceptive advice & supplies. Clinics open Mon 9.45-11.30 am; Tue 2-4 pm & 5.15-7 pm; Wed 9.45-11.30 am (appointment necessary) & 1.45-3.30 pm.

Hunter Street Health Centre
8 Hunter Street
London WC1N 1BN
T 0171 530 4300 F 0171 530 4301
Free contraceptive advice & supplies. Clinics on Mon 5.30-7 pm (appointment necessary); Wed 9.30-11.30 am and 1-3 pm; Fri 1.30-3.30 pm (appointment necessary).

Kentish Town Health Centre
2 Bartholomew Road
London NW5
T 0171 530 4700

Free contraceptive advice & supplies. Clinics on Tue 9.30-11.30 am & 1.15-3.30 pm; Wed 5.30-7 pm.

Solent Road Health Centre
9 Solent Road
London NW6
T 0171 530 2550
Free contraceptive advice & supplies. Clinic on Thurs 5.15-7 pm.

COUNSELLING AND THERAPY

Camden Centre
Sheryle Geen
95 Leighton Road
London NW5 2QJ
T 0171 482 4450
Psychotherapy & counselling with women therapists.

Camden Psychotherapy Unit
Instument House
207-215 King's Cross Road
London WC1X 9DB
T 0171 837 5628 F 0171 837 5731
Phone enquiries: Mon & Wed 9.30 am-2 pm; Tue 9.30 am-6 pm; Thurs 9.30 am-5 pm. Free or low cost psychotherapy services to people living in Camden who are experiencing psychological difficulties.

Women's Therapy Link
Helen Carroll or Mary Sarjeant
P O Box 2704
London NW5 2LW
T 0171 916 0123
Counselling & therapy offered to women. Qualified & experienced therapists have practices throughout London & home counties. Sliding scale of charges. Professional supervision, training, etc.

DISABILITY

Artsline
Roger Robinson
54 Chalton Street
London NW1 1HS
T 0171 388 2227 F 0171 383 2653
London's information & advice service for disabled people on arts & entertainment. Produces access guides to cinemas, theatres, tourist attractions. Mobile library service supplying videos & talking books.

Disability Arts in London (DIAL)
34 Osnaburgh Street
London NW1 3ND
T 0171 916 6351 F 0171 916 5396
Minicom 0171 916 6350. Provides monthly magazine acting as a voice for disabled artists & includes details of new access facilities in theatres, cinemas & other arts venues in London. Free to disabled people.

London Disability Arts Forum
34 Osnaburgh Street
London NW1 3ND
T 0171 916 5484
Above phone number is on minicom. For disabled working in partnership with DIAL (see separate entry) to promote disability arts & identification of a disability culture.

ETHNIC MINORITIES

Asian Leisure and Arts Planners (ALAAP)
Nasim Khan
25 Platts Lane
Hampstead
London NW3 7NP
T 0171 794 9640 F 0171 431 6073
nasim.khan@MCRI.poptel.org.uk
A consultancy made up of women of mainly Asian orgin that offers a specialist service to the public sector around Asian issues.

Asian Women and Families Project
Rezina Khaleque
Holborn Community Centre
Bedford House
35 Emerald Street
London WC1N 3QL
T 0171 405 2370
Open Mon-Fri 10 am-7 pm. Under 5s group; ESOL; sewing classes (Fri).

Asian Women's Group
Mary Kells
Kingsgate Community Centre
107 Kingsgate Road
London NW6 2JH
T 0171 328 9480 F 0171 624 8067
Open Tue 10 am-4 pm. Informal drop-in centre providing benefits advice & support relating to domestic violence. Health seminars, outings, advocacy work. Translations available. Asian newspapers.

Asian Women's Group - West Hampstead (HENNA)
Abbey Community Centre
222 Belsize Road
London NW6 4DJ
T 0171 624 1000

Bangladeshi Women's Health Project
Rezina Khaleque
Holborn Community Centre
35 Emerald Street
London WC1N 3QL
T 0171 405 2370
Open Thurs. Advice on general health matters. Women seen by a GP & if necessary sent to an appropriate clinic. Also women in groups.

Bengali Women's Health Forum
Kawser Zannath
C/o Bengali Women's Health Project
King's X Neighbourhood Centre
51 Argyle Street
London WC1H 8EF
T 0171 837 4025
Meets every two months. Advancing Bengali women's health in London.

Bengali Women's Health Project
M Ahmed
C/o Hopscotch Asian Women's Centre
42 Phoenix Road
London NW1 1TA
T 0171 388 1231
Sessions are held in various centres in Camden & Westminster. Incontinence advice sessions held at Hopscotch Asian Women's centre on second Thurs of each month 11 a.m-1 pm, etc.

Bengali Workers' Association
Aziz Choudhury
Surma Community Centre
1 Robert Street
London NW1 3JU
T 0171 388 7313 F 0171 387 8731
Open Mon-Fri 10 am-5.30 pm; Sat 12.30-5.30 pm. Helping all members of the Bengali community in Camden. Girls' & young women's groups aged 8-25 on Tue 3.30-7.30 pm & Sat 11 am-3 pm.

Camden Asian Young Women's Groups
Tahmina and Prabhat
C/o Camden Young Women's Centre
4 Caversham Road
London NW5 2DU
T 0171 267 2898
Two groups. One meets on Fri 3-5.30 pm at Parliament Hill School and the other on Sat

10 am-2 pm at Abbey Road Community Centre. Phone above number for further details.

Camden Black Sisters
2c Falkland Road
London NW5 2PT
T 0171 284 3336
For African/African Caribbean women living/working in Camden. Open Mon-Thurs 10 a.m-5 pm; Fri by appointment only. Counselling, support, advice, information, workshops, seminars. Library. Support groups.

Camden Chinese Community Centre
May Tsaney
173 Arlington Road
London NW1 7EY
T 0171 267 3019 F 0171 485 4108
Open Mon-Fri 9.30-5 pm. Nursery service, advice & information, women's group, elderly group, ESOL classes, housebound projects, youth club. Promoting equal opportunities for Chinese in Camden.

Camden Cypriot Women's League
Koula Ioannou, Coordinator
94 Camden Road
London NW1 9EA
T 0171 267 7194
For Cypriot women living in Camden. Drop-in centre with information on health, housing, welfare rights, legal advice. Young girls' group; mothers' & toddlers' group; elderly group. Open Mon-Thurs 10 am-5 pm.

Commission of Filipino Migrant Workers
Mary Jane de Belen
57 Charlton Street
London NW1 1HY
T 0171 388 5845 F 0171 383 7520
Open Mon-Fri 10 am-6 pm (Wed 10 am-3.30 pm) Community development centre for Filipinos: advice on immigration, health, employment, family law, domestic violence. Counselling seminars. Phone for appt.

Family Connections (FACO)
Ronke Jomo-Coco
Prosper House
146-154 Kilburn High Road
London NW6 4JD
T 0171 328 7251 F 0181 933 3767
To provide practical care, emotional & spiritual support for women & children of African descent who are living with HIV/AIDS &/or any other communicable diseases. Open Mon-Fri 10 am-6 pm.

Latin American Women's Rights Service
Patricia Garcia
4 Wild Court
London WC2B 4AU
T 0171 831 4145 F 0171 831 9710
Provides referral & advice service on health, education, housing, immigration & welfare rights for Latin American women living in London. Counselling service. By appointment only.

Refugee Mothers' Group
Etse Hiywet
Camden Family Service Unit
St Margarets
25 Leighton Road
London NW5 2DQ
T 0171 267 9717 F 0171 485 3301
Meets Thurs 11.30 am-1 pm. An open-ended group for refugee women who live in Camden. Advice, referral if necessary to other agencies. Outings. Visits to other women's groups.

Somali Women Drop-in Centre
Women and Health
4 Carol Street
London NW1 0HU
T 0171 482 2786

West Hampstead Asian Women's Group
Rukhsana Chishti
C/o West Hampstead Women's Centre
55 Hemstal Road
London NW6 2AD
T 0171 328 7389
Meets Wed 11 am-3 pm. Social group with emphasis on education, training & health. There is also an Asian girls' group at the Centre.

West Hampstead Somali Women's Group
Rukhsana Chishti
West Hampstead Community Centre
55 Hemstal Road
London NW6 2AD
T 0171 328 7389
Meets Fri 10 am-4 pm. ESL. Sewing classes.

GIRLS/YOUNG WOMEN

Alone in London Service
Dawn Brecken/Jenny Izekor
188 King's Cross Road

London WC1X 9DE
T 0171 278 4224 F 0171 837 7943
Drop-in Mon-Fri 9.30 am-1 pm Thurs by appt only. Information, advice, short-term counselling & referral for homeless aged up to 25. Help with finding accommodation. Wheelchair access - phone for assistance.

Brandon Centre
26 Prince of Wales Road
London NW5 3LG
T 0171 267 4792 F 0171 267 5212
For young people aged 12-25 depressed, anxious, in difficulties with families, etc & who are unable to find or cope with paid work. Bereavement counsellor; two women doctors; contraceptive advice & supplies.

Calthorpe Project Children's and Youth Groups
258-274 Gray's Inn Road
London WC1X 8LH
T 0171 837 8019
Girls' group for 8-14 year olds on Tue 5-7.30 pm

Holborn Community Centre's Girls' and Young Women's Project
Caroline Walker
Holborn Community Centre
Bedford House
35 Emerald Street
London WC1N 3QL
T 0171 405 2379
Wed 6.30-9 pm girls aged 12+, Thurs 4-7 pm young women with learning difficulties; Sat 12-3 pm. Asian girls & young women's group aged 11+.

HEALTH

Camden and Islington Drug Services
Michael Orr, Outpatient's Co-ordinator
Outpatient Drug Services
122 Hampstead Road
London NW1 2LT
T 0171 530 3086 F 0171 530 3085
Help with drug problems. Open Mon, Wed, Thurs 9 am-1 pm & 2-5 pm; Tue 9 am-1 pm & 2-7 pm; Fri 9 am-1 pm & 2-4 pm. Counselling & group therapy. Alternative drug prescribing. Self-referrals.

CASA Alcohol Services
Ella Risi/Hazel Jordan
55 Fortress Road
London NW5 1AD

T 0171 485 1945 F 0171 428 0318
Open Mon-Fri 10 am-5 pm. Individual counselling & group work at centre to anyone in Camden, Islington & Westminster with alcohol problems. Wheelchair access. Women's group on Wed afternoons.

Centrepeace
Eaine Kelly
3 Gloucester Avenue
London NW1 7AS
T 0171 267 8316
Tue 11 am-4 pm women's drop-in. Where people affected by HIV/AIDS can meet, find support, share experiences. Lunch, art therapy, relaxation, massage, Shiatsu, aromatherapy. Befriending.

Department of Genito-Urinary Medicine (GUM)
Royal Free Hospital
Pond Street
London NW3 2GT
T 0171 830 2047
Open Mon-Fri 9 am-7 pm (Wed 2-6 pm) Screening, STDs, smears, HIV testing, hepatitis testing, free condoms, emergency contraception, safer sex advice, sexual counselling. Phone for appointment.

Ian Charleson Day Centre
Pond Street
London NW3 2QJ
T 0171 830 2062
Helpline: 0171 431 0970 open Mon-Fri 9 am-5 pm. Bed ward & rooms offering full range of treatment & care for people living with HIV/AIDS. Same day testing.

Link, The - Camden
Esme Madiee
7 Church Studios
North Villas
London NW1 9AY
T 0171 267 1100 F 0171 267 0400
Minicom 0171 267 7440. Centre for people with HIV/AIDS & carers. Women & children only Thurs 10 am-3 pm, otherwise open Mon-Fri 10 am-6 pm. Counselling, legal advice, nurse specialists, support groups.

London Hazards Centre
Interchange Studios
Dalby Street
London NW5 3NQ
T 0171 267 3387

Open Mon, Tue, Thurs & Fri 10 am-12 pm & 2-5 pm. Provides information, advice, & training to trade unions & community groups in London on VDUs & other hazards. Publications.

Margaret Pyke Centre
Sarah Raynor
73 Charlotte Street
London W1P 1LB
T 0171 530 3600 F 0171 436 8394
NHS women's health: pregnancy testing, contraception, infertility, smear testing, psycho-sexual counselling, sterilisation & infertility. Drop-in Mon-Fri 9 am-3.30 pm; clinic appts Mon-Fri 9 am-6.15 pm

Mortimer Market Centre (UCH)
Capper Street
London WC1E 6AU
T 0171 530 5055
STDs & HIV testing. Clinics on Mon, Wed & Thurs 9 am-6 pm Tue 9 am-12 pm & 3.45-7 pm, Fri 9 am-2.45 pm.

Royal Free Hospital Menstrual Problem Clinic
Dept of Obstetric/Gynaecology
Royal Free Hospital
Pond Street
London NW3 2QG
T 0171 794 0500
Investigation of menstrual problems such as heavy periods, bleeding in between periods, bleeding after intercourse, after menopause, etc. Free service.

Royal Free Hospital Osteoporosis Scan
Roayl Free Hospital
Pond Street
London NW3 2QG
T 0171 794 0500 F 0171 830 2469
For women over aged 40. Free testing for osteoporosis. Appointments through GPs.

Women and Health
Daniele Lanarche
4 Carol Street
London NW1 0HU
T 0171 482 2786
Open Mon-Thurs 10 am- 8 pm, Fri 10 am-5 pm. Provides low cost health care for women who live or work in Camden. Groups, workshops & classes open to women regardless of geographical area.

Women's Health Forum
Sandra van der Feen
Interchange
Dalby Street
London NW5 3NQ
T 0171 837 8037
A forum set up to act as link between local health groups & authorities on women's health issues.

INTERNATIONAL

Empowerment Projects
Judith Crossland
48 Belsize Grove
London NW5 4TR
T 0171 586 8293 F 0171 586 8293
A consultancy that creates & coordinates projects that benefit women through self-employment activities in developing and redeveloping countries.

IRISH WOMEN

London Irish Centre
Vivien Harvey
50-52 Camden Square
London NW1 9XB
T 0171 916 2222 F 0171 916 2638
Community advice centre for Irish people living in London. Welfare, housing, advocacy, legal service. Open Mon-Fri 9.30 am-12.30 pm & 2-4 pm (Closed Wed morning & Fri afternoon.)

Solas Anois - Irish Women's Domestic Violence Project
Development Office
52 Camden Square
London NW1 9XB
T 0171 813 0595
Integrated service, including refuge provision for Irish women & their children escaping domestic violence.

JEWISH WOMEN

Jewish Gay and Lesbian Group (JGLG)
BM-JGLG
London WC1N 3XX
T 0181 905 3531 F 0181 905 3531
106257.3510@compuserve
Social group for all ages including women's focus evenings & lesbian visibility pub nights. Open Mon & Thurs 7-10 pm.

LONDON - CAMDEN

LARGER/TALLER WOMEN

Fat Women's Group
Diana Pollard
The Wheel
4 Wild Court
London WC2B 5AU
Meets on first Wed of each month. Newsletter: 'Fat News'. A non-dieting size-acceptance group for women providing advice & support.

Sixteen 47 Ltd/French & Teague
Susie Burgin, PR Officer
69 Gloucester Avenue
London NW1 8LD
T 0171 483 4174 F 0171 722 1627
Shop open Mon-Sat 10 am-6 pm. Office (0171 483 0733) open Mon-Fri 10 am-6 pm. Dawn French & Helen Teague's shop providing fashionable, high quality, big clothes for women.

LEGAL MATTERS

Burton Judith & Co
Museum House
25 Museum Street
London WC1A 1JT
T 0171 491 0048 F 0171 493 9241
Lesbian solicitors. Commercial/residential conveyancing; wills & probate; landlord & tenant; company & partnership; family; civil actions; employment law; debt; personal injury. Accepts legal aid work.

Camden Community Law Centre
2 Prince of Wales Road
London NW5 3LG
T 0171 485 6672 F 0171 267 6218
Drop-in Mon, Tue, Wed 10 am-5 pm; Fri 10 am-4 pm. Phone Mon-Fri 10 am-6 pm (Tue 2-6 pm) Advice on housing, immigration, employment, family matters, welfare, legal representation. Wheelchair access.

Free Representation Unit
49-51 Bedford Row
London WC1R 4LR
T 0171 831 0692
Arranges volunteer free representation for hearings before tribunals in emplyment, social security, criminal injuries compensation, immigration, rent & council tax. Takes cases via CAB, solicitors, etc.

Gay and Lesbian Legal Advice (GLAD)
Room D
10-14 Macklin Street
London WC2B 5NF
T 0171 831 3535
Minicom 0171 831 3555. Open Mon-Thurs 7-9 pm, otherwise ansaphone. Free & confidential legal advice & referrals to appropriate/sympathetic solicitors or other organisations.

Immunity Legal Centre
First Floor
32-38 Osnaburgh Street
London NW1 3ND
T 0171 388 6776 F 0171 388 6371
Enquiries Mon-Fri 10 am-1 pm & appointments 10 am-1 pm & 2-5 pm. Free & confidential legal advice & information for anyone with, or affected by, HIV/AIDS. Wheelchair access.

Mary Ward Legal Centre
Cheryl Allen
26-27 Boswell Street
London WC1N 3JZ
T 0171 831 7079 F 0171 831 5431
Free initial legal & debt advice, mainly in evening. Phone for an appt (Mon-Fri 9.30 am-7.30 pm). Languages offered. Wheelchair access.

LESBIAN

West Hampstead Black Lesbians 35+
Jean Cross
West Hampstead Women's Centre
55 Hemstal Road
London NW6 2HD
T 0171 328 7389
A social group meeting on first Sun of month 3-6 pm

LESBIAN AND BISEXUAL

Accommodation Address Service
66 Castle Road
London NW1 8SN
T 0171 267 7887
Open Mon-Sat 9.30 am-7 pm & Sun 10 am-1 pm. Confidential service for lesbians & gay men who choose not to receive their mail where they live. Straight women also welcome.

Box
Seven Dials 22
Monmouth Street
Covent Garden
London WC2H 9DA

LONDON - CAMDEN

T 0171 240 5828
Lesbian & gay cafe & bar. Open Mon-Sat 11 am-11 pm Sun noon-10.30 pm. Lesbian only Sunday evening (Box Babes). Covent Garden tube.

First Step
B M Box 1992
London WC1N 3XX
T 0181 461 4112
Lesbian & gay support group for young people in south London. Advice & information. Meets Mon 7.30-10 pm

Gay and Lesbian Humanist Association
Conway Hall
25 Red Lion Square
Holborn
London WC1
Meets second Fri of each month at above address.

Gay's The Word
66 Marchmont Street
London WC1N 1AB
T 0171 278 7654
Bookshop with lesbian, gay & bisexual publications. Open Mon-Wed, Fri & Sat 10 am-6 pm; Thurs 10 am-7 pm; Sun 2-6 pm

Gay's The Word Discussion Group
66 Marchmont Street
London WC1N 1AB
T 0171 278 7654
Discussion group for lesbians Wed 8 pm. Support, discussion, etc.

London Bisexual Helpline
BM BI
London WC1N 3XX
T 0181 569 7500
Telephone service: counselling, information & support for all bisexual people. Line open Tue & Wed 7.30-9.30 pm & Sat 10.30 am-12.30 pm

London Lesbian Line
Mary Rogan
BM Box 1514
London WC1N 3XX
T 0171 251 6911
Minicom: 0171 253 0924. Help, advice, support, information phoneline for lesbians & women exploring their sexuality & others affected by this. Helpline open Mon & Fri 2-10 pm; Tue, Wed, Thurs 7-10 pm.

London Lesbian Parenting Group
Anne
T 0171 249 9951
Support group for all lesbians who are parents or who are planning to be parents.

Older Lesbian Network
C/o The Wheel
4 Wild Court
London WC2B 4AU
For lesbians aged 40+. Meets on third Sat of each month 12.30-5.30 pm in Community Rooms, 50 Millman Street, London WC1 (Camden). For more information, write to above address.

Regard
Kath Gillespie Sells
BM Regard
London WC1N 3XX
T 0171 738 8097 F 0171 738 8097
A campaigining & befriending group for disabled lesbians & gay men. Quarterly newsletter.

Salsa-Rosada
7 Wakefield Street
London WC1
T 0171 813 4831
Salsa classes for lesbians & gay men. Classes on Wed. Beginners 7-8 pm; intermediates 8-9 pm & 9-10 pm.

Salsa-Rosada
Stephanie Lipton
11 Woburn Court
Bernard Street
London WC1N 1LA
T 0171 813 4831 F 0171 837 3752
Salsa club & salsa classes for lesbians & gay men.

West Hampstead Lesbian Umbrella
West Hampstead Women's Centre
55 Hemstall Road
London NW6 2AD
T 0171 328 7389
Meets every third Sunday in the month from 3-6 pm. Planned activity with outings, including trips out of London.

Young Lesbian Group
Joanna/Liz/Theresa
Camden Young Women's Centre
4 Caversham Road
London NW5 2DU

T 0171 267 2898
Meets Mon 6-9 pm at above address.

Libraries/Archives
Stephanie Colasanti
Stephanie Colasanti
38 Hillside Court
409 Finchley Road
London NW3 6HQ
T 0171 435 3695 F 0171 435 9995
Photo-stock library. Medium format. World travel. 50,000 transparencies in stock.

Manual Trades
Camden Training Centre
57 Pratt Street
London NW1 0DP
T 0171 482 2103 F 0171 284 2340
Open Mon-Fri Training courses for people with few or no educational qualifications. Specialist techniques in painting & decorating - women only - 18 months five days a week. Limited wheelchair access.

Media
Capital Radio Helpline Services
Euston Tower
London NW1 3DR
T 0171 388 7575
Lines open Mon-Fri 10 am-10 pm; Sat 8 am-8 pm; Sun 10 am-4 pm. Confidential off-air advice & information from counsellors with wide range of experience & expertise. Referral to other organisations.

Paradise Pictures
Anya Camilleri
2 Hillside
Highgate Road
London NW5 1QT
Film production company. Develops moves for television & for the big screen.

Older Women
Care Alternatives
College House
4a New College Parade
Fincley Road
London NW3 5EP
T 0171 586 6800 F 0171 586 6952
Provides flexible care at home for elderly or disabled people. Can assist with both personal care & domestic tasks. Care workers do induction training & are thoroughly vetted.

Greater London Pensioners' Association
the secretary
Interchange Studios
Dalby Street
London NW5 3NQ
Meets last Fri each month at Camden Town Hall, Euston Road, NW1. Defends interests of pensioners by all means possible, including pensions, health care, free & safe travel, old people's homes, home helps, etc.

SPH Care and Repair
St Richard's House
110 Eversholt Street
London NW1 1BS
T 0171 209 9203
Service for older & disabled people who are owner-occupiers or private tennants. Works in Camden, Islington & City. Advice on repairs & adaptations their homes may need. Organises finances & technical support.

Photography
Ritva Raitsalo Photographer
Ritva Raitsalo
11 Glenmore Road
London NW3 4BY
T 0171 586 6906
Highly original style of manipulating photographs. Commissions for bookjackets by major publishers. Exhibitions include Helsinki Arts Festival, Whitechapel Open Studios; Association Gallery; etc.

Pregnancy/Childbirth
Camden and Islington Community Midwives' Serivce
2nd Floor Obstetric Hospital
Huntley Street
London WC1E 6AU
T 0171 380 9696 F 0171 380 9565
Available Mon-Fri 8.30 am-4.30 pm. In-labour telephone enquiries 0171 380 9567.

Prisoners/Prisoners' Wives
Creative and Supportive Trust (CAST)
Petronella Davis
37-39 King's Terrace
London NW1 0JR
T 0171 383 5228 F 0171 388 7252
Open Mon-Fri 10 am-5 pm. Helps women prisoners, women ex-offenders, women who

have been in psychiatric, drug & alcohol rehabilitation. Advice on housing, child custody benefits. Training & education, etc.

PUBLISHERS/PUBLICATIONS

Compendium Women's Desk
234 Camden High Street
London NW1 8QS
T 0171 485 8944   F 0171 267 0193
Also phone 0171 267 1525. Open Mon-Sat 10 am-6 pm & Sun 12-6 pm. Feminist, lesbian, women's health interests, etc.

Diva
Gillian Rodgerson, Editor
Millivres Ltd, Ground Floor
Worldwide House
116-134 Bayham Street
London NW1 0BA
T 0171 482 2576
diva@gaytimes.co.uk
Lesbian bi-monthly news & style magazine.

Loki Books Ltd
Marion Baraitser, Director
38 Chalcot Crescent
London NW1 8YD
T 0171 722 6718   F 0171 722 6718
all@lokibooks.u-net.com
Small press specialising in fiction/drama by new Israeli women wirters. Aims to discover & bring into the English language new, exciting texts from minority languages.

Silver Moon Women's Bookshop
64-68 Charing Cross Road
London WC2H 0BB
T 0171 836 7906   F 0171 379 1018
Open Mon-Sat 10 am-6 pm (Thurs until 8 pm); Sun 12-6 pm. Large selection of titles by or about women. World-wide mail order service. Wheelchair access to ground floor. Events held.

RACIAL EQUALITY

Camden Health and Race Group
Marueen Brewster
Instrument House
207-215 King's Cross Road
London WC1X 9DB
T 0171 713 0522
Identifying issues of concern relating to health & community care needs of Black & other ethnic minority communities; lobbying & campaining to improve services; forum for information sharing & networking, etc.

SERVICES

Capital Careers
78 Parkway
London NW1
T 0171 482 3996
Open Mon-Fri 9.30 am-4.30 pm. Offers careers guidance, help with cvs, information & help with getting a job. For Camden residents. Phone for further details.

Women's Resource Centre
The Wheel
4 Wild Court
London WC2B 4AU
T 0171 405 4045
WIRE (Women's Information & Referral Exchange) advice line open 11 am-4 pm four days a week; resource library open Tue 10 am-12 noon; Thurs 4-6 pm; crisis referral system for women in emergencies, etc.

SEXUAL ABUSE/RAPE CRISIS

In Support of Sexually Abused Children (ISO-SAC)
Angela Rivera
P O Box 526
London NW6 1SY
T 0171 284 2125
Helpline open Mon-Fri 10 am-4 pm. Telephone counselling for mothers of sexually abused children. Short-term counselling for adult survivors of child sexual abuse from a feminist perspective.

London Rape Crisis Centre
P O Box 69
London WC1X 9NJ
T 0171 916 5466   F 0171 916 5519
0171 837 1600 free counselling Mon-Fri 6-10 pm & Sat & Sun 10 am-6 pm Run by women for women & girls who have been raped/sexually assaulted at any time in their lives. Legal & medical advice/information.

London Rape Crisis Training Project
P O Box 69
London WC1X 9NJ
T 0171 916 5519   F 0171 916 5519
Training (in house) & courses about rape & sexual violence issues for women working in voluntary, statutory & private sectors. Phone for details about prices as they vary according to income.

Survivors of Incest Anonymous
The Wheel

4 Wild Court
London WC2B 5AU
T 0171 831 6946
Meets Sat 5.30-7 pm. Open survivors' group for women.

West Hampstead Incest Survivors' Group
Jean Cross/Rukhsana Chishti
55 Hemstal Road
London NW6 2AD
T 0171 328 7389
Meets on Mon. A self-help support group.

Women Against Rape London
Lisa Longstaff
Crossroads Women's Centre
230a Kentish Town Road
London NW5 2AB
T 0171 482 24496
Phone Mon-Fri 10 am-12.30 pm & 1.30-4 pm; Thurs 5-7 pm. Centre open Tue & Wed 12-4 pm; Thurs 5-7 pm Mail: P O Box 287, London NW6 5QU. Counselling, support, legal advice, information, campaigning.

Social

Drill Hall Women's Bar
Julie Parker
The Drill Hall
16 Chenies Street
London WC1E 7EX
T 0171 631 1353 F 0171 631 4468
admin@drillhall.co.uk
The Drill Hall Women's Bar runs every Mon evening. Very friendly & a great place for women new to the London scene to make contacts. Reasonably priced bar & friendly staff.

Hampstead Women's Club
Joyce Diamond
T 0181 458 5127
Provides a networking/social organisation for north American women in London for a few years usually because of a husband's transfer & who have chosen not to work while in the UK.

Spirituality/Ecofeminism

Wood and Water
77 Parliament Hill
London NW3 2TH
Goddess-centred, feminist influenced pagan quarterly. Mixed collective. Articles, fiction, poetry, reviews, news.

Sports and Leisure

Sequinpark Women's Health Club and Gym
81-84 Chalk Farm Road
London NW1 8AR
T 0171 284 0004
Open Mon-Thurs 7.15 am-10 pm; Fri 8.30 am-9 pm; Sat & Sun 8.30 am-4 pm. Women-only gym. All-day aerobics. Steam. Running club.

Women's Football Project
Mary Kells
Kingsgate Community Centre
107 Kingsgate Road
London NW6 2JH
T 0171 328 9480 F 0171 624 8067
Meets Tue 5-6 pm. A group of women play football informally ... and have fun.

Support

Camden Mediation Service
11-17 The Marr
Camden High Street
London NW1 0HE
T 0171 383 0733 F 0171 383 7110
Open Mon-Fri 10 am-5 pm. Free, confidential dispute resolution servides provided by trained volunteers living/working in Camden to Camden residents experiencing difficulties with neighbours.

Desert Winds
Mary Ward House
5 Tavistock Place
London WC1H 9SN
T 0171 387 9681
To help the emotional, physical & spiritual well-being of people living with & affected by HIV/AIDS. Retreats, counselling, support.

Doorstep
Kim Smith
13a Broadhurst Gardens
London NW6 3QX
T 0171 372 0413
Drop-in centre for families with children in temporary accommodation. Play sessions, free laundry facilities, children's clothing. Advice on welfare, housing, etc. Under 5s session Mon 10.30 am-12 pm

MIND in Camden
Deltine Patterson
9-15 Camden Road
London NW1 9LQ

LONDON - CAMDEN

T 0171 911 0822 F 0171 911 0825
Supports emotionally stressed people.
Women's group offers assertiveness training, relaxation, food & self-image workshops, art & counselling. Mon 11 am-4.30 pm women's day centre (phone 0171 911 0820).

People First of the London Boroughs
Alice Etherington, Coordinator
Instrument House
207-215 King's Cross Road
London WC1X 9DB
T 0171 713 6400 F 0171 883 1880
Open Mon-Fri 9.30 am-5 pm. Offers advice/ information to people with learning difficulties, service providers/ employers. A campaigning project, run by people with learning difficulties.

Women First
Alice Etherington, Coordinator
C/o People First of the London Boroughs
Instrument House
207-215 King's Cross Road
London WC1X 9DB
T 0171 713 6400 F 0171 883 1880
Offers special advice on health, personal safety, etc to women with learning difficulties & teaches people without learning difficulties about the rights & needs of people with learning difficulties.

TRAINING

Boyden Howard Associates
Anne Howard or Tina Boyden
26 Raglan Street
London NW5 3DA
T 0171 482 4299
Training & consultancy providing training for women on finance & self-development. One hour's free consultancy to readers of this directory.

Women's Training Link
L Jean-Baptiste
4 Wild Court
London WC2B 4AU
T 0171 242 6050 F 0171 430 1506
Training courses for women, including driving instructor's course. Counselling course. Also ESOL, training in childcare & education, guidance & career counselling. Drop-in Thurs 1-5 pm. Wheelchair access.

TRANSPORT

Camden Community Transport
Arlington Road Works Depot
B Block
211 Arlington Road
London NW1 7HD
T 0171 911 0958 F 0171 916 0229
Provides transport to community groups & individuals at low cost. Office open Mon-Fri 9.30 am-5 pm. Trains minibus drivers (0171 911 0955). Runs driving school. Provides women drivers on request to women.

VIOLENCE AGAINST WOMEN

First Step Centre
Rosemary
218 Eversholt Street
London NW1 1BD
T 0171 383 2876 F 0171 383 0851
24-hour helpline: 0171 267 1917. Open Mon-Fri 9.30 am-8 pm; Sat 12.-3 pm. Offering legal advice & referral on domestic violence, child abuse, harassment to vulnerable women & children. Wheelchair access.

Monica Tuohy
London
T 0171 328 9117 F 0171 372 3642
Helpline Mon-Fri 10 am-4 pm. For women experiencing domestic violence. No wheelchair access.

Multi-Agency Domestic Violence Forum
Annette Webb
193-195 Kentish Town Road
London NW5 2JU
T 0171 267 6744 F 0171 284 2355
Meets every four months. Developing an inter-agency strategy on domestic violence in Camden. A domestic violence action group meets monthly.

West Hampstead Domestic Violence Support Group
Jean Cross or Rukhsana Chishti
West Hampstead Women's Centre
55 Hemstal Road
London NW6 2AD
T 0171 328 7389
Meets Tues 11 am-1 pm. Support for women given by women.

WORKING WOMEN

English Collective of Prostitutes
Niki Adams
Crossroads Women's Centre
230a Kentish Town Road
London NW5 2AB

T 0171 482 2496 F 0171 209 4761
Phone lines open Mon-Fri 10 am-4 pm.
Network of women working at various levels of the sex industry. Campaigning for sex workers to be recognised as workers legal, economic & civil rights. Help & support.

Corporation of London

Accommodation

Women's Link - Women's Housing Advice in London
1st Floor Suite
8-9 Giltspur Street
London EC1A 9ED
T 0171 248 1200 F 0171 248 1570
Open Mon-Thurs 10 am-4 pm; Fri 1-4 pm.
Accommodation advice service for women, Londonwide. Phone for an appointment. Runs ex-offenders project with London prisons. Publications.

Counselling and Therapy

Just Ask Counselling and Advisory Service Ltd
Davina Lilley
46 Bishopsgate
London EC2N 4AJ
T 0171 628 3380 F 0171 628 3370
Open Mon-Thurs 10 am-6 pm, Fri 10 am-5 pm. Free information, listening & referral help line, open to everyone. Free counselling for young people up to age 35 who are homeless, unemployed, low waged.

Finance

Berkeley Morgan Ltd
Shaheena Pall
Hulton House
161-166 Fleet Street
London EC4A 2DY
T 0171 936 2408 F 0171 353 1404
Independent financial adviser; financial advice to individuals & corporations. Areas include pensions, mortgages, insurance, investment, tax & estate planning. Contactable Mon-Fri 9 am-7.30 pm.

Health

Barts Sexual Health Centre
St Bartholomew's Hospital
West Smithfield
London EC1A 7BE
T 0171 601 8090
Screening for STDs, HIV testing, contraceptive advice & supplies, cytology, psychosexual counselling (phone for durther details). Drop-in service on Mon, Thurs & Fri 9 am-3 pm & Tue & Wed 2-6.30 pm.

St Bartholomews Sexual Health Centre
West Smithfield
London EC1A 7BE
T 0171 601 8888
Drop-in clinic, STDs testing, HIV testing, contraceptive advice & supplies. 'Women for women' on Tue mornings. Clinics on Mon, Thurs & Fri 9 am-3 pm & Tue & Wed 2-6.30 pm.

Croydon

Arts and Crafts

Ringway Needlecraft Class
Mrs J Hetherington
15 Rectory Park
Sanderstead
Croydon CR2 9JQ
T 0181 857 7980
Meets Wed 10 am-12 pm at Ringway Centre, 268 Baring Road, Grove Park SE12 0DS. Tuition in many aspects of needlecraft: lacemaking, cross-stitch, tatting, embroidery, canvas work. Beginners welcome.

Child Care and Family

Tumble Tots Croydon
Karen McGee
18 Canal Walk
Croydon CR0 6BZ
T 0181 406 5200
Physical, pre-school activity for children aged 6 months to 5 years. Gym for babies. Meets Mon-Fri at different centres: Kenley, Coulsdon, South Croydon, Thornton Heath & central Croydon.

Contraception/Well Woman

Broad Green Centre
1-3 Lodge Road
Croydon CR0 2PD
T 0181 665 7485
Free contraceptive advice/supplies. Clinics Mon 12-2 pm & 5.30-7.30 pm; Wed 12-2 pm; Thurs 5.30-7.30 pm; Fri 9.30-11.30 am Well woman by appt Thurs 9 am-1 pm. Blood pressure & breast checks & info.

Parkway Health Centre
Parkway
New Addington
Croydon CR0 0JA
T 01689 842117

Contraceptive advice/supplies. Clinics on Mon 2-4 pm & Thurs 5.30-7.30 pm. Free service.

Purley Community Health Clinic
62 Whytecliffe Road North
Purley CR8 2AR
T 0181 660 3549
Free contraceptive advice & supplies. Clinics on first, third & fifth Mon of each month 5.30-7.30 pm.

Sanderstead Clinic
40 Rectory Park
Sanderstead
Croydon CR2 9JN
T 0181 651 5122
Free contraceptive advice & supplies. Clinics on second & fourth Mon of each month 5.30-7.30 pm & Tue 9.30-11.30 am.

Shirley Clinic
135 Shirley Road
Shirley
Croydon CR0 7LR
T 0181 655 2041
Free contraceptive advice & supplies. Clinics on Tue 5.30-7.30 pm.

Shrublands Clinic
Shrublands Youth & Community Centre
Shrublands Avenue
Shirley
Croydon CR0 8JA
T 0181 777 8239
Free contraceptive advice & supplies Tue 1-3 pm.

Thornton Heath Health Centre
61a Gillett Road
Thornton Heath CR7 8RL
T 0181 684 2424
Free contraceptive advice & supplies. Clinics on Wed 5.30-7.30 pm.

COUNSELLING AND THERAPY

Croydon Community Unit and Counselling Centre
R St Elmo-Ross
118 Windmill Road
Croydon CR0 2XQ
T 0181 684 1715
Counselling, elderly lunch club, refugee matters. Family group for women on Thurs 11 am-3.30 pm Wheelchair access.

ETHNIC MINORITIES

Asian Mother and Child Group
Hansa Shah
81 Galpins Road
Thornton Heath CR7 6EN
T 0181 689 4173
Meets Mon 1-3 pm in term time. For mothers with children. Playgroup with creche workers. Cooking, craftwork, speakers.

Croydon Asian Women's Organisation
Mrs Jahangir
38 Broadgreen Avenue
Croydon CR0 2ST
T 0181 684 8739 F 0181 689 6015
Meets at Eldon House, 78 Thornton Road, Thornton Heath, CR7 6BA on Fri 6-8 pm. For Asian women aged 18-60. For women to meet & discuss various issues. Health seminars, cookery classes, etc.

Jagruti Asian Women's Group
Mrs Madhu Patel, Coordinator
Eldon House
78 Thornton Road
Thornton Heath CR7 6BA
T 0181 689 8492
Meets on Tue & Thurs 1-4 pm at Winterbourne Youth Centre, Winterbourne Road, Thornton Heath. Activities include: yoga, exercise, Diwali, Christmas party, day trips, readings. Speakers are invited.

New Addington Sangum
Mrs Charu Patel
Goldcrest Community Centre
Goldcrest Way
New Addington CR0 0PL
T 01689 849074
Meets at the Centre on Wed 1-3 pm. Social support group for Asian women. Social, cultural, educational & recreational activities. Several Asian languages spoken.

Turkish Youth and Community Association
Nilay Emek
14 Willis Road
Croydon CR0 2XX
T 0181 665 0425 F 0181 665 1977
Women only health session Tue 12.30-3 pm. Creche Mon, Tue, Thurs & Fri. Women's health discussion Sat 12-2 & 2-4 pm. Outings for women only to combat isolation. English language classes.

LONDON - CROYDON

GIRLS/YOUNG WOMEN

Goldcrest Youth Centre
Goldcrest Way
New Addington CR0 OLP
T 01689 843333
A young women's group meets on Thurs 12-3 pm. A safe environment for women to meet & gain empowerment through peer support. Creche. Talks on health & First Aid.

Samuel Coleridge-Taylor Centre
Mrs E Miller
194 Selhurst Road
Croydon CR25 6XX
T 0181 653 3449 F 0181 653 7886
After school club 3.30-5 pm; counselling Mon, Wed & Fri 2-4 pm; centre for young people Mon-Fri 7-10 pm: computers, library, art/drama classes, photography, health education. Girls' group Thurs 7-10 pm

HEALTH

Drug Concern Croydon
Keith Thomas
76a Southbridge Road
Croydon CR0 1AE
T 0181 681 8113 F 0181 686 1038
Open Mon-Fri 9.30 am-5.30 pm. Drug counselling, advice/information to drug users & friends. Self referral. Family support group; needle exchange; assessment for rehabilitation; home visits to disabled.

Fairfield Club - MIND in Croydon
Sally or Mike
10 Altyre Road
Croydon CR0 5LA
T 0181 688 1210
Women only group for women with mental health problems meets Fri 1.30-4.30 pm.

Genito Urinary Medicine (GUM) Clinic
Mayday University Hospital
Mayday Road
Thorton Heath CR7 7YE
T 0181 401 3002
Health adviser 0181 401 3004. Clinic for women only Tue 9-11 am; Mon & Thurs 2-5 pm Sexual health screening & advice; referral to other agencies if required. HIV testing & counselling; hepatitis vaccine.

LARGER/TALLER WOMEN

Long Tall Sally
Unit 1, Peterwood Way
Beddlington Farm Road
Croydon CR0 4UQ
T 0181 649 9119 F 0181 649 9449
Clothes for the taller woman sizes 12-20.
Open Mon-Sat 9.30 am-5.30 pm; Sun 10 am-4 pm. For mail order phone 0181 649 9009.

OLDER WOMEN

ARP Over 50 - Croydon and Purley Centre
J R Rose
65 Buxton Lane
Caterham CR3 5HL
T 01883 344292
Meets first Wed of each month 2 pm. Different venues weekly for aerobics, knitting for Red Cross, classical music, rambles, pub lunches, etc. Newsletter. No women only events but mainly women participants.

Parchmore Tuesday Club
Jean Lammond
4 Limpsfield Avenue
Parchmore CR7 6BE
T 0181 684 3553
For women aged 45+. Group meets at Parchmore Church & Community Centre, Parchmore Road, Thornton Heath on Tue 2-4 pm. Speakers. Wheelchair access.

PRISONERS/PRISONERS' WIVES

Outmates
Anne Lockett
C/o South East London Probation Service
Church House
Old Palace Road
Croydon CR0 1AX
T 0181 686 6551 F 0181 688 4190
Emotional & practical support for the partners & families of prisoners. Creche facilities available.

RELIGIOUS ORGANISATIONS

Salvation Army - Croydon
Captain Mrs M Dockerill
Women's Fellowship
Booth Road
Croydon CR0 1XY
T 0181 688 2038
Women's Fellowship meets Mon 7-8.30 pm for younger women members (up to aged 50): cake & flower decorations etc. Also Home League for older women retired members meets Wed 10.30 am Wheelchair access.

St Philip's Women's Fellowship
Marion Crawley, President
3 Namton Drive
Thornton Heath CR7 6EP
T 0181 689 4593
Meets at St Philip's Church Hall, Beech Road, Norbury usually on fourth Wed on each month at 8 pm. Church based group but open to any woman living in parish or beyond. Speakers, outings, Christmas party.

SEXUAL ABUSE/RAPE CRISIS

Rape and Sexual Abuse Support Centre
Trish Stokes
P O Box 383
Croydon CR9 2AW
T 0181 239 0099 F 0181 239 0101
Open Mon-Fri 12-2.30 pm & 7-9.30 pm & Sat & Sun 2.30-5 pm. Helpline 0181 239 1122. Free support & counselling. Escort service. Talks & training.

SINGLE PARENTS

Christian Family Concern
Hazel Taylow, Chief Exectuive
42 South Park Hill Road
Croydon CR2 7YB
T 0181 688 0251 F 0181 686 7114
Drop-in centre for mothers & their children, open Mon-Thurs 10 am-2 pm. Also a scheme for pregnant women & their children, if any.

Croydon Playcare Company
Paula Carter/Del Wilson
Gingerbread Corner
Grenaby Avenue
Croydon CR0 2EG
T 0181 683 1183 F 0181 665 6876
All services offered to one parent families. Day nursery 8 am-6.30 pm. Out of school: 7.45 am-school start/school end-6.30 pm. Holidays: 8 am-6.30 pm.

Croydon Welcare
Eileen King
1 Ramsey Court
Church Street
Croydon CR0 1RF
T 0181 688 5151 F 0181 686 7185
Social work agency working with lone parents & their children, offering practical & emotional support. Information & advice on a range of issues, including parenting, relationship issues, family violence.

SOCIAL

Caterham Women's Guild of Friendship
Mrs G D Phillips
33 Homestead Road
Caterham CR3 5RN
T 01883 343011
Meets on third Wed of each month 7.30-10 pm at Douglas Brunton Day Centre, Park Road, Caterham. Social club with speakers. Outings to theatres, restaurants, etc.

Coulsdon Ladies Guild
Mrs J Owen, Secretary
116 Woodcote Grove Road
Coulsdon CR5 2AF
T 0181 660 5313
Meets on third Tue of each month from 2-4 pm from September-July each year at the John Saunders Room, Coulsdon Methodist Church, Brighton Road, Coulsdon.

SPORTS AND LEISURE

Croydon Camogie Club
40 Nova Road
Croydon CR0 2TL
T 0181 688 4941
Meets at Purley Way playing fields on Wed 7.30 & Sun 12-2 pm. Camogie is an Irish women's field sport. Modified version of Hurling; team sport with 12 aside. Looking for new players: women of any age welcome.

Redoubtables Women's Cricket Club
Mrs C Driver, Secretary
2 Manor Way
Purley CR2 3BH
T 0181 668 3061

TRANSPORT

Before and After Dark - Croydon Women's Safe Transport
Berni Excell
Cornerstone House
14 Willis Road
Croydon CR0 2XX
T 0181 665 0861 F 0181 665 1972
For women living in the London borough of Croydon. Service runs Mon-Thurs 6.30-11 pm. Book up 24 hours in advance. Daytime service by arrangement. Wheelchair access on vehicles. Also phone 0181 665 0918.

Croydon Community Transport
Marjorie Grindrod
Cornerstone House

14 Willis Road
Croydon CR0 2XX
T 0181 665 0137
Open Mon-Fri 8 am-2 pm Minibus hire to voluntary groups in Croydon & for people who cannot use public transport. Three buses for wheelchairs.

Ladycars
Sue Hutchinson
49 Shirley Road
Croydon CR0 7ER
T 0181 655 3959
Operates 7.30 am-12.30 am Mon-Wed & 7.30 am-3 amThurs-Sat. Minicab service for anyone who prefers to travel with a female driver.

EALING

ARTS AND CRAFTS

Ogressers, The
Anne F Johnson
28 Dorset Road
Ealing
London W5 4HU
T 0181 579 7651
Storytellers, poets, musicians.

Skin You're In, The
Anne F Johnson
28 Dorset Road
Ealing
London W5 4HU
T 0181 579 7651
Storytellers, poets & musicians.

Society of Women Artists, The
Barbara Tate, President
Willow House
Ealing Green
Ealing
London W5 5EN
Annual open exhibition at Westminster Gallery.

BUSINESS SUPPORT SCHEMES

City Women's Network
P O Box 353
Uxbridge
London UB10 0UN
T 01895 272178
To promote active networking on a business, professional & social level; for members to exchange views on business issues & other areas of interest; to promote professional & personal contacts, etc.

Sharma Associates
Nita Sharma
47 Hessel Road
London W13 9ER
T 0181 346 0611
Runs 'Women in Business' course of five workshops (run three times a year). Free. For women thinking to start a business or for those who have been doing so for 18 months.

CONTRACEPTION/WELL WOMAN

Marie Stopes Parkview Clinic
Sue Baldock, Manager
87 Mattock Lane
London W5 5BJ
T 0181 567 0102 F 0181 567 3636
Pregancy advice (helpline 0171 388 4843); general healcare/contraception (helpline 0171 388 0662); sterilisation services (helpline 0171 388 5554); well woman clinics; abortion clinics; menopause clinics; etc.

COUNSELLING AND THERAPY

Ealing Youth Counselling Information Service (EYCIS)
55 High Street
Acton
London W3
T 0181 992 8182
Youth counselling service for women aged 14-25. Counselling available Mon & Tue 2-5 pm & 6.30-9.30 pm; Wed 10 am-1 pm, 2-5 pm & 6-9.30 pm. Fri 2-5 pm. Drug users Thurs 10 am-12 noon & 2-5 pm.

TASHA in Ealing
Pat Howerd
24 Uxbridge Road
Ealing
London W5 2BP
T 0181 579 7475
Open Mon-Fri 9.30 am-5.30 pm. Confidential information, advice, support, counselling, holistic health care to individuals affected by tranquillisers, sleeping pills, stress, anxiety, depression, agoraphobia.

ETHNIC MINORITIES

Armenian Information and Advice Centre
Hayashen
105 Mill Hill Road
Acton
London W3 8JF
T 0181 992 4621
Open Mon-Fri 9.30 am-4.30 pm. Information & advice for women, especially refugee

women. English language classes for older refugees. Interpretation & translation in Armenian, Russian & Farsi.

Indian Workers' Association
P S Khabra
112a The Green
Southall
Middlesex UB2 4BQ
T 0181 574 7283
Provides advice & casework in Asian languages on various matters such as housing, employment, immigration, domestic violence & welfare rights.

Society of Afghan Residents in the UK
Ahmad Karwani, Coordinator
West Acton Community Centre
Churchill Gardens
Acton
London W3
T 0181 993 8168
Advice & information on immigration, welfare benefits, housing, health, legal problems & education. There is a women's group. Also a full range of social, religious & cultural activities.

Somali Women's Refugee Centre
Amina Ali
Priory Community Centre
Acton Lane
London W3 8NY
T 0181 896 0566 F 0181 896 0566
Promoting any charitable purpose for the benefit of women & their children of Somali origin. Also phone 0181 752 1787.

Southall Black Sisters
52 Norwood Road
London UB2 4DW
T 0181 571 9595 F 0181 574 6781
Provides information & resources for Black women, particularly those experiencing domestic violence. Expertise on the needs of Asian women. Language interpreting available in Hindi, Punjabi & Gujerati.

Southall Day Centre
Mrs Santofh Kanwar
20 Western Road
Southall
Middlesex UB2 5DX
T 0181 574 0902
Open every day 10 am-7 pm. For Asian women of all ages. Companionship, mutual support, information, advice, counselling, recreational & cultural activities. Transport for older, disabled & housebound women.

HEALTH
Ealing Spectrum
P O Box 8242
Ealing
London W5 4WJ
T 0181 758 1351
Self-help group for people affected by HIV/AIDS, providing holistic health care programme designed to improve health & lifestyle. Referral agency.

LARGER/TALLER WOMEN
Bra Box, The - Taplin's Ltd
Mrs Taplin
26c Broadway
West Ealing
London W13 0SU
T 0181 567 6152
Bras in all sizes from 32-48 with cup fittings B-GG. Open Mon, Tue, Thurs, Fri & Sat 9.30 am-5 pm. Catalogue available.

PHOTOGRAPHY
Acton Community Arts Workshop
Norma Constable
T 0181 992 5791
Formerly Bottom Drawer Exhibitions. A women's arts organisation promoting the production & exhibition of women's photography/mixed media work.

RELIGIOUS ORGANISATIONS
Norwood Road Sisterhood Southall
Miss V R Puttick
St John Ambulance Hall
Norwood Road
Southall
Middlesex
T 0181 574 7641
Aims to win people for Jesus Christ. Promoting the practical expression of religion. Encouraging the exercise of Christian citizenship. Meets Wed 2-4 pm.

Women's Guild - Ealing
Mrs Margaret Hunter
Pitshanger Methodist Church
Pitshanger Lane
London W5 1QP
T 0181 997 3230

Meets first Wed of each month (except August) at 8 pm. Devotional meetings.

SERVICES

Lighthouse Marketing
Uta Grieser
3a Shakespeare Road
Hanwell
London W7 1LT
T 0181 840 9627   F 0181 840 9647
Individual marketing consultancy services; marketing workshops; practical help with implementation; business coaching; management & leadership training; NLP-based training.

SOCIAL

Dolphin Women's Club
Mrs P Agate
7th Greenford Scout Hall
Greenford Road
Greenford
Middlesex
T 0181 578 0157
Meets Wed 8-10 pm. Social club for women aged 18+.

SPORTS AND LEISURE

Alpha Women's Amateur Rowing Club
Mrs Nina Padwick
12 Woodville Road
Ealing
London W5 2SF
T 0181 997 5671   F 0181 997 5671
Open for training on Thurs eve, Sat afterns & Sun morns. Facilities based at Mortlake. Club welcomes beginners & will take them through from that stage to International representation. There is a blind section.

TRANSPORT

Dial-A-Ride
Capricorn House
The Bilton Centre
Walmgate Road, Perivale
Middlesex UB6 7LR
T 0181 970 0090
Provides transport for carers if person cared for is unable to use public transport to get to dentist or a hospital. All vehicles wheelchair accessible. A charge is made for the distance travelled.

Gainsborough Cars
Claire/David
173 South Ealing Road
Ealing
London W5 5TE
T 0181 568 3333
Female cab service covering all London areas.

West London Dial-A-Ride
Capricorn House, Bilton Centre
Walmgate Road
Perivale
Middlesex UB6 7LR
T 0181 970 0090
Door-to-door service for disabled people who can't use public transport. Seven days 8.30 am-11.30 pm. Fares similar to bus fares. Covering Hounslow, Hill'don, Harrow, Brent, Ealing, parts of Ham. & Fulham.

ENFIELD

ALTERNATIVE THERAPIES

Phoenix Therapy Centre, The
Maureen Jackson
Phoenix House
12 Overton Road
Oakwood
London N14 4SY
T 0181 360 7019
Past life regression & healing; hypnotherapy & psychotherapy - relationships - confidence - panic attacks - fears - phobias - stress - eating disorders, etc. Counselling. Specialists in women's issues.

ARTS AND CRAFTS

Electra Strings
Sonia Slany
100 Village Road
Enfield
London EN1 2EX
T 0181 360 4975
Mobile 0973 159563. An all-woman string quartet. Plays for parties, conferences, weddings. Also a studio quartet with 8 years recording experience in pop, jazz & rock music.

CENTRES FOR WOMEN

Enfield Women's Centre
Debbie Dean, Publicity Officer
31a Derby Road
Enfield
London EN3 4AJ
T 0181 443 1902

For women & their families in Enfield. Counselling for women & 11-17-year-olds; training courses in eg assertiveness, interview skills/cvs; survivors of sexual abuse group, eating disorders group, etc.

CHILD CARE AND FAMILY

Hanlon Centre
Jack Lyons
Hanlon Centre
Lawrence Road
Edmonton
London N18 2HN
T 0181 803 8292
Youth club. After school care. Under 5s playgroup. Wheelchair access. Open 9-6 daily.

Moorfields Family Centre
Joyce Hammersley
2 Moorfield Road
Enfield
London EN3 5TU
T 0181 805 6313
Drop-in on Wed 9.30-11.30 am Parents to stay with their children. Range of activities supervised by qualified staff. Aromatherapy for babies Thurs 2-3.30 pm. Toy library 9.30-11.30 am.

CONTRACEPTION/WELL WOMAN

Bowes Road Clinic
Dr Hampton
269 Bowes Road
London N11 1BD
T 0181 368 2051
Well woman health checks: blood pressure, weight checks, urine tests, etc on alternate Fri 9.30 am-12 pm. Phone for an appointment. Wheelchair access.

Clinic 4
Chase Farm Hospital
The Ridgeway
Enfield
London EN2 8JL
T 0181 366 6600
Free contraceptive advice & supplies: pills, coils, diaphrams, condoms, etc contraception on Tue & Thurs 9.30-11.30 am Outside these hours the clinic is a woman's health centre for gynaecological problems.

Edmonton Central Clinic
Plevna Road
Edmonton
London N9 0BU
T 0181 807 1632
Free contraceptive advice & supplies: pills, coils, diaphrams, condoms etc, & well woman health checks - blood pressure, urine tests, etc on Mon & Wed 6.30-8.30 pm & Sat 9.30-11.30 am Wheelchair access.

Forest Road Health Centre
2a Forest Road
Edmonton
London N9 8RX
T 0181 805 1429
Free contraceptive advice & supplies: pills, coils, diaphrams, condoms & emergency (after sex) contraception & well woman health checks - blood pressure, urine tests, etc on Wed 1-3.30 pm Wheelchair access.

Ian McDonald Ward
North Middlesex Hospital
Sterling Way
London N18 1QU
T 0181 887 2540
Contraceptive advice & supplies Tue 6.30-8 pm; Fri 9.30-11 am Hysterectomy group last Sun of every month 3 pm. Endometriosis group.

Lincoln Road Clinic
Bush Hill Park
Enfield
London EN1 1LJ
T 0181 363 1949
Free contraceptive advice & supplies: pills, coils, diaphrams, condoms & emergency (after sex) contraception on Mon & Thurs 6.30-9 pm; Fri 9.15-11.30 am Wheelchair access.

Merryhills Clinic
118 Enfield Road
Enfield
London EN2 7HL
T 0181 363 8228
Free contraceptive advice & supplies: pills, coils, diaphrams, condoms, & emergency (after sex) contraception on Wed 6.30-8.30 pm. No appointment required. Wheelchair access.

Moorfield Road Health Centre
Moorfield Road
Enfield
London EN3 5PS
T 0181 805 1632

Free contraceptive advice & supplies: pills, coils, diaphrams, condoms, etc & well woman health checks (blood pressure, urine tests, etc) on Mon 6.30-8.30 pm; Wed 9.15-11.45 am; Sat 10 a.m-12.30 pm.

North London Nuffield Hospital, The
Cavell Drive
Uplands Park Road
Enfield
London EN2 7PR
T 0181 366 2122
Well woman screen. Full female health assessment. Phone for up-to-date price lists.

Ridge House Clinic
Church Street
London N9 9JT
T 0181 360 6456
Free contraceptive advice & supplies: pills, coils, diaphrams, condoms & emergency (after sex) contraception on Tue 6.30-8.30 pm.

Silver Street Clinic
Sterling Way
Edmonton
London N18 1QU
T 0181 807 8321
Free contraceptive advice & supplies: pills, coils, diaphragms, condoms & emergency (after sex) contraception & well woman health checks, blood pressure, urine tests on Tue 6.30-8.30 pm Wheelchair access.

St Stephen's Clinic
St Stephen's Road
Enfield
London EN3 5UH
T 0181 804 1074
Free contraceptive advice & supplies: pills, coils, diaphrams, condoms & emergency (after sex) contraception & well woman health checks, blood pressure, urine tests etc on Tue 6.30-8.30 pm Wheelchair access.

COUNSELLING AND THERAPY

Enfield Counselling Service
Julia Darmon
St Paul's Centre
102a Church Street
Enfield
London EN2 6AR
T 0181 367 2333
Phone to make an appointment Mon-Fri 10 am-12 pm & 6-8 pm Woman counsellor can be requested. Reasonably priced. No wheelchair access.

Jocelyn Barker
Jocelyn Barker
45 Elmcroft Avenue
Wanstead
Enfield
London E11 2BN
T 0181 530 3858
Counselling & psychotherapy for individuals - person-centred, integrative approach. Daytime or evening sessions. Fees negotiable. Experienced in long- & short-term work, including counselling in primary care.

ETHNIC MINORITIES

African Women's HIV Support Group
Pippa McNicol
The House, Enfield HIV Centre
17 Chase Side Crescent
Enfield
London EN2 0JA
T 0181 363 6660
For African women who are positive & for family. Group meets Sun 3.30 p.m once a month. Free. Creche. The House is for anyone affected by HIV/AIDS who can receive care according to their particular needs.

Asian Day Care Centre
Mrs Rhaja
129-139 South Street
Ponders End
Enfield
London EN3 4PX
T 0181 443 1197
Open Tue, Wed & Fri 9 am-4 pm. Day care facilities, health programmes, diet talks, breast screening, keep fit for elderly Asian women. Free services & free transport to the centre. Wheelchair access.

Community Aid Asian Project
S N Shansad
Ponders End Area Office
Curlew House, 4 Napier Rd
Enfield
London EN3 4QW
T 0181 443 4361
Drop-in Centre Thurs 11 am-4 pm & ESOL Thurs 1-3 pm at 31a Derby Road, Ponders End women only, phone 0181 443 1902; talks for women: health issues; women's only swimming on Sat, Edmonton Leisure centre.

LONDON - ENFIELD

Enfield Bangladesh Women's Society
Mrs Bakar
33 Ashridge Gardens
London N13 4JA
T 0181 245 5909
The group meets every 5-6 weeks at different venues providing support with children. Translation.

Enfield Saheli
Community House
311 Fore Street
Edmonton
London N9 0PZ
T 0181 345 5904
Meets daily 9.30 am-5.30 pm, plus 24 hour ansaphone. Group for all Asian women providing advice on social, cultural, civic life in Enfield. Workshops, coffee mornings. Wheelchair access. Phone first.

Greek & Greek Cypriot Women of Enfield
Litsa Worral
Community House
311 Fore Street
Edmonton
London N9 0PZ
T 0181 803 3600
Office open Mon-Fri 10 am-3 pm. Drop-in Thurs 3-7 pm. Provides advocacy, benefits help and community care to all Greek and Greek Cypriot women living in Enfield. Wheelchair access.

MIND Asian Women's Group - Enfield
Sufia Rahman/Shirley Scott
5 St James Chambers
North Mall
Edmonton Green
London N9 0UD
T 0181 807 0977
Drop-in for Asian women suffering mental health problems/emotional distress on Tue 12.30-4 pm. Sewing classes, refreshments, health education, keep fit, outings.

Nehanda
C/o Enfield Women's Centre
31a Derby Road
Enfield
London EN3 4AJ
T 0181 443 1902
For African/Caribbean women & dependants in Enfield. Meets Fri 7-9 pm. Information, advice, support through formal & informal discussions. Also speakers, training & workshops covering eg education & health.

Ponders End Youth Centre
129-137 South Street
Enfield
London EN3 4PX
T 0181 804 5908
Muslim Girls' Group "Sisters of Islam" & other groups. Phone for further details.

Tamil Refugee Centre
Community House
311 Fore Street
Edmonton
London N9 0PZ
T 0181 887 0644
Open Mon-Fri 10 am-4 pm. Drop-in for women who want advice about health matters, benefits & education. Catering to women's & children's needs. All services are free. Wheelchair access.

HEALTH

Enfield and Haringey Breast Screening Service
Mrs Etuk
North Middlesex Hospital
Sterling Way
Edmonton
London N18 1QU
T 0181 887 2135
Open Mon-Fri 9 am-5 pm. Breast screening only. No charge for service. Wheelchair access.

Enfield Community Drug Team
Mary McDermott
2a Forest Road
Edmonton
London N9 8RX
T 0181 443 3272
Open Mon-Thurs 9 am-1 pm & 2-5 pm. Fri 9 am-1 pm & 2-4 pm. On-site needle exchange. Referrals for detox. & rehab. Advice on safer sex/safe drug use. Crisis intervention. Free service, etc.

LESBIAN AND BISEXUAL

Enfield Lesbian & Bisexual Group
C/o Enfield Women's Centre
31a Derby Road
Enfield
London EN3 4AJ
T 0181 443 1902
Meets weekly at Centre. Open to all women questioning their sexuality. A forum for women to discuss topics of mutual interest;

an opportunity for women to meet others who have similar life experiences, etc.

OLDER WOMEN

Bullsmoor Ladies' Fellowship
Mrs V Webb
St John's Methodist Church
Jews' Avenue
Enfield
London EN1
T 01992 760533
Meets Wed 2-3.30 pm. For women aged 60+. Telephone first to confirm meeting. Wheelchair access.

RELIGIOUS ORGANISATIONS

Women's Fellowship
Mrs Urwin
Methodist Church
Park Drive
Winchmore Hill
London N21
T 0181 360 5654
Meets Tue 2.30 pm. Speakers, entertainment, devotional activities. Wheelchair access.

SOCIAL

Co-op Ladies' Friendly Group
Mrs Hodgkins
Co-Operative Hall
444 Hertford Road
Enfield
London EN3 5QH
T 0181 363 6242
Meets Tue 7.30 pm. Speakers, quizzes, bingo, outings. Wheelchair access.

First Tuesday Group
Miss W Sansbury
Christ Church Hall
Chase Side
Enfield
London EN2
T 01992 719590
Meets first Tue of each month at 1.30 pm Mainly for older women. Speakers on various subjects, eg reflexology, cake decorating, etc.

SPORTS AND LEISURE

1.45 Women's Club
Cheryl
The Church in the Orchard
Grange Park
London N21
T 0181 360 5759
Meets Wed 1.45 pm. Keep fit, yoga, speakers, demonstrations. Wheelchair access.

Exercise to Music
Southgate Leisure Centre
Winchmore Hill Road
London N14
T 0181 967 9534
Women only exercise to music 9.45-10.45 am Phone above number to book sessions.

Middlesex Women's Hockey Association
Miss Jan Kirkland, President
50 Bush Hill Road
Winchmore Hill
London N21 2DT
T 0181 364 1752
Organisation of hockey in Middlesex from the age of 8 upwards to adults. 28 clubs in the county are affiliated to Middlesex, together with over 30 schools. Coaching of players & umpires provided.

Women Only Swimming
Arnos Pool
Bowes Road
New Southgate
London N11
T 0181 967 9534
Women only swimming 9-9.30 am & 9.30-10 am Also at Albany Pool, Hertford Road, Enfield NE3 on Wed 9-9.30 pm & 9.30-10 pm. Phone above number to book sessions.

Yoga for Women
Southgate Leisure Centre
Winchmore Hill Road
London N14
T 0181 967 9534
Yoga for women only Tue 10 am Yoga for women only also at Edmonton Leisure Centre, Plevna Road, London N9 on Thurs 9.45-10.30 am Phone above number to book sessions.

TRAINING

Enfield College - ESOL Unit
Ros Staines
Enfield Women's Centre
31a Derby Road
Ponders End
London EN3 4AJ
T 0181 805 5694

Teaching English to refugees/asylum seekers. Home tutor scheme, mainly for women with small children. No charge for part-time classes which are four hours per week.

Simpson Training Services
Judyth E Simpson
8 Abbotts Crescent
Enfield
London EN2 8BT
T 0181 372 8365   F 0181 372 8365
First aid at work training; specialist first aid training (eg women motorists, etc), training in specific hazards (oxygen therapy, cyanide poisoning, hydrofuoric acid burns); basic training in food hygiene.

TRANSPORT
North London Dial-A-Ride
Units C/D
Regents Avenue Industrial Est
Palmers Green
London N13 5UR
T 0181 829 1200
Door-to-door service for people with disabilities unable to use public transport. Seven days a week 8.30 am-11.30 pm. Fares similar to bus fares. Operating in Enfield, Barnet, Hackney, Islington & Haringey.

VIOLENCE AGAINST WOMEN
Enfield Domestic Violence Unit
Sergent Sue Reed
Enfield Police Station
41 Baker Street
Enfield
London EN1 3EU
T 0181 345 1465
Condidential support & advice for people in close relationships & carers. Open Mon-Sat 8 am-4 pm.

GREENWICH

ALTERNATIVE THERAPIES
Greenwich Natural Health Centre
Ren Harding
Neptune House
70 Royal Hill
Greenwich
London SE10 8RT
T 0181 691 5408
Open from 9 am daily. Sat 10 am-12 p.m/ drop-in & counselling session for women only on general health matters. Payment by donation. Therapies include aromatherapy, reflexology, counselling, Shiatsu.

ARTS AND CRAFTS
Greenwich Dance Agency
Debbi Christophero
The Borough Hall
Royal Hill
Greenwich
London SE10 8RT
T 0181 293 9741   F 0181 858 2497
The agency runs community dance activities, performances and professional training. Its classes are predominantly attended by women and its Raqs Sharqi (Egyptian dance) classes are for women only.

Spare Tyre
Clair Chapman
West Greenwich House
141 Greenwich High Road
London SE10 8JA
T 0181 305 2800   F 0181 305 2800
Women's theatre company providing theatrical training for both women & men. Some women-only groups, particularly older women, catered for.

BUSINESS SUPPORT SCHEMES
Greenwich Enterprise Board
Jane Holman
26 Burney Street
Greenwich
London SE10 8EX
T 0181 305 2222   F 0181 858 7010
Provides start-up business advice & training to people living in Greenwich, Lewisham, Bexley & Bromley. Free services to clients (by appointment only). Women-only returners' courses.

Women's Business Network, Greenwich and S E London
Shirley Porter
C/o Greenwich Enterprise Board
26 Burney Street
Greenwich
London SE10 8HA
T 0181 305 2222   F 0181 858 7010
To promote business & employment opportunities for women living & working in south east London. Also to raise the profile of women in business, the arts & public life.

CARERS
Greenwich Carers
Miss Jaqueline Evans
Unit E38
Macbean Centre

Macbean Street
London SE18 6LW
T 0181 316 7866 F 0181 316 1171
Information, advice, practical support to carers (people looking after friends/relatives at home with disabilities & illnesses) in Greenwich. Open Mon-Fri 9 am-4.30 pm 24-hour helpline: 0181 316 7866.

CENTRES FOR WOMEN

Greenwich Asian Women's Centre
Daljeet Lall
45 Hare Street
Woolwich
London SE18 6NE
T 0181 317 4141
Advice, support, assistance & guidance to Asian women. Case work on benefits, emotional support. Prioritises domestic violence cases. Mother tongue classes on Sat.

CHILD CARE AND FAMILY

Eastcombe Avenue Respite Care Centre
79 Eastcombe Avenue
London SE7
T 0181 858 2178
Provides respite and day care for children with a severe learning disability in Greenwich.

Greenwich Playcare Ltd
Jennie Wolfe
C/0 St Mary's Chuirch
Greewich Street
Woolwich
London SE18 5AR
T 0181 317 3194
Mobile creche providing creches for meetings, conferences, seminars, open days, etc. Any time, any day. Open to all children aged 3 months to 12 years. Managed by a workers' cooperative. Qualified childcarers.

CONTRACEPTION/WELL WOMAN

Abbeywood Clinic
186 Eynaham Drive
London SE8
T 0181 310 2360
Contraceptive advice & supplies Fri 1.30-3.30 pm. Emergency contraception also available.

Charton Lane Clinic
82 Charlton Lane
London SE7
T 0181 317 9415
Contraceptive advice & supplies Wed 9.45 am-1 pm & 1.30 -3.30 pm. Emergency contraception also available.

Garland Road Clinic
30 Garland Road
Plumstead
London SE18
T 0181 855 2372
Contraceptive advice & supplies on second, third & fourth Wed of each month & every Thurs 10 am-12 noon. Emergency contraception also available.

Greek Road Clinic
19 Greek Road
Deptford
London SE8
T 0181 32 9483
Contraceptive advice & supplies Tue 10 am-12 noon. Emergency contraception also available.

Greenwich District Hospital
Reception Area 6
Outpatients' Department
London SE10
T 0181 858 6141
Contraceptive advice & supplies Fri 6-8 pm.

Kidbrooke Health Centre
10 Telemann Square
Ferrier Estate
London SE8
T 0181 856 9604
Contraceptive advice & supplies Mon 6.30-8.30 pm; Tue 6.30-8.30 pm; Wed 9-11 am Emergency contraception also available.

Langton Way Clinic
175 Langton Way
Blackheath
London SE3
T 0181 858 8898
Contraceptive advice & supplies. Youth advisory clinics on Mon & Tue 7-9 pm. Emergency contraception also available.

Market Street Health Centre
16-20 Market Street
Woolwich
London SE18
T 0181 317 9415
Contraceptive advice & supplies. Drop-in youth advisory service Mon 4-8 pm & Thurs 7-9 pm. Contraception clinics for all ages

Wed 7-9 pm. Emergency contraception also available.

Plumstead Health Centre
Tewson Road
London SE18
T 0181 816 7374
Contraceptive advice & supplies Tue 5.30-7.30 pm & Thurs 6.30-8.30 pm. Emergency contraception also available.

St Marks Health Centre
Wrotleslay Road
London SE18
T 0181 317 3297
Contraceptive advice and supplies Tue 9.30-11.30 am Emergency contraception also available.

Disability

Greenwich Assn. of Disabled People's Ctr. for Independent Living
Christchurch Forum
Traflagar Road
London SE10 9EQ
T 0181 305 2221
Minicom 0181 858 9307. Open Mon-Fri 10 am-4 pm. Welfare night Wed. Advice & information on welfare, preparing own care package. Advocacy for disabled people aged 16-25. Counselling. Training project.

Environment

Greenwich Sustainable Millenium Network
David Sharman
55 Mayhill Road
London SE7 7JG
T 0181 305 2196 F 0181 305 2196
A network of people who care about Greenwich & the community & who want to do something to improve it for the next millennium. Sets out to bring people together around key issues to work towards common ground.

Ethnic minorities

Greenwich Asian Women's Art Group
Arti Prashar
C/o Greenwich Young People's Theatre
Burrage Road
London SE18 7JZ
T 0181 317 4904
A community arts organisation in the educational sector promoting Asian women.

Creates awareness & access of arts to women.

Sahara - Asian Careers' Project
Sahida Awan, Project Manager
Unit F2
MacBean Centre
MacBean Street
London SE18 6LW
T 0181 855 0172
Open Mon-Fri 9.30 am-5 pm. Supports Asian carers in the community with advice, drop-in centre, seminars & discussion groups, home care in Greenwich, young Asian carers.

Health

Beresford Drugs Project
Madeline Long
8 Beresford Square
London SE18 6BB
T 0181 854 9518
Open Mon-Fri 9 am-5 p.m and drop-in Wed 1.30-5.30 pm. Drug counselling, support, advice and information. Needle exchange. Interpreters available.

Genital Urinary Medicine (GUM) Clinic
Greenwich District Hospital
London SE10
T 0181 312 6056
Clinics Mon & Thurs 8.30 am-7 pm; Tue, Wed & Fri 8.30 am-5 pm. Emergency contraception & sexually transmitted diseases. Phone for an appointment.

Greenwich and Bexley Council on Alcohol and Drugs
1 Woolwich New Road
London SE18 6EX
T 0181 316 5958 F 0181 854 7689
Open Mon-Fri 9.30 am-4.30 pm. & some weekday evenings & daytime weekends. Counselling & treatment of alcohol & drug problems. There is a women's group. Residential rehabilitation hostel.

Larger/Taller Women

Seconde Choix
Beryl Mason
30 The Village
Charlton
London SE7 8UD
T 0181 856 0606
Ladies' dress agency, specialising in sizes 16+ with some selected sizes 14 & under. Also provides beauty therapies: chiropody,

holistic massage, reflexology, Bach flower consultations.

OLDER WOMEN
Age Exchange Reminiscence Centre & Theatre Trust
Pam Schweitzer
11 Blackheath Village
London SE3 9LA
T 0181 318 9105 F 0181 318 0060
Open Mon-Sat 10 am-5.30 pm. Performs reminiscence theatre & provides workshops, mostly with pensioners. Community cafe and museum where people can come to record their memories. Full wheelchair access.

PHOTOGRAPHY
Rogues Gallery
Susie Monkhouse
3 Mell Street
Greenwich
London SE10 9TU
T 0181 853 1545
A Greenwich-based professional portrait photographer.

PREGNANCY/CHILDBIRTH
Crisis Pregnancy Centre - Greenwich
Mrs J Church
316 Plumstead High Street
London SE18 1JT
T 0181 854 3615
Open Mon-Fri 9.30 am-5.30 pm. Free pregnancy testing, counselling & support for women with unplanned pregnancies. Post abortion/miscarriage counselling. Phone for appt.

PUBLISHERS/PUBLICATIONS
Women & Children First
14 The Market
Greenwich
London SE10 9HZ
T 0181 853 1296
Open Mon-Fri 10 am-5 pm, Sat & Sun 10 am-5.30 pm. Bookshop with large collection of children's books & women's books.

RACIAL EQUALITY
Greenwich Action Committee Against Racist Attacks
1-4 Beresford Street
London SE18 6BB
T 0181 855 4343
Open Mon-Fri 9 am-5 pm. 24-hour helpline 0956 921901. Campaigns against racial attacks. Carries out individual case work. Monitors racial attacks & police & council responses. English, Hindi, Punjabi, Urdu.

RETAILING
Cotton Moon Ltd
Suzanne Youles
P O Box 280
London SE3 8DZ
T 0181 305 0012 F 0181 319 8345
Mail order company selling 100 % cotton clothing for children from 0-8 years old. Emphasis on casual & comfortable easy care garments. Also a selection of gifts. Phone for up-to-date catalogue.

SERVICES
Ann-O-Gram
Annie King
11 Wycherley Close
Vanbrugh Park Road West
London SE3 7QH
T 0181 853 6368 F 0181 853 6368
Corporate hospitality, events, gift finding, staff-incentives, unusual venues, historic buildings, theatre visits. Particularly events for the millenium celebrations.

SPORTS AND LEISURE
Nexus Netball Club
A Asante
80 Pinto Way
Kidbrooke
London SE3 9NN
T 0181 319 2930
Training sessions held at Blackheath Wanderers Sports Ground, Eltham Road, Lee, SE12 on Mon 7.30-9 pm. Women only & looking for women to join. Contact phone number above.

VIOLENCE AGAINST WOMEN
Support and Befriending Services (SABS)
Clockhouse Community Centre
Definace Walk
Woolwich Dockyard Estate
London SE18 5QL
T 0181 317 0088
24 hour helpline outside office hours. For women & children victims of abuse. Trained counselling service by appointment & crisis

LONDON - HACKNEY

drop-in. Support group meets 11 am-12 noon for victims to meet others.

HACKNEY

ACCOMMODATION

Ackee Housing Project
Angela Clinkett
103 Stoke Newington Road
London N16 8BX
T 0171 254 5159
Temporary accommodation for Black single women aged 17-21.

ALTERNATIVE THERAPIES

Clissold Park Natural Health Centre
154 Stoke Newington Church Street
London N16 0JU
T 0171 249 2990
Open Mon-Fri 9 am-7 pm (closed 1-2 pm) & Sat 9 am-5 pm. Homoeopathic drop-in clinic on Mon, Wed & Fri 5 pm. Acupuncture, Alexander Technique, aromatherapy, counselling/psychotherapy, etc.

Clissold Park Natural Health Centre - Courses
154 Stoke Newington Church Street
London N16 0JU
T 0171 249 2990
Year-round courses for women only, eg Astrology for Women, Anger - Friend or Foe?, Reflexology for women, Aromatherapy for women.

ARTS AND CRAFTS

Ashwin Furniture Workshop
Charlotte Everett
The Printhouse
18 Ashwin Street
Dalston Junction
London E8 3DL
T 0171 241 3825 F 0171 275 9914
Five women in a collective run the Workshop, making both their own designed craft work and wooden furniture to commission. Temperate hardwoods rather than tropical woods are used.

Fagments and Monuments
Anna Birch
117 Milton Grove
London N16 8QX
T 0171 241 0555
A.Birch@herts.ac.uk
Women's theatre company producing visual & physical text-based theatre.

MVL Designs
Valerie Lee/Mary Vassallo
41a Walford Road
London N16 7BP
T 0171 241 4108
We have a small business signuturing/designing for restaurants/pubs, etc. We always visit potential customers to have a look at the job & give a quote, etc. Pricing is dependent on the individual job.

Women's Eye Co-op
Unit 4
1 Bodney Road
London E8
T 0181 885 6596
Independent, multidisciplinary work as professional artists experienced in education & community arts work, art therapy, as curators & in the organisation of exhibitions.

BUSINESS SUPPORT SCHEMES

Hackney Business Venture
Tracy Maylath
277 Mare Street
London E8 1HB
T 0181 533 4599 F 0181 533 6996
For unemployed in Hackney by helping them become self employed. 2 courses for women: MatchMaker (6 weeks for women returners) & Business Breakthrough Workshops (7 days). All services free. Open 9 am-5.30 pm.

CENTRES FOR WOMEN

Asian Women's Centre
161 Mare Street
London E8 3RH
T 0181 986 4804
Open Mon-Fri 10 am-3 pm. Advice on housing, welfare rights, immigration, & domestic violence. Counselling available. Wheelchair access. Bengali, Gujerati, Urdu, Punjabi & Hindi spoken.

Hackney Women's Centre
20 Dalston Lane
London E8 3AZ
T 0171 254 2980
Open Mon-Fri 10 am-5 pm. Drop-in advice & support to all women in Hackney on welfare rights, education, immigration & housing. Counselling & optical services provided. A resource for women's groups.

London Irish Women's Centre
Maggie O'Keeffe

59 Stoke Newington Church Street
London N16 0AR
T 0171 249 7318 F 0171 923 9599
Open Tue, Wed & Thurs 10 am-1 pm & 2-5 pm. Housing, welfare advice, information & references. Counselling service. Outreach work with travellers. Publications. Services available to women of Irish descent.

CHILD CARE AND FAMILY

Northumberland Park Women and Children Centre
Ilse Amlot, Coordinator
Somerford Grove
Tottenham
London N17 0PG
T 0181 808 9117
Amenities for women and children in north east Tottenham. Welfare provision and playgroups.

COMPUTERS/IT

Central Hackney Computer Project
The Forum
Units 24-32 Independent Place
Shacklewell Lane
London E8 2HD
T 0171 275 8195
Computer training for people who live in Hackney. Targets women returners but doesn't offer any specific course for women. Pays for childcare whilst women study.

Finsbury Park Community Trust
Dolly or Ronshi
Park Gate House
306 Seven Sisters Road
London N4 2AQ
T 0181 211 0121 F 0181 211 0234
IT, childcare courses, return to work, social care courses - all for women only.

Hackney Tenants Telecentre
1 Kingsland High Street
London E8 2JS
T 0171 275 6740
Computer networking facilities, including Internet, for Hackney residents. Computer training, desktop publishing, cv design. Free to Hackney tenants.

CONTRACEPTION/WELL WOMAN

Shoreditch Brook Centre
Shireditch Health Centre
210 Kingsland Road
London E2 8EB
T 0171 301 3130
Open Mon 4.30-6.30 pm; Sat 2-4 pm. To make an appointment outside opening hours, phone 0171 580 2991. Free, confidential contraceptive advice. Free condoms & other contraceptive supplies. Pregnancy tests.

COUNSELLING AND THERAPY

City and Hackney MIND
8-10 Tudor Road
London E9 7SN
T 0181 533 6220
Provides free general counselling service to residents of Hackney and City of London boroughs. Phone above number for counselling line & for details of other counselling services.

Grove Project
23 Hackney Grove
London E8 3NR
T 0181 986 5222
Counselling, advice, young mothers' groups & outreach work on local estates. Telephone for opening hours.

Hurst Associates
Hannah Hurst
62 Winston Road
London N16 9LT
T 0171 254 7288
Psychotherapist. Management development consultant: team building, non-managerial supervision, support group facilitator. Courses individually developed with/for clients. Working in equal opportunity framework.

Shoreditch Centre
2 Dawson Street
London E2 8JU
T 0171 739 4102
Counselling; art therapy. Child care available. Turkish counsellor Tue 5-8 pm. Occasional women-only sessions (phone above number for further details).

Synthesis
Kris Barbara Black
London
T 0171 275 9449
Humanistic integrative arts psychotherapist in training offers services to women. Counselling for women: short- & long-term

work. Areas covered: N16, WC1, N1. First consultation is free.

Disability

Choice Hackney
C/o Disability Resource Centre
St Leonards Hospital
Nuttall Street
London N1 5LZ
T 0171 613 3206
Free advocacy service run by & for people with disabilities. Wheelchair access.

Equal Play Adventure Park
Sue Codling
Spring Lane Project
Spring Lane
London E5 9HQ
T 0181 806 6149
Project for young people with disabilities aged 5-25. Women's youth group, ages 13-25, runs on Wed 6.30-10.30 pm. Youth groups, social education, art projects & games.

Ethnic minorities

Asian Women's Business Administration
Ronshi or Dolly
Finsbury Park Community Trust
Park Gate House
306 Seven Sisters Road
London N4 2AQ
T 0181 211 0121 F 0181 211 0234
Courses for Asian women only. Business Administration NVQ levels 1 & 2. Certificate at end of training. Courses run for 6 months. To help Asian women improve their job prospects.

Asian Women's Group
Purinma Chakraborty
C/o Asian Resource Centre
229 Seven Sisters Road
London N4 2DA
T 0171 263 3182 F 0171 561 9844
Open Thurs 11-4 pm. Advice on welfare & immigration issues. Keep fit & embroidery classes. Health services. Advice on social & emotional issues that affect the day-to-day lives of Asian women.

Asian Women's Support Group
Poppy Banerjiee
18 Ashwin Street
London E8 3DL
T 0171 241 1986

Counselling facilities; advice on welfare; family credit; income support; ESOL facilities.

Asian Women's Support Group
Zohra Ali Zubar
31b Chatsworth Road
London E5 0LH
T 0181 986 4804
Housing & other welfare support; problems with immigration; ESOL. Mobile phone: 0956 505764. Counselling & support to Asian women suffering mental distress. Phone for details of sessions. Wheelchair accessible.

Claudia Jones Organisation
103 Stoke Newington Road
London N16 8BX
T 0171 241 1646
Open Mon-Fri 10 am-5.30 pm & Sat 10 am-2 pm. A space for Afro-Caribbean women. Concerned with education, women's health issues & older women. Counselling available. Women's health support groups.

Cultural Society of Women
39 Leswin Road
London N16 7NX
T 0171 241 2551
Open Mon-Fri 10 am-4.30 pm. Advice given on welfare rights, children, health, housing & violence against women. Bengali, Hindi & Urdu spoken.

Hackney Muslim Women's Council
101 Clapton Common
London E5 9AB
T 0181 809 0993
Counselling, advisory service: domestic violence, marriage problems, welfare rights & health. Training, classes, playgroup. Open Mon & Tue 9 am-7 pm, Wed & Thurs 9 am-6 pm, Fri 9 am-4.30 pm

Hackney Pakistan Women's Welfare Centre
Mrs Qureshi, Coordinator
25 Martaban Road
Hackney
London N16 5SJ
T 0181 809 7039
Mianly for older Asian women. Luncheon club, health & elderly project, social activities for older women. Mother tongue project, Asian craft project. Urdu & English spoken. Open Mon-Fri 9.30 am-5 pm.

LONDON - HACKNEY

North London Muslim Youth Club
Saleh Gajia
68 Cazenove Road
London N16 6AA
T 0181 806 1147
Special classes for girls/young women on Sun 2-6 pm. Cooking, sewing, keep fit, computing, language skills.

Pakistan Women's Welfare Association
Mrs Mian, Coordinator
20 Blackstock Road
London N4 2DW
T 0171 226 4427
Open Mon-Fri 10 am-6 pm. Various activities & lunch clubs.

Turkish Cypriot Community Association - Women's Group
Turkay or Handan
117 Green Lanes
London N16 9DA
T 0171 359 5231
Open Mon-Fri. Offers advice sessions & discussion groups. Seminars on Thalassaemia, child psychology. Cultural & social activities. Refugee advice centre. Domestic violence unit. ESOL. Mothers & children group.

Turkish Cypriot Cultural Association
14a Graham Road
London E8 1BZ
T 0171 249 7410
Advice on range of issues including some very relevant to women: welfare rights, domestic violence, health advice, education, training. Luncheon club. Open Tue-Fri 10 am-4 pm. Transport for older women.

Ujamaa Women's Project
30 Cavendish Mansions
Clapton Square
London E5 8HR
T 0181 986 0915
Education & training in the arts, fashion design, textile, Black dance. Phone for further details of courses.

Union of Muslim Families
55 Balfour Road
London N5 2HD
T 0171 226 0934
Advice on welfare rights, immigration, childare, carers, housing, domestic violence. Open 1-5 pm. Urdu, Bengali, Arabic & French spoken.

Upper Clapton Muslim Welfare and Women's Association
66 Detmold Road
London E5 9NJ
T 0181 806 6536
Meetings. Advice on a range of issues including welfare rights, childcare, education, training. Language classes for children aged 5-15.

GIRLS/YOUNG WOMEN

Centerprise
Emmanuel Amevor
136-138 Kingsland High Street
London E8 2NS
T 0171 254 9632 F 0171 923 1951
CNPR@demon.co.uk
Open Mon-Fri 10 am-5 pm. Young girls' (13-16) writing group. Community centre with bookshop & cafe. Regular events such as advice sessions Tue 10 am-noon; Thurs 6.30-7.30 pm. Wheelchair accessible.

Community Education Project - Hackney Girls & Young Women
Glynnis Flood-Coleman
Stoke Newington School
Clissold Road
London N16 5EU
T 0171 254 0089
Concerned with girls & young women in Hackney. Runs groups in different venues. Phone for further details.

Leaving Care Project
8 Marcon Place
London E8 1ND
T 0171 249 1010
For young women & men leaving care: training, support, advice, accommodation.

Off Centre
25-27 Hackney Grove
London E8 3NR
T 0181 985 8566
Free, confidential counselling for young women & men aged 13-25. Individual/group work. Self-referral or referral by agency. Can choose to have a woman counsellor. Also phone 0181 986 4016.

HEALTH

Candida Support Group
Antigone Coghill-Ellis
Clissold Park Natural Health Centre
154 Stoke Newington Church St

LONDON - HACKNEY

London N16 0JU
T 0171 249 2990
Meets second Sun of each month 3-5 pm. Free. Sharing day-to-day difficulties of living with Candida Albicans. Practical tips & recipes exchanged & results brought to meetings to sample.

Community Drug Team
62 Kenworthy Road
London E9 5RA
T 0181 986 0660
Information, advice about drugs & drugs services. Helpline open 10 am-5 pm. Drop-in, support & counselling Mon, Wed & Fri 9.30 am-12 noon.

Department of Sexual Health
Homerton Hospital
Homerton Row
London E9 6SR
T 0181 919 7989 F 0181 919 7978
Drop-in service for STDs/HIV Mon-Fri. Check ups, treatments, contraceptive information, advice & supplies. Cytology, smears, psychosexual counselling for women. Can request to see a woman doctor.

Drug Dependency Unit
Homerton Hospital
Homerton Row
London E9 6SR
T 0181 919 5555
Counselling, prescribing for people having problems with drug use. HIV/AIDS counselling & testing.

Homerton Hospital Department of Sexual Health
Homerton Row
London E9 6SR
T 0181 919 7989
Sexual health screening, contraceptive advice & supplies, HIV testing, HIV outpatient care, psychosexual counselling, dietary advice. Drop-in clinics. Phone for opening times.

Lorne House Turning Point
126-128 Lower Clapton Road
London E5 0QR
T 0181 533 5700
Alcohol & drug rehabilitation residential service for young women & men aged 15-25.

MIND Tranquilliser Project
City and Hackney MIND
8-10 Tudor Road
London E9 7SN
T 0181 533 6565
For people with problems using tranquillisers and anti-depressants. Information, counselling, support groups.

INTERNATIONAL

Beijing Action Partnership
Margaret Page
7 Palatine Avenue
London N16 8XH
T 0171 254 4957

North to South
Diane Pungartnik
80 Quantock House
Lynmouth Road
London N16 6XW
T 0181 806 5401
Non-profit fund collecting money for women's shelters, centres & self-help projects in Africa, Asia & South America.

IRISH WOMEN

Irish Women's Housing Action Group
Angie Birtill
P O Box 85
LIWC
59 Stoke Newington Church St
London N16 0AR
T 0171 249 7318
Campaigns on housing issues relevant to Irish women. The group meets on a regular basis.

JEWISH WOMEN

Beis Chana: Jewish Women's Centre
19 Northfield Road
London N16 5RL
T 0181 809 6508
A women's centre for all Jewish women. Open Mon-Thurs 9.30 am-4 pm; Sun 10 am-1 pm.

Lubavitch Women's Group
19 Northfield Road
London N16 5RL
T 0181 809 6508
A range of services is provided for Jewish women of all ages, eg Jewish learning group, City & Guilds childcare course, counselling & advice. Open Sun-Thurs.

Lubavitch Youth Club
Yehudis Ives
107-115 Stamford Hill
London N16 5RP
T 0181 800 0022
Wed evening youth group for girls only 6.30-9.30 pm.

Yad Voezer Home
Mrs E Greenblatt, Family Welcare Officer
80 Queen Elizabeth Walk
London N16 5UQ
T 0181 809 4203
Welfare support organisation for Orthodox Jewish people. Clubs, holiday schemes for families. Residential home providing respite & welfare care for Jewish women with learning difficulties.

Legal Matters

Hackney Community Law Centre
236-238 Mare Street
London E8 1HE
T 0181 985 8364 F 0181 533 2018
Legal advice about employment, police misconduct, landlord & tenant, immigration. Legal education & legal representation. Phoneline open Mon-Fri 10 am-1 pm. Emergency phone number: 0181 986 9891.

Hoxton Trust Legal Advice Service
156 Hoxton Street
London N1 6SH
T 0171 613 4174
Free, confidential impartial legal advice on eg benefits, housing, debt, consumer problems, employment, personal injury. Open Mon, Tue, Thurs, & Fri 10.30 am-12.30 pm.

Media

Girls' Own Pictures
Louise Wadley, Director
227 Glyn Road
London E5 0JP
T 0181 985 4805 F 0181 985 4805
louwadley@ad.com
Women's production company for film & TV. Small scale. Aims to promote & make lesbian & women's films.

Older Women

Hackney Pensioners' Convention
15 Brougham Road
London E8 4PD
T 0171 249 1402

Campaigning group for better rights for pensioners. Meetings held at Pitcairn House, E9. Wheelchair accessible. Toilet facilities for disabled people.

Woodberry Down Estate Over 60s Project
5 Chattenden House
Woodberry Down
London N4 2SG
T 0181 800 9973
Social activities for over 60s in Hackney. Outings, bingo, card games, Asian Milap club, drop-in. Wheelchair accessible.

Photography

Hoxton Hall
Sophia Bardsley
130 Hoxton Street
London N1 6SH
T 0171 739 5431 F 0171 729 3815
Community arts centre running music, drama & visual arts classes. Women only photography workshop & women only creative workshop. Playgroup, cafe, free legal advice. Events programme available.

Publishers/Publications

Saks Media
Kadija George
42 Chatsworth Road
Hackney
London E8 2NS
T 0181 985 3041 F 0181 985 9419
Publishing - Burning Words, Flaming Images - annual anthology for writers of African descent. Specialised holidays - writers' HotSpot. Creative writing holidays to The Gambia/USA/India, etc.

Racial Equality

Refugee Women's Association
2nd Floor
18 Ashwin Street
London E8 3DL
T 0171 923 2412
Provides free service to refugee women: education, training, ESOL classes, requalification advice. Open Mon-Fri 10 am-5.30 pm.

Retailing

Sh!
43 Coronet Street
London N1 6HD

LONDON - HACKNEY

T 0171 613 5458
Open Mon-Sat 11.30 am-6.30 pm (8 pm on Thurs). Women's sex shop (lesbian & straight).

SERVICES

Kate French Associates
Kate French
10 Kersley Road
London N16 0NP
T 0171 249 7459 F 0171 249 7459
Consultant in organisation development interested in gender issues. Consultancy work covers organisational audits, strategic planning, team development sessions, individual/group consultancy, etc.

SEXUAL ABUSE/RAPE CRISIS

Hackney Sexual Abuse Project
C/o Hackney Women's Centre
20 Dalston Lane
London E8 3AZ
T 0171 254 1594
Open Mon-Fri 10.30 am-5 pm. Run by & for women who have experienced child sexual abuse. Information for women about how to access services such as counselling, group work, legal advice & therapy.

Rape Awareness Project (RAP)
Kris Black
C/o 55a Carysfort Road
London N16 9AD
T 0171 275 9449
Low cost face-to-face counselling & group work for women survivors of rape/child sexual abuse for those in north/cental London. Fees on sliding scale. Training, consultancy, advice to groups & individuals.

Spectrum Incest Intervention Counselling Research Project
Clare Kavanagh
7 Endymion Road
London N4 1EE
T 0181 348 0196 F 0181 340 0426
Providing fixed-term focussed counselling to women survivors of childhood sexual abuse. Counselling, both individual & group work is offered free of charge London-wide. Office staffed Mon & Tue 11 am-4 pm

SPORTS AND LEISURE

Amazon Fitness for Women
134 Newington Church Street

Hackney
London N16 0JU
T 0171 241 1449
Open Mon, Wed, Fri 7.30 am-10 pm; Tue & Thurs 9 am-10 pm; Sat & Sun 8.30 am-4 pm. Women-only gym, sauna, jacuzzi. Classes available.

Britannia Leisure Centre
40 Hyde Road
London N1 5JU
T 0171 729 4485
Women only Wed 6-10 pm. Badminton, weights, squash, table tennis, leisure pool, jacuzzi, sauna, solarium, football, volleyball, basketball, aerobics, keep fit, gym facilities.

Haggerston Pool
111 Whiston Road
London E2 8BN
T 0171 739 7166
Women only: Tue 5-7 pm - swimming; Thurs 6.15-7.15 - water aerobics.

King's Hall Leisure Centre
39 Lower Clapton Road
London E5 0NU
T 0181 985 2158
Women only Thurs 6-9 pm 6 pm - aerobics, weight circuit, aqua-woggle; 7 pm step intermediate, supervised weights, aqua aerobics; 8 pm step beginners, supervised weights, aqua aerobics. Swimming & sauna.

SUPPORT

Agudas Women's Group
97 Stamford Hill
London N16 5DN
T 0181 800 6688
Advice provided about welfare rights, immigration, carers, education & training, employment & housing. Phone for when open.

Coldline
31 Dalston Lane
London E8 3DF
T 0171 241 0440
Help given to pensioners, parents with children under 5 & people with disabilities. Help with repairs to heating systems, fuel debts, emergency heaters. 24-hour helpline 0171 241 2299. Wheelchair access.

FamilyLine
Vanessa Wiseman, Coordinator

501-505 Kingsland Road
London E8 4AU
T 0171 923 9200 F 0171 249 5443
A confidential telephone helpline for all the family. Wed-Fri 3-8 pm, Sat & Sun 12-6 pm. To provide an immediate response to callers, offering information, guidance & support.

Finsbury Park Homeless Families Project
Alexander National House
330 Seven Sisters Road
London N4 2PJ
T 0181 802 7426
Provides services for homeless families. Women only Mon & Wed 10 am-12 pm. Drop-in centre for homeless families Mon-Fri 10 am-4 pm at St John's church, Gloucester Drive N4. Women only sewing classes.

Huddleston Centre
30 Powell Road
London E5 8DJ
T 0181 985 8869
Turkish women's group; Asian women's group; playgroup; parent support group; youth group; etc. Phone for further details & opening hours.

Incontinence Laundry Service
Environmental Health Depot
Millfields Road
London E5 0AR
T 0181 985 5930
Free laundry service for people who are incontinent.

Training

Margaret Page Associates: Training Consultancy Research
Margaret Page
7 Palatine Avenue
London N16 8XH
T 0171 254 4957 F 0171 254 4957
mnpmlp@bath.ac.uk
International women's networker & consultant to managers in the public & not for profit sectors. Expertise is in consultancy to management teams or individuals working on organisational change; etc.

Transport

Hackney Community Transport
Hertford Road Depot
2-8 Hertford Road
London N1 5SH
T 0171 275 0012

Voluntary organisation providing door-to-door transport for disabled & elderly people. Minibus hire for community groups. Advice/training on transport matters to community groups.

Ladycabs
London
T 0171 254 3501
Women's transport using women-only drivers in Stoke Newington & Hackney. Phone also 0171 254 3314 and 0171 923 2266. Disabled users catered for, with advance notice required. Quotes for journeys provided.

Violence against Women

Domestic Violence (Housing) Advice Service
London
T 0181 525 2854
Advice & counselling service for all women in Hackney suffering, or who have suffered, domestic violence. Emotional support, legal, housing & benefit advice. Telephone staffed Mon, Tue, Thurs, Fri 9 am-5 pm

Women's Aid

Asian Women's Aid
P O Box 1558
N16 5JJ
T 0171 392 2092
A refuge providing Asian women with a neutral ground away from distressed circumstances & an escape from domestic violence. Accommodation for up to 15 women & their children.

Hackney Women's Aid
P O Box 6566
London E8 3ST
T 0171 392 2092
Offers support, advice & temporary emergency accommodation to women, with or without children, experiencing domestic violence. Wheelchair accessible. Turkish spoken.

Hammersmith & Fulham

Accommodation

Women's Pioneer Housing Ltd
Janet Davies
227 Wood Lane
London W12 0EX
T 0181 749 7112 F 0181 749 9843
Provides housing for women in need. There are 920 flats in management & 70 sold under

long leases. About 30 new homes are currently being built. Works with seven local authorities.

ALTERNATIVE THERAPIES

Sonja Vanderdol
Sonja Vanderdol
106 Colehill Lane
Fulham
London SW6 5EJ
T 0171 731 4856
Nutritional/weight management products: Klamath Lake blue-green algae. Registered nutritionist & aromatherapist. Open Mon-Fri 9 am-7 pm. Experience with digestive problems, PMS, candida albicans.

ARTS AND CRAFTS

Eleventh Hour Arts
Debbie Golt
113 Cheesemans Terrace
Star Road
London W14 9XH
T 0171 385 5447 F 0171 385 5447
Music & arts consultancy association promoting female musicians. Festival programming, especially if women performers; press campaigns undertaken; arts consultancy; occasional journalism.

Wednesday Women Writers' Group
Josie Pearce
Fulham Cross Centre
Caroline Walk
London W6 8EW
T 0181 969 0943
Meets Wed 10.30 am-12.30 pm Women writers' group for beginners & experienced women writers. Encouraging women of all ages & educational backgrounds to write. Workshops to write & discuss writing.

Women & Words
Anne Cotgreave
C/o Community Education
Riverside Studios
Crisp Road
London W6 9RL
T 0181 600 2308
Meets Sat 10 am-12 pm. Drop-in for women who write. For women of all ages, backgrounds & styles. Varied programme of writers' circle, workshop & discussion sessions. Emphasis on support & encouragement.

COUNSELLING AND THERAPY

Bridge - Centre for Women's Emotional Well-Being
Merle Joseph
129 Bloemfontein Road
Shepherds Bush
London W12 7DA
T 0181 749 9451 F 0181 749 9451
For women in Hammersmith and Fulham who have mental health problems. One-to-one counselling & group counselling.

Hammersmith Counselling Centre
Robert Timmerman
182 Hammersmith Road
Hammersmith
London W6 7DJ
T 0181 741 3335 F 0181 741 3335
Counselling for people of all ages, especially aged 16 -25. Can request woman therapist. Women's support group. Open Tue & Fri 2-4 p.m; Thurs 3.30-5.30 pm. No appointment necessary. Library.

MIND - Hammersmith and Fulham branch
Mark Logan
153 Hammersmith Road
London W14 0QL
T 0181 741 0661 F 0181 563 8186
Open Mon-Fri 9.30 am-1 pm & 2-5 pm
Women's group Wed 10 am-1 pm. Low-support homes, home support project, property maintenance training project, counselling service, advocacy, etc.

Women's Action for Mental Health (WAMH)
Janet Brown/Susannah Lopez
131 Bloemfontein Road
White City Estate
London W12 7DA
T 0181 749 9446
Free counselling for women in Hammersmith & Fulham. Waiting list. Creche. Phone for appointment or be referred by GP. Counselling & advocacy service for women aiming to help those who are depressed or anxious.

ETHNIC MINORITIES

Arab Women's Group
Zina Hassan
123 King Street
Hammersmith
London W6 9JG
T 0181 563 0850 F 0181 563 0850

Open 9.30 am-5 pm daily. Advice & counselling on wide range of issues for Arab-speaking women: welfare rights, housing, health, translation. Outings & events. Training courses: IT, business English, etc.

Asha Bangladeshi Women's Project
Irfat Tarafdar, Coordinator
Room 16, 1st Floor
Bishop Creighton House
378 Lillie Road
London SW6 7PH
T 0171 386 1881   F 0171 386 1881
Open Mon-Fri 9.30 am-5 pm. Group sessions run Tue & Wed from 11 am-1 pm. A service for Bengali women's emotional wellbeing & support. One-to-one counselling, outings. To combat loneliness.

Asian Women Outreach Support Service
Merle Joseph
Bridge
129 Bloemfontein Road
Sherpherds Bush
London W12 7DA
T 0181 749 9451   F 0181 749 9451
Counselling for Asian women.

Muslim Women's Organisation
Mrs M Aftab
66 Rosebury Road
London SW6 2NG
T 0171 731 5455   F 0171 746 2701
Supports Asian women in Hammersmith & Fulham. Raises issues about Asian women, helping to alleviate problems. Supplementary School on Sat at Shepherd's Bush Library for 4-16 year olds in mother tongue classes.

GIRLS/YOUNG WOMEN

Hammersmith Girls' and Women's Project
Clare Douglas
Edward Woods Community Centre
60-70 Norland Road
Edward Woods Estate
London W11 4TX
T 0171 371 1690
Open Tue & Thurs 3-7 pm Wheelchair access. Various activities, eg cookery, dance, keep-fit, maths & English workshops.

Maya Project
Patricia Howcroft, Administrator
45 New King's Road
London SW6 4SD
T 0171 736 0688

For girls & young women aged 11-17 living in Hammersmith & Fulham. Offers facility to learn about your rights. Information & advice, meeting other women, helping to identify needs & resolve problems, etc.

Rainbow, Brownies, Guides and Rangers
Mrs Marjorie Kipling
T 0171 228 4993
For girls from the age of 5 & upwards. Phone for further information.

HEALTH

ACCEPT
Barbara Elliot, Director
724 Fulham Road
London SW6 5SE
T 0171 371 7477
For women (and men) with alcohol problems, their families and friends. Free non-medical day treatment. Individual counselling. One women only group and other mixed drop-in groups. Relatives & friends groups.

Bernhard GUM Clinic
Department of Genito-Urinary Medicine
Charing Cross Hospital
Fulham Palace Road
London W6 8RF
T 0181 846 7606
Clinic Hours: Mon, Tue 9.30 am-12.30 pm Thurs & Fri 2-5 pm Wed 1-5 pm & 5.30-7 pm. Clinic for lesbians. Screening for sexually transmitted infections. Result line 0181 748 3456.

Breast Screening
Charing Cross Hospital
Fulham Palace Road
London W6 8RF
T 0181 846 1139
Mammography breast screening for women over the age of 50 on Mon, Tue, Thurs & Fri. A mobile breast screening unit is also available. Phone for further details.

River House
Furnival Gardens
London W6 9DJ
T 0181 741 4772   F 0181 846 9745
Open Tue, Wed & Fri 10 am-5 pm. Drop-in centre for people affected by HIV/AIDS. Women only Thurs 12-4.30 pm - African, Caribbean & Asian. Social work advice sessions. Black people's support service.

West London Community Counselling
27 Hammersmith Grove
London W6 7EN
T 0181 846 9888
Free, short- & long-term counselling to people infected & affected by HIV/AIDS.

Women's Sexual Health - Naz Project
Parminder Sekhon, House Coordinator
Palinswick House
241 King Street
London W6 9LP
T 0181 741 1879 F 0181 741 9841
Open Mon-Fri 9 am-5 pm Working with south Asian & Turkish women on HIV prevention. A support group called 'HER'.

Irish Women

Irish Support and Advice Service
Fionnular O'Hare
Blacks Road
Hammersmith
London W6 9DT
T 0181 741 0466
Support group for Irish residents of Hammersmith & Fulham only. Open Fri 11 am-1 pm Wheelchair access.

Legal Matters

Fulham Legal Advice Centre
Pam Donohue
679a Fulham Road
London SW6 5BZ
T 0171 731 2401
Provides free legal advice Mon, Tue & Thurs from 6.30 pm onwards. Welfare advice & general advice Mon, Tue & Thurs 10 am-12 pm & 2-4 pm.

Hammarsmith and Fulham Community Law Centre
142 King Street
London W6 0QU
T 0181 741 4021
Free legal advice mainly for people living in Hammersmith & Fulham. Referral by phone Mon-Fri 2-5 pm & Mon, Wed Thurs morning 10 am-1 pm; women's advice session (by appointment) Wed 10 am-1 pm; etc.

Lesbian and Bisexual

Amach Linn! Irish Lesbians and Gay Men in London
Dara de Burca
Hammersmith & Fulham Irish Centre
Black's Road
Hammersmith
London W6 9DT
Advancing social/cultural welfare of Irish lesbians/gay men in London & providing awareness of the experience of being Irish & lesbian/gay. Regualr social events & monthly meetings. New members welcome.

Bernhard GUM Clinic
Department of Genito-Urinary Medicine
Charing Cross Hospital
Fulham Palace Road
London W6 8RF
T 0181 846 1576
Clinic on Wed 2-7 pm for lesbians only. Only women doctors. Phone for an appointment. Confidential service offering cervical smears, STD testing, breast checks, HIV testing, sexual health counselling, etc.

Hammersmith Young Lesbian Group
London
T 0181 748 4910
For all young women aged 16-25 who think they are/might be lesbian.

Health, Education, Rights (HER)
C/o the Naz Project (London)
Pallingswick House
241 King Street
London W6 9LP
T 0181 741 1879 F 0181 741 9609
Support & information on sexuality, safer sex, safer drug use, HIV & sexual health for women who have sex with women from south Asian, Middle Eastern & north African communities.

Libraries/Archives

Dominic Photography
Catherine Ashmore
4b Moore Park Road
London SW6 2JT
T 0171 381 0007 F 0171 381 0008
Photographer & entertainments library: 1956-present day. Theatre, opera, dance, musicals, personalities: UK, USA, Russia, Europe.

Manual Trades

Gilmour Painters
Paula Gilmour
P O Box 6150
Fulham
London SW6 5LL

T 0171 610 9841   F 0171 610 9841
Painting & decorating. Basic painting & specialist paint effects (stencilling, colour washes, marbling, graining, etc). Private homes, offices, businesses & painted furniture. Small professional team.

OLDER WOMEN

Bishop Creighton Women's Club
Mrs B Barber, Secretary
39 Delorme Street
London W6 8DS
T 0171 381 1270
Club for women aged 40 +. Meets occasional Mon 8-10 pm Wheelchair access.

Older Women's Health Group
Andy White, Centre Manager
Bishop Creighton House
378 Lillie Road
London SW6 7PH
T 0171 385 9689
Open Thurs 10 am-12 pm. For women pensioners. Information & discussion group about health matters. Phone for further information.

PLACES TO STAY AND EAT

Reeves Hotel for Women
Carole Reeves
48 Shepherds Bush Green
London W12 8PJ
T 0181 740 1158   F 0181 740 1158
Secure, comfortable hotel for women. Open all year. Good transport links. Phone for up to date price list.

PREGNANCY/CHILDBIRTH

British Pregnancy Advisory Service - West London
160 Shepherds Bush Road
London W6 7PB
T 0171 602 2723
Daily clinic for women to discuss all aspects of contraception, sexual health, pregnancy, & referral for termination of pregnancy. Comprehensive well woman service. Free contraceptives & preganancy tests.

Successful Nannying
Jackie Nancey
323 North End Road
London SW6 1MM
T 0171 386 9688

A service for post-natal mothers. Initial two-hour consultation & subsequently maternity nurse offered. Phone for price list.

SERVICES

Anne Woodhead Electrolysist
Anne Woodhead
67 Rannoch Road
London W6 9SS
T 0171 385 4904   F 0171 385 4904
Hair removal for women. Home visits.

Capital Careers
181 King's Street
London W6 9JU
T 0181 741 2441
Open Mon-Fri 9.30 am-4.30 pm. Offers careers guidance, help with cvs, information & help with getting a job. For residents of Hammersmith & Fulham. Phone for further details.

Typographics
Eugenie Dodd
1 Coulter Road
London W6 0DJ
T 0181 748 9565   F 0181 748 4594
Graphic design consultancy specialising in creative communication & typography for information. Particular interest in promoting women's businesses.

SPORTS AND LEISURE

Fulham Pools, The
Normand Park
Lillie Road
London SW6 4PL
T 0171 385 7642
Women only Fri 6-8.30 pm. Lane swimming, wave pool, sauna, sunbeds.

Janet Adegoke Centre
Bloemfontein Road
White City
London W12 7DH
T 0181 743 3401
Women only Thurs 6-10 pm. Swimming, fitness classes, gym, steam room, sunbeds.

Lillie Road Fitness Centre
Lillie Road
London SW6 7PN
T 0171 381 2183
Women only Tue 5-7 pm. Aerobics 6 pm; gym 5-7 pm.

Sands End Community Sports Hall
Miss Taylor
59-61 Broughton Road
London SW6 2LA
T 0171 736 1504
Women only events on Tue & Thurs 10 am-12 pm. Step aerobics (Tue), aerobics & body conditioning (Thurs). Creche.

West London Women's Self-Defence Association
Fulham Cross Centre
Caroline Walk
London SW6
T 0171 385 7339
Facilitates provision of self-defence training for women. Provides professional forum for women self-defence instructors who teach women: able-bodied, disabled girls, older women, Black & Asian women, etc.

SUPPORT

Baron's Court Project
Mike Farrow
69 Talgarth Road
Baron's Court
London W14 9DA
T 0171 603 5232
Drop-in free service for people who are isolated & lonely. Women only drop-in Fri 10 am-12 pm for support & talk about women's issues.

Colebrooke Women's Association
Colebrooke Social, Cult. & Welfare Assn
51 Hugon Road
London SW6 3ER
T 0171 736 8329
Women any age & nationality talk about issues affecting women, especially pre-retired & retired women, such as health, loneliness & bereavement. Courses on health; outings. Meets Tue 11 am-2 pm.

TRANSPORT

Ladys West Cars
154 Shepherds Bush Road
London W6
T 0171 602 5511
Also 0171 602 6952. Provides a special minicab service for women to reduce their anxieties at night. Male & female drivers with women drivers at night for women by request.

VIOLENCE AGAINST WOMEN

Domestic Violence Intervention Project
Jane Stavart
P O Box 2838
London W6 9ZE
T 0181 748 6512
Above phone number for women only, open 10 am-8 pm most weekdays. Advice & support for women experiencing violence or abuse from partners. Short-term counselling, safety strategy planning, support groups.

HARINGEY

ACCOMMODATION

Beacon Lodge Charitable Trust
Kea Byer, Manager
35 Eastern Road
London N2 9LB
T 0181 883 4468 F 0181 883 4065
Accommodation for women with children staffed 24 hours a day.

Girls Alone Project
Julie Leonie
77 Lansdowne Road
London N17 0NN
T 0181 493 0239
Support & accommodation for girls and young women aged 16-21. Referrals only.

Patchwork Community Ltd
7a Willoughby Road
London N8 0HK
T 0181 348 1075
Open Mon-Fri 9 am-5 pm. Above telephone is for north office. For south office phone 1071 252 6280. Accommodation for disabled women, lesbians, Asian women, ex-offenders, etc. Some mother & baby units.

ACCOUNTANCY

Rose Book-keeping Service
Victoria Watts
76A Northview Road
London N8 7LL
T 0181 341 5473 F 0181 348 3335
Personal book-keeping for small businesses & self-employed people. Set-ups, VAT, PAYE.

ALTERNATIVE THERAPIES

Delcia McNeil
Delcia McNeil
Flat 2
56 Queen's Avenue

Muswell Hill
London N10 3NY
T 0181 442 0391
Psychotherapist & healer & specialises in working with women around the issues of self-esteem, personal crisis, relationship & work problems. Runs a women's therapy group. Also runs courses (not women only).

ARTS AND CRAFTS

Deliverance Theatre Company
Gillian Roberts/Esca Francis
C/o 12 Ivor Court
Crouch Hill
London N8 9EB
T 0181 347 8153
Committed to new writing and promoting the work of women theatre practitioners.

Therese Wassily Saba
Therese Wassily Saba
6 Thirlmere Road
Muswell Hill
London N10 2DN
T 0181 442 1489 F 0181 442 1489
106665.3500@compuserve.com
Freelance music journalist (concert programme notes, CD liner notes, music dictionary entry research work also undertaken); News Editor of Classical Guitar Magazine; professional classical guitarist.

Vanessa Lake Carpenter & Joiner
Vanessa Lake
153 Quill Street
London N4 2AE
T 0171 503 5390
Carpenter & joiner of traditional & freestyle woodwork for kitchens, studies, bedrooms. Also shelving, doors, locks, windows, glazing, flooring & general repair & maintenance.

BUSINESS SUPPORT SCHEMES

In-House Training Services
Lesley Howard
Unit WS2
Grove Business Centre
560-568 High Road
London N17 9TA
T 0181 801 0555 F 0181 365 0224
Consultancy & training in the areas of communication skills & business. Works with individuals & companies. Some courses subsidised by government grants & therefore free to participants.

CENTRES FOR WOMEN

Bangladesh Women's Association in Haringey
Mrs R A Islam
Mitalee Centre
Stanley Road
London N15 3HB
T 0181 365 7498
Open Mon-Fri 9 am-5 pm. Improving conditions of life for Bangladeshi women in Haringey, & promote education & vocational training. Language classes, day seminars, recreational activities. Help & advice.

Haringey Women's Forum
628 High Road
London N17 9TP
T 0181 885 4705
Advice & information agency. Open Mon-Thurs 10.30 am-1 pm.

CHILD CARE AND FAMILY

Haringey Childcare and Training Project
Janet Bryan
Annex B
Tottenham Town Hall
Town Hall Approach Road
London N15 4RY
T 0181 365 1812 F 0181 808 7445
Part of Haringey Council social services pool of creche & respite workers. For organisations & groups by referral. Will go to homes & collect children from school, etc.

COMPUTERS/IT

Connexions
Athol Brown
33 Winkfield Road
Wood Green
London N22 5RP
T 0181 365 7435
IT training for people with disabilities. Open Mon-Thurs 9.30 am-4.30 pm & Fri 9.30 am-12.30 pm

I Can Do It
Selby Centre
Selby Road
London N17 8JL
T 0181 365 0032
To help women, mainly Asian women, gain confidence & experience using computers. A number of women only groups.

LONDON - HARINGEY

CONTRACEPTION/WELL WOMAN

Alexandra Surgery
125 Alexandra Park Road
London N22 4UN
T 0181 888 2518
Open Mon-Fri 9 am-noon; 4.30-6.30 pm (not Wed). Well woman clinics, contraceptive clinics. Woman doctor & woman practice nurse fully trained in contraception & cytology (cervical smears). Phone for appt.

COUNSELLING AND THERAPY

Avril Hollings, Psythotherapist
Avril Hollings
Spectrum
7 Endymion Road
London N4 1EE
T 0181 341 7214
Humanistic psychotherapist working with individuals and groups.

ETHNIC MINORITIES

Asian Women's Action Group
Parminder or Aniz
30 Willoughby Road
Hornsey
London N8 0JG
T 0181 341 3802
For young Asian women. Runs on Sat from 2-5. Drama work, poetry, photography, project day trips.

Asian Women's Forum
D Shah, Project coordinator
2nd Floor
Nursery Premises
50 Mayes Road
London N22
T 0181 888 2446
Open Mon-Fri 10 am-5 pm. Helps women & children with housing benefits & mental health problems. Advocacy work. Refers clients to single B&B accommodation.

Asian Women's Friends' Network
Dr Jethwani
P O Box 9504
London N17 6SH
T 0181 801 5976
Informal get together for Asian women to discuss problems & to try to help each other with problems. Meets once a fortnight at various places.

Cypriot Community Centre
Chris Stylianou
Earlham Grove
Wood Green
London N22 5HJ
T 0181 881 7828 F 0181 881 7894
Open seven days a week 9 am-11 pm. For women only: ESOL Tue 6-8 pm; Greek classes; Cypriot dancing Wed 7-9 pm. Special groups by arrangement. Wheelchair access.

Greek Cypriot Women's Organisation
Afendra Eleftheriou
Social, Cultural & Health Centre
Denmark Road
London N8 OD2
T 0181 348 9011
Open Mon-Fri 10 am-4 pm & Tue & Thurs 7-9 pm. English classes, keep fit, yoga, counselling, playgroup. Wheelchair access.

Haringey Turkish Cypriot Women's Project
Miss Aziz
6a Hampden Road
Hornsey
London N8 0HX
T 0181 340 3300
Open Mon, Tue, Thurs, Fri 9.30 am-4.30 pm to all Turkish speaking women. Information & advice & problem solving with such issues as welfare, benefits, health, domestic violence.

Ijeoma Black Women's Alcohol Counselling Project
Gay Fletcher
628 High Road
Tottenham
London N17 9TP
T 0181 885 5227
Open Mon-Fri 10 am-1 pm. Advice, information & counselling on alcohol-related issues for Black women. Wheelchair access.

Ugandan Community Relief Association
Selby Centre
Selby Road
London N17 8JN
T 0181 808 6221
Open Mon-Fri 9.30 am-5.30 pm. Advice & help on immigration, welfare rights, HIV/AIDS, other health issues & women's issues. Wheelchair accessible & toilet facilities for disabled people. Creche.

HEALTH

Alcohol and Drug Abuse Drop-In Centre
590 Seven Sisters Road
Tottenham
London N15 6HR
T 0181 800 6999
Open Mon-Fri 11 am-5 pm Women only all day Wed.

Drug Advice Service in Haringey (DASH)
80 Stroud Green Road
Finsbury Park
London N4 3EN
T 0171 272 2757
Advice and information on all aspects of drug-related matters.

Foundation for AIDS Counselling Treatment and Support (FACTS)
23-25 Western Park
London N8 9SY
T 0181 348 9195   F 0181 340 5864
Out patients' clinic seven days a week. Specialised care for people affected by HIV/AIDS. Range of non-medical services. Gym & cafe.

Gail Mincher Nutrition Consultant
Gail Mincher
2 Thirlmere Road
London N10 2DN
T 0181 444 1780
Initial consultations last one hour & follow-up consultations half an hour. Good nutrition advice helps to prevent ageing, maintains optimum weight, increases fertility & reduces risk of disease.

St Ann's Sexual Health Centre
St Ann's Hospital
St Ann's Road
London N15 3TH
T 0181 442 6000
Mon-Fri drop-in for women. Victim support service with psychologists & counsellors. Sexual assault support & advice. Contraceptive advice & supplies Fri 5-7 pm. Full sexual health screening.

Women and Medical Practice (WAMP)
Christa Moeckli
40 Turnpike Lane
London N8 0PS
T 0181 888 2782   F 0181 365 8157
HIV line 0181 365 8285. Open Mon-Thurs 10 am-5 pm. For women in Haringey. Free health advice/information. Counselling & therapy. Pregnancy testing. Free HIV counselling. Befriending, etc.

IRISH WOMEN

CARA - Irish Housing Association
Caroline O'Neill
339 Seven Sisters Road
London N15 6RD
T 0181 800 2744
Provides homes for single Irish people. Research on health & housing for Irish people. Open Mon-Fri 9.30 am-5.30 pm Welcomes lesbians & has lesbian staff.

Haringey Irish Centre
Francis Baker
Pretoria Road
London N17 8DX
T 0181 885 3490
Open daily 9 am-5 pm. Irish women's group meets Wed 12.30-3 pm. A cultural & community centre. Wheelchair access.

Haringey Irish Women's Group
Bernie McGee
Haringney Irish Cultural & Community Ctr
Pretoria Road
Tottenham
London N17 8DX
T 0171 272 7594
Support group meeting on Wed 12-3 pm. Two creche workers are available & a hairdresser. Dental care available & aromatherapy.

LARGER/TALLER WOMEN

Rita Models
L Fox
6 Turnpike Parade
Green Lanes
London N15 3EA
T 0181 888 6234   F 0181 958 7921
Fashion shop specialising in fashion for the fuller figure lady - up to size 28.

MANUAL TRADES

Plumbline
Annabel Hands
47a Belmont Road
London N15 3LU
T 0181 889 3921   F 0181 889 3921
Domestic plumbing & heating business working in north east London area. Employs both female & male plumbers.

OLDER WOMEN

Grace (Afro/Caribbean Elders)
Mrs Marsh
Whitehall & Tenterden Community Centre
Whitehall Street
London N17 8BP
T 0181 808 0718
Open Mon-Fri 9 am-4 pm. Day care centre for elderly & housebound people. Transport service available. Wheelchair access.

PLACES TO STAY AND EAT

Women's Health Cafe
Christa Moeckli
Women and Medical Practice
40 Turnpike Lane
London N8 0PS
T 0181 888 2782 F 0181 365 8157
Open Tue, Wed and Thurs 11 am-3 pm. Cheaply priced.

PREGNANCY/CHILDBIRTH

Association of Radical Midwives North London Branch
Suzanne Colson
C/o Flat 2
125 Crouch Hill
London N8 9QN
T 0181 341 7394
Midwives challenging attitudes in maternity services. Journal 'Midwifery Matters'.

North London and Hertfordshire Independent Midwives
Rachel Lewis
54 Denton Road
Hornsey Vale
London N8 9NT
T 0181 347 9039
Group practice of independent midwives covering N & W London, Herts, Harrow & Beds. Provides individualised care for women seeking home or hospital births. Experience in homoeopathy, birth education, yoga, etc.

SERVICES

Daphne Trotter
Daphne Trotter
2 Thirlmere Road
London N10 2DN
T 0181 883 8533
Proofreading, copy-editing: fiction, non-fiction, bilingual dictaionaries, phrase books, travel guides.

SPORTS AND LEISURE

Seqinpark Women's Health Club and Gym
17 Crouch Hill
London N4 4AP
T 0171 272 6857
Open Mon, Wed, Fri 7.30 am-10 pm; Tue & Thurs 9.30 am-10 pm; Sat & Sun 8.30 am-4 pm. Women-only gym. Relaxation area, sauna & steam. Treatment area: massage & reflexology.

TRANSPORT

Ladycabs
London
T 0171 272 3019
Women's transport using women-only drivers in Haringey. Disabled users catered for, with advance notice needed. Quotes for journeys provided.

VIOLENCE AGAINST WOMEN

Justice for Women - London
Jinny Keatinge
55 Rathcoole Gardens
London N8 9NE
T 0181 340 3699 F 0181 340 3699
Set up to campaign against discrimination within the legal system towards women subjected to male violence. Campaigning for changes in the law so that women's experiences of male violence are taken seriously.

WOMEN'S AID

Asian Women's Aid
P O Box 2604
London N22 6TL
T 0181 888 6936
Refuge for Asian women & their children (if any) who are suffering domestic violence or sexual abuse from their partners.

Haringey Women's Aid
P O Box 915
London N8
T 0181 341 4665
Refuges for women & their children (if any) who are suffering from domestic violence or sexual abuse from their husbands or partners.

Tottenham Women's Aid
P O Box 945
London N15 4TN

T 0181 802 8614
A safe house for women & their children (if any) who are suffering from domestic violence from a partner.

HARROW

ARTS AND CRAFTS

Harrow and District Flower Group
Mrs M Spanner
53 Lucas Avenue
Harrow
Middlesex HA2 9UH
T 0181 868 7836
Flower demonstrations on second Thurs of month except August. Meets at St Mary-The-Virgin Church Hall, Kenton Road, Harrow.

BEREAVEMENT

National Association of Widows - Harrow branch
Mrs P M Brooker
61 Highmead Crescent
Wembley
Middlesex HA0 4ED
T 0181 903 2084
Support service for widows run by widows, to alleviate injustices faced by widows. Help, advice & comfort whenever & wherever needed. Meetings held Tue 7.30 pm in members' homes. Socials, outings, films.

CARERS

Carers' Support Harrow
Red Cross Centre
39 Sheepcote Road
Harrow
Middlesex HA1
T 0181 427 0711   F 0181 427 0711
Information for carers relating to services available to them and the people they care for; training for carers; counselling; support; advocacy; networking with existing carer groups.

CENTRES FOR WOMEN

Sangham Association of Asian Women
210 Burnt Oak
Broadway
Edgware
Middlesex HA9 0AP
T 0181 952 7062
Advice centre for housing, benefits, immigration, employment & homelessness. Legal advice sessions on Tue, Fri & Sat. Also an elderly Asian women's group.

Women's Centre, The
Jan
99C Hindes Road
Harrow
Middlesex HA1 1RX
T 0181 863 4500
Open Mon 10am-4 pm; Wed 10 am-3 pm; Fri 10 am-3 pm; Sat 10 am-12 noon. Legal advice Wed 2 pm with women solicitors; pregnancy testing Sat morning; one-to-one counselling. Meeting room, courses.

COUNSELLING AND THERAPY

WPF Counselling NW Middlesex
1 Oxley Court
Greenford Road
Sudbury Hill, Harrow
Middlesex HA1 3QD
T 0181 423 8454
Counselling for people with difficulty coping with emotional problems: relationships, home, work, or who are depressed, suffering loss, separation. One-to-one psycho-dynamic counselling by trained counsellors.

ETHNIC MINORITIES

Asian Parents Group
Hussain Akhtar, Chairperson
26 Wellesley Road
Harrow
Middlesex HA1 1QN
T 0181 427 1751   F 0181 427 1751
Working towards racial equality in educational matters & helping parents & children. Representing them at all levels. Meets monthly at various venues.

Harrow Women's Association
60 Wilson Gardens
West Harrow
Middlesex HA1 4DZ
T 0181 422 2677
Free & confidential counselling service for Asian women of all ages relating to their mental health problems. Stress, strain, depression, sexual abuse, suicide attempts, domestic violence.

Milap Mandal
Mrs Badiani
87 Ravenswood Crescent
Rayners Lane
Harrow
Middlesex HA2 9JL
T 0181 864 4696

Promoting social & cultural activities for Asian women. Meets in Victoria Hall, Sheepcote Road, Harrow on second Wed of each month.

Pakistan Women Association
Mrs Farrukh Mahmood
417 Pinner Road
Harrow
Middlesex HA1 4HN
T 0181 427 1481 F 0181 427 6892
Aims to end the isolation of very many Pakistani & other Muslim women. Information & guidance in all matters relating to women. Cultural & sports activities. Mother tongue classes & religious festivals.

SETV
Honeypot Lane Clinic
Honeypot Lane
Stanmore
Middlesex HA7 1AT
Free & confidential counselling service for Asian women. Open Mon 9 am-1 pm, Tue, Fri 9 am-5 pm, Wed, Thurs 1-5 pm. Counselling offered on one-to-one or in small groups. Drop-in during the week.

Somali Community of North West London Assn
Aisha Ahmed
373 Greenrigg Walk
Chalk Hill
Wembley
Middlesex HA9 9UL
T 0181 908 6274 F 0181 908 6274
Offers advice & support on various issues such as housing & welfare rights. Translation provided. There is a women's association. Phone for further details.

UK Asian Women's Conference (1)
Asma Sutenwalla
St Peter's Centre
Sumner Road
West Harrow
London HA1 4BX
T 0181 423 4186 F 0181 423 5367
Interpreting & translation scheme connected to mental health for Asian women. Referrals from hospitals & social workers. Open Mon-Thurs 9 am-5 pm; Fri 9 am-1 pm.

UK Asian Women's Conference (2)
Illa Bhuva
Vaughan Centre
Wilson Gardens
West Harrow
Middlesex HA1 4EA
T 0181 423 6731
Informs advises & involves Asian women on issues affecting their daily lives. Drop in Tue & Thurs 11 am-2 pm; mental health support group Mon 10-11.30 am

Yakeen Counselling Service
Yakeen
C/o DAWN
1 St Kildas Road
Harrow
Middlesex HA1 1QD
T 0181 427 6796
Free counselling available to all Asian women experiencing depression, loneliness, marital problems, cultural alienation, domestic violence etc. Counselling provided by professionally trained counsellors.

JEWISH WOMEN

League of Jewish Women - North Harrow branch
Frankie Zeitlin
60 Elm Croft Crescent
North Harrow
Middlesex HA2 6HN
T 0181 836 1424
Home visiting, meals on wheels, shopping, hospital visiting, & transporting people in need without regard to race, creed or colour. Monthly evening meetings.

League of Jewish Women - Stanmore branch
Carol Rose, Welfare Officer
24 Dalkeith Grove
Stanmore
Middlesex HA7 4SG
T 0181 958 8146
Home visiting, meals on wheels, shopping, hospital visiting & transporting people in need, without regard to race, creed or colour. Monthly evening meetings.

LEGAL MATTERS

Ogilvie's
Rashida Ogilvie
34 Landers Drive
North Harrow
Middlesex HA2 7PB
T 0181 429 2589
Women solicitors covering all aspects of marital breakdown. Legal aid offered. Phone for further details.

Pregnancy/Childbirth

Harrow Home Birth Support Group
Mary Lou Watts
39 Talbot Road
Wealdstone
Middlesex HA3 7QQ
T 0181 424 8364
Meets first Wed of each month & sometimes daytime (phone for details). Offers information, support & encouragement to those thinking of having their babies at home.

National Childbirth Trust - Harrow branch
Alison Whitehead
65 Yeading Avenue
Harrow
Middlesex HA2 9RL
T 0181 429 2358
Information & support in pregnancy, childbirth & early parenthood & enables parents to make informed choices. Ante-natal classes, postnatal exercise & discussion classes & support, telephone helpline, etc.

National Childbirth Trust - Harrow branch
Judith, Secretary
Middlesex
T 0181 428 5924
Offers information & support in pregnancy, childbirth & early parenthood & aims to enable every parent to make informed choices. Antenatal classes, Breastfeeding information & bras, postnatal support.

Racial Equality

Racial Harassment Support Group
Mr T P Suchak
98 Blenheim Road
North Harrow
Middlesex HA2 7AF
T 0181 863 0061
Help available in connection with racial harassment. Group meets Wed morning at Wealdstone library.

Religious Organisations

Harrow Gayatri Satsang Mandel
Mrs Kusumben Patel /Mrs Veenaben Lavingia
305 Byron Road
Wealdstone
Harrow
Middlesex HA3 7TE
T 0181 863 3847
For older women aged 65+. Meets Tue & Thurs for prayers for two hours at the Community Centre, Grant Road, Wealdstone, Harrow 1-3 pm. Also meets elsewhere from 1-4.30 pm

Trinity Church Women's Thursday Guild
Miss Lillian Eggleton
Welldon Centre
Welldone Crescent
Harrow
Middlesex HA1 2QL
T 0181 427 6691
Meets Thurs 10.30 am for coffee & biscuits, followed by programmes of speakers & slides. Devotional activities.

Women's Fellowship
Mrs Maud Hollidge
53 Peel Road
Wealdstone
Middlesex HA3 7QX
T 0181 863 2887
A Christian group meeting weekly on Mon afternoon, affiliated to Wealdstone Baptist Church. Speakers & refreshments.

Sexual Abuse/Rape Crisis

Harrow Survivors of Sexual Abuse
Mrs Lorraine Warren
2 Rosslyn Crescent
Harrow
Middlesex HA1 2ST
T 0181 424 2846
Self-help group for women adult survivors of child sexual abuse.

Social

815 Club
Mrs Vivien Spiteri
10 Regent Close
Kenton
Middlesex HA8 8AB
T 0181 907 1756
Meets second Tue of each month at 8.15 pm at members' houses to discuss topics of interest to women such as theatre trips, meals out, darts, videos, etc. New members from all age groups welcome.

Women's Guild
Mrs Rachel Windsor
6 Chester Road
Northwood
Middlesex HA6 1BQ
T 01923 822752

Meets on first & third Tue afternoons of each month. Speakers & tea. Phone for further details.

TRANSPORT

Shop Mobility
Office (level 3)
St George's Centre
Harrow
Middlesex HA1 1HS
T 0181 861 2282
Also 0181 427 1200. Free service for people with difficulty getting around town centre shops. Help with short-term loan of electrically powered wheelchair/scooter or manual wheelchair. Special needs facilities.

WOMEN'S AID

Harrow Women's Aid
C/o HAVS
The Lodge
64 Pinner Road
Middlesex HA1 4HZ
T 0181 251 6537
Provides temporary refuge for women & their children who have suffered mental or physical harassment. A support groups maintains an emergency 24-hour call system.

HAVERING

ALTERNATIVE THERAPIES

Ladies' Yoga
Mrs J Benham
Spencers
North Road
Havering-atte-Bower
Romford RM4 1PP
T 01708 728245
Meets at North Romford Community Centre, Collier Row On Fri at 9.30 am and at Rise Park Infants School on Wed at 8 pm.

BEREAVEMENT

Havering and Brentwood Bereavement Service
Maureen Kolgour, Coordinator/Secretary
C/o St Francis Hospice
The Hall
Havering-atte-Bower
Romford RM4 1QH
T 01708 734239

CARERS

Carers' National Association - Havering branch
Mrs Fincham
13 Evansdale
Rainham
T 01708 559186
Meets at Mencap Hall, Victoria Road, Romford usually on third Thurs of each month at 7.45 pm.

CHILD CARE AND FAMILY

Chase Cross Baptist Church Mother & Toddler Group
Mrs G Turner
14 Judith Avenue
Romford RM5 2PL
T 01708 734814
Meets on Tue at Chase Cross Baptist Church 1.15-3 pm (term time only).

Harold Park Baptist Church Mother & Toddler Club
Sue Galliers
T 01708 381775
Meets at Harold Park Baptist Church, Harold Court Road, on Tue 1-3 pm (term time only).

Salvation Army Mother and Toddler Group
Mrs J Goldsmith
42 Herbert Road
Hornchurch RM11 3LT
T 01708 445342
Meets at the Salvation Army, Petersfield Avenue, Harold Hill on Thurs 10-11.30 am.

St Edward's Mother and Baby Group
Jenny Card
T 01708 746221
Meets on Thurs 9.30-11.30 am at Wykeham Hall, Market Place, Romford.

Upminster Methodist Church Mother and Toddler Group
Mrs N Holland, Leader
T 01708 250960
Meets on Tue 10.30 am-12 noon.

CONTRACEPTION/WELL WOMAN

Annie Prendergast Clinic
Ashton Gardens
Chadwell Heath
T 0181 599 2435

Comprehensive contraceptive & cytology services available. Emergency contraception, pregnancy testing, condoms, the pill, coil, cap, etc. Smear tests. Clinics Wed 5-8 pm; every other Sat 9 am-noon.

Elm Park Clinic
Abbs Cross Lane
Hornchurch
T 01708 443681
Blood pressure checks, urine tests, pregnancy testing, weight checks, cervical cytology (smear tests). Female doctor/nurse available. Clinics on Fri 9 am-noon.

Harold Hill Health Centre
Gooshays Drive
Harold Hill
T 01708 377004
Comprehensive contraceptive & cytology services available. Emergency contraception, pregnancy testing, condoms, the pill, coil, cap, etc. Smear tests. Clinic on Wed 1.30-4.30 pm.

Harold Wood Clinic
Gubbins Lane
Harold Wood
T 01708 340022
Contraceptive & cytology services available. Emergency contraception, pregnancy testing, condoms, the pill, coil, cap, etc. Smear tests. Clinics on Mon 5.30-8.30 pm; third Wed of each month 9 am-noon.

Hornchurch Clinic
Westland Avenue
Hornchurch
T 01708 440315
Comprehensive contraceptive & cytology services available. Emergency contraception, pregnancy testing, condoms, the pill, coil, cap, etc. Smear tests. Clinic on Tue 5.30-8.30 pm.

Lynwood Medical Centre
4 Lynwood Drive
Collier Row
T 01708 743244
Comprehensive contraceptive & cytology services available. Emergency contraception, pregnancy testing, condoms, the pill, coil, cap, etc. Smear tests. Clinic Thurs 4-7 pm.

Marks Gate Clinic
Lawns Farm Grove
Chadwell Heath
T 0181 590 9181
Comprehensive contraceptive & cytology services available. Emergency contraception, pregnancy testing, condoms, the pill, coil, cap, etc. Smear tests. Clinic on Mon 6-8 pm.

North Street Medical Centre
274 North Street
Romford
T 01708 757628
Comprehensive contraceptive & cytology services available. Emergency contraception, pregnancy testing, condoms, the pill, coil, cap, etc. Smear tests. Clinics Mon 6-8.30 pm; Sat 9-11.30 am.

Petersfield Surgery
70 Petersfield Avenue
Harold Hill
T 01708 343113
Comprehensive contraceptive & cytology services available. Emergency contraception, pregnancy testing, condoms, the pill, coil, cap, etc. Smear tests. Clinic on Fri 6-8 pm

Rainham Health Centre
Upminster Road South
Rainham
T 01708 552187
Comprehensive contraceptive & cytology services available. Emergency contraception, pregnancy testing, condoms, the pill, coil, cap, etc. Smear Tests. Clinic on Wed 5.30-7.30 pm.

Romford Clinic
Main Road
Romford
T 01708 742507
Blood pressure checks, urine tests, pregnancy testing, weight checks, cervical cytology (smear tests). Female doctor/nurse available. Clinics on second & fourth Fri of each month 9 am-noon.

Rosewood Medical Centre
1 Rosewood Avenue
Elm Park
T 01708 449100
Comprehensive contraceptive & cytology services available. Emergency contraception, pregnancy testing, condoms, the pill, coil, cap, etc. Smear tests. Clinic on Mon 6.30-8.30 pm.

LONDON - HAVERING

South Hornchurch Clinic
Southend Road
Rainham
T 01708 552821
Blood pressure checks, urine tests, pregnancy testing, weight checks, cervical cytology (smear tests). Female doctor/nurse available. Clinics on second and fourth Tue of each month 9 am-noon.

Surgery, The
39 Frederick Road
Rainham
T 01708 552738
Comprehensive contraceptive & cytology services available. Emergency contraception, pregnancy testing, condoms, the pill, coil, cap, etc. Smear tests. Clinic on Sat 9.30-11.30 am.

The Surgery
75 Sunnyside Gardens
Upminster
T 01708 640713
Comprehensive contraceptive & cytology services available. Emergency contraception, pregnancy testing, condoms, the pill, coil, cap, etc. Smear tests. Clinic on Wed 3-5 pm.

The Surgery
382 Upminster Road
Rainham
T 01708 556767
Comprehensive contraceptive & cytology services available. Emergency contraception, pregnancy testing, condoms, the pill, coil, cap, etc. Smear tests. Clinic on Mon 8-10 pm.

Upminster Clinic
St Mary's Lane
Upminster
T 01708 226170
Blood pressure checks, urine tests, pregnancy testing, weight checks, cervical cytology (smear tests). Female doctor/nurse available. Clinics on second & fourth Tue of each month 9 am-noon.

Western Road Medical Centre
99 Western Road
Romford
T 01708 757558
Contraceptive & cytology services available. Emergency contraception, pregnancy testing, condoms, the pill, coil, cap, etc. Smear tests. Clinic on Thurs 6.30-8.30 pm. For appt. phone between 11.30 am-3 pm.

HEALTH

Barking, Havering and Brentwood Alcohol Advisory
Mr C Rutter
Victoria Centre
Pettits Lane
T 01708 740072
Open Mon-Fri 9 am-5 pm or by appointment. 24-hour answering service. Support group for carers of those suffering from alcohol abuse.

LARGER/TALLER WOMEN

Big Is Beautiful
Dianne Rolph
164 Rush Green Road
Romford RM17 0GH
T 01708 745379
Ladies' outsize fashion sizes 16-36, including casual wear blouses. Friendly, helpful service.

POLITICS

Hornchurch Constituency Labour Party - Women's Section
the secretary
The Labour Hall
11 Park Lane
Hornchurch RM11 1BB
T 01708 742674

Romford Conservative Women's Constituency Committee
Mrs M Ramsey
85 Western Road
Romford RM1 3LS
T 01708 761583

PREGNANCY/CHILDBIRTH

Havering Home Birth Support Group
Tracy Moran
T 01708 703180

Women Together
Barbara Maskens
T 01708 454220
Havering post natal support group for women. Meets Fri 10 am-12 noon (creche open 9.30 am-12 noon). YMCA Rush Green Road, Romford. Phone above number in the evening.

Services

Joya Consultants
Lynda Edwards
23 Sussex Avenue
Harold Wood RM3 0TA
T 01708 377282
Training & consultancy, specialising in career consultancy incorporating personal presence & confidence skills, customer care, appraisal interview training, telephone techniques, assertiveness training.

Social

Avon Club
Mrs D Beaney
Cranham Community Centre
Marlborough Gardens
Upminster
T 01708 227456
Meets on alternate Wed 8 pm.

Deyncourt Ladies' Probus Club
Miss D Griffiths
17 Abington Court
Hall Lane
Upminster RM14 1BA
T 01708 224324
Meets in the Masonic Hall, Deyncourt Cardens, Upminster on third Wed of each month 11 am-2.30 pm.

Havering Ladies
Mrs P Tyrell, Chairman
7 Upland Court Road
Harold Wood
Romford RM3 0TT
T 01708 370220
Meets at United Reformed Church, Western Road, Romford on first Thurs of each month at 1.30 pm.

Rosewood Club
Mrs H Fisher
35 Ambleside Avenue
Elm Park
Hornchurch RM12 5ES
T 01708 450219
Meets at St Nicholas Church Hall, Eyhurst Avenue, Elm Park on Wed 7.30-9.45 pm.

South East Essex Association of Women's Clubs
Mrs Chittick
T 01708 450960
To find your nearest club, phone above number (evenings).

Sports and Leisure

Clockhouse Ladies' Bowling Club
Mrs Jean Saw
75 Park Drive
Upminster RM14 2AS
T 01708 228891
Meets at St Mary's Lane, Upminster.

Collier Row Ladies' Football Club
Mrsw J Setford
146 Machiters Walk
Romford RM1 4BU
T 01708 768185
Meets on Wed evenings. Phone above number for further details.

Cranham Ladies' Keep Fit Class
Mrs C S Robinson
33 Chelmer Road
Upminster RM14 1QT
T 01708 226708
Meets at Cranham Social Centre, Front Lane, Cranham on Wed 2-3.30 pm.

Elm Park Ladies Swimming and Life Saving Club
Mrs J Roberts
16 Nelmes Way
Hornchurch RM11 2QZ
T 01708 448174
Meets at Hornchurch Sportcentre, Harrow Lodge Park, Hornchurch on Thurs from 12 noon.

Elm Park Ladies' Bowls Club
Mrs P Miller
120 Saunton Road
Hornchurch RM12 4HB
T 01708 437538
Meets at Upper Rainham Road, Hornchurch on Tue, Wed, Thurs & Fri.

Haynes Park Ladies' Bowling Club
Mrs S Fishlock
135 Osborne Road
Hornchurch RM11 1HF
T 01708 448645
Meets at Haynes Park, Slewins Lane, Hornchurch on Tue & Thurs at 2 pm from May-September.

Keep Fit Group - Classes in Aerobics
Jean Madden
13 Primrose Court
King's Road
Brentwood

T 01277 224895
Meets at Harold Wood Neighbourhood Centre on Thurs 10.30-11.30 pm.

Langtons Keep Fit Club for Ladies
Mrs R Warnes
28 Beverley Gardens
Hornchurch RM11 3PA
T 01708 447638
Meets at Langtons Junior School, Westland Avenue, Hornchurch on Thurs 7.30-9.30 pm.

Liberty of Havering Ladies' Bowling Club
Mrs C O'Connor
27 Stafford Avenue
Hornchurch RM11 2EU
T 01708 472293
Ladies' bowling club. Open from end of April to end of September.

Nu-Trend Slimming and Nutrition Club
Mrs E Goldsmith
43 Albany Road
Hornchurch RM12 4AE
T 01708 447429
Meets at Seabrook Hall, Fidlers Roundabout, Dagenham on Thurs 7 pm.

Saffron Ladies' Keep Fit
Mrs Julia Pagram
7 Lynwood Close
Collier Row
Romford RM5 2QU
T 01708 757678
Meets Tue 8-9.30 pm at Cranfield junior school, White Hart Lane, Collier Row, Romford. Women's Keep Fit Association. Fitness through movement, exercise and dance.

South Essex Keep Fit Association
Heather Deacon, Hon Secretary
36 West Malling Way
Hornchurch RM12 5RS
T 01708 550617
Provides ongoing training for current Keep Fit Association teachers. Teacher training courses. Provides all members, teachers & class members with opportunity to take part in keep fit & various social events.

SUPPORT

Havering Agoraphobic Society
Margaret Kingston
T 01708 767738

TRANSPORT

Shopmobility
Keith Billingham
Angel Way Centre
1-3 Angel Way
Romford RM1 4JH
T 01708 739431
Phone between 9.30 am and 4.45 pm.

HILLINGDON

CENTRES FOR WOMEN

Hillingdon Women's Centre
333 Long Lane
Hillingdon
Middlesex UB10 9JU
T 01895 259578
Open Mon, Thurs 9 am-5 pm, Tue, Wed 9 am-4.30 pm. Free pregnancy testing, legal advice (Mon 6-7.15 pm, Wed 2-4 pm), one-to-one counselling, outings, acitivites, campaigning, resources, speakers.

CONTRACEPTION/WELL WOMAN

Hayes Brook Centre
Minet Clinic
Avondale Drive
Hayes
Middlesex UB3 3PF
T 0181 813 7050
Open Tue 5-7 pm; Sat 9.30-11.30 am To make an appointment outside opening hours, phone 0171 580 2991. Free confidential contraceptive advice. Free condoms & other contraceptive supplies.

Uxbridge Brook Centre
1st Floor
Fountains Mill
81 High Street
London UB8 1JR
T 01895 813595
Open Sat 2-4 pm. To make an appointment outside opening hours, phone 0171 580 2991. Free, confidential contraceptive advice. Free condoms & other contraceptive supplies. Pregnancy testing & quick results.

ETHNIC MINORITIES

Hillingdon Women's Communication Service
C/o Hillingdon Women's Centre
333 Long Lane
Hillingdon
Middlesex UB10 9JU
T 01895 259578

For Black & Asian women: interpretation, translation (mainly Hindi, Gujarati, Urdu, Punjabi & Bengali), counselling, legal advice, pregnancy testing. General support & advice. Open Sat 1-3 pm.

HEALTH

Hillingdon Anorexics, Bulimics & Compulsive Eaters' Group
Maureen
T 01923 823441
Phone between 7.30 and 9.30 pm on Mon or Wed.

LESBIAN AND BISEXUAL

Amazon Group
C/o Hillingdon Women's Centre
333 Long Lane
Hillingdon
Middlesex UB10 9JU
T 01895 259578

OLDER WOMEN

Older Women's Group
C/o Hillingdon Women's Centre
333 Long Lane
Hillingdon
Middlesex UB10 9JU
T 01895 259578
Meets at the Women's Centre on alternate Tue 1.30-3.30 pm. Offers practical & emotional support & occasional speakers.

SEXUAL ABUSE/RAPE CRISIS

Phoenix Group
C/o Hillingdon Women's Centre
333 Long Lane,
Hillingdon
Middlesex UB10 9JU
T 01895 259578
Self-help support group for women survivors of sexual abuse. Meets weekly at the Centre.

SPORTS AND LEISURE

Academy Netball Club
Sally Exxex
177b Swakeleys Road
Ickenham
Uxbridge
Middlesex UB10 0AE
T 01895 675993
Plays in Greater London & National leagues. For women only. New members are welcome, provided they are reasonably good players.

HOUNSLOW

ACCOMMODATION

Asian Women's Refuge
T 0181 843 2333
Also 0181 572 8656 & crisis line 0800 374 618 (free phone). Contact also through London Women's Aid 0171 251 6537. Offers refuge, support & advice for Asian women & children.

Homelessness Unit
London Borough of Hounslow
Civic Centre, Lampton Road
Hounslow
Middlesex TW3 1DR
T 0181 862 5280
For people seeking housing. Assessment of needs & eligibility for housing & referral to Housing Advice Service.

Housing Equalities Team
housing department
London Borough of Hounslow
Civic Centre, Lampton Road
Hounslow
Middlesex TW3 1DR
T 0181 862 5280
Support & advice to women experiencing racial harassment &/or domestic violence. Wheelchair accessible. Signing & minicom available. Interpretation services in most languages.

Integrated Care Ltd - 'L'attitudes'
Norman Harknett, Manager
13 Bolton Road
Chiswick
London W4 3TE
T 0181 994 1272 F 0181 995 8925
Unit for young women with challenging behaviours, staffed 24 hours a day.

ARTS AND CRAFTS

Arts Team
Civic Centre
Lampton Road
Hounslow
Middlesex TW3 4DN
T 0181 862 5804
Offers wide range of arts events and ensures that activities for women are represented in the community. Provides safe transport for women and creche facilities. Wheelchair accessible.

LONDON - HOUNSLOW

Navrang Theatre
Chand Sherma
45 Kirton Close
Chiswick
London W4 5UQ
T 0181 994 2965
Uses drama to help women in assertiveness training and to develop an understanding of issues related to their position in society. Runs workshops and after-show discussions including the audience.

Paul Robeson Theatre
Centre Space
24 Treaty Centre, High Street
Hounslow
Middlesex TW3
T 0181 577 6969
Organises women's cabaret events and encourages local women to get involved. Organises plays, concerts of interest to women and children's theatre workshops. Events during holiday periods.

Women Writers' Network
Susan Kerr
55 Burlington Lane
Chiswick
London W4 3ET
T 0181 994 0598
Making contact with women writers & editors. Over 200 members with wide range of writing interests - journalism, fiction, non-fiction, poetry, drama, etc. Monthly meetings with editors or agents. Newsletter.

BEREAVEMENT

Bereavement Services for Hounslow
Thanet House
191 High Street
Brentford
Middlesex TW8 8LB
T 0181 568 6776
One-to-one counselling service for the recently bereaved in their own homes. Monthly group meeting for ongoing support for the bereaved. Support for people with Asian languages.

BUSINESS SUPPORT SCHEMES

Cranford Training Group - Women's Project
Kim Bennett
Cranford Community School
High Street
Cranford
Middlesex TW5 9PD
T 0181 897 6609
Offers women courses in business skills, eg RSA Administration NVQ levels 1,2, & 3; Women for Management RSA level 4. Free training lasting between 3 months to a year. Weekly training allowance. Creche.

CARERS

Carers' National Association - Hounslow Branch
The Lodge
The Grove
Isleworth
Middlesex TW7 4JD
T 0181 570 6990
Help and support to carers of disabled people. Advice on welfare benefits and other services helpful to disabled people and their carers.

Hounslow Crossroads Care Scheme
28 The Butts
Brentford
Middlesex TW8 8BL
T 0181 568 2022
A scheme for caring for carers. Relieves stress experienced by carers of people with physical, mental or sensory impairments by providing trained care attendants in the home free of charge.

CENTRES FOR WOMEN

Asian Women's Centre
Manjeet Mangat
86 Hibernia Road
Hounslow
Middlesex TW3 3RN
T 0181 577 6325 F 0181 577 2381
Facility for Asian women, classes, workshops, clubs, special events, outings, social groups. It is a community centre & space is hired out. Computing facilities.

COMPUTERS/IT

Heston Adult Education Centre
Anne Lloyd
Heston Community School
Heston Road
Heston
Middlesex TW5 0QR
T 0181 577 1166
Offers women part-time & evening classes, such as keyboarding, word processing, counselling, British Sign Language, soft furnishing & upholstery. Most word

processing tutors can speak some Asian languages.

COUNSELLING AND THERAPY

Star Centre
65 Bell Road
Hounslow
Middlesex TW3 3NU
T 0181 572 4211   F 0181 814 0311
Offers counselling & help/support for people with problems. Referrals necessary. Advice on welfare benefits & advocacy. Women's groups & women's befriending.

TASHA in Hounslow
Chi Maher
West Middlesex Hospital, R Block
Twickenham Road
Isleworth
Middlesex TW7 6AF
T 0181 569 9933   F 0181 568 0062
Open Mon-Fri 9.30 am-5.30 pm. Confidential information, advice, support, counselling, holistic health care to individuals affected by tranquillisers, sleeping pills, stress, anxiety, depression, agoraphobia.

ETHNIC MINORITIES

African-Caribbean Evenings
London
T 0181 847 6245
Social group offering mutual support for Black women & their families. Focuses on issues relevant to African & Caribbean women living in the community. Drama groups, cultural activities & social outings.

Anjuman-E-Khawateen
Muktaben Shah
28 Lansdowne Road
Hounslow
Middlesex TW3 1LQ
T 0181 572 3599
Meets Tue at Oxley Centre, Montague Road, Hounslow. Lectures on various issues covering women's health, social & religious requirements.

Ashra Asian Carers Project
5th Floor, Holdsworth House
65-73 Staines Road
Hounslow
Middlesex TW3 3HW
T 0181 814 0838

Supports Asian carers caring for physically disabled, frail & housebound Asian elderly people.

Asian Talkback
Ashi Dhillon
12 School Road
Hounslow
Middlesex TW3 1QZ
T 0181 577 3226
Confidential support group for Asian young women who may feel conflict between their experience at home, school or social life. One-to-one counselling & family mediation. Recreational activities.

Asian Women's Counselling Service
Dr L Patel
5th Floor, Holdsworth House
65-73 Staines Road
Hounslow
Middlesex TW3 3HW
T 0181 570 6568
Open Tue-Thurs 9 am-5 pm. Confidential counselling service, mainly for Asian women. Trained women counsellors offer cultural sensitivity. Self-help support groups also available.

Asian Women's Group
Feltham Child and Family Centre
Danesbury Road
Feltham
Middlesex TW13 5AL
T 0181 890 3816
Helps Asian women to get together, tackle depression & isolation, make friends, share ideas, interests, pursue skills. Outings. Translation in Urdu & interpretation in Urdu, Punjabi, Gujarati & Hindi.

Cranford Language Class
Cranford Public Library
Bath Road
Cranford
Middlesex
T 0181 384 2009
Free conversation practice to help mainly Asian women prepare for ESOL courses in English.

DOSTI
Brentford Child and Family Centre
No 1 The Butts
Brentford
Middlesex
T 0181 560 8041

Also 0181 577 0017. A social group empowering Asian women to get together, tackle depression & isolation, make friends, share ideas, interests, etc. Outings & recreation.

EKTA (Heston/Cranford) Older Women's Group
62 Westway
Heston
Middlesex TW5 0JG
Self-help group for older Asian women. Meets two afternoons a week. Discusses issues of interest to women. Workshops, outings, holidays. Facilities for disabled women.

EKTA Women's Social Group
Chiswick Child and Family Centre
Hogarth School, Chiswick
London W4
T 0181 862 6573
Activities for Asian women with young children. Opportunities to make friends, tackle isolation, share problems & pursue skills. Recreations. Hindi/Punjabi translation & interpretation service available.

Feltham Asian Women's Group
Mina Thakraz
Feltham People's Centre, Riverside
High Street
Feltham
Middlesex TW13 4AH
T 0181 751 4618
Aims to provide a safe meeting place for Asian women of all ages to share their experiences & socialise. Recreational activities, information sessions & advice surgeries supported by professionals.

Horn of Africa Somali Women's Association
Samiya Aden
12 School Road
Hounslow
Middlesex TW3 1QZ
T 0181 577 3226
Addresses the welfare & well-being of Somali women & their children. Advice & counselling relating to immigration, housing, social security, employment, training & women's refugee rights. Creche.

Hounslow Project, The
Ashi Dillon
12 School Road
Hounslow
Middlesex TW3 1QZ
Advice & casework in five Asian languages on issues such as housing, employment, immigration, domestic violence & welfare rights. Helps to develop self-help groups in the Asian communities, eg women's groups.

Maa Aur Bachhe
Jas Montini
Feltham Child and Family Centre
Danesbury Road
Feltham
Middlesex TW13 5AS
T 0181 893 7816
A social group for Asian women with young children with an opportunity to meet other women to reduce isolation. Various recreational & cultural activities such as keep fit, art workshops, etc.

Millan Asian Women's Group
Mrs S K Sharma
91 Barrack Road
Hounslow Heath
Middlesex TW4 6AN
T 0181 230 9571
Meets every Thurs 11 am-2 pm at Montague Hall, Hounslow. Various activities such as discussions & exercises. Help & support to women. Care for elderly, disabled & housebound women.

Mulakaat
Child and Family Centre
Nantley House
33 Lampton Road, Hounslow
Middlesex TW3 1JG
T 0181 577 0017
Asian women's social group for women to tackle depression & isolation, make friends, share ideas, interests, etc. Outings. Translation available in Urdu & interpretation in Urdu, Punjabi, Gujarati & Hindi.

Pakistan Welfare Association
Voluntary Action Centre
12 School Road
Hounslow
Middlesex TW6 2JA
T 0181 577 3226
Offers advice, information on immigration, housing, matrimonial issues, domestic violence and benefits. Help & support to single mothers. Organises language classes.

SAHIL - Single Asian Mothers' Association
Jameel Lone
C/o The Multicultural Centre
49-51 Derby Road
Hounslow
Middlesex TW3 3UQ
T 0181 577 2702
Self-help group providing advice, discussion, counselling. Social, educational & recreational activities. Provides help to women such as decorating homes, removals, help with getting to hospitals, legal advice.

SANGHAM (Single and Young Asian Women's Group)
Mrs Parveen Gulzar
23 Concorde Close
Hounslow
Middlesex TW3 UDG
T 0181 570 0161
Provides emotional support in distressing situations to young girls & young Asian unemployed mothers. Information & advice on health & safety. Celebration of national & international events.

GIRLS/YOUNG WOMEN

Hounslow Youth Counselling Service
78 St John's Road
Isleworth
Middlesex TW7 6RU
T 0181 568 1818
Free, confidential counselling to women & men aged 14-25. Issues relating to domestic violence, sexual harassment, divorce, teenage pregnancy & drug & alcohol abuse.

HEALTH

Ethnic Alcohol Counselling in Hownslow (EACH)
Zaibby Shaikh, Director
Holdsworth House
65-73 Staines Road
Hownslow
Middlesex TW3 3HW
T 0181 577 6059 F 0181 577 6573
Open Mon-Fri 9.30 am-5.30 pm, Wed 9.30 am-7.30 pm. Free confidential counselling to people with drink or other problems. Women's group. Information on HIV & AIDS. Appts preferred but can drop in.

Hounslow HIV/AIDS Unit
Policy Office
Civic Centre
Lampton Road
Middlesex TW3 4DN
T 0181 862 5004
Open daily 9.30-11 am Resource centre providing information on HIV/AIDS, sexual health, drugs & related services.

LEGAL MATTERS

Hounslow Law Centre Ltd
51 Lampton Road
Hounslow
Middlesex TW3 1JG
T 0181 570 9505
Open Mon-Fri 10 am-1 pm; Thurs 6-7 pm. Free legal advice on issues such as domestic violence, divorce, employment, immigration, housing, benefits, welfare rights. Drop-in; no need for an appointment.

SEXUAL ABUSE/RAPE CRISIS

Hounslow Rape and Crisis Support Group
P O Box 315
Hounslow
Middlesex TW3 4DN
T 0181 572 0100
Helpline listed above operates Mon 7-9 pm. Free counselling & support by trained women for girls & women who have been raped or have experienced abuse in any form. Also information on health & legal matters.

Survivors of Sexual Abuse
The Open Door Project
Boundaries Road
Feltham
Middlesex TW13 5DT
T 0181 890 4732
Three facilitated self-help groups; referral agency. The facilitators are survivors. Phone for details of the groups.

SOCIAL

Cranford Women's Group
Sheila Kanwal
43 Woodfield Road
Cranford
Middlesex TW4 6LL
T 0181 897 9333
Social & educational women's group offering encouragement to women to meet other women in the community & to know what goes on in their community. Discusses local & national issues. Outings.

SPORTS AND LEISURE

Barnes Bridge Ladies' Rowing Club
the captain
Civil Service Boathouse
Riverside Drive
Dukes Meadow
London W4 2SH
T 0181 994 0025
Rowing for women novices to senior levels. Boats sculling to Eights. Leisure & competitive rowing. Meets Tue & Thurs evenings & Sat & Sun mornings.

Brentford Fountain Leisure Centre
658 Chiswick High Road
Brentford
Middlesex TW8 0HJ
T 0181 994 9596
Open for women only Wed 5.45-9 pm for sauna, jacuzzi & steam room, badminton, swimming, aerobics, aqua aerobics & step aerobics. Tue & Thurs 9-10 am aerobics for women only. Phone for further details.

Feltham Airparcs Leisure Centre
Uxbridge Road
Hanworth
Middlesex TW13 5EG
T 0181 894 9156
Women's leisure (aerobics, aquafit, squash, circuits, swimming, sauna, steam, exercise suite & creche Thurs 9.30 am-12.30 pm & Tue 6-10 pm; health suite Tue & Thurs 10 am-9 pm; swimming lessons Wed.

Heston Community Sports Hall
Heston Road
Heston
Middlesex TW5 0QR
T 0181 570 6544
Open Mon-Fri 6-10 pm & Sat -Sun 9 am-9 pm Women only body conditioning/ training Fri 7-8 pm. Activities for older people. Facilities for disabled women (mixed groups). Basketball Wed 6-8 pm

Heston Pool
New Heston Road
Heston
Middlesex TW5 0LW
T 0181 571 4396
Open every day. Women only activities: Wed 9 am-noon - swimming, aerobics, gym, sauna. Mon 5-9 pm same as above plus aquafit classes, Sat 3-5 pm women only swimming, with women only lifeguards.

Hownslow Community Recreation Outreach Team
Jo Valks, Recreation Development Officer
Heston Road
Heston
Middlesex TW5 0QR
T 0181 569 5867
To increase participation & quality of recreation provision for women. Information on women's sports activities in the borough of Hounslow.

Isleworth Recreation Centre
Twickenham Road
Isleworth
Middlesex TW7 7EU
T 0181 560 6855
Open Mon, Wed, Fri 9 am-9 pm; Tue & Thurs 12-9 pm Wed 9 am-12 pm & Fri 5-9.30 pm for women only: Keep fit, gym, circuit training, sauna. Ladies only swimming Fri 5-6 & 8-9.30 pm

New Chiswick Pool
Edensor Road
Chiswick
London W5 2RG
T 0181 747 8811
Open Mon, Wed & Fri 9 am-10 pm; Tues & Thurs 12 noon-10 pm; Sat & Sun 9 am-6 pm Women only leisure: Thurs 6-10 pm & Fri 10 am-noon. Free creche. Ante-natal & post-natal courses available.

Southville Centre, The
Jo Valks, Recreation Development Officer
Southville Road
Bedfont
Middlesex
T 0181 751 4229
Women only workout Wed 1-2 pm. Free creche. Parent & toddler group, over 50s activities, youth club programme, classes for parents with children.

SUPPORT

Cranford Good Neighbours Scheme
654 Bath Road
Cranford
Middlesex TW5 9TN
T 0181 384 2009
Offers help & support to anyone who is isolated from community life. Mother & toddler group. English conversation classes. Ante- & post-natal exercise classes. Confidential counselling.

Violence Against Women

Hounslow Monitoring Project - Women's Support Project
Kiran Ballay
5th Floor, Holdsworth House
65-73 Staines Road
Hounslow
Middlesex
T 0181 572 8656
Free 24-hour helpline: 0800 374 618. Free legal advice, practical & moral support for women suffering from domestic violence & related problems. Support group meets weekly from 3-7 pm. Creche.

Islington

Accommodation

Homeless Action and Accommodation
52-54 Featherstone Street
London EC1Y 8RT
T 0171 251 6783 F 0171 251 3361
Temporary accommodation for single homeless women. Runs 30 houses in London with places for around 160 women. Campaigning for increased housing provision for single women.

Agriculture

Morrigan Garden Services
Fiona Morrigan
134 Downham Road
Islington
London N1 3HJ
T 0171 226 7477
Qualified & experienced gardener can provide advice, planning, site clearance & preparation, planting & maintenance. One-off jobs or regular service. Also rubbish removal. Medium sized van. Own tools.

Alternative Therapies

Spiral Centre
Aleine Ridge/Julie Walkling
208-209 Upper Street
London N1 1RL
T 0171 359 0187
aleine@spiral.u-net.com
An all women practice, founded by two women, offering counselling, homoeopathy, osteopathy, etc.

Arts

Black Women in the Arts
Lola Aroun/Beverley Davis
Metropolitan Business Centre
Unit B20, 1st Floor
Kingsland Road
London N1 5AZ
T 0171 923 7658
Supporting & promoting Black women visual & performing artists. Agency services, management of artists, supply/support conferences & special functions, publications, training, educational programmes, etc.

Arts and Crafts

Ambache Chamber Orchestra & Ensemble
Heather Baxter, General Manager
9 Beversbrook Road
London N19 4QG
T 0171 281 7880 F 0171 263 4027
Professional chamber orchestra & ensemble specialising in music of Mozart & contemporaries. Also known for pioneering revival of music by women composers from 18-20th centuries. Diana Ambache Musical Director.

Art and Soul
Rebecca Bramwell
Unit G
14 Belgravia Workshops
157-163 Marlborough Road
London N19 4NF
T 0171 263 0421 F 0171 263 0421
A framing service for artists, designers & photographers.

Islington Arts Factory
2 Parkhust Road
London N7 0SF
T 0171 607 0561
Open Mon-Thurs 10 am-10 pm, Sat 2-6 pm & Fri 10 am-7 pm. Classes & courses in dance, music, visual arts, photography & writing. Vegetarian cafe. Dark room. Rehearsal facilites. Wheelchair accessible.

Lesley Craze Gallery
Lesley Craze
34 Clerkenwell Green
London EC1R 0DR
T 0171 608 0393 F 0171 608 0393
Contemporary jewellery gallery with non precious work in craze & precious work. Also new contemporary textile gallery at 33 Clerkenwell Green. Opening hours for all gallery areas Mon-Sat 10 am-5.30 pm

LONDON - ISLINGTON

Maple Carpentry
Ruth Thomson
18 Cloudesley Road
Islington
London N1 0EQ
T 0171 833 5890
An all-round carpenter/joiner. Furniture making. Builds customised cupboards, doors, locks, wondows. Phone above number for further information.

Signwriting
Yasemin Sami
23b Grosvenor Avenue
Highbury
London N5 2NP
T 0171 226 4403
Signwriting. Specialist painting techniques. Stencilling, wood-graining, marbling, stucco, sponging, stippling, gilding, etc.

Titus Davies
Titus Davies
6 Lambert Street
Islington
London N1 1JE
T 0171 609 7200
Specialises in small, free-standing furniture such as chairs & tables. Also fitted work. Uses non-tropical hardwoods. Sculptures in wood. Part of the Ashwin Furniture Workshop.

Velvet Fist
Tara Tierney
6 Carleton Gardens
Brecknock Road
London N19 5AQ
T 0171 267 1071
graham@sodom.demon.co.uk
A cappella singing group of 12 female voices, singing for peace, trade union representation and international socialism. Affiliated to MANA (Musicians Against Nuclear Armaments).

BUSINESS SUPPORT SCHEMES
Islington Enterprise Agency
64 Essex Road
London N1 8LR
T 0171 359 8982 F 0171 3354 1518
Offers Women into Business Management Certificate training; refugee training programme; 40-week programme covering ESOL, literacy, numeracy, IT & small business development.

CARERS
Islington Carers' Forum
C/o Carers Co-Ordinator
Room 313, Highbury House
3 Highbury Crescent
London N5 1RW
T 0171 278 6645
Run by carers for all carers in Islington. Networking, supoort, information & assistance. Meetings held at Town Hall. Wheelchair accessible & toilet for people with disabilities.

Islington Crossroads
91 Upper Street
London N1 ONP
T 0171 359 7169
Respite support for carers of people with physical/learning disabilities; dementia respite scheme for carers of people with dementia/Alzheimers; special project scheme providing direct support.

CENTRES FOR WOMEN
Bangladesh Women's Organisation
Rozina or Aleya
58 Hanley Road
London N4 3DR
T 0171 263 7005
Open Mon-Fri 10 am-4 pm. Courses in English, sewing, music & cookery. Day trips for mothers & children. Help & advice on housing, social security, unemployment benefit, pensions, widows' allowance, etc.

Manor Gardens Centre
6-9 Manor Gardens
London N7 6LA
T 0171 272 4231 F 0171 263 0596
Open Mon-Fri. Health/community centre with many different women's organisations: AGLOW, RSI group, special housing project (SHAD), groups for Benglai, Asian & Turkish/Kurdish women, couselling for women, etc.

Tindlemanor
52-54 Featherstone Street
London EC1Y 8RT
T 0171 608 0929
Open Mon-Fri. The base for many women's groups, including Women's Health, London Women and Munual Trades, Rights of Women, etc. Wheelchair accessible & toilet facilities for disabled people.

CHILD CARE AND FAMILY

Accident Prevention Loan Scheme
6-9 Manor Gardens
London N7 6LA
T 0171 272 4231 F 0171 263 0596
Open Mon, Wed, Thurs 9.30 am-2.30 pm
Reducing incidence of preventable accidents occurring to young children. Free safety equipment for low income parents, eg fireguards, safety gates, harnesses.

Community Education Service
Ian Spencer
Islington Council
Laycock Street
London N1 1TH
T 0171 457 5646
Under Fives' workers. Responsible for registration of childminders & can supply list of registered childminders. Provides range of paycentres, play schemes, after school provision & youth clubs.

Friends United Network
Francesca Weinberg
404 Camden Road
London N7 0SJ
T 0171 609 5444 F 0171 609 5470
Provides long-term friends & mentors for emotionally & socially disadvantaged children & teenagers (aged 5-16 on referral) in Camden & Islington.

Islington Under 3s Group
Block i
The Barnsbury Complex
Offord Road
London N1 1QH
T 0171 457 5916
Parent & toddler support group providing jump-around equipment, soft play equipment, toy library & training opportunities for those setting up & running parent & toddler groups. Free for Islington residents.

National Council of Voluntary Child Care Organisations
Unit 4
Pride Court
81-82 White Lion Street
London N1 9PF
T 0171 833 3310

Transcend
61 Banner Street
London EC1Y 8PX
T 0171 490 1696

Open Mon-Fri 9 am-5 pm Referral agency for disabled children & families. Holiday weekend trips. Playscheme. Wheelchair accessible & toilet facilities for disabled people.

Whittington Park Community Centre
Yerbury Road
London N19 4RS
T 0171 272 1847 F 0171 281 4890
Full time nursery provision Mon-Fri 9 am-4 pm; morning playgroup Mon-Fri 9.30 am-12.30 pm; drop in session Mon-Fri 1-3 pm. Pensioners' lunch/social club/ keep fit; rooms available for hire, etc.

CONTRACEPTION/WELL WOMAN

Barnsbury Clinic
Carnegie Street
London N1
T 0171 530 4100
Free contraceptive advice & supplies. Clinics on Tue & Thurs 9.30-11 am.

Bath Street Health Centre
60 Bath Street
London EC1V 9JX
T 0171 530 2700
Free contraceptive advice & supplies. Clinic on Thurs 9.30-11 am Well woman clinic Fri 9.30-11.30 am.

Finsbury Health Centre
Pine Street
London EC1
T 0171 530 4200
Free contraceptive advice & supplies. Clinics on Tue 9.30 am-1.30 pm & 5-6.45 pm; Thurs 5-6.45 pm; Fri 3-5.30 pm; psychosexual counselling Fri 1-2.30 pm.

Goodinge Health Centre
Goodinge Close
North Road
London N7 9EW
T 0171 530 4900
Free contraceptive advice & supplies. Clinics Wed 5-6.45 pm; Sat 9.30-11.30 am (appt necessary). Well woman clinic Tue 9.30-11.30 am.

Highbury Grange Health Centre
Highbury Grange
London N5 2QB
T 0171 530 2888

LONDON - ISLINGTON

Free contraceptive advice & supplies. Clinics on Mon 9.30-11.30 am; Tue 5-6.45 pm; Wed 9.30-1.30 am; Thurs 5-6.45 pm. Well woman clinic on Tue 9.15-11.15 am.

Hornsey Rise Health Centre
Hornsey Rise
London N19
T 0171 530 2400
Free contraceptive advice & supplies. Clinics on Mon 5-6.45 pm; Thurs 9.30-11.30 am.

Islington Brook Centre
Manor Gardens Centre
6 Manor Gardens
Holloway Road
London N7 6LA
T 0171 272 5599
Open Tue 1.15-3.15 pm; Thurs 4.30-6.30 pm. For appointment outside opening hours, phone 0171 580 2991. Free, confidential contraceptive advice. Free condoms & other contraceptive supplies. Pregnancy tests.

Manor Gardens Health Centre
6-9 Manor Gardens
London N7 6LA
T 0171 272 4231
Free contraceptive advice & supplies. Clinics Mon 9.30-11 am; Tue 5.15-7 pm; Wed 5-6.45 pm Well woman clinic Thurs 9.30-11.30 am.

River Place Health Centre
River Place
Essex Road
London N1 2DE
T 0171 530 2900
Free contraceptive advice & supplies. Clinics Tue & Thurs 5-6.45 pm; Fri 9.30-11.30 pm Well woman clinic Thurs 9.30-11.30 am.

COUNSELLING AND THERAPY

Highbury Counselling Centre
28 Highbury Grove
London N5 2EA
T 0171 226 2190
Offers free, short-term counselling for unwaged. Low rates for waged.

Islington MIND
Manor Gardens Centre
8 Manor Gardens
London N7 6LA
T 0171 272 6797
Advice information support & counselling services. Campaigns for improved mental health services. Drop-in centre open six days a week. Women only day Thurs. No creche. Lesbian & gay mental health support group.

Islington Women's Counselling Centre
Joanna Best
Eastgate Building
131b St John's Way
London N19 3RQ
T 0171 281 2673 F 0171 281 2673
Free counselling for women who live or work in Islington, have an income of less than £4,000 p.a., have not had counselling/therapy before, & have not had the opportunity to study at degree level. Training.

Nuala White
Nuala White
10 Alexander Road
London N19 3PQ
T 0171 263 2076
Psychotherapy for individuals & groups.

Stress Project, The
Shelburne House
2 Shelburne Road
London N7 6DL
T 0171 700 3938 F 0171 607 6961
Counselling, advice, information & support to enable young people, women & people from minority ethnic groups to develop & maintain good mental, emotional & psychological health. Alternative therapies.

DISABILITY

Women With Disabilities Support Group
Finsbury Neighbourhood Office
85 Central Street
London EC1V 8DT
T 0171 251 1661
Counselling for people with disabilities having sexual or relationship difficulties. Information, support for carers/professionals. Study days/workshops. Wheelchair accessible & toilet for disabled people.

ENVIRONMENT

BTCV
80 York Way
London N1 9AG
T 0171 278 4293
Conservation group with a lesbian, bisexual & gay section.

EQUAL OPPS
Women's Committee and Women's Equality Unit
Islington Council
Town Hall
Upper Street
London N1 2UD
T 0171 477 3133
Working to improve the lives & opportunities of women & girls in Islington. Provides information, advice & training to local women, women's groups, etc. Seeks external funding for resources for women, etc.

ETHNIC MINORITIES
African Refugee Women's Group
African Refugee Housing Association
Unit 1, 1st Floor
36-40 York Way
London N1 9AB
T 0171 278 3358
Contact the women's group via the housing association.

African Women's Information and Research Agency (AWIRA)
Wanguri Wa Goro
11b Waterloo Terrace
London N1 1TQ
T 0171 704 1153   F 0171 704 1153

African Women's Welfare Association
Maureen Okwu
Unit 14
321 Essex Road
London N1 3PS
T 0171 226 3899   F 0171 226 3899
Meets on one Sat a month at noon. Advice, information, counselling & support to African women living anywhere in London. Igbo, Swahili & Yoruba spoken.

Anglo Asian Women's Association
Mrs Siddiqui
25 Eversholt Road
London N4 3DG
T 0171 272 7031
Legal & welfare rights advice, including advice on housing, education & social services. Counselling, support & visits to disabled people, pensioners & people in hospital. Telephone Sun, Mon & Thurs mornings.

Arachne Greek Cypriot Women's Group
Tina Refenes/Eleftheria Constantinidou
3rd Floor
67-83 Seven Sisters Road
London N7 6BU
T 0171 263 6261   F 0171 263 6261
Open 10 a.m-3 pm & some evenings. Mon: keep fit, Pitman English; Tue: mother & toddler group, ESOL with creche, young women's group; Wed: computer & exercise classes, ESOL; Fri: ESOL & dance classes.

Asian Resource Centre
Purima Chakravorty
229 Seven Sisters Road
London N4 2DA
T 0171 263 3182
Women only Thurs 12 pm onwards. Craft & design classes, informal talks, discussion groups. Free entry. Wheelchair access.

Association of Blind Asians
322 Upper Street
London N1 2XQ
T 0171 226 1950
Open Mon-Fri 9 am-5 pm. Support, training, social activities to visually impaired Asians & other people who are partially sighted or blind. Meetings held at Royal National Institute for the Blind (RNIB).

Bengali Women's Group
Orkney House
199 Caledonian Road
London N1 0SQ
T 0171 278 9500
Open Mon & Fri 10.30 am-5 pm. Cultural functions & classes in the mother tongue. Legal work & referrals for welfare, advice & information. The welfare of children is taken into consideration.

Bengali Women's Group
Manor Gardens Centre
6-9 Manor Gardens
London N7 6LA
T 0171 272 4231   F 0171 263 0596
Open Wed morning. Information, support & activities for local Bengali women. Creche. Wheelchair access.

Black Women on the Move
Celina Smith
C/o Reel Life Television
9 Cynthia Street
London N1 9JF
T 0171 713 1585   F 0171 713 1603
Promoting networking, social events & debate among interested Black women. All

women, regardless or age or profession are welcome. Newsletter, organised meetings, auctions. Supporters welcome.

Eritrean Mothers' Project
C/o The Eritrean Community in the UK
266-268 Holloway Road
London N7 6NE
T 0181 749 3173
Open Mon-Fri 10 am-5 pm. Support, advice & information on housing, immigration, education & health. English classes. Support group for Eritrean women to meet & share experiences. Wheelchair accessible.

Finsbury Bengali Women's Group
community worker
Finsbury Neighbourhood Office
85 Central Street
London EC1V 8DT
T 0171 251 1661
Meets Wed 2-3.30 pm. Social activities, outings, speakers on topics of interest to Bengali women. Wheelchair access & toilet facilities for people with disabilities.

Greek and Cypriot Cultural, Community and Youth Centre
178a Seven Sisters Road
London N7 1PX
T 0171 263 6445   F 0171 263 6445
Provides a range of activities for Greek & Cypriot women: European exchange scheme, writing group, medical advice, child rearing, re-habilitation for women returning to work, schemes for elderly women.

Iranian Community Centre - Women's Section
266-268 Holloway Road
London N7 6NE
T 0171 700 0477   F 0171 700 3248
Advice & information on immigration, housing welfare rights, health, education & employment. Women-only drop-in Mon & Wed. Telephone advice on Tue, Thurs & Fri am Social events & cultural activities.

Islington Chinese Association - Women's Group
33 Giesbach Road
London N19 3DA
T 0171 263 5986
Open Mon & Fri 10.30 am-5 pm. To promote awareness of needs, rights and welfare of Chinese women & their families.

Kurdish Information Centre
129 St John's Way
London N19 3RQ
T 0171 272 9499
Open Mon-Fri 10 am-5 pm. Information, support & advice for Kudish community. English classes for women; music & dance; employment & training work experience & job Placement; sports sessions.

Lambo Day Centre
48 Despart Road
London N19 5NW
T 0171 263 3046
Open Mon & Wed 10 am-4.45 pm; Tue & Thurs 10 am-7.45 pm. Women's group Tue 2.30-4 pm. Keep fit (mixed) Thurs 11-12; alternative therapies; for African/Caribbean people with mental health problems.

NAFSIYAT
278 Seven Sisters Road
London N4 2HY
T 0171 263 4130
Counselling to all Black & ethnic minority people in over 23 different languages. Women only groups. Phone above number for further details.

Orisha
Glenor Roberts
Manor Gardens Centre
7-9 Manor Gardens
Holloway Road
London N7 6LA
T 0171 700 4588   F 0171 263 0596
Providing services to Black families that facilitate celebration & healing of relationships in those families. Counsellors & therapists; courses; publications; training, consultancy & research.

Turkish Speaking Women's Group
2 Newington Green Road
London N1 7RX
T 0171 354 1359   F 0171 226 7599
Open Mon-Fri 10 am-1 pm & 2-5 pm Wed appt only. Provides advice, support, advocacy to Turkish speaking women. Covers welfare, legal issues, immigration, domestic violence, housing etc. Social events.

Turkish/Kurdish Women's Group
Manor Gardens Centre
6-9 Manor Gardens
London N7 6LA

T 0171 272 4231 F 0171 263 0596
Open Wed afternoon. Support, information, activities for local Turkish/Kurdish women. Creche. Transport to the centre can be arranged. Wheelchair accessible & disabled toilet facilities. Minicom 0171 272 4231.

Women of Colour Against Pornography
11 Goodwin Street
London N4 3HQ
T 0171 263 1833

Girls/Young Women

Barnados Young Women's Project
Libby Fry, Project Leader
354-356 Goswell Road
London EC1V 7LQ
T 0171 837 5939 F 0171 833 4858
Open Mon, Tue, Thurs, Fri 1-5 pm; Wed 1-8 pm. For young women aged under 21 in need of housing. Health advice, counselling, housing & welfare rights advice.

City Roads Youth Counselling
202 City Road
London EC1V 2PH
T 0171 250 1829
Individual counselling to 16-25 year olds across the London area. Contribution according to means. Self-referral by phone. Approximately two weeks waiting time for assessment & 4-6 weeks to see counsellor.

Eden Grove Youth Project Trust
Eden Grove community Centre
62 Eden Grove
London N7 8EN
T 0171 607 5176
Girls' night (12 +) on Thurs 5.30-8.30 pm. After school provision Mon, Wed 3.30-6 pm. Youth provision (14+) Mon 6.30-9.30 pm & Wed & Fri 6-9 pm for 11-16 year olds. Wheelchair accessible.

Holloway Neighbourhood Group
Old Fire Station
Mayton Street
London N7 6QT
T 0171 607 9794
Open Mon-Fri. Community & youth centre with nearby nursery. Young lesbian group, creche, girls' groups, keep fit & yoga classes. Hall for hire.

Islington Elfrida Rathbone Association
34 Islington Park Street
London N1 1PX
T 0171 359 7443
Young women's group. School leaver's group at Samuel Rhodes school to help young women through transitional periods. Women's group for over 16s who are educationally disadvantaged. Parents' group for women.

Islington Project
White Lion Youth Centre Site
White Lion Street
London N1 9PW
T 0171 833 0775
Open Mon-Fri. Detached youth work project working with Asian, Greek & Turkish young women. Wheelchair accessible.

King's Corner Project
104 Old Street
London EC1V 9AY
T 0171 253 6776
Workers helping young people develop their skills through projects they initiate themslves. Offers employment, housing advice, sports & leisure activities, weekends away. Women-only sports events.

Mayville Community Centre
Heather Hark, Outreach Worker
Woodville Road
London N16 8NS
T 0171 249 8286 F 0171 477 3983
Mon 7.30-9.30 pm women's night; Mon 6.30-9 pm girls/young women-only youth club. Mon 7-9 pm photography for girls only. The Centre is managed by Islington Council.

Venus Project, The
The Old Laundry
Hornsey Road
London N7 7QT
T 0171 281 2121
Counselling for young people aged 11-21, & up to age 25 if disabled or lesbian. Counselling on sex education & drugs education in groups. Individual counselling on an ongoing basis for up to two years.

Youth Services
Community Education
Islington Council
Laycock Street
London N1 1TH
T 0171 457 5641

LONDON - ISLINGTON

Runs clubs, centres & projects, many of which have separate provision for girls/young women.

HEALTH

Angel Drug Project
38-44 Liverpool Road
London N1 0PU
T 0171 226 3113 F 0171 359 4644
Open Mon, Wed, Fri & Sat 2-5 pm & Tue & Thurs 2-7 pm. Free confidential services for people with drug related problems & partners & friends. Advice, information, support, etc. Women only Wed afternoons.

Archway Sexual Health Clinic
Archway Wing
Wittington Hospital
Highgate Hill
London N19 5NF
T 0171 530 5800
Appts necessary: STDs, cytology, HIV testing, HIV counsellors. Clinics on Mon 9 am-5 pm, Tue 2-7 pm, Wed 9 am-5 pm, Thurs 1.30-7 pm, Fri 8.30 am-4 pm; women only Thurs 1.30-3.30 pm.

Greater London Association of Alcohol Services (GLAAS)
30-31 Great Sutton Street
London EC1V 0DX
T 0171 253 6221
Open Mon-Fri 9 am-5 pm. Networking organisation.

Healthy Islington
159-167 Upper Street
London N1 1RE
T 0171 477 3035 F 0171 477 3057
Open Mon-Fri. Promotes health for all. Runs small grants scheme for projects promoting health. Coordinates the Islington Women's Health Group. Runs Islington Health and Race Forum.

Impact Project
67-69 Cowcross Street
London EC1M 6BP
T 0171 251 5860
Early interventions in drug use for young people living in Islington.

Islington Community AIDS Resource (ICARE)
23-26 St Alban's Place
London N1 0NX

T 0171 359 7829 F 0171 359 8247
Supports people with HIV/AIDS in Islington. Welfare benefits & housing advice. Counselling. Medical & social support. Emotional & practical support for carers, relatives, friends of those affected by HIV/AIDS.

Mental Health Resource Centre
10 Corsica Street
London N5 1JD
T 0171 354 0414
Open Mon, Tue, Wed, Fri & alternative Sun. Community-based drop-in service providing mental health services for the community. Women only service Tue 9.15 am-54.45 pm. Wheelchair access.

Milton House
495-497 Liverpool Road
London N7 8NS
T 0171 700 6177 F 0171 700 6232
Community-based drug rehabilitation project with residential & after-care service. Support, social acitivities, counselling, training, education. Specific work with women & women with children.

North East London Drugs Prevention Team
8-9 Angel Gate
City Road
London EC1V 2PT
T 0171 837 7477
Advice & grants for local people & organisations to set up drugs prevention projects.

Women's Alcohol Centre
Diane Goldman
66a Drayton Park
London N5 1ND
T 0171 226 4581 F 0171 354 8134
Open Mon-Fri 9.30 am-5 pm. Assessments for new clients 9.30-11 am Variable day programme. Groups, massage, acupuncture. Lesbian counsellor available. Creche Tue & Thurs. Children's services available.

Women's Mental Health Crisis Project
Shirley McNicholas, Manager
32 Drayton Park
London N5 1PB
T 0171 607 2777 F 0171 607 3777
Health crisis project for women who might otherwise be admitted to hospital, linking women with community services.

IRISH WOMEN

Irish Women's Abortion Support Group
C/o Women's Health
52-54 Featherstone Street
London EC1Y 8RT
T 0171 251 6580
Open Mon, Wed, Thurs & Fri 11 am-5 pm. Support for Irish women coming to England for an abortion.

Irish Women's Project
Islington Women's Counselling Centre
Eastgate Building
131b St John's Way
London N19 3RQ
T 0181 281 2673 F 0181 281 2673
Free counselling to Irish women who live in Islington, are unemployed or who are on a low income. One-to-one & group counselling available.

LARGER/TALLER WOMEN

Big Girl (UK) Ltd
Beverley
139a Fonthill Road
London N4 3HF
T 0171 277 608 F 0171 281 9111
Wholesale & retail for the outsize fashion, sizes 16-34. Open 9.30 am-6 pm every day.

LEGAL MATTERS

North Islington Law Centre
161 Hornsey Road
London N7 6DU
T 0171 607 2461 F 0171 700 0072
Advice on legal rights: employment, education, housing, immigration, racial harassment & violence. Open Mon & Wed 10.30 am-2.30 pm; Thurs 1.30-5.30 pm; Fri 9.30 am-1.30 pm; Thurs 7-9 pm appt only.

LESBIAN AND BISEXUAL

GALOP
Unit 2G
Leroy House
436 Essex Road
London N1 3QP
T 0171 704 6767
Offers assistance to lesbians, gay men & bisexuals in dealing with homophobic violence & the police. Gives callers the option of talking to lesbian or gay men. Helpline 0171 704 2040, called the shoutline.

Gender and Sexuality Alliance (G&SA) - London
Simon Dessloch/Zac Nataf
6-9 Cynthia Street
London N1 9JF
T 0171 498 5965
GayGnSA@aol.com
Local chapter of non-sectarian national group working on the politics of gender/sexuality & their transgression.

Islington Lesbian and Gay Committee
Islington Council
Town Hall
Upper Street
London N1 2UD
T 0171 477 3260
Promotes equality for & non-discrimination against lesbians & gay men & monitors Council policies to ensure the needs & interests of lesbians & gay men are being met. Meetings are open to all.

Islington Young Lesbian Group
The Fire Station
84 Mayton Street
London N7 6QT
T 0171 700 4658
Minicom 0171 609 4059. Meets Wed 7-10 pm. Open to all women aged 16-25 who identify as lesbian, bi-sexual or who wish to explore their sexuality. Information, advice & support. Wheelchair access.

Lesbian A A Group
C/o London Friend
86 Caledonian Road
London N1 9DN
A group of lesbians with alcohol problems meets Sat 3-4.30 pm at London Friend.

Lesbian and Gay Fostering and Adoption Network
C/o London Friend
86 Caledonian Road
London N1 9DN

Lesbian at Friend on Sundays (LAFS)
London Friend
86 Caledonian Road
London N1 9DN
T 0171 833 1674 F 0171 833 1674
Free, twice-monthly socialising for all lesbians. Speakers, discussions, videos. Meets 6-8.30 pm on first & third Sun of each month.

LONDON - ISLINGTON

Lesbian Network for Women Affected by Cancer
C/o CancerLink
11-21 Northdown Street
London N1 0DN
T 0171 833 2818 F 0171 833 4963
Information & support for lesbians with cancer, their partners, relatives & friends.

London Bisexual Group
P O Box 3325
London N1 9EQ
London Bi@bi.org
Meets Fri 8 pm at London Friend, 86 Caledonian Road, N1. Social /discussion group for bisexual men & women, their friends & partners.

London Friend Lesbian Helpline
86 Caledonian Road
London N1 9DN
T 0171 837 2782
Helpline open Sun-Thurs 7.30-10 pm.

London Lesbian and Gay Switchboard
Katherine, Information Group
P O Box 7324
London N1 9QS
T 0171 837 6768 F 0171 837 7300
Helpline: 0171 837 7324. Phones are answered 24 hours a day by highly trained volunteers. Holds the largest computer database of lesbian & gay related information in Europe.

London Lesbian and Gay Teenage Group
6-9 Manor Gardens
London N7 6LA
T 0171 263 5932
Open to all young women under 25 who are lesbian, bi-sexual or wish to explore their sexuality. Support, socialising & discussion group. The group meets Wed 7-10 pm & Sun 3-7 pm. Wheelchair accessible.

New Beginnings
2nd Floor Meeting Room
C/o Central Station
37 Wharfdale Road
London N1 9SE
T 0181 981 3621
Meets Sat at the Central Station 8 pm. Lesbian, gay bisexual. Discussion group for people coming to terms with their sexuality. Outings.

North London Line Lesbian
London
T 0171 607 8346
General advice & information for all young lesbians. One-to-one counselling for young lesbian & bisexual young women available for 12 weeks. Young lesbian group meets Tue 6-9 pm (contact Vicky or Jo).

Pain and Strength
C/o The Wheel
4 Wild Court
London WC2B 5AU
T 0171 831 1492
Support group for lesbians who are or who have been in violent relationships with other lesbians.

Project for Advice, Counselling & Education (PACE)
Julienne Dickey
34 Hartham Road
London N7 9JL
T 0171 700 1323 F 0171 609 4909
Minicom: 0171 609 5028. Counselling, crisis & HIV, for lesbians & gay men. All female counsellors are lesbian. Open Mon-Fri 10 am-5 pm 12-week counselling. Free for unemployed, low waged contributions.

Stonewall Immigration Group
London
T 0171 336 0620
For same-sex couples with immigration problems.

Manual Trades

Crosscut Carpentry & Joinery
Rossi Stohr
34 Nicholay Road
London N19 3EZ
T 0171 263 8226
Carpentry & joinery business. Maintenance, conversions, shelving, built-in kitchens, wardrobes, doors, windows, fencing. Tutoring on self-build sites with timber-framed houses.

London Women and Manual Trades
Mavis Williams
52-54 Featherstone Street
London EC1Y 8RT
T 0171 251 9192 F 0171 251 9193
Open Mon-Fri 10 am-5 pm. Self-employment classes, training information, employment opportunities, conferences for tradeswomen,

LONDON - ISLINGTON

works register, training manual, newsletters, library. Drop in office hours.

PHOTOGRAPHY

Caroline Mardon (Photographer)
Caroline Mardon
19 Crossley Street
Islington
London N7 8PE
T 0171 700 6981   F 0171 700 6981
Freelance photographer: portraiture, editorial, corporate, location, documentary, film & TV stills. Mobile 0831 461979.

PLACES TO STAY AND EAT

Duke of Clarence
140 Rotherfield Street
London N1 3DA
T 0171 226 6526
Open Mon-Fri 6-12 pm Sat opens 7 pm Sun opens 3 pm. Pub, beer garden & pool room, plus food. Women only bar & mixed gay bar.

POLITICS

Womanactive (Democratic Left Women's Network)
Kate More
6-9 Cynthia Street
London N1 9JF
T 01642 224617   F 01642 224617
CousinKat@aol.com
Successor group to the Communist Party of Great Britain's Women's Network.

PREGNANCY/CHILDBIRTH

Active Birth Centre
Janet Balaskas
25 Bickerton Road
London N19 5JT
T 0171 561 9006   F 0171 561 9007
Classes & workshops: yoga & breathing, water birth workshop, etc, complementary therapies, parenting your baby, resuscitation & first aid. Postnatal programmes. Publications.

PRISONERS/PRISONERS' WIVES

Prisoners' Wives and Families
Marie Maynard
254 Caledonian Road
Islington
London N1 0NG
T 0171 278 3981   F 0171 278 3981
Open Mon-Thurs 10 am-5 pm; Fri 10 am-1 pm. Advice, support, referral for family & friends of inmates/offenders.

PUBLISHERS/PUBLICATIONS

Pink Paper
13 Hercules Street
London N7 6AT
T 0171 272 2185
Lesbian & gay newspaper. Free. Articles, news, extensive listings.

Women and Her Sphere
Elizabeth Crawford
5 Owen's Row
London EC1V 4NP
T 0171 278 9479
Secondhand books by & about women.

RACIAL EQUALITY

Race Equality Unit
Islington Council
Islington Town Hall
Upper Street
London N1 2UD
T 0171 477 3241
Open Mon-Fri 9 am-5 pm. Developing policies on all aspects of race relations in Isligton & trying to ensure that the Council's own policies do not discriminate against groups or individuals.

Race On The Agenda
Marina Ahmad
356 Holloway Road
London N7 6PA
T 0171 700 8135   F 0171 700 0099
Policy development, research & information service for London's Black voluntary sector & other organisations working with Black communities.

SERVICES

Delights
Debbie and Julie
58C Tollington Road
Holloway
London N7
T 0956 158269
Catering for weddings, Christenings & funerals. Deliveries possible. Food is versatile. Phone for further information.

LONDON - ISLINGTON

Equality Works
Jane Farrell
328 Upper Street
London N1 2XQ
T 0171 704 8002 F 0171 704 1644
Consultants in training organisations run by women within an equal opportunity framework. Consultancy/training to public/voluntary sector organisations on management development appraisal, team-building, etc.

Queen's Nursing Institute, The
Mrs P Bagnall
3 Albemarle Way
London EC1V 4JB
T 0171 490 4227 F 0171 490 1269
qni1@aol.com
Offers professional guidance & expertise in the field of primary health care. Reference materials. Library. Promotes excellence in community nursing.

SPORTS AND LEISURE

Crouch Hill Recreation Centre
83 Crouch Hill
London N8 9EG
T 0171 263 0293 F 0171 263 0293
Open all week. Runs lots of activities for women, eg keep fit, belly dancing, yoga, mother & toddler groups, table tennis. Space also available for women's groups. Wheelchair accessible.

Keinja Okussa Women's School of Self Defence
Josey Allen
C/o 59c Mildmay Park
London N1
T 0181 248 5343
Classes at Kentish Town Methodist Church, Fortress Road, NW1 on Mon 7-9 pm & in Islington. Body & mind art incorporating health, fitness & deep breathing to manage stress.

Sequinpark Women's Health Club and Gym
240 Upper Street
Islington
London N1 1RU
T 0171 704 9844
Open Mon-Thurs 7.15 am-10.15 pm; Fri 7.15 am-9 pm; Sat 8.30 am-4 pm; Sun 8.30 am-7 pm. Women-only gym. Steam, sauna, over-50s classes.

Women's Gym, The
Thuvia Jones, Coordinator
Sobell Leisure Centre
Hornsey Road
London N7 7NY
T 0171 700 1141 F 0171 700 3094
Mon-Fri 9 am-10.30 pm; Sat & Sun 10 am-9 pm. Run by women for all London-based women. Very wide range of health activities. Charitable organisation independent of the Sobell Centre.

SUPPORT

Caxton House Community Centre
129 St John's Way
London N19 3RQ
T 0171 263 3151
Open Mon-Fri 9 am-5.30 pm. Promotes equal opportunities. Runs playgroup, women's fitness & football, parents & toddler drop in, toy library, Kurdish women's group, Asian elderly group. Dark room facilities.

Hackney and East London Family Mediation Service
74 Great Eastern Street
London EC2A 3JL
T 0171 613 1666
Open Mon, Wed & Fri 11 am-4 pm. Offers professional help to parents who are separating or divorcing & help for their children.

Repetitive Strain Injury (RSI) London Support Group
C/o Islington CHC
6-9 Manor Gardens Centre
London N7 6LA
T 0171 263 7207
Support & advice on all aspects of RSI & information. The group meets last Thurs of each month.

Siren Project
Imogen Ashby
Elfrida Society
34 Islington Park
London N1 1PX
T 0171 359 7443
Open Mon-Fri. Women's issues group Tue 4-6 pm. For adults with learning difficulties. Creche. Basic education sessions: literacy & numeracy.

LONDON - KENSINGTON & CHELSEA

Women's Royal Voluntary Service - South East Division
Carole Mayers, Divisional Director
99 White Lion Street
London N1 9PE
T 0171 837 1132 F 0171 837 5281
The areas are: Downlands, Thames, North Chilterns, Anglia, Norfolk, Herts & Essex, Solent, The Weald. Meals on wheels, meals in lunch clubs, hospital projects, family contact centres, family holidays, etc.

TRAINING

City and Islington College
Shepperton Road
London N1 3DH
T 0171 226 6001
Open Mon-Fri. Offers many courses for women at various sites. Women's Day on Fri; Tue 9.30-12.30 women only wood carving; Fri 9.30-12.30 women only drawing for design.

TRANSPORT

Ladycabs
London
T 0171 272 3019
Women's transport using women-only drivers in Islington. Diabled users caterd for, with advance notice required. Quotes for journeys provided.

WOMEN'S AID

London Women's Aid
London
T 0171 251 6537 F 0171 251 1399
Domestic violence helpline for women & their children experiencing physical, psychological, emotional or sexual violence. Can refer women to safe refuge accommodation. Advice & information.

KENSINGTON & CHELSEA

ACCOMMODATION

Capital Housing Project
Bina Gardens Hostel
2-4 Bina Gardens
London SW5 0LA
T 0171 370 4869 F 0171 259 2061
Mixed short-stay (maximum 12 weeks) hostel central London for 16-25 year olds. Referral by professional agency. Level of support medium to low. One third Black, one third ex-offenders, one quarter lesbian/gay.

Havengrove - Grove House
Wendy Simpson
12 Chesterton Road
London W10 5LX
T 0181 968 0943 F 0181 968 0943
Temporary accommodation for homeless mothers & babies. Aims to relieve poverty, sickness & distress.

ALTERNATIVE THERAPIES

Caroline Reynolds Seminars
Caroline Reynolds
4 Cambridge Gardens
London W10 5UB
T 0181 968 8163 F 0181 968 8163
NLP practitioner, marketing & personal development consultant for the Virgin group & a member of the self-esteem network. Self-empowerment & motivational seminars & workshops.

ARTS AND CRAFTS

Adelle Corrin
Adelle Corrin
42 Arundel Gardens
London W11 2LB
T 0171 221 1136
A designer-maker who designs and fabricates stain glass - original designs. Primarily works to commission.

CHILD CARE AND FAMILY

West London Action for Children
Lady Dawson
Ashburnham Community Centre
Tetcott Road
London SW10 0SH
T 0171 352 1155
Supports families at risk. Social work support for children & their families. Counselling; family therapy.

COMPUTERS/IT

AVIVA
Kate Burke
41 Royal Crescent
London W11 4SN
T 0171 602 0140 F 0171 371 6315
kateb@aviva.org
An international women's listing magazine on the internet. Free entry to editorial (news/reviews/interviews/letters); listings (groups/resources); events (arts/theatre/dance/film/music).

LONDON - KENSINGTON & CHELSEA

CONTRACEPTION/WELL WOMAN

Basement Project
Catherine Holland
Basement Project
4 Hogarth Road
London SW5 0PT
T 0171 373 2335 F 0171 259 2085
Well woman clinics for young women aged 16-30 on Thurs 1-3.30 pm & 8-10.30 pm.

Raymede Clinic
Telford Road
North Kensington
London W10 5SH
T 0181 960 0942
Drop-in Mon-Thurs 9.30 am- 4 pm; Fri 9.30 am-2 pm Wed 5.30-7.30 pm; appt Mon, Tue, Thurs 5.30-7.30 pm. Well woman Wed 1.30-3.30 pm (appt); psycho sexual & vasectomy counselling by appointment.

Violet Melchett Clinic
Flood Walk
London SW3
T 0181 846 6677
Audiology, chiropody, parent & toddler group, ante-natal classes. Contraception services/well woman clinics: Mon 6.30-7.30 pm; Tue 5.30-5.45 pm; Wed 9.30-10.45 am; Fri 1.30-2.30 pm.

Walmer Road Clinic
Eastry House
226 Walmer Road
London W11 ET4
T 0171 243 0296
Drop-in/appointment contraception & postnatal clinic Thurs 1.30-3.30 pm. Free, confidential services. Advice & information. All contraceptive methods & emergency contraception provided.

COUNSELLING AND THERAPY

Kenginton and Chelsea MIND
Mary Fotheringham
4th Floor
153-155 Kensington High Street
London W8 6SU
T 0171 376 1000 F 0181 964 9345
Women-only day Wed 10 am-4 pm. Lunch, women's therapy group, art.

ETHNIC MINORITIES

Al-Hasaniya Moroccan Women's Project Ltd
Aisling Byrne, Coordinator
Bays 1 and 5
Trellick Tower
Golborne Road
London W10 5PL
T 0181 969 2292 F 0181 964 8843
Open Mon-Fri 9.30 am-5 pm. Classes in English, sewing, sessions & focus groups on health aspects. Part-time creche, lunch club, outings. Mental health project. Working with Moroccan & Arabic-speaking women.

Bangla Group, The
Queen's Park Family Service Unit
604 Harrow Road
London W10 4NJ
T 0181 960 3266 F 0181 960 3267
Meets Tue 10 am-12 pm on a drop-in basis. For Bangladeshi mothers & under 5s who are isolated, overcrowded & living in poverty. Women & children have space to meet, share ideas, play together.

Commission of Filipino Migrant Workers
St Francis Centre
Pottery Lane
London W11 4NQ
T 0171 221 0356 F 0171 792 3060
Open 10 am-6 pm all week. Community development centre for Filipinos. Advice on immigration, health, employment, family law, domestic violence. Peer counselling seminars. Phone for appt.

Somali Women's Group
Catherine Holland
Basement Project
4 Hogarth Road
London SW5 0PT
T 0171 373 2335
Meets Thurs 10 am-12 pm. For young Somali women aged 16-30.

Sudanese Women's Group
Nadia Abdalla
74 5th Avenue
London W10 4DB
T 0181 964 9527
Advice & support for Sudanese refugees. Help with domestic problems, job searches, etc.

LONDON - KENSINGTON & CHELSEA

GIRLS/YOUNG WOMEN

Basement Project
Catherine Holland
4 Hogarth Road
London SW5 0PT
T 0171 373 2335 F 0171 259 2085
For 16-30 year olds. Advice on issues such as housing, benefits, education, employment, health & legal matters. Drop-in for women on Thurs 12-4 pm. Needle exchange, advice & counselling.

HEALTH

Alcoholics Anonymous (AA) - London
1st Floor
11 Redcliffe Gardens
London SW10 9BQ
T 0171 352 3001
London-wide service. Phoneline open 10 am-10 pm daily, otherwise ansaphone. Self-referral. Anyone who wishes to stop drinking is welcome at an AA meeting. A local contact will be arranged for new members.

Care and Resources for People Affected by HIV/AIDS (CARA)
178 Lancaster Road
London W11 1QU
T 0171 792 8299
Drop-in Tue 12.30-2.30 pm. Monthly Sun lunch. Wed women's day drop-in 12.30-2.30. Offers non-judmental, spiritual, emotional & practical support to those affected by HIV/AIDS. Complementary therapies.

Red Admiral Project
51a Philbeach Gardens
London SW5 9EB
T 0171 835 1495 F 0171 373 1935
Open Mon-Fri 10 am-6 pm. Free counselling for people affected by HIV/AIDS. Individuals, couples & group work.

LARGER/TALLER WOMEN

Cocoon
110 Kensignton Church Street
London W8 4BH
T 0171 221 7000
Retailing fashionable rain wear. Any size, any length.

LESBIAN AND BISEXUAL

West London Lesbian and Gay Bridge Club
Andy
Devonshire Arms
Pembridge Road
London W8
T 0181 903 9893
Meets Mon 7.30 pm

MANUAL TRADES

Women's Education in Building (WEB)
Wendy Ryan
12-14 Malton Road
Ladbroke Grove
London W10 5UP
T 0181 968 9139 F 0181 964 0255
Training unemployed women in painting & decorating, plumbing, carpentry & joinery, electrical installation. NVQ & evening classes. Employment support. Financial assistance with childcare, travel & lunch costs.

PREGNANCY/CHILDBIRTH

Perfectly Happy People (PHP)
105 Freston Road
London W11 4BD
T 0171 221 0041
Produces Kooshies, washable nappies & baby products.

PRISONERS/PRISONERS' WIVES

Women Prisoners' Resource Centre
Florence Bruce-Annan
Office 1a
Canalside House
383 Lanbrooke Grove
London W10 5AA
T 0181 968 3121 F 0181 960 3898
Open Mon-Fri 9.30-5.30 or ansaphone. Staff go to London prisons to meet needs of women prisoners returning to London on release. Advice on housing, education, training, welfare & legal rights, benefits, etc.

RELIGIOUS ORGANISATIONS

Chelsea Methodist Church
Women's Fellowship
155a King's Road
Chelsea
London SW3
T 0171 823 3301

Meets for devotions Tue 2.30-4 pm. Speakers.

Services
Capital Careers
19-27 Young Street
London W8 5EH
T 0171 938 5311
Open Mon-Fri 9.30 am-4.30 pm. Offers careers guidance, help with cvs, information & help with getting a job. For residents of the borough of Kenginston & Chelsea. Phone for further details.

Gender Identity Consultancy Services
Fran Springfield
10 Warwick Road
Earls Court
London SW5 9UH
T 0171 244 6090 F 0171 244 0900
GICS@aol.com
Aims to help all those who come for assistance to find solutions to the problems posed by the impact of gender identity issues on their lives. Self- or professional referrals. Counselling, facilitation, etc.

Social
FOCUS Information Services
Pam Drobnyk, Chair
13 Prince of Wales Terrace
London W8 5PG
T 0171 937 7799 F 0171 937 9482
An organisation for ex-pats to meet, socialise, exchange info. Emphasis is on job resources & settling into the UK. Over 90 per cent of the membership is female but does not bar men.

Kensington Chelsea Women's Club
London
T 01426 933348
Meets first Thurs of each month at Kensington Roof Gardens, 99 Kensington High Street. A social women's group with many different activities.

Support
Blenheim Project
321 Portobello Road
London W10 5SY
T 0181 960 5599
Open Mon-Fri 10 am-5 pm. Women's day: Wed; drop-in Fri 1-4 pm. Needle exchange; alternative therapy; counselling. Emphasis on meeting women's needs. London-wide support, counselling, advice, publications.

Training
Third Feathers Club
Ammi Karlsson-Pye
17 Bramham Gardens
London SW5 0JJ
T 0171 373 2681
Wokshops for women. Free creche.

Kingston Upon Thames
Accommodation
Bhavan Ltd
Fatima Mirza/Hina Patel
P O Box 368
Kingston upon Thames KT2 6YS
T 0181 399 8087
Asian women's refuge & for dependants - males up to age 11; females up to age 16. A safe house for single Asian women aged 16-25. Referrals accepted via London Women's Aid & Women's Aid Federation.

Alternative therapies
Health for Life
Mariela Angel
15 Queen Elizabeth Road
Kingston upon Thames KT6
T 0181 549 5038
Homoeopathy and Polarity therapies.

Arts
Conquest
Mrs Ursula Hulme
3 Beverley Close
East Ewell KT17 3HB
T 0181 393 6102
Teaching art to disabled women and men.

Business support schemes
Women in Management - Kent, Surrey, Sussex branch
Winifred Cummins
10 Bickney Way
Fetcham KT22 9QQ
T 01372 459996
Monthly events on an ad hoc basis to promote training for individual women - low cost for unemployed & returners. Marketing/advertising workshops, internet workshops, networking.

CARERS

Kingston Carers' Network
Room 5
35 Coombe Road
Kingston upon Thames KT2 7BA
T 0181 547 1614

CENTRES FOR WOMEN

Hillcroft College
South Bank
Surbiton KT6 6DF
T 0181 399 2688 F 0181 390 9171
An education & training centre for women only. Women's studies courses; IT; etc. Caters particularly for women returners.

Kingston Women's Centre
Susan/Cathy/Hazel
169 Canbury Park Road
Kingston upon Thames KT2 6LG
T 0181 541 1964
Open Mon-Thurs 10 am-5 pm. Run by women for women. Information & support about housing benefits &, if necessary, referral to other agencies. Crisis counselling by appointment. Legal help Thurs evenings.

CONTRACEPTION/WELL WOMAN

Acre Road Clinic
204 Acre Road
Kingston upon Thames
T 0181 546 5812
Contraceptive clinic, advice and free supplies for under 21s only on Mon 3.30-6.30 pm.

Forum, The
Walton Road
West Molesley
T 0181 979 6464
Contraceptive clinic on Thurs 7-9 pm.

Hawks Road Clinic
Kingston upon Thames
T 0181 546 1115
Contraceptive advice & supplies & well woman clinics Tue 6.30-8.30 pm.

Mercer Close
Watts Road
Thames Ditton
T 0181 398 0914
Contraceptive advice & supplies & well woman clinics on first and third Mon of each month 9.30-11.30 am.

Oakhill Health Centre
Oakhill Road
Surbiton KT6 6EM
T 0181 390 6755
Contraceptive advice & supplies & well woman clinics on Fri 9.30-11.30 am.

Roselands Clinic
163 Kingston Road
New Malden KT3 3NN
T 0181 942 0800
Contraceptive advice & supplies Mon 6.30-8.30 pm.

EDUCATION

Association of Women Graduates - Croydon & Reigate Branch
Winifred Cummins
10 Bickney Way
Fetcham KT22 9QQ
T 01372 459996
Monthly meetings on, for example, international affairs, debt collection. Social events. Meets different times and different places each week. Phone for further details.

HEALTH

Women's Health Concern - Surbiton
June Ower, Senior Nurse Counsellor
Oakhill Health Centre
Oakhill Road
Surbiton KT6 6EN
T 0181 399 9359
Phone Tue 3.15-5.15 for an appointment. Free counselling for all women about their health problems & concerns.

JEWISH WOMEN

League of Jewish Women - Kingston & Wimbledon branch
Hilda Sinclair
T 0181 399 0269
Meets second Mon of each month.

LARGER/TALLER WOMEN

Something Extra
Sarah L Hunt
94 High Street
Esher KT10 9QJ
T 01372 466991
Women's clothing retail. Specialist in larger sizes up to 30. Middle price range. Open Mon-Sat 9.30 am-5.30 pm

PREGNANCY/CHILDBIRTH

Ante-Natal Caesarian Birth Classes
Fiona Barlow
39 Fullers Avenue
Tolworth KT6 7TD
T 0181 391 1144
Ante-natal caesarian birth classes. Also provides advice & information about caesarians for pregnant women.

Born Too Soon
Pauline Woods, Fund-raising Administrator
Neo-natal Unit
Kingston Hospital
Galsworthy Road
Kingston upon Thames KT2 7QB
T 0181 974 9157
Promoting awareness about the problems of giving birth prematurely. Support & fund-raising.

National Childbirth Trust - Kingston branch
Penny D'Souza
Kingston upon Thames
T 0181 549 5331

RELIGIOUS ORGANISATIONS

Berrylands Women's Club
Mrs Beryl Jewell-Smith
12 Fairmead
Tolworth KT2 9BA
T 0181 390 1722
Meets Mon evening at Elgar Hall, United Reformed Church, Elgar Avenue, Tolworth.

St James' Church Women's Guild
Mrs C Thomas
109 Bodley Road
New Malden KT3 5QJ
T 0181 942 1909
Meets twice monthly at St James' Church Hall, Bodley Road, New Malden.

SOCIAL

Buckland Women's Club
Mrs P M Stickley
414 Leatherhead Road
Malden Rushett
Chessington
T 01372 724237
Meets Thurs evenings at Guide HQ, Buckland Road, Chessington.

Surrey Association of Women's Clubs
Mrs S Stevens-Stratten, Secretary
40 Fairfield Way
Ewell
Epsom KT19 0EF
T 0181 393 6880
Coordinating 12 clubs in Surrey - non-political, non-religious, any age group.

Worcester Park Women's Club
Mrs Jo Evans, Secretary
17 Hill Crescent
Worcester Park KT4 8NB
T 0181 337 6582
Meets at Cheam Common Junior School, Kingsmead Avenue, Worcester Park on Fri 7.30-9.30 pm. Membership open to women aged 18+. Affiliated to the National Association of Women's Clubs.

WOMEN'S AID

Kingston Women's Aid
P O Box 240
Kingston upon Thames KT1 3AY
T 0181 390 8431
Provides a safe house for women & children (if any) fleeing domestic violence. Help, support & information for issues around domestic violence. 24-hour ansaphone.

LAMBETH

ACCOMMODATION

CCP
housing management team
25 Camberwell Grove
London SE5 8JA
T 0171 703 6545
Open 10 am-5 pm Resettlement & housing for single women aged 21-55 with special needs.

Central and Cecil Housing Trust (CCHT)
Ms B Gould, Manager
Cecil House
266 Waterloo Road
London SE1 8RF
T 0171 928 5752
Provides direct access accommodation (two hostels) for single women aged 16-60.

Centrepoint Vauxhall
11 Bondway
Vauxhall
London SW8 1SN
T 0171 735 7999

Hostel for homeless. Caters for 60 people. Maximum stay six months. Lesbian & gay quota.

Drink Crisis Centre - Women's Services
Bernie Cahill/Judy Watchman
15 Rydal Road
Streatham
London SW16 1QF
T 0181 696 0148
Residential project offering up to two years' low-support accommodation to homeless women with support needs (five-bed unit) & to women who are currently drinking problematically (36-bed unit).

Drink Crisis Centre - Women's Services
Bernie Cahill/Emma Sandys
110 Knollys Road
Streatham
London SW16 2JO
T 0181 664 7477
Residential project offering support & resettlement for up to 12 months to women who have undergone treatment for their drinking or drug use. Houses six women. Low support, staffed 2 1/2 days per week.

Heama Hostel
32 Gauden Road
Clapham
London SW4 6LT
T 0171 627 4005 F 0171 627 4007
6 bed spaces for young single homeless women with an age range of 16 to 20. Supervision in office hours only.

Homeless Action
Lincoln House
2nd Floor
1 Brixton Road
London SW9 6DE
T 0171 735 2062
Housing organisation managing houses for housing associations. Single women aged 18-60 who are homeless or are threatened with homelessness are provided with temporary accommodation.

Housing for Women
Margaret Moran/A Lander/Caroline Allen
353 Kennington Road
London SE11 4QE
T 0171 582 7605 F 0171 793 0050
Charity supplying housing mainly for single women. Self-contained flats & some sheltered accommodation. Open Mon-Fri 9 am-1 pm & 2-5 pm. Information about housing problems. Wheelchair accessible.

Kabo
32 Saltoun Road
Brixton
London SW2 1EP
T 0171 733 9466
7 bed spaces for young single homeless women aged between 16 & 20. Two rooms are shared. Another 3 bed spaces are reserved for young women on probation.

Nyalia Hostel
47-51 Barrington Road
Brixton
London SW9 7JG
T 0171 738 3335 F 0171 274 7376
11 Bed spaces for young mothers with an age range of 13 to 23 & their babies. 5 bed spaces for single women aged between 16 & 20. For young, single homeless women. 24-hour care. Usually referred.

ALTERNATIVE THERAPIES

Jacky Chapman
Jacky Chapman
99 Barrow Road
Stretham
London SW16 5PB
T 0181 677 8254
Offers reflexology (Ingham method). Hours are 10 am-8 pm.

Kathleen Beegan MRSS
Kathleen Beegan
41 Stanthorpe Road
Streatham
London SW16 2DZ
T 0181 769 3613 F 0181 969 3613
Provides Shiatsu therapy, Vini yoga classes and ante-natal exercise and relaxation classes.

Medical Herbalist, Healing Massage
Marilena Hettema
127 Elmhurst Mansions
Edgeley Road
Clapham
London SW4 6EX
T 0171 622 0164 F 0171 622 0164
Herbalist & holistic massage. Concessions available.

Sandra Zarafis
Sandra Zarafis
7 Woodcote Villas
West Norwood
London SE27 0UQ
T 0181 761 9582
Therapeutic massage or aromatherapy. Helps stress-related problems and assists chronic conditions on a one-to-one basis. Appointments can be made any day of the week between 10 am-10 pm.

Arts and Crafts

198 Gallery - Education and Training Centre
Natasha Anderson
194-198 Railton Road
Herne Hill
London SE24 0LU
T 0171 978 8309
Works with artists from differing cultural backgrounds at a culturally diverse visual arts centre. Open Tue-Sat 11 am-7 pm. Free entry, wheelchair access.

Cath Tate Cards
Cath Tate
Unit 1
45 Morrish Road
London SW2 4EE
T 0181 671 2166 F 0181 678 1119
Produces and distributes postcards, greeting cards, T-shirts, mugs and a Women's Diary with a feminist profile. Specialises in the work of women cartoonists.

Circle Eight Square and Round Dance Club
Betty Freddi
63 Dulwich Road
Herne Hill
London SE24 0NJ
T 0171 733 4512
Teaches American Square Dancing and Line Dancing as well as American Round Dancing. Afternoon classes for over 50s - social dancing. No women only events. Phone for further details.

Lambeth Ladies Choir
Mrs M H Price
99 Downton Avenue
Streatham Hill
London SW2 3TU
T 0181 674 5095
Meets on Fri 2-4 pm at Chatsworth Baptist Church Hall, Chatsworth Way, West Norwood. Two public concerts a year and other performances given to hospitals, residential homes, etc.

Lisa Perry Upholstery
Lisa Perry
391 Clapham Road
Clapham North
London SW9 9BT
T 0171 326 1266
Self-employed sole trader in traditional and modern upholstery (not loose covers or curtains). Free estimates. Open 9 am-5 pm.

Carers

Lambeth Carers' Project
Carers' Coordinator
St Anne's Hall
Venn Street
London SW4 0BW
T 0171 627 0227
Focal point for carers of all ages in Lambeth. Information on welfare benefits, respite care, local services. Aims to raise awareness of carers' needs. Umbrella organisation for carers of all age groups.

Lambeth Crossroads - Care Attendant Scheme
coordinator
Laburnham Court
Palace Road
London SW2 3NS
T 0181 671 6188
Provides a trained care attendant to take over from carers.

Support One Group for Carers
C/o 24 Kirstall Road
London SW2 4HF
T 0181 671 9270
Open Tue 6.30-8.30 pm. Support and advice for carers of people with HIV/AIDS.

Centres for Women

Asian Women's Resource Centre - Asha Collective
Yasmin Asaria-Lakhani
27 Santly Street
London SW4 7QF
T 0171 274 8854 F 0171 733 3525
Counselling & advice for women suffering domestic violence. Advice & information on housing & benefits. Advocacy work undertaken.

CHILD CARE AND FAMILY

ABC Children's Centre
Ms E Carr
48 Chapel Road
West Norwood
London SE27 0UR
T 0181 766 0246
Private nursery for 65 children aged 3 months to primary school age. Open 7 am-6 pm

Cabin, The
Ivy Gordon
131 Lyham Road
London SW2 5PY
T 0181 674 3521
Day nursery. Places for 20 children aged 2-5. Open Mon-Fri 8.15 am-5.45 pm

Connect
Sue Manning
T 0181 674 0213
A mothers' and toddlers' group which meets most Tue 9.45-11.30 am during term time at New Park Road Baptist Church, New Park Road, Streatham Place, London SW2 4UP.

Family Friends
Molly Evans
34 Brixton Water Lane
Brixton
London SW2 1PE
T 0171 274 4295   F 0171 274 4295
Out of school facilities for children aged 4-8 and children with special needs. Advocacy service. Also young women's workshop (aged 16-20), a self-help group engaging with personal development strategies.

Family Link
Alison Pritchard, Coordinator
256 Brixton Hill
Brixton
London SW2 1HF
T 0181 671 8939
Provides family based respite care for children with disabilities. Saturday club and teenage club for children and teenagers with disabilities that meet once a month.

Fatemah Day Nursery
53 Buchleigh Road
Streatham
London SW16 5RY
T 0181 764 8657
A nursery for children aged 2-4 open 8 am-6 pm

Knight Hill Day Nursery
Eleanor Kelman
24 Eden Road
West Norwood
London SE27 0UB
T 0181 761 7338
For single parents who are working or who are at college. Open 8 am-6 pm. Day nursery for children aged 2 to 5. Provides care and education through child learning, including aspects of multiculturalism.

Montgomery Hall Community Centre
Mrs Starr
58 Kennington Oval
London SE11 5SW
T 0171 582 5613
Mothers' and toddlers' group meets on Thurs 10 am-12 pm

Myatts Field Mobile Creche
45 Foxley Square
London SW9
T 0171 735 7495
Drop in 2-hour creche facilities in various community centres in the Myatts Field estate area.

Penworth Manor Playgroup
Eugene Delcanto
14 White Hart Street
Kenningsway
Kennington Lane
London SE11 4EP
T 0171 735 2029
Open Mon-Fri 9.30 a.m-12 noon. For 18 children aged between two-and-a-half to five.

St Cecilia's Nursery
Di Farley
Christ Church Vicarage
Union Grove
London SW8 2QJ
T 0171 720 0827
Open Mon-Fri 8 am-5.30 pm. Non-profit making teaching nursery. Help for those with poor English. Free legal advice once a month Sat 10.30 am-2.30 pm. Help with form filling Tue & Thurs 5.30-7 pm.

COMPUTERS/IT

Baytree Centre
Marie-Claire Irwin
300 Brixton Road
London SW9 6AE
T 0171 733 5283   F 0171 737 2368

Open Mon-Wed 9.30 a.m-8 pm; Thurs and Fri 9.30 am-5.30 pm. Women only. Computer skills course, ESOL classes, youth activities for girls aged 8-16 & adult evening classes.

CONTRACEPTION/WELL WOMAN

Brixton Brook Centre
53 Acre Lane
London SW2 5TN
T 0171 274 4995
Open Mon 10.30 am-12.30 pm & 4.30-6.30 pm; Wed 10.30 am-12.30 pm & 4.15-7 pm; Fri 3.30-5.30 pm; Sat 9.30-11.30 am Free, confidential contraceptive advice & supplies. Help with sexual problems.

Manor Health Centre, The
86 Clapham Manor Street
London SW4
T 0171 622 2293
Contraception & well woman clinics Tue & Thurs 5-7.30 pm; Fri 1-3.30 pm. Free advice & information on contraception & free contraceptive supplies. Free blood pressure checks, urine tests, breast checks.

Marie Stopes Raleigh Centre
Ground Floor
Unit 5, Arodene Court
Arodene Road
London SW2 2JZ
T 0181 671 1541 F 0181 678 1662
Pregancy advice (helpline 0171 388 4843); general healcare/contraception (helpline 0171 388 0662); sterilisation services (helpline 0171 388 5554); well woman clinics; abortion clinics; menopause clinics; etc.

Marie Stopes Raleigh Clinic
Francoise Armstrong, Manager
1a Raleigh Gardens
Buxton Hill
London SW2 6AB
T 0181 671 1542 F 0181 674 3173
Pregancy advice (helpline 0171 388 4843); general healcare/contraception (helpline 0171 388 0662); sterilisation services (helpline 0171 388 5554); well woman clinics; abortion clinics; menopause clinics; etc.

Mawbey Brough Health Centre
38 Wilcox Close
London SW8
T 0171 627 4444
Well woman clinic Wed 1-6 pm.
Contraception advice, information & supplies.

Blood pressure & breast checks, advice about menopause & HRT, etc.

Moffat Health Clinic
Charity Duah
65 Sancroft Street
London SE11 5NG
T 0171 735 4169
Well woman clinics Mon 5.30-7.30 pm; Tue 9-11.30 am; Thurs 5-7.30 pm.

Railton Road Clinic
143-149 Railton Road
Herne Hill
London SE24 0LT
T 0171 274 1083 F 0171 733 6028
Open 9 am-5 pm. Contraception clinics Wed 5.30-7.30 pm & Fri 3-5 pm. Parent & baby groups Wed 11 am-1 pm. Well women clinics are also provided.

Raleigh Nursing Home
1a Raleigh Gardens
Brixton Hill
London SW2 6AB
T 0181 671 1541
Well woman clinic. Phone for an appointment. Advice & information on health matters such as how to stop smoking, menopause, HIV/AIDS. Free health checks: blood pressure, urine tests, breast examinations, etc.

Rose McAndrew Community Health Services Clinic
Beale House
Lingham Street
London SW9
T 0171 274 5777
Contraception & well woman clinics on Tue 9-11.30 am No appointment necessary. Free advice & information about contraception & free contraceptive supplies. Free urine tests, blood pressure checks, etc.

St Thomas' Brook Centre
Harrison Wing, 2nd Floor
Lambeth Wing, St Thomas' Hos.
Lambeth Palace Road
London SE1 7EH
T 0171 928 9292
Open Mon 9.30 am-4.30 pm. For appointment outside opening hours, phone 0171 703 9660. Free confidential contraceptive advice. Free condoms & other contraceptive supplies. Pregnancy testing & quick results.

St Thomas' Hospital
Third Floor
Lambeth Wing
Lambeth Palace Road
London SE1
T 0171 922 8026
Contraception & well woman clinics Tue 1-3.30 pm. Free advice & information about contraception & free contraceptive supplies. Free blood pressure checks, urine tests, information on health matters, etc.

Streatham Common Community Health Services Clinic
293 Streatham High Road
London SW16
T 0181 764 5268
Contraception & well woman clinics Mon 5.30-8 pm; Tue 1.30-4 pm& 4.30-7 pm. Free advice & information about contraception & free contraceptive supplies. Free blood pressure checks, urine tests, etc.

Streatham Hill Community Health Services Clinic
24 Kirkstall Road
London SW2
T 0181 674 7178
Contraception & well woman clinics Thurs 1-3 pm & 5-7.30 pm. Free advice & information about contraception & free contraceptive supplies. Free blood pressure checks, urine tests, breast examinations, etc.

COUNSELLING AND THERAPY

Lambeth Wel-Care
Vilma Maduro
St John The Divine Community Centre
19 Frederick Crescent
London SW9 6XN
T 0171 735 9130 F 0171 735 9168
Counselling for single parents & pregnant women. Lone parent groups & self-help training groups. Play therapy. Surrogate grandparent scheme using local people aged over 50 to provide support for young families.

Lovewell
Jacqui Love
2 Rosethorn Close
Thornton Road
London SW12 0JP
T 0181 671 6306
Mobile 0958 468212. Counselling/therapy for individuals, couples & groups. Training consultancy. Relationships, sex/sexuality, HIV/AIDS, self-esteem, assertiveness, personal development, lifeskills workshops.

Myatts Community Project
Cathy Towers/Donna Burrowes
5 Baldwin Crescent
London SE5 9LQ
T 0171 733 6291 F 0171 924 0975
Provides free one-to-one counselling for women aged over 18 or groupwork (eg parenting skills, survivors of childhood sexual abuse, health and fitness etc). Reception service available Mon-Fri 9.30 am-5 pm.

Shanti Women's Psychotherapy Service
1a Dalbury House
Edmundsbury Court
Ferndale Road
London SW9 8AP
T 0171 733 8581 F 0171 783 3496
Open Mon-Fri 10 am-5 pm. For women only within the west Lambeth community. Self referral. Free counselling covering a range of topics from racism, through abuse to depression. By appointment only.

DISABILITY

Greater London Association for Disabled People (GLAD)
information department
336 Brixton Road
London SW9 7AA
T 0171 274 0107
Telephone enquiries taken during office hours. Publications. A number of disabled women's groups are affiliated to GLAD.

ETHNIC MINORITIES

Africa Research and Information Bureau - Women's Group
Phyllis Thomas, Chairperson
5 Westminster Bridge Road
London SE1 7XW
T 0171 928 8728 F 0171 620 1431

Ashram
Lambeth Asian Elderly Day Centre
13 Shrubbery Road
London SW16 2AS
T 0181 677 4133
Day centre for Asian women & older Asian people. Open Mon-Fri 9 am-5 pm. Health sessions for Asian women only throughout the week. Keep fit for Asian women only on Mon morning & Wed. Sewing classes on Wed.

Blackliners
Unit 46
Eurolink Business Centre
49 Effra Road
London SW2 1BZ
T 0171 738 7468
Helpline: 0171 738 5274 open Mon-Fri 10 am-6.30 pm. Drop-in Thurs 12-4 pm.
Counselling, care & support for people affected by HIV/AIDS who are of African, Asian or Caribbean descent.

Eritrean Community in Lambeth
Habteab Fessaha/Kiflom Mebrahtu
365 Brixton Road
London SW9 7DA
T 0171 738 4059   F 0171 738 4059
Open 9.30 a.m-5.30 pm. Advice on immigration, welfare, housing & benefits. Provides training, enterprise & employment. Support for elderly bereaved women.

Pada Women's Forum
Dr E U Etim
21 Addington House
Stockwell Road
London SW9 0TZ
T 0171 274 5252   F 0171 233 1747
Open Mon-Fri 9 am-5 pm. A network for Black women of various interests. Training available.

Refugee Women's Group
Janet Basley
C/o Myatts Community Project
Family Service Unit
46 Foxley Square
London SW9 7RX
T 0171 733 6291   F 0171 924 0975
For women who are refugees & asylum seekers. Discussion & support group. Oral history. By referral only.

GIRLS/YOUNG WOMEN

Dick Sheppard Youth and Community Centre
Lee Parker
Tulse Hill
London SW2 2QA
T 0181 674 2168
Open Mon-Fri 4-6 pm & 6-10 pm. After school programme 5-7 pm Sun 2-8 pm. Young women only throughout the week. Women unemployed programme. For health & education contact Helen Knox.

Lambeth Young Women's Project
Loz Broughton and Anne Lawrence
166a Stockwell Road
Brixton
London SW9 9TQ
T 0171 326 4447   F 0171 326 4513
Community education information & resource project for young women aged 14-25. Offers advice, information, counselling, training. Aims to initiate, develop & promote work with Lambeth women. Creche.

HEALTH

Alcohol Recovery Project
174 Kennington Park Road
London SE11 4BT
T 0171 735 6217   F 0171 357 6712
Support for all people experiencing difficulties with alcohol. Women and children unit. An access point for four hostel in Lambeth.

Health Shop, The
LSLHC
1 Lower Marsh
London SE1 7NT
T 0171 716 7000   F 0171 716 7039
Open for drop in Mon-Fri 10 am-4 pm. Telephone helpline 0171 716 7078 Mon-Fri 9 am-5 pm. Health information centre for Lambeth, Southwark & Lewisham. Information on a wide range of medical facilities.

Landmark, The
47 Tulse Hill
London SW2 2TN
T 0181 678 6686   F 0181 678 6825
Drop-in centre for people with HIV/AIDS. Open Mon-Fri 1-5 pm. Women only evening Wed 5-9 pm. Free service, wheelchair access. Complementary therapies available: shiatsu, massage & reflexology.

Lydia Clinic for Sexually Transmitted Diseases
St Thomas' Hospital
1st Floor, Lambeth Wing
Lambeth Palace Road
London SE1
T 0171 928 9292
Clinics for sexually transmitted diseases Mon, Wed, Thurs, Fri 8.30 am-6 pm; Tue 8.30 am-4 pm. No appointment necessary - just drop in.

Moffat Health Clinic
Charity Duah
65 Sancroft Street
London SE11 5NG
T 0171 735 4169
Open 9 am-5 pm. Post natal group Mon 2-4 pm; toddler groups Wed 2-4.30 pm & Fri 10 am-12.30 pm; baby clinics Tues 9.30-11.30 am.

Positive Partners/Positively Children
Ruth Tamplin
Unit F7
Shadespeare Commercial Centre
245a Coldharbour Lane
London SW9 8RR
T 0171 738 7333 F 0171 501 9382
Set up by & for people directly affected by HIV/AIDS. Mixed support groups, face-to-face or telephone support, individual counselling, information & advice, massage, aromatherapy.

Rathmell Health Centre
9a Rathmell Drive
Clapham
London SW4 8JG
T 0181 674 7400 F 0181 671 6618
Open Mon-Fri 9 a.m-5 pm. Baby clinics Mon 1.30-3.30 pm & Wed 9.30-11.30 am Toy library Thurs 1.30-3.30 pm.

LEGAL MATTERS

Brixton Community Law Centre
506-508 Brixton Road
London SW9 8EN
T 0171 737 0440
Free legal advice for people living in the Brixton area & SW2, SE5 & part of SE24. Open Mon, Thurs, Fri 10.30 am-12.30 pm; Tue 6-8 pm

Gold, Lerman and Muirhead
43 Streatham Hill
London SW2 4TP
T 0181 671 6611 F 0181 674 8004
Open Mon-Fri 9 am-5.30 pm. Solicitors: divorce; family law; domestic violence; crime; housing; personal injury; company & commercial; wills & probate; conveyancing. Accepts legal aid work.

Lifeline
Alan Goddard
30 Woodland Hill
London SE19 1NY
T 0181 670 1980
Meets 1st & 3rd Sat of month, Upper Norwood Library, also first Sat of month, Berridge Road Church Centre, Berridge Road Estate, Berridge Road. Free advice: legal, benefits, welfare, unemployment law.

Stockwell and Clapham Community Law Centre
57-59 Old Town
Clapham Common
London SW4 0JQ
Free legal advice, representation in courts/tribunals for people in SW4 & SW8. Advice on housing, education, employment. Lines open 10 am-1 pm. Drop-in Wed 6.30-8 pm; Thurs 2-4 pm; Fri 10.30-12.30.

Vetti & Co
Mrs Miriam Sarmany
400-402 Brixton Road
London SW9 7AW
T 0171 274 0100
Open 9.30 am-6 pm. Solicitors depending purely on legal aid work. Green form advice & assistance forms the major part of the work. Also criminal law & litigation.

LESBIAN

Black Lesbian and Gay Centre
Room 113
5-5a Westminster Bridge Road
London SE1 7XW
T 0171 620 3885
Open Sat 2-5 pm. Drop-in. Telephone advice & information Mon 10 am-5 pm; Tue 3-6 pm; Fri 1-5 pm. Counselling, social groups & activities. Conference facilities. Referrals for housing associations.

LESBIAN AND BISEXUAL

Brixton Cycles
435-437 Coldharbour Lane
London SW9 8LN
T 0171 733 6055
Cycle shop. Accessories & repair service. Lesbian & gay friendly.

Lesbian and Gay Alcohol Counselling Project
Fiona or Darren
34 Electric Lane
Brixton
London SW9 8JT
T 0171 737 3579 F 0171 737 2719

Individual & group counselling for lesbians & gay men. Several venues. Free service.

Lesbian and Gay Pride Organising Committee
Unit 28
Eurolink Centre
49 Effra Road
London SW2 1BZ
T 0171 738 7644
Open Mon-Fri 10 am-6 pm. Organises & raises funds for the annual carnival parade & festival of lesbian & gay pride.

Red Hot AIDS Charitable Trust
Unit 32
Eurolink Business Centre
49 Effra Road
London SW2 1BZ
T 0171 924 0385 F 0171 738 6354
Fundraises from music industry for HIV/AIDs prevention work. Sponsors fundraising. Provides HIV/AIDS education.

LIBRARIES/ARCHIVES

Christine Osborne Pictures
Christine Osborne
53A Crimsworth Road
London SW8 4RJ
T 0171 720 6951 F 0171 720 6951
Stock photo library: 50,000 images. Commissions undertaken for women at work & social events.

MANUAL TRADES

Lambeth Women's Workshop
Caroline Tomiczek
Unit C22
Park Hill Trading Estate
Martell Road
London SE21 8EA
T 0181 670 0339 F 0181 670 0339
Open Mon-Fri 9.30 a.m-4.30 pm. Provides accredited training in carpentry & joinery for women aged 17+ who have had little chance of training. Courses are free. Child care and travel allowance are available.

MEDIA

Lambeth Video Ltd
E M Kirkpatrick
Unit G11
245a Coldharbour Lane
London SW9 8RR
T 0171 737 5903

Offers production & training experience in video equipment to women & ethnic minorities. Some projects are for women only.

Platinam Media Services
Tina Attoh-Baidoo
3 Woodgate Drive
London SW16 5YP
T 0181 765 1980 F 0181 765 1980
International freelance film maker. Documentaries & cultural affairs. 'Caste in Half': five women working together, based on culture.

OLDER WOMEN

Friendly Almshouses
the secretary
167 Stockwell Park Road
London SW9 0TL
T 0171 274 7176
Sheltered housing for women of modest means aged 60 & over.

Older Women's Group
Mrs Olive Burrage
New Park Road Baptist Church
New Park Road
Streatham Place
London SW2 4UP
T 0181 674 2680
Meets Wed 2.30-3.30 pm for Christian worship. For further details, contact Mrs Burrage on above number or Mrs Bridget Smith on 0181 671 2800.

PHOTOGRAPHY

Monocrone Women's Photography Collective
Sonia Mullings, Administrator
Clapham Pool
Clapham Manor Street
London SW4 6DB
T 0171 926 0703
Photography classes for beginners, intermediate, refreshers. Community darkroom. Commissioned work. Hiring of commercial equipment. Open Tues-Thurs 12-6 pm, Tues & Thurs 6.30-9.30 pm Sat 11 am-5 pm.

PLACES TO STAY AND EAT

Number 7 Guesthouse
7 Josephine Avenue
Brixton

London SW2 2JU
T 0181 674 1880
Lesbian & gay guesthouse. Brixton tube.
Phone for up to date price list.

Pregnancy/Childbirth

Crossroads Pregnancy Crisis Centre
Marcia Buxton
Arowdene Road
Brixton Hill
London SW2 2BH
T 0181 678 0900
Open Tue & Fri 10 am-12 noon; Wed 5-7 pm.
Free pregnancy testing, counselling &
support for women with unplanned
pregnancies. Post abortion & miscarriage
counselling. Phone for an appt. 24-hour
ansaphone.

Infertility - IVF Unit
Churchill Clinic
80 Lambeth Road
London SE1 7PW
T 0171 928 5633   F 0171 401 9942

Prisoners/Prisoners' Wives

HALOW (London)
Julie Robertson
193 Brook Drive
London SE11 4TG
T 0171 793 7484   F 0171 793 7230
Open 10 am-5 pm Mon-Sat. For prisoners,
ex-prisoners, familes & partners. Counselling,
advocacy, escort service with children. A bus
service to prisons. Telephone help line open
Mon-Sat 9 am-5 pm.

Services

London Heatcare
Valerie Taylor
3 Windsor Grove
London SE27 9NT
T 0181 761 7193   F 0181 761 7448
Insulation & energy efficiency services for low
income households in London.

Marsh & Associates
Jackie Marsh
37 Killyon Road
London SW8 2XS
T 0171 622 3265   F 0171 622 3265
Editorial packaging service: whole magazine,
from commissioning & design to disks for
repro; contract magazines, brochures, one-off
projects commissioned, edited & designed;
subbing & proofreading service.

Sexual Abuse/Rape Crisis

Family Welfare Assocation
area director
Brixton Family Centre
27 Josephine Avenue
London SW2 2JY
T 0181 671 5414
Deals primarily with child abuse. Support to
families. Also provides a social work service to
individuals, couples & groups.

Sports and Leisure

Brockwell Park Ladies Bowling Club
Mrs Sheila Jenkins
Brockwell Park
Herne Hill
London SE24
T 0171 926 0105
The Club day is Wed pm but play on most
days. Prospective new members should
contact Mrs Jenkins on 0181 670 2903.
Almost all the women are pensioners.

Transport

Lambeth Dial-A-Ride (LAMDAR) Ltd
George Clarke
1 Barstow Crescent
Palace Road
London SW2 3NS
T 0181 678 7242
Provides transport service to people with
mobility difficulties who cannot use public
transport. Open 9.30 a.m-5 pm.

Violence Against Women

Towards A Safer Brixton
Beverley Campbell
Safety Unit
164 Clapham Park Road
London SW4 7DQ
T 0171 926 7771   F 0171 926 7797
A project promoting community safety
initiatives in the Brixton City Challenge area.

Women's Aid

Asian Women's Aid
C/o Asian Women's Resource Centre
27 Santley Street
Brixton
London SW4 7QF

T 0171 274 8854
Counselling & advice for Asian women suffering domestic violence. Temporary accommodation offered.

Lambeth Women's Aid
P O Box 3791
London SW24 0ER
T 0181 674 1864
Helpline open Mon-Fri 9 am-5 pm. Ansaphone at all other times. For women & their children (if any), female relatives & friends fleeing or suffering from domestic violence.

LEWISHAM

ACCOMMODATION

Marsha Phoenix Memorial Trust
Mrs Sybil Carey
90-92 Tressillian Road
Brockley
London SE4 1YD
T 0181 691 5911 F 0181 691 9056
Residential accommodation & support for young women provided. Counselling, group work & the teaching of life skills.

New Cross Circle Projects
53 Deptford Broadway
London SE8 4PH
T 0181 692 7551
Open Mon-Fri 9 am-5.30 pm. Housing with support workers for women aged 18-55 who are homeless, including housing for lesbians and Asian women escaping domestic violence. Tenants stay for 1-2 years.

ARTS

Caribbean Women Writers' Alliance (CWWA)
Joan Anim-Addo
Caribbean Studies Centre
Goldsmiths College
New Cross
London SE4 6NW
T 0171 919 7397 F 0171 919 7397
ceaOljaa@scorpio.gold.ac.uk
Promotes voice and visibility for Caribbean women writers. Disseminates information about the work of Caribbean women writers, stimulates creative writing, facilitates networking & develops a forum.

ARTS AND CRAFTS

Leah Thorn
Leah Thorn
14 Lind Street
London SE8 4JE
T 0181 692 4104
Performance poet, working in theatres & poetry venues nationally & internationally. Workshops for women which explore use of performance poetry as means of empowerment & self-expression.

Rockbourne Printing Project
Sere Trew/Gary Bricklebank
41a Rockbourne Road
Forest Hill
London SE23 2DR
T 0181 291 4808
Sat morning session for women only 10 am-1 pm. Wheelchair access. Very reasonable charges for materials. Creche.

BEREAVEMENT

Lewisham Bereavement Counselling
Pamela Austin, Coordinator
C/o Deptford Methodist Mission
1 Creek Road
Deptford
London SE8 3BT
T 0181 692 6252
Provides one-to-one bereavement counselling, usually in people's homes. Core hours 10 am-1 pm Mon-Thurs. Referrals taken by phone. The service is free.

CONTRACEPTION/WELL WOMAN

Albion Street Health Centre
87 Albion Street
London SE16 1JX
T 0171 231 2296
Well woman clinic on Wed 5.15-7.45 pm. Free, confidential service for women run by women. Advice & information on health topics, eg vaginal infections, menopause. Blood pressure/urine checks, etc.

Bermondsey Health Centre
108 Grange Road
London SE1 3BW
T 0171 237 2826
Well woman clinic on Thurs 1.30-4 pm. Free, confidential service for women run by women. Advice & information on health topics, eg vaginal infections, menopause. Blood pressure/urine checks, etc.

Boundfield Road Clinic
Goldsmiths Community Centre
Castillon Road

London SE6 1QD
T 0181 698 3585
Free contraceptive advice & supplies. Clinics on Wed 10 a.m-12.30 pm; Thurs 6.30-9 pm.

Central Lewisham Health Centre
410 Lewisham High Street
London SE13 6LL
T 0181 690 3922
Free contraceptive advice/supplies. Clinics Mon 9.30-11.30 am & 6.30-8.30 pm; Wed 6.30-8.30 pm; Thurs 9.30 am-12 noon. Well woman Fri 1.15-3.15 pm. Free, confidential service for women run by women.

Deptford Brook Centre
Waldron Health Centre
Stanley Street
London SE8 4BS
T 0181 691 0417
Open Fri 3-5 pm. To make an appointment outside opening hours, phone 0171 703 9660. For young people aged 19 & under. Free, confidential contraceptive advice, condoms & other contraceptive supplies.

Heathside Clinic
Landale Court
Sparta Street
Lewisham Road
London SE10 8DQ
T 0181 692 8115
Free contraceptive advice & supplies. Clinic on Thurs 10 am-12 noon.

Jenner Health Centre
201 Stanstead Road
London SE23 1HU
T 0181 690 2231
Well woman clinic on Fri 9.30-11.30 am Free, confidential service for women run by women. Advice & information on health topics, eg vaginal infections, menopause. Blood pressure/urine checks, etc.

Lee Health Centre
2 Handen Road
London SE12 8NP
T 0181 852 1772
Well woman clinic on Thurs 6.15-8.15 pm. Free, confidential service for women run by women. Advice & information on health topics, eg vaginal infections, menopause. Blood pressure/urine checks, etc.

Lewisham Brook Centre
Central Lewisham Clinic
410 Lewisham High Street
London SE13 6LL
T 0181 690 3922
Open Tue 5.30-7.30. To make an appointment outside opening hours, phone 0171 703 9660. Free, confidential contraceptive advice. Free condoms & other contraceptive supplies. Pregancy testing & quick results.

Sydenham Green Health Centre
26 Holmshaw Close
London SE26 4TG
T 0181 659 6616
Well woman clinic on alternate Tue 9.15-11.45 am Free, confidential service for women run by women. Advice/information on health topics, eg vaginal infections, menopause. Blood pressure/urine checks, etc.

Waldron Health Centre
Stanley Street
London SE8 4BS
T 0181 691 5796
Well woman clinic on Tue 5.15-7.45 pm. Free, confidential service for women run by women. Advice/information on health topics, eg vaginal infections, menopause. Blood pressure/urine checks, etc.

COUNSELLING AND THERAPY

Pride Counselling
Ann Bromley
35 Mount Ash Road
Sydenham
London SE26 6LY
T 0181 699 1159
Psychotherapy & counselling for individuals, couples, groups.

Suneith Psychotherapist
Suneith
124 Wellmeadow Road
London SE6 1HP
T 0181 698 6312
An attachment-based psychotherapist in private practice in south east London. Appointments by arrangement. Working individually with women & men in depth usually over a number of years over issues of trauma.

Ethnic Minorities

Black HIV/AIDS in South London (BASEL)
Andrea Enisuh
P O Box 7953
London SE4 1ZA
T 0181 694 6639
Drop-in for HIV positive women/men on Fri 4-7 pm Wheelchair access. There is a female outreach worker who attends to Black women.

South East London Bangladeshi Women's Association
Mrs Suphia Ali
51 Ashmead Road
Deptford
London SE8 4DY
T 0181 691 2782
Provides a forum for Bangladeshi women in Lewisham to exchange ideas & information. Provides a support network, advice & counselling. English & Bengali spoken. Bengali classes for children.

Girls/Young Women

Catford Women's Group
Sonia
Catford Centre for Unemployed
20 Holbeach Road
Catford
London SE6 4QX
T 0181 690 8427
A group of young unemployed women & those on low incomes meet on Wed. Helps to advance education. Facilities are provided in the interests of social welfare for recreation & leisure time.

Forest Hill Youth Project - Platform 1
Elaine Lamont
2-4 Devonshire Road
Forest Hill
London SE23 3TT
T 0181 291 2428 F 0181 699 4036
Woman's group meets on Wed 11 am-3 pm: counselling, advice, information, training, support & resources. Mixed groups Mon, Thurs 12-4 pm; Tue 10 a.m-4 pm. A woman worker always available to talk to.

Young Women's Resource Project
Sharon Long
308 Brownhill Road
Catford
London SE6 1AU
T 0181 698 6675 F 0181 695 1552
lywvp@gn.apc.org

For young women aged 8-25. Black women's goup, open door young lesbian group, Lewisham lesbian mothers' group, young mothers' drop-in service & young women with special needs. Workshops in schools.

Health

Alcohol Recovery Project
Delores Young
318 New Cross Road
London SE14 6AF
T 0181 691 2886
Open Mon-Fri 9.30 am-12.30 pm. On Wed women only - drop-in. Afternoons appointment only. Counselling for all young people with alcohol problems. Alternative phone number 0181 691 5975.

Bromley Health Home Care and Respite Care
C/o St Christopher's Hospice
51-59 Lawrie Park Road
London SE26 6DZ
T 0181 778 9252
24-hour emergency cover. Home care, respite care & day care for people affected by HIV/AIDS, cancer & motor neurone disease.

Drugline Ltd
Margaret Moses
9a Brockley Cross
London SE4 2AB
T 0181 692 4975 F 0181 692 9968
Provides advice & support to drug users & their families. Offers an outreach service to women & children. Counselling. Educates the public, particularly young people, on the dangers of drugs & their misuse.

Manual Trades

Solar Plumbing and Heating
Viviene Bish
143 Foxborough Gardens
Brockley
London SE4 1HT
T 0181 314 0141 F 0181 314 0141
Qualified, competent plumbers working in domestic plumbing & small industrial plumbing. Works covered include all types of domestic plumbing & central heating. Working 24 hours, covering inner & outer London.

OLDER WOMEN

Older Women's Network, Lewisham
Henriette Dodd
29a Burghill Road
Sydenham
London SE26 4HJ
T 0181 778 8064
own@lewisham.gov.uk
Run by older women for older women. Affiliated to OWN Europe. Involved in research, having published a health survey in 1994 and a survey on housing in 1997.

Pensioners' Link
Charlie Woods
74 Deptford High Street
London SE8 4RT
T 0181 691 0938
Open Mon-Fri 9.30 am-1 pm. Fortnightly social meetings for older women with different activities. Welfare advice, home visits, befriending. There is an older black women's group. Wheelchair access.

PREGNANCY/CHILDBIRTH

Dorothy Norris
Dorothy Norris
13 Newquay Road
London SE6 2NR
T 0181 698 3266
Independent midwife offering full pregnancy, birth & post-natal care. Birth may be in hospital or at home, working with doctors, homeopaths or other practitioners as women choose. Phone for price list.

Home Birth Support Group (Lewisham and Greenwich)
Susan Robinson
83 Bargery Road
Catford
London SE6 2LP
T 0181 244 3732
Free information, support & a forum for discussion for those interested in or having a home birth. Meets in Catford last Mon of each month (except August & December) 8-10 pm. Phone for more details.

Nappies Direct
Maxine Alexander
P O Box 11709
London SE14 5BU
T 0171 635 7000
Mail order postal service for nappies. Some terry towling; some squares. Also essential oils for aromatherapy.

RETAILING

Nicole Manter Couture
Nicole Manter
The Conservatory
95 Belmont Hill
London SE19 5DY
T 0181 552 7307
Exclusive made to measure ladies garments, ranging from 'one off' couture to business wear (day and evening wear).

SERVICES

Carol-Ann Walters
Carol-Ann Walters
344D Brownhill Road
Catford
London SE6 1AY
T 0181 697 0887 F 0181 697 0887
PR & production services.

Interior Solutions
Caroline Davies
25 Pincott Place
London SE4 2ER
T 0171 277 8752 F 0171 277 8752
Interior design for homes & businesses. Aims to provides environments that people want to live & work in. Prices based on percentage of the contract amount. Phone any time.

SOCIAL

New Cross Circle Club
Irene Wright
308 New Cross Road
London SE14
T 0181 691 3381
A women-only social club for women in south London. Meets Mon 2-6 pm. No wheelchair access.

SPORTS AND LEISURE

Blackheath Ladies' Hockey Club
Janet Gainey
Rubens Street
Catford
London SE6 4DH
T 0181 699 2423
Youth coaching & training run by qualified coaches. Competitive & friendly hockey. Hockey for over 35s also available.

Dacre Morris
Sarah Crofts
7 Northbrook Road

LONDON - MERTON

London SE13 5QT
T 0181 331 8383
Women-only Morris Dance team. Traditional dancing in & around south east London. Member of Morris Federation. Meets Mon 8-9.30 pm at Kingswood Hall Annexe, Kingswood Hall, Kingswood Place, SE12.

In The Swim
Ann Bromley
35 Mount Ash Road
Sydenham
London SE26 6LY
T 0181 699 1159
Swimming lessons, specialising in water-phobic & non-swimmers. Learn to swim at your own pace. Swimming for disabled people.

Millwall Lionesses Football Club
C/o Millwall Football Club
Zampa Road
London SE16 3LN
T 0171 231 0379
Meets Fri at Ladywell Lodge, Dressington Avenue, Brockley, SE4. Women only from aged 9 onwards. Contact Millwall football club to which it is affiliated for further details.

Women's Inner Natural Strength for Self Defence (WINS)
Shirley Henry
38 Kender Street
New Cross
London SE14 5JG
T 0171 252 9351
Classes available in afternoon & evenings. Self defence movements & steps taught while individual encouraged to become non violent & non aggressive while using unique breathing method to balance energy levels.

SUPPORT

Women's Group - Lewisham
Dawn Henry
C/o Lewisham Way Centre
138 Lewisham Way
New Cross
London SE14 6PD
T 0181 692 1577
Meets Tue 6.30-9 pm. Self-programming, issue-based group. Educational & recreational activities during the year to help women develop knowledge & build up their confidence to challenge problems in society.

TRAINING

Adun Society
Patricia Collins
62 Deptford High Street
London SE8 4RT
T 0181 694 1951 F 0181 694 1083
Open Mon-Fri 9.30 am to 5.30 pm. A registered charity providing training & support for women.

VIOLENCE AGAINST WOMEN

Police Domestic Violence Unit
41-43 Nightingale Grove
Hither Green
London SE13 6DY
T 0181 284 5855
Open Mon-Fri 8 am-4 pm. Free & confidential service for women only. Will if necessary refer caller to other agencies. Leaflets available in Turkish, Vietnamese, Cantonese, Urdu, Bengali, Gujerati, Somali.

MERTON

ACCOMMODATION

Bhavan Ltd
Hansa Dave
P O Box 552
London SW19 4XP
T 0181 540 8819
Asian women's refuge & for dependants (males up to age 11 - female up to age 16). A safe house for single Asian women aged 16-25. Referrals accepted via London Women's Aid & Women's Aid Federation of England.

ALTERNATIVE THERAPIES

Christina Maria Langley Polarity Therapist
Christina Maria Langley
16a Canon Hill Lane
Wimbledon Chase
London SW20 9EP
T 0181 542 9476

Homoeopathic Mother and Baby Clinic
Barbara Geraghty
77 Kenilworth Avenue
Wimbledon Park
London SW19 7LP
T 0181 946 4950
Open Mon 3-6 pm. Phone for an appointment - no drop-in.

Wimbledon Children's Homoeopathic Clinic
Wimbledon Community Centre

St George's Road
London SW19
T 0181 857 4612
Homoeopathic treatment for children.

ARMED FORCES

Women's Royal Army Corps Association - Wimbledon branch
Miss B E Wright, Chairman
58 Rokeby House
Lochinvar Street
Balham
London SW12 8PX
T 0181 673 3662
Ex-servicewomen meet at Community Centre, St George's Road, Wimbledon on second Fri (third in October) of each month (except January & August). Talks & promoting friendship between serving & ex-service members.

BUSINESS SUPPORT SCHEMES

Altrusa Club of London For Business and Professional Women
Miss Margaret Rowbottom, Secretary
22 Glendale Drive
Wimbledon
London SW19 7BG
T 0181 947 0848

CARERS

Carers' Support Merton
Helen Barns, Coordinator
The Vestry Hall
London Road
Mitcham CR4 3UD
T 0181 640 4159
Provides information and supports existing carers' groups. Identifies carers & raises awareness of the needs of all carers in Merton.

CONTRACEPTION/WELL WOMAN

Family Planning Clinic
Nelson Hospital
Kingston Road
Merton
London SW20 8DB
T 0181 770 8000
Contraceptive & well woman clinics Thurs 6.15-8 pm. Free contraceptive advice & supplies; pregancy testing; well woman screening; menopause counselling. Phone 0181 770 8080 outside clinic times.

Family Planning Clinic
Amity Grove
Wimbledon
London SW20 1LG
T 0181 770 8000
Contraceptive & well woman clinic Tue 6.15-8.15 pm. Free contraceptive advice & supplies; pregnancy testing; well woman screening; menopause counselling. Phone 0181 770 8080 outside clinic hours.

Family Planning Clinic - The Surgery
58 High Street
Colliers Wood
Wimbledon
London SW19 2BY
T 0181 770 8000
Contraceptive & well woman clinic Tue 9.30-11.30 am Free contraceptive advice & supplies; pregnancy testing; well woman screening; menopause counselling; phone 0181 770 8080 outside clinic hours.

Patrick Doody Clinic
79 Pelham Road
Wimbledon
London SW19 1NX
T 0181 770 8000
Contraceptive & well woman clinics on Mon, Wed & Fri 6.15-8.15 pm & Tue 1-3.30 pm. Free contraceptive advice & supplies; well woman; menopause counselling. Youth contraceptive clinics Tue 3.30-4.30.

COUNSELLING AND THERAPY

TherapyWorks
Ruthmoyra St John
Tranquil Cottage
156b Merton Road
Wimbledon
London SW19 1EB
T 0181 543 3903 F 0181 543 3903
Woman to woman counselling. Specialises in alcohol & drug abuse, eating disorders, self-esteem, relationship. Also provides reflexology, aromatherapy, holistic massage (on-site massage) & healing.

ETHNIC MINORITIES

Bengali Women's Association of Merton
Mrs Choudhury
MREC
36 Colliers Wood High Street
Wimbledon
London SW19
T 0181 540 7386

Aims to help members of the Asian community & Bengali women in particular. Advice on DSS & housing. Runs a mother tongue school & various religious activities.

Merton Asian Women's Association
Shibani Basu
C/o Mitcham Library
Lonton Road
Mitcham CR4 2YR
T 0181 648 4070
Meets third Sat of each month at Mitcham library. Educational & cultural programmes. Aims to motivate individual members to integrate with the local society. The group runs a local catering cooperative.

Pregnancy/Childbirth

National Childbirth Trust - Wimbledon and Wandsworth branch
Lisa Khalil
15 Ellerton Road
Wimbledon
London SW20 0ER
T 0181 946 6650
Support/information in pregnancy, childbirth, early parenthood. Ante natal/post natal classes. Breastfeeding counselling. Post-natal support network. Helpline. Presses for improvements in local maternity care.

Single Parents

Merton Welcare Association
Mary Budden, Social Worker
28 St Mark's Road
Mitcham CR4 2LE
T 0181 640 5506
Advice & information for single parents regarding pregnancy, coping with isolation, parenting, housing & benefits. Advises on safety, health, development of children aged under 8 of single parents.

Social

Pollards Hill Ladies' Association
Evelyn Mayes
22 Conway Gardens
Mitcham CR4 1QA
T 0181 764 2466
Social club. Meets on second & fourth Mon of each month at 7.30 pm at Pollards Hill Community Association. Speakers, discussions, etc.

Wimbledon Women's Club
Mrs B A L Hilyer, Secretary
1 Harcourt Road
Wimbledon
London SW19 1LS
T 0181 540 2322
Meets alternate Thurs evenings at Sir Cyril Black Community Centre, St George's Road, Wimbledon, SW19 8-10 pm. Speakers & social activities.

Sports and Leisure

Raynes Park Women's Hockey Club
Michelle Baldock, Secretary
84 Amity Grove
West Wimbledon
London SW20 0LJ

Wimbledon Ladies' Hockey Club
Claire Bennett
55 Southway
Raynes Park
London SW20 9JH
T 0181 543 8633
Trains regularly on Thurs 7.30-9.30 pm throughout the year. Runs five teams - first team in first division of national league.

Transport

South London Dial-A-Ride
45 Weir Road
Wimbledon
London SW19 8UG
T 0181 784 6016
Door-to-door service for people with disabilities unable to use public transport, every day 8.30 am-11.30 pm. Fares similar to London busses. Areas: Lamb., Wandsw'th, Mert., Kings., Richmond, Croyd., Sutton.

Newham

Accommodation

Eastwards Trust Ltd
Rajni Kaur
London Borough of Newham
19-25 Carlton Road
London E12 5BG
T 0181 514 7730 F 0181 514 7730
Provides sheltered accommodation for older Asian women. 12 self-contained flats. Housing needs & caring are provided. The organisation campaigns for further needs & resources.

Arts and Crafts

Bryony Lavery
Bryony Lavery
17 Maitland Road
London E15 4EL
T 0181 534 5364
Playwright, director, performer & teacher of playwriting. Plays include, The Two Marias, Witchcraze, Kitchen Matters & Her Aching Heart. Was Artistic Director of her own company Female Trouble.

Centres for Women

East London Black Women's Organisation (ELBWO)
P Smith
ELBWO Centre
Clinton Road
Forest Gate
London E7 OHD
T 0181 534 7545
Service provision includes skills training for jobless women, child care, an after school club, a holiday play scheme, creche, supplementary school, advice, information & counselling.

Women's Health Centre
Kris McKenna/Arun Mushiana/Anne Parker
Stratford Advice Arcade
107-109 The Grove
Stratford
London E15 1HP
T 0181 221 0311   F 0181 221 1996
For women only. Advice, information for pregnant women & mothers, well-women clinics, contraception, complementary therapies, counselling, health visitor advisory clinics. Health information 0181 221 0411.

Computers/IT

Newham Women's Training & Education Centre (NEWTEC)
Nicola Ingle
22 Deanery Road
Stratford
London E15 4LP
T 0181 519 5843   F 0181 519 9704
NEWTEC@newtec.demon.co.uk
Open Mon-Fri 9 am-5 pm. Free courses for unemployed women in East London, mainly new technology, computing & language support courses from basic to degree level. Help with travel & childcare facilities.

Contraception/Well Woman

Lord Lister Health Centre
121 Woodgrange Road
Forest Gate
London E7
T 0181 552 8828
Clinic on Wed 1.45-3.30 pm. Free, confidential contraceptive advice & supplies; pregnancy testing & advice; emergency contraception; cervical smears.

Margaret Scott Clinic
Appelby Road
London E16
T 0181 552 8828
Clinic on Mon 2-3.30 pm. Free contraceptive advice & supplies; pregnancy testing & advice; emergency contraception; cervical smears.

Newham Brook Centre
West Ham Lane Clinic
84 West Ham Lane
Stratford
London E15 4PT
T 0181 519 1150
Open Wed 4.30-6.30 pm; Sat 9.30-11.30 am
To make an appointment outside opening hours, phone 0171 580 2991. Free, confidential contraceptive advice. Free condoms & other contraceptive supplies.

Shrewsbury Road Health Centre
East Ham
London E7
T 0181 552 8828
Clinics on Tue 9.30-11 am & 6.30-8 pm; Wed 6.30-8 pm. Free & confidential contraceptive advice & supplies; pregnancy testing & advice; emergency contraception; cervical smears.

Tollgate Health Centre
Tollgate Road
Beckton
London E6
T 0181 552 8828
Clinic on Thurs 6.30-8 pm. Free, confidential contraceptive advice & supplies; pregnancy testing & advice; emergency contraception; cervical smears.

West Beckton Health Centre
Lawson Close
London E16
T 0181 552 8828

LONDON - NEWHAM

Clinic on Mon 6.30-8 pm. Free, confidential contraceptive advice & supplies; pregnancy testing & advice, cervical smears; emergency contraception.

West Ham Lane Clinic
84 West Ham Lane
London E15
T 0181 552 8828
Clinics Tue 6.30-8 pm; Thurs 6.30-8 pm. Free, confidential contraceptive advice & supplies; pregnancy testing & advice; emergency contraception; cervical smears.

Women's Health Centre, The
The Stratford Advice Arcade
107-109 The Grove
Stratford
London E15 1HP
T 0181 221 0311
Drop-in Wed 9.30-11.30 am Free, confidential service provded by female doctor & nurse team. Free creche: phone 0181 221 0311. Contraceptive advice & supplies, referrals for abortion, emergency contraception.

COUNSELLING AND THERAPY

Newham Independent Counselling Service
Hazel Hickson
365 High Street North
Manor Park
London E12 4PG
T 0181 470 9900
Free, confidential counselling. Specialist areas: HIV, bereavement, sexual abuse. Asian languages spoken: Hindi, Urdu and Gurjerati. Also Turkish & French speaking counsellors.

Private Health Centre
Mrs P Steel
37 Green Street
Forest Gate
London E7 8DA
T 0181 472 0170
Stress, anxiety, sexual abuse counselling. (Not free.) Psychotherapy & hypnotherapy. One-to-one counselling. Languages: Hindi, Gujarati, Punjabi, Urdu. Open Mon-Fri 9.30 am-12 pm & 5.30-7.30 pm.

DISABILITY

Asian Deaf Women's Association
Sarla Meisuria
Stratford Advice Arcade
107-109 The Grove
London E15 1HP
T 0181 221 0581 F 0181 221 0582
Supports Asian women & girls who are deaf or hard of hearing. Training workshops provided. Volunteer training, advocacy & support, welfare advice, counselling & a social club. Minicom: 0181 555 9680.

ETHNIC MINORITIES

Apna Ghar
Sudarshan Bhumi
Community Links
105 Barking Road
Canning Town
London E16 4HQ
T 0171 473 2270 F 0171 473 6671
24-hour helpline: 0171 474 1547. Free, confidential service for Asian women who are experiencing or have experienced domestic violence. Helps with welfare benefits, housing, legal matters, emergency shelter.

Asha Women Support Group
Afshan Khan
365 High Street North
Manor Park
London E12 6EG
T 0181 470 9900
Meets at Trinity Centre, Manor Park, East Avenue, on Mon 1-2.30 pm. For women who have suffered domestic violence or who are isolated, single parents, have language difficulties or are experiencing separation.

Asian Parents Advocacy Group
Iram Mukhtar
Cleves Primary School
Arragon Road
London E6 1QP
T 0181 472 6298 F 0181 471 2589
Open Fri 10 am-12.30 pm for Asian parents who want assistance for their children with special needs. Brings Asian parents with special needs children together.

Asian Women's Advice & Activities Service (AWAAS)
Atia Malik
Friendship House
St Bartholemew's Road
East Ham
London E6
T 0181 470 3017 F 0181 471 6967
A free service for Asian women, providing general counselling, support, advice & information. One-to-one counselling; also by

telephone. Also support groups. Befriending, stress, family concerns.

East London African & Caribbean Counselling Service (ELACCS)
Dee Crawford, Co-ordinator
2 Windmill Lane
Stratford
London E15 1PG
T 0181 221 1233   F 0181 221 1233
Free counselling on sexual abuse, stress relationship breakdown, childhood experiences, loss & bereavement & racial discrimination. Also a refugee counselling service. Staffed by Black professional workers.

Newham Asian Women's Project
Anita Kirpal
661 Barking Road
Plaistow
London E13 9EX
T 0181 472 0528   F 0181 503 5673
Provides emergency refuge & support to Asian women & children fleeing domestic violence. Practical & emotional support & advice on debt issues. Training in computing, book-keeping & other areas.

Newham West African Women's Organisation
Catherine Heroe
5 Wolffe Gardens
Stratford
London E15 4JJ
T 0181 519 0811
Run by women to promote the health of women & their families, especially those of African descent. To educate people about sexually transmitted diseases, domestic violence, drugs. Phone between 4-6 pm.

Shree Kutch Leva Patel Community - Women & Girls' Group
Mrs Vijaya M Patel
35 Helnham Road
East Ham
London E6 2JL
T 0181 471 4760
Cultural & religious activities. Health & support group for victims of domestic violence. Counselling & educational classes; wlefare rights advice. Arts & crafts. Child care/child protection support group, etc.

Sohali Group
Balbir Kaur
C/o Shalom Employment Action Centre
395 High Street North
Manor Park
London E12 6TL
T 0181 472 3571   F 0181 552 0762
An Asian women's support group. Meets on Thurs 1.30-4 pm. Enables women to obtain advice on a variety of issues, eg education & training, counselling, information about services available.

Somali Women's Development Project
C/o Newham Somali Association
728 Romford Road
Manor Park
London E12 6BT
T 0181 514 6683
Meets at the Newham Somali Association on Fri 12-5 pm. Activities include learning about Somali traditional culture.

Trinity Community Centre
Ms I Osman
East Avenue
Manor Park
London E12 6SJ
T 0181 472 8947
Asian women's counselling/support Mon 1-2.30 pm; Trinity girls' group (ages 11-16) Wed 3-4.45 pm; Milan Ashram (Asian older women) Tue 1-4 pm; ESOL classes for girls Tue, Wed, Thurs 10 am-12 pm

Young Muslim Women's Project
B Meman
640 Barking Road
London E13 9JY
T 0181 472 9657
Classes are run on Sat mornings from 10.30 am to 12.30 pm at Lister Community School, St Mary's Road, Plaistow, London E13 in sewing, cake-decorating & cooking.

GIRLS/YOUNG WOMEN

Liveline
Jan Marr
London
T 0500 585850
A telephone counselling service for women (& men) under 21, providing support on any problem or concern. On-going counselling, referral agency & in-school support, providing information & support.

LONDON - Newham

Youth Information and Advice Service
Verena Thompson
51 The Broadway
Stratford
London E15 3AF
T 0181 221 0802   F 0181 221 1347
Information, advice & counselling for young people under 25. Lifeskill workshops. Self-defence classes for young women. Drop-in Tue, Thurs, Fri 2-5 pm; Wed 4-7.30 pm; Sat 11 am-3 pm.

Health

Cancer - You Are Not Alone (CYANA)
Pam Iveson/Cathy Applegate
31 Church Road
Manor Park
London E12 6AD
T 0181 553 5366
Provides support, advice & information on all cancer-related issues & problems free of charge to all women in Newham. Children's library. Home. hospital & hospice visiting. 24-hour telephone service.

Genito Urinary Medicine (GUM) Clinic
Newham General Hospital
Glen Road
Plaistow
London E13 8RU
T 0171 363 8146
Genito-urinary clinic on daily basis. HIV/AIDS service, STD screening, contraception. Dealing with any type of sexual health problem. Psychology service. Wheelchair access.

London East AIDS Network (LEAN)
35 Romford Road
London E15 4LY
T 0181 519 9545   F 0181 519 6229
Advice & support services for people affected by HIV/AIDS. Staff provide welfare/housing advice, legal advice, advocacy service, housing, prevention & care issues, etc.

Newham Alcohol Advisory Service
Maeve Malley
Capital House
134-8 Romford Road
London E15 4LD
T 0181 257 3068
Free service for women worried about their drinking or that of someone close to them. Lesbians can see a lesbian counsellor. Face-to-face for individuals, couples, families. Also group work (0181 221 0821).

Newham Drugs Advice Project
Julie Jarvis
361 Barking Road
Plaistow
London E13 8EE
T 0171 474 2222   F 0171 473 5899
Open Mon, Wed, Thurs, Fri 10 am-5.30 pm; Tues 6-8.30 pm; Wed is for women only. Free counselling on drug use & resulting issues on a one-to-one basis. Women can ask for a woman counsellor. Female nurse.

Sexual Health Advisors (GUM Dept)
Newham General Hospital
Glen Road
London E13 8SL
T 0171 363 8146
Free HIV/AIDS pre- & post-test counselling. Appointment necessary. One-to-one counselling, by phone or in groups. Advice & information given on all aspects of sexual health.

Lesbian and Bisexual

Vicarage Lane Community Centre
Govier Close
Stratford
London E15 4HW
T 0181 519 0235
Provides priority to community groups serving lesbians & gay men.

Manual Trades

Cowling Contracting
Andrea Cowling
24 Buxton Road
East Ham
London E6 3NB
T 0181 548 9760   F 0181 548 9760
Carries out work for housing associations, lettings agents, special needs housing. Main trades: painting & decorating, carpentry, cleaning, clearance, carpet cleaning, garden maintenance. Some plumbing, etc.

Pregnancy/Childbirth

Alternatives Crisis Pregnancy Centre
Mrs Julia Acott
415 Barking Road
Plaistow
London E13 8AL
T 0171 476 8215
Free pregnancy tests. Crisis pregnancy counselling. Ongoing support/practical help for women who decide to keep their babies.

Miscarriage & post-abortion counselling.
Open Mon-Fri 9.30 am-9.30 pm.

New Beginnings Midwifery Practice
Clare Winter
65 Lonsdale Avenue
London E6 3JZ
T 0181 470 2885
Providing continuity of midwifery care, specialising in home births, water births. Main aim is to help women to achieve the birth of their choice.

Pregnancy Counselling Services (Newham Healthcare)
Zella Greenland
Pregnancy Advice Clinic
St Andrew's Hospital
Devons Road, Bow
London E3 3NT
T 0171 363 8247
Free short-term crisis counselling for women thinking about abortions. Also issues around planned & unplanned pregnancies, sexual health & contraception. Post-abortion support.

SERVICES

Health Eastenders
Kay Balogun
114 Atkinson Road
London E16 3LS
T 0171 476 4007
Health care, dress making, training. Exporter of new & used medical aids, eg wheelchairs, commodes, beds. Open 9 am- 9pm Mon-Sat. Promotes equality in healthcare & helping local people get decent jobs.

SEXUAL ABUSE/RAPE CRISIS

Ann Marney
Ann Marney
97 Crofton Road
Plaistow
London E13 8QT
T 0171 474 1297
Individual short- & long-term counselling for sexual abuse, stress, phobias, bereavement, depression, relationship problems, etc.
Counselling times: Mon, Tues, Wed, Fri 9.30 am-2.30 pm; Wed 7-9 pm.

SINGLE PARENTS

Holiday Endeavour for Lone Parents (HELP) - Newham

Ms F Morris
5 Wall End Road
East Ham
London E6 2NP
T 0181 475 0375
Provides low cost family holidays for lone parents who are brining up children on their own from May-December. Phone for further details.

SOCIAL

Ladies' Guild of Friendship
Mrs J Prinelle
44 Southchurch Road
East Ham
London E6 4DZ
T 0181 472 6901

SPORTS AND LEISURE

Atherton Leisure Centre
189 Romford Road
Stratford
London E15
T 0181 519 5731
Swimming: women only swimming lessions. Wed Asian Women's Club 12-1 pm; Thurs women only 9-10 pm; Sat women & girls only 12.30-3 pm. Fitness: women only induction Thurs 6.30-8.30 pm.

Balaam Leisure Centre
Balaam Street
Plaistow
London E13 8AQ
T 0171 476 5274
Women only swimming lessions & fitness induction sessions - phone for further details. Women & girls' swimming Tue 10-11 am; legs, bums & tums Tue 8-9 pm.

Newham Leisure Centre
281 Price Regent Lane
Plaistow
London E13 8SD
T 0171 511 4477
Women only sessions: Mon 7.30-10.30 pm; Wed & Fri 10 am-12 pm. Swimming, fitness, aerobics, sauna/steam & sunbed suite, supervised play area. Women only swimming lessions & induction to fitness centre.

Newham Women's Football Club
Diane Shaw
39 Meads Court
Carnarvon Road
Stratford

London E15 4LB
T 0181 519 2014
Training on Tue & Thurs 6.30-8.30 pm.
Encourages football for all women & girls: playing, coaching, managing, administering, watching, coordinating & deciding to do any of these as they choose.

Support

Community Links Centre
Community Links advice team
105 Barking Road
Canning Town
London E16 4HQ
T 0171 473 2270
Free open door advice sessions Mon-Thurs 9.30 am-12.30 pm: welfare benefits, disability benefits, housing, immigration, etc. Free pregnancy testing. Home visiting. Appeals & tribunal worker representation.

Powerhouse
Bridget O'Shea
P O Box 10450
London E16 1RF
T 0171 473 5321
For women with learning difficulties organised by women with learning difficulties. User-led services enabling women to make informed choices and have control over their lives.

Training

Shalom Employment Action Centre (SEAC)
Balbir Kaur
395 High Street North
Manor Park
London E12 6TL
T 0181 472 3571 F 0181 552 0762
Drop-in 10 am-12.30 pm & 1.30-4 pm.
Courses in garment making, office skills, computing, woodwork, everyday English, everyday maths, spoken English. Aims to provide free childcare. Mother & toddler group.

Transport

Newham Women's Safe Transport
Bee Burgess
Hallsville Road Depot
Hallsville Road
Canning Town
London E16 1EE
T 0171 473 6100
Offers lifts on Wed, Thurs and Fri evenings between 6-11 pm. A door-to-door service.

Accessible to women in wheelchairs. Also offers advice & training courses.

Violence Against Women

Newham Action Against Domestic Violence (NAADV)
Emma Mortoo
St Marks Community Centre
Tollgate Road
London E6 4YA
T 0171 473 3047 F 0171 511 5520
Open Mon-Fri 9.30-5.30. Practical & emotional support for women experiencing domestic violence.

Redbridge

Accountancy

El-Jai Consulting
Lisa Jensen
41 Rectory Court
189 High Road
South Woodford
London E18 2PE
T 0181 504 3585 F 0181 504 3522
ELJAI@vossnet.co.uk
Offering large & small businesses quick, cost-effective & no hassle approach to streamlining company accounts using Sage Accounting Software. Companies charged on an hourly basis to benefit smaller businesses.

Alternative Therapies

Josephine Haworth
Josephine Haworth
76 Clavering Road
Wanstead
London E12 5EX
T 0181 989 7142
Acupuncturist, using Traditional Chinese Medicine techniques; psychotherapist, using a psychodynamic approach.

Child Care and Family

Play Pen Out of School Club
Sandra Taku or Angela Brouet
38 Uphall Road
Ilford IG1 2JF
T 01956 630858
Caters for children aged 5-12. Open Mon-Fri 3.30-6.30 pm. Qualified and experienced staff. Club based at Aldborough Hatch Community Centre, Aldborough Road North, Newbury Park, Ilford IG5 7SR.

CONTRACEPTION/WELL WOMAN

Redbridge Brook Centre
John Telford Clinic
Cleveland Road
Ilford IG1 1EE
T 0181 478 6982
Open Thurs 5-7 pm; Sat 2-4 pm. To make an appointment outside opening hours, phone 0171 580 2991. Free, confidential contraceptive advice. Free condoms & other contraceptive supplies. Pregnancy tests.

COUNSELLING AND THERAPY

Counselling Practice
Frances Wiseman
22 Lavender Place
Ilford IG1 2BE
T 0181 478 5730
Short & long-term general counselling. Person-centred, integrative approach for individuals. Weekends & evenings.

One Stop
Pat Walton/Pauline Turner
Eastwood Medical Centre
Eastwood Road
South Woodford
London E18 1BN
T 0181 491 7077   F 0181 518 8728
Free counselling for women suffering perinatal loss & other bereavement. Sliding scale fee for counselling (sexual abuse) & psychotherapy. Office hours for initial contact are Mon-Fri 8.30 am-7.30 pm.

Private Counselling Practice
Anne Robertson
54 Uphall Road
Ilford IG1 2JF
T 0181 478 1856
Short- and long-term individual counselling: relationships, bereavement, health, sexual abuse, general. Open to all from aged 8 onwards. Person-centred, integrative.

Redbridge Counselling Services
Qulsoom Inayat
6 Arlington Road
Woodford Green IG8 9DE
T 0181 498 9780
24-hour ansaphone. Urdu & Punjabi spoken. Account taken of specific needs of ethnic minority groups. Counselling for victims of sexual abuse; bereavement counselling; counselling for older women, etc.

ETHNIC MINORITIES

Asian Women's Association
Mrs Parhar
40 Argyle Road
Ilford IG1 3SN
T 0181 518 0725   F 0181 518 3039
Open 9 am-5 pm weekdays; 24-hour answering service. Aims to enhance quality of life for Asian women & girls in the Redbridge area. Counselling, advice, information & representation. Social functions.

LARGER/TALLER WOMEN

Women At Large
95 George Lane
South Woodford
London E18 1AN
T 0181 989 5133
Clothes for women sizes 14-32.

PHOTOGRAPHY

Cosine Graphics
Jane Shemilt
16 Cowslip Road
South Woodford
London E18 1JW
T 0181 530 6874   F 0181 530 8291
jshemilt@macline.co.uk
Self-employed medical photographer. Areas covered include medico-legal photography, plastic surgery. 35mm slide presentation production computer.

SERVICES

Aurora Moon Communications
Aurora Moon
29 St Anthony's Avenue
Woodford Green IG8 7EP
T 0181 505 2860   F 0181 505 2860
Promotes personal developers & peak performace trainers to teach women how to break through the walls of life's limitations & achieve high levels of excellence, emotionally, physically & financially.

Egere Public Relations
Carol O'Callaghan
146a Empress Avenue
Ilford IG1 3DF
T 0181 554 2457   F 0181 554 0153
Public relations including media relations. Issues management, crisis management, internal communications, events, exhibitions. Consultancy & implementation.

Share-Bernia Associates
Joanne Share
68 Clayhall Avenue
Clayhall IG5 OLF
T 0181 550 4440 F 0181 551 2478
Chartered occupational organisational psychologist. Stress management workshops, individual counselling/therapy, mentoring support programmes for HR departments, executive development.

Transport
Dial-A-Ride
400 Roding Lane South
Woodford Green IG8 8EY
T 0181 498 8200
Door-to-door service for disabled people unable to use public transport, all week 8.30 am-11.30 pm. Fares similar to London busses. Covers T. Hamlets, New'm, Redbr'ge, Bark. & Dag., Havering, Waltham Forest.

Richmond Upon Thames

Centres for Women
Women's Information and Resource Centre
91 Queen's Road
Twickenham
Middlesex TW1 4EU
T 0181 744 9888
Open Mon 10 am-3 pm, Thurs 3-8 pm, Fri 10 am-3 pm. Women's group; domestic violence support group; topical discussion group. Speakers on women's interests on Thurs 6-7.30 pm. Free creche. Drop-in.

Counselling and Therapy
Mediation in Divorce
13 Rosslyn Road
East Twickenham
Middlesex TW1 2AR
T 0181 891 6860
Open Mon-Fri 9.30 am-1 pm. Helps couples affected by separation/divorce to meet face-to-face & communicate constructively to reach joint decisions about children, etc. Short-term counselling.

TASHA in Spelthorne
Chi Maher
Community Link Centre
Council Offices Building
Knowle Green
Middlesex TW18 1XD
T 01784 440128

Open Mon-Fri 9.30 am-5.30 pm. Confidential information, advice, support, counselling, holistic health care to individuals affected by tranquillisers, sleeping pills, stress, anxiety, depression, agoraphobia.

Disability
Keep Able Ltd
11-17 Kington Road
Staines
Middlesex TW18 4QX
T 01784 440044 F 01784 449900
Sells aids & equipment for the elderly & disabled. There are also stores in Mill Hill & Sydenham.

Health
Alcohol Counselling Service
Richmond Royal Hospital
Richmond
T 0181 940 7542
Telephone line open Mon, Thurs, Fri 10 am-5 pm, Tue 10 am-8 pm, Wed 10 am-9 pm. Drop-in service Mon-Fri: 0181 891 5488. Free service offering one-to-one counselling & support to family & friends.

Older Women
Thursday at Three
Mrs Betty Carr, Leader
69 Cowley Road
Mortlake SW14 8QD
T 0181 878 1120
Meets at St Mary's Church Hall, Mortlake High Street, Mortlake on first Thurs of each month at 3 pm. A social club with speakers.

Photography
Ancient Lights
Glenda Colquhoun
21 Northcote Road
St Margarets
Middlesex TW1 1PB
T 0181 891 1704
Freelance photographer. Course coordinator for HNC Photography & Electrical Imaging & G&G 9231 Photography, Richmond Upon Thames College, Photographic Section, Egerton Rd, Twickenham TW2 7SJ 0181 607 8208.

LONDON - RICHMOND UPON THAMES

RACIAL EQUALITY

Ethnic Minorities Advocacy Group (EMAG)
1 Princes Street
Richmond TW9 1ED
T 0181 332 2911
Support for people facing racial disadvantage. Free service. Wheelchair access.

RELIGIOUS ORGANISATIONS

All Hallows Twickenham Monday Group
Mrs Burdon, Leader
158 Wills Crescent
Whitton TW3 2JD
T 0181 894 7573
Meets at the Long Room, All Hallows Church, Erncroft Way, Twickenham on Mon fortnightly at 8 pm Speakers, questions, discussions.

British League of Unitarian and Other Liberal Christian Women
Mrs Hilda M Tuckman, Secretary
23 Alton Gardens
Twickenham TW2 7PD
T 0181 898 6546
Meets at Holland Road Free Church, Ormond Road, Richmond on first Tue of each month 2 pm. Aims to quicken religious life of churches & to bring Unitarian/other liberal Christian women into closer fellowship.

St Philip & St James' Women's Group
Jean Pettitt
Whitton
T 0181 570 0917
Meets at St Philip & St James' Church Hall, Hounslow Road, Whitton on third Thurs of each month at 8 pm. Aims to provide an outside interest for wives & mothers in parish affairs. Raises funds for the church.

SERVICES

Career Development for Women
Linda Greenbury
97 Mallard Place
Twickenham
Middlesex TW1 4SW
T 0181 892 3806 F 0181 892 3806
Personalised career planning & counselling for adult women. Fee paying. By appointment only.

SOCIAL

Hampton Methodist Ladies Guild
Mrs Joan O'Brien, Secretary
14 Cleves Way
Hampton TW12 2PL
T 0181 287 7401
Meets at the Small Hall, Methodist Church, Percy Road, Hampton on alternate Tue 8 pm. Outings, speakers, bazaars, etc.

St Augustine's Thursday Club
Mrs B N Hopkins, Secretary
67 Lincoln Avenue
Twickenham
Middlesex TW2 6NH
T 0181 898 9269
Meets at St Augustine' Church Hall, Hospital Bridge Road, Whitton, TW2 on first & third Thurs of each month at 8 pm. Talks, demonstrations, theatre visits. Women of all ages welcome.

Teddington Women's Luncheon Club
Miss Barbara Macmahon, Secretary
25 Bushy Park Road
Teddington TW11 9DQ
T 0181 977 4965
Meets at the Stable Room in the Lion, Wick Road, Teddington on second Wed of each month at 12.30 pm

SPORTS AND LEISURE

Whitton Netball Club
Mrs Mary Turner
16 Strathearn Avenue
Whitton TW2 6JU
T 0181 894 5478
For women of all ages. Plays in two leagues. Matches on Sat. Training on Wed evenings.

WINNERS
Angela Francombe, Chair
c/o 146 Petersham Road
Richmond TW10 6UX
T 0181 831 6133
Women's Information Network News Education Recreation and Sport. A London-wide networking process to share ideas about sport for women and girls. Coordinating London-based activities.

Women's Football Association
Miss A Mason
15 Ferry Road
Teddington TW11 9NN
T 0181 977 3658

Greater London Regional Women's Football League.

Support

Richmond and Kingston Missing Persons Bureau
Roebach House
284-286 Upper Richmond Rd West
East Sheen SW14 7JE
T 0181 392 2000
Freephone 0500 700700.

Southwark

Accommodation

Cecil House
Brenda Gould
266 Waterloo Road
London SE1 8RF
T 0171 928 5752 F 0171 261 9059
A hostel for homeless women aged 16 to 60. Both referred & self-referral.

Drink Crisis Centre - Women's Services
The Community Alcohol Service
177 Southwark Bridge Road
London SE2 0ED
T 0171 357 0090
Three residential projects for women with alcohol problems, & homeless women.

Drink Crisis Centre - Women's Services
Bernie Cahill/Manuella Mezzanotte
54 Peckham Road
Camberwell
London SE5 8PX
T 0171 252 6900 F 0171 701 8253
Residential project offering a three-six month programme or group & one-to-one therapy to women with drug & alcohol problems.
Houses up to seven women, staffed by two workers. Office hours Mon-Fri.

Key South
48-54 Denmark Hill
London SE5 8RZ
T 0171 737 7888
Open Mon-Fri 10 am-5 pm. Housing for single homeless people aged 18-55. Policy of allowing 35-65 % of bed spaces for lesbians & gay men.

Sojourner Housing Association
5 de Crespingny Park
London SE5 8AB
T 0171 703 8085 F 0171 252 6463

Accommodation for young homeless women. Priority to women in Southwark's Black & Asian community & students. Long stay young women's hostel aged 16-21. Shared housing for Black women on low incomes.

Alternative Therapies

Holos Dulwich Clinic
Imelda Leahy
206 Lordship Lane
East Dulwich
London SE22 8LR
T 0181 693 3356
Imelda is qualified in massage & aromatherapy. She uses a range of soft tissue techniques, including manual lymphatic drainage & remedial massage work.

Holos Massage School
Imelda Leahy, Director
206 Lordship Lane
East Dulwich
London SE22 8LR
T 0181 693 3355
Based in Old Street, London EC1 (enquiries to above adddres/phone number). Introductory weekends in massage & aromatherapy a prerequisite to Professional Training in Massage Therapy. Lesbian teaching staff.

Arts and Crafts

Maskarray
Brige Bidell
213 Rotherhithe New Road
Southwark
London SE16 2BA
T 0171 231 3827
Women's art group which forms pieces of art, both visual and time-based, that identify & communicate issues pertinent to women. Workshops to help share skills. On tour to various organisations.

See Saw Carpenters
Shirani Situnayake
30 Bethersden House
Kinglake Street
London SE17 2LH
T 0171 703 8868
Women carpenters. All carpentry work & glazing & fencing. Also decorating & gardening work. Works for women's organisations in particular. Free quotes,

reasonable rates. London-wide work. Women-friendly.

Stream Record/Fish Out of Water
Genie Cosmas
77a Hindmans Road
East Dulwich
London SE22 9NQ
T 0181 299 2998 F 0181 693 0349
Stream Records distributes via mail order recordings made by disabled artists and integrated bands. Consultancy for live music events. Fish Out of Water an integrated band playing original jazzy blues music.

BUSINESS SUPPORT SCHEMES
Phase One
Chris Dove
405 Baltic Quay
Sweden Gate
Surrey Quays
London SE16 1TG
T 0171 394 1011 F 0171 394 3360
chris-dove@compuserve.com
Business development consultancy specialising in securing local authority Department of Trade & Industry & European Commission funding for business support/project finance etc for small/medium sized companies.

CENTRES FOR WOMEN
Southwark Black Women's Centre
Margaret Haynes
76 Elsted Street
Walworth
London SE17 1QG
T 0171 708 1643
Open Mon-Fri 10 am-5.30 pm. Provides a variety of support services, including counselling & advice services on a range of issues. All services are free. Wheelchair access on ground floor only.

Southwark Phoenix Women's Health Organisation
Dr Pat Adjin Tettey
Sally Mugabe House
69 Bellenden Road
London SE15 5BH
T 0171 732 0658 F 0171 635 6115
Open 10 am-6 pm Mon-Fri. Phone for appt or drop in Mon & Tue 10 am-5 pm. Counselling, workshops, befriending for young mothers, housing/benefits advice, advice to deaf women, free pregnancy testing, etc.

CHILD CARE AND FAMILY
Colby Road Nursery
Mary Chowdhury
9b Colby Road
Upper Norwood
London SE19 1HA
T 0181 761 3482
Open 8 am-6 p.m for children aged one-and-a-half to five. Ten places. Also runs an after school care from 3-6 pm. Children can be collected from school.

COMPUTERS/IT
Coyne Mycrosystems
Carol Coyne
45 Stradella Road
London SE24 9HL
T 0171 733 5702
Computer programming services to various industries, including publishing & typesetting. Databases a speciality.

CONTRACEPTION/WELL WOMAN
East Street Brook Centre
A McFarlane
153a East Street
London SE17 2SD
T 0171 703 7880 F 0171 277 2103
Open Mon-Thurs 9.30 am-7.30 pm; Fri 9.30 am-2.30 pm; Sat 9.30-11.30 am For an appointment outside opening hours, phone 0171 703 9660. Free, confidential contraceptive advice/supplies. Pregnancy tests.

Rotherhithe Brook Centre
Albion Street Health Centre
87 Albion Street
London SE16 1JX
T 0171 231 2296
Open Thurs 5-7 pm. To make an appointment outside opening hours, phone 0171 703 9660. Free, confidential contraceptive advice. Free condoms & other contraceptive supplies. Pregnancy testing & quick results.

COUNSELLING AND THERAPY
Charterhouse Women's Project
Patricia McDade, Project Manager
40 Tabard Street
London SE1 4JU
T 0171 403 4367 F 0171 357 8379
Drop-in classes & individual counselling for women in Southwark. Classes include

quilting, dressmaking, art & fitness. Most activities supported by creche. Phone for up-to-date timetable.

ENVIRONMENT

Centre for Accessible Environments
Nutmeg House
60 Gainsford Street
London SE1 2NY
T 0171 357 8182 F 0171 357 8183
Open Mon-Fri 9 am-5 pm. Works to improve the built environment to accommodate all users, including older disabled people. Offers information & advisory service on design & technical matters. Publications.

ETHNIC MINORITIES

Bengali Women's Group
Rockingham Community Centre
Rockingham Street
London SE1 6RQ
T 0171 357 0623
Open Mon & Tue 10 am-3 pm; Wed 2-6 pm; Thurs 10 am-6 pm; Fri 10 am-3 pm. Bengali development project: Tue & Thurs 10 am-12 noon; mothers' & toddlers' groups Thurs 1-3 pm; ESOL; Bengali Classes.

East Dulwich Community Work Project
Eyullahemaye Miller
The Albrighton Centre
37 Albrighton Road
East Dulwich
London SE22 8AH
T 0171 326 4803 F 0171 326 4803
Open Mon-Fri 9.30 am-5.30 pm. Black women's group. Sewing, childcare, dancing, ESOL classes. "Lowest possible cost, if not free activities for the local community."

Mauritius Association of Women
Mrs Ameena Fakira
21 Manchester House
East Street
Walworth
London SE17 2DW
Social activities, welfare, cultural & religious events, sports, educational activities for women residents of UK, their families, relatives & friends of Mauritian origin & those interested in Mauritius.

Southwark Muslim Women's Assocation Family Centre
Zafar Iqbal
Ground Floor
Bellenden Old School
Bellenden Road
London SE15 4DG
T 0171 732 8053 F 0171 277 7320
Self-help group assisting women & their families with particular problems faced by Muslim ethnic Asians. Counselling, ESOL classes & creche. Computer classes & creche. Workshops. Youth project for school girls.

ZARA Women's Group
Suk Gill
Thomas Catton Community Education Centre
Alpha Street
Peckham
London SE15 4NX
T 0171 358 0697
Open Wed & Fri 10 am-4 pm. Aims to develop self-confidence, self-esteem, self-sufficiency & independence of Asian & Muslim women. Support, information, advice on welfare rights, health issues, training.

GIRLS/YOUNG WOMEN

Charterhouse Young People's Centre
Rainbow Building
32 Crosby Row
London SE1
T 0171 403 1676
Girls' group meets on Mon 5-8 pm. For girls aged 11-15.

Focus at Teenage Information Network (TIN)
102 Harper Road
London SE1 6AQ
T 0171 403 2444 F 0171 207 2982
Open Mon-Fri - phone for times. Advice, information, counselling. Resource centre. Drop-in Mon 2-4 pm, Wed 5-7 pm, Thurs 3-5 pm. Sexual health, housing benefits, counselling. Lesbian, gay, bisexual groups.

Geoffrey Chaucer Youth Club
Yvette Okafort
C/o Geoffrey Chaucer School
Harper Road
London SE1 6AG
T 0171 378 0207
Girls-only lunchtime group on Thurs & Thurs evening women only sessions for girls aged 11-16.

Salmon Youth Centre
43 Old Jamaica Road

London SE16 4TE
T 0171 237 3788
Provides opportunities for young women aged 10-22 to participate in a range of activities in a non-threatening environment.

HEALTH

Alcohol Recovery Project
Sue Millman, Director
68 Newington Causeway
London SE1 6DF
T 0171 403 3369
Open Mon-Fri 9 am-5 pm. Housing & counselling for people with drink problems in London. Hostels for women only & for women with children offering therapeutic support, parenting skills, etc.

Community Drug Project
Dyanne Allen
146 Camberwell Road
London SE5 0EE
T 0171 703 0559
Open Mon-Fri 2-5 pm. Drop-in - no appointment needed. Practical support & counselling. Needle exchange. Total confidentiality.

Kings Health Care Menopause Clinic
Sister Nicky Colville/Kathy Morris
Menopause Clinic
King's College Hospital
Denmark Hill
London SE5 9RS
T 0171 737 4000
An NHS clinic, open Mon-Fri 9 am-5 pm with GP referral. For women from anywhere in the UK.

Menopause Clinic - St Thomas' Hospital
Lambeth Palace Road
London SE1A 7EH
T 0171 922 8026
NHS clinic with GP referral. Open Mon-Thurs 9 am-5 pm; Fri 9 am-4.45 pm.

LARGER/TALLER WOMEN

June Anderson
June Anderson
55a Chadwick Road
Peckham
London SE15 4RA
T 0171 639 1653 F 0171 639 9559
Any size catered for.

LEGAL MATTERS

Gold, Lerman and Muirhead
New London Bridge House
25 London Bridge Street
London SE1 9TW
Open Mon-Fri 9 am-5.30 pm. Solicitors: divorce & family, domestic violence, crime, housing, personal injury, company & commercial, wills & probate, conveyancing. Accepts legal aid work.

LIBRARIES/ARCHIVES

Feminist Library
5 Westminster Bridge Road
London SE1 7XW
T 0171 928 7789
Open Tue 11 am-8 pm; Sat & Sun 2-5 pm. Books, pamphlets, journals, published & unpublished research. Specialist collections. Meeting rooms for feminist activities.

MANUAL TRADES

Phoebe Caldwell
Phoebe Caldwell
22 Martin House
Falmouth Road
Elephant & Castle
London SE1 6QP
T 0171 610 9841 F 0171 610 9841
Painting & decorating: quality work & reasonable prices. Basic painting & special paint finishes. Interior work preferred. Will travel. References available.

PHOTOGRAPHY

Gill Orsman
Gill Orsman
The Stable
6-8 Cole Street
London SE1 4YH
T 0171 378 1867 F 0171 357 6909
Professional photographer specialising in flowers & still life. Advertising, design & editorial commissions.

SERVICES

Brige Bidell
Brige Bidell
213 Rotherhithe New Road
Southwark
London SE16 2BA
T 0171 231 3827
Tarot & astrology, especially for women.

SPORTS AND LEISURE

Women's Self Defence Clasees
Dash Studio
215-16 Upper Floor
Elephant & Castle Shopping Ctr
London SE1
T 0171 701 9383
Teachers women to defend themselves through physical & mental training. Thurs 6-7 pm.

TRAINING

Headstart
Angela Hancock, Development Worker
St James Hall
30 St James Road
London SE16 4QR
T 0171 231 9248   F 0171 231 9248
Pre-vocational administration training with work placements. Literacy with computers. Cultural & social events for women & children. Opening times vary so phone to check.

WOMEN'S AID

Southwark Women's Aid
16 Relf Road
London SE15 4J5
T 0171 732 1986
Refuge for women. Advice, welfare rights, housing, immigration. Appointments only.

SUTTON

ARTS AND CRAFTS

Lady Barber Shop Harmony Club
Mrs Beryl Haines
98 Surrey Grove
Sutton SM1 3PN
T 0181 644 2605

Wallington Floral Art Group
Jane Miller
43 Park Hill Road
Wallington SM6 0SA
T 0181 647 8624
Meets first Wed of each month at Wallington Public Hall, Stafford Road 7.45 pm. Floral demonstrations, flower arranging classes, decoration of local churches & other buildings, etc.

BEREAVEMENT

Sutton Bereavement Service
Mrs Yvonne Herber, Coordinator
St Helier Hospital
Wrythe Lane
Carshalton SM5 1AA
T 0181 641 8682
Trained volunteer bereavement counsellors who offer counselling to the bereaved either within their own home or at the above address.

CARERS

Sutton Borough Volunteer Bureau - Help Service
Pauline Kimantas, Manager
31 West Street
Sutton SM1 1SJ
T 0181 770 4860
Provides a range of practical & social support services to carers, the elderly & disabled members of the community in their own homes. Befriending, wheelchair pushing, easy DIY, gardening, odd jobs, etc.

CENTRES FOR WOMEN

Sutton Women's Centre
Marian and Irene
3 Palmerston Road
Sutton SM1 4QL
T 0181 661 1991
Drop in, crafts, women's rights, women's health, lending library, tutored courses, free legal advice for women (once a month), trips to theatre/cinema, walks, social evenings, massage. Phone for more details.

CHILD CARE AND FAMILY

Cystic Fibrosis Mother and Toddler Group
Mrs Lin McGraw
Queen Mary's Hospital
Wrythe Lane
Carshalton SM5 1AA
T 0181 296 3076
Meets first Wed of each month during term time. Enabling parents to share with each other their feelings, problems & information about having young children with cystic fibrosis.

Mother and Baby Group, Sutton
Linda
C/o Sutton Women's Centre
3 Palmerston Road
Sutton SM1 4QL
T 0181 661 1991
For mothers with children under aged 2. Meets Thurs 1.30-3.25 pm. All children must be supervised by their mothers.

Preschool Playgroups Association - Sutton branch
Brenda Barron, Chair
Glastonbury Centre
Glastonbury Road
Morden SM6 6NZ
T 0181 660 1921
Promoting community situations in which parents can make the best use of their own knowledge & resources in the development of their children & themselves.

Small Steps Parents' Support Group
Mrs Jenny Kendrick, Chairman
North Cheam Baptist Church
Ridge Road
Sutton SM3 9LY
T 0181 540 1491
Meets on first & third Thurs of each month in term time 10.30 am-12 noon for coffee & chats while the children play. Parents of children with special needs, disabilities, etc are welcome.

Sutton Area Childminding Association
Mrs A J Saunderson, Chairperson
105 Abbotts Road
Cheam SM3 9ST
T 0181 644 6911
Providing the best day care in a family environment for the children minded whilst parents are at work. Age range 0-8 years, though some are older.

CONTRACEPTION/WELL WOMAN

Family Planning and Reproductive Health Services
Dr Ruth Clancy, Consultant
1 Damson Way
Orchard Hill
Fountain Drive
Carshalton SM5 4NR
T 0181 770 8000
Contraceptive services; vasectomies; menopause advice; psychosexual counselling; domiciliary service; young people's services; training for doctors/nurses; phone sexual helpline for information: 0181 770 8080.

Green Wrythe Lane Clinic
Middleton Roundabout
Carshalton
T 0181 770 8000
Contraceptive & well woman clinics Mon 1.30-3 pm. Free contraceptive advice & supplies. Well woman screening; pregnancy testing; menopause counselling. Phone 0181 770 8080 outside clinic times.

Health Centre - Roundshaw
Mollison Drive
Roundshaw
T 0181 770 8000
Contraceptive & well woman clinics on Thurs 1.30-3.30. Free contraceptive advice & supplies; well woman screening; menopause counselling; pregancy testing. Phone 0181 770 8080 outside clinic times.

Priory Crescent Clinic
Cheam
T 0181 770 8000
Contraceptive & well woman clinics Tue 7-8.30 pm & Wed 2-3.30 pm. Free contraceptive advice & supplies; pregnancy testing; well woman; Menopause counselling. Phone 0181 770 8080 outside clinic times.

Shotfield Health Centre
Wallington
T 0181 770 8000
Contraceptive & well woman clinics on Tue 1-3.30 pm & Fri 6-7.45 pm. Young people's clinics Tue 9.30 am-7.30 pm. Free contraceptive advice & supplies; well woman screening; menopause counselling.

St Helier Hospital
Outpatients' Department
Wrythe Lane
Carshalton
T 0181 770 8000
Contraceptive & well woman clinics Wed & Thurs 6.30-8 pm. Youth Clinic Mon 7-8.15 pm. Free contraceptive advice & supplies; well woman; menopause counselling. Phone 0181 770 8080 outside clinic times.

Sutton Hospital Outpatients' Department
Sutton Hospital
Brighton Road
Sutton
T 0181 770 8000
Contraceptive advice & supplies & well woman clinics on Mon & Wed 7-9 pm. Free contraceptive advice & supplies; well woman screening; menopause counselling. Phone 0181 770 8080 outside clinic times.

DISABILITY

Dorothy Chapman Trust
Mrs Joan Christopher

LONDON - SUTTON

9 Woodcote Green
Wallington SM6 9NN
T 0181 647 3824
Provision of low cost holidays for disabled people & their families at King's Park, Eastbourne. Self-catering.

Ethnic Minorities
Jawani
The Century Youth Centre
Fellows Road
Carshalton SM5 2SX
T 0181 647 3627
For young Asian women aged 11-21. Meets Fri eves. Arts, crafts, drama, outdoor activities, sports, discussions, cultural activities & outings.

Sutton Ashiyana
Raj Mittal
19 Wilbury Avenue
Sutton SM2 7DU
For Asian women of all ages. Meets at the Friend's Meeting House, Cedar Road, Sutton on Mon 1-3 pm. Yoga, speakers, health issues, welfare benefits, first aid. Outings.

Health
Sutton Community Drug Helpline
Dorothea Bickerton, Co-ordinator
20 Woodcote Road
Wallington SM6 0NN
T 0181 773 9393
Free & confidential help to all drug users in Merton & Sutton. Counselling, group work, needle exchange & support. Advice & help to families, partners & friends. 24-hour helpline on 0181 647 6169.

Lesbian and Bisexual
Lesbian Support Group - Sutton
C/o Sutton Women's Centre
3 Palmerston Road
Sutton SM1 4QL
T 0181 661 1991
Meets on first & third Fri of each month 8-10 pm. Phone above number for further details.

Pregnancy/Childbirth
Merton Community Midwives
Maternity Unit
Community Centre
St Helier Hospital
Carshalton

T 0181 644 4343

Sexual Abuse/Rape Crisis
Breaking Free
Samantha Rowe
C/o Flat 2
66 Cheam Road
Sutton SM1 2SU
T 0181 770 7533 F 0181 685 0246
Support group for women survivors of child sexual abuse. Helpline (as above) open 9 am-12 pm daily. Weekly support groups. Support by letter. Information & referral agency. Talks & training.

Sutton Survivors
C/o Sutton Women's Centre
3 Palmerston Road
Sutton SM1 4QL
T 0181 661 1991
Women survivors of incest & childhood sexual abuse. All female survivors welcome to give each other support & understanding. Meets first & third Mon of each month at above address.

Single Parents
Sutton Gingerbread
Margaret Evans, Secretary
Rosehill Community
Rosehill
Sutton SM1 3HD
T 01372 811502
Self-help group for lone parents meeting twice monthly. Friendship & advice. Outings. Monthly newsletter.

Social
Clyde Women's Club
Mrs T Browne, Secretary
102b Carshalton Park Road
Carshalton SM5 3SG
T 0181 669 4470
Meets Thurs 8-10 pm at Sutton West Centre (Day Centre Hall), Robin Hood Lane, Sutton. Members of the National Association of Women's Clubs.

Renaissance
Nancy Paul
35 Lind Road
Sutton SM1 4PP
T 0181 770 0465 F 0181 770 0468
A group of professional women from all kinds of organisations & walks of life. Meets 3-4

Transport

Sutton Borough Volunteer Bureau - Transport
Mrs Una Rennard
31 West Street
Sutton SM1 1SJ
T 0181 770 4858
Transport provided by volunteers using their own cars for frail, elderly & disabled people, people with learning difficulties, carers & disadvantaged children. All new users assessed except for one-off trips.

Sutton Shopmobility
Samantha Edwards, Coordinator
3rd Floor Car Park
St Nicholas Centre
Sutton SM1 1AY
T 0181 770 0691
Provides free loan of manual & powered wheelchairs & scooters to enable people with either a temporary or permanent problem to visit the centre of Sutton. Open Mon-Fri 10 am-5 pm

Women's Aid

Merton Women's Aid
Barbara Davidson, Social Worker/Manager
P O Box 402
Sutton SM1 3TG
T 0181 542 8791
Refuge for women & children & 24-hour counselling/advice service. Aims to relieve suffering experienced by women who have been gravely/persistently maltreated or sexually abused by men.

Sutton Women's Aid
Mrs Joyce Crump, Secretary
31 West Street
Sutton SM1 1SJ
T 0181 669 7608
Providing help for battered women & their children (if any). Providing emotional support & welfare; advice & information. There is refuge space for victims of domestic violence.

Tower Hamlets

Accommodation

Aluna Court
Grimwade Close
Evalina Road
Nunhead
London E15 3HN
T 0171 732 6003 F 0171 277 5674
6 bed spaces for mothers & their babies.

Step Ahead
Elissa Palser, Project Manager
St Margaret's House
21 Old Ford Road
London E2 9PL
T 0181 981 7582 F 0181 981 7582
Setting up the first women only club house in UK. Providing a service for women with mental health problems where members are active in running club house with support of a small staff team.

Alternative Therapies

Bodywise Natural Health Centre
Dharanasri
119 Roman Road
Bethnal Green
London E2 0QN
T 0181 981 6938
Provides a wide range of complementary therapies, counselling service, yoga classes & a massage school. Open Mon-Fri 9 am-9 pm; Sat 9 am-1 pm.

Feel Good Factor, The
Ann Craddock
Last But Not Least Unit, ASDA
151 East Ferry Road
Isle of Dogs
London E14 3BT
T 0171 537 1114 F 0171 537 1115
Beauty salon, alternative health centre and aromatherapy shop. Open Mon-Thurs 9 am-8 pm; Fri 9 am-9 pm; Sat 8.30 am-6 pm; Sun 11 am-3 pm. Chiropody, osteopathy, naturopathy, etc.

Arts and Crafts

Alternative Arts
Maggie Pinhorn
47a Brushfield Street
London E1 6AA
T 0171 375 0441 F 0171 375 0484
Arts organisation run by women. Provides platform for new arts. Makes arts accessible to public. Programme of events & exhibitions in Westminster & Tower Hamlets. Work plays vital role in urban regeneration.

Chisenhale Dance Space
Justine Simons
64-84 Chisenhale Road

London E3 5QZ
T 0181 981 6617 F 0181 980 9323
Dance organisation supporting new developments in dance through a programme of workshops/training/performances. Phone for brochure.

Half Moon pty Ltd
Penny Clayton
43 Whitehorse Road
London E1 0ND
T 0171 265 8138 F 0171 702 7220
Working for and with young people in London; promoting, encouraging & supporting new writing for & by young people; challenging all forms of prejudice; promoting women's art.

Theatre Centre
Jo Hammant
Units 7 & 8
Toynbee Workshops
3 Gunthorpe Street
London E1 7RQ
T 0171 377 0379 F 0171 377 1376
Produces new plays for young people aged between 5-18, performed by professional actors in schools and theatres. Positively discriminates in favour of women and people of colour.

BUSINESS SUPPORT SCHEMES

Gaynor Walker Real Estate
Gaynor Walker
Suite Two, Ensign House
Admiral's Way
Isle of Dogs
London E14 9RN
T 0171 712 0500 F 0171 712 0400
Personal service to major international companies relocating to city & docklands - sales & lettings. Also secures the right type of property for existing clients in other parts of London.

HEBA women's Project
Janice Djelloul, Coordinator
170 Brick Lane
London E1 6RV
T 0171 247 5401
Open Mon-Sat 9.30 am-3.30 pm & 5-8 pm
Women's enterprise project to help women in the community to use their skills in a small community business. Ethnic clothes made. Sewing & computer training. Creche.

VFL Ltd
Ann M Muldowney
1 Park Place
Canary Wharf
London E14 4HJ
T 0171 538 2223 F 0171 987 5030
Financial awareness training & management skills training for people in business. Full CPE programme for accountants. Technical newsletter. Hotline on accountacy & auditing.

Women in Docklands
Anna Moffatt
C/o Kall Kwik, Unit 4
Riverpark Trading Estate
108 Westferry Road
London E14 8QP
T 0181 980 8870 F 0171 538 8640
Aims to promote & encourage businesses, networking & training opportunities for its members & to raise the profile of women working or living in Docklands & east London.

CARERS

Tower Hamlets Carers
Eileen Lowe
The Prince's Royal Trust Carers' Centre
21 Brayford Square
London E1 0SG
T 0171 790 1765 F 0171 790 7073
Open Mon-Fri 9 am-5 pm. Raising awareness & profile of carers to service providers & to carers themselves. Free service for people connected with the borough. Advice & support for carers.

CENTRES FOR WOMEN

African Women's Welfare Association
Theresa Shiyanbola
Celestial Church of Christ
Northumbria Street
London E14 6LF
T 0171 987 0371
Open Mon-Fri 10 am-5 pm 24-hour ansaphone. Advice, information & referrals. Works with African families in the community on issues like training, education, employment, immigration, matrimonial problems.

Jagonari Women's Centre
Yasmin Hoque
183-185 Whitechapel Road
London E1 1DW
T 0171 375 0520

For local women run by women. Priority for Bangladeshi, Somali women & women with disabilities but all women are welcome. Playgroup, advice, information, textile art & craft workshop, ESOL, girls' group, yoga.

Computers/IT

East London Advanced Technology Training
Heather Finch
The Davenant Centre
179-181 Whitechapel Road
London E1 1DW
T 0171 375 0114 F 0171 375 1374
h.finch@pfim.demon.co.uk
Training in all aspects of IT. Training for disadvantaged groups, including women. Women-only courses. Our trading company, THATT Services Ltd, can provide IT training for the private sector.

Contraception/Well Woman

Barkantine Clinic
95-137 Westferry Road
Isle of Dogs
London E14 8JH
T 0171 515 6161
Tue 1.30-3.30 pm well woman & contraception clinics: cytology (cervical smears) screening; breast & blood pressure checks; advice on all women's health issues; contraceptive advice & supplies. Free services.

Bethnal Green Health Centre
Florida Street
Bethnal Green
London E2 0AS
T 0171 739 1440
Free contraceptive advice & supplies. Clinic Fri 1.30-3.30 pm. Pills, injectables, coils, caps, condoms, natural family planning, pregancy tests, fertility advice, rubella tests, emergency contraception.

Greenwood Clinic
Peel Grove
Bethnal Green
London E2 9LR
T 0181 980 5865
Well woman Tue 9.30-11.30 am cytology (cervical smears) screening, breast & blood pressure checks, advice on all women's health issues; Thurs 9.30-11.30 am contraceptive advice & supplies. Free services.

Leopold Street Clinic
Burdett Road
London E3 4LA
T 0171 987 3252
Free contraceptive advice & supplies. Clinic Mon 5-7 pm. Pills, injectables, coils, caps, condoms, femidoms, natural family planning, pregnancy tests, fertility advice, rubella tests, emergency contraception.

Newmill Clinic
Empson Street
London E3 3LS
T 0171 987 1334
Contraceptive advice & supplies on 1st, 3rd & 5th Thurs of each month 9.30-11.30 am: emergency contraception, pills, injectables, coils, caps, condoms, femidoms, natural family planning & pregnacy testing.

Ruston Street Clinic
Ruston Street
London E3 2LR
T 0181 980 1036
Free contraceptive advice & supplies on 1st, 3rd & 5th Thurs of each month 5-7 pm. Emergency contraception, pills, injectables, coils, caps, condoms, fremidoms, natural family planning, pregnancy testing, etc.

Spitafields Health Centre
9-11 Brick Lane
London E1 6PU
T 0171 247 8251
Contraceptive advice & supplies Wed 9.30 am-11.30 a.m & Fri 1.30-3.30 pm: free emergncy contraception, pills, injectables, coils, caps, condoms, femidoms, natural family planning, pregnancy testing.

Stepney Green Clinic
Stepney Green
London E1 3JX
T 0171 790 3594
Well woman Mon 2-4 pm; contraceptive advice & supplies Wed 5-7 pm. Free cytology testing, breast & blood pressure checks, advice on all women's health issues. Free services.

Wellington Way Centre
Wellington Way
Bow
London E3 4NE
T 0181 980 3510
Well woman Fri 1.30-3.30 pm; contraceptive advice & supplies Fri 9.30 -11.30 am Free

cytology (cervical smears) testing; breast & blood pressure checks; advice on all women's health issues. Free services.

COUNSELLING AND THERAPY

Cedar Centre
Helen Menezes
17 Arden Crescent
Isle of Dogs
London E14 9SW
T 0171 538 4600   F 0171 537 2283
helen@c-link.demon.co.uk
Multi-cultural cooperative centre, open 46 hours a week. Counselling, advice, employment, education, playgroup, healing, volunteering. Most activities free of charge. Many languages spoken.

Elizabeth Sutherland
Elizabeth Sutherland
Blondin Street
Bow
London E3 2TR
T 0181 981 1553
Psychotherapy & counselling to individuals in Bow, Bethnal Green & London Bridge. BAC accredited & on UKCP register.

Kameleon
Pat Justice
14 Landons Close
Jamestown Harbour
Prestons Road
London E14 9QQ
T 0171 538 8228   F 0171 515 3887
Counselling for stress and anxiety, identity, eating disorders, sexual abuse, incest survivors, children & family problems. Sliding scale costs. Counselling provided one-to-one, in groups, by phone.

Marijke de la Motte
Dr Marijke de la Motte
The London Independent Hosptial
Beaumont Square
Stepney Green
London E1
T 0171 537 9418
Psychotherapist specialising in occupational & personal life stress, eg depression & self-image problems. Cognitive-behavioural psychotherapy. Brief solution therapy & hypnotherapy. Times: 9.30 am-7 pm.

MIND in Tower Hamlets
Val Ford
13 Whitethorn Street
London E3 4DA
T 0171 537 7£04   F 0171 537 7944
Open Mon-Fri 10 am-5 pm. Wheelchair access. Women's group, Bengali women's group, Somali women's woodwork group. Provides 'Open House' community mental health centre: drop-in therapeutic groups, etc.

ETHNIC MINORITIES

Bangladesh Welfare Association
Farhan Begum, Information and Advice Officer
39 Fournier Street
London E1 6QR
T 0171 247 7960
Farhan Begum works with Bangladeshi women only, providing information & advice on welfare & training for Bangladeshi women.

Bangladeshi Women's Association
Mrs Asghar
196 Canterbury Road
Leyton
London E10 6EH
T 0181 556 4969
The group meets for English classes two days a week at the Marshall Centre, Leyton High Road. Creche workers. Wheelchair access.

East London Asian Family Counselling
Anwar Dewan
183-185 Whitechapel Road
London E1 1DW
T 0171 377 8640
Counselling for Asian women & families, especially domestic violence victims. Free service for women in the borough, but a charge for women living outside. Open mon-Fri 9.30 am-5 pm for crisis work.

London Black Women's Health Action Project
Shamis Dirir
Cornwall Community Centre
1 Cornwall Avenue
London E2 0HU
T 0181 980 3503   F 0181 980 6314
Open Mon-Fri 9.30 am-5 pm. Counselling & advice to young women, parents & families concerning female health problems & HIV/AIDS. Workshops on health-related issues.

Positive Care Link
Charles Mayombwe
4 Paradise Row
Bethnal Green
London E2 9LE
T 0171 613 7700
Services for African people with HIV. Office hours: Mon-Fri 9.30 am-5.30 pm. Extra hours on weekends can be arranged. Emotional support, home help, childcare.

HEALTH

493 Project
493 Cambridge Heath Road
Bethnal Green
London E2 9BU
T 0171 729 2070
Women's clinic, needle exchange, health care, outreach projects, HIV testing, pharmacy scheme, probation satelites. Counselling. Drop-in. Free needle exchange & free condoms. General health advice.

Ambrose King Centre GUM Clinic
Turner Street
London E1 1BB
T 0171 377 7306
Screening for STDs, HIV-testing, contraceptive advice & supplies, counselling. Rose clinic for sexually assaulted women (appts required). Drop-in clinics Mon-Fri 9.30 am-5.30 pm. Thurs until 2.30 pm. only.

Cable Street Day Programme
Top Floor
71 Johnson Street
London E1 0AQ
T 0171 790 9960
Structured education & training programme for drug users & drug using offenders. Practical skills are provided such as how to prepare a cv & apply for a job. Health education & help with relapse prevention.

College of Health
Marianne Rigge, Director
St Margaret's House
21 Old Ford Road
London E2 9PL
T 0181 983 1225   F 0181 983 1553
enquiry@tcoh.demon.co.uk
Runs the regional health information service in NE Thames & S Thames on 0800 665544. Has a wide range of health topics on tape for women that callers can listen to 24 hours a day.

Community Women's Health Services for Tower Hamlets
1st Floor, Alderney Building
Mile End Hosptial
Bancroft Road
London E1 4DG
T 0171 377 7898

Docklands Dental Centre
Seema Sharma, Dent Surg/Theresa Thompson, Practice Manger
27 Skylines
Marsh Wall
London E14 9X2
T 0171 538 9990   F 0171 338 9991
Gentle dental care at affordable prices. Offers early, late & lunchtime appointments. A check up costs £10.

Euromedia plc
Lorna Stent, Research Manager
5 Raleigh House
Admiral's Way
Waterside
London E14 9SN
T 0171 538 5164   F 0171 538 8362
International executive search in healthcare.

Globe Centre
159 Mile End Road
London E1 4AQ
T 0171 791 2855   F 0171 780 9551
Day centre for people affected by HIV/AIDS. Gym, hydrotherapy pool, cafe, meeting place, day care. Drop-in advice.

London Independent Hospital
Gerri Watts, Marketing Executive
1 Beaumont Square
Stepney Green
London E1 4NL
T 0171 790 0990   F 0171 265 9032
Providing confidential consultation with female doctor on aspects of women's health which may be causing concern such as premenstrual tension, menstrual disorders, HRT, etc. Phone for up to date price list.

Mildmay Mission Hospital
Hackney Road
London E2 7NA
T 0171 739 2331   F 0171 729 5361
Comprehensive palliative care service for people affected by HIV/AIDS. 28 individual rooms with leisure & relaxation areas. Family care centre, etc.

LONDON - TOWER HAMLETS

Tower Hamlets Community Drug Team
71 Johnson Street
London E1 0AQ
T 0171 729 8008
First point of contact for drug users. Drop-in, advice & information, referrals, service networks. Liaising with GPs. Asian outreach scheme. Needle exchange. Counselling.

Tower Hamlets Sickle Cell and Thalassaemia Centre
Olumide Abidemi
St Margaret's House
15a Old Ford Road
London E2 9PL
T 0181 981 9603
Open Mon-Fri 10 am-5 pm. Information, raising awareness, support & education to cope with sickle cell anemia. Women-only classes with children on Tue 10 am-1 pm. Creche.

Women's Health and Family Services
The Brady Centre
192-6 Hanbury Street
London E1 5HU
T 0171 377 8725 F 0171 377 1064
Health advocacy. Works with clients with first language not English: Somali Bengali, Chinese, Vietnamese. Housing/welfare advice & medical advocacy. Keep fit. Parents' advice. Open Mon-Fri 9 am-5 pm.

LEGAL MATTERS

Tower Hamlets Law Centre
341 Commercial Road
London E1 2PS
T 0171 791 0741 F 0171 702 7301
Free service to anyone living/working in Tower Hamlets. Specialist areas: housing, welfare rights, immigration, employment, education. Open Mon-Fri 10 am-1 pm; 2-4 pm. Phoneline open to 5 pm (not Tue).

LESBIAN AND BISEXUAL

Audre Lord Clinic
Ambrose King Centre
Royal London Hospital
Whitechapel
London E1 1BB
T 0171 377 7312
Drop-in clinic for lesbians staffed by women only on Fri 10 am-5 pm. Screening for STDs, cervical smears, advice/counselling on sexual matters; free dental dams/gloves; breast examinations; HIV testing; etc.

MEDIA

Four Corners Film Workshop
Carla Mitchell
113 Roman Road
Tower Hamlets
London E2 0HU
T 0181 981 4243 F 0181 983 4441
Film production training course for women from the refugee community. Ten-week training in 16mm film production. Eight fully subsidised places; free travel & child care; tuition in technical language.

Paradise Beach (Productions)
Carole Thomas
45 Caravel Close
Tiller Road
London E14 8PD
T 0171 987 0210 F 0171 537 7682
Design for print & multi-media. Design & print production of brochures, leaflets, directories, promotional & sales literature, corporate identity, educational publications, books & magazines.

OLDER WOMEN

Bethnal Green Pensioners' Action Group
Len Aidis
18 Club Row
London E2 7EY
T 0171 739 8066 F 0171 729 5172
The group meets on Wed 10 am-2 pm. Discussions. Lobbying. Campaigns for pensioners' rights.

PHOTOGRAPHY

Network Photography
Vanessa
426 Roman Road
Bow
London E3 5LU
T 0181 983 6900 F 0181 983 6899
Commercial photographers. Competent in press, PR, sports, industrial, etc. London & regional network of photographers in more than 150 cities nationwide. Print & processing on site.

PLACES TO STAY AND EAT

Cherry Orchard, The
241 Globe Road
London E2 0JD
T 0181 980 6678

A restaurant run by Buddhist women. Open Mon 11 am-3 pm; Tue-Fri 11 am-7 pm. There are a lot of private functions.

Pregnancy/Childbirth
Ali Herron
87 Coborn Road
Bow
London E3 2DG
T 0181 983 3617
Independent midwifery services providing continuity of care, full antenatal delivery & postnatal care offered including water births. Encourages active births & home births. Links with alternative therapists.

Publishers/Publications
Cherry Orchard Bookshop
241 Globe Road
London E2 0JD
T 0181 980 6678
Run by Buddhist women. Open Tue & Wed 10.30 am- 7 pm; Mon, Thurs, Fri & Sat 10.30 am- 5.30 pm. Mainly self-help & children's books. There is a large feminist section.

Religious Organisations
RC Caucus of Lesbian & Gay Christian Movement
C/o L GCM
Oxford House
Derbyshire Street
London E2 6HG
T 0171 739 1249 F 0171 739 1249
Counselling helpline: 0171 739 8134 open Wed & Sun 7-10 pm RC Caucus phone 01443 406940. Believes that human sexuality is gift of God & therefore entirely compatible with Christian faith to be lesbian/gay.

Services
Promotion for Growth
Carol Brooks
33 Plymouth Wharf
Saunders Ness Road
Isle of Dogs
London E14 3EL
T 0171 987 8084 F 0171 377 1093
Management consultancy specialising in book-keeping for sole practitioners solicitors & other small business. Also property management, public relations, marketing & event organisation.

Sports and Leisure
Arena Racquet and Sports Club
Katy Holden
Limeharbour
London E14 9TH
T 0171 515 8040 F 0171 515 1244
A woman-run health & fitness club in the heart of the Isle of Dogs. Facilities include gymnasium, fitness classes, squash, indoor tennis, badminton, sunbeds, sports injury clinic & massage.

Docklands Leisure Management Ltd
Eleri Wyn Morgan
11 Rembrandt Close
London E14 3UZ
T 0171 538 2461
Health & fitness consultants: corporate fitness facility management, personal training, classes, health & fitness assessments.

London Community Association Women's Cricket
Jenny Wostrack
Room 102
London Fruit and Wool Exchange
Brushfield Street
London E1 6EX
T 0171 247 4177
Promotion of women's cricket covering the whole of Greater London.

Support
Oxford House
Saad Shire
Derbyshire Street
London E2 6HG
T 0171 739 9001
Advice/information for women. Free English language classes for Somali women Mon-Thurs 10 am-12.30 pm. Sewing classes Mon & Wed 1-3 pm. Women-only English language class Tue & Thurs 6.45-8.30 pm.

Training
Pentland Training and Consultancy
Karen Barr
31 St Anthony's Close
St Katharine By the Tower
London E1 9LT
T 0171 481 8519 F 0171 488 1638
101620.1656@compuserve.com
Training & consultancy in the areas of self, people & organisational management & development covering both private & public

sectors. Programmes can be run internally or externally at affordable costs.

Women's Development Trust, The
Margaret Mukama
St Margaret's House
21 Old Ford Road
London E2 9PL
T 0181 983 3761 F 0181 981 9213
Open Mon-Fri 10 am-5 pm. Training & employment activities for women.

WALTHAM FOREST

ALTERNATIVE THERAPIES

Victoria Leach
Victoria Leach
61 Chestnut Avenue South
Walthamstow
London E17 9EJ
T 0181 925 8034
Therapeutic massage for women with aromatherapy oils. Available afternoons and evenings.

BEREAVEMENT

Circle Bereavement Support Service
Julia Griffiths
Unit 1
The Mews
2a Truro Road
London E17 7BY
T 0181 521 2975
For all people under aged 60. Waltham Forest referrals only. Confidential one-to-one support for bereaved people. Unlimited times. For further information contact above number.

CARERS

Waltham Forest Carers Association
Nick Boston
St Andrew's Centre
St Andrew's Road
Walthamstow
London E17
T 0181 531 9652
Advice & support to carers in the borough. Carers welfare rights & advice worker. The Association facilitates a carers' consultation group that meets monthly. Free service.

CENTRES FOR WOMEN

African/Caribbean Women's Development Centre
Berlyn Baptiste
603 High Road
Leyton
London E10 6RF
T 0181 556 4053 F 0181 923 9323
Women's centre with domiciliary homecare service. Advice service. Elderly group. Keep fit sessions. Computer courses. Health seminars on social/welfare issues. After school club. Educational support classes.

CONTRACEPTION/WELL WOMAN

Comely Bank Clinic
Ravenswood Road
London E17
T 0181 521 8742
Or phone 0181 520 8971 ex 2196; 0181 521 8742 clinic times. Contraception Fri 9.30-11.15 am Free services/supplies. Well woman Wed 1.45-3.15 pm. Under 21 sex advice Wed 3.30-4.30 pm

Granleigh Health Clinic
Trinity Close
London E11
T 0181 535 6794
Or phone 0181 520 8971 ex 2196; 0181 539 8565 clinic hours. Contraception Thurs 6.15-8.30 pm. Free services/supplies. Well woman Thurs 6.15-8.30 pm

Langthorne Health Centre
13 Langthorne Road
London E11
T 0181 535 6794
Or phone 0181 520 8971 ex 2196; 0181 558 7821 clinic hours. Contraception Mon 6.15-8.30 pm & Tue 1.45-3.15 pm. Free services/supplies. Well woman Mon 6.15-8.30 pm; under 21 sex advice Tue 3.30-4.30 pm

Leyton Green Clinic
Leyton Green Road
London E10
T 0181 535 6794
Or phone 0181 520 8971 ex 2196; 0181 539 8646 clinic hours. Contraception Fri 6.15-8.30 pm. Free services/supplies. Well woman Fri 6.15-8.30 pm; under 21 sex advice Mon 4.45-6.15 pm

Silverthorn Centre
Chingford Hospital
Larkshall Road
London E4
T 0181 535 6794

Or phone 0181 520 8971 ex 2196; 0181 529 3706 clinic hours. Contraception Mon 6.15-8.00 pm & Wed 6.15-8 pm. Free services/supplies; under 21 sex advice Fri 3.30-4.30 p.m; well woman Mon & Wed 6.15-8 pm

St James' Health Centre
St James' Street
London E17
T 0181 535 6794
Or phone 0181 520 8971 ex 2196; 0181 520 3476 clinic hours. Contraception Wed 6.45-8.30 pm & Sat 9.45-11.45 am Free services & supplies.

Counselling and Therapy
Cathy Towers
Cathy Towers
1 Norlington Road
London E11 4BE
T 0181 539 5216 F 0181 539 5216
Private service for individuals & organisations, providing short- & long-term counselling & psychotherapy, supervision & counsultancy, small groupwork & introductory courses in psychosynthesis.

Sarah Jack
Sarah Jack
61 Chestnut Avenue South
Walthamstow
London E17 9EJ
T 0181 509 9751
Available mornings & afternoons. Practising attachment-based psychoanalytic psychotherapy, working with individuals & couples.

Disability
Disability Youth Work Unit
Stephen Richardson
Youth & Community Service
Davies Lane
London E11 3DR
T 0181 556 7202 F 0181 558 6533
There are a number of groups for young disabled people in Waltham Forest, including young disabled women's groups. Phone above number for further details.

Waltham Forest Association of Disabled People
Units 13-14
Alpha Business Centre
South Grove
London E17 7NX
T 0181 509 0812
Minicom number above. Waltham Forest disability association, working with statutory authorities ensuring disabled people get services they need. Disabled Asian women's disabled project last Tue of month.

Ethnic Minorities
All-Asian Girls' Group
Mrs K Alamgir
Children's Community Centre
114 Fairlop Road
Leytonstone
London E11
T 0181 539 3873
Social & educational group for young Asian women & girls aged 11-25. Asian music. Issues of concern are discussed & evaluated. Meets Sun afternoons.

Asian Women's Group
Sally Mehta
C/o Family Service Unit
344 Hoe Street
Walthamstow
London E17 9PX
T 0181 509 0119 F 0181 520 7180
Open to all Asian women in Waltham Forest. A range of activities offered including cooking, sewing & English classes. Creche. Urdu & English spoken. Open Wed 1-3.30 pm

Asian Women's Society
Mrs Meher Hashni/Mrs Shahida Hashni
C/o 5 Antlers Hill
Chingford
London E4 7RT
T 0181 524 0618
Welfare & general advice for Asian women & girls. Social, cultural & educational events. Classes in Asian Culture, customs & dress. Urdu, Hindi & Punjabi spoken.

Bengali International Women's Section
Mrs Ali
242 Francis Road
Leyton
London E10 SNJ
T 0181 558 8403
Open Tue 9.30-11.30 am; Thurs 1-3 pm. ESOL; creche; advice for Bengali women with problems. Mothers' & toddlers' group. Sewing classes. Dress cutting classes.

LONDON - WALTHAM FOREST

Bengali Women's Welfare project
Mrs Alamgir
Children's Community Project
114 Fairlop Road
London E11
T 0181 539 3873
Open Fri & Sun 3-6 pm. Advice, family counselling, housing, mothers' & toddlers' group, translation, help with form filling.

Muslim Ladies' Circle
228 Francis Road
Leyton
London E10 SNJ
T 0181 550 2849
Advice & help centre. Housing, education, income support, benefits, family matters, battered wives, HIV/AIDS, elderly women, welfare rights, disability problems, help with form filling, cultural identity.

Muslim Women's Sports Club
Mrs Nusrat Dar
19 Shortlands Road
Leyton
London E10 7AH
T 0181 556 4689
Currently little activity but hopes to expand. Contact between 4.30-5.30 pm weekdays.

Muslim Women's Welfare Association
Mrs Meher Khan
425 Lea Bridge Road
Leyton
London E10 7EA
T 0181 539 7478
Mon 5-7 pm. Asian dress-making; Tue & Thurs 1.15-3.15 pm. ESOL; Fri outreach work, assisting people with DSS, doctors, hospitals, etc. Fri 5-7 pm health & beauty classes. Advice on domestic violence, etc.

Pakistani Women's Welfare Association
Mrs Khan
William Morris Community Centre
Greenleaf Road
Walthamstow
London E17 6QQ
T 0181 521 7871
Open Mon-Fri 1-4 pm. Advice sessions, health activities. Children/toddlers' group (Fri). Dress-making classes, keep fit. All services are free. Wheelchair access.

West Indian Women's Association - Young Mothers' Project
Cavelle Davis

William Morris Community Centre
Greenleaf Road
Walthamstow
London E17 6QQ
T 0181 521 4456
Open Mon-Fri 9 am-5 pm. Advice/information for young single Afro-Caribbean women (mainly single mothers). Drop-in Fri 7-9 pm for keep fit, etc. Benefits advice; sewing classes Tue 1-3 pm & Wed 7-9 pm.

HEALTH

National Asthma Campaign - Waltham Forest Branch
Mrs Hazel Thomas
101 Chingford Avenue
Chingford
London E4 6RG
T 0181 529 0885
Organises events with GPs to discuss asthma-teaching process for doctors & patients. Fundraising events.

Waltham Forest Alcohol Counselling Service
Fiona Dunwoodie, Business Administrator
1 Beulah Road
Walthamstow
London E17 9LG
T 0181 509 1888 F 0181 509 1888
Open Mon 9.30 am-8.30 pm, Tue-Fri 9.30 am-4 pm. 24-hour helpline. Full-time therapy programme - appt only. Women's group & separate full-time service for relatives of alcoholics, phone 0181 509 2255.

OLDER WOMEN

MIND in Waltham Forest
The Marshall Centre
388-392 High Road
Leyton
London E10 6QE
T 0181 556 9621 F 0181 539 1770
Women's group for women aged 50+. T & S club meets Tue 2-5 pm. Outings & discussions. (Not necessarily for women with mental health problems.)

PREGNANCY/CHILDBIRTH

Choices Crisis Pregnancy Counselling
16 Epping Glade
Chingford
London E4 7PQ
T 0181 523 9699
Open Tue evenings & Sat mornings. Free pregnancy testing, counselling & support for

women with unplanned pregnancies. Post abortion & miscarriage counselling. Phone for an appt. 24-hour ansaphone.

Sexual Abuse/Rape Crisis

Jan Hawkings Person-Centred Workshops
376 Hale End Road
Highams Park
London E4 9PB
T 0181 531 9760   F 0181 531 9760
Person-centred workshops & individual therapy for survivors of all types of childhood abuse. Trains accredited counselling diploma course for workers working with survivors of abuse.

Wandsworth

Accommodation

Annesley House
Sue Dodd
2 Princes Way
Wimbledon
London SW19 6QE
T 0181 788 9737
Student hostel for women who are full-time students, very reasonably priced. Phone for up-to-date price list.

Subira Hostel
40-42 Ansell Road
London SW17 7LS
T 0181 767 1498   F 0181 767 1498
6 bed spaces for young mothers & babies with an age range of 13 to 23. For young, single homeless women, generally referred by DHS. 24-hour care.

Arts and Crafts

Sheela-Na-Gig
Jeanne Rathbone
123 Lavender Sweep
London SW11 1EA
T 0171 228 2327
Comedienne for short performance or one-woman show, usually at arts centres/festivals/private parties.

Bereavement

Wandsworth Bereavement Services
66 Theatre Street
Wandsworth
London SW11 5NF
T 0171 223 3178
Free & confidential bereavement counselling service. Office open Mon-Fri 9.30 am-5.30 pm. Home visits or rooms available at the office.

Child Care and Family

Wandsworth Child Minders' Association
Pam Jones
66 Theatre Street
Wandsworth
London SW11 5NF
T 0171 228 7182
Support for childminders on any issue. Advice on childminding for parents. Vacancy scheme.

Contraception/Well Woman

Balham Health Centre
120 Bedford Hill
Wandsworth
London SW12 9HP
T 0181 700 0600
Contraception & well woman clinics on Tue 6-8 pm; Thurs 9.30-11.30 am; Fri 5-7 pm Wheelchair access. Free contraceptive advice & supplies; blood pressure checks; urine tests; breast screening; etc.

Bridge Lane Health Centre
20 Bridge Lane
Wandsworth
London SW11 3AD
T 0171 441 0730
Contraception & well woman clinics on Tue 6-8 pm & Fri 2-4 pm Wheelchair access. Free contraceptive advice & supplies; blood pressure tests, urine tests, breast screening, pregnancy testing, etc.

Brocklebank Health Centre
249 Garratt Lane
Wandsworth
London SW18 4DU
T 0181 870 1341
Contraception & well woman clinics Mon 1-3 pm & 5-7 pm; Wed 5.30-7.30 pm Wheelchair access. Free contraceptive advice & supplies, blood pressure checks, urine tests, pregnancy tests, etc.

Doddington Health Clinic
311 Battersea Park Road
Wandsworth
London SW11 4LU
T 0171 622 6463
Contraception & well woman clinics on Wed 5.30-7.30 pm. Free contraceptive advice & supplies; blood pressure checks, urine tests,

breast checks, pregancy testing, etc.
Wheelchair access.

Eileen Lecky Clinic
2 Clarendon Drive
Wandsworth
London SW15 1AA
T 0181 788 2236
Contraception & well women clinics Tue 6.30-8.30 pm; Wed 1.30-3.30 pm & 6.30-8.30 pm Wheelchair access. Free contraceptive advice & supplies; blood pressure checks, urine tests, breast checks, etc.

Linnet House Clinic
Charlbert Street
St John's Wood
London NW8 7BT
T 0171 586 4044
Appt/drop-in contraception clinics Tue 5.30-7.30 pm. Free, confidential services. Advice & information. All contraceptive methods & emergency contraception provided.

St Christopher's Clinic
Wheeler Court
Plough Road
Wandsworth
London SW11 2AX
T 0171 441 0770
Contraception & well woman clinics on Wed 1.30-3.30 pm; Fri 5-7 pm. Free contraceptive advice & supplies, blood pressure checks, breast checks, urine tests, pregancy testing. Wheelchair access.

St George's Hospital Ante-Natal Clinic
Coutyard Clinc
Blackshaw Road
Wandsworth
London SW17 0QT
T 0181 672 1255
Clinic for contraceptive advice & supplies Thurs 6.15-7.45 pm Wheelchair access.

Stormont Health Clinic
Antrim House
5-11 Stormont Road
Wandsworth
London SW11 5EG
T 0171 228 4104
Contraception & well woman clinic Thurs 6.30-8.30 pm. Free contraceptive advice & supplies; breast screening, blood pressure checks, urine tests, pregnancy testing, etc.

Tooting Health Clinic
63 Bevill Allen Close
Amen Corner
Wandsworth
London SW17 0PX
T 0181 700 0400
Contraception & well woman clinics on Mon 6-8 pm; Wed 9.30-11.30 am & 6.30-8.30 pm; Fri 5-7 pm; Sat 10 am-12 pm Wheelchair access. Free contraceptive advice & supplies; blood pressure checks, etc.

Tudor Lodge Health Centre
8c Victoria Drive
Wimbledon
London SW19 6AE
T 0181 788 1525
Contraception & well woman clinics Thurs 6.30-8.30 pm & Fri 10 am-12 pm Wheelchair access. Free contraceptive advice & supplies; breast checks, blood pressure checks, urine tests, etc.

Walworth Clinic
Larcom Street
London SW17 1RY
T 0171 703 3262
Well woman clinic on Tue 9.15-11.45 am Free, confidential service for women run by women. Advice & information on health topics, eg vaginal infections, menopause. Blood pressure/urine checks, etc.

ETHNIC MINORITIES

African Women's League (Wandsworth)
Mrs Ogumley
28 Upper Tooting Park
Wandsworth
London SW17 7ST
T 0181 946 7603
Meets second Sat of each month.
Discussions & support group for women.

Aisha Women's Group
Faye Harry
C/o Wandsworth Asian Community Centre
57-59 Trinity Road
London SW17 7SD
T 0181 871 7774
Meets Thurs 10 am-12 pm for general discussions on social, religious matters.

Asian Women's Association - Elderly Care Project
Nasirm Chughtai/Sarwat Butt
Mantle Court

Mapleton Road
Wandsworth
London SW18 4AU
T 0181 875 9465
Social day centre luncheon club & activities for women only on Mon-Wed 10.30 am-2.30 pm Wheelchair access.

Islamic Youth Group
Tajwar Hussain
73 Falcon Road
Wandsworth
London SW11 2PG
T 0171 223 5965
A girls' group meets Thurs 6-9 pm & Sat-Sun 10 am-1 pm. For girls & young women aged 11-19. Indoor & outdoor activities.

Mushkil Aasaan
Nasseem Aboobaker
Community Care for Families in Crisis
1 Idlecombe Road
Tooting
London SW17 9TD
T 0181 672 6581   F 0181 672 6581
Support & advice for Asian families in crisis: counselling, advocacy, home support. Approved provider with Wandsworth Council for domiciliary care. Open Mon-Fri 10 am-5 pm.

Wandsworth Somali Women and Children's Association
Simone Farr
MSW Health Promotion
Wilson Hospital
Cramer Road
Mitcham
T 0181 648 3021
Aims to promote health & social well being amongst Somali women & children in Wandsworth & to empower women to take control over their own lives through skills development & employment.

HEALTH

Stop Smoking Service
Jeanne Rathbone
123 Lavender Sweep
London SW11 1EA
T 0171 228 2327
A stop smoking service offering group workshops & an individual service consisting of an initial preparation session in person, followed by three telephone counselling sessions after quitting.

PHOTOGRAPHY

Patricia Townsend
Patricia Townsend
48 Wandle Road
London SW17 7DW
T 0181 672 4277
Photographer & artist. Work used on a number of book covers. Black & white only. Special area: issues concerning gender.

PREGNANCY/CHILDBIRTH

Birth Centre, The
Caroline Flint
37 Coverton Road
Tooting
London SW17 0QW
T 0181 767 8294   F 0171 498 0698
midwifecf@aol.com
Private birth centre. Women have own midwife throughout pregnancy, labour & post-natal period. Waterpools in every room. Some women funded by their GPs to come here. Next door to a high tech maternity unit.

PRISONERS/PRISONERS' WIVES

Rescue Foundation Centre
62-64 Culvert Road
Battersea
London SW11 5HR
T 0171 924 3974
London-wide assistance given to individuals & families who have difficulties with police, prisons or who are on remand. Pre-release courses & after release training for work. CGLI certificates.

Wandsworth Visitor Centre
Chris
17 Heathfield Road
London SW18 3HR
T 0181 874 4377
Works with familes, partners, friends of inmates in prison. Enquires, information, listening ear, children's play area, coffee bar. Open Mon-Sat 8 am-4 pm; Sun 12-4 pm.

SERVICES

Anne Radford
Anne Radford
Warriner House
140 Battersea Park Road
London SW11 4NB
T 0171 622 7011   F 0171 498 6769
AnneLondon@aol.com

Self-employed consultant. Services to women's organisations include team & management effectiveness skills, mediation & conflict resolution assistance, coaching women managers to improve performance.

British Humanist Association Ceremonies Officiant
Jeanne Rathbone
123 Lavender Sweep
London SW11 1EA
T 0171 228 2327
A trained British Humanist Association non-religious officiant for ceremonies of rites of passage such as baby naming, weddings, gay unions, funerals.

BVY Associates
Beverley P Bramwell
30 Kettering Street
Steatham
London SW16 6PZ
T 0181 769 6370   F 0181 769 6370
KAD67@dial.pipex.com
Management consultancy & training. Clients include local authorities, voluntary agencies, community organisations. Beverley Bramwell is a Black woman with extensive experience in both private & public sectors.

Tango Management Consultancy
Alison Bowditch
9 Langroyd Road
London SW17 7PL
T 0181 767 0247   F 0181 767 0247
Individual & organisation development, helping to create environments where people can flourish. Consultancy, facilitation, personal & organisation development plans.

Tooting Tutors
Jan Samson
40 Idlecombe Road
London SW17 9TB
T 0181 767 1038   F 0181 767 0138
Home tuition service in south London covering all school subjects. A chartered educational psychologist offering assessments of general intelligence, learning difficulties & dyslexia.

SINGLE PARENTS

Wandsworth One Parent Family Centre
Tina Walsh
102 Earlsfield Road
Wandsworth
London SW18 3DR
T 0181 870 3207
Childcare for one-parent families for children aged 3-11. Collects from certain local schools - ends at 6.15 pm. All day care during school holidays (0 am-6.15 pm). Phone for up-to-date price list.

SPORTS AND LEISURE

Streatham Park Bowling Club
Mrs Carter
Pringle Gardens
Ullathorne Road
Wandsworth
London SW16
T 0181 672 4769
Season starts end of April/beginning of May. Plays matches, both home & away. Two women coaches for tuition.

WOMEN'S AID

Shanti Women's Aid
Kauser Yousaff
P O Box 407
Wandsworth
London SW18 2TP
T 0181 874 7262
Helpline open Mon-Fri 9 am-5 pm. Provides temporary sheltered accommodation & support to Asian women & their children.

WESTMINSTER

ACCOMMODATION

St Louise's Hostel
sister in charge
Irish Centre Housing Ltd
33 Medway Street
London SW1P 2BE
T 0171 222 2071   F 0171 976 0569
Hostel & self-catering for young women aged 18-25 who have newly arrived in London. All women of any nationality welcomed. Unlimited stay.

ARTS AND CRAFTS

Barbara Card
BWB Moorings
16 South Wharf Road
London W2 1PQ
T 0171 724 2920
Signwriter: traditional lettering & gilding. For windows and canal decoration.

Ranjana Sidhanta Ash
Ranjana Sidhanta Ash

Flat 9
43 Moscow Road
London W2 4AH
T 0171 727 2667
Freelance lecturer & critic on South Asian literature. Interested in diasporic Asian women writing in Britain; literature in translation.

BEREAVEMENT

Pagan Hospice and Funeral Trust
BM Box 3337
London WC1 3XX

CONTRACEPTION/WELL WOMAN

Covent Garden Health Centre
8-12 Neal Street
London WC2H 9LZ
T 0171 240 8484
Appt/drop-in contraception clinics Tue 9.30-11.30 am Free, confidential services. Advice & information. All contraceptive methods & emergency contraception provided.

Hallfield Clinic
Pickering House
Hallfield Estate
London W2 6HF
T 0171 723 5071
Appt/drop-in contraception clinics Mon (postnatal only) 9.30-11.30 am Appt only clinics: Tue & Thurs 5.30-7.30 pm. Free, confidential services. All contraceptive methods & emergency contraception provided.

Lisson Grove Health Centre
Gateforth Street
London NW8 8EH
T 0171 724 2391
Appt/drop-in contraception clinics Mon 5.30-7.30 pm. Free, confidential services. Advice & information. All contraceptive methods & emergency contraception provided.

Marie Stopes House
Deborah Russell, Manager
108 Whitfield Street
London W1P 6BE
T 0171 388 2585 F 0171 383 7196
Pregancy advice (helpline 0171 388 4843); general healcare/contraception (helpline 0171 388 0662); sterilisation services (helpline 0171 388 5554); well woman clinics; abortion clinics; menopause clinics; etc.

Medical Centre, The
7e Woodfield Road
London W9 3XZ
T 0171 286 5111
Drop-in/appt contraception clinics Mon & Fri 2-4 pm; Wed 1.30-3.30 pm Thurs 5-7 pm (appt only). Well woman drop-in Wed 1.30-3.30 pm. Free, confidential services. All contraceptive methods provided.

Queen's Park Health Centre
Dart Street
London W10 4DL
T 0181 968 8899
Appt/drop-in contraception clinics Tue 1.30-3.30 pm & Fri 9.30-11.30 am Wed 5-7 pm (appt only). Free, confidential services. Advice & information. All contraceptive methods & emergency contraception.

Tottenham Court Road Brook Clinic
233 Tottenham Court Road
London W1P 9AE
T 0171 323 1522
Open Mon-Thurs 9.30 am-7.30 pm; Fri 9.30 am-2.30 pm; Sat 12-2 pm. To make an appointment phone 0171 580 2991. Free, confidential contraceptive advice. Free condoms & other contraceptive supplies.

Upper Montagu Street Clinic
64 Upper Montagu Street
London W1H 1FP
T 0171 935 0706
Appt/drop-in contraception clinics Fri 9.30-11.30 am Free, confidential services. Advice & information. All contraceptive methods & emergency contraception provided.

COUNSELLING AND THERAPY

London Marriage Guidance Council
Renate Olins, Director
76a New Cavendish Street
London W1M 7LB
T 0171 580 1087 F 0171 637 4546
Counselling for couples & individuals in distress about their relationships, whether married or unmarried. Group & sex therapy. Open Mon-Fri 8.30 am-8.30 pm. Phone for an appointment.

DISABILITY

London Transport Disabled Passenger Unit
172 Buckingham Palace Road
London SW1W 9TN

LONDON - WESTMINSTER

T 0171 918 3312
Information & advice about transport for the disabled & for disabled people using London transport.

EQUAL OPPS
Fair Play London
Jennifer Keirl, Coordinator
Government Office for London
4th Floor
Riverwalk House
London SW1P 4RR
T 0171 217 3376 F 0171 217 3288
Positive action equalities project. A government EOC initiative to stimulate partnerships which improve opportunities for women to realise their full potential in education, employment & the community.

ETHNIC MINORITIES
Friday Group, The
Queen's Park Family Service Unit
604 Harrow Road
London W10 4NJ
T 0181 960 3266 F 0181 960 3267
A women & children's group. For women who are isolated in their new environment & are unable to communicate in English. Meets Fri 10 am-12 pm. Sharing ideas & skills.

FINANCE
Allied Dunbar Assurance plc
Anne de Suiza
Haymarket House
26-28 Haymarket
London SW1Y 4SP
T 0171 839 5555 F 0171 930 6098
Financial planning & general financial advice, mostly for women. Self-employed, working under the aegis of Allied Dunbar.

GIRLS/YOUNG WOMEN
London Connection, Advice, Counselling and Streetwork Team
Colin Glover
12 Adelaide Street
London WC2N 4HW
T 0171 930 3451 F 0171 839 6277
Counselling for young, single homeless 16-25 aged group. Streetworkers in West End, emergency service, long-term service. Help on housing & welfare. Open Mon-Fri 9.30 am-1.30 pm for visits & home enquiries.

HEALTH
Dr A Coxon
Dr A Coxon
78 Harley Street
London W1N 1AE
T 0171 486 2534
Woman doctor. Private medical practice only.
Open Mon-Fri 9 am-6 pm

Hungerford Drug Project
32a Wardour Street
London W1V 3HJ
T 0171 287 8743 F 0171 287 1274
Open Mon-Fri 10 am-1 pm & 2-5 pm for drop-in. Wed 6-9 pm by appt only. Advice, information, counselling for people using drugs & their partners, families, friends. Education on HIV/AIDS & drugs, etc.

Needle Exchange Project (NEP)
Peter Simmons
16a Cleveland Street
London W1P 5FA
T 0171 530 4580 F 0171 530 4584
Open Mon-Fri 10 am-12 pm & 12.30-2.30 pm. Self-referral project for people with drug problems. Needle provider. Health education, etc.

LARGER/TALLER WOMEN
Long Tall Sally
21 Chiltern Street
London W1M 1HG
T 0171 487 3370
Clothes for the taller woman sizes 12-20.
Open Mon, Tue, Wed, Fri & Sat 9.30 am-5.30 pm; Thurs 10 am-7 pm; Sun 11 am-5 pm.

Rita Jarvis
Rita Jarvis
16 Queen's Grove
London NW8 6EL
T 0171 722 1127
Sizes 16+. Mail order catalogue.

Ronnie's
Mr Salomon
25 Margaret Street
London W1N 7LB
T 0171 436 5253 F 0171 436 9967
Open Mon-Fri 10 am-6 pm. Ladies' fashion in sizes 14-32. Phone for up-to-date price list.

LEGAL MATTERS

Central London Community Law Centre
19 Whitcomb Street
London WC2 7HA
T 0171 839 2998 F 0171 839 6158
Open Mon 2-5.30 pm, Tue-Fri 10 am-5.30 pm. Free legal advice on employment, immigration, landlord & tenant law, homelessness. Referral by appt only, taken from other local agencies.

Gillian Bull
Gillian Bull
50 Wendover Court
Chiltern Street
London W1M 1PG
T 0171 486 1559 F 0171 486 1559
Solicitor & writer. Information & communication systems a speciality within the law.

LESBIAN AND BISEXUAL

Freedom Cars
60-62 Old Compton Street
Soho
London W1V 5PA
T 0171 734 1313 F 0171 734 4834
fameed@freedomcar.win-uk.net
Lesbian & gay taxi services.

Lesbian Link
The GLI Agency
Room 401
29 Margaret Street
London W1N 7LB
T 0171 627 4960 F 0171 627 4970
Open Mon-Sat 9.30 am-6 pm. Lesbian introduction agency for one-to-one friendships only.

Salsa-Rosada
229 Great Portland Street
London W1
T 0171 813 4831
Salsa club for lesbians & gay men. Phone above number for more details.

MEDIA

Lynn Davis Film Editing
Lynn Davis
Lexington Post
52-53 Poland Street
London W1V 3DF
T 0171 437 4045 F 0171 439 7808
Avid editing for commercials, promos, TV dramas & documentaries, feature films. Quotations on request.

PHOTOGRAPHY

Hilary Shedel Photography
Hilary Shedel
14a Dufour's Place
London W1V 1FE
T 0171 734 3374 F 0171 287 0126
Photographer specialising in dance & movement shots. Works on location & in central London studio.

POLITICS

Project Parity
Lesley Abdela
46 Portland Place
London W1N 3DG
T 0171 631 1545 F 0171 631 1544
Carrying our training in democracy/good government in seven central European nations.

PUBLISHERS/PUBLICATIONS

Virago Press
Little, Brown
London WC2E 7EN
T 0171 911 8000 F 0171 911 8101
Large backlist of books by women. Feminist titles.

RELIGIOUS ORGANISATIONS

Men Women & God
Rhiannon Jones
C/o London Intute Contemp Christianity
St Peter's Church
Vere Street
London W1M 9HP
Providing opportunities for women & men to work through issues raised by feminism from Christian perspective. Exploring changing roles, relationships & ministries of women & men in the church.

SERVICES

Capital Careers
3-4 Picton Place
London W1M 5DD
T 0171 487 4504
Open Mon-Fri 9.30 am-4.30 pm. Offers careers guidance, help with cvs, information

& help with getting a job. For residents of Westminster. Phone for further details.

Elisabeth Brooke
Elisabeth Brooke
101 Great Titchfield Street
London W1P 7AG
T 0171 580 7911
Astrologer: medical astrology & general psychological astrology. Tarot readings, non-fatalistic with psychological/feminist perspectives. Postal readings & workshops. Author of books on Wicca, herbalism, etc.

Eyecatcher Associates
Lesley Abdela
46 Portland Place
London W1N 3DG
T 0171 631 1545 F 0171 631 1544
Equal opportunities, journalism, research consultancy.

SOCIAL

Canadian Women's Club
2 Audley Square
London W1
T 0171 408 2459
Social club for Canadian women ex-pats living in London.

SUPPORT

Junior League of London
Barbara Ilias
9 Fitzmaurice Place
London W1X 6JD
T 0171 499 8159
Club for women committed to promoting voluntary service. Office open Mon & Thurs 9.30 am-1.30 pm Mandatory training before joining. Helping elderly people. Fundraising. Produces 'Living in London' booklet.

Samaritans - Central London Branch
46 Marshall Street
London W1V 1LR
T 0171 734 2800
Phone line open 24 hours a day. Confidential telephone befriending for the suicidal, despairing & those going through personal crises. Drop-in at centre between 9 am-9 pm

TRANSPORT

Central London Dial-A-Ride
Hathaway House
7d Woodfield Road
London W9 2BA
T 0171 266 6100
Door-to-door service for disabled people who can't use public transport. Seven days a week 8.30 am-11.30 pm. Fare similar to bus fares. Covering Westminster, Camden, Ham. & Fulham, Kensington & Chelsea.

SCOTLAND

ABERDEEN AND GRAMPIAN

ACCOMMODATION

Aberdeen Cyrenians - Women's Hostel
Norma McQuade
69-71 Crown Street
Aberdeen AB11 6EX
T 01224 580411
Provides medium to long-term residential care for homeless women. To enable women to work through problems & increase their self-esteem within a supportive environment to be more independent.

Aberdeen Soroptimist Housing Society Ltd (ASHS)
1 Golden Square
Aberdeen AB9 8BH
T 01224 740746
Provides 14 self-contained flats for single women over 60 years old & 1 dwelling for a disabled women & her carer.

Richmondhill House
Diane McCabe
18 Richmondhill Place
Aberdeen AB2 4EP
T 01224 634158
Residential accommodation & care for up to 9 unsupported mothers who find it difficult to care for their children alone. Staff offer support 24 hours a day. Communal kitchen, living room, playroom.

BEREAVEMENT

Aberdeen Area Cot Death Support Group
Yvonne Veltman
12 Ferryhill Place
Aberdeen
T 01224 581182
Local support group of the Scottish Cot Death Trust

Miscarriage Association Support Group
23 St Nathalan Crescent
Banchory AB31 3YU
Local Miscarriage Association Support group. Send sae for information.

Miscarriage Association Support Group
65 Forest Park
Stonehaven AB3 2GF
Local contact for Miscarriage Association. Send sae for information.

Miscarriage Association Support Group
20 Bydand Gardens
Whitetrees
Inverurie AB51 9FL
Local contact for Miscarriage Association. Send sae for information.

War Widows of Great Britain Association (Aberdeen)
Mrs C Littlejohn
76 Bankhead Avenue
Bucksburn
Aberdeen AB2 9EY
T 01224 713563
Mrs Littlejohn is the regional organiser for this association which was formed to improve conditions for all war widows & their dependants. Works with governments departments & other organisations.

CENTRES FOR WOMEN

Aberdeen Women's Centre
Babs Greenwood
Shoe Lane
Aberdeen AB10 1AL
T 01224 625010 F 01224 625777
Open Mon-Fri 9.30 am-4 pm. Working with women & women's groups in Aberdeen. The Centre is a safe, women-only space providing information, meeting rooms & other resources. Wheelchair accessible.

COUNSELLING AND THERAPY

Aberdeen Counselling and Information Service
The ACIS Centre
100 Crown Street
Aberdeen AB1 2HJ
T 01224 573892
Open 9.30 am-5 pm Mon-Fri and 6-8 pm Mon, Tues and Thurs. Closed Wed afternoons. Counselling & information for those with personal, emotional or mental health problems, anxiety, depression or stress.

DISABILITY

Deaf Women's Health Project
Kathleen Cameron
13 Smithfield Road
Aberdeen AB2 2NR
T 01224 481414
Aims to improve deaf women's access to health information & health education materials in British Sign Language. Trains

women to offer support & information to other deaf women.

EDUCATION

Aberdeen Association of Graduate Women
Mrs Caroline Green
30 Desswood Place
Aberdeen AB25 2DH
T 01224 644080
c.green@abdn.ac.uk
Aberdeen branch of BFWG. Meets third Wed evening of each month from September-May. Talks of general interest. Occasional lunches, theatre visits, etc. A support network of graduate women.

ETHNIC MINORITIES

African Women's Support Group
Kemi Adebayo, Publicity Officer
C/o Aberdeen Women's Centre
Shoe Lane
Aberdeen AB1 1AG
T 01224 625010 F 01224 625777
The main aim of the group is to reduce isolation & loneliness of African women in Aberdeen & to share information about matters such as employment, health, welfare rights, etc. Meets once a month.

Chinese Women Health Awareness Group
Kay Halderman, Chair
97 Thistle Drive
Aberdeen AB12 4QU
T 01224 1782840
Aims to further the health of the Chinese community in Aberdeen. Tai chi & aerobics classes, health talks, meetings, outings.

GIRLS/YOUNG WOMEN

Aberdour with Tyree Young Women's Group
Mrs Aileen Irvine
Sauchentree
New Aberdour
Fraserburgh AB43 7LN
T 01346 561296
Meets at New Aberdour School from March to October on the last Wed of each month at 7.30.

Fordyce Parish Young Woman's Group
Mrs Dawn Gould
Sandineuk
Sandend

Banff AB45 1BE
T 01261 843343
Meets at the Church Hall, Seafield Street, Portsay on Tue at 10 am or 2 pm from September to March in term times only.

Marnoch Young Wives
Mrs P Gray
9 Smith Crescent
Aberchirder
Huntly AB54 8FX
T 01466 780342
Meets at the Church Hall, Main Street, Huntly on the first & third Tue of each month from 2-3.30 pm.

HEALTH

Alcohol Advisory & Counselling Service
Janis McDonald
62 Dee Street
Aberdeen AB1 2DS
T 01224 573887
Open Mon-Thurs 9 am-9 pm; Fri 9 am-5 pm. Advice, counselling & information for people with alcohol problems, their families & friends. Special self-help groups for women.

Association for Mental Health in Banff & Buchan
Phil Hitchen, Development officer
Grampian House
86-88 Commerce Street
Fraserburgh AB43 5LP
T 01346 514966 F 01346 510620
Open 9 am-1 pm and 24-hour ansaphone. Women's group, drop-in, Wednesday Club, befriending scheme, counselling, phobic groups, manic depression fellowship, relaxation therapy, domestic visits, information.

Crown Street Day Centre
Roberta Buchan, Manager
112 Crown Street
Aberdeen AB1 2HJ
T 01224 591652
Offers group therapy, individual & couple counselling for those whose difficulties are expressed through their use of alcohol, & their families.

Drugs Action
Carol Calderwood, Secretary
48a Union Street
Aberdeen AB1 1BB
T 01224 624555 F 01224 620907

Open Mon 2-4 pm; 5-7 pm; Tues, Wed, Fri 10 am-1 pm; 2-5 pm; Thurs 2-5 pm. Women only sessions Tues 2-5 pm; drop in Wed 2-5 pm. Confidential support and advice provided; all services are free.

Grampian Osteoporosis Self Help Group
Hilda Glennie, Secretary
51 Rosewell Gardens
Off Summerhill Road
Aberdeen AB15 6HZ
T 01224 325162
Advises sufferers from osterporosis & those concerned to prevent the condition. To educate & to raise money to fund research into ostoporosis. A branch of the National Osteoporosis Society.

Hysterectomy-Menopause-HRT Support and Self Help Group
Mrs Carol Weatherall
C/o Ardeer
Forres
Rafford IV36 0RU
T 01309 673178
Meets bimonthly at various venues. To encourage better communication between women & their GPs & to inform women about what is hapening to their bodies with regard to hysterectomies, menopause & HRT.

Input Nutrition
Dr Christine Fenn
19 Craigton Court
Aberdeen AB15 7PF
T 01224 316814 F 01224 324181
Dr Fenn is an accredited nutritionist & professional speaker. Presents her own seminars & short courses in nutrition. She gives advice to a wide range of societies & business organisations.

Mastectomy Association for Grampian
Mrs E Dorothy Lawrie, Honorary President
28 Covenanters Drive
Aberdeen AB12 5AB
T 01224 875011
To support mastectomy patients both before & after their operation. Also for women who have an understanding of & interest in the problems involved. Regular meetings & a weekly swimming class.

NAPS Aberdeen PMS Support Group
Margaret Clark
61 Jesmond Avenue North
Bridge of Don
Aberdeen AB22 8WJ
T 01224 821393
Support group for women suffering from PMS. Meets every first & third Thurs 7.00-8.00 pm in the Community Education Centre, 17a Belmont Street. Support, advice & information provided.

National Osteoporosis Society - Aberdeen
Department of Rheumatology
City Hsopital
Urquhart Road
Aberdeen AB9 8AU
T 01224 681818
Information & advice about osteoporosis.

LARGER/TALLER WOMEN

Long Tall Sally
123 George Street
Aberdeen AB25 1HU
T 01224 638273
Clothes for the taller woman sizes 12-20. Open Mon, Tue, Wed, Fri & Sat 9.30 am-5.30 pm; Thurs 10 am-7 pm; Sun 11 am-5 pm.

LESBIAN AND BISEXUAL

Aberdeen Lesbian Group
Babs Greenwood
C/o Aberdeen Women's Centre
Shoe Lane
Aberdeen AB10 1AL
T 01224 625010 F 01224 625777
The group meets weekly from 8-10 pm on Wed at the Women's Centre. It is open to all lesbians & to bisexual women who wish to be in a lesbian-centred environment. Social events, discussions, etc.

Lesbian Gay and Bisexual Switchboard
P O Box 174
Aberdeen AB9 8UZ
T 01224 633500
Open Wed and Fri 7-10 pm. To provide help, information & someone to talk to for lesbians & bisexual women, their families, friends & relatives. HIV/AIDS & safer sex information. Counselling.

PLACES TO STAY AND EAT

B&B Glenbrae
Jean Fraser
Glenbrae
Gailoch IV21 2AH
T 01445 712279

B&B double room. Full breakfast. Vegetarians & vegans catered for; no smoking. Tea/coffee-making facilities; own bathroom. Beaches, windsurfing, boat hire, golf course. Phone for up-to-date price list.

Pregnancy/Childbirth

Association for Post Natal Illness
Claire Lai
24 Rosebery Street
Aberdeen AB2 4LL
Aberdeen area coordinator, offering information for mothers suffering from postnatal depression on a one-to-one basis.

Caesarean Support Network
Lyn Byers
1 Cairnequheen Gardens
Aberdeen AB2 4HJ
T 01224 317082
Provides education & information on all matters relating to caesarean delivery. Reassurance provided for caesarean mothers who hope to have a vaginal delivery in the future. Literature available.

Lifeline Pregnancy Counselling and Care (Aberdeen)
Margaret House
132 Huntly Street
Aberdeen
T 01224 640266
Open Mon, Tues, Thurs and Fri 11 am-3 pm; Wed 2-6 pm. Provides free professional pregnancy counselling & care service to help pregnant women facing problem pregnancies. Confidential help.

Nest Support Group
Assisted Reproduction Unit
Dept of Obstetrics & Gynae
Foresterhill
Aberdeen AB9 2ZD
T 01224 681818 F 01224 684880
A support group for couples who are having or who have had problems with fertility. Meets once a month to discuss relevant treatment available. Speakers.

Religious organisations

Forglen United Free Church Women's Association
Mrs M Low
The Neuk
Bridgend Terrace
Turriff AB53 4ES
T 01888 562229
Meets at the Church Hall in Turriff approximately three times a year.

Fraserburgh Baptist Church Women's Auxilliary
Mrs Alice Buchan
11 Charleston
St Combs
Fraserburgh AB43 8YT
T 01346 582736
Meets at Fraserburgh Baptist Church on Thurs at 7.30 pm.

Retailing

Body and Face St Cyrus Ltd
Anna Pirie
Units 4-6
Laurencekirk Business Park
Aberdeen Road
Laurencekirk AB30 1EY
T 01561 378811 F 01561 378292
Manufactuers of natural skin care, hair care & aromatherapy products. Also quality gifts including colour co-ordinated beauty preparations in glass bottles.

Sexual abuse/rape crisis

Aberdeen Rape Crisis
P O Box 123
Aberdeen AB9 8NX
T 01224 620768
Open Mon and Thurs 7-9 pm. Free & confidential counselling for women & girls who have been raped & sexually abused. Both telephone & face-to-face counselling are available.

Adult Survivors Project (ASP)
Morag Fraser, coordinator
Office 1
79 High Street
Banff AB45 1AN
T 01261 818330
A phoneline on Thurs 7-9 pm for the Banff & Buchan areas for survivors of sexual abuse.

Grampian Action Against Sexual Abuse
10-16 Exchequer Row
Aberdeen AB1 2BW
T 01224 593381
Open Mon-Thurs 9 am-5 pm; 24-hour on-call service. Support counselling on a one-to-one basis to women who are victims of rape & mothers of children who have been sexually abused. There is a refuge.

SCOTLAND - DUMFRIES, GALLOWAY & BORDERS

SPORTS AND LEISURE

Aberchirder Ladies Keep Fit Group
Mrs D Knox
12 Deveron Road
Turriff AB53 7BB
T 01888 562227
Meets at Aberchirder from Easter to June on Thurs 8-9 pm.

Broch Ladies Badminton Group
Calvin Little
Alexandra Terrace
Fraserburgh AB43 9pp
T 01346 518788
Meets on Mon 10 am-12 noon at the Fraserburgh Community Education Centre.

Deveron Ladies Hockey Club
Jacqui Kelly
Clova
9 Ogilvie Street
Whitehills
Banff AB45 2NQ
T 01261 861588

Gardenstown Ladies Badminton Club
B Wain
26 Seatown
Gardenstown
Banff AB45 3YQ
T 01261 851749
Meets on Tue at 1.30 pm at Gardenstown village hall.

SUPPORT

Aberdeen Friendship Group
Norma Duncan, Chairperson
C/o Aberdeen Women's Centre
Shoe Lane
Aberdeen AB1 1AG
T 10224 590388
Meets on Tues 7.30-9.30 pm at the Women's Centre. There is a mother's group on the last Tues of the month. Support network for women survivors sexually, emotionally or physically abused in childhood.

Whitehills Ladies' Lifeboat Guild
Mrs Peter Lovie
31 Knock Street
Whitehills
Banff AB45 2NW
T 01261 561331
Meets at Whitehills Public Hall approximately four times a year. Supports the RLNI by fundraising.

WOMEN'S AID

Aberdeen Women's Aid
66 The Green
Aberdeen AB11 6PE
T 01224 591577
3 emergency rooms for women; 17 family places & 7 places for women with children. 24-hour answerphone. Advice, support & refuge for women & children, victims of physical, sexual & emotional abuse.

Aberdeenshire Women's Aid
P O Box 11851
Turriff AB53 4YA
T 01885 562241
Office open Mon-Fri 10 am-4 pm. Providing support & refuge to women with or without children who have suffered any form of domestic violence by either male or female perpetrators.

Grampian Women's Aid
10-16 Exchequer Row
Aberdeen AB1 2BW
T 01224 593381
Open 9 am-5 pm Mon-Fri. 24-hour helpline for emergency assistance. Advice, support & refuge to women & children who are victims of domestic abuse. One-to-one counselling service for women.

DUMFRIES, GALLOWAY & BORDERS

AGRICULTURE

Gillian R Scott
Gillian R Scott
Falla
Jedburgh TD8 6RN
T 01835 840247 F 01835 840247
Mobile: 0374 428973. Work varies from farm work, horsesitting to basic office work. I also work for the Agricultural Training Board organising short courses for farmers.

ALTERNATIVE THERAPIES

Dr Dominique Davis
Dominique Davis
The Library
Abbey St Bathans House
Duns TD11 3TX
T 01361 840340 F 01361 840284
Medical doctor and herbalist with alternative medical practice and holistic approach to health. Listens to patients. Advice on lifestyle, nutrition. Provides natural therapies, including use of medicinal plants

Teacher of the Alexander Technique
Eleanor Boeing
Innerleithen
Tweeddale
T 01896 831208
Teaches the Alexander Technique which is a gentle process which can improve poise, self-presentation, voice and performance. It can also help with backpain, stress and many chronic conditions. Member of ATN.

BEREAVEMENT
Borders Cot Death Action Group
Mr J Gill
3 Abbotsford Terrace
Darnick
Melrose TD6 9AD
T 01896 823072
Befriending for families suffering cot deaths.

Dumfries and Galloway Cot Death Support Group
Mrs Margaret Findlater
2 MacDonald Loaning
Heathhall
Dumfries
T 01387 64286
A local support group of the Scottish Cot Death Trust.

Eastern Borders Stillbirth and Neonatal Death Society
Mrs Susan Bryson
Peel View
Lennel Mount
Coldstream TD12
T 01890 883574
Offers support when a baby dies during pregnancy or around the time of birth or shortly afterwards.

Miscarriage Association Support Group
Sarah Pearson
33 Eskdail Street
Langholm DG13 OBG
T 01387 381131
Advice, support & information given about miscarriages. Open Mon, Tues, Wed & Fri in the evenings before 10 pm.

BUSINESS SUPPORT SCHEMES
Broderline Business Agency
Helen Pope
Blythbank
Station Road
Duns TD11 3EJ
T 01361 883633 F 01361 884117
Employment agency specialising in secretarial temporary staff in the Scottish borders.

Contact
Pauline Williams, Co-ordinator
3 New Belses
Ancrum
Jedburgh TD8 6UR
T 01835 870380 F 01835 870380
panda@sol.co.uk
For women active in business or the professions in the Scottish borders. Provides members with a business & social forum to meet, exchange ideas & personal development. Networking; training.

J A Consultancy
Jacqui Beaton
Avonlea
68 Edinburgh Road
Peebles EH45 8EE
T 01721 720539
To help small & large businesses realise their true potential & show them how to maximise efforts & results. Also how to acquire more customers with little or no risk & double sales from existing customers.

CARERS
Care Connect
Mrs Sarah Fraser
Nenthorn House
Kelso TD5 7RY
T 01573 226868 F 01573 226105
Provides domiciliary care to persons in their own homes, hourly, daily or live-in. Optional supporting services available to maintain independence.

CONTRACEPTION/WELL WOMAN
Hay Lodge Health Centre
Dr Young and partners
Neidpath Road
Peebles EH45 8JG
T 01721 720380 F 01721 733430
Well woman clinic: Wed 3 pm; antenatal clinic: Mon 11 am Also Dr Love & partners, tel 01721 720601, fax 01721 723430, antenatal clinic Tue 2-3.30 pm; well woman clinic Thurs 12-1 pm.

Health Centre - Castle Douglas
Castle Douglas
T 01387 244013

Well woman & contraception clinics first & third Fri of each month at 2 pm.

Health Centre - Earlston
Dr Burns & Partner
Kidgate
Earlston TD4 6DW
T 01896 849273 F 01896 848192
Well woman clinic: any time by appointment. Antenatal clinic: Thurs 2 pm.

Health Centre - Eyemouth
Dr Fenty and partners
Houndlaw Park
Eyemouth TD14 5DA
T 01890 750599 F 01890 751749
Well woman/cervical cytology: alternative Wed & Fri; antenatal clinic: Wed.

Health Centre - Galashiels
Dr Frame and partners
Currie Road
Galashiels TD1 2UA
T 01896 754833 F 01896 751389
Antenatal clinic: Wed 3-4 pm; Thurs 3 pm onwards; Fri 1.30 pm onwards; also Dr Johnston & partners, tel 01896 752419, fax 01896 751389, well woman clinic weekly by appt; antenatal clinic Fri 2-3 pm.

Health Centre - Hawick
Dr Oliver and partners
Teviot Road
Hawick TD9 9DT
T 01450 372550 F 01450 371025
Antenatal clinic: Thurs by appt; well women clinics: Tue, Wed, Thurs 5-6 pm. Also Dr Suttie & partners, tel 01450 372076, fax 01450 377387, antenatal clinic: Thurs 1.30 pm; well woman clinic: by appt.

Health Centre - Kelso
Dr Mooney and partners
Inch Road
Kelso TD5 7LF
T 01573 224424 F 01573 226388
Well woman clinic by appointment.

Health Centre - Melrose
Dr McDonald and partners
St Dunstan's Park
Melrose TD6 9RX
Antenatal clinic: Tue 2-3 pm; well woman clinic: Thurs 10 am

Health Centre - Selkirk
Dr Fiddes and partners
Viewfield Lane
Selkirk TD7 4LJ
T 01750 21674 F 01750 23176
Antenatal clinic: Mon 2-4 pm; well woman/cytology: Tue 9 am-1 pm.

Health Centre - St Boswells
Dr McDonald and partners
Orchard Park
St Boswells TD6 0AL
T 01835 822269
Well woman clinic: Thurs 3 pm; antenatal clinic: Thurs 2 pm.

Health Clinic - Annan
Charles Street
Annan
T 01461 2022017
Well woman & contraception clinics Tue 6.40 pm; second Fri of each month 2 pm.

O'Connell Street Medical Centre
Dr Brogan and Partners
Hawick TD9 9HU
T 01450 372276 F 01450 371564
Cytology & well woman clinics: Tue & alternative Thurs 4.30-6 pm; antenatal clinics Mon & Wed 1.30-3 pm & Tue 2-3.15 pm.

St Ronan's Health Centre
Dr Cumming and Partner
Angle Park
Innerleithen EH44 6PG
T 01896 830203 F 01896 831202
Well woman clinic: Wed 2-3.30 pm; antenatal clinic Thurs 9-11 am

ENVIRONMENT

Exterior Design Associates
Charlotte Cottingham
2 East End Cottages
Maxton
St Boswells TD6 0RL
T 01835 823836 F 01835 823836
Commissions in the fields of design, contract management, landscape & environmental impact assessment. Contracts vary from small-scale garden design to landscape consultancy for national organisations.

SCOTLAND - Dumfries, Galloway & Borders

Health

Amarant Trust - Hawick
Grace Phillips
11 Sandbed
Hawick TD9 0HE
Information & advice about the menopause.

Dumfries Amarant Trust
Joan Hutchinson
29 Castle Street
Dumfries DG1 DL
T 01387 251830
Provides information for women who are having problems with the menopause.

Dumfries Breast Care Group
Elizabeth J Maxwell
23 Auchenkeld Avenue
Heathhall
Dumfries DG1 3QY
T 01387 263058
Provides help advice & information for women who have undergone breast surgery.

Eating Disorders Self-help Group
Fiona Houston
3a Roxborgh Street
Galashiels
T 01896 754445
Meets at the Borders General Hospital on alternate Wed 7.30-9. am

Eildon Surgery
Dr McDonald and Partners
Auction Mart
Newtown St Boswells TD6 0PP
T 01835 822777
Antenatal clinic Mon 2 pm.

Health Centre - West Linton
Dr Pollock and partner
Deanfoot Road
West Linton EH46 7EX
T 01968 660808 F 01968 660856
Antenatal clinics: Tue and Wed 2-3 pm.

Memorial Medical Centre
Dr Crombie-Smith and partners
Edinburgh Road
Lauder TD2 6TW
T 01578 722267 F 01578 718667
Antenatal clinic on Wed 4-5 pm.

Premenstrual Syndrome Support
Mary Armour

Community Nursing Department
Annandale House
Crichton Royal Hospital
Dumfries
T 01387 255301

Photography

Rown Ballantyne Photographic
Penny Davies
9 Tower Street
Selkirk TD7 4LR
T 01750 20521 F 01896 750023
Also on 01896 750023. Commercial & social photographers offering creative & high quality images for corporate & advertising organisations. Fully equiped studio. Location work in UK & Europe.

Pregnancy/Childbirth

Antenatal & Post-Natal Clinics
Dr Auld and Partners
The Knoll
Duns TD11 3EL
T 01361 882186
Antenatal & post-natal clinics: Wed 2 pm.; cervical smear clinic: Wed 9 am

Services

Clare Gilmore Beauty Clinic
Elcho Street
Brae
Peebles EH45 8HU
T 01721 724420
Provides manicures, pedicures, facials, eye treatments, make ups, lash & brow tints, eyebrow trims. Phone for up-to-date price list.

Dale Designs
Ruth C Miller
Moray House
Main Street
St Boswells TD6 0AP
T 01835 822853 F 01835 822853
Interior design business offering wallpaper, fabrics & a complete design service for homes, offices & hotels. All work is personally supervised by a qualified interior designer.

J M & D B Hicks
Jean Hicks
Birghamhaugh House
Coldstream TD12 4NE
T 01890 830247 F 01890 830600

A consultancy offering a multi-disciplinary approach to marketing communications particularly relevant to the needs of smaller companies under direct management of an owner/principal.

Pat Mosel
Pat Mosel
Bedrule
Hawick TD9 8TE
T 01450 870644   F 01450 870644
Editorial & copywriting. Integrated creative services in preparation for publication.

Tuff Food Consultants
Catherine Tuff
Greenhouse Farm
Lilliesleaf
Melrose TD6 9EP
T 01835 870250   F 01835 870250
Working with the food industry, providing expertise on Scottish food & drink, new product research & recipe development, assessment of hotels & restaurants for guides & competitions, etc.

Women's Aid

Borders Women's Aid
10 Exchange Street
Jedborough TD8 6BH
T 01835 863514
Office open Mon-Fri 9 am-4 pm. 24-hour telephone answering service. A refuge for five women & their children. Support, information & advice for abused women.

Dumfries Women's Aid
12 Whitesands
Dumfries DG1 2RR
T 01387 263052
Open Mon, Tues, Wed, Fri 10 am-4 pm; Thurs 1-4 pm. A refuge for seven families. Advice, support, information & counselling given to abused women & their children.

Newton Stewart Women's Aid
C/o Welfare Rights Office
Cree Bridge
Newton Stewart
T 01671 404284
Consultations Fri 11.30 am-2.30 pm. Information, support & advice given to battered women.

Wigtownshire Women's Aid
8 St John's Street
Stranraer DG9 7EL
T 01776 703104
Open Mon-Fri 10 am-4.30 pm. A six-base refuge. Advice, support, counselling for abused women & their children (if any). 24-hour on call service Rape referrals & contact for incest/child abuse survivors.

Dundee, Tayside & Fife

Accountancy

CAP Services
Anne Tremble
4 Katrine Drive
Crossford
Dunfermline KY12 8XR
T 01383 729295   F 01383 729295
Tremble@compuserve.com
Provides a bookkeeping & payroll service to small businesses. Training given on Sage Sterling & Sage Instant.

Winton & Co
Lynn Winton
16 Hamilton Street
Broughty Ferry
Dundee DD5 2NR
T 01382 477193   F 01382 730800
Chartered accountants: audits, accountancy, bookkeeping, tax advice, general business advice. Hours of business: Mon-Fri 9 am-6 pm; Sat 10 am-12.30 pm.

Alternative Therapies

Allergy Therapist Kinesiologist
Jean Wallace
30 Lammerton Terrace
Dundee DD4 7BL
T 01382 461165
Allergy work; kinesiology; Touch for Healthy Instructor work. Phone for up-to-date price list.

Health and Harmony
Jan Killan
Polomouth
Old Montrose
Montrose DD10 9LJ
T 01674 810346   F 01674 810346
Relexology, stress, management, counselling (individuals & groups). Home visits & workshops.

Molly McCombes
Molly McCombes
Flat 1 Beaumont House
15 St John's Place
Perth PH1 5S2

SCOTLAND - DUNDEE, TAYSIDE & FIFE

T 01738 637565
Yoga teacher, reflexologist, Reiki master, offering classes in yoga, relaxation & meditation, therapies & classes in reflexology & introductions, therapies & attunements in Reiki.

Natural Alternative, The
Aileen Cameron Brannen
Ronvale Cottage
2 Chamberfield Road
Dunfermline KY12 0DN
T 01383 726982
106313,3652@compuserve
A herbal supplement & nutritional distribution company, selling products targeted to build the immune system & to help prevent disease.

Natural Health Care/Chiropractic Clinic
Patricia Waite
15 Wallace Street
Dundee DD4 6AN
T 01382 461081 F 01382 461081
Chiropractitioner. Also state registered physiotherapist. Works Mon, Tue, Wed, Fri 10 am-5.30 pm; Thurs 11.30 am-5.30 pm. Also works two half days in Aberfeldy - phone 01887 820199.

Sheelagh Cameron
Sheelagh Cameron
Dean House
11 High Street
Kirriemuir DD8 4EY
T 01575 573214 F 01575 573214
Reflexology, hypnotherapy & muscular body therapy. Works Mon-Fri 9 am-8 pm.

Sheila Caldwell
Sheila Caldwell
Abbotsford
30 James Street
Pittenweem KY10 2QN
T 01333 311468
Trained in Bowen Therapy, reflexology, aromatherapy, intuitive healing & stress management. Also a colour & image consultant, offering private or corporate consultations, selling skin therapy, etc.

Twa Acres Natural Therapy Centre
Vicky Watson
Newton Villa
Newton Terrace
Blairgowrie PH10 6HG
T 01250 874384 F 01250 874384

Training school for National Society of Professional Hypnotherapy; certificated training courses in hypnotherapy & hypno analysis; workshops in relaxation, stress management & self-hynosis; individual appts.

Westbank Natural Health Centre
Mrs Wendy MacManaway
Strathmiglo KY14 7QP
T 01337 860233 F 01337 860233
Wendy MacManaway practises aromatherapy, reflexology, yoga & releasing of trapped nerves. Courses on alternative therapies. Phone above number any weekday 9 am-12 noon for further information.

ARMED FORCES

Dundee and District Wrens Association
Mrs Barbara Rickmann, Secretary
53 Strathmore Street
Broughty Ferry
Dundee DD5 2PA
T 01382 738385
Meets last Tue of month 2.15-4 pm at 27 Crichton Street, YWCA Rooms, Dundee DD1 3AR. Annual reunions. Gives to charities, mostly naval but also hospices and disabled.

ARTS AND CRAFTS

Alison and Roy Murray
Alison Murray
4 Balbirnie Craft Centre
Glenrothes KY7 6NE
T 01592 753743 F 01592 753743
Design & manufacture of jewellery using precious metals & stones. Commissions a speciality. Open Mon-Sat 10 am-5 pm; Sun 2-5 pm.

Margaret Evans Art Courses - Shinafoot Studios
Margaret Evans
Shinafoot Studios
Auchterarder PH3 1DU
T 01764 663639 F 01764 663843
All-year-round programme of art courses, painting holidays, in Scotland, rest of UK and abroad. Margaret Evans is the resident artist, tutor, author, demonstrator.

Mari Donald Knitwear
Mari Donald
Graiglea
Pudding Lane
Comrie PH6 2DS

T 01764 670150 F 01764 670150
MariDonald@lineone.net.uk
Small craft workshop making & selling knitwear for adults & children from own original designs, using pure wool & other natural yarns. Open all year - phone to check opening times.

Repocast Scotland Ltd
Philomena M Alexander, Managing Director
Clickham House
Milnab Terrace
Crieff PH7 4ED
T 01764 653660
Providing stoneware quality products with refreshing & innovative designs at very reasonable prices.

BEREAVEMENT

Friends of Scottish Cot Death Trust - Central and West Fife
Miss Dawn Thomson
Dumbryden
Links Road
Leven
T 01333 426852
Local contact for Scottish Cot Death Trust.

Miscarriage Association Support Group
138 Townhill Road
Dunfermline KY12 0BP
T 01383 720811

Miscarriage Association Support Group
Leuchars
St Andrews KY16 03Z
T 01334 888846

National Association of Widows - Cupar branch
Judy Harris, Advisory Worker
11 Westport Place
Cupar KY15 4AL
Offering comfort, support & advice to all widows.

BUSINESS SUPPORT SCHEMES

Fife Women in Business
Irene Dick
C/o Fife Chamber of Commerce & Industry
Wemyssfield House
Wemyssfield
Kirkcaldy KY1 1XN
T 01592 201932 F 01592 641187
enquiries@fifecham.demon.co.uk

Providing a forum for business women in the Fife area. Monthly evening meetings.

Smart Training & HR Consultant
Lexi Smart
Slioch
12 McCulloch Drive
Forfar DD8 2EB
T 01387 464330 F 01387 464330
Offers a management training service to businesses who use external resources/freelance.

South Fife Business Shop
Linda Fitzsimmons
Dunfermline Business Centre
Izatt Avenue
Dunfermline KY11 3B2
T 01383 626626 F 01383 620641
Helping individuals to start up their own business. Help with raising finance, marketing advice, accounts, market research, advice on premises, exporting advice, sales training, ISO 9000, legal matters, etc.

Zaragow Ltd
Davina Reid
5 Fordell Gardens
Hillend
Dunfermline KY11 5EZ
T 01383 417744 F 01353 414111
zaragon.ital@virgin.nql
CAD/IT consultancy, training, technical support. Hardware & software sales - leasing or invoice.

CENTRES FOR WOMEN

Dundee International Women's Centre (DIWC)
Annette Miller, Community Education Worker
49 Lyon Street
Dundee DD4 6RA
T 01382 462058
Keep fit, singing, art group, swimming, Urdu study group, cookery, ESOL, Koran reading, Baha'i children's group & other activities. Drop in morning Thurs fortnightly 1 am-12 pm. Local unit of YWCA.

Dundee Women's Resource Collective
P O Box 6863
Dundee DD1 5ZZ
Committed to sharing information about & with women's organisations & individual women. A resource centre for information,

networking, socialising & sharing. A small, friendly group; new members welcome.

CHILD CARE AND FAMILY

Abacus Day Nursery
Joyce Moyes
8 Lethnot Street
Barnhill
Dundee DD5 2QS
T 01382 774915
3 nurseries, education in play, safe play areas, lunch/snacks, from birth-aged 11. St Peter St, Perth Road, Dundee, 01382 660161; 8 Lethnot St, Barnhill, Dundee 01382 774915; 84 North St, Forfar 01307 461961.

Partnership in Child Care Project
Siobhan Wilks
14 Moss Way
Hillend Industrial Estate
Dalgety Bay KY11 5JS
T 01383 821970 F 01383 821970
Quality childcare provision for children aged three months to five years. Open all year. Prices are based on income.

Rascals Pre-School Nursery
Pat Hughes
The Old School House
26 Hill Street
Cowdenbeath KY4 9DE
T 01383 513318
Open Mon-Fri 8 am-6 pm. Staff ratio to children: 1:3.

COMPUTERS/IT

Dunfermline Women's Technology Centre
Nancy McDonald
Unit 10
Elgin Industrial Estate
Dickson Street
Dunfermline KY12 7SL
T 01383 621038 F 01383 621159
100673.2536@compuserve.com
High quality training in computing & electronics for women. Concentrates on technician level electronics & computer programming. Training over a 40-week period, 7 hours a day Mon-Fri. One-to-one tuition.

Fife Training Information Services
Chris Simpson
9-10 Flemington Road
Glenrothes KY7 5QT
T 01572 611231 F 01572 611232
Free information on education & training. Opportunities for women living or working in the telephone enquiry service 0800 243 260 & signposting to public access computers containing the national Scotia.

JEM Computer Systems
Jennifer Martin
Second Floor
Granary Business Centre
Cupar KY15 5YQ
T 01334 652681
Woman-owned company providing hardware & software & training in computing. Phone between 9 am-5 pm for further details.

Perfect Training
Amanda Darroch
9 Dean Ridge
Gowkhall
Dunfermline KY12 9PE
T 01383 851114 F 01383 851114
Software trainer: Microsoft office; Lotus smart suite; Perfect office.

Writeword Business Services
Miss Eleanor Rowe
1 River View
Dalgety Bay KY11 5YE
T 01383 824490 F 01383 824490
Computer-based business services comprising business printing, promotional printing & publishing.

COUNSELLING AND THERAPY

Carol Bagnall
Carol Bagnall
24 Well Street
Monifieth DD5 4AT
T 01382 533291
c.s.bagnall@norcol.ac.uk
Person-centred counselling; counselling supervision; trainer in counselling skills, assertiveness & stress management.

Ladybank Counselling Service
Jane Hoffman
64 Commercial Road
Ladybank KY15 7JS
T 01337 831669 F 01337 831725
106115.1062@compuserve.com.uk
Professionally qualified counsellors for one-to-one, group or supervision work. Person-centered approach. Brochure on request.

Zinaida Lewczuk
Zinaida Lewczuk
88 Hepburn Gardens
St Andrews KY16 9LN
T 01334 474745
Freelance counsellor & therapist. Particular areas of expertise are stress, self-esteem, relationships, bereavement, sexual abuse, eating disorders. Fees depend of financial circumstances. Available by appt.

EDUCATION

Dundee Association of Women Graduates
Mrs Hilary Nimmo
4 Duntrune Terrace
West Ferry
Dundee DD5 1LF
T 01382 477364
Meets once a month on Tue evenings at Methodist Church, 20 Marketgait, Dundee. Aims to foster friendship among university women in the world. Encourages research & stimulates interests of university women.

ETHNIC MINORITIES

Muslim Women Group
Mrs Shamim Akhtar Saleem
68 Barclay Street
Cowdenbeath KY4 9LD
T 01383 511705
Encouraging Muslim women & girls to be active in the community; introducing Muslim culture to younger generations.

FINANCE

Douglas & Price Associates
Roberta Goodall
13 Meldrum Road
Kirkcaldy KY2 5LD
T 01592 595333 F 01592 595890
Advising on investments, savings, pensions, protection contract & mortgages. Providing a full financial planning service, either on a fee or commission basis. Open Mon-Fri 9 am-5 pm; Sat 9.30 am-12 noon.

Judy Hume Financial Services
Judy Hume
19a Barossa Place
Perth PH1 5HH
T 01738 627515 F 01738 441315
Independent financial advisor. Professional & confidential advice on investments, pensions, life assurance & financial planning. Specialist advice for teachers, lecturers & professional women.

HEALTH

Breast Care Service
SOPD Victoria Hospital
Hayfield Road
Kirkcaldy KA2 5AH
T 01592 643355
Psychological/emotional care & support. Breast prosthesis. Home visits. Self help group.

Coping with Hysterectomy and Menopausal Problems (CHAMP)
DCVS
2 Halbeath Road
Dunfermline
Meets third Thurs of each month at above address. For women who have had hysterectomies or suffer from menopausal problems.

Dundee Menopause Support Group
Marion Campbell, Health Education Officer
Health Education Unit
7 Dudhope Street
Dundee DD1 1JX
T 01382 228213
Meets Sat mornings at six-week intervals at Kandahar House, Meadowside, Dundee. Aim is to afford women facing the menopause the opportunity to share their experiences with others in the same position.

Dunfermline Osteoporosis Society
83 Wedderburn Crescent
Dunfermline KY11 4RY
T 01383 729829

Premenstrual Support Group
DCVS
14 Halbeath Road
Dunfermline
Support for PMS sufferers.

Road to Recovery Breast Cancer Support Group
Red Cross Centre
Maygate
Dunfermline
Self-help group for women having undergone breast surgery. Meets last Thurs of each month at above address.

Women's Health and Family Project
Sheena Keeley, Coordinator
1 Russell Place
Hilltown

SCOTLAND - DUNDEE, TAYSIDE & FIFE

Dundee DD3 7RU
T 01382 810230
Open Mon-Thurs 9 am-4 pm; Fri 11 am-4 pm. Free, anonymous, confidential help. Healthy eating group, sexuality surgery, money advice, girls' group, well woman, contraceptive advice & supplies, etc.

LEGAL MATTERS

Calders Solicitors
Miss Mary Crighton
10 Whitehall Street
Dundee DD1 4AQ
T 01382 2224391 F 01382 202924
Open Mon-Fri 9 am-5 pm; Sat 9 am-noon.

Fords Solicitors
Irene Dick
15 Tolbooth Street
Kirkcaldy KY1 1RW
T 01592 640630 F 01592 640622

Kippen Campbell W. S.
Deirdre A Beaton/Susan J Wightman
48 Tay Street
Perth PH1 5TR
T 01738 635353 F 01738 643773
Solicitors. Open Mon-Fri 9 am-5 pm & at other times by arrangement. All legal work including matrimonial, business start-up, etc.

Lynn Herbert
Lynn Herbert
4 Mitchell Street
Leven KY8 4HJ
T 01333 429007 F 01333 424800
Open Mon-Fri 9 am-5 pm. Solicitors & notaries. Family law, civil & criminal court work, industrial tribunals, accident claims, debt recovery, conveyancing, wills. Legal aid & free initial interview.

LESBIAN AND BISEXUAL

Fife Friend
Emma
P O Box 19
Kirkcaldy KY1 3JF
T 01592 266688
Telephone helpline & social activities for lesbians, gay men & bisexual women & men.

MEDIA

Catchline Public Relations Ltd
Pamela Caira

40 High Street
Kirkcaldy KY1 1LU
T 01592 643200 F 01592 643201
catchline@fife.ac.uk
Public relations consultancy staffed by 18 specialists in media relations. Event management, publication of in-house newspapers & magazines. Design of corporate literature & strategic communications, etc.

PLACES TO STAY AND EAT

Nova Suite, The
Joan N Keith
3 Scott Street
Brechin DD9 7BZ
T 01356 622381 F 01356 622381
Function suite, concentrating on weddings, dinners & dances. Private parties.

Sunflowers - Coffee Shop & Wine Bar
Ms Linda Butcher
39 Whytes Causeway
Kirkcaldy KY1 1XY
T 01592 646266
Open Mon-Sat 8.30 am-4 pm. Vegetarian food. Homebaking. Soups, toasties, baked potatoes, vegetarian specialities, freshly ground coffee & speciality teas, calorie-counted meals, snacks & cakes.

POLITICS

Women's Citizens Association
Mrs M Chalmers, Secretary
47 Baldovan Terrace
Dundee DD4 6NJ
T 01382 454186
Meets Mon 2-3.30 at Glasite Hall, St Andrew's Church, King Street, Dundee DD1 2JB. To foster citizenship in women; education in political, civic & economic matters; to represent women's interests & experiences.

PREGNANCY/CHILDBIRTH

Caesarian Support Network
8 Henderson Street
Kingseat
Dunfermline
T 01383 733323
Education & information on all matters relating to caesarean delivery. Reassurance for those who have had caesarians who hope to have a vaginal delivery in the future.

SCOTLAND - DUNDEE, TAYSIDE & FIFE

RETAILING

Crescent Health and Beauty Salon
Susan Fraser
76 High Street
Aberdour
Burntisland KY3 0SW
T 01383 860842
Open Tue, Wed, Fri 9 am-6 pm; Thurs 9.30 am-8 pm; Sat 9 am-3 pm. Darphin facials, perfector therapy, manicures, pedicures, electrolysis, waxing, eye treatment, sunbed, massage, aromatherapy.

Edward & Stewart Ltd
Maggie Stewart
439 Clepington Road
Dundee DD3 8RX
T 01382 810728 F 01382 810738
Seat dealers & Citroen specialists; sales of new/used cars & light vans & parts. Servicing of all makes of cars. Open Mon-Fri 8 am-5.30 pm. Late night Thurs 7.30 pm Sat 10 am-4 pm; Sun 2-4 pm.

Pinnochios
Amanda Milton
110 Gray Street
Broughty Ferry
Dundee DD5 2DN
T 01382 480418
Retail outlet: wooden toys, gifts, clothes, bedroom furniture, etc. for children. Open Mon-Sat 9.30 am-5 pm.

Scotia Designer Oils
30 Lammerton Terrace
Dundee DD4 7BL
T 01382 461165
Provides range of oils designed to treat spinal & other problems arising from spinal damage. Can make up blends to suit individual requirements. Sports & foot oils also available & special oils for children.

Scottish Everlastings Ltd
M Louise Carstairs
Carnbee
Anstruther KY10 2RU
T 01333 720318 F 01333 720353
Grower & wholesale supplier of dried flowers. We supply arrangements, silk flowers, basket-ware & import the exotics. We also preserve our own foliage.

SERVICES

Alternative Marketing and Design
Elizabeth S Miller
Edison House
Fullerton Road
Glenrothes KY7 5QR
T 01592 610076 F 01592 610094
alternative@sol.co.uk
Marketing & design, including design & production of promotional material - newsletters, brochures & corporate identities. Copywriting, public relations, advertising, direct mail & telesales, etc.

Aztec Marketing
Miss Brigid Doherty, Partner
57-59 Viewforth Street
Kirkcaldy KY1 3DJ
T 01592 651600 F 01592 651800
aztecmar@aol.com
Business development & marketing company providing strategic planning, marketing strategy, public relations, advertising & design services. Multi-media tools to enhance the corporate image.

Bridg-It Graphics Ltd
Miss Brigid Doherty, Managing Director
57-59 Viewforth Street
Kirkcaldy KY1 3DJ
T 01592 652435 F 01592 650435
Graphic design & marketing consultancy supplying graphic design, advertising & print facilities, corporate identity, illustration, brochures, newsletters, leaflets, signage, packaging, annual reports, etc.

Earnside Enterprises
Linda MacDougall
Number Five
Dunira Street
Comrie PH6 2LJ
T 01764 670762 F 01764 670920
earnside@amslink.demon.co.uk
Open Mon-Fri 9 am-5 pm. Providing professional secretarial service for those without equipment or experience. Photocopying, wordprocessing, spreadsheets, fax transmissions, etc.

Holmes and Holmes
Joan Robertson
127 Albert Street
Dundee DD4 6PR
T 01382 452900 F 01382 454212
Estate agents, mortgage brokers. Open Mon-Fri 9 am-5 pm; Sat 9 am-1pm.

SCOTLAND - DUNDEE, TAYSIDE & FIFE

Jane Mulholland
Jane Mulholland
2 Atholl Place
Perth PH1 5ND
T 01738 621112 F 01738 621155
Employment agency for temporary & permanent position in admin, clerical, secretarial & accounts. Secretarial service: invoicing, payroll, letters, dissertations, etc. For small businesses, students, etc.

Lawside Graphics
Elizabeth Kay
8 Panmure Terrace
Dundee DD3 6HP
T 01382 226426
Artwork & graphic design services for local businesses within a 25-mile radius of Dundee.

Re-Dress Designer Dress Agency
Pauline Smith
43 New Row
Perth PH1 5QA
T 01738 444447
Middle to up-market range of clothing. Wedding outfits with hats & accessories. Day wear. Separates. Evening wear. A haven to rummage in. Open Mon-Sat 10 am-4.30 pm.

SEXUAL ABUSE/RAPE CRISIS

Dundee Rape Crisis Centre
P O Box 83
Dundee DD9 9PF
T 01382 201291
Open Wed and Fri 7-9 pm. Otherwise a 24-hour answering machine. Messages will be returned asap. Appointments can be made. Support & advice for women who have been raped or sexually abused.

Dunfermline Incest Survivors' Group
Maureen Magee
Bruce Street Hall
Bruce Street
Dunfermline KY12 8BS
T 01383 739084 F 01383 622261
Women's group; parents of survivors' group; befriending; counselling. Open to both men & women.

Young Women's Project
Laurie Matthew
Dundee Rape Crisis Centre
P O Box 83
Dundee DD1 9PF

T 01382 206222
Free & confidential support & advice for young women & girls who have been sexually abused. Telephone helpline Thurs 6-8 pm. 24-hour answerphone. Confidential, support, pregnancy testing.

SINGLE PARENTS

Whitfield Project
Lynda Sawers, Administrator
101 Whitfield Drive
Whitfield
Dundee DD4 0DX
T 01382 501972
Part of One Parent Families Scotland network, to enable lone parents to achieve their full potential as individuals or parents. Women's group Tue 6.30-8.30 pm; girls' group Thurs 3.30-4.30 pm. Free creche.

SOCIAL

Monifieth Ladies Circle
Marion Brooksbank, Secretary
8 Palnackie Road
Monifieth
Dundee DD5 4TZ
T 01382 535775
Meets second & fourth Thurs of the month at Monifieth Hotel, Albert Street, Monifieth, Dundee DD5 4JR.

University of Dundee Ladies Club
Mrs Beth Fletcher, President
7 Home Street
Broughty Ferry
Dundee DD5 1DX
T 01382 778144
Social club for wives & female members of staff. Meets about twice each academic term.

SPORTS AND LEISURE

Camperdown Ladies Golf Club
Mrs I Edgar
42 Strathbeg Place
Broughty Ferry
Dundee DD5 3HQ
T 01382 774147
Meets at Camperdown House, Camperdown Park, Dundee. Aims to promote women's golf in the area. Competitions.

Menzieshill Ladies Hockey Club
Veronica Scott, Secretary
3 Blairfield Terrace
Birkhill

Dundee DD2 5PP
T 01382 580802
Trains Mon Ardler Community Centre 8.30-9.30 pm; Tue at Gussie Park 6-7.30 pm; Thurs at Harris Academy Annexe 7-9 pm. Aims to promote hockey & to encourage women of any age & ability to participate.

Support

Ladies Lifeboat Guild
Mrs E Mussen, President
6 Douglas Terrace
Broughty Ferry
Dundee DD5 1EA
T 01382 779923
Meetings are held twice a year at the above address. Aims to raise funds for the local lifeboat. House to house collections & coffee mornings.

Ladies Speakers Club, Dundee
Mrs Vivien Smith, Secretary
Old Smiddy House
Cupar KY15 4NU
T 01337 870259
Meets at the Royal Tay Yacht Club, 34 Dundee Road, Broug, Dundee on alternate Mon evenings at 7.35 pm. Aims to increase women's self-confidence & to improve communication between women.

Zonta Club
Dr H Duguid, President
1 Collingwood Place
Broughty Ferry
Dundee DD5 2UG
T 01382 778678
Meets first Tue of each month 7.15-9.45 pm. Aims to advance the status of women socially, politically & economically.

Training

Craig Young Training Services
Pat Young
7 Fordell Bank
Dalgety Bay
Dunfermline KY11 5NP
T 01383 824857 F 01383 824857
106067.2535@compuserve.com
Provides personal development training programmes for small to medium enterprises. Particularly interested in designing & conducting training for women.

d'Artagnan Training Ltd
Karen Mackenzie

Dunfermline Conference Centre
Halbeath
Dunfermline KY11 5DY
T 01383 722674 F 01383 722665
An approved centre where trainees are trained to recognised national standards & certification. Assessors & verifiers who support the NVQ/SVQ qualifications are also trained.

Fife Adult Guidance and Education Services
Anne Macintyre
Auchterderran Centre
Woodend Road
Cardenden KY15 0NE
T 01592 414738 F 01592 414750
Free, independent advice & information service on education, training & employment. Workshops specifically for women on career development.

LFA Ltd
Lorna Ann Finlay
7 Bennochy Avenue
Kirkcaldy KY2 5QE
T 01592 640878 F 01592 640878
Training consultancy. Training for success in health & safety, SCOTVECs in care, assessor training, investors in people advice, bespoke training.

Mid Fife Business Trust Ltd
Elizabeth Dosso
Mid Fife Business Shop
Enterprise Centre
Mitchelston Drive
Kirkcaldy KY1 3NF
T 01592 652552 F 01592 650550
Enterprise trust, providing information, advice & training for business start-ups & small businesses, including specialist programmes for 'women into business'.

School of Colour, The
Mrs Jean Braes
Woodhead Farm
Culross KY12 8ET
T 01383 880270 F 01383 880465
Image consultancy training school. Further details on application.

Women's Aid

Angus Women's Aid
Tayside
T 01241 431659

Advice & support for battered women & their children. Refuge for four families. Covers a large rural area.

Dundee Women's Aid
First Floor
2 Union Street
Dundee DD1 4BH
T 01382 202525
24-hour phone number for advice & support: 01382 202525. Office hours are Mon-Fri 10 am- 4 pm. Information, support & safe refuge to abused women & any accompanying children. Free & confidential.

Dunfermline Women's Aid
73 Campbell Street
Dunfermline KY12 0QW
T 01383 732289 F 01383 625718
Providing refuge, information & support to women & their children (if any) who have suffered domestic abuse. Office opening times Mon-Fri 9 am-3 pm. On-call service out with office times.

Kirkcaldy District Women's Aid
Barbara McCormack
15 Nicol Street
Kirkcaldy KY1 1NY
T 01592 261008

Perth Women's Aid
9 York Place
Perth PH2 8EP
T 01738 639043
24-hour telephone for information & support. A refuge for abused women & their children. Office hours are Mon & Fri 9.30 am-12.30 pm; Wed 10 am-4 pm.

EDINBURGH & LOTHIANS

ACCOMMODATION

Brenda House - Aberlour Child Care Trust
Wendy Pretswell, Deputy Project Leader
7 Hay Road
Edinburgh EH16 4QE
T 0131 669 6676 F 0131 657 4768
For women with drug & alcohol dependencies & their children. Three core service phases: residential rehabilitation, non-residential services & supportive/respite accommodation. Referrals from any source.

Edinburgh Lodging House Association
the staff
Cranston Street Hostel
2 Cranston Street
Edinburgh EH8 8BE
T 0131 669 2315 F 0131 557 2338
Offers temporary emergency accommodation to homeless women aged 18+. Six self-catering flats providing single bedrooms with shared kitchen & bathrooms for up to 20 women. One is wheelchair accessible.

Pathway Project
ask for project worker
77 Buccleuch Street
Edinburgh EH8 9LS
T 0131 662 4166
Provides long-term shared accommodation for young women affected by sexual abuse. A safe house with strictly confidential address. A two-year time limit on stay. Available to women aged 16-21 years.

ARTS AND CRAFTS

Msfits Theatre Company, The
Fiona Knowles
119 Marchmont Road
Edinburgh EH9 1HA
T 0131 447 1197 F 0131 447 1197
msfits @argonet.co.uk
One-woman shows. Scottish feminist. Funny. Workshops for women's groups in assertiveness and confidence building. The main aim of the company is to encourage women to value themselves.

Pomegranate Women's Writing Group
Mary McCann
14/1 Dinmont Drive
Edinburgh EH16 5RF
T 0131 666 0158
An Edinburgh-based women's writing group meeting regularly in each others' homes to give criticism & support. Poetry, short stories, plays & songs. Everyone has been published in anthologies & magazines.

CENTRES FOR WOMEN

Number 20 - Women & Children's Centre
Zoe Hoppe/Sally Lynch
20/1 Muirhouse Park
Edinburgh EH4 4RR
T 0131 336 4804
A centre for women of all ages, with or without children. Open Mon-Fri 9 am-4 pm. Counselling, welfare rights, groups & activities, confidential advice & support, drop-in, creche, snacks & teas.

SCOTLAND - EDINBURGH & LOTHIANS

Ratho Community Centre
Lynne Rae, Management Committe Secretary
School Wynd
Ratho EH28 8TT
T 0131 333 1055 F 0131 333 1293
Open Mon-Fri, daytime & evenings. Broad range of educational, social & recreational opportunities for women of all ages. Women's discussion group, women's development project, keep fit, 50+ exercise, etc.

Womanzone
Jean McEwan, Coordinator
49/2 Greendykes Road
Edinburgh EH16 4EJ
T 0131 652 0182
Women's health project. Open Mon-Thurs 9.30 am-4.30 pm.; Fri 9.30 am-1 pm. For all women aged 14 + living in the Craigmillar area. Promoting health & well-being & use of preventative health care, etc.

CHILD CARE AND FAMILY

Craigmillar Out of School Project
George Burgoyne
23 Niddrie Marischal Gardens
Edinburgh EH16 4LX
T 0131 669 5432 F 0131 669 5432
Provides primary school age childcare before & after school, & throughout school holidays for working parents/parents returning to education. Aims is to provide a warm, safe, fun environment for the children.

CRY-SIS
Pauline Peat
21 Falkland Gardens
Edinburgh EH12 6UW
T 0131 334 5317
Another tel no: 0131 539 1533. For women living in Edinburgh. Support & advice with crying babies, temper tantrums, food allergies, sleep disorders.

Homeline
Michele Flockhart
The Patch
Sighthill Primary School
5 Calder Park
Edinburgh EH11 4NF
T 0131 538 7400
Open Mon-Thurs (am-5 pm; Thurs 9.30 am-5 pm. A range of services for parents that aims to give support & build up confidence, including activity groups, individual counselling, Pal a Parent service.

COMPUTERS/IT

BrainPool
Isabel Willshaw
1 Admiral Terrace
Edinburgh EH10 4JH
T 0131 229 1576
isabel.willshaw@brainpool.co.uk
International network & learning community for people exploring new ways of working & being. Organizes workshops & events which stimulate creativity, self-development & new approaches to work.

Edinburgh Women's Training Centre
Christine Doherty
5 Hillside Crescent
Edinburgh EH7 5DY
T 0131 557 1139 F 0131 557 8167
Open Mon-Fri 9 am- 5 pm. Training for Edinburgh women aged 25 & over who are unemployed with few or no qualifications. Computing, electronics, personal development.

CONTRACEPTION/WELL WOMAN

Family Planning and Well Woman Services
Dr Anna Glasier, Director
C/o Edinburgh Healthcare NHS Trust
18 Dean Terrace
Edinburgh EH4 1NL
T 0131 3332 7941 F 0131 332 2931
Operates in 20 locations throughout Lothian. Phone above number for local clinic. All services free & confidential. Provision includes contraception, referral for termination of pregnancy, well woman screening.

Lothian Brook Advisory Centre
Dr Val McGregor
2 Lower Gilmore Place
Edinburgh EH3 9NY
T 0131 229 3596 F 0131 221 1486
Contraception, sexual health advice & counselling for young people. Open Mon, Tue, Fri 9.15-11.50 am, Mon (drop-in nurse) 3-4.30 pm, Sat 9.30-11.50 am, Thurs 12.30-3 pm, Mon-Wed 7-9 pm, Thurs 6-8 pm.

COUNSELLING AND THERAPY

Children's Counselling Service
Hazel Dorey/Sally Lynch
C/o Number 20 Women & Children's Centre
20/1 Muirhouse Park
Edinburgh EH4 4RR

T 0131 336 4804
Counselling for school age children & their families living in north west Edinburgh run by Family Care. To make contact, write or phone or contact the centre direct. Meetings ususally take place at the centre.

Cullen Centre
Maggie Gray, Jean Saddler
29 Morningside Park
Edinburgh EH10 5HF
T 0131 537 6000
For people with eating & other non-psychotic disorders such as depression, post-traumatic stress disorder. Use of behaviour therapy on a day-patient & out-patient basis. Therapy for childhood sexual abuse.

Wellspring
Anita Alexander
13 Smith's Place
Edinburgh EH6 8NT
T 0131 553 6660 F 0131 553 4506
Psychotherapy & counselling. Trained counsellors/therapists working for people with stress, anxiety, depression. Charges on a sliding scale. Office hours Mon-Fri 9.30 am-4 pm. Not only for women.

DISABILITY

Grapevine Disability Information Service
Morag Holden
8 Lochend Road
Edinburgh EH6 8BR
T 0131 555 4200 F 0131 554 1661
Open Mon-Fri 9 am-5 pm., & 24-hour ansaphone. Free, confidential service provided to anyone in the Lothian region. Information on eg sheltered housing, orange badges, wheelchairs, form filling, etc.

Lothian Coalition of Disabled People
Barbara Howie
8 Lochend Road
Edinburgh EH6 8BR
T 0131 555 2151 F 0131 554 1661
A group of disabled people aiming to bring about changes in services to disabled people & challenge stereotyped images. There is a women's group which has compiled positive images of women with disabilities.

EDUCATION

Adult Learning Project, The
Joan Bree
184 Dalry Road
Edinburgh EH11 2EP
T 0131 337 5442 F 0131 337 9316
Encourages active participation in the learning process. Women-only classes include: Scottish women, past & present; Women & folksong; women's mixed instrument workshop; women's writing group.

Kirkliston Community Education Centre
Brian Kennedy, Community Education Worker
Queens Ferry Road
Kirkliston EH29 9AR
T 0131 333 4214
SCOTVEC & further education classes specifically targetted at women, young mothers & women returners. Also tea time club, keep fit, parents & toddlers, step class, toy library, senior club & art group.

Lothian Women's Forum
Barbara Smith
C/o WEA Scotland
Riddle's Court
322 Lawnmarket
Edinburgh EH1 2PG
T 0131 226 3456
A women's education forum aiming to put on courses to meet the needs of women, & to open up the debate on women's education generally. New members welcome.

Norwood Community Education Centre
Brian Kennedy, Community Education Worker
Ratho Station Road
Ratho Station
Newbridge EH28 8PT
T 0131 333 1021
SCOTVEC & further education classes specifically targetted at women, young mothers & women returners. Also tea time club, toy library, senior club, keep fit, parent & toddlers & step classes.

ETHNIC MINORITIES

All Pakistan Women's Association
Mrs Ghazala Farooq, Chair
22 Buccleuch Street
Edinburgh EH8 9JR
T 0131 557 9262 F 0131 557 2062
For the welfare of isolated Pakistani ladies. For them to meet each other by holding talks & seminars. Social & cultural events to promote our culture. Annual outings. Charity work. Tel 0131 667 7550 evenings.

Black Community Development Project
Khalida Hussain/Agnes Kinnaird
Room D6
Craigroyston High School
Pennywell Road
Edinburgh EH4 4HP
T 0131 467 7990 F 0131 467 7991
Main aim is to combat racism. Office open from 9 am- 5 pm during school term times. There is a women's group which meets on Thurs from 12.30-2.30 pm.

Bonnyrigg Ethnic Minority Women's Group
Shamin Joshi
7 Bellfield Avenue
Eskbank
Dalkeith EH22 3JT
T 0131 663 9248
Meets Mon & Wed 9.30-11.30 am ESOL (Scotvec module). Also computing, cooking & art.

Canopy
Tara McLaren or Kieran Kutwaroo
C/o Lothian Racial Equality Council
14 Forth Street
Edinburgh EH1 3LH
T 0131 556 0441
A forum for Black & minority ethnic women in the Lothian area. Does not meet on a regular basis.

Leith Sikh Community Groups
Trishna Singh/Mary Hastie
19 Smith's Place
Leith
Edinburgh EH6 8NT
T 0131 553 4737 F 0131 553 4737
Aims to promote the education & well-being of sikh women & children by providing support, learning & educational opportunities. Office Hours Mon-Fri 10 am-4 pm.

Nari Kallyan Shangho
Naina Minhas
Darroch Annexe
7 Gillespie Street
Edinburgh EH3 9NH
T 0131 221 1915 F 0131 221 1915
Open Mon-Fri 9 am-4 pm. Main aim is to alleviate deprivation & isolation experienced by South Asian women & children living in Edinburgh.

Saheliya
Saheliya staff
10 Union Street
Edinburgh EH1 3LU
T 0131 556 9302 F 0131 556 9302
Black & ethnic minority women's health organisation. Counselling & one-to-one support, group support, complementary therapies, befriending (home visits, hospital visits, outings), etc.

Sisterhood (Edinburgh)
Miss Shamina Vehalil
400 Ferry Road
Inverleith
Edinburgh EH5 2AA
T 0131 552 0218 F 0131 447 2062
For young Muslim ladies. Meets Sun 12-2 pm. Religious (Islamic) activities. Other functions and festivals are organised. Badminton classes are held for group members.

Wester Hailes Against Racism Project
Nasra Nabi
16/1 Murrayburn Place
Edinburgh EH11 3RR
T 0131 458 4135
Black community development project. A female development worker develops initiatives to meet the needs of local Black women. Black women's group & young Black women's group (aged 10-14).

GIRLS/YOUNG WOMEN

Fort Community Wing
Kenny Pringle
Fort Primary School
North Fort Street
Leith
Edinburgh EH6 4HF
T 0131 553 1074
Children & youth clubs. Various women's groups, which always operate with a creche.

Lothian Girls' Work Group
Heather Muchamore
Dunford House
7 Boroughloch Lane
Edinburgh EH8 9NL
T 0131 667 1828 F 0131 667 9862
Support to workers & groups involved in work with girls & young women. Meetings, forums, resource base, information, networking, events. To enable girls & young women in Lothian to develop their full potential.

SCOTLAND - EDINBURGH & LOTHIANS

Pilmeny Development Project
Carol Scarth/Anne Munro
19/21 Buchanan Street
Leith
Edinburgh EH6 8SQ
T 0131 553 2559 F 0131 554 8671
For young people aged 16-25. Advice on welfare rights; recreational activities; occasional outings. Also women's groups, eg in 1997 a women & health group, looking at smoking & health.

Pilton Youth Programme
Gilly Hainsworth
42 Ferry Road Avenue
Edinburgh EH4 4AT
T 0131 332 9815 F 0131 538 7268
Offers support, counselling, groupwork & informal education to young people aged 12-18. There are a number of girls-only resources & the importance of female only environments is emphasised.

Stepping Stones for Young Parents
Pat Haikney
126 Crewe Road North
Edinburgh EH5 2NE
T 0131 551 1632
Offers individual support & group activities to young parents & their children who live in the greater Pilton area of Edinburgh. Also caters for pregnant teenagers. Open Mon-Thurs 9 am-4 pm.

Stopover
Orlean Harbinson
9 Mayfield Gardens
Newington
Edinburgh EH9 2AX
T 0131 667 2068
An emergency accommodation project for homeless 16-21-year-olds. Six bed are always kept free for women.

HEALTH

Body Positive (Lothian)
37-39 Montrose Terrace
Edinburgh EH7 5DJ
T 0131 652 0754 F 0131 661 9100
Support for those living with HIV/AIDS. Advice & information; support groups; one-to-one support; welfare advice; legal advice; complementary therapies, etc. Phone for times of opening or for an appointment.

Buddy Service
Jenny Heath
C/o Waverely Care Trust
4a Royal Terrace
Edinburgh EH7 5AB
T 0131 556 3959 F 0131 556 5045
For people who are HIV positive or have an AIDS diagnosis. Confidential one-to-one befriending service. Emotional support with everyday living. If you want a Buddy, contact the Buddy Service Coordinator.

Edinburgh & Lothian Council on Alcohol
Meichelle Walker
40 Shandwick Place
Edinburgh EH2 4RT
T 0131 225 8888 F 0131 220 4090
Provides a one-to-one counselling service, information & advice for anyone affected by their own or someone else's alcohol problem, throughout the Lothians.

Harm Reduction Team
Jim Chanley, Team Leader
The Spittal Street Centre
22-24 Spittal Street
Edinburgh EH11 2HY
T 0131 537 8326 F 0131 537 8303
Open Mon, Wed, Thurs Fri 10 am-4 pm, Tue 1-6 pm. Free, confidential service offering HIV, safer sex & safer drug use advice. Needle exchange, free condoms & pregnancy testing throughout Lothian.

LIBRA - Women and Alcohol Project
Justine Dickson
4 Norton Park
Edinburgh EH7 5RS
T 0131 661 0111
Open Mon-Thurs, day & evening. Appointments. Help for women concerned about their own or someone else's drinking. Free one-to-one counselling, self-help & support groups. Training, alcohol awareness workshops.

Marie Curie Cancer Care
Sarah Grotrian
21 Rutland Street
Edinburgh EH1 2AH
T 0131 229 9214 F 0131 229 9887
Providing free nursing care & support for people with cancer & their families. Care is backed up by an education programme & research.

SCOTLAND - EDINBURGH & LOTHIANS

Milestone House
Ruth Murie
113 Oxgangs Road North
Edinburgh EH14 1EB
T 0131 441 6989 F 0131 441 6989
Offers residential care for all people infected with HIV & support for carers. Purpose-built hospice & respite care centre with interdisciplinary team. Arts programme available. Some child care also available.

Wester Hailes Health Project
Cath Elliot, Coordinator
6 Hailesland Place
Edinburgh EH14 2SL
T 0131 442 4387
Open Mon, Wed 9.30 am-4.30 pm; Tue 9.30 am-9.30 pm; Thurs 9.30 am-8 pm; Fri 9.30 am-1 pm. Promotes awareness of health issues in Wester Hailes. First aid courses, assertiveness training, etc.

Women and HIV/AIDS Network
Hazel Dawson, Administrator
13a Great King Street
Edinburgh EH3 6QW
T 0131 557 5199 F 0131 556 5722
Training & information sessions: HIV - prevention of infection, general information, sexuality, safer sex & issues for women, loss & bereavement, talking with children. Newsletter. Information resource bank.

LARGER/TALLER WOMEN

Big Ideas
Rosemary McKinnel
96 West Bow
Edinburgh EH1 2HH
T 0131 226 2532 F 0131 226 2532
Large size fashion from Scandanavia, USA, Italy & Germany. Open Mon-Sat 10 am-5.30 pm. Sizes 14-30.

Cocoon
28 Victoria Street
Edinburgh EH1 2JW
T 0131 226 2327
Fashionable rain wear, any size, any length.

Long Tall Sally
1 Victoria Street
The Grassmarket
Edinburgh EH1 2HE
T 0131 225 8330

Clothes for the taller woman sizes 12-20.
Open Mon, Tue, Wed, Fri & Sat 9.30 am-5.30 pm; Thurs 9.30 am-7 pm.

LESBIAN AND BISEXUAL

Edinburgh Bisexual Group
C/o Lesbian, Gay and Bisexual Centre
58a-60 Broughton Street
Edinburgh EH1 3SA

Lesbian and Gay Switchboard
P O Box 169
Edinburgh EH1 3UU
T 0131 557 0751

Lesbian, Gay and Bisexual Centre
Ian Dunn
58a-60 Broughton Street
Edinburgh EH1 3SA
T 0131 557 1662 F 0131 558 1683
Office space & meeting room for use by various organisations.

LGB Community Project Ltd
Kate Fearnley
LGB Centre
60 Broughton Street
Edinburgh EH1 3SA
F 0131 558 1683
Community centre for lesbian, gay & bisexual people, their families & friends. Cafe (licensed), gift shop, meeting-room. Pride Scotland HQ. Bisexual phoneline: 0131 557 3620 - Thurs 7.30-9.30 pm.

Lothian Lesbian Line
Justine Dickson, Deputy Coordinator
P O Box 169
Edinburgh EH1 3UU
T 0131 557 0751

Pride Scotland
Laura Norris, Human Resources Manager
58a Broughton Street
Edinburgh EH1 3SA
T 0131 556 8822
pridescotland@drink.demon.co.uk
Organises annual lesbian, bisexual & gay men festival in Scotland. Aims to create a focus through which lesbians, bisexuals & gay men of Scotland can project their unity, diversity, dignity & right to equality.

Student Lesbian Gay and Bisexual Society
C/o Lesbian, Gay and Bisexual Centre

58a-60 Broughton Street
Edinburgh EH1 3SA

LIBRARIES/ARCHIVES

Ethnic Library Service of Edinburgh City Libraries
Shahida Allanddin
McDonald Road Library
2 McDonald Road
Edinburgh EH7 4LU
T 0131 529 5643 F 0131 529 5646
For women in Edinburgh. Open Mon, Wed 10 am-8.30 pm; Tue, Thurs, Fri 10 am-4.30 pm; Sat 9 am-1 pm. To provide people from minority ethnic communities with access to written and/or visual material.

MEDIA

Catchword
Gail Purvis
680 Old Dalkeith Road
Edinburgh EH22 1RR
T 0131 654 2459
gail@mabig.demon.co.uk
Industrial & business journalist & editor specialising in computers & electronics. Freelance writing, market research & public relations. Has founded three weekly IT & electronic papers.

OLDER WOMEN

Edinburgh & Leith Age Concern
Mrs Penny Fleming, Coordinator
Dalry House
15 Orwell Place
Edinburgh EH11 2AD
T 0131 467 7118
Open Mon-Fri 10 am-4 pm. Aims to improve quality of life for older people. Information, befriending housebound, socially isolated & frail older people in Edinburgh, & counselling.

PLACES TO STAY AND EAT

Amaryllis Guest House
Lynne Melrose
21 Upper Gilmore Place
Edinburgh EH3 9NL
T 0131 229 3293
Women-friendly guest house run by women. 3 family rooms, 1 double room & twin en suite. Phone for up-to-date price list.

Aries Guest House
Stella Robertson
5 Upper Gilmore Place
Edinburgh EH3 9NW
T 0131 229 4669
Woman-owned & woman-friendly guest house. 2 double, 2 twin, 1 single bedroom. 2 shared bathrooms, TV. Vegetarians catered for; children & disabled women welcome; no pets. Phone for price list.

Armadillo Guest House
P O'Donnell
12 Gilmore Place
Edinburgh EH3 9NQ
T 0131 229 6457
Woman-owned & women-friendly guest house. CH, TV, bath/shower rooms. Full Scottish breakfasts/late breakfasts. Phone for up-to-date price list.

Stonewall Cafe-Bar
Lesbian, Gay and Bisexual Centre
58a-60 Broughton Street
Edinburgh EH1 3SA
Open seven days a week from noon-9.30 pm (Sun until 5.30 pm) Serves wholesome & reasonably priced meals & snacks. Offers a place for lesbians, bisexuals, gay men & transsexuals to meet.

POLITICS

Scottish Women's Action Network
Sarah Morton
87 Joppa Road
Edinburgh EH15 2HB
T 0131 669 1971

PREGNANCY/CHILDBIRTH

Breast Feeding Support Group
Margaret Lancaster and Mary Miller
296b Colinton Road
Edinburgh EH13 0LB
T 0131 441 1906
Meets Mon 11.30 a.m-12.30 pm. No charge. For breast feeding mothers to support each other.

Lifeline Pregnancy Counselling and Care
Mrs Sarah Home
7a Albany Street
Edinburgh EH1 3PY
T 0131 557 2060
Free, confidential counselling to women with an unwanted pregnancy, miscarriage, infertility, post abortion trauma, etc. Free pregnancy tests. Open Mon-Fri 9.30 am-3.30 pm. Also telephone counselling.

Lothian Home Birth Support Group
Sarah Morton
87 Joppa Road
Edinburgh EH15 2HB
T 0131 669 1971
Sarah-Morton@ccis.org.uk
Supports women who want to have home births. Campaigns for better access to home birth in the Lothian area. Support is provided by telephone & monthly meetings.

RACIAL EQUALITY

YWCA Roundabout Centre
Kate Betney
4b Gayfield Place
Edinburgh EH7 4AB
T 0131 556 1168
Committed to the eradication of racism. Under 5 multicultural creche. Cantonese speaking women's group. Drop-in women's group. Women's summer project. Music & drama group for Punjabi/Urdi speaking women.

RELIGIOUS ORGANISATIONS

Quest
C/o Lesbian, Gay and Bisexual Centre
58a-60 Broughton Street
Edinburgh EH1 3SA
An organisation that meets at the centre for lesbian and gay Catholics.

RIGHTS

Rights Office, The
P O Box 12775
Edinburgh EH8 9YG
T 0131 667 6339
Open for advice & information on welfare, disability, housing & employment rights, debt counselling, etc Southside Community Centre, 117 Nicolson Street, Edinburgh Mon & Wed 10 am-12.30 pm. Free service.

SERVICES

Champfleurie Consultants
Hazel Bech
Champfleurie School House
Kingscavil by Linlithgow
West Lothian EH49 6NA
T 01506 842476 F 01506 846476
Consultancy firm specialising in management development. Occupational psychologists.

Grant Chiropody
E Dawn Grant
The Tower
36 Braehead
Bo'ness EH51 9DW
T 01506 826286
Professional service for people's feet.

Information Service, The
Kay Goodall
12 Craiglockhart Drive North
Edinburgh EH14 1HT
T 0131 4433645 F 0131 455 8802
100653.162@compuserve.com
Publishing; database design & management; research; listings services. Publishes publicity material, staff newsletters, compiles directories & reference books, produces tailor-made company diaries.

SEXUAL ABUSE/RAPE CRISIS

Edinburgh Rape Crisis Centre
Lily Greenan
P O Box 120
Brunswick Road
Edinburgh EH17 5XX
T 0131 557 6737 F 0131 557 6737
101670.27@compuserve.com

SINGLE PARENTS

Joint Parenting Support Group
C/o One Parent Families Scotland
13 Gayfield Square
Edinburgh EH1 3NX
T 0131 556 3899 F 0131 557 9650
Meets on first & third Thurs of each month 7.30-9 pm. For separated & divorced parents sharing parenting of children with ex-partners experiencing practical /emotional difficulties. For one partner only.

SOCIAL

Bo'ness Women's Groups
Yvonne Dougall
139 North Street
Bo'ness EH51 9ND
T 01506 778551
Both groups meet for educational, recreational needs & to discuss current topics of interest. One group meets Tue 8-10 pm & the other Fri 10 am-12 noon. Both meet at the Bo'ness Recreation Centre.

SCOTLAND - EDINBURGH & LOTHIANS

Sports and Leisure

Norwood Women's Group
Karen Grubb
Norwood Community Wing
Station Road
Ratho Station EH28 8PT
T 0131 333 0121
Outdoor activities & informal learning on subjects of interest to the women as decided by the women themselves, eg Alexander Technique, self-hypnosis, golf, skiing, etc.

Support

Colinton Mother & Baby Group
Margaret Lancaster and Joyce Tibbuht
Colinton Surgery
296b Colinton Road
Edinburgh EH13 0LB
T 0131 441 1906
For first-time mothers. A six-weekly session of informal topics, chosen by group members. Attendance by invitation. Meets at Colinton Parish Church. No charge. Aims to offer support & provide information.

Oasis Women's Support Group
Jane Hislop
40 Shandwick Place
Edinburgh EH2 4RT
T 0131 225 8508 F 0131 220 0028
Meets at Gilmerton Community Centre, Drum Street on Mon, Thurs, Fri 10 am-12 pm & Wed 2-4 pm. For women run by women. Free creche. Provides support/self-help for women who are lonely or stressed.

Women's Royal Voluntary Service - Scottish Division
19 Grosvenor Crescent
Edinburgh EH12 5EL
T 0131 337 2261 F 0131 346 8364
Services are divided into family, hospital, food & emergency services. They include meals on wheels, hospital shops, tea & coffee bars, contact centres, family holidays & lunch clubs.

Training

IMS Training and Development
Ian Ramage, Chief Executive
107 McDonald Road
Edinburgh EH7 4NW
T 0131 557 3796 F 0131 557 9151
Training, advice & counselling to help people who are unemployed & promoting economic development.

Quirk-Co
Lesley Quirk
39 Palmerston Place
Edinburgh EH12 5AU
T 0131 527 6060 F 0131 527 6070
100256.3374@compuserve.com
Consultancy, training & development for women & organisations employing women.

Scottish Birth Teachers Association (SBTA)
Nadine Edwards
40 Leamington Terrace
Edinburgh EH10 4JT
T 0131 229 6259 F 0131 229 6259
Occasional two-year training courses (part time). Birth groups run by SBTA members focus on preparation for normal birth where possible. Limited 'doulba' service available. Occasional study days available.

Women and New Directions
Natalie Robertson
Craigroyston Community High School
Pennywell Road
Edinburgh EH4 4QP
T 0131 332 5541 F 0131 332 5541
fr81@dial.pipex.com
For women living in the greater Pilton area of Edinburgh. One-to-one guidance & short courses for women who want to change their lives. Free childcare (creche & childminding). Open Mon-Thurs 10 am-4 pm.

Women Onto Work
Jennifer Goodman
137 Buccleugh Street
Edinburgh EH8 9NE
T 0131 662 4514 F 0131 662 0989
Runs courses for unemployed women in Great Pilton, Craigmillar & Wester Hailes housing estates & city-wide courses for black minority ethnic women & women with disabilities.

Women's Aid

Edinburgh Women's Aid
97 Morrison Street
Edinburgh EH3 8BX
T 0131 229 1419
Drop-in Mon-Fri 10 am-3 pm. Six refuges in Edinburgh. Provides accommodation, support, information & counselling for women & their children (if any) who are suffering or who have suffered domestic abuse.

SCOTLAND - FALKIRK & CENTRAL

Shakti Women's Aid
Jacinta J Barker
31 Albany Street
Edinburgh EH1 3QN
T 0131 557 4010 F 0131 556 3284
Run by black women for black women & their children escaping domestic violence. Works for women to challenge & campaign against violence against women. Open Mon-Fri 9.30 am-5 pm. Ansaphone 5 pm-9 am

FALKIRK & CENTRAL

ACCOMMODATION

Falls Retirement Home
Mrs Hilary Martin
Main Street
Killin FK21 8UW
T 01567 820237
24-hour care for elderly people.

ACCOUNTANCY

Ann Fraser
Ann Fraser
4 Manor Steps
Alloa Road
Stirling FK9 5QJ
T 01786 470280
Book-keeping, VAT, wages for small businesses. Tailored systems to suit individual requirements.

ALTERNATIVE THERAPIES

Clinical Aromatherapy
Jennifer Booth
8 Alexandra Drive
Alloa FK10 2DQ
T 01259 218057
Clinical aromatherapy, treatments with essential oils to promote physical and mental well being. Personal consultations to provide best treatment.

Healing Touch
Carol Lloyd
Yetts O' Muckhart
Dollar FK14 7JT
T 01259 781349
Complementary/alternative practitioner. Therapeutic/remedial massage, clinical aromatherapy and reflexology. By appointment only.

Rhona Campbell
Rhona Campbell
12 Dalmorglen Park
Stirling FK7 9JL
T 01786 478121 F 01786 478121
Provides SHEN therapy for positive emotional change and growth as it helps with chronic pain, eating disorders, depression, migraines, pre-menstrual distress, blocked sexual feelings, sexual abuse, etc.

ARTS AND CRAFTS

Camelon Community Project Women's Group
S McLernon
156 Glasgow Road
Camelon FK1 4JA
T 01324 634 090
Meets twice a week 9.30-11-30 am at Camelon Education Centre, Camelon FK1 4AA. The aims are to get together & learn new skills & crafts such as silk screen painting, aromatherapy, & jewellery making.

Falkirk Women Writers
Rene Richards, Tutor
26 Hanover Grange
Grangemouth FK3 8LF
T 01324 474448
Meets Fri 2.30-4 pm from April to December inclusive at Community Education Building, Park Street, Falkirk. Tutoring, critique on members' work, discussions.

Inidvidual Ceramics
Caroline Gage
37 Balfour Street
Alloa FK10 1RU
T 01259 213003
Small, solo business making pottery/ceramics of a very unique & individual type, mainly wall hangings, bells & small jewellery. Most unusual pieces are ceramic bowler hats!

Joyce Macphail, Dressmaker
Joyce Macphail
44 Inverallan Drive
Bridge of Allan FK9 4JP
T 01786 833304
Made-to-measure bridal wear, evening wear and daywear. Curtains and soft furnishings. Fashion alterations. Theatrical and fancy dress costumes made to order.

Langlees Creative Group
Cathy Knox
Langlees Family Centre
26-32 Dunkeld
Langlees FK2 7UD
T 01324 638080

SCOTLAND - FALKIRK & CENTRAL

Meets Mon and Thurs afternoons at above address. Creative arts for women: painting, dancing, music, etc.

Rostrum Promotions
Fiona Paterson
4 Ferniebank Brae
Bridge of Allan FK9 4P5
T 01786 834449   F 01786 833949
An arts management organisation offering total artist management, festival administration, organising tours, etc, mainly in the classical music field and also in the jazz scene.

Share-A-Craft
Moira Weir
165 Bowhouse Road
Grangemouth FK3 0EX
T 01324 666021
Meets Wed 9.30 am-12.30 pm at Community Education Unit, Grangemouth Sports Complex. For women only to exchange craft skills and develop new skills.

BUSINESS SUPPORT SCHEMES
Compact Business Services
Loretta Waddell
17a High Station Road
Falkirk FK1 5LP
T 01324 623400
Administration for small businesses. Self-assessment, setting up book-keeping/computer systems with support. VAT, payroll, tax returns, end of year returns & accounts. Calls at clients' premises free of charge.

Independent Business Women in Scotland (IBIS)
Mrs Alexis Rigby, President
Travail
6 Allanbank Road
Dunblane FK15 0NH
T 01786 823183   F 01786 464837
Meet last Mon of each month in Stirling Management Centre, University of Stirling, Stirling. To promote & support independent/self-employed women.

Stirling Enterprise
Mrs Evelyn Paterson, Enterprise Manager
John Players Buildings
Stirling FK7 7RP
T 01786 463416   F 01786 479611

Enterprise trust offering advice/ support in starting a business, expanding current business, advice on grants & loans, marketing, business development, personal development training. Free for local people.

Women's Enterprise Unit
Christina Hartshorn
Scottish Enterprise Foundation
University of Stirling
Stirling FK9 4LA
T 01786 467353   F 01786 450201
christina.hartshorn@stir.ac.u.
Promoting & enabling women to create & manage more effective enterprises. Research & consultancy; post-graduate certificate in Small & Medium Enterprise Management.

CENTRES FOR WOMEN
Clackmannon District Women's and Girls' Resource Project
Pauline Douglas
Unit 1
Claremont Business Centre
Claremont
Alloa FK10 2DE
T 01259 219891   F 01259 211986
Open Mon-Fri 10 am-4 pm. Provides resource information on women's issues. Educational group work, issue-based on subjects such as breastfeeding, self-defence, etc. Computer access. Free service.

CHILD CARE AND FAMILY
Acrewood Nursery
Cathy Ritchie or Samantha Smith
C/o Forthbank Stadium
Springkewe
Stirling FK7 7UW
T 01786 462621   F 01786 446541
Private children's nursery, school holiday club and after school care. Open Mon-Fri 8 am-6 pm. For children aged 2 months-12 years.

Rosemount Nursery School and Out of School Club
Mrs E Flanagan
4 McNabb Street
Dollar FK14 7OJ
T 012259 742571   F 01259 742571
ETPlan@aol.com
Open 8 am-6 pm. Aim is to promote development of children within a secure, safe, healthy & happy environment. Holiday clubs run during school holidays except during Christmas period.

COMPUTERS/IT

ACE Secretarial Services
Eva Gardiner
Alloa Business Centre
Alloa Business Park
Alloa FK10 3SA
T 01259 721454 F 01259 217303
Alloanew@Post.Almac.Co.UK
Short/long-term qualified computer & secretarial staff.

Alloa Women's Technology Centre
Pam Courtney
14 Bank Street
Alloa FK10 1HP
T 01259 211180 F 01259 721347
Provides 12-month full-time training courses for 12 women. Training includes computing, programming, software production & application systems. Training & travel allowances & childcare provided.

Falkirk Women's Technology Centre
Kate Robertson
Unit H
Newhouse Business Park
Newhouse Road
Grangemouth FK3 8LL
T 01324 471000 F 01324 471774
fwtc@zetnet.co.uk
Offers a one-yr full time course to 15 local women. Training develops advanced skills in information technology SVQ level 2. There is a training allowance & childcare allowance. Travel costs are reimbursed.

Prospects Training Centre Ltd
Margaret Silver
Unit 149
Stirling Enterprise Park
Stirling FK7 7RP
T 01786 450380 F 01786 450623
100432,2077@compuserve.com
Workshops offering certificated training to lead industry body standards in: office skills; computing; management; welding; joinery. Assessment of ability to occupational areas for people with disabilities.

Stirling Women's Technology Centre
Anne Marie Gardner, Co-ordinator
The Stirling Arcade
King Street
Stirling FK8 1DN
T 01786 450980 F 01786 448054
Provides one-year full-time courses in computing for unemployed women over the age of 18. Areas of study include data processing principles, programming design, networks, 'C' programming & spreadsheets.

COUNSELLING AND THERAPY

Psychotherapy, Training and Supervision
Benekikte Uttenthal
3 Mount Hope
Bridge of Allan FK9 4RL
T 01786 832768
Individual therapy, couple therapy, family therapy. Practice consultancy & supervision. Training in counselling & interpersonal skills.

ENVIRONMENT

Stirling Women and the Environment
Vivien Roberts
Old Mill Farmhouse
Craigforth
Stirling FK9 4UH
T 01786 461623
For women who care about environmental issues. Meets first Mon of each month 8 pm in the Stirling area. Aims to educate members & local public on sound environmental practice.

EQUAL OPPS

Women in Focus
Carey Sinclair
33 Kerse Gardens
Falkirk FK2 9DY
T 01324 636622
The Forum campaigns for sex equality in all fields, organises events & provides information & networking opportunities for women. Meets once a month Tue 6.30 at a central Falkirk location.

ETHNIC MINORITIES

Asian Women's Group - Falkirk
Nasreen Malik
25 Millar Place
Stirling FK8 1XD
T 01786 462722
Meets every Mon during the daytime at Camelon Education Centre. Educational, support & networking group.

FINANCE

Financial Planning Scotland Ltd
Jean Band
Suite 13 Stirling Enterprise Park
Player Road

SCOTLAND - FALKIRK & CENTRAL

Stirling FK7 7RP
T 01786 450336 F 01786 447604
Financial planning services. Representative of Asa Equity & Law, offering sound advice on pensions, life assurance, savings, investments, PEPS, unit trusts & mortgages.

GIRLS/YOUNG WOMEN

Girls' Group
Nicky Ferguson
Grange Community Centre
Redding Road
Brightons
Falkirk FK2 0AA
T 01324 715921
Meets Thurs 7.30-9.30 pm at above address. Support, integration & networking group for teenage girls with special needs.

Teenage Mums' Group
Mary Hewins
Grange Community Centre
Redding Road,
Brightons
Falkirk FK2 0AA
T 01324 715921
Meets Fri 1.30-3.30 pm at above address. For young women & girls who are either pregnant or who have babies. Opportunity for personal & social development. Access to formal & informal education.

Young Women's Group
Nicky ferguson
Grange Community Centre
Redding Road
Brightons
Falkirk FK2 0AA
T 01324 715921
Meets Tue 1-3.30 pm at above address. Support, networking & activity group for young women.

HEALTH

Aberlour Child Care Trust
Mary McKellar
36 Park Terrace
Stirling FK8 2JR
T 01786 450335 F 01786 473238
Aim is to provide care, help & support for children, young people & families in Scotland whose development or well-being is threatened by disadvantage. Drug & alcohol dependency units & family centres.

Genital Urinary Medicine (GUM) clinic
Falkirk & District Royal Infirmary
Falkirk
T 01324 24000
Phone above number for health advice or 01324 24000 ext 5785 for an appointment. Open Mon, Wed, Thurs 2-5 pm & Tue & Fri 9.30 am-12.30 pm.

MEDECO
Helen Colquhoun
North Lodge of Orchil
Braco
Dunblane FK15 9LG
T 01764 681312 F 01764 681312
medeco@perth.almac.co.uk
Provides medical consultancy to the pharmaceutical & medical device industries. Services include advice about clinical development, design of clinical trials, setup & monitoring of clinical trials.

Orchard House Health Centre
Stirling
T 01786 463448
Phone the above number for health advice or 01786 463448 ext 152 for an appointment. Open Mon, Wed & Thurs 9.30 am-12.30 pm & Tues 2-4 pm.

Stirling Women and Health Project
Sandra, Anne, Sharon
Spittals House
61 Baker Street
Stirling FK8 1DB
T 01786 451770
Aims to empower & improve the well-being of women in the Stirling area. Key elements are empowerment, respect for the individual & intervention work. Drop-in on Tue & Wed 1.30-3.30 pm.

Watt Physiotherapy Clinic
Joan M Watt
Devonvale Crescent
Tillicoultry FK13 6NR
T 01259 750960 F 01259 750960
General out-patient physiotherapy practice with rehabilitation gymnasium. Specialists in orthopaedics & sports injuries. Sports-specific advanced rehabilitation.

LEGAL MATTERS

Allan Grant
Eva Comrie
61 Stirling Street

SCOTLAND - FALKIRK & CENTRAL

Alva FK12 5ED
T 01259 760224
01259 769670
Private practice of solicitors providing general advice regarding all aspects of Scottish law. Eva Comrie is a specialist in family law in matters relating to children & their welfare.

Jardine Donaldson, Solicitors
Fiona Dearing
18-22 Bank Street
Alloa FK10 1HP
T 01259 724411 F 01259 213064
Solicitors' practice covering all aspects of legal work. Open Mon-Fri 9 am-5 pm. Sympathetic to women.

OLDER WOMEN

40+ Women's Group
Eileen Thorburn
67 Main Street
Bonnybridge FK4 1AL
T 01324 814660
Meets fortnightly every second Thurs 1-3 pm at Bonnybridge Community Educational Centre, Bridge Street, Bonnybridge FK4 1AA. Speakers, demonstrations, outings & day trips.

Ladies 50+ Group
Hilda Cumpstey
70 Muirhead Road
Stenhousemuir FK5 4JD
T 01324 554143
Open to any woman over 50. Meets Thurs at the Tryst Community Centre, Stenhousemuir 2-3.30 pm. Provides entertainment & companionship. Annual membership allows use of the facilities of the centre.

PLACES TO STAY AND EAT

Easterhill Farm Trekking Centre
Liana Louie
Easterhill Farm
Gartmore FK8 3SA
T 01877 382875
Trekking & riding centre. Open all year. Lessons, hacking, trekking. Pony rides for children. Fun days & summer camps.

Gean House
Debbie Millar
Tullibody Road
Alloa FK10 2HS
T 01259 213827

Woman-owned & women-friendly. Small country house hotel (4 crown deluxe), open all year. Phone for up-to-date price list.

Riverway Restaurant
Mrs Barbara Bell
Kildean
Stirling FK9 4AN
T 01786 475734 F 01786 446648
Restaurant specialising in functions, weddings dinner dances for all occasions. Open Tue-Sun for lunches & Scottish high teas. Wonderful views to the Ochil hills & Wallace monument.

PUBLISHERS/PUBLICATIONS

Profiles: The Women's Business Directory
Maria Craig
1 Netherton Court
Bridge of Allan FK9 4NE
T 01786 834640 F 01786 832787
profiles@cqm.co.uk
Maria Craig publishes women's business networking directories.

RETAILING

Blossoms
Katrina Scott
3 The Steadings
Redhall Farm
Kerse Road
Stirling FK7 7LU
T 01786 470080
Florist business. Aims to run a quality business at prices people can afford.

Celebration Station
Elizabeth Cowan
1 Station Road
Dunblane FK15 9ET
T 01786 823714
Makes & sells celebration cakes & sweets.

Creative Stencil Designs
Sarah Gleave
Flanders Moss
Station Road
Buchlyvie FK8 3NB
T 01360 850389 F 01360 850565
Manufacturers of stencils for the bakery & DIY home deocrating market. Cad Cam technology. Laser cutting cuts intricate designs in a wide range of materials, including polyester, acrylic, vinyl, wood, paper.

SCOTLAND - Falkirk & Central

Dorothy Brookes
Dorothy Maxwell
7 Princes Street
Falkirk FK1 1LS
T 01324 612460
Retailer of high quality ladies' fashions. Also retails high quality ladies' fashions & gifts at 280-282 Stonelaw Road, Burnside, Glasgow G73 3RP. Phone for more details.

Dressing Up Box, The
Mrs F Hamilton
64 Henderson Street
Bridge of Allan FK9 4HS
T 01786 832090
Ladies' dress & hat hire & sale. Also sells & hires top quality costume jewellery.

Happymeats
Paloma Sire
Blairingone Mains Farm
Dollar FK14 7NT
T 01259 742962 F 01259 742962
Production of traditional, fruit-fed, free-range pork & bacon for sale to top chefs & gourmet customers with the aim of encouraging commercial but non-intensive rearing of rare breed pigs.

Impromptu
Liz Hallam
11 Upper Craigs
Stirling FK8 2DG
T 01786 472948
Ladies quality shoe shop selling shoes, boots, handbags & belts. Open Mon-Sat 9.30 am-5 pm.

J & M Stationers
Mrs Margaret Galloway
8 Baker Street
Stirling FK8 1BJ
T 01786 462156 F 01786 462156
Stationers open Mon-Sat 9 am-5.30 pm. Aims to satisfy customer requirements & to grow steadily over the next 10 years. 10% off list prices to small businesses.

L-J Designs
Linda-Jane
25 Islay Court
Grangemouth FK3 0HA
T 01324 485929
L-J designs provide a high quality bespoke tailoring & design service for all occasions.

Mad Tarts Clubwear
L-J
25 Islay Court
Grangemouth FK3 0HA
T 01324 485929
Provides exclusive, outrageous & delicious clubwear for babes with attitude. We supply wholesale to funky retail outlets or direct to our customers by mail order & party nights.

Scottish Samplers
Frances Rankin
6 Bishops Gardens
Dunblane FK15 0AW
T 01786 824272 F 01876 824272
Design & marketing of high-quality, well researched embroidery kits, both traditional & contemporary. Wholesale & mail order.

Servisart
16 Pine Court
Doune FK16 6JE
T 01786 841005 F 01786 841005
Picture framing; original paintings. Open almost any time - just phone first.

Village Glass
Karen Young
Queen's Lane
Bridge of Allan FK9 4NY
T 01786 832137 F 01786 834431
Decorative glassware. Open Mon-Fri 9 am-5 pm.

Services

A & A Imaging Services
Mrs Anne Park
Unit 1
Dalderse Avenue
Falkirk FK2 7EF
T 01324 624173 F 01324 624173
Microfilming of plans & paperwork ; C D rom; optical disk; plan copying while you wait. New & used equipment. Suppliers.

A-Z Typing Services
Susan Gillon
6 Ochilview
Kincardine-on-Forth
Alloa FK10 4QG
T 01259 730504 F 01259 730816
101464.1235@compuserve.com
A one-person business offering a word-processing, audio-typing & temping service.

SCOTLAND - FALKIRK & CENTRAL

Bartering Company Scotland Ltd
Jean Band
Suite B
Stirling Enterprise Park
Player Road
Stirling FK7 7RP
T 01786 463214   F 01786 447604
Bartering of goods & services.

Beauty Care
Mary E Gillies
12 Holding
Longcroft
Bonnybridge FK4 1SX
T 01324 841226
Mobile beauty treatment. Appointments available Mon-Sat during the daytime & evenings. To help people with health & beauty in the comfort of their own homes.

Fountain Management Services
Pamela McGibbon
47 Fountain Road
Bridge of Allan FK9 4AU
T 01786 833752   F 01786 833752
Management services/business advice undertaken on a full-time or temporary basis. Computer work; dtp; industrial liaison work a speciality.

FPS Mortgage Division
Jean Band
Suite 13
Stirling Enterprise Park
Player Road
Stirling FK7 7RP
T 01786 446263   F 01786 447604
Mortgage brokers.

Grant Chiropody
E Dawn Grant
14 Kerse Lane
Falkirk FK1 1RQ
T 01324 621809
Professional feet treatment.

Initial Approach
Sandra Menoni
4 Beech Road
Dunblane FK15 0LA
T 01786 825777   F 01786 825777
100747.3412@compuserve.com
Introduction & social agency, tailored exclusively for Scots. Two services: 'Introductions' & 'Occasions'. Someone available to take calls from Mon-Fri 10 am-9 pm.

ITC Communicators Club
Marion Graham
8 McLachlan Avenue
St Ninians
Stirling FK7 0PL
T 01786 812261
Helps members gain confidence, develop communication & leadership skills through a programme of practice & constructive evaluation in a friendly & supportive atmosphere.

Margaret Griffith
Margaret Griffith
Croftfoot House
Main Street
Polmont FK2 0PS
T 01324 711105
Beauty therapy.

R E Geddes - Optometrist
Rhona E Geddes
70 High Street
Dunblane FK15 0AY
T 01786 825826
NHS & private eye examinations. Choice of spectacle frames. Contact lens fitting. Open Mon, Thurs and Fri 9 am-1 pm & 2-5.30 pm; Tue 9 am-1 pm & 2-7 pm; Wed & Sat 9 am-1 pm.

SEXUAL ABUSE/RAPE CRISIS

Central Scotland Rape Crisis Group (1)
P O Box 48
Stirling FK8 1YG
T 01786 471771
Free, confidential support for women who have been raped or suffered sexual abuse. Face-to-face counselling. 24-hour answering service. Crisis line: Tue 11 a.m-1 p.m, Thurs 7-9 pm, Sat 1-3 pm.

Central Scotland Rape Crisis Group (2)
P O Box 28
Falkirk FK2 9DG
T 01786 471771
Free & confidential support for women who have been raped or who have suffered sexual abuse. 24-hours answering service. Face-to-face counselling provided.

Open Secret
Catriona Laird
Open Secret
22 Newmarket Street
Falkirk FK1 1JQ

SCOTLAND - FALKIRK & CENTRAL

T 01324 630100 F 01324 635650
Provides a confidential service to adult survivors of childhood sexual abuse. Training for other agencies & support to workers. There is a large resource library. Works in a way which empowers survivors.

SINGLE PARENTS
Maddiston Family Centre Women's Group
Eileen Ward
Maddiston Family Centre
68-70 Forgie Crescent
Maddiston
Falkirk FK2 0LZ
T 01324 711271
Meets Wed 10 am-12 noon at Maddiston Family Centre. An interest group for women attending the Centre, in particular for single mothers. Discussion of topical issues particularly pertaining to women.

SOCIAL
Slamannan Women's Group
Ann Lacey
Slamannan Community Centre
Bank Street
Slamannan FK1 3EZ
T 01324 851548
Meets weekly on Tue 10 am-12 noon at Slamannan Community Centre. Women meet informally to discuss viewpoints & to work to broaden interests & experiences.

SPORTS AND LEISURE
Falkirk Ladies Health Club
J Dunn (Mr)
4/8 Callander Road
Falkirk FK1 1XQ
T 01324 612391 F 01324 612391
Women only 7 days a week, open 9 am-10 pm. Sauna, jacuzzi, steamroom, ladies' gym, toning tables, universal contour wrap. There is a beautician & face perfector.

Stirling Volleyball Club
Shiona Finn
31 Creteil Court
Falkirk FK1 1UL
T 01324 612601
Two ladies' national teams. Training Thurs 7-10 pm. Matches on Sat from September to March.

SUPPORT
Avonbridge Women's Group
Ann Lacey
Slamannan Community Centre
Bank Street
Slamannan FK1 3EK
T 01324 851548
Meets on Wed 930-11.30 am at Avonbridge Welfare Hall. Provides women with skills & confidence to remove perceived barriers & the chance to broaden interests & experience.

Hallglen Women's Group
Christine Christie
Community Education Service
Park Street
Falkirk FK1 1RE
T 01324 611385
Meets Thurs 10 am-12 noon at Ettrickdochart Community Centre, Hallglen. An educational group with discussions & raising of awareness.

Westfield Park Women's Group
Wilma Wolstenholme
Westfield Park Community Centre
Westfield Street
Falkirk FK2 1DT
T 01324 611768
Offers support to women & promotes their well-being. Training, activities of interest & speakers.

Women's Discussion Group
Susan Stewart, Assistant Project Leader
Langlees Family Centre
26-32 Dunkeld
Langlees FK2 7UD
T 01324 638080
Meets Tue 9.30-11.30 am. Speakers on various topics such as sexual abuse, women's aid, money matters, complementary & alternative medicine, etc.

TRAINING
Forth Directions
Lyn Baird
33 High Street
Falkirk FK1 1ES
T 01324 429998 F 01324 429987
Runs courses for women returners covering topics such as confidence building, interview techniques, stress management. Open Mon-Fri 9.30 am-5 pm. Also provides career information & guidance.

Women's Aid

Clackmannan Women's Aid
Sally Pitt/ Jennifer Syire
Greenfield Lodge
Parkway
Alloa FK10 1AF
T 012259 721407
Open 9.30-4.30. Out of hours on-call service via ansaphone. Offers information, support & safe refuge accommodation to abused women with or without children.

Falkirk Women's Aid
8 West Bridge Street
Falkirk FK1 5RQ
T 01324 635661
Provides information, support & refuge to abused women & their children. Open Mon, Wed, Thurs & Fri 10 am-12.30 pm & 1.30-4 pm Tue 10 am-12.30 pm.

Stirling Women's Aid
Anne Shaw
1st Floor
29-31 Friar Street
Stirling
T 01786 470897 F 01786 472674
We provide a comprehensive service of information, support, refuge & follow-up to abused women & their children.

Glasgow & Strathclyde

Accommodation

Hemat Gryffe Drop-in Centre
Famida Ali
Flat 0/1
24 Willow Bank Street
Glasgow G3
T 0141 353 0859 F 0141 647 3421
Provides temporary refuge for women & children of Black, Asian & other ethnic minority groups who have suffered abuse. A 24-hour service. Any messages left on ansaphone are always returned.

Say Women
Carol Fair, Kirsh Hay
1st Floor
19 Waterloo Street
Glasgow G2 6BQ
T 0141 226 3622 F 0141 204 5405
Safe housing for three young women aged 16-25. Up to two-year stay. Crisis counselling/support for survivors. Support/consultancy for staff working with survivors.

Accountancy

Accounting & Bookkeeping Services
Mrs C Richmond
244 Bath Street
Glasgow G2 4JW
T 0141 331 1871 F 0141 332 8986
Accounting and bookkeeping. Financial Accounts. All aspects of maintenance of books of original entry, ie cash book, purchase and sales ledger, trial balance. Income tax, VAT and PAYE.

Andrew Business Services
Liz Andrew
67 Auchenlodment Road
Elderslie
Renfrewshire PA5 9PA
T 01505 323369 F 01505 323369
Provides a service to small businesses in the area. Computerised accounts, payroll, invoicing, credit control, VAT preparation and typing.

Anne G Hansen & Co
Ann G Hansen
3 South Road
Busby
Glasgow G76 8JB
T 0141 644 5486 F 0141 644 1431
Accountants.

Barry Moore & Co
Anne E Moore
43 Woodhead Crescent
Thorywood Grove
Uddingston G11 GLR
T 01698 817819 F 01698 817599
Chartered accountants and chartered taxation advisors.

Bell Barr & Co
Louise D Thomson
2 Stewart Street
Milngavie
Glasgow G62 6BW
T 0141 956 4454 F 0141 956 5660
Chartered accountants.

Martin Aitken & Co
Jayne Clifford
1 Royal Terrace
Glasgow G3 7NT
T 0141 332 0488 F 0141 332 6688
100645.2014@compuserve.con
Chartered accountants and business advisors providing a comprehensive range of services, including tax planning, computer

consultancy, bookkeeping and payroll services for own-managed businesses.

R A Woollard Chartered Accountant
Rosalind
19 Annetyard Drive
Skelmorlie PA17 5BN
T 01475 520699   F 01475 522900
Accountants. Our aim is to help small businesses grow.

Sloan & Co
Jean Sloan
20 Lynton Avenue
Glasgow G46 7JP
T 0141 638 1688
Chartered accountants aiming to provide a personal service to individuals and small businesses.

ALTERNATIVE THERAPIES

Alexander Technique
Hilary Dalby
23 Muirpark Way
Drymen G63 0DX
T 01360 660427   F 01360 660397
The Alexander Technique helps to learn about unecessary tension and to become aware of balance, posture and freedom of movement in everyday activities. Hilary Dalby also teaches in Bridge of Allan.

College of Holistic Medicine
Judith Bolton, Administrator
4 Craigpark
Glasgow G31 2NA
T 0141 554 5808   F 0141 554 9036
Part-time professional diploma courses in therapeutic massage, counselling and psychotherapy. Phone for up-to-date price list.

Complementary Medicine Centre
Ruth Chappell, Clinic Director
11 Park Circus
Glasgow G3 GAX
T 0141 332 4924   F 0141 353 3783
Natural therapy centre providing acupuncture, herbal medicine, homoeopathy, allergy testing, remedial massage and counselling.

Healing Sound Centre
Sundara Forsyth
10 Doune Gardens
Glasgow G20 6DJ
T 0141 946 9764
Sundara Forsyth works as a humanistic counsellor, Shiatsu practitioner & craniosacral therapist. She also works with women who are often severely traumatised.

Irene P MacDonald LCSP (Phys)
Irene P MacDonald
Yatama
61 Graffham Avenue
Glasgow G46 6EH
T 0141 637 8659
Therapies available for RSI, sports injuries, muscular and joint problems, general stress management, spinal and peripheral joint problems. Treatments structured to suit individuals. By appointment.

Linda Bates Clinic, The
Linda Bates
14 Findhorn Place
Troon KA10 7DJ
T 01292 316820   F 01292 316820
Therapies include hypnotherapy, psychotherapy and counselling for pain control, stress, stopping smoking, weight, confidence. Linda Bates is available Mon-Fri, including evenings; weekends in emergencies.

Natural Therapy
Jean Barnes Humble
230 Wedderlea Drive
Glasgow G52 2SB
T 0141 883 4084
Aromatherapy massage to relieve stress, nervous tension, insomnia, depression, etc. Home visits arranged. Phone for up-to-date price lists.

ARTS AND CRAFTS

Bubblyjocks
Laura Wilson
Wellpark Enterprise Centre
120 Sydney Street
Glasgow G31 1JF
T 0141 550 4994   F 0141 550 4443
We design and maufacture printed giftware using natural and traditional themes with a contemporary look. Current products include stationery and nursery gifts.

Elizabeth Henderson School of Dancing
Elizabeth Ann Henderson
6 North Gardner Street
Glasgow G11 5BT

SCOTLAND - GLASGOW & STRATHCLYDE

T 0141 339 8116
Classes for children aged two-and-a-half upwards in ballet, modern theatre and tap dancing. Exams with the Imperial Society of Teachers of Dancing. Adult classes in ballet, tap and Scottish country dance.

Sheila Findlay (Art & Ceramics)
Sheila Findlay
15 Rannoch Avenue
Newton Mearns
Glasgow G77 6LN
T 0181 639 6418 F 0181 639 6418
Painting and individually designed and handbuilt ceramics by Sheila Findlay. Commissions undertaken.

Bereavement

Ayrshire and Arran Support Group
Mrs Anne Marie Conlan
34 Whitelees Court
Ardrossan
T 01294 68926
Local support group of the Scottish Cot Death Trust.

Cot Death Support Group
Ayrshire Central Hospital
Irvine KA12 8SS
T 01294 274191
Counselling & support to parents suffering a cot death.

Glasgow Stillbirth and Neonatal Death Society (SANDS)
29 St Ives Road
Moodiesburn
Glasgow G69 0PE
T 01236 873001
Support to parents when a baby dies during pregnancy or around the time of birth or shortly afterwards.

Miscarriage Assocation Support Group
Mary Couttie/Margaret Smith
Kyle and Carrick Women's Centre
14 Green Street
Ayr KA8 8AD
T 01292 268284

Miscarriage Association Support Group
Rosemary Connor
Irvine
T 01294 215978
Local contact for the Miscarriage Association. Phone before 10 pm.

Miscarriage Association Support Group
Christine Gebbie
16 Burnbank Street
Darvel KA17 0DY
T 01560 321959
Local Contact for the Miscarriage Assocation.

National Association of Widows - Cumnock branch
Mrs J Baird
15 River View
Lugar
Cumnock
Contact for the Cumnock branch of the National Association of Widows, offering comfort & support to all widows.

Paisley Cot Death Support Group
Mrs Sue Palmer
19 Corsebar Drive
Paisley
T 0141 889 2827
Local Support group of the Scottish Cot Death Trust.

Business support schemes

GAP Communications
Jo Lloyd
55 Loudoun Road
Newmilns KA16 9H5
T 01560 322396 F 01560 322396
mail@gapcomm.demon.co.uk
Provides marketing & public relations services to a wide variety of engineering & technology companies.

King Personnel Services
Lynn Fearnside
Media House
Dunnswood Road
Cumbernauld
Glasgow G67 3ET
T 01236 736059 F 01236 458377
Employment agnecy, owned by Lynn Fearnside. Services local businesses with temps & permanent staff.

Learning Partnership, The
Zeta Anich
The Learning Partnership
175 Yokermill Road
Glasgow G13 4HS
T 0141 951 4633 F 0141 951 4633
zanich@learningpartnership.co.uk
Human resource consultancy: change management; management development;

investors in people; organisational development. Special interest in team development in manufacturing.

Office Helpline
Mrs Catherine Russell
106 Main street
Alexandria G83 0PB
T 01389 767373 F 01389 753935
Recruitment agency & suppliers of secretarial services.

Personnel Solutions
Marie Docherty
604 Clarkston Road
Netherlee
Glasgow G24 3SQ
T 0141 637 3065 F 0141 637 3065
Advisory service to assist small to medium-sized companies to manage their staff. Provides an ongoing service in the areas of recruitment, relocation, personnel services & legislation.

Scribe Marketing and Communications
Lara Bayley
50 Wellington Street
Glasgow G2 6HJ
T 0141 221 2150 F 0141 221 2152
scribe@scribe.co.uk
Creative PR & corporate communications programmes focussed on achieving business objectives. Specialist in buisness-to-business & high tech sectors.

Westwood Associates
Fiona A Westwood
4 Kirklee Gardens
Glasgow G12 0SY
T 0141 339 0240 F 0141 339 0315
Management & training consultancy, specialising in business planning, facilitation, investors in people support & professional firms support.

CARERS

Newark Caring Services
Linda Coyle
Nicolson Business Centre
18 Nicolson Street
Greenock PA15 1JU
T 01475 730896 F 01475 888097
24 hour private homecare. Care assistants and home helps to assist the elderly, disabled, etc. in their own homes. Tailored to meet all individual requirements.

CENTRES FOR WOMEN

Barrhead Women's Centre
Kath Gallagher
Water Road
Barrhead G78 1SQ
T 0141 876 1824 F 0181 876 1825
Provides a wide range of services to women in a non-threatening environment. Cafe & library open Mon-Fri. Also evenings & weekend groups. Drop in, self-help groups, arts classes, discussions groups, etc.

Centre for Women's Health
Jenni Campbell, Rosina McCrae
6 Sandyford Place
Sauchiehall Street
Glasgow G3 7NB
T 0141 211 6700 F 0141 211 6702
cfwl@cqm.co.uk
Drop-in Tue, Wed, Thurs 10 am-9 pm; creche Tue, Wed, Thurs 10 am-4 pm & 6-9 pm; lesbian health service Thurs 5.30-8.30 pm; menopause support group, peer counselling for disabled women, etc.

Greater Foxbar Women's Centre
Fran Walsh
1 Lyon Road
Foxbar
Paisley PA2 ONA
T 01505 814953 F 01505 816066
Access to training & employment to local women & to provide somewhere to meet socially in a safe environment. Open Mon, Tue, Wed 8.45 am-4.45 pm; Fri 8.45 am-3.45 pm. Money advice, women's aid. Cafe.

Maryhill Women's Centre
women at the centre
Shawpark Street
Maryhill
Glasgow G20 9DA
T 0141 946 4215
Aims to bring women together & enable them to tackle issues of importance & to find practical ways of improving their situation. Advice, information, back-to-work courses, ceilidh dancing, Sunday walks.

Meridian Black and Ethnic Minority Women's Centre
Selma Rahman, Coordinator
58 Fox Street
Glasgow G1 4AU
T 0141 221 4443 F 0141 204 4325
Open Mon-Fri 9 am-5 pm. Information & resource centre for Black & ethnic minority women in Scotland. Educational & leisure

centre. English classes, yoga, ethnic dancing, employment-related courses. Creche.

Shanti Bhavan
Swarsha Rehan, Project Coordinator
1 La Belle Place
Glasgow G3 7LH
T 0141 332 2412
Resource centre for Asian women, open Mon-Fri 8.45 am-4.45 pm. The languages used are mainly English, Hindi & Punjabi.

South Ayrshsire Women's Centre
Mary Couttie
14 Green Street
Ayr KA8 8AD
T 01292 268284
Open Mon-Fri 10 am-4 pm. Drop-in for women. Day room, TV, laundry facilities, playroom, free, confidential pregnancy testing service, baby changing facilities, social events, support groups, snack bar.

CHILD CARE AND FAMILY

Barlanark Out of School Care
Margaret Halferty
C/o Barlanark Community Education Centre
33 Burnmouth Road
Barlanark
Glasgow G33 4RZ
T 0141 771 7690
Operating from 8 am-6 pm. Childcare provision to dual and single parent families returning to employment/ training/ further education. Children offered educational and recreational activities.

Castlemilk Play Forum
Angela McHale, Development Worker
123 Castlemilk Drive
Castlemilk
Glasgow G45 9UG
T 0141 634 5016
Brings together groups, agencies and individuals concerned with children in Castlemilk to share information, discuss issues affecting children, coordinate their work and provide support in working for children.

Centre for Residential Childcare
Lymehurst
74 Southbrae Drive
Glasgow G13 1SU
T 0141 950 3683 F 0141 950 3681

Aims to improve the quality of residential child care through information, training, publications, etc.

Claythorn Kindergarten
Kate Barrett
11 Whittingehame Drive
Glasgow G12 0XS
T 0141 339 1019
Montessori school for children aged 2 to 5. Open Mon-Fri 8 am-6 pm. Phone for up-to-date price list.

Govanhill Action for Parents
Suzanne Audrey, Co ordinator
Govanhill Neighbourhood Centre
6 Daisy Street
Glasgow G42 8JL
T 0141 424 0448
Mobile creche service. Aims to fill gap in childcare provision in Govanhill and increase community safety. Service operates 7.15-9.00 am and 2.30-6.15 pm; all day in school holidays. There is a small fee.

Jeely Piece Club Resource Centre
Carol Cooper
39 Arnprior Road
Castlemilk
Glasgow G45 9EX
T 0141 634 7305 F 0141 634 5646
Provides a cafe, creche for under 5s, printing services, meeting rooms, three holiday playschemes run in the school breaks, the 'play it safe' project. Open 9 am-4 pm. A small charge for the creche.

Kelvinside Kindergarten
Kate Barrett
17 Lancaster Crescent Lane
Glasgow G12 9SJ
T 0141 334 1124
For babies and children up to the age of 3. Open Mon-Fri 8 a.m-6.30 pm. Phone for up-to-date price list.

Kid Care Ltd
Eileen
C/o Wellpark Enterprise Centre
120 Sydney Street
Glasgow G31 1JF
T 0141 353 2333
Open 8.30 am-5.30 pm. Childcare for babies to age 5. 31 places available.

Learning Tree Nursery
Elaine McCarvill/Patricia Brown
3 Claremont Terrace
Charing Cross
Glasgow G3 7XR
T 0141 353 1234
Open 7.30 am 6.30 pm Mon-Fri. A nursery school for infants and children pre aged 5.

SASCA
Rita Hopper
55 Renfrew Street
Glasgow G2 3BD
T 0141 333 1434
Open Mon-Fri 9 am-5 pm. To promote and support the development and maintenance of out-of-school care schemes through the provision of development work, training, information and advice.

Southside Communication Disorder Support Group
Jean Humble/Alison Millar/Angela Bruce
Berryknowes Centre
14 Hallrule Drive
Cardonald
Glasgow G52 2HH
T 0141 883 9181
Offers support to parents & carers of children & young people with communication disorders. Enjoy a chat & a coffee. Every second Wed. Evening phone number is 0141 883 4084.

Thistle Day Nursery
Linda Craig
Glasgow College of Nautical Studies
21 Thistle Street
Glasgow G5 9XB
T 0141 420 3944 F 0141 420 1690
Open from 8 am-6 pm. 52 weeks of the year. Closed on public holidays. Phone for up-to-date price list.

COMPUTERS/IT

Glasgow Women's Technology Centre
35 Springfield Road
Glasgow G40 3EL
T 0141 550 7301 F 0141 580 1468
Open 9.30 am-4.30 pm. Training for 20 women. Year-long computer studies' course: business numeracy & assertiveness training. For women in the East End, Greater Easterhouse, Castlemilk & Drumchapel areas.

Rainbow Rhythm
Mary Rose Ruhl
Wellpark Enterprise Centre
120 Sydney Street
Glasgow G31 1JF
T 0111 550 4994 F 0141 550 4443
Ruhl@Rainbow Rhythm.co.uk
Rainbow Rhythm designs, develops & provides training in multimedia applications for the business sector. Services include web site design, getting a company on-line & setting up e-mail, internet training.

CONTRACEPTION/WELL WOMAN

Family Planning and Sexual Health Centre
Dr Alison Bigrigg
2 Claremont Terrace
Glasgow G3 7XR
T 0141 211 8135 F 0141 211 8139
Open Mon-Thurs 9 am-9 pm, Fri 9 am-4 pm, Sat 9.30 am-12.30 pm. Services include: contraception, pregnancy testing, abortion counselling, well women and menopause clinics, incest and rape counselling.

Glasgow Nuffield Hospital, The
25 Beaconsfield Road
Glasgow G12 0PJ
T 0141 334 9441
Well woman screen. Full female health assessment. Phone for up-to-date price lists.

COUNSELLING AND THERAPY

Phoenix (Scotland) Trust
Anne Shearer, Director
278 High Street
Glasgow G4 0QT
T 0141 553 2353
Aims to relieve stress in all its forms. Works with women on post-natal depression. Also relaxation, stress management, illness prevention, assertiveness training, self counselling. Not only for women.

Wellpark Enterprise Centre
120 Sydney Street
North Gallowgate
Glasgow G31 1JF
T 0141 550 4994 F 0141 550 4443
Information, advice, counselling for women-owned businesses & women starting up in business; training for current & potential women entrepreneurs; marketing; outreach counselling ; on-site childcare services.

Women's Counselling and Resource Service
31 Stockwell Street
Glasgow G1 4RZ
T 0141 552 5483 F 0141 552 7982
Free services. Counselling in the following: unplanned pregnancies, rape, sexual assault, post-abortion, sexual abuse. Also training, consultation & information provided. Women-centred; open to all women.

Education

Glasgow Association of Women Graduates
Dr Janet M Warren
5/5 Victoria Circus
Glasgow G12 9LB
T 0141 334 3004 F 0141 211 4829
To perfect the art of friendship & promote the interests of women graduates. To enable them to make their views known to government & to the UN & EU. Meets regularly during the academic year.

Inverclyde Association of Women Graduates
Dr H S Dunsmore
5 Drumslea
Greenock PA16 7SJ
T 01475 723553 F 01475 723553
To perfect the art of friendship. To promote the interests of all women. To support & encourage women in all their endeavours. Meetings are held in Greenock on Thurs evenings.

Environment

Anderson Christie Architects
Karen Anderson
25 St James Street
Paisley PA3 2HQ
T 0141 842 3133 F 0141 842 3278
Architectural consultancy, interior design, space planning, landscape design & feasibility studies. Experienced in community-based projects & in residential & special care work.

Dallman Johnstone Architects
Lillian Johnstone
28 Russell Drive
Bearsden
Glasgow G61 3BD
T 0141 942 3025 F 0141 942 8777
Award winning architectural practice which is gaining a reputation for good design.

Natural Resource Consultancy
Carol Crawford
26 Miller Road
Ayr KA7 2AY
T 01292 280800 F 01292 280900
Works at interfaces of development, agriculture, forestry, promoting nature conservation, sustainable land-use. Specialises in environmental impact assessment, ecological surveys, native woodland restoration.

PCR Architects & Energy Consultants
Kathleen Robertson
1 Princes Terrace
Glasgow G12 9JW
T 0141 357 5850 F 0141 357 5850
Architectural services & energy analysis. Working at building performance in terms of fabric & material performance, comfort & energy use.

Tennant Garmory Partnership
Nicola Garmory
Wellpark Enterprise Centre
120 Sydney Street
Glasgow G31 1JF
T 0141 550 3553 F 0141 550 3553
Landscape architectural consultancy.

Equal Opps

Fair Play Scotland
Anne Meikle, Coordinator
Equal Opportunities Commission
Stock Exchange House
Nelson Mandela Place
Glasgow G2 1GW
T 0141 248 5833 F 0141 248 5834
Positive action equalities project. A government EOC initiative to stimulate partnerships which improve opportunities for women to realise their full potential in education, employment & the community.

Ethnic Minorities

Asian Women's Action Group
Nasreen Latif
Annette Street Primary School
29 Annette Street
Govanhill
Glasgow G42 8YB
T 0141 423 0192
Meets every Wed at above address 1.15-3.15 pm. Sewing & language classes.

SCOTLAND - GLASGOW & STRATHCLYDE

Counselling for Asian and Chinese Women
C/o Women's Clling. & Resource Service
31 Stockwell Street
Glasgow G1 4RZ
T 0141 552 5483 F 0141 552 7982
Counselling & group work for Asian & Chinese women.

Darnley Street Family Centre
175 Darnley Street
Pollokshileds
Glasgow G41 2SY
T 0141 424 3920
Multicultural, multiracial family centre, with majority of Asian users. Women's groups, children's playgroups, women's health groups, etc.

NCH Action for Children San Jai Chinese Project
Dorothy Neoh, Project Manager
53 Rose Street
Glasgow G3 6SF
T 0141 332 3978 F 0141 332 2665
Open Mon-Thurs 9.30 am-5 pm; Fri 9.30 am-4 pm. Counselling, advice & information to the Glasgow Chinese community. Women's group.

Pakistani Women's Welfare Association
Mrs Tasneem Karim, General Secretary
15 Keir Street
Glasgow G41 2NP
T 0141 429 2418 F 0141 429 2418
Provides religious, cultural education for the women, young girls & children of Pakistani families. Temporary shelter provided to women faced with domestic violence. Counselling; get-togethers; Urdu taught.

FINANCE

Personal and Corporate Solutions
Linda Morpurgo
84 Downanhill Street
Glasgow G12 9EG
T 0141 339 2299 F 0141 337 6570
Independent financial advisers. Established IFA practice providing a personal & comprehensive service. Specialist areas are pensions, investments, protection & savings.

GIRLS/YOUNG WOMEN

City Centre Initiative
196 Bath Street
Glasgow G2 4HH

T 0141 227 6767
Working with young women at risk from exploitation & prostitution.

Teens 'n' Tots
Claire Hanlon or Myra Murray
Chapelside Centre
Waddell Street
Airdrie ML6
T 01236 751538 F 01236 756570
Meets Tue 7-9 pm. Free creche. A group of teenage mums offering support & an interesting programme of activities to others in the same situation.

HEALTH

Aberlour Child Care Trust
Myra Patterson
Scarrel Road Project
5 Scarrel Road
Castlemilk
Glasgow G45 0DR
T 0141 631 1504 F 0141 634 7133
Open 24 hours a day. First & second stage rehabilitation projects for women who are drug/alcohol misusers and their children. Referrals from Strathclyde region only.

AIDS Care Education and Training (ACET) - Scotland
Margaret Gillies
P O Box 725
Glasgow G20 9PX
T 0141 945 5286 F 0141 945 5486
Provides practical help to women who are HIV positive, their partners & carers. Also has a child & family support worker & an education officer. Office hours are Mon-Fri 9 am-5 pm Respite breaks arranged.

Body Positive Strathclyde
Sian Cox
The Body Positive Centre
3 Park Quadrant
Glasgow G12 8NT
T 0141 332 5010 F 0141 332 4285
6pstrathclyde@enterprise.net
Information concerning HIV/AIDS. Self-help, aromatherapy & other complementary therapies; women's activities; respite, creche, social events.

Breast Cancer Care (Glasgow)
Fiona Sandford
Suite 2/8
65 Bath Street

Glasgow G2 2BX
T 0141 353 1050 F 0141 353 0603
Open Mon-Fri 9.30 am-4.30 pm. Free help & information to anyone concerned about breast cancer. Literature, prosthesis fitting service & a network of trained volunteers. Nationwide freeline 0500 245 345.

Elspeth L Harte
Elspeth L Harte
7 Macpherson Drive
Bothwell
Glasgow G71 8QP
T 01698 853041
Accredited addiction counsellor counselling & training to help to prevent alcohol addiction & help people cope with others drinking; trainer in various workshops.

Glasgow HIV/AIDS Carers Support Group
Jacqui Pollock
Suite 226
Baltic Chambers
50 Wellington Street
Glasgow G2 6HJ
T 0141 221 8100 F 0141 221 8100
Self-help group for carers of those with HIV/AIDS. Free support, advice & practical help. Office open: Mon-Fri 10 am-2 pm. Support night Wed 7-10 pm. Bereavement group Tue 7-9 pm.

National Association for Premenstrual Syndrome - Glasgow branch
Renfield St Stephen's Church Centre
260 Bath Street
Glasgow
T 01236 874501
Support & information to PMS sufferers about diet. Meets second Thurs of each month 7.30 pm at above address.

National Osteoporosis Society - Glasgow branch
P O Box 485
Clarkston
Glasgow G76 7EE
Glasgow self-help group offering advice & information to sufferers.

Prevention of Illness, Nervous Tension & Stress (POINTS)
Margaret Rutherford
105 Stirllinfauld Place
Gorbals
Glasgow G5 9BY
T 0141 429 3345 F 0141 429 3345

Reducing isolation & dependency on local health care. Assertiveness training, budget cooking, alternative therapies. Free or minimal charge for those living in Gorbals area. Women's group.

LARGER/TALLER WOMEN

Cocoon Coats
William Macdonald
Lomond Industrial Estate
Alexandria G83 0TL
T 01389 755511
Makes & retails a wide range of fashionable rainwear. Any size, any length. Mail order catalogue. Shops in London, Edinburgh & Alexandria (factory shop).

Long Tall Sally
43 West Nile Street
Glasgow G1 2PF
T 0141 221 8474
Clothes for the taller woman sizes 12-20. Open Mon, Tue, Wed, Fri & Sat 9.30 am-5.30 pm; Thurs 9.30 am-7 pm; Sun 11 am-5 pm.

LEGAL MATTERS

Dickson, Haddow & Co
Annabel MacNicoll Goldie
100 Berkley Street
Glasgow G3 7JX
T 0141 248 3020 F 0141 248 6915
General practice, dealing with general advisory matters, conveyancing, wills, executry administration etc. Sympathetic to women.

Macdonald-Henderson
Morinne Macdonald
5 Royal Exchange Square
Glasgow G1 3AJ
T 0141 248 4957 F 0141 248 4986
Corporate & commercial lawyers. Provides commercial legal services at reasonable cost & with a personal touch. Sympathetic to women.

Messrs Brechin Robb
Karen S Brodie
24 George Square
Glasgow G2 1EE
T 0141 248 5921 F 0141 204 0135
Business & court lawyers, offering services to both individuals & businesses. Sympathetic to women.

SCOTLAND - GLASGOW & STRATHCLYDE

T F Reid & Donaldson
Marianne Mair
48 Causeyside Street
Paisley PA1 1YH
T 0141 889 7531
0141 887 3380
Provision of general legal services, including house purchase, commercial lease, matrimonial or commercial dispute, business start up or sale. Sympathetic to women.

LESBIAN AND BISEXUAL

Glasgow Lesbian Line
The collective
P O Box 686
Glasgow G3 7TL
T 0141 552 3355
Information & support to women who are or think they may be lesbian. Telephone open Wed 7-10 pm. Monthly women-only discos. Monthly quizzes. Newsletter. Befriending.

Strathclyde Lesbian and Gay Switchboard
Development Officer/Co-ordinator
P O Box 38
Glasgow G2 2QF
T 0141 332 8372
Counselling, advice & information on sexuality, sexual health, relationships & numerous other topics. Sexuality training. Icebreakers: monthly social for women & men. Counselling 7-10 pm daily.

LIBRARIES/ARCHIVES

Glasgow Women's Library
Sue John, Kate Henderson, Adele Patrick
4th Floor
109 Trongate
Glasgow G1 5HD
T 0141 552 8345
Reference & lending library, archive & information resource. Open Tue-Fri 1-6 pm & Sat 2-5 pm. Women in Profile is part of the Glasgow Women's Library.

MEDIA

Ailsa Productions Ltd
Doreen McArdle
3rd Floor
34 Albion Street
Glasgow G1 1LH
T 0141 552 0888 F 0141 552 0888
Open 10 am-6 pm. Main aim is to produce documentaries & drama. Can also provide a script to screen service for corporate videos.

For staged events a script & cast can be provided.

PLACES TO STAY AND EAT

Copthorne, The
Mandy Scott, General Manager
George Square
Glasgow G2 1DS
T 0141 332 6711 F 0141 332 4264
A four-star city centre hotel, renowned for exceptional standards of customer care; awarded 'Investors in People' (January 1996). Caters for business women travellers. Special corporate & weekend rates.

Garth House
Margaret Bryan
Garth
Bankend Road
Bridge of Weir PA11 3EU
T 011505 614414
A woman-owned & women-friendly B&B. There are single & twin rooms & a double with en suite. Phone for an up-to-date price list.

Holiday Caravan
Shirley Risdon or Helen Varley
Kilantringan House
Glenapp
Ballantrae KA26 0PE
T 01465 831211
Holiday caravan. Sleeps three. Quiet, rural, coastal location. Ideal for walkers, gardeners, birdwatchers, golfers. Plus pottery & plants business. Open daily except Tue. Phone for up-to-date price list.

PREGNANCY/CHILDBIRTH

Ayrshire Infertility Support Group
Sheena Young
17 Laurieland Avenue
Crosshouse
Kilmarnock KA2 0JQ
T 01563 543082
Support group for women & couples with fertitlity problems. Meets first Wed of each month at 7 pm in Committee Room, Administration Block, Ayrshire Central Hospital, Irvine. Publications.

Baby Milk Action - Dunbartonshire
Ginny Graham
8 Marguerite Gardens
Lenzie G66 4HV
T 0141 775 0034

Baby Milk Action area contact.

British Pregnancy Advisory Service (BPAS) - Glasgow
Jacqueline Houston
245 North Street
Glasgow G3 7DL
T 0141 248 9370 F 0141 248 9370
National action line, 7 days a week: 0345 304030. Confidential pregancy counselling & abortion referral. Termination referrals without GP involvement up to 24 weeks gestation. Post-abortion counselling.

Postnatal Depression Group
Community Mental Health Team
The Arran Centre
Bridgeton
Glasgow G40 2QA
T 0141 550 3324
For mothers with postnatal depression.

Society of the Innocents
Jon P Mc Grory
272 St Vincent Street
Glasgow G2 5RL
T 0141 221 3700
24-hour help line on 0141 204 0001. Pregnancy testing & counselling. Open Mon-Fri 10 am-4 pm & 7-9 pm. Assistance with material requirements & accommodation. A pro-life charity.

Retailing

Aroshi
Annie Robertson
Cuilt Farm
Blanefield
Glasgow G63 9AN
T 01360 770479 F 01360 770001
New & nearly new designer clothing. Personal service.

Barnes Textiles
Mrs Anne C Calder
23 Rosyth Road
Glasgow G5 0YD
T 0141 429 7151 F 0141 420 1032
Wholesale upholstery fabric & sundry suppliers. Open Mon-Thurs 8 am-5 pm; Fri 8 am-4.30 pm.

Bizzarre
Pat Haliburton
86 West Clyde Street
Helensburgh G84 7AF
T 01436 67111
gail@mabig.demon.co.uk
Gifts, clothing & jewellery at affordable prices. A quarterly newsletter highlights latest offerings. Occasional talks organized on topics ranging from jewellery manufacture to colour consultancy.

Dorothy Brookes
Dorothy Maxwell
280-282 Stoneland Road
Burnside
Glasgow G73 3RP
T 01324 612460
Retailer of high quality ladies' fashions & unusual gifts.

Elizabeth Bruce
Mrs Elizabeth Bruce
15 Moidart Avenue
Kirklandneuk
Renfrew PA4 9BT
T 0141 886 3588
Manufactures quality tartan gifts, fishing fly gifts & various styles of dog coats.

Elspeth Gardner Ceramics
Elspeth Gardner
Flat 2
13 Laird Interchange
Swanston Street
Glasgow G40 4HW
T 0141 554 3914 F 0141 554 3914
Design & manufacture of hand-made & decorated tiles, sold as gifts through a range of retail outlets. Also designed & made to order.

F T C Contracts
Margaret Robertson
Unit 3
Elderpark Workspace
100 Elderpark Street
Glasgow G51 3TR
T 0141 445 1222 F 0141 337 2300
Manufactures custom-made curtains & soft furnishings for trade customers.

Hamilton and Lilly Business Gifts
Mairi Hamilton
26 East Argyle Street
Helensburgh G84 7RR
T 01436 679020 F 01436 679043
Printers, designers & suppliers of printed promotional gifts & incentives. Artwork service provided, storage & control.

SCOTLAND - GLASGOW & STRATHCLYDE

Lightbox (UK) Ltd
Wendy Hosie
Unit 24
42 Dalsetter Avenue
Glasgow G15 8SL
T 0141 944 2647 F 0141 944 1604
General lighting wholesale. Specialist full spectrum lighting division. Agents for phototherapy units for treatment of Seasonal Affective Disorder (SAD). Own branded fluorescent lamp 'The Daystar'.

Lomond Activities
I Georgeson
Hope House
Main Street
Drymen G63 0BG
T 01360 660066 F 01360 660066
Mail order & delivery throughout Scotland of toys, games & sports. Opening hours: 9 am-5 pm seven days a week.

Mary Anderson
Mary Roberts
Aldessan House
Clachan of Campsie
Glasgow G65 7AB
T 01360 312100 F 01360 312100
Manufactuers of a range of garments in own designs for children & adults. Also offer a cut, make & trim, that is, making up customers' designs in their own fabric.

McFarlanes (Milngavie)
Andrea McFarlane
5 Mugdock Road
Milngavie
Glasgow G62 8PD
T 0141 956 4597
Cook shop & ironmongers. Up-market, quality goods in many kitchen lines.

Oasis Florist
Karen O'Hagan
13 Inverkip Street
Greenock PA15 1SX
T 01475 721709
Fresh, dried & silk flowers for all occasions. Wedding flowers a speciality. A member of Teleflorist.

Redress
Vicky Judd and Valerie Lawrence
51 Eastwoodmains Road
Williamwood
Glasgow G46 6PW
T 0141 6385090

Nearly new designer clothes & accessories for women. Open 9.30 am-5.30 pm Mon-Sat.

Ross & Romeo Ltd
Karen Ross and Mary Romeo
Unit 5
Glenpark St Industrial Estate
Dennistoon
Glasgow G31 1NU
T 0141 554 2814
Manufacturers of quality hand-made & hand-packed Scottish tablet for retail, catering & customised corporate gifts. Sisters-in-law operate the business from producing/packing to selling/delivery.

Tri-Em Exports Ltd
Jaki Stevenson
Unit 2
Griffon Centre
Vale of Leven Industrial Est.
Dumbarton G82 3PD
T 01389 721186
Manufactures childrenswear. Produce ranges of basic vests & petticoats & recently lauched a range of fashion clothing.

Windowbox, The
Karen Tidswell
Antartex
Lomond Estate
Alexandria G83 0TP
T 01389 721800
Floral art sundries, flowers for all occasions. Open Mon-Sat 10 am-5 pm; Sun 11 am-4.30 pm. Special designs for special occasions such as weddings, births, etc.

RIGHTS

Maryhill Representation Unit
Freda McMutrie
76 Dunar Street
Maryhill
Glasgow G20
T 0141 945 5125
Free representation for all members of the public, at appeals, tribunals & reviews. Benefits advice & information. Training for community & voluntary organisations.

SERVICES

1st Impressions Typing & Secretarial Service
Mrs Lyndsay McIntosh
35 Lynnhurst
Uddingston

SCOTLAND - GLASGOW & STRATHCLYDE

Glasgow G71 6SA
T 01698 814099 F 01698 813230
Typing & secretarial services which include wordprocessing, desk top publishing, presentations & proposal documents. Audio or copy typing. Out of hours service available.

A M Editorial
Anne Marr
14 Hillcrest Drive
Newton Mearns
Glasgow G77 5HH
T 0141 639 1912
Editorial services: producing leaflets, brochures, newsletters, etc. Desk top publishing. Press releases & media liaison available. Training offered in how to produce effective literature. Annual reports.

Andrews Administration
Jean Andrews
295 Eldon Street
Greenock PA16 7QN
T 01475 632199 F 01475 632199
Provides a secretarial service, temping services & full book-keeping & management account service.

Astrology and Counselling
Anne Whitaker Halliburton
259 Garrioch Road
Glasgow G20 8QZ
T 0141 946 5426
Birth chart readings to develop self-awareness. Beginners & advanced astrology classes. Personal counselling & supervision. Member of BAC & AHP (Britain) with MA, DipEd & CQSW qualifications.

Beauty For All Seasons
Rosemary Sedgwick
118 Beech Avenue
Newton Mearns
Glasgow G77 5BL
T 0141 639 7477 F 0141 639 9666
Colour & image consultants. Corporate & private work undertaken. Seminars & presentations available.

Bryce Curdy Productions
Margaret Curdy
P O Box 400
Ayr KA7 4EE
T 01292 443398 F 01292 443398
Event management consultants; product launches; fashion shows; new products launches.

Carol Craig Associates
Dr Carol Craig
Old Edenkiln
Strathblane
Glasgow G63 9EF
T 01360 770967 F 01360 770967
Management & training consultancy specialising in equality issues & managing diversity.

Commands
Maureen Dunlop
Unit 6
Duntreath Avenue
Great Western Business Park
Glasgow G5 6SA
T 0141 944 3900 F 0141 944 4227
Direct marketing services.

Dunning Design
Claire Dunning
51 Queen Mary Avenue
Glasgow G42 8DS
T 0141 422 1251 F 0141 422 1251
Range of services offered covers most aspects of design from slide presentations through to colour brochure design. Also offers various marketing & design audit services.

E L M Essentials
Muriel Campbell
The Accounting House
2 Argyle Street
Greenock PA15 1XE
T 01475 733332 F 01475 733332
Bookkeeping services.

Equine Services
Lynn Bryan Bhsai
16 South Street
Greenock PA16 8UE
T 01475 781050 F 01475 781050
Comprehensive service provided for the horse owner which includes lessons on owners' own horses, exercising, clipping & turnout for shows.

Essence Health and Beauty Salon, The
Roslyn Docherty
4 Renfrew Street
Renfrew PA4 8RW
T 0141 885 1166
Full range of beauty treatments using Susan Molyneux range of products. Open Mon 9.30 a.m-5 pm., Tue 9.30 am-1 pm, Wed & Thurs 9.30 a.m-7 pm, Fri 9.30 am-6 pm, Sat 9.30 am-5 pm.

SCOTLAND - GLASGOW & STRATHCLYDE

Face the Future
Pauline Logue
71 Torburn Avenue
Glasgow G46 7QZ
T 0141 621 0182
Provides collage replacement therapy, non surgical face lifts & body tuning.

GLS Language Services
Dagmar Fortsch and Hildegard Pesch
Pentagon Centre
Suite 215
36 Washington Street
Glasgow G3 8AZ
T 0141 226 8440 F 0141 226 8441
106071.2110@compuserve.com
Translations, interpreting, language courses, telephone/telemarketing & video voice-over services.

Graphic Design for Publishing
Janet Watson
85 Monteith Drive
Clarkston
Glasgow G76 8NX
T 0141 637 1724 F 0141 637 1724
Provides graphic design for publishing companies.

House of Colour
Denise Winton
Roseneath
6 Montgomery Drive
Giffnock
Glasgow G46 6PY
T 01141 638 2877
Image consultancy: personal style & image consultations; colour analysis; make-up; executive top-to-toe's; wardrobe planning; corporate image - tailor-made programmes. Consultations by appointment.

House of Colour
Allison Brownlie
Earnockmuir Farm
Hamilton ML3 8RL
T 01698 424423
Image consultancy. Personal classes in colour, body shape, personality, skin care & make-up. Also corporate work, all bespoke: Perception, successful first impressions, dress code rules, etc.

Jan Torrance
Jan Torrance
14 Cormorant Avenue
Houston PA6 TLW
T 01505 614325 F 01505 614325
Consultant in marketing services marketing project consultancy specialising in direct marketing.

KHS Hair Design
Kellie Stirling
39 High Street
Johnstone PA5 8AJ
T 01505 383188
Hairdressing salon open Mon, Tue, Wed, Fri 9 am-6 pm, Thurs 9 am-7 pm, Sat 9 am-5 pm.

Mary Warnock DRE FIG
Mary Warnock
20 Belhaven Terrace
Wishaw
N. Lanarkshire ML2 7AY
T 01698 355581
Electrolysis for the permanent removal of superfluous hair. Open from Tues-Sat all day. Mary Warnock is a Fellow of the Institute of Electrolysis.

McLaurin Public Relations
Katherine McCudden or Sharon McEwan
P O Buildings
Greenhill Avenue
Glasgow G46 6QX
T 0141 621 0424 F 0141 621 0424
PR consultancy services for clients to increase sales, improve client reputation, create business opportunities, profile the company's brand & increase staff morale.

Model Team Scotland
Shelagh Davis
180 Hope Street
Glasgow G2 2UE
T 0141 332 3951 F 0141 332 1915
Model agency.

Murgitroyd & Co
Dr Caroline Sincock
373 Scotland Street
Glasgow G5 8QA
T 0141 307 8400 F 0141 307 8401
murgitroyd.co.uk
Intellectual property specialists, dealing with trade marks, copyright, patents, designs & confidential information, including searches & protection. Free initial consultation. Open Mon-Fri 9 am-5 pm.

SCOTLAND - GLASGOW & STRATHCLYDE

Pet and Home Comforts
Rose O'Doherty
Flat 1/1
252 Aikenhead Road
Glasgow G42 0QJ
T 0141 423 3025
Provides a daily care service for pets in owners' own homes, as well as care of unoccupied houses. Service available all year round. The response to this new Scottish venture has been very positive.

Petersons
Debra Peterson
The Stables
Glenlora
By Lochwinnoch
Renfrewshire PA12 HDN
T 01505 842292 F 01505 842292
Communications, consultancy: publicity, interim management, mentoring.

Pitch Perfect
Lesley Boyd
5 Aytoun Road
Pollokshields
Glasgow G41 5RL
T 0141 423 5577 F 0141 423 5544
An event-management company specialising in unusual venues, catering & entertainment: musicians (of all kinds), traditional after-dinner speakers, jugglers to magicians.

PMG Event Consultants
Patricia McGhee
Coatbridge Business Centre
204 Main Street
Coatbridge
Lanarkshire ML5 3RB
T 01236 434535
Event organisers. Themed dinners, corporate hospitality.

R P M Interior Design
Margaret Robertson
Unit 4
Elderpark Workspace
100 Elderpark Street
Glasgow G51 3TR
T 0141 445 1222 F 0141 337 2300
Interior designers & consultants; specialists in showrooms. Projects of all sizes undertaken, both commercial & domestic.

Rae Livingstone Associates
Rae Livingstone
6 Kelvinside Gardens East
Glasgow G20 6BD
T 0141 946 4983 F 0141 946 4983
Specialist consultants: European programmes, employment initiatives, research, evaluation, management training. Promoting practical solutions & innovative programmes.

Sally-Ann Geary
Sally-Ann Geary
1 Farmfield Terrace
West Kilbride
Strathclyde KA23 9ED
T 01294 829750 F 01294 829750
100737,100@compuserve.com
Translating, interpreting, tutoring services in Spanish & Portuguese.

Smith & Paul Design Associates
Doreen Smith
Balgonie House
Acer Crescent
Paisley PA2 9LN
T 0141 884 22114 F 0141 884 7802
Works on one-to-one basis with clients. Undertakes part/complete projects, from initial design through layout, photography, typesetting, illustration, copy writing & printing to final delivery.

Yam Publications
Grace Franklin
Suite 9, Second Floor
73 Robertson Street
Glasgow G3 2QD
T 0141 226 4898 F 0141 226 4708
Journalist led, small publishing & public relations company.

SEXUAL ABUSE/RAPE CRISIS

Ayr Incest Support Centre
P O Box 45
Ayr KA8 8BT
T 01292 611301
Open Mon-Thurs 9 am-4 pm; Fri 9 am-12 noon; Wed 6-9 pm. Support & advice for women survivors of child abuse. Group on Wed 7-9 pm. Also group for mothers of abused children. Counselling: 01292 611301.

Ayr Rape Crisis
P O Box 45
Ayr KA8 8BT
T 01292 611298
Open Mon-Thurs 9 am-4 pm; Fri 9 am-12 noon; Wed 6-9 pm. 24-hour ansaphone.

Counselling line: 01292 611301.
Advice/support for women who have been raped or sexually abused.

Glasgow Rape Crisis Centre
Marion Corooran
P O Box 53
Glasgow G2 1YR
T 0141 331 1955 F 0141 331 1922
Crisis line is 0141 331 1990. Free & confidential support to women and girls who have been raped, sexually assaulted or abused at any time during their lives. Telephone, letter or face to face counselling.

Kilmarnock Rape Counselling and Resource Centre
P O Box 23
Kilmarnock KA1 1DP
T 01563 541769 F 01563 544686
A women's organisation supporting female survivors of rape & sexual abuse. Also supports mothers whose children have been abused. Face-to-face & phone counselling & support groups.

North East Women's Support Services
Flat 12
30 Sunnylaw Street
Possilpark
Glasgow G22 6AQ
T 0141 336 8810
Linked with Glasgow City Council social work services. Offers information & support to women survivors who have been sexually abused. Group work provided.

Sexual Abuse Line for Women (SAL)
78-8- West Blackhall Street
Greenock PA19 1XG
T 01475 888110
A helpline for women who have been or are being sexually abused. Line open on Tue 10 am-12 noon with follow-on counselling if desired.

SINGLE PARENTS

Flexicare Service for Single Parents
Margaret McAlpine, Project Coordinator
72-74 Main Street
Alexandria G83 0PB
T 01389 755251
Child care/support for single parents. Open Mon-Fri 9 am-5 pm. Priority for those living in Haldane & Renton areas. Children cared for in their own homes; the service is free. Also a creche. Must book.

Garthamlock Lone Parents Projects
Pauline Docherty
7 Inverlochy Street
Garthamlock
Glasgow G33
T 0141 774 6105 F 0141 774 4086
Informal meeting place for women, with creche facilities as & when groups are active (ie training, groupwork).

SUPPORT

Castlemilk Umbrella Group - Women's Sub Group
Allison Connell
Glenwood Business Centre
141 Castlemilk Drive
Glasgow G45 9UG
T 0141 634 2651 F 0141 634 2608
Main aims & objectives are to involve local people in local decision-making structures & actively encourage people in regeneration strategy. The women's sub group looks at specific issues for local women.

Home-Start UK - Scotland
84 Drymen Road
Bearsden
Glasgow G61 2RH
T 0141 942 3450 F 0141 942 3479
Support, befriending, practical help to young families; helping to prevent crisis & breakdown.

Women's Information and Support Project
Sheila Doharty, Project Coordinator
16 Shandwick Street
Easterhouse
Glasgow G34 9BP
T 0141 771 8403
Open Mon-Fri 9 am-3.30 pm; Tue, Wed Thurs evenings. Provides safe atmosphere for women in Easterhouse area. First aid & counselling courses, workshops, mother & toddler groups. Outreach worker available.

TRAINING

Adept Training Services
Anna Drummond
28 Locksley Avenue
Cumbernauld G67 4EN
T 01236 722499 F 01236 722499
Specialist training in avoiding/handling aggression & violence at work. Practical

health focus oriented stress management training & personal performance consultancy.

Elizabeth Lawrence Consultancy and Training
Elizabeth Lawrence
The Flat
Old Ballikinrain
Balfron by Glasgow G63 0LL
T 01360 440162
Course for empowerment/personal development. Assertiveness training & courses on mediation-conflict resolution. Particularly interested in working with teachers & pupils in schools. Fees to be negotiated.

Glasgow North Ltd
Kathleen Lees, Business Information Officer
St Rollox House
130 Springburn Road
Glasgow G21 1YL
T 0141 552 5413 F 0141 552 0886
Offers a women-only business training course, New Enterprise for Women.

Isabel Macinnes-Manby
Isabel Macinnes-Manby
Kilmaronock Castle
Gartocharn G83 8SB
T 0136 0660351 F 0136 0660351
Personal & professional development.

McKinnon-Long Partnership, The
Dr K Long
32 Skirving Street
Glasgow G41 3AA
T 0141 636 0490 F 0141 649 9179
Courses on stress management, NLP, confidence building & autogenic training run by qualified physicians Drs Hetty McKinnan & Kathleen Long. Prices vary as courses tailored to client need.

Organize
Andrea McHugh
T/L 9 Ashburn Gardens
Gourock PA19 1BT
T 01475 639184
Time management training & consultancy. Flexible training to help manage the work/home balance. Practical, workable solutions to time management problems. Solutions that suit individual working styles.

Scotacs
Marilyn Christie/Catherine McMaster
201a Bath Street
Glasgow G2 4H2
T 0141 226 4373 F 0141 204 4115
Training in counselling skills (RSA & COSCA certificates; RSA advanced diploma in counselling & group work). Training in food hygiene - health care packages. Also training in personal effectiveness.

Tessa Simpson Associates
Tessa Simpson
Hillpark House
Rostan Road
Newlands
Glasgow G43 2XD
T 0141 637 2273 F 0141 637 2273
Training in management development motivation & women returners. Career counselling on a one-to-one basis. Founder & past President of East & West of Scotland Business Women's Clubs.

TRANSPORT

Margaret's School of Motoring
Margaret Campbell
Flat 10
The Old Church Hall
Spinner Street
Balfron G63 OTN
T 01360 440402
Teaching to the highest standards for both practical driving & theory tests. Advanced driving available. Phone for up-to-date price list.

VIOLENCE AGAINST WOMEN

Community Safety Centre
Ann Fenilly
The Old Fire Station
347 Blytheswood Court
Glasgow G2 7PH
T 0141 226 4782 F 0141 248 8651
Working in partnership to develop safe communities for women. The Centre runs ASSERT, personal safety & self-defence training courses for women.

Safe & Secure in Renfrew
Eleanor Thomson
3 Silk Street
Paisley PA1 1HG
T 0141 848 6262 F 0141 848 9442

SCOTLAND - GLASGOW & STRATHCLYDE

Open 9 am-4.30 pm. An urban aid project set up to address issues of community safety within priority areas in Renfrewshire.

Women's Safety Centre
Frances or Elizabeth
120 Sydney Street
Glasgow G31 1JF
T 0141 554 7676 F 0141 550 4443
Qwerty 0141 554 7979. Addresses women's experiences & fears of crime through self-defence & personal safety courses. Information & advice about all areas of safety & violence against women.

Women's Support Project
Jan Macleod
31 Stockwell Street
Glasgow G1 4RZ
T 0141 552 2221 F 0141 552 1876
Qwerty phone 0141 552 9979. Working against male violence: domestic violence, rape, sexual assault, child sexual abuse, incest. Services include: library, information, support, training, consultancy.

WOMEN'S AID

Clydebank Women's Aid
T 0141 952 8118
Drop-in Mon-Fri 10 am-4 pm. Space for six women & their children. Accommodation, support, information & counselling for women & their children (if any) who are suffering or who have suffered domestic abuse.

Cumnock and Doon Valley Women's Aid
Susanne Russell
30a Ayr Road
Cumnock KA18 1EE
T 01290 423434 F 01290 423434
Support, information to abused women & their children (if any). A refuge is also provided if required. Office open to women from Mon-Fri 10 am-3 pm & 24-hour 7-day a week on call service is provided.

Drumchapel Women's Aid
Camus Place Centre
2 Camus Place
Drumchapel
Glasgow G15 7EW
T 0141 944 0201 F 0141 944 0201
Office hours Mon-Fri 10 am-3 pm on-call 24 hours. Drop-in/support group Wed 11 am-1 pm. Offers support & emergency accommodation to women & their children (if any) suffering domestic abuse.

Dumbarton Women's Aid
T 01389 751036
We provide support &/or refuge accommodation for women experiencing male violence in their homes. Office hours are Mon-Fri 9.30 am-4.30 pm. The first contact is usually by phone.

East Dunbartonshire Women's Aid
Mary Donnelly/Lorraine McKenzie
4 Freeland Place
Kirkintilloch
Glasgow G66 1ND
T 0141 776 0864
Offers information, support & refuge to women & children who have been abused. Open Mon-Fri 9.30 am-3.30 pm, & we operate a 24-hour on-call service.

East Kilbride Women's Aid
Patricia Doran
The Hut
Torrance Road
East Kilbride G74 1AR
T 01355 249897
Offers support, information & help to any woman & her children who have been mentally, physically or sexually abused. Open Mon and Fri 10 am-2 pm, Wed 1.30-3.30 pm. 24-hour ansaphone.

Glasgow Women's Aid
Fourth Floor
30 Bell Street
Glasgow G1 1LG
T 0141 248 2989
Drop-in Mon-Fri 9.30 am-1 pm. Phone line open Mon-Fri 9.30 am-4.30 pm. Refuge, support, information, counselling for women & their children (if any) who are suffering/have suffered domestic abuse.

Greater Easterhouse Women's Aid
5 Kildermorie Path
Glasgow G34 9EJ
T 0141 773 3533 F 0141 781 0820
Open Mon-Fri 10 am-1.30 pm, afternoons by appointment. Free service. Information, support & refuge for abused women & their children (if any). Agencies phone: 0141 781 0230.

Hamilton Women's Aid
74 Burnbank Centre (above library)
Hamilton ML3 0NA
T 01698 891498
Support, information & refuge to women & their children who are suffering domestic abuse. Open Mon-Fri 10 am-4 pm. Legal service by appointment Mon 2-4 pm. Emergency on-call Mon-Thurs 6 pm-8 am

Hemat Gryffe Women's Aid
Famida Ali
24 Willowbank Street
Glasgow G3
T 0141 353 0859
Providing temporary refuge accommodation for Black, ethnic women & their children (if any) who have experienced domestic abuse. 24-hour call out service. Counselling, after care service, interpreting, etc.

Inverclyde Women's Aid
78-80 West Blackhall Street
Greenock PA19 1XG
T 01475 781689
Helpline 01475 888505. For women & their children (if any) who have suffered/are suffering from domestic abuse. Open 10 am-4 pm. Counselling. Pagers for women within the refuge.

Kilmarnock Women's Aid
Hazel Bingham
66 John Finnie Street
Kilmarnock KA1 1BS
T 01563 536001 F 01563 574917

Monklands Women's Aid (1)
11a Bank Street
Coatbridge ML5 4AG
T 01236 432061
Aims to help abused women & their children (if any) & to end such abuse against women. 24-hour support, information, a safe place to stay. Office open Mon-Fri. Encourages women to determine their own future.

Monklands Women's Aid (2)
Resource Centre
Anderson Street
Airdrie
T 01236 754150
To help abused women & their children (if any) & to end such abuse against women. Office open Mon-Fri. Offers support, information & help. National children's workers available.

North Ayrshire Women's Aid
Anne Paton
87-89 New Street
Stevenston KA20 3HD
T 01294 602424 F 01294 601415
Offers refuge, information & support to abused women & their children (if any).

Paisley & District Women's Aid
Marie Lewis
57 Kilnside Road
Paisley PA1 1RP
T 0141 561 7030
Open Mon, Tue, Wed 9 am-4 pm; Thurs 10 am-1 pm; Fri 9 am-3.30 pm. Provides a temporary refuge for women & their children (if any) where the women have suffered mental, physical or sexual abuse.

South Ayrshire Women's Aid
Helen Alexander
14 Green Street
Ayr KA7 8AD
T 01292 266482 F 01292 618399
Open Mon-Fri 9 am-4 pm. On call: Sat & Sun, 24 hours on call. (Open 9 am-4 pm) Support, information, accommodation (where possible) for women/children who have been mentally/physically/sexually abused.

INVERNESS, H & I

BEREAVEMENT

Forres Cot Death Monitor Fund
Singapore
Leask Road
Forres IV36 0AA
T 01309 676225
Local support group of the Scottish Cot Death Trust.

Highland Cot Death Support Group
Mrs Val Dunford
Reiskmore
Delney Muir
Invergordon
T 01349 852485
Local support group of the Scottish Cot Death Trust.

Miscarriage Association Support Group
Amanda Floyd
4 Muirfield Drive
Brora KY9 6QQ
T 01408 621196
Provides information & support to women who have experienced a miscarriage. Please

phone before 10 pm. Can provide details of local support groups.

Miscarriage Association Support Group
Maureen Frere
42 Bank Row
Wick
T 01955 604549
Provides information & support to women who have expereinced a miscarriage. Can supply details of local support groups. Please phone before 10 pm.

Miscarriage Association Support Group
Alison Lindsay
Lhanbryde IV30 3PG
T 01343 843105
Provides information & support to women who have experienced a miscarriage. Please phone Mon-Fri mornings & Mon & Wed evenings.

Miscarriage Association Support Group
Jane Campbell
19 Birch Place
Culloden
T 01463 791398
Provides support & information to women who have experienced miscarriages. Please phone before 10 pm.

Miscarriage Association Support Group
Sarah Munro
Foulis Mains
Evanton IV16 9UX
T 01349 830366
Information & support for women who have had miscarriages. Please phone before 10 pm.

Miscarriage Association Support Group
Anne Cottage
The Old Schoolhouse
Clava
Culloden
Inverness
T 01463 793130
Provides information & support to women who have experienced a miscarriage. Please call before 10 pm.

CHILD CARE AND FAMILY

Inverness Central - Playgroups
Sandra Tucker
26 Morlich Crescent
Achareidh
Nairn
Contact the above name and address for information about playgroups in the central region of Inverness.

Inverness East - Playgroups
Ailsa Charlton
84 Smithton Park
Inverness
T 01463 792409
Contact the above number or address for information about playgroups in the eastern area of Inverness.

Inverness West - Playgroups
Sheila Wallace
Mossfield
Kiltarlity
T 01463 741382
Contact the above address or number for information about playgroups in the western area of Inverness.

Spectrum Centre Creche
Mrs Brenda Luke
Spectrum Community Centre
1 Margaret Street
Inverness
Open Mon-Fri 10 am-12 noon. For children of pre-school age.

Spectrum Centre Playgroup
Mrs B Strain, Playleader
2 Cradlehall Gardens
Inverness IV1 2FW
Playgroup at Specrum Community Centre, 1 Margaret Street, Inverness. Open Mon-Fri 10 am-12 noon.

CONTRACEPTION/WELL WOMAN

Highland Brook Centre
77 Church Street
Inverness IV1 1ES
T 01463 242434
Free confidential contraceptive advice. Help with emotional and sexual problems. Free condoms and other contraceptive supplies. Pregnancy tests and quick results, etc. Phone for opening times.

EDUCATION

Workers' Educational Association
Hilary Lawson
57 Church Street
Inverness IV1 1DR

T 01463 710577
Offers a wide range of learning opportunities, including women & health groups. Phone above number for details of courses in the Highland region.

Runs courses on women's health issues, diet, nutrition, contraception, menopause, HRT, stress, osteoporosis, cancer, assertiveness, drugs & other addictions, first aid, confidence skills, parenting, etc.

Health

Highland Breast Care and Mastectomy Association
Irene Gillespie, Secretary
137 Old Edinburgh Road
Inverness IV2 3BX
T 01463 238889
Support for women who are undergoing/have undergone surgery & treatments for breast cancer. Hospital visits & confidential one-to-one meetings. Meets second Mon of month at Cummings Hotel, Church St, Inverness.

HMM Group
Mrs Carol Wetherell
Ardeer
Rafford
Forres IV36 0RU
T 01309 673178
Hysterectomy, menopause & HRT support group, encouraging better communication between women & their GPs. An information service about hysterectomy, menopause & HRT & recommended reading lists.

Osteoporosis Society
Mrs Lorna Young
5 Eastfield Avenue
Culcabock
Inverness
T 01463 235026

Ross-shire Health Protection Trust - Tain Breast Scanner
Mrs Stone
6 Stafford Street
Tain
T 01862 893339
Helps to detect breast cancer at an early stage but does not use X-rays. Leave name & telephone number on ansaphone. Trained nurses available.

Women's Health Groups
Mandy Mepham
21 West
Balnakeil
Durness
By Lairg IV27 4PT
T 01971 511389

Lesbian and Bisexual

Out and About
P O Box 91
Inverness IV1 2GJ
A lesbian social group offering support & friendship to lesbians living in the highlands of Scotland. Regular meetings, social events & outings throughout the area.

Places to Stay and Eat

ABB Cottage
Ms K E Storrar
11 Douglas Row
Inverness IV1 1RE
T 01463 233486
B&B. Woman-owned & woman-friendly. Access for wheelchairs. Special diets catered for. No smoking. Children over age 12 welcome. Phone for up-to-date price list.

Bed and Breakfast
Penny Ross Browne
3 Castle Terrace
Ullapool IV2 62XD
T 01854 612409
Vegetarian B&B in friendly house. Spectacular scenery, mountain walks, boat trips, sea birds, seals, golf & swimming pool on doorstep. Philosophy dispensed on demand!

Ceilidh Place, The
Jean Urquhart
West Argyle Street
Ullapool IV26 2TY
T 01854 612103 F 01854 612886
Woman-run & women-friendly. Two cottages, a shed & a bunk house. Wide range of prices. Licensed, vegetarian - but meat-eaters welcome. Special diets catered for. Phone for up-to-date price list.

Croit Mo Sheanair
Lynn Bennett-Mackenzie
29 Strath
Gairloch IV21 2DA
T 01445 712389
Woman-run & women-friendly crofthouse. One double, two twin, both with whb; no smoking. Views of Gairloch Bay & Skye.

SCOTLAND - INVERNESS, H & I

Four Lephin
Janet Kernachan, Proprietor
Glendale
Isle of Skye IV55 8WJ
T 01470 511376 F 01470 511376
Woman-owned & women-friendly B&B in modern crofthouse on small working croft with view to outer Hebrides. 1 double, 2 twin bedrooms; separate shower & WC. No smoking. Phone for up-to-date price list.

Glendale Vegetarian Guest House
Michele Roberts
Mandally
Invergary PH35 4HP
Mother & daughter-owned house; women friendly. Open fire, books, maps. CH. Vegetarian; vegan food on request; disabled access & facilites; special diets catered for; phone for up-to-date price list.

Invercassley Cottage
Pam Menzies
Rosehall
Laig IV27 4BD
T 01549 441288
Woman run & women-friendly B&B. Set in own ground in Rosehall village, it overlooks Strathoykel. Phone for up-to-date price list.

Ladysmith Guesthouse and Scottish Larder Restaurant
Lauri Chltern
24 Pulteney Street
Ullapool IV26 2UP
T 01854 612185 F 01854 612185
Woman-run & women-friendly guesthouse & licensed restaurant. B&Bs with a wide range of prices. Disabled access. Vegan food available but meat eaters also welcome. Special diets catered for.

Langdale House
Myra Macgregor
Waterloo
Breakish
Isle of Skye IV42 8QE
T 01471 822376
Woman-run & women-friendly licensed house. 2 double twin rooms en suite. No smoking; special diets catered for; vegetarian meals on request. Sea & mountain views. Phone for up-to-date price list.

Little Lodge
Di Johnson and Inge Ford
North Erradale
Gailoch IV21 2DS
T 01445 771237
Women-owned, women-friendly guest house. Three bedrooms, 1 twin & 2 double, en suite. Four-course 'taste of Scotland' dinner at 7 pm. Traditional Scottish or continental breakfast. Phone for price list.

Minton House
Judith Meynell or Ruth Corner
Findhorn Bay
Forres
Moray IV36 0YY
T 01309 690819 F 01309 691583
minton@findhorn.org
B&B. Available all year in double, twin or single rooms. Long-term accommodation at special rates during winter. Retreats & workshops. Phone for up-to-date price list.

Rua Reidh Lighthouse Holidays
Chris Barrett/Fran Cree
Rua Reigh Lighthouse
Gairloch IV21 2EA
T 01445 771263 F 01445 771263
ruareidh@netcomuk.co.uk
Women-run B&B holiday centre. Guided walking holidays, multi-activity holidays, weeks & short breaks, B&B/hostel accommodation. Phone for up-to-date price list.

Seafood Restaurant
Jann Macrae and Andrea Mathson
Railway Buildings
Kyle of Lochalsh
T 01599 534813 F 01599 577230
Seafood restaurant serving local produce in a cosy atmosphere.

Seagreen Restaurant and Bookshop
Fiona Begg
Plockton Road
Kyle of Lochalsh IV40 8DA
T 01599 534388
Specialises in local seafood & wholefood dishes. Garden wholefood shop. Exhibition space. Traditional music. Local interest literature. Open every day except from mid January to the end of March.

Shieling, The
Ann Worthy
The Shieling

Culran
Ardgay IV24 3DW
T 01549 421211
A non-smoking B&B run by a woman, open from April to September & women-friendly. A homely base for walkers, bird watchers, artists or for those who just want to relax. Phone for up-to-date price list.

The Schoolhouse
Sonia or Sue
Lochyside
Fort William PH33 7NX
T 01397 702267
Women only B&B. Open all year. Water skiing; snow skiing. No smoking, no children or pets. Advance booking & deposit essential. Phone for up-to-date price list.

Two Glen
Paula Williams
An T-ob - Leverbrough
Harris HS5 3TY
T 01859 520319
Woman-owned & women-friendly converted crofthouse. 2 twin, 1 family rooms; own dining room & sitting room with open fire. Vegetarian food available; special diets catered for. Phone for price list.

PREGNANCY/CHILDBIRTH

Baby Milk Action - Inverness
Daphne Meacock
Bridge House
Resaurie
Inverness IV1 2NH
T 01463 792549
The Baby Milk Action area contact.

Caesarian Support Network (1)
Lynda Muir
Ballichnoch Farm House
Cawdor
Nairn IV12 5XZ
T 01667 404749
Education & information on all matters relating to caesarean delivery. Provides reassurance for women who have had caesarian births & who hope to have a vaginal delivery in the future.

Caesarian Support Network (2)
Lynda Muir
Corner House
Cromartie Buildings
Strathpeffer IV14 9DS
T 01997 421947
Education & information on all matters relating to caesarean delivery. Reassurance to women who have had caesarian births & who hope to have a vaginal delivery in the future.

Childlessness Overcome Through Surrogacy (COTS)
Lairg IV27 4EF
T 01549 402401 F 01549 402401
A voluntary organisation assisting birth childless couples & surrogates.

Foresight Association for Promotion of Preconceptual Care
Dr Cornelia Fellner
5 Bank Lane
Forres IV36 0NU
T 01309 690934
Working to promote best health in both parents prior to conception. List of publications sent on request. Send sae for further information.

Inverness Crisis Pregnancy Centre
Mrs Catherine MacInnes
3 Gordon Terrace
Inverness IV2 3HD
T 01463 713999
Free pregnancy testing, counselling, maternity, baby clothes & furniture. Temporary accommodation. Referral for adoption or foster care; counselling. Open Mon 10 am-12 noon; Wed 2-4 pm; Fri 12-2 pm.

National Childbirth Trust - Inverness and District branch
Sheila MacIver
T 01463 792588
Ante-natal classes for couples; breastfeeding counsellors; breastpump hire; Mava bras measuring & fitting service; valley cushion hire; post-natal support; library; newsletter.

SEXUAL ABUSE/RAPE CRISIS

Highlands and Islands Rape and Abuse Line
P O Box 10
Dingwall IV15 9LH
T 01349 865316
Offers confidential support to anyone who has been raped or sexually abused. Phone

line, correspondence address or face to face support. Phone line open 7-10 pm every evening.

SPORTS AND LEISURE

Highland Ladies' Curling Club
Mrs Shirley Shepherd, Secretary
11 Druim Avenue
Inverness IV2 4LG
T 01463 235217
Meets regularly at Inverness Ice Rink throughout the winter. To foster & improve the ancient game of Scottish curling.

WOMEN'S AID

Inverness Women's Aid
Liz McCaffray
6 Nelson Street
Inverness IV3 6BY
T 01463 220719 F 01463 234110
Office open Mon-Fri 9 am-5 pm; Sat 9 am-12 pm. 01463 220710 for 24-hour on call service. Free, confidential. Advice, support, refuge to women (& their children) who are victims of domestic abuse.

Ross-Shire Women's Aid
T 01349 863568
Offers information, support & refuge to abused women & their children (if any). Office & refuge on a 24-hour number. Office hours Mon-Fri 10 am-5 pm.

Western Isles Women's Aid
53a Bayhead
Stornoway
Isle of Lewis HS1 2DZ
T 01851 704750 F 01851 706958
Information, support & counselling for battered women & their children. A refuge, comprising three family rooms & one single room.

WALES

ABERYSTWYTH AND MID WALES

ACCOMMODATION

Montgomeryshire Women's Centre
J Richardson, Community Support Coordinator
321 Maesyrhandir
Newtown SY16 2ZZ
T 01686 629114
Drop-in five days a week for advice, counselling, support or a talk. 24-hour on call service. Three-bedroomed refuge for women & their children (if any) who are suffering abuse: physical, mental or sexual.

ARTS AND CRAFTS

Silverweed
Hanna Lindenberg
Parc-y-Rhos
Cwmann
Lampeter SA48 8DZ
T 01570 423254
Jewellery making courses for women only. Week & weekend residential courses. Individual tuition. Also jewellery for sale at the workshop. Phone for up-to-date price list.

PLACES TO STAY AND EAT

Fachwen Ganol
Jo Groves
Llwydiarth
Llangadfan SY21 0QG
T 01938 820595
Women's vegetarian guesthouse. Seventeenth-century farmhouse set in one-&-a-half acres with stream & ponds. Open all year. Non smoking. Can pick up from Welshpool. Phone for up-to-date price list.

Silverweed
Hanna Lindenberg
Parc-y-rhos
Cwmann
Lampeter SA48 8DZ
T 01570 423254
B&B for women only. Vegetarian breakfast. No smoking. Cats in the house. Near the Cambrian mountains & 16 miles from the sea. Phone for up-to-date price list.

PUBLISHERS/PUBLICATIONS

Honno Cyf/ Welsh Women's Press
Rosanne Reeves
Penroc Rhodfa'r Mor
Aberystwyth SY23 2AZ
T 01970 623150
Editorial office. Open 30 hours a week. Phone for further information.

SPIRITUALITY/ECOFEMINISM

Soul & Spirit - Women's Wilderness Walking Experiences
Michele Leslie
Rhiwlas
Taliesin
Machynlleth SY20 8JG
T 01970 832105
Walking & camping trips. Striving towards wholeness. Getting back in touch with nature, the earth, ourselves, others & the cosmos through walking, sharing silences, meditating, drawing, poetry, writing, etc.

WOMEN'S AID

Aberystwyth Women's Aid
P O Box 38
Aberystwyth SY23 1AA
T 01970 625585
24-hour on-call. Refuge: always a space. Time, support for women escaping domestic abuse. Women's Aid Information Centre: 4 Pound Place, Aberystwyth; 01970 612225. Open Mon 1-4.30 pm; Thurs 10 am-10 pm.

Radnor Women's Aid
P O Box 26
Llandrindod Wells LD1 5AA
T 01597 824655
24-hour on call service. Four-roomed refuge. Support, information, advice for women suffering from domestic abuse: sexual, mental, physical. Floating support project for women in housing association properties.

Welsh Women's Aid
4 Pound Place
Aberystwyth SY23 1LX
T 01970 612748 F 01970 627892
Open Mon-Fri 9.30 am-4 pm. Aims to relieve need, distress & suffering experienced by women of limited financial means who have been gravely or persistently maltreated by men in mid-Wales.

BANGOR AND NORTH WALES

ARTS AND CRAFTS

Art for Women
Kath Kelly
Dewis Cyfarfod

Llannderfel
Y Bala LL23 7DR
T 01678 530243

Business support schemes
Wrexham Enterprise
Morag Murphy
Wrexham ITEC
Unit 19
Whitegate Industrial Estate
Wrexham LL13 9UG
T 01978 350775 F 01978 358643
Wrexham.ITEC@tbn.wales.com
Women's enterprise centre. Helping people start up their own businesses. Provides a seven-day start-up course. Bookkeeping advice.

Contraception/Well woman
Family Planning Association Cymru - North Wales
Bangor
T 01248 352176 F 012248 371138
106353,125@compuserve.com
Information & advice Mon-Fri 9 am-5 pm on all aspects of sexuality, contraception, abortion, clinic information; leaflets & resources; education & training; consultancy & project work.

Education
Bangor & North Wales Assn of Women Graduates
Mrs Hilda Cronin
6 Bryn Avenue
Old Colwyn LL29 8AL
T 01492 516947
Has a yearly programme of speakers & lunches in members' homes. Promotes postgraduate research by provision of scholarships; professional networks for support, encouragement & exchange of ideas, etc.

Services
Linda Harper - Equality Through Diversity
Linda Harper
Hafod
Bryn-y-Garreg
Flint Mountain
Flint CH6 5QU
T 01352 761262 F 01352 761262
1011463.1212@compuserve.com
Freelance consultant, trainer & counsellor specialising in equal opportunities & managing diversity as enablers of organisation change. Wide experience in local government & education sector.

North Wales Heatcare
Mark Bruce
6a Somerset Street
Llandudno LL30 2LH
T 01492 860956 F 01492 872209
Insulation & energy-efficiency services for low income households in north Wales.

Sexual abuse/rape crisis
Dyfed Rape Crisis
Ty Cerrig
Llanwnnen SA48 7JU
T 01570 480247
Helpline open most days.

North West Wales Rape Crisis Line
Abbey Road Centre
7-9 Abbey Road
Bangor LL57 1EA
T 01248 354885
Helpline open Tue 6-9 pm 24-hour answering service. Telephone support & information by trained women volunteers for women & girls (16-18) who have been raped or have experienced any form of sexual abuse.

Spirituality/ecofeminism
Wild Women Gatherings
Fiona Fredenburgh
Pen-y-Craig
Croesor
Penrhyndeudraeth LL48 6SS
T 01766 771460
Wild women gatherings every three months in Snowdonia. Usually 3-4 days residential with week's camp in tipi in mountains. Aims to celebrate, share, heal & empower women. Support for other wild women groups.

Support
Cawn Cymru
Pat Daniel
24 Carneddi Road
Bethesda LL57 3RY
T 01248 600908 F 01248 602669
ems0lb@bangor.ac.uk
Promotes links between women in Wales & women in Central America. The Wales branch of the Central America Women's Network.

TRAINING

PDQ
Patricia Daniel
24 Ffordd Carneddi
Bethesda LL57 3RY
T 01248 600908 F 01248 602669
ems0lb@bangor.ac.uk
Advisory/consultancy training relating to bilingualism, language planning, staff development & women's development/equal opportunities. Terms negotiable depending on the assignment.

VIOLENCE AGAINST WOMEN

Rhyl Safer Cities Project
Julie Hartless
155 Wellington Road
Rhyl LL18 1LE
T 01745 360006 F 01745 360384
Government-funded community safety partnership with NACRO promoting local initiatives to prevent crime & make places safer.

WOMEN'S AID

Aberconwy Women's Aid
P O Box 1052
Llandudno
Conwy
T 01492 872992
Or phone 01492 872202. Refuge & support for women & children escaping domestic violence. 24-hour on-call helpline.

Bangor and District Women's Aid
P O Box 873
Bangor LL57 2QN
T 01248 370877
Drop-in Mon, Tue, Thurs & Fri 10 am-2 pm. Otherwise 24-hour ansaphone. Refuge for six families. For women & their children (if any) who have suffered domestic abuse.

Blaenau Ffestiniog Women's Aid
P O Box 59
Blaenau Ffestiniog LL41 3BY
T 01766 830878 F 01766 830878
Offering support to women & their children (if any) suffering domestic abuse. Operating a 24-hour on-call service.

Colwyn Women's Aid
Metropole Buildings
Penrhyn Road
Colwyn Bay

T 01492 534705
24-hour on call service. Office open Mon, Thurs & Fri 12-2 pm. Safe accommodation for women escaping domestic abuse. Offers a drop-in centre & outreach service working with women in the community.

Delyn Women's Aid
P O Box 1103
Holywell CH8 7WJ
T 01352 712150
Phoneline open 24 hours a day. Providing confidential support, information & where necessary a refuge for women & their children experiencing domestic abuse, whether physical, sexual or emotional.

Glyndwr Women's Aid
12-14 Hall Square
Denbigh LL16 3NU
T 01745 814494 F 01745 813279
Helping women who are or have suffered domestic abuse. Refuge, support & 24-hour on-call service. Also provide training to volunteers & training on various aspects of the work to other organisations.

Welsh Women's Aid
26 Wellington Drive
Rhyl LL18 1BN
T 01745 334767 F 01745 331502
Open Mon-Fri 9.30 am-4 pm. Aims to relieve need, distress & suffering experienced by women of limited financial means who have been gravely or persistently maltreated by men in north Wales.

Wrexham Women's Aid
8a Grosvenor Road
Wrexham LL11 1BU
T 01978 310203
Office open Mon, Wed & Fri 10 am-2 pm. 24-hour on call service. Support for women & children suffering domestic violence.

CARDIFF AND SOUTH WALES

ACCOMMODATION

Cardiff Single Women's Housing Group
4 Ninian Park Road
Riverside
Cardiff CF1 8HZ
T 01222 667871 F 01222 664100
Temporary support & accommodation for single homeless women aged 16-60. Open Mon-Fri 9 am-5 pm. Self-referral or statutory agencies' referral.

WALES - CARDIFF AND SOUTH WALES

ARTS AND CRAFTS

Permanent Waves
Nancy Pickard
Carfiff Resource Centre
Wroughton Place
Ely Bridge
Cardiff CF5 4AB
T 01222 569800 F 01222 578110
Women's arts association. For amateur & professional women of all ages & abilities to realise creative potential. Annual women's arts festival; practical workshops; skills register; low cost reprographics.

BUSINESS SUPPORT SCHEMES

Business and Professional Women (BPW) - Cardiff
Judith Marsh
14 The Green
Radyr
Cardiff CF4 8BR
T 01222 842729
Encouraging business & professional women to achieve their full potential by encouraging & training them to take an active part in public life & decision-making at all levels, etc.

Made & EDP Ltd
Mrs Patricia Turner
MADE Enterprise Centre
The Gadlys
Abadare CF44 8DL
T 01685 882515 F 01685 882806
Business skills seminars held in over 20 subjects & tailor-made courses for individual business needs.

CARERS

Caerphilly Care for Carers Ltd
Jean M Noble, Care Services Officer
18 Windsor Street
Caerphilly CF83 1FW
T 01222 882663 F 01222 851351
CAERCARE@baynet.uk.co
Free service; information about support services; provides a listening ear to distressed carers; respite sitting service between 8 am-10.30 pm 7 days a week. The centre is open Mon-Fri 11 am-3 pm.

CENTRES FOR WOMEN

Swansea Women's Training and Resource Centre
Alison Morris
228 High Street
Swansea SA1 1NY
T 01792 467365
A women-only safe space, open Mon-Fri 10 am-2 pm. Training courses to enable women to build confidence & knowledge. Information on areas relevant to women, eg sexual, mental, physical abuse, health issues.

CHILD CARE AND FAMILY

South Glamorgan Playbus Association
Kim Rees
Harwich House
Colchester Estate
Colchester Avenue
Cardiff CF3 7AP
T 01222 470775
Provides mobile play service with specially converted double-decker & single-decker bus. Play sessions are free of charge. Sessions run Mon-Fri in areas of Cardiff where there are little or no play provisions.

COMPUTERS/IT

Dove Workshop
Mair Francis
Banwen Community Centre
Roman Road
Banwen
Neath SA10 9LW
T 01639 700024 F 01639 701528
ad345@dial.pipex.com
Provision of adult education from confidence-raising, self-awareness to information technology & part-time degree schemes. A Women & Technology course free for women unemployed for more than six months.

South Glamorgan Women's Workshop
Marie Sloan
Clarence House
Clarence Road
Cardiff CF1 6JB
T 01222 493351 F 01222 482122
Free training for women aged over 25 in information technology. Free on-site childcare. Courses run during school terms. The courses include elements of personal & career development & workplacement.

CONTRACEPTION/WELL WOMAN

Family Planning Association Cymru - South Wales
Gilly Stoddart
4 Museum Place
Cardiff CF1 3BG
T 01222 655034 F 01222 644306

106353,125@compuserve.com
Information & advice Mon-Fri 9 am-5 pm on all aspects of sexuality, contraception, abortion, clinic information; leaflets & resources; education & training; consultancy & project work.

Counselling and Therapy

Cardiff Women in MIND
Helen Prior
22 Moira Terrace
Adamsdown
Cardiff CF2 1EJ
T 01222 482224   F 01222 493363
Run by women for women. To meet the mental & emotional health needs of women in Cardiff. Produces a pink list of accredited women counsellors & therapists in Cardiff; limited free counselling service, etc.

Education

BFWG - Swansea & District Association
Dr Elizabeth Rhodes, Hon President
47 Summerland Park
Upper Killay
Swansea SA2 7HX
T 01792 201172
bfwg@swansea.ac.uk
Meets monthly usually third Mon of each month September-June at University of Wales, Swansea. Lectures & talks of general as well as women's issues & educational topics. Lunches, study groups, national events.

Equal Opps

Chwarae Teg (Fair Play in Wales)
Jane Hutt, Director
Main Block
Ty Oldfield, Llantrisant Rd
Llandaff
Cardiff CF5 2YT
T 01222 563360   F 01222 562202
chwarteg@celtic.co.uk
Positive action equalities project. A government EOC initiative to stimulate partnerships which improve opportunities for women to realise their full potential in education, employment & the community.

National Federation of Women's Institutes - Wales
Rhiannon Bevan
19 Cathedral Road
Cardiff CF5 1LZ
T 01222 221712   F 01222 387236

A democratic & social organisation, offering women the opportunity of learning & working together to improve the quality of life in the community, particularly in rural areas.

Ethnic Minorities

Black Association of Women Step Out (BAWSO)
Mutale Nyoni
P O Box 270
Cardiff CF1 8YY
T 01222 343154
Support for Black women experiencing domestic violence from black & ethnic backgrounds. Promoting their rights & to freely participate in society & live in a safe supportive environment.

Pakistan Women Association
Zakia M Ahmed
14 Eskdale Close
Lady Mary Estate
Cardiff CF2 5LF
T 01222 764218
Phone in the evenings. Direct service for Pakistani women & their children in positive recognition of the disadvantage suffered by this community. ESOL classes, skills training, parents' crafts, etc.

Health

Glan Hafren NHS Trust Osteoporosis Service
Claire Quontock
St Woolos Hospital
Newport NP9 4SZ
T 01633 238289   F 01633 212582
Health service osteporosis service. GP referral required. Consultation, bone density testing if required. Treatment options, life style advice. Counselling. Information on HRT. Telephone helpline for patients.

National Endometriosis Society - South Wales
Mrs Pat Supple
127 St Helens Road
Swansea SA1 3UN
T 01792 645752
Information & support to anyone with endometriosis, their family or friends. Sharing feelings & problems associated with endometriosis, including treatments & side effects. 10 meetings held per year.

National Osteoporosis Society - Cardiff Group
10 Hawthorn Close
Dinas Powys
Vale of Glamorgan CF64 4TD
T 01222 512675
Raising awareness of the condition of osteoporosis, its prevention & treatment. Supporting sufferers. Keeping the bone densitometer at full capacity.

Self Help Group for Women with Rheumatoid Arthritis
Sian Morgan
10 Edgeware Road
Uplands
Swansea SA2 0NA
T 01792 518973
A women only group for sufferers of rheumatoid arthritis & other similar related illnesses. Meets on a three-weekly basis on Fri between 2-4 pm. Befriending, supporting, speakers, outings. Leaflets.

LARGER/TALLER WOMEN

Cappella Fashions
Mrs Maxine Pell
32 Clytha Park Road
Newport NP9 4NZ
T 01633 220082
Ladies' fashions sizes 12-28. Middle to upper price range. Beautiful clothes for any occasions. Model silk hats for hire, accessories & selected dress agency. Open Mon-Fri 10 am-4 p.m & Sat 9 am-2 pm

PHOTOGRAPHY

Courses for Women
Tina
Nr Llandysul
West Wales
T 01559 362843
Women only photography courses, for absolute beginners to very experienced enthusiasts. Courses on wild funghi with experienced mushroom collector. Gormet cookery courses. Places to stay.

PLACES TO STAY AND EAT

Brenda and Millie's Place
Brenda
The Glen
Red Lodge Lane
Brockweir
Chepstow NP6 7NQ
T 01291 689767

Lesbian-owned women-only country cottage in lower Wye valley, overlooking river. Phone for up-to-date price list.

L'Amuse
Kate Cole
2 Woodville Road
Mumbles
Swansea SA3 4AD
T 01792 366006
Women-owned restaurant serving French food. Open Tue-Sat 12.30-2.15 & 7-9 pm. Set price menu. Situated west of Swansea.

Women Only Farmhouse
Tina
Nr Llandysul
West Wales
T 01559 362843
For women only. 1 double bedroom. Shared bathroom. Sittingroom. Lounge. Log fires. Garden. Lunch & dinner; vegetarians catered for. Organic produce. Open all year. Phone for up-to-date price list.

PREGNANCY/CHILDBIRTH

Crisis Pregnancy Centre - Merthyr Tydfil
Leighton Rees
147a High Street
Merthyr Tydfil CF47 8DP
T 01685 377060
Open Mon-Fri 10 am-3 pm. Evenings by appt only. Free pregnancy testing, counselling & support for women with unplanned pregnancies. Post abortion & miscarriage counselling. 24-hour ansaphone.

Crisis Pregnancy Centre - Newport
Margaret Travis
The Beresford Centre
7 Beresford Road
Newport NP9 0AU
T 01633 212320
Open Mon, Tue & Wed 10 am-2 pm; Fri 7-9 pm; Sat 10 am-12 noon. Free pregnancy testing, counselling & support for women with unplanned pregnancies. Post abortion & miscarriage counselling.

Fertility Clinic
Princess of Wales Hospital
Coity Road
Brigend CF31 1RQ
T 01656 752752 F 01656 752593

WALES - CARDIFF AND SOUTH WALES

National Childbirth Trust - Cardiff branch
Meriel Jones
69 Marlborough Road
Roath
Cardiff CF2 5BU
T 01222 489553
Information & support in pregnancy, childbirth & early parenthood. Helpline: 01222 461590 operating 24 hours a day, providing information about NCT services in Cardiff.

SERVICES

South Wales Heatcare
Cliff Davies
Unit 5
Tonmawr 2000 Industrial Estate
Heol Hamdden, Tonmawr
Port Talbot SA12 9PB
T 01639 631757 F 01639 645246
Insulation & energy efficiency services for low income households in south Wales.

SEXUAL ABUSE/RAPE CRISIS

Mid Glamorgan Rape and Sexual Abuse Support Service
development worker
C/o The Fountain Centre
147a Lower High Street
Merthyr Tydfil CF47 8DP
T 01685 379310
Development worker on Mon, Tue & Fri 9 am-5 pm. Otherwise 24-hour ansaphone. Women are seen almost immediately they make contact. Helpline counselling Wed & Sun 7-9 pm. Also for women & men survivors.

Rape and Sexual Abuse Line (South Wales) Ltd
Sue Turbervill/Kath Mills
P O Box 338
Cardiff CF1 3TY
T 01222 373181
Helpline open Mon & Thurs 7-9.30 pm. Providing practical & emotional support to any woman or girl or anyone supporting someone who has been, or is being raped or sexually abused or harassed.

SUPPORT

Penarth Adapt
Shirley Murphy
35 Penlan Road
Llandough
Vale of Glamorgan CF64 2LT
T 01222 350313

Supporting women suffering from emotional stress at any age in the Vale of Glamorgan. Meets Wed 1.30-3.30 in the Dove Centre, Windsor Road, Penarth, Vale of Glamorgan. Additional phone no: 01222 350320.

Relate Dyfed
Mrs Helen Thomas
The Lodge
1 Penlan Road
Carmarthen SA31 1DN
T 01267 236737
Confidential counselling service for people who have difficulties or anxieties in their marriage or in other personal relationships. For an appt contact Jeanne on above number Mon-Fri 9 am-5 pm.

Women's Royal Voluntary Service - Welsh Division
6 Cleeve House
Lambourne Crescent
Llanishen
Cardiff CF4 5JG
T 01222 747717 F 01222 747796
Services are divided into family, hospital, food & emergency services. They include meals on wheels, hospital shops, tea & coffee bars, contact centres, family holidays & lunch clubs.

WOMEN'S AID

Bawso Women's Aid
Mutale Nyoni
109 St Mary's Street
Cardiff CF1 1DX
T 01222 343154
Provides secure, temporary accommodation, advice & counselling to Black & ethnic minority women & children suffering domestic violence. Open Mon-Fri 10 am-4 pm 24-hour on-call system after office hours.

Cardiff Women's Aid
20 Moira Terrace
Adamsdown
Cardiff CF2 1EJ
T 01222 460566 F 01222 484097
Office open 10 am-2.30 pm. 24-hour on call service. Four refuges. Supporting all women who live with the fear of violence or abuse in their homes. Offers advice, information & a safe place to stay.

WALES - CARDIFF AND SOUTH WALES

Cardigan Women's Aid
P O Box 5
Cardigan SA43 1LE
T 01239 615385
24-hour on-call service. Office hours 9 am-5 pm. Provides safe refuge, places always available, for women who have to leave home because of domestic violence. Advice, support, information & a listening ear.

Carmarthen Women's Aid Information Centre
10 Water Street
Carmarthen SA31 1PY
T 01267 238410
Open Mon, Wed & Thurs 10 am-1 pm. Refuge for women & their children (if any). 24-hour on call in emergency. At information centre information, advice & counselling on women-related issues (eg sexual abuse).

Lliw Valley Women's Aid
P O Box 503
Pontardawe
Swansea SA8 4WN
T 01792 862035
Helpline open Mon-Fri 9 am-5 pm & 6 pm-9 am 24-hour ansaphone. Refuge for six families, women & their children (if any), who are suffering domestic violence. Support, information & outreach worker.

Neath Women's Aid
P O Box 5
Neath SA11 9PS
T 01639 633580
24-hour on call service. Office open Mon-Fri 10 am-5 pm. 7-bedroomed refuge for women & children (if any) suffering domestic abuse. Information, support & advice. A women's centre opened late 1997.

Newport Women's Aid
56 Stow Hill
Newport NP9 1JG
T 01633 840258
24-hours on-call service. Refuge for 8 familes & an information centre. Emergency accommodation for women & their children (if any) who are suffering from physical or/and mental violence.

North Gwent Women's Aid
P O Box 13
Blackwood NPA 0YA
T 01495 220180

Offers a 24-hour on-call service. Providing a place of safety for women & their children (if any) escaping physical, mental or sexual violence from their partner.

Ogwr Women's Aid
P O Box 26
Bridgend CF31 3YJ
T 01656 766139
24-hour on call service. Two refuges for eight families. Temporary crisis accommodation & support for women & their children (fi any) who are suffering somestic abuse, either sexual, physical or emotional.

Pembrokeshire Women's Aid
P O Box 201
Haverfordwest SA61 1BF
T 01437 769564
24-hour on-call service. Refuge for five families. For women & their children (if any) who have suffered physical, mental or sexual abuse in the home.

Pontypridd Women's Aid
3 Church Street
Pontypridd CF37 2TH
T 01443 491528 F 01443 492879
Providing temporary refuge accommodation to women & their children who are experiencing domestic violence.

Port Talbot Women's Aid
P O Box 20
Port Talbot
T 01639 894864
Line open 24 hours a day. Office hours 9 am-5 pm. Refuge for six families. Information, advice & support for women & their children (if any) who have suffered/are suffering physical, mental, sexual abuse.

Rhondda Women's Aid
P O Box 1
Ferndale CF43 3YD
T 01443 731445
24-hour on call service. Refuge for nine familes; self-contained flats. Counselling & support for women who have or who are suffering domestic, physical, verbal or sexual abuse.

Rhymney Valley Women's Aid
34 Cardiff Road
Caephilly CF8 1JP
T 01222 860255

Line open 24 hours a day Mon-Fri. At weekends the same number gets through to the police station. There are three refuges for a total of 11 women. For women & their children (if any) suffering domestic abuse.

Tarian Women's Aid
P O Box 3
Merthyr Tydfil CF47 0AD
T 01685 373148
Telephone helpline open 24 hours a day. Refuge for five family spaces. Also provides support for women in their own homes. Drop-in Mon-Fri 12-3.30 pm. Phone for directions.

Vale of Glamorgan Women's Aid
222 Holton Road
Barry CF63 4HS
T 01446 744755
Information centre open Mon-Fri 10 am-3 pm. Otherwise an on-call 24-hour service providing advice & emergency accommodation for women & their children (if any) fleeing domestic violence.

Welsh Women's Aid
38-48 Crwys Road
Cardiff CF2 4RY
T 01222 390874 F 01222 390878
Open Mon-Fri 9.30 am-4 pm. Aims to relieve need, distress & suffering experienced by women of limited financial means who have been gravely or persistently maltreated by men in south Wales.

EIRE

DUBLIN

BUSINESS SUPPORT SCHEMES

Women Managers Network for the Civil Service
Kilda Taylor
Ctr for Management & Organisation Devlmt
Landsdowne House
Landsdowne Road
Dublin 4
T 01 604 5051 F 01 668 5506
Network of women managers in the Irish civil service at middle & senior levels. Networking & support; training & development in a women only forum; promoting equal opps for all women in the civil service.

CENTRES FOR WOMEN

Women's Education Research and Resource Centre
Ailbhe Smyth, Director
Room F104B, Arts Building
University College Dublin
Belfield
Dublin 4
T 01 706 8571 F 01 706 1195
WERRC@ollamh.ucd.ie
Open Mon-Fri 9.30 am-5.30 pm. WERRC office F104B & WERRC resource room F104A. Phone for an appointment. Events & publications. Studying women's historical & contemporary roles, etc.

CONTRACEPTION/WELL WOMAN

Family Planning Services
67 Pembroke Street
Dublin 8
T 01 668 1108

Marie Stopes Reproductive Choices Clinic
Dr Jim Loughran
Dublin
T 01 676 7852 F 01 661 8545
Offering contraceptive advice & supplies, well woman clinics, menopause checks, HRT, confidential, non-judgemental & non-directive counselling for women with unplanned pregnancies.

South City Centre
59 Synge Street
Dublin 8
T 01 478 0712

Tallaght Medical Centre
Level 3
The Square Shopping Centre
Blessington Road
Dublin 24
T 01 459 7686

Well Woman Centre
Ann Broekhoven
73 Lower Leeson Street
Dublin 2
T 01 678 9204 F 01 661 4618
Services include: menopause clinic, pregnancy testing, contraception, smear & breast screening, post abortion check ups, adolescent gynae clinics, PMS clinics, counselling. Free to medical card holders.

Well Woman Centre
35 Lower Liffey Street
Dublin 1
T 01 872 8051 F 01 872 8466
Services include: menopause clinic, pregnancy testing, contraception, smear & breast screening, post abortion check ups, adolescent gynae clinics, PMS clinics, counselling. Free to medical card holders.

Well Woman Centre
Northside Shopping Centre
Coolock
Dublin 5
T 01 848 4511 F 01 848 4264
Services include: menopause clinic, pregnancy testing, contraception, smear & breast screening, post abortion check ups, adolescent gynae clinics, PMS clinics, counselling. Free to medical card holders.

Well Woman Education Department
Ann Broekhoven
73 Lower Leeson Street
Dublin 2
T 01 662 1497 F 01 661 4618
Provides courses, training workshops & talks on all aspects of women's health, sexuality & assertiveness.

EDUCATION

Dublin University Women Graduates Association
Miss C M Lysaght, Hon Sec
Trinity College
Dublin 2
Seeks to promote & develop the interests of women graduates of the university. Meetings

with speakers. Weekly poetry session. Public speaking competition for girls at secondary level school.

WERRC Degrees and Awards
Ailbhe Smyth, Director
Room F104B, Arts Building
University College Dublin
Belfield
Dublin 4
T 01 706 8571 F 01 706 1195
WERRC@ollamh.ucd.ie
Certificate in Women's Studies, open to non-graduates. BA (Modular) degree; Women's Studies may be taken as a full module, levels 2 & 3. MA degree & postgraduate diploma in Women's Studies. PhD research degree.

Environment

Comhaontas Glas/The Green Party
Mary Bowers
5a Upper Fownes Street
Dublin 2
T 01 679 0012 F 01 679 7168
greenpar@iol.ie
Office open Mon-Fri 10 am-5 pm.

Irish Women's Environmental Network (IWEN)
Carmichael House
North Brunswick Street
Dublin 7
T 01 873 2600 F 01 873 5737
Irish branch of the Women's Environmental Network.

Girls/Young Women

Irish Girl Guides
Linda Peters, Chief Executive Officer
Trefoil House
27 Pembroke Park
Dublin 4
T 01 668 3898 F 01 660 2779
trefoil@igg.iol.ie
Non-denomiational voluntary organisation for girls & young women: ladybirds, brownies, guides, rangers & young leaders.

Health

Reach To Recovery
Olwyn Ryan, Support Group Coordinator
5 Northumberland Road
Dublin 4
T 01 668 1855 F 01 668 7599
admin@irishcancer.ie

Support group for women who have had breast cancer.

International

Banulacht - Irish Women For Development
C/o National Youth Federation
20 Lower Dominick Street
Dublin 1
T 01 872 6952 F 01 872 4183
banulach@iol.ie
A network of women working to promote awareness of the links between development issues that affect people both locally & globally.

Legal Matters

AIM Family Services
Marie Therese Naismith
6 D'Olier Street
Dublin 2
T 01 670 8363 F 01 670 8365
Family law information, counselling & mediation centre. Drop-in open Mon-Fri 10 am-1 pm. Mediation & ongoing counselling by appt. Providing people with accurate up-to-date information on family law.

Lesbian and Bisexual

Dublin Lesbian Line
Carmichael House
Brunswick Street North
Dublin 7
T 01 872 9911
Line open Thurs 7-9 pm. Otherwise 24-hour ansaphone.

First Out
C/o LOT
5-6 Capel Street
Dublin 1
T 01 872 7770 F 01 872 0460
leanow@indigo.ie
Meets first Wed & third Sat of each month at 7.15 at above address. For women exploring their sexuality.

Media

Women in Film and Television - Ireland
Anne Burke, Director
5 Gilford Court
Sandymount
Dublin 4
T 01 706 7035 F 01 283 0060
anne.burke@ucd.ie

Networking & training. Meets last Thurs of each month 6.30 pm.: Irish Film Centre, 6 Eustace Street, Temple Bar, Dublin 2; in July meets in Galway with film festival & October meets in Cork with film festival.

PLACES TO STAY AND EAT

Dunsany Bed & Breakfast
Anne Murphy or Maureen Smyth
7 Gracepark Gardens
Drumcondra
Dublin 9
T 01 857 1362
Woman-run B&B. Full breakfast, tea & coffee all day. Reduction on stays of three or more nights. Phone for up-to-date price list.

POLITICS

Women's Political Association, The
Vonnie Roche, Chairwoman
11 Foxfield Heights
Foxfield
Dublin 5
T 01 831 5734 F 01 831 5734
Encouraging/promoting participation of women in all areas of public & political life & addressing issues of concern to women. Training & encouraging women committed to integrating gender perspectives.

PUBLISHERS/PUBLICATIONS

F/M
Mary Montaut/Clare Toolan
C/0 WERRC
University College Dublin
Belfield
Dublin 4
T 01 269 3244
Feminist magazine. Feminist social & political analysis; psychoanalysis; women's studies; literature; journalism; theatre; film & media. Aimed at women who read, write, teach & study.

RETAILING

Lunasa
Stephanie Smith
6 Crow Street
Temple Bar
Dublin 2
T 01 677 1974
A one-woman business selling cards, gifts & crafts.

SEXUAL ABUSE/RAPE CRISIS

Dublin Rape Crisis Centre
70 Lower Sesson Street
Dublin 2
T 01 661 4911 F 01 661 0073
rec@indigo.iol.ie
Open Mon-Fri 8.30 am-7 pm & Sat 9.30 am-4 pm. Otherwise 24-hour ansaphone service. Freefone 1800 778 888. Counselling/therapy for women & men who are victims of rape, sexual assault & child sexual abuse.

SUPPORT

Manufacturing Science and Finance Union - Women's Committee
15 Merrion Square
Dublin 2
T 01 661 1063 F 01 661 1738

North West Inner City Women's Network
19 Manor Street
Dublin 7
T 01 671 7284 F 01 677 5741

Rowlagh Women's Group
Neilstown Road
Clondalkin
Dublin 22
T 01 623 0574
Meets Mon-Fri 10 am-1 pm. Bringing women who are isolated in their homes together & training in arts & crafts. Self-esteem courses. Free creche but places are limited.

Tallaght Women's Support Project
the supervisor
TCU, St Dominic's Hall
Main Street
Tallaght
Dublin 24
T 01 451 7500 F 01 451 7500
Supporting women in the community to break down isolation; Information on education grants, creche facilities, training locations; information on women's health issues & services available; etc.

VIOLENCE AGAINST WOMEN

Rathmines Refuge 24-hour Crisis Line
C/o Dublin Women's Aid
P O Box 791
Dublin 1
T 01 496 1002

EIRE - OUTSIDE DUBLIN

Women's Aid
Dublin Women's Aid
Roisin McDermott
P O Box 791
Dublin 1
T 01 874 5302 F 01 874 5525
waiddub@iol.ie
Open Mon-Fri 10 am-10 pm; Sat 10 am-6 pm. Information, support & accommodation to women & children who are physically, emotionally & sexually abused in their own homes. Free helpline: 1800 341 900.

Working women
Women's Health Project for Women in Prostitution
Mary O'Neill
Baggot Street Clinic
19 Haddington Road
Dublin 4
T 01 660 2227 F 01 668 0050
Drop-in medical service for women in prostitution & outreach programme. Free, confidential clinic- & work-based serivces, including condom distribution, referral for drug treatment, STD clinics.

Outside Dublin

Accommodation
Adapt Kerry Ltd
Kerry Women's Refuge
Killeen Road
Tralee
County Kerry
T 066 27836
The line is open 24 hours a day. Temporary crisis accommodation available. Six appartments. Child care unit. Panel of counsellors available.

Donegal Women's Refuge Group
C/o P O Box 55
Letterkenny
County Donegal
T 074 26267
Open Mon-Fri 9.30 am-5 pm. Otherwise 24-hour ansaphone. Refuge for 2 families & 1 single woman. Drop-in centre. Court accompanying service. Crisis counselling. Referrals to Letterkenny Women's Centre.

Irish Federation of Women's Refuges
Rosmen
Kells
County Meath
T 046 40158

Mayo Women's Refuge and Support Services
Pavilion Road
Castlebar
County Mayo
T 094 25409
Open Mon-Fri 9.30 am-5.30 pm. Otherwise 24-hour ansaphone service. Information, advice, support & counselling for women living with domestic violence.

Arts and Crafts
Weaving Dreams
C/o Shanty Educational Project
The Shanty, Glenaraneen
Brittas
County Dublin
T 01 458 2194 F 01 458 2194
An enterprise project for women on a sheep farm. Eight women who are trained in spinning & weaving demonstrate how they make their crafts from wool.

Centres for women
Letterkenny Women's Centre
Nora Newell
Port Road
Letterkenny
County Donegal
T 074 22895
Offers a women's health & family planning clinic, generic counselling, education courses, networking with other groups. Open Mon-Fri 9 am-5 pm. Women's health clinic on Tue 5-8 pm.

Tralee Women's Resource Centre
Evelyn Browne, Coordinator
3 The Mall
Tralee
County Kerry
T 066 20622 F 066 20817
Umbrella for locally-based women's groups in & around Tralee. Information on counselling & training courses. Drop-in centre open Mon-Fri. Photocopying, typing cvs for women. All services are free.

Contraception/Well woman
Cork Family Planning Clinic
23 Tuckey Street
Grand Parade
Cork
T 021 277 906
Family Planning Services
78a Lower Georges Street

EIRE - OUTSIDE DUBLIN

Dun Laoghaire
County Dublin
T 01 284 1666

Galway Family Planning Clinic
Medicare Services, Lisboyle House
Augustine Street
Galway
County Galway
T 091 562 992

Limerick Family Planning Clinic Ltd
27 Mallow Street
Limerick City
T 061 312 026
Clinics & female doctors Mon & Tue 2-4.30 pm; Thurs 11.30 am-2 pm; Fri 5-7.30 pm. Female nurse provides breast checks & advises on gynaecological problems. Free to medical card holders. Self-referral.

Navan Family Planning Clinic
37 Watergate Street
Navan
County Meath
T 046 28140

Newcastle West Family Planning Clinic
1 North Quay
Newcastle West
County Limerick
T 069 62933

Sligo Family Planning Clinic
12 Stephen Street
Sligo
T 071 46315

Tralee Family Planning Clinic
14 Ashe Street
Tralee
County Kerry
T 066 25322
Open Mon-Fri 9.30 am-12.30 pm.
Counselling 7-9 pm.

Well Woman Centre
15 Church Street
Athlone
County Westmeath
T 0902 73550 F 0902 73684
Services include: menopause clinic, pregnancy testing, contraception, smear & breast screening, post abortion check ups, adolescent gynae clinics, PMS clinics, counselling. Free to medical card holders.

Wexford Family Planning Clinic
Glena Terrace
Spawell Road
Wexford
County Wexford
T 053 43040

Women's Health Clinic
Nancy Murphy
North Quay
Newcastle West
County Limerick
T 069 62933
birt@indigo.ie
Well woman clinics: smear tests, menopausal clinics, pregnancy testing, ante-natal classes, contraceptive advice & supplies. Open Tue, Wed, Thurs, Fri 10 am-1 pm; Mon, Wed, Fri 7-9 pm. Free advice.

COUNSELLING AND THERAPY

Forum - Women's Working Group
Cathy Keane
Letterfrack
Connemara
County Galway
T 095 41117 F 095 41198
connemara@indigo.ie
The women's section of a community development organisation, supporting ten women's groups in the area. Provides a locally-based counselling service.

EDUCATION

Kilkenny Women's Studies Group
Anne Smart
C/o Adult Education Office
Ormond College, Ormond Road
Kilkenny
T 056 61145 F 056 61145
rotel@indigo.ie
Weekly meetings for women in Kilkenny. Courses for women related to personal development. Talks & workshops.

Shanty Educational Project
Carmel Habington
The Shanty
Glenaraneen
Brittas
County Dublin
T 01 458 2194 F 01 458 2194
Provides 30 courses, mainly for women: a one-year personal development course; a two-year women's studies course; women's

cultural exchange course; media communications (mixed); creative writing (mixed); etc.

UCC Women Graduates' Association
Deirdre O'Shea, President
8 Tracton Avenue
Montenotte
County Cork
T 021 503 251   F 021 302 304
Draws membership from university graduates. Monthly meetings from September to May which are both educational & social. Speakers, annual dinner in December. New members are very welcome.

University College Galway Women's Studies Centre
Vivienne Batt
University College
Galway
County Galway
T 091 750 455   F 091 750 549
wsc@ucg.ie
Promoting the teaching of women's studies; fostering debate on issues affecting women; encouraging research into & documentation of women's experiences; linking up with other women's organisations; etc.

HEALTH

Women's Health Action Group
C/o The Community Contact Centre
Partnership Court, Park Street
Dundalk
County Louth
T 042 37642
Part of a women's network discussing issues around the delivery of a health service in the Republic of Ireland. Involved in a government strategy relating to women's health issues.

LESBIAN AND BISEXUAL

Galway Gay Helpline
St Augustine Street
Galway
County Galway
T 091 566 134
Helpline open Tue 8-10 pm. Otherwise 24-hour ansaphone.

Lesbian Health Project
The Other Place
Lesbian & Gay Resource Centre
8 South Main Street
Cork
T 021 278 470   F 021 278 471
lesgay@indigo.ie
Open Tue 10 am-2 pm; Wed & Thurs 10 am-5.30 pm; Fri 10 am-2 pm. Free & confidential service: lesbian drug & alcohol recovery group; annual lesbian health day; sexual health, drug awareness, etc.

The Other Place
Geraldine McCarthy
8 South Main Street
Cork
T 021 278 470   F 021 278 471
esgal@indigo.ie
Lesbian & gay community centre. comprising bookshop, cafe, information & resource centre. Resource offices open Mon-Fri 10 am-5.30 pm; cafe & bookshop open Mon-Sat 10 am-5.30 pm.

PLACES TO STAY AND EAT

Amazonia
Penny Rainbow
Coast Road
Fountainstown
County Cork
T 021 831 115
Women-only guesthouse. Open all year round. Free tea/coffee all day. Kayaks, bikes, snorkelling equipment. Collection from air/ferry port. Breakfast served until noon. Vegetarian meals available.

Mon Bretia B&B
Lynn O'Donoghue
Mont Bretia
Adrigole
Skibbereen
County Cork
T 028 33663
Women run B&B. Women friendly. Open all year round. Phone for up-to-date prices.

SEXUAL ABUSE/RAPE CRISIS

Athlone (Midland) Rape Crisis Centre Ltd
4 Roselevin Court
Athlone
County Westmeath
T 0902 73815
Freefone 1800 306 600. Face to face, & telephone crisis counselling. Counselling for women & men & support for families. Open Mon-Fri 10 am-1 pm & Mon 7-10 pm.

EIRE - OUTSIDE DUBLIN

Carlow and Kilkenny Rape Crisis Centre
5 Dean Street
Kilkenny
County Kilkenny
T 056 51555
Freefone 1800 478 478. Line open Tue & Wed 10 am-5 pm; Thurs 10 am-2 pm & 4-8 pm; Fri 10 am-4 pm. Otherwise 24-hour ansaphone. Counselling for victims of sexual abuse, rape & sexual harassment.

Clonmel Rape Crisis Centre
20 Mary Street
Clonmel
County Tipperary
T 052 27677
Open Mon-Fri 9 am-5 pm otherwise 24-hour ansaphone service. Freefone 1800 340 340. Counselling for adult survivors of rape & sexual abuse, for both women & men. Also provides a mothers' support service.

Cork Rape Crisis Centre
Mary Crilly
5 Camden Place
Camden Quay
County Cork
T 021 505 577 F 021 504 690
corkrcc@indigo.ie
Open Mon-Fri 9 am-5 pm. Counselling services to victims of rape & sexual abuse. Information & advice provided.

Galway Rape Crisis Centre
Agnes Warren
3 St Augustine Street
Galway
County Galway
T 091 564 983
Open Mon-Fri 10 am-1 pm & 3-5.30 pm. 24-hour ansaphone outside these hours. Support for female survivors of rape & sexual abuse. CallSave 1850 355 355.

Kerry Rape Crisis Centre
11 Denny Street
Tralee
County Kerry
T 066 23122 F 066 20247
Open Mon-Fri 10 am-4 pm. Otherwise 24-hour ansaphone. Freefone 1800 633 333.

Kilkenny Rape Crisis Centre
South Leinster
Waterford Road
Kilkenny
County Kilkenny
T 056 51950
Open Mon & Wed 10 am-4 pm; Thurs 7-9 pm. Otherwise 24-hour ansaphone service. Freefone 1800 727 737.

Letterkenny Rape Crisis Centre
C/o Letterkenny Women's Centre
Port Road
Letterkenny
County Donegal
T 074 22895

Limerick Rape Crisis Centre
Dorothy Morrissey
11 Mallow Street
Limerick City
T 061 311 511 F 061 312 682
Freefone 1800 311511. Open Mon-Sat 9.30 am-5 pm. Evening appointments by prior arrangement. 24-hour emergency service. Free, confidential counselling of survivors of rape, child sexual abuse & incest.

Mayo Rape Crisis Centre
Nicola Rowntree/Ruth McNeely
Ellison Street
Castlebar
County Mayo
T 094 25657
Free phone 1800 234 900.

Sligo Rape Crisis Centre
The Manse
Wine Street
Sligo
T 071 71188
Freefone 1800 750 780. Helpline as above open Mon, Tue, Wed & Thurs 10-11 am

Tullamore Rape Crisis Centre
P O Box 105
Tullamore
County Offaly
T 1800 323 232
Freefone helpline as above.

Waterford Rape Crisis Centre
2a Waterside
Waterford
County Waterford
T 051 873 362 F 051 850 717
Open Mon-Fri 9.30 am-5.30 pm & Sat 11 am-1 pm. Otherwise 24-hour ansaphone service. Freefone 1800 296 296. Counselling for

victims of sexual abuse & rape & transsexual abuse. For women & men aged 16+.

SOCIAL

Ballybofey and Stranorlar Women's Group
Nuala Murphy
Edenmore House
Ballybofey
County Donegal
T 074 31167 F 074 31167
edenmore@iol.ie
Meets regularly for relaxation & stress management. Swimming, raising self-esteem. Talks & speakers.

SPIRITUALITY/ECOFEMINISM

Fellowship of Isis, The
Olivia Robertson
Clonegal Castle
Enniscorthy
Publications related to matriarchy studies & The Goddess. Contact Cesara Publications.

SUPPORT

Blessington Women's Community Group
Anne Cowie
Education Centre
Blessington
County Wicklow
T 045 865 970 F 045 891 099
Open 9.30 am-1 pm. Courses, Mother & toddler group. Information centre for women. Community-run playgroup. Vocational education centre.

Challenge
Jane Dillon Byrne
Silchester House
Glenageary
County Dublin
T 01 280 1624
Works in the field of social issues, for example, taxation & health, on behalf of women.

Clare Women's Network
Liney Seward/Sarah Mortimer
C/o East Clare Community Co-Op Centre
Main Street
Scarriff
County Clare
T 061 921 737 F 061 921 271
Meets monthly. Coordinates women's groups throughout County Clare. Produces a women's directory. Gathers & disseminates information on all issues affecting women's lives. Newsletter: 'Clare Wide'.

Cork Federation of Women's Organisations
Unit 9, Thompson House
McCurtain Street
Cork
T 021 509 274 F 021 273 557
The umbrella group for women's organisations in Cork. Has produced a women's directory.

Western Women's Link
Breda Cahill
Eglinton House
34 Lower Dominick Street
Galway
County Galway
T 091 568 974 F 091 568 974
Office open Tue, Wed, Thurs & Fri 10 am-2 pm. Information, resources, newsletter, workshops, seminars. Support start up of women's groups. Networks with national agencies. Umbrella for 66 women's groups.

TRAINING

Limerick Federation of Women's Organisations
Helen O'Donnell, Coordinator
B1 Wellesley Court
Limerick City
T 061 417 929 F 061 417 929
Umbrella organisation for 18 women's organisations in Limerick. Training.

Women of the North West
Marion Flannery
Moygownagh Community Centre
Ballina
County Mayo
T 096 31900 F 096 31900
Women in leadership training course. Concerned with economic development for women. Research on women & work.

WOMEN'S AID

Dundalk Women's Aid
P O Box 60
Dundalk
County Louth
T 042 33245
Helpline: 042 33244 available Mon & Fri 10 am-2 pm; Tue & Thurs 7-10 pm. Otherwise 24-hour on call service. Refuge for five women. Provides advice, information, support & safe accommodation for women.

NORTHERN IRELAND

Belfast

Business Support Schemes

Links Women's Group
Donna Spence
Tullycarnet Family Project
Tullycarnet Primary School
King's Road
Belfast BT2 7EH
T 01232 419069
Promoting women's development in Tullycarnet. Meets Thurs 10 am-12 noon. Courses in arts & crafts: needlework, paint effects, etc.

Centres for Women

Ballybeen Women's Centre
Anne Graham
34 Ballybeen Square
Dundonald
Belfast BT16 0QE
T 01232 481632 F 01232 484077
Open Mon-Fri 9 am-4 pm. Education & training; health education & promotion for women & young people; pre-school groups for children & creche; drop-in for women.

Downtown Women's Centre
30 Donegall Street
Belfast BT1 2GQ
T 01232 243363 F 01232 237884

Fall's Women Centre
Oonagh Marrow
173 Fall's Road
Belfast BT12 7LY
T 01232 327672 F 01232 333566
Open Mon-Thurs 9.30 am-5 pm; Fri 9.30 am-2.30 pm. Provides secure, welcome women-only environment in west Belfast; training & educational facilities; confidential advice, counselling & referral service.

Footprints Women's Centre
Gillian Gibson
6 Colin Road
Poleglass
Belfast BT17 0LG
T 01232 625083
Open Mon-Fri 9 am-4 pm. Offers support, advice, drop-in facility & education/training for local women. Creche. Aims to support women & help them grow in confidence & self-esteem.

Newtownards Road Women's Group
Christine Hagen
The Carew Centre
Tamar Street
Belfast BT4 1HS
T 01232 451730 F 01232 460882
The women's group owns & manages family centre in E Belfast. Facilities: pre-school playgroup; afterschool club, toddlers' club, women's group (Fri mornings), adult education classes + creche, holiday schemes.

Shankill Women's Centre
Anne McVicker/Heather Floyd
151-157 Shankill Road
Belfast BT13 1FD
T 01232 240642 F 01232 310632

Shankill Women's Forum
Pheme Brown, Development Worker
250 Shankill Road
Belfast BT13
T 01232 314404
Open Mon-Thurs 9 am-5 pm; Fri 9 am-1 pm. Open network of women in the greater shankill area providing information, networking support & development services. A lobbying body for action on women's needs.

Windsor Women's Centre
Joy Poots/Eleanor Jordan
136-144 Broadway
Belfast BT12 6HY
T 01232 235451 F 01232 230684
Open Mon-Thurs 9 am-4 pm; Fri 9 am-1 pm. Community based centre providing education & training programmes, advice & information. Fully registered daycare, youth groups, young mothers & elderly groups.

Child Care and Family

Ionad Uibh Eachach
Sue Pentel
34a Ineagh Crescent
Belfast BT12 6AT
T 01232 329180 F 01232 319369
Irish language pre-school parents' centre providing 96-place pre-school playgroup, mother & toddler/creche facility; adult Irish language classes; courses for women; after school programme for children.

Ligoniel Family Centre
Rosaleen Donaghy

NORTHERN IRELAND - BELFAST

4 Millview Court
Belfast BT14 8PY
T 01232 721008
Self-help project in north Belfast. Open Mon-Fri 9 am-5 pm & two nights per week 6.30-9.30 pm. Creche, playgroup for children aged 3-5, after school homework project, girls' group (aged 13-18), etc.

Ligoniel Parents and Toddlers Group
Terri McCallum
Ligoniel Community Centre
144 Ligoniel Road
Belfast BT14 8DT
T 01232 719337 F 01232 716906
Meets Tue 11 am-2 p.m & Thurs 10 am-1 pm. Talking with other mothers, play with children, outings by minibus, speakers, small summer scheme. Occasional lunches & dinners.

CONTRACEPTION/WELL WOMAN

Belfast Brook Centre
29a North Street
Belfast BT1 1NA
T 01232 328866
Free, confidential contraceptive advice. Help with emotional and sexual problems. Free condoms and other contraceptive supplies. Pregnancy tests and quick results, etc. Phone for times of opening.

Ulster Pregnancy Advisory Association Ltd
Mrs Joan Wilson, Director
719a Lisburn Road
Belfast BT9 7GU
T 01232 381345 F 01232 826288
For information about where to have abortions in the UK; counselling; contraceptive advice and supplies; emergency contraception information. Supporting women who have unplanned pregnancies.

EDUCATION

Centre for Women's Studies
Dr Myrtle Hill, Director
Queen's University Belfast
8 College Park East
Belfast BT7 1LQ
T 01232 245133 F 01232 325651
M.Hill@qub.ac.uk
BA degree. Modules offered: Introduction to women's studies: sexuality; women & social policy; gender & psychology; women, culture, texts; women in Irish society; popular culture & politics of gender; etc.

Irish Association for Research in Women's History
Mary O'Dowd
School of Modern History
Queen's University
Belfast BT7 1NN
T 01232 335101 F 01231 314611
M.ODOWD@qub.ac.uk
Association for research into women's history in Ireland. Newsletter & annual conference.

EQUAL OPPS

Making Belfast Work
Briege Lewis
North City Business Centre
2 Duncairn Gardens
Belfast BT15 2GG
T 01232 744022
Government initiative to improve education & training leading to skills enhancement; expand existing job base; promote opportunities for women to enter the labour market etc in 11 deprived areas within Belfast.

Women Working for Change
Co UNISON
Fortwilliam Business Park
Belfast BT3 9JZ
T 01232 770813

ETHNIC MINORITIES

Ethnic Minority Women's Development Project
Nooshin Agahi
Multi-cultural Resource Centre
12 Upper Crescent
Belfast BT7 1NT
T 01232 244639 F 01232 329581
Open Mon-Fri 9 am-5 pm.

GIRLS/YOUNG WOMEN

Contact Youth Counselling and Information Service
Phyllis Twamley, Director
2a Ribble Street
Belfast BT4 1HW
T 01232 457848 F 01232 455656
Helpline 01232 456654 open 12 hours Mon-Fri. One-to-one counselling; one-to-one information; information resource specialising in substance abuse; consultancy for

employment/training/educational opportunities.

Ligoniel Young Women's Group
Terri McCallum
Ligoniel Community Centre
144 Ligoniel Road
Belfast BT14 8DT
T 01232 719337 F 01232 716906
Meets Wed 7-9 pm. For girls aged 12-16. Personal development exercises, sports, arts & crafts, boardgames, outings, etc.

Upper Andersrown Young Women's Group
Emma Groves/Pauline Moore
Tullymore Commercial Complex
Tullymore Gardens
Belfast BT11 8NS
T 01232 622201
For the general advancement of young women.

HEALTH

Cancer Helpline
Cancer Information Service
Ulster Cancer Foundation
40-42 Eglantine Avenue
Belfast BT9 6DX
T 01232 663439
Helpline open Mon-Fri 9 am-5 pm. Information, counselling, support to help cope with cancer & fill gaps in knowledge. Resource library. For patients, relatives, friends, general public, health professionals.

PMS and PND Support
Julia Crawford
C/o 113 University Street
Belfast BT7 1HP
T 01232 653209
Providing information & support to sufferers of premenstrual syndrome & post natal depression. Regular support group. Women directed to other local groups, if such exist, should distance be a problem.

Ulster Cancer Foundation
Community Services Department
40-42 Eglantine Avenue
Belfast BT9 6DX
T 01232 663281 F 01232 66081
info-ucf@unite.net
Breast cancer support service from diagnosis to post surgery advice & support. Fitting service by appt, offering advice on clothing & fitting medical supplies & prostheses. Also ovarian cancer support service.

LARGER/TALLER WOMEN

Long Tall Sally
73 Royal Avenue
Belfast BT1 1FE
T 01232 327710
Clothes for the taller woman sizes 12-20.
Open Mon, Tue, Wed, Fri & Sat 9.30 am-5.30 pm; Thurs 9.30 am-7 pm.

POLITICS

Women Into Politics
Joanne Vance
30 Donegall Street
Belfast BT1 2GQ
T 01232 243363 F 01232 237884
Supports women who wish to take the first step into political life. Informs women of how political power is held & how decisions are made & empowers them to participate in political debate; etc.

PREGNANCY/CHILDBIRTH

Crisis Pregnancy Centre - Belfast
Deirdre Galbraith
227 Crumlin Road
Belfast BT13 7DY
T 01232 351652
Open Mon, Wed & Sat 10 am-12 noon; Wed 3.30-5.30 pm; Thurs 6-8 pm. Free pregnancy tests, counselling & support for women with unplanned pregnancies. Post abortion/miscarriage counselling. Phone for appt.

SEXUAL ABUSE/RAPE CRISIS

Nexus Institute
Dominica McGowan
119 University Street
Belfast BT7 1HP
T 01232 326803 F 01232 237392
Open Mon-Thurs 8.45 a.m-5.15 pm., Fri 9 am-4 pm. Counselling, education & research in the area of sexual abuse of both females & males over the age of 17.

Rape Crisis and Sexual Abuse Centre
Eileen Calder
29 Donegall Street
Belfast BT1 2FG
T 01232 321830

Phone 01232 249696 on crisis line Mon-Fri 10 am-6 pm. Counselling, support & information for adult survivors of rape & sexual abuse. Immediate, confidential & free. Advice on legal & court proceedings, etc.

SOCIAL

Belvoir Women's Group
Jessie Greer
8 Grays Park Gardens
Belfast BT8 4QG
For women to get together & embark on various projects of interest, eg photography, Irish history, sign language. Women of all ages are most welcome & would enjoy & benefit from joining our group.

Newhill Women's Support Group
Old Whiterock Road
Belfast BT12 7FX
T 01232 236241
Meets Mon-Fri 10 am-2 pm. Outings, speakers, talks & other social activities.

SUPPORT

Ainsworth Community Centre
May Robinson
117 Mayo Street
Belfast BT13 3AZ
T 01232 232077
Aims to improve the quality of life in the Ainsworth area of Belfast which is an area of deprivation, particularly for the elderly, women & young children.

Ardmonagh Family & Community Group
C/o 46 Ardmonagh Gardens
Turf Lodge
Belfast BT11 8DY
T 01232 245943
Open every day. Play group. After school activities for children. Youth groups. Mothers' & toddlers' group. Women's group. Phone 01232 233354 in evening. To empower people to have some control over their lives.

Ballynafeigh Women's Group
Nuala Moynagh
BCDA
283 Ormeau Road
Belfast BT7 3GQ
T 01232 491161 F 01232 492393
Meets Mon, Wed & Fri 11 am-1 pm. Support to local women & children from Protestant & Catholic communities. Courses & workshops

of own choice & safe/caring environment with structured play for children.

Divis Women's 'Stretch' Personal Development Project
Claire McKeever
Divis Community Centre
Ardmoulin Place
Divis Flats
Belfast BT12 4RT
T 01232 242551 F 01232 313924
Meets twice weekly. Free. To help women from a disadvantaged area build self-esteem, enjoy a 'feel-good' factor about themselves & their local community. Hopefully creating a positive ripple effect in the area.

Greenway Women's Group
Janette Moule/Julie Murray
Greenway Women's Centre
19 Greenway
Cregagh
Belfast BT6 0DT
T 01232 799912 F 01232 799912
Open Mon-Fri 9 am-5 pm + some evenings. To empower & support women, encouraging them to develop potential through holistic alternative to mainstream provision. Education, personal development, creche, etc.

Lower Ravenhill Women's Project
Helen Smith
The Bridge Community Centre
135-139 Ravenhill Road
Belfast BT6 8DR
T 01232 459000 F 01232 739099
Support group for women in the Lower Ravenhill area providing information, education & contact with other relevant groups & organisations.

Newhill Youth and Community Centre Association
Chrissie McAuley, Development Worker
231 Old Whiterock Road
Belfast BT12 7FX
Provides range of services & projects based on specific needs of local community. Women's groups; training for women; childcare & pre-school provision. Open for activities 7 days a week from 9.30 am-11 pm

Pastoral Outreach, The
Clare O'Mahony
Sussex Place
Belfast BT2 8LN

NORTHERN IRELAND - OUTSIDE BELFAST

T 01232 249953
Outreach work to individuals: mothers & toddlers & women in prostitution. Hospitality, counselling & outreach home visits.

Sandy Row Community Centre
Gabi Mornmingweg, Community Development Worker
63-75 Sandy Row
Belfast BT12 5ER
T 01232 325403 F 01232 313956
To enable local people to become involved in groups & to influence decision-making processes. Provides rooms available to local people at low cost. Education classes for women; mother & toddler groups, etc.

Sussex Place Family Services
Sr Clare O'Mahony
Sussex Place
Belfast BT7 3LA
T 01232 249953
Supporting & regular visits to families; special care for single parent familes, families undergoing stress or bereavement; senior citizens' group; youth work; outreach to women involved in prostitution.

Upper Anderstown Women's Group
Maura McCatter
Tullymore Commercial Complex
Tullymore Gardens
Belfast BT11 8NS
T 01232 622201
For the general advancement of women.

Women's Support Network
Marie Mulholland, Coordinator
30 Donegall Street
Belfast BT1 2GA
T 01232 236923 F 01232 319879

TRAINING

Belfast Women's Training Services
Judith Willoughby
30 Lower Bonegall Street
Belfast BT1 2GQ
T 01232 323904 F 01232 319879
Amalgamation of locally based women's centres with aim to run pre-vocational return to work courses in women's centres during family friendly hours. Full creche facilities & cash bonus on completion of courses.

Glen Parent Women's Group
Catherine Morris
41a Suffolk Road
Belfast BT11 9PE
T 01232 611225
Open to women who are looking for the first link back to training, education & employment. Courses are run two/three times a week 10 a.m-2 pm. A broad range of courses offered. Creche.

WOMEN'S AID

Belfast Women's Aid
Central Office
129 University Street
Belfast BT7 1HP
T 01232 249041 F 01232 239294
Helplines: 01232 662385; 01232 757607; 01232 491407. Advice & support centre 01232 666049. 24-hour on call service. Support & advice for women & their children (if any) suffering domestic violence.

OUTSIDE BELFAST

ALTERNATIVE THERAPIES

Therapy Centre, The
Karen Gannon
312a Antrim Road
Glengormley
Newtownabbey
County Antrim BT36 8EG
T 01232 865986
Provides hypnotherapy, psychotherapy and laser therapy for smoking cessation, weight loss, stress and assistance with any problem where psychological or emotional forces are involved.

ARTS AND CRAFTS

CKS Women's Group
Carmel Mc Anulla
CKS Community Centre
O'Kare Park BT78 5AB
T 01552 247560
Meets every Wed for arts and crafts & Thurs for adult training 11 am-1 pm. Run on a friendly, no demand framework. Open to any woman.

Dolly Mixtures
Philomena Gallagher
147 Drumbeg North
Craigavon
County Armagh BT65 5AE
T 01762 344211
Women's creative writing group writing on the 'Troubles' in N I & women's issues, also fiction. Two anthologies published.

NORTHERN IRELAND - OUTSIDE BELFAST

Coordinates creative writing classes & gives presentations/talks throughout UK.

BEREAVEMENT

Friend of Foundation for Study of Infant Death NI
Kathleen Savage, Nurse Manager
Glengormely Health Centre
40 Carnmoney Road
Newtownabbey
County Antrim BT36 6HP
T 01232 342151 F 01232 838944

CARERS

Newry and Mourne Carers' Association
Sue Cunningham
Ballybot House
22 Corn Market
Newry
County Down BT35 8BG
T 01693 69015 F 01693 69122
Open Mon-Fri 9 am-2 pm. Information, support, training, advocacy, counselling to carers. Mutual support groups in Newry, Kilkeel, Crossmaglen, Newtownhamilton, Belleeks, Rathfriland, Dromintee, Warrenpoint.

CENTRES FOR WOMEN

Chrysalis Women's Centre
Theresa Watson
520-523 Burnside
Brownlow
Carigavon
County Armagh BT65 5DE
T 01762 341846 F 01762 341846
Open mon-Fri 9.30 am-4.30 pm & 7-10 pm. Promoting opportunities for growth of women in the Craigavon area. Education programme; drop-in; meeting space for local groups; creche; young women's group; etc.

Lisburn Women's Centre
Fidelma Carolan
57 Bridge Street
Lisburn
County Antrim BT28 1XZ
T 01846 605806
Comfortable space for women to meet, talk, learn, get advice, exchange information & develop skills. Educational courses. Support group for women affected by domestic violence. Open Mon-Fri 9 am-5 pm.

Women's Centre
Theresa Kelly/Margaret Logue
24 Pump Street
Londonderry BT48 6JG
T 01504 267672 F 01504 266766
Resource & information centre; advice & referral; creche; classes in assertiveness, English, maths, psychology, sociology, creative writing, conversational Irish; drop-in for women to meet, sit, chat, etc.

Women's Centre, The (CWA)
Avril A Watson
3 & 3a Abbey Street
Coleraine
County Antrim BT52 1DS
T 01265 56573
Outreach support project of Coleraine Women's Aid. Advice, support, self-development opportunities & drop-in centre available to all vulnerable women regardless of whether or not they have accessed the Refuge.

CHILD CARE AND FAMILY

Creggan Parent and Toddlers' Association
Louise McIntyre
13a Cromore Gardens
Creggan
Creggan BT48 9TF
T 01504 267060
Parent & toddler organisation. Also runs playgroup for 3-5 year olds. Also short-term courses for women. There are now 10-12 courses running, including GCSEs & RSA stages I & II (Cregan Women's Activity Group).

Naiscoil Rosbhile (Pilot's Row)
Rionach Ni Scolai
An Gaelaras
34 Great James' Street
Londonderry BT48 7DB
T 01504 264132 F 01504 269292
Irish nursery education for children aged 3-4. Aim is to prepare children for entry into Irish medium primary education. Open Mon-Fri 10 am-12.30 pm. Very reasonable fees.

NiPPA - The Early Years' Organisation - NW Region
37 Glendermott Road
Londonderry BT48 7ET
T 01504 313004 F 01504 313004
Provides play-based, quality learning environments for all young children; partnership with parents & other agencies;

coordinated & holistic approach to young children's learning & development.

NiPPA - The Early Years' Organisation - SW Region
61a Market Street
Campsie
Omagh
County Tyrone BT79 0AA
T 01662 245678 F 01662 250104
Provides play-based quality learning evnironments for all young children; partnership with parents & other agencies; coordinated & holistic approach to young children's learning & development.

Omagh Childminding Group
Doris Birney
40 Beltany Road
Omagh
County Tyrone BT78 5NF
Meets once a month as a support group for all registered childminders. Runs courses, eg first aid, speech therapy, and anything the child minding group might benefit from.

CONTRACEPTION/WELL WOMAN

Derry Well Woman
Karen Meehan
17 Queen Street
Londonderry BT48 7EQ
T 01504 360777 F 01504 370103

Family Planning Association
Evelyn Kerr
14 Magazine Street
Londonderry BT48 6HH
T 01504 260016
Information service for contraception; community education workshops; pregnancy testing & counselling service; training & development for professionals. Free service.

EQUAL OPPS

Coleraine Standing Conference of Women's Organisations
Mrs Irene M Leacock
127 Moycraigh Road
Mosside
Ballymoney
County Londonderry BT53 8QZ
T 012657 31081
Meets four times annually plus one fundraising event for a local good cause, mostly for women. To exchange information on matters of public welfare, especially those affecting women & children in the area.

GIRLS/YOUNG WOMEN

New Mossley Women's Group
Elizabeth McClenaghan
C/o New Mossley Youth Centre
New Mossley
Newtownabbey
County Antrim BT36 5UW
T 01232 839078 F 01232 839078

PREGNANCY/CHILDBIRTH

Brownlow Breastfeeding Support Group
Clare Mc Cann
520 Burnside
Brownlow
Craigavon
County Armagh BT65 5DE
T 01762 341846 F 01762 341846
Providing support, advice & information to women wishing to, or currently, breastfeeding. Lobbies for improvement in facilites which support breastfeeding mothers, also for changes in government policy.

Crisis Pregnancy Centre - Lurgan
Diane Davison
39 Union Street
Lurgan
County Armagh BT66 8DY
T 01762 329900
Open Mon-Sat 10 am-12 noon; Mon & Thurs 2.30-5 pm; Mon, Tue, Thurs 7.30-9.30 pm. Free pregnancy testing/counselling for women with unplanned pregnancies. Post abortion/miscarriage/bereavement counselling.

SOCIAL

Armagh BPW Lunchtime Club
Mrs Norah McCabe
22 Victoria Street
Armagh
T 01861 523697
Meets in Charlemont Arms Hotel, English Street, Armagh on first Thurs of each month 12.30-2 pm.

SUPPORT

Cullyhanna Women's Group
Mrs Teresa Nugent
67 Slatequarry Road

NORTHERN IRELAND - OUTSIDE BELFAST

Cullyhanna
Newry
County Down BT35 0PU
T 01693 878010
Benefiting women of Cullyhanna by promoting general community projects of a social & economic nature with the object of improving their conditions of life. The group meets on Wed evenings September-May.

Daisy Women's Group
Mrs Angela Dickson, Women's Development Worker
26 Yoan Road
Enniskillen
County Fermanagh BT74 6EL
T 01365 327808 F 01305 327808
Meets Tue 10.30 am-12.30 pm. Classes in aromatherapy, reflexology, women & children's health promotion, healthy eating, drug/alcohol awareness seminars, etc. Providing a warm, supportive outlet for women.

Family helpline
T McGarvey
P O Box 32
Larne
County Antrim BT40 1RF
T 01574 260206
24-hour telephone helpline.

Fermanagh Women's Network
Marie Crawley
Belmore Mews
2 New Street
Enniskillen
County Fermanagh BT74 6AH
T 01365 328998 F 01365 323355
Providing women in Fermanagh with opportunities, skills & knowledge to advance their position in their homes, communities, public life by supporting & encouraging them to work together openly & inclusively.

Kilcooley Women's Group
Norma Johnston
45 Carrickmannin Gardens
Kilcooley Estate
Bangor
County Down BT19 1SX
T 01247 472556
Meets Tue 9.30 am-12 pm.

Knocks Women's Group
Anne McElroy
Knocks

Lisnaskea
County Fermanagh BT92 5AS
T 013657 21074
Small rural women's group aiming to improve the lot of women in this area of high deprivation by a programme of education classes & social activities.

Newtonabbey Women's Group
Rosaleen McAlister
20a The Diamond
Rathcoole
Newtownabbey
County Antrim BT37 9B5
T 01232 854041 F 01232 854041
Offers women from what has been described as a socially & economically deprived area a place where they & their children can overcome their feelings of isolation, improve social lives & attend workshops, etc.

Rostrevor Women's Group
Barbara Wendel-Sands
50 Shore Road
Rostrevor
County Down BT34 3EW
T 016937 38015 F 016937 38015
Providing support, information & stimulation to local women. Meets Mon 8 pm at Harmony Hill hall, Rostrevor. Workshops & courses for women covering wide range, from clay sculpturing to women's health issues.

Trillick Women's Group
Maria King
Trillick Enterprise Resource Centre
71-73 Main Street
Trillick
County Tyrone BT78 3ST
T 013655 613835 F 013655 61878

TRAINING
Bellaghy Women's Group
Sheilagh Murphy
Community Hall
Tamlagatduff Park
Bellaghy
County Londonderry BT45 8JR
T 01648 386861
Aims to alleviate poverty through providing courses for the community, leading to employment. Open Mon-Thurs 9 am-4.30 pm; Fri 9 am-1 pm

NORTHERN IRELAND - OUTSIDE BELFAST

Greencastle Women's Group
C/o Millgreen Youth Centre
19a Newton Gardens
Newtownabbey
County Antrim BT36 7DB
T 01232 364534 F 01232 364534
Open Mon-Fri 10 am-12 pm. Improving quality of life for women & children & for community regeneration in the Greencastle area. Education & training for women. Creche facilities for project members.

Strathfoyle Women's Activity Group
Catherine McGinty, Development Officer
12 Bawnmore Place
Strathfoyle
Strathfoyle BT47 1XP
T 01504 860733 F 01504 860733
Open Mon-Fri 9.30 am-4 pm. Parent & toddler groups Mon & Thurs. Maths, cookery, flower arranging, aerobics, machine knitting, crafts, GCSE English Language, Art. Tuition in reading, writing & counting.

WOMEN'S AID

Ballymena Women's Aid
Ballymena
County Antrim
T 01266 632135
24 helpline & on-call service. 24-hour helpline 01232 331818. Support & advice for women & their children (if any) who are suffering domestic violence. 24-hour emergency accommodation.

Bangor Women's Aid
South East Office
6 Hamilton Road
Bangor
County Down
T 01247 272520
24-hour helpline & on-call service 01232 331818. Support & advice for women & children suffering domestic violence. 24-hour emergency accommodation service.

Coleraine Women's Aid
North West Office
2C Abbey Street
Coleraine
County Antrim BT52 1DS
T 01265 320270
24-hour on call service 01265 58999. Advice & support centre 01265 65673. 24-hour helpline 01232 331818. Support & advice for women & their children (if any) suffering domestic violence.

Cookstown & Dungannon Women's Aid
County Tyrone
T 016487 69040
24-hour helpline/on-call service. Advice/support centre 016487 69300. 24-hour emergency helpline 01232 331818. Support/advice for women & children suffering domestic violence. 24-hour emergency accommodation.

Craigavon Women's Aid
Denise Murphy
323 Westacres
Brownlow
Craigavon
County Armagh BT65 4BD
T 01762 348755
Also 01762 343256. Advice, advocacy, information, practical help & safe accommodation. Providing temporary refuge to women & children suffering mental, physical or sexual abuse within the home.

Fermanagh Women's Aid
Fermanagh
T 01365 328898
24-hour helpline & on-call service: 01232 331818. Support & advice for women & children suffering domestic violence. 24-hour emergency accommodation service.

Foyle Women's Aid
Foyle
County Derry
T 01504 263174
Also phone 01504 312803. 24-hour helpline & on-call service 01232 331818. Support & advice for women & their children (if any) who are suffering domestic violence. 24-hour emergency accommodation service.

Newry Women's Aid
Newry
County Down
T 01693 67174
24-hour helpline & on-call service. Advice & support centre: 01693 250765. 24-hour helpline 01232 331818. Support & advice for women & their children (if any) who are suffering domestic violence.

North Down Women's Aid
County Down
T 01247 463608
24-hour helpline & on-call service. Advice & support centre 01247 273196. 24-hour helpline 01232 331818. Support & advice for

NORTHERN IRELAND - OUTSIDE BELFAST

women & children suffering domestic violence. 24-hour emergency accommodation.

Omagh Women's Aid
Omagh
County Tyrone
T 01662 245998
24-hour helpline & on-call service. Advice & support centre 01662 241414. 24-hour helpline 01232 331818. Support & advice for women & their children suffering domestic violence. 24-hour emergency accommodation.